ALEXANDRA MUNROE
WITH JON HENDRICKS

WITH ESSAYS BY
David A. Ross
Murray Sayle
Jann S. Wenner

CONTRIBUTIONS BY
Bruce Altshuler
Kevin Concannon
Edward M. Gomez
Chrissie Iles
Joan Rothfuss
Kristine Stiles
Reiko Tomii
and others

YES YOKO ONO

Japan Society, New York
and Harry N. Abrams, Inc., Publishers

GENERAL EDITORS:
Reiko Tomii and Kathleen M. Friello

FOR JAPAN SOCIETY:
MANAGING AND PHOTO EDITOR:
Annie Van Assche

FOR HARRY N. ABRAMS, INC.:
PROJECT MANAGERS:
Nicole Columbus and Margaret Chace

PRINCIPAL PHOTOGRAPHY:
John Bigelow Taylor

DESIGN:
Miko McGinty

This volume accompanies the exhibition YES YOKO ONO, shown at the Japan Society Gallery, New York, from October 18, 2000, through January 14, 2001.

YES YOKO ONO is made possible in part by major support from NTT DoCoMo, Inc.

Generous assistance from Apple Computer, Inc.; EMI Recorded Music, EMI Records Ltd., and Capitol Records, Inc.; EMI Music Publishing; Signatures Network, Inc.; The Andy Warhol Foundation for the Visual Arts; the E. Rhodes and Leona B. Carpenter Foundation; The David Geffen Foundation; and Marilyn and Jeffrey Katzenberg is also gratefully acknowledged. Programs at Japan Society Gallery are supported in part by the Lila Wallace–Reader's Digest Endowment Fund and the Friends of Japan Society Gallery.

EXHIBITION SCHEDULE:

Walker Art Center, Minneapolis
March 10–June 17, 2001
www.walkerart.org

Contemporary Arts Museum, Houston
July 13–September 16, 2001
www.camh.org

MIT–List Visual Arts Center, Cambridge, Mass.
October 18, 2001–January 6, 2002
web.mit.edu/lvac/www

Art Gallery of Ontario, Toronto
February 22–May 20, 2002
www.ago.on.ca

San Francisco Museum of Modern Art
June 22–September 8, 2002
www.sfmoma.org

Other venues in North America and Asia to be announced

LIBRARY OF CONGRESS CATALOGING-IN-PUBLICATION DATA

Munroe, Alexandra.
Yes Yoko Ono / Alexandra Munroe with Jon Hendricks ; with essays by David A. Ross, Murray Sayle, Jann S. Wenner ; contributions by Bruce Altshuler ... [et al.].
p. cm.
Includes bibliographical references and index.
ISBN 0-8109-4587-8 (Abrams: cloth) /
ISBN 0-913304-45-X (Japan Society: pbk.)
1. Ono, Yâko—Exhibitions. 2. Conceptual art—United States—Exhibitions. 3. Ono, Yâko—Criticism and interpretation. I. Ono, Yoko. II. Hendricks, Jon. III. Altshuler, Bruce. IV. Title

N6537.O56 A4 2000
700'.92—dc21 00-40146

Published in 2000 by Harry N. Abrams, Incorporated, New York

Printed in Italy

JAPAN SOCIETY
Japan Society Gallery
333 East 47th Street
New York, N.Y. 10017
www.japansociety.org

ABRAMS
Harry N. Abrams, Inc.
100 Fifth Avenue
New York, N.Y. 10011
www.abramsbooks.com

Front cover: Photograph by Iain Macmillan.
© YOKO ONO, Courtesy LENONO PHOTO ARCHIVE, New York

Back cover: Photograph by George Maciunas, intended as poster for *Works by Yoko Ono* at Carnegie Recital Hall, 1961. The Gilbert and Lila Silverman Fluxus Collection, Detroit

Contents

Preface

For nearly a century, Japan Society has been active as a private, nonprofit organization fostering more enlightened relations between Japan and the United States. The Society's cultural programs have always been committed to the belief that better awareness of the great riches of Japanese art and thought enhance American life and that these riches can take on many guises. Often, through a creative encounter with modern international art, what we think of as traditional Japanese culture is transformed and interpreted, thereby opening new worlds of artistic expression.

Yoko Ono is one such "transformer." Born in Japan and raised partly in the United States, where she has lived on and off since 1952, she bridges the cultural and intellectual brilliance of high Japanese art with the postwar global avant-garde. To show that unique "combustion" and its enduring influence is what this exhibition, YES YOKO ONO, is all about.

Ms. Ono has a long history with Japan Society. As a young artist in lower Manhattan from the late 1950s through the mid-1960s, she earned a modest living demonstrating the traditional arts of Japan at numerous Japan Society events. Her husband at the time, avant-garde composer and pianist Ichiyanagi Toshi, would occasionally accompany her as they turned a tea ceremony, *haiku* class, or other event into a mild display of Fluxus-like performance art. It is with a sense of greeting a good friend that we welcome Ms. Ono back to Japan Society.

Our sincere thanks to the corporate sponsors, foundation grantors, and individuals who made the exhibition, its North American tour, and this ambitious publication possible. We are grateful for the major support provided by NTT DoCoMo, Inc.

Assistance from Apple Computer, Inc.; EMI Recorded Music, EMI Records Ltd., and Capitol Records, Inc.; EMI Music Publishing; and Signatures Network, Inc. also contributed significantly to the project. We also appreciate grants from The Andy Warhol Foundation for the Visual Arts; the E. Rhodes and Leona B. Carpenter Foundation; The David Geffen Foundation; and Marilyn and Jeffrey Katzenberg. Additionally, we offer special gratitude to Peter Shukat, who assisted in our funding efforts. Finally, we want to acknowledge the Lila Wallace–Reader's Digest Endowment Fund and the Friends of Japan Society Gallery, whose ongoing support of Japan Society Gallery programs is invaluable.

YES YOKO ONO has been organized by Japan Society Gallery under the direction of Alexandra Munroe in consultation with the artist's curator, Jon Hendricks. Both deserve acknowledgment for producing a spectacular show and this scholarly publication, whose contribution goes beyond the study of Ms. Ono's art to encompass the East-West history of modern and contemporary art.

This ambitious project would not have been possible without the abiding support and cooperation of Ms. Ono and Sam Havadtoy. We offer our tremendous thanks for all they have done to help us realize this important venture.

Michael I. Sovern
Chairman, Japan Society

William Clark, Jr.
President, Japan Society

Acknowledgments

The guiding inspiration of this exhibition and publication, YES YOKO ONO, has been to construct a useful and illuminating survey of Ono's art in all media over a crucial period in the history of late modernism. Such an undertaking would have been impossible to achieve without the generous cooperation of the artist herself. I am grateful for the unwavering faith that Yoko has shown toward me and this project since we first began working together in 1995. Over the years, she has shared her insights and reminiscences and provided extraordinary background on the forces that have shaped her work. Her keen perception and wonderful humor have enriched our discussions, as has her boundless intellectual spirit and sense of the supernaturally divine. Yoko also gave tremendous attention to the authors during the research of their texts—an accessibility that has assured this book lasting authority.

Ono once said that a dream you dream alone is only a dream, but a dream we dream together is reality. Sam Havadtoy has made this project possible at every stage and at all levels of production, and I thank him for his constant support, leadership, and creative input. His dedication to Yoko Ono's art is the mainstay of YES.

Jon Hendricks, who has worked with Ono as curator and archivist since 1989, first revealed Yoko's seminal conceptualism to me while I was researching an earlier exhibition of postwar Japanese art. His profound and detailed knowledge of her work has informed this exhibition and book and has inspired numerous discoveries. It has been a rare privilege to work with Jon as consulting curator on this project. His essay here on Yoko Ono and Fluxus sheds light on Yoko's Fluxus history, and his compilation of the Anthology of artist's writings offers rich and provocative testimony to Yoko's unique artistic vision. Jon guided the authors through the artist's archives, suggested directions for research, and his manuscript reviews helped fine-tune each author's thinking, including my own. In thanking Jon we are appreciative as well of Joanne Hendricks and Aurora Hendricks. We also thank Sara Seagull for her assistance in many ways.

This exhibition draws primarily from three collections: the artist's collection, New York; The Gilbert and Lila Silverman Fluxus Collection, Detroit; and the Gilbert and Lila Silverman Collection, also in Detroit. We are grateful to these collections for their generous loans. We also acknowledge the Collection Archiv Sohm, Staatsgalerie, Stuttgart, and Jon and Joanne Hendricks for lending important work to this show.

At the artist's Lenono Photo Archive, Karla Merrifeld supplied with marvelous calm and order a seemingly endless request for press clippings, broadcast recordings, and photographs representing Ono's entire career. Her assistance with many aspects of this book's research contributed to the success of our production. Curt Fritzeen also facilitated our work at the artist's office, Studio One. We thank them for their support and cooperation.

Shows have a way of being conceived simultaneously as books, and YES was from the start an Abrams publication. I am grateful to publisher Paul Gottlieb for his enthusiastic support of this project and for his vision of the book's significance. A monograph of this scope could not have been accomplished without the talents of Margaret Chace, Vice President and Managing Editor, and Nicole Columbus, editor, who supervised its publication. At Japan Society Gallery, Annie Van Assche compiled the photographs—a daunting task—and oversaw all new photography, scanning, and photo research. She worked tirelessly in coordinating many aspects of this project. General Editors Reiko Tomii and Kathleen M. Friello did a masterful job of compiling the manuscripts, editing this book, and working closely with its eighteen authors. Dr. Tomii was instrumental in conceptualizing and organizing the Yoko Works section. We were fortunate to engage John Bigelow Taylor and Diane Dubler to produce new photography of Yoko Ono's objects and ephemera that are featured throughout. In Jerusalem, Oded Lobl photographed several works on view at the Israel Museum, for which we are most grateful. All other photographers who contributed to this book are listed under photography credits. Our thanks also go to Lisa Overton of Big Pink for her assistance on the scanned material. I am grateful also to research assistants Fergus McCaffrey and Midori Yoshimoto, and to translators Dr. Tomii and Ms. Yoshimoto for making so many previously unknown Japanese texts available to us. The book's superb design is the work of Miko McGinty. Rachel Tsutsumi assisted Miko in organizing the photographic material and in typesetting.

The range of Yoko Ono's work demanded an equally wide range of expertise. YES YOKO ONO features essays and contributions by leading scholars and critics in the visual arts, film, music, performance studies, and cultural history, and we are indebted to the following individuals for their important texts on Ono. For Part II, On Yoko: David A. Ross, Director, San Francisco Museum of Modern Art; Murray Sayle, writer on Japan for *The New Yorker*; and Jann S.

Wenner, Publisher of *Rolling Stone* magazine. For Part III, Yoko Works: Bruce Altshuler, Director of Studies for Graduate Programs, Christie's Education; Kevin Concannon, Adjunct Professor, Virginia Commonwealth University; Edward M. Gomez, critic and novelist; Chrissie Iles, Curator of Film and Video, Whitney Museum of American Art; Joan Rothfuss, Associate Curator of Visual Arts, Walker Art Center; Kristine Stiles, Associate Professor, Duke University; and Midori Yoshimoto, Ph.D. Candidate, Department of Art History, Rutgers University. This section, arranged in catalogue raisonné format, provides an in-depth history and appreciation of Ono's work that should inspire a serious re-appraisal not only of her art but of conceptualism itself. Special thanks are due to these authors for their scholarly expertise. Global perspectives on Ono's recent work have been supplied by curators who have first-hand experience presenting her projects: Kai Bauer, former commissioner of visual arts programming, Langenhagen, and currently independent curator, Stuttgart; Achille Bonito Oliva, independent curator, Rome, and 1993 commissioner of the Venice Biennale; Nanjō Fumio, independent curator, Tokyo; Pablo J. Rico, independent curator, Spain; and Lars Schwander, Curator, Fotografisk Center, Copenhagen. Part IV represents an extensive documentary and research effort on the part of Jon Hendricks and the team of Kevin Concannon and Reiko Tomii.

This exhibition travels to several venues in North America. I am grateful to David Ross, Director of the San Francisco Museum of Modern Art, for his early and abiding interest in this show and to each of my colleagues who signed up early for the tour: Kathy Halbriech, Director, and Joan Rothfuss, Associate Curator, Walker Art Center; Marti Mayo, Director, and Dana Friis-Hansen, former curator, Contemporary Art Museum, Houston; and Jane Farver, Director, MIT List Visual Arts Center, Cambridge. We look forward to watching Yoko Ono's art and thought expand with new meaning in today's world.

When I assumed the directorship of Japan Society Gallery in spring 1998, my plans for this exhibition were well underway. I am grateful to Ambassador William Clark, Jr., President of Japan Society, for his enthusiastic embrace of this project and for his belief in its importance within the overall programming of the Society. John Wheeler, Vice President, and Carl Schellhorn, Vice President and Treasurer, have also provided support throughout. Each of the following individuals contributed to Japan Society's presentation: Elizabeth Costa, Director, and Diana Foster, Assistant Director, Development; Paula Lawrence, Director, Performing Arts; Kyoko Hirano, Director, Japan Society Film Center; Kate Cohen, Director, Communications, and Ruth Kaplan, press consultant; Ruri Kawashima, Director, and Katharina Belting, Senior Program Officer, U.S.-Japan Program.

In the Gallery, Assistant Director Jane Rubin superbly managed every aspect of this exhibition and its ambitious tour. As I struggled with my new balancing act of directing a museum and curating an exhibition, Jane compiled much of the object research that forms the basis of this show. Together with Curator of Education, Annie Van Assche, they have made YES everything we ever dreamed of. Others whose hard work helped realize this project are Assistant to the Director, Takahide Tsuchiya, and Gallery interns Cynthia Elden, So Young Lee, Mori Oda, and research associate Hyunsoo Woo.

The Gallery benefits from its Art Advisory Committee, chaired by Samuel Sachs, II, and the Friends of Japan Society Gallery. I am thankful for their support and encouragement of new directions and scholarship in the field of Japanese art.

Alexandra Munroe
Director, Japan Society Gallery
and Exhibition Curator

Notes to the Reader

Japanese, Korean, and Chinese names are given in the traditional order, surname first, except in the case of individuals who primarily reside outside their native countries and adopt the Western system (e.g., Yoko Ono, Nam June Paik).

Macrons have been used to indicate long vowels in Japanese names and words (e.g., Sōgetsu). Commonly known city names and words adapted into English have been given without macrons (e.g., Kyoto, Shinto).

Unless otherwise noted, all works reproduced are by Yoko Ono.

As a rule, the date given for Yoko Ono's work indicates its initial realization; where double dates are given (e.g., 1955/1962), the first date indicates that of initial conception or score, and the second, that of its specific realization.

Dimensions of works are given, unless otherwise noted, in order of height by width, for two-dimensional objects; and height by length by depth, for three-dimensional objects.

In citations of musical recordings, the name of the featured performer precedes the song title (e.g., Plastic Ono Band, "Give Peace a Chance").

In cross-references, "no." refers to entries in "Yoko Works"; "pl." refers to plates in "Yoko Works," including "Yoko Now"; and "fig" refers to all other illustrations. "Anthology" refers to works in "Anthology: Writings by Yoko Ono."

For frequently cited books, exhibition catalogues, and periodical and newspaper articles, as well as titles of exhibitions, concerts, and events, extensive abbreviations are employed. Full data can be found in the Chronology and Bibliography.

Authors for "Yoko Works":

Bruce Altshuler (BA)
Kevin Concannon (KC)
Edward M. Gomez (EG)
Chrissie Iles (CI)
Joan Rothfuss (JR)
Kristine Stiles (KS)
Midori Yoshimoto (MY)

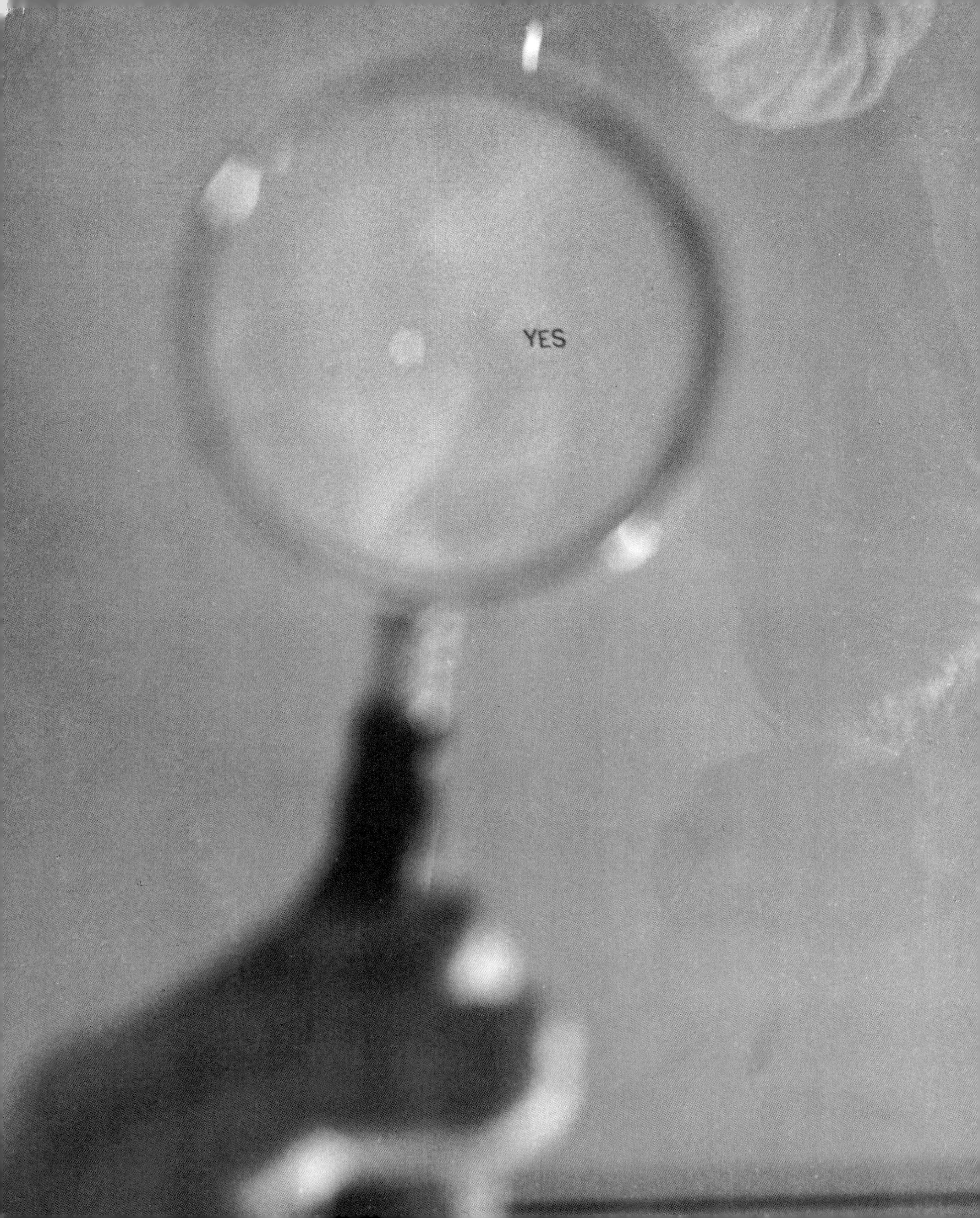
YES

Spirit of YES: The Art and Life of Yoko Ono

ALEXANDRA MUNROE

Yoko Ono. What comes to mind?

Extremes of opinion have shaped the public's idea of Yoko Ono since she first emerged in the New York art world in the early 1960s. While her work has often confounded critics, her faith in the power of art to open and uplift the mind has touched millions. As an artist, poet, and composer working alternatively at the fringe and mainstream of culture, she has irked those who resist boundary-crossing. Yet she emerges, over and over, as a forerunner of new art forms that mix and expand different media. Her work as an antiwar activist, like the global ads for peace that she orchestrated with her husband, John Lennon, have offered a kind of public instruction that carries a profoundly positive and transformative message: Imagine.

For decades, people around the world have celebrated her meaning while critics looked on, perplexed.

Why, one wonders—despite recent attempts that focus on her contribution to Fluxus—has the canon of postwar modernism been slow to accept Yoko Ono's art? Originally, the difficulty of categorizing her work, the ambiguities of her insider/outsider status to contemporary art movements such as Conceptualism, and the unprecedented diversity of her artistic worlds all presented obstacles. As a Japanese woman artist emerging at a time when neither Asians nor women had much place in modernism's history, Ono had little framework for sustained critical support. And what potential she had to establish her standing was all but destroyed by the torrent of popular press that attended her life with "Beatle John." Although she was always admired as an "artist's artist," few critics have traced her travels among the underground art worlds of New York, Tokyo, and London to recognize the importance of what she had to transmit, and fewer still fathomed the complexity of Ono's cultural lineage that shaped her seemingly cryptic ideas of art.

Even in the 1990s, as Ono became more and more active in the international exhibition arena, her sheer range of artistic expression and her poetic and intellectual style continued to puzzle the art establishment. The terminology to describe Ono's mind-transformative art had yet to be found or agreed upon; and the cataloguing, collecting, or display of her mostly ephemeral works remained a challenge most curators found daunting. The modern museum system, wherein artists are categorized by traditional media (e.g. painting) and where performance art, film, and music are too often separated from museum studies altogether, did not apply to Ono's work—which is by nature beyond and between genres, open, unorthodox, and inventive rather than fixed in any conventional sense. At a time when the art world was ensnared in the politics of multiculturalism and its polemics of difference, Ono's aspirations for one world, one mind seemed fey and sentimental, too wishful for the divisive world that artists so sensationalized at the end of the millennium.

FIGURE 1.1
CEILING PAINTING (YES PAINTING), 1966.
DETAIL

This is what Lennon meant when he remarked that Yoko was the world's "most famous unknown artist. Everybody knows her name, but nobody knows what she does."[1]

YES refers to the title of a 1966 work by Yoko Ono (fig. 1.1; no. 7), shown at Indica Gallery, London. Like so much of her art, it is instructional and like so many of her instructions, it offers affirmation. John Lennon got it, on his first meeting with Yoko: when he climbed the ladder to peer at the framed paper on the ceiling, he encountered the tiny word YES. "So it was positive. I felt relieved."[2]

Ono's art is directed at transformation, a faith in the mind's power to realize good through the act of visualization. She uses language—minimal, epigrammatic, poetic—to instruct us to dream, to wish, to imagine, to think YES. Linguistic devices like paradox, antisense, and humor provoke mystery, and mystery in turn provokes us to question the nature of ourselves and the world. Hers is a social art that relies on participants—not just to be appreciated in the abstract, but to be actually made real, completed. In her 1967 work *Glass Keys to Open the Skies* Ono transforms ordinary keys into a Shinto-like votive object and leaves the mind a box waiting to be unlocked (no. 23). On a different scale, the text of her and Lennon's 1969 billboard campaign, "War Is Over! / If You Want It," suggests that the possibility to overcome belligerance lies in our own imagination (no. 39). For Ono, the purpose of art is to push the mind to become the ultimate "fabricator of truth."[3] These aspects of her art and thought—ephemerality, metaphysics, interactive participation—have guided her prolific production in a range of media over four decades.

Yoko Ono's strategies reflect the discourse on art and life that has dominated much of twentieth-century avant-garde culture. To break down the boundaries between high art and everyday life has been the object of radical art and thought since Marcel Duchamp took an ordinary porcelain urinal and exhibited it as a Readymade sculpture entitled *Fountain* in 1917. But unlike so many artists who have framed the discourse in terms of the dichotomy of art and life, who aim to take art off its pedestal to look and behave like everyday things or events, Yoko has maintained that art and life are neither opposing nor synonymous. Her work is not about simulating life, as in many of Allan Kaprow's Happenings and Chris Burden's performances. Rather, she aims to assimilate the consciousness of art into the fabric of ordinary living through operations she calls "rituals…to rationalize the irrationality in us, humans."[4]

On insound

IN: like really in-within-inner-non-un-insane-crazed...
Insound is a practice rather than music.
Most of the insound pieces are spread by word of mouth.
The following is one of the insound pieces.

Stay in a room for a month.
Do not speak.
Do not see.
Whisper at the end of the month.

A word-of-mouth piece, a strip-tease piece and an audience piece will be performed in this concert.

On instructure

Something that emerged from instruction and yet not quite emerged-not quite structured-never quite structured... like an unfinished church with a sky ceiling.

The instructures will be exhibited in the lobby.

FIGURE 1.2
ON INSOUND AND *ON INSTRUCTURE* IN PROGRAM, *CONTEMPORARY AMERICAN AVANT-GARDE MUSIC CONCERT,* YAMAICHI HALL, KYOTO, 1964

The origins of Yoko Ono's art are linked to Fluxus, an avant-garde movement that developed in lower Manhattan during the late 1950s and early 1960s. Ono was central to its early history and remained closely associated with its community of artists and revolutionary aesthetics. The conditions of Fluxus were twofold: everyday existence is the site of art; and dynamic intermedia, rather than static form, is art's truest medium.[5] Arising from a Duchampian Dadaism, Fluxus opposed the institutionalization and commodification of art, advocating an alternative state of improvisation that is "non-art, anti-art, nature, reality."[6] The wide-ranging impact of John Cage's ideas on contemporary aesthetics—that art and the means for its creation lie all around us—further promoted an open environment where borders between music, poetry, performance, and the visual arts no longer existed. To Fluxus founder George Maciunas, rainfall, a flight of a butterfly, and the babble of a crowd are manifestations of "concrete" life that ultimately surpass the "artificial world of abstraction" found in the fine arts.[7] Ono's instructions for music, paintings, events, objects, and film—many of which were compiled in her influential 1964–71 anthology, *Grapefruit*—established the primacy of concept, language, and participation that was central to Fluxus as well as to Conceptual Art.

Through Maciunas, who adored Yoko, her Eastern sensibility helped shaped such Flux-ideas as minimalism, poetics, and the investigation of the simple and habitual acts of everyday life and their inherent relation to art. Indeed, Ono's experiential and intuitive art played a key role in the transmission of Eastern aesthetics to an international avant-garde trained in postwar existential thought. From Düsseldorf to New York, artists of all media looked to the East—Japan especially—for an alternative structure and practice of existence that art could make transparent. Building on a complex intellectual history with roots in such modern thinkers as Friedrich Nietzsche, Henri Bergson, and Suzuki Daisetz Teitarō (D. T. Suzuki), the postwar generation repudiated the vestiges of modern Western positivism and embraced an ontology lovingly informed by Daoism and Zen. The reformulation of those philosophical and deeply cultural traditions is one of the greatest—and least examined—forces of modern art. Cage's influence is legendary, but he was by no means the sole medium or catalyst. Yoko Ono, whose work extends from Buddhist thought as well as from *haiku* and Noh poetics—with their emphasis on minimalist form and suggestive (conceptual) imagery—was also a powerful embodiment of those non-Western aesthetics that ultimately transformed the course of contemporary art. Her seminal texts "On Insound" and "On Instructure," which accompanied her 1964 exhibition and concert in Kyoto, reveal her approach to both music and object-making as a *practice*, an unfinished *process* of concept transmission. Although her reliance on text is partly Fluxus, her reliance on the spiritual imagination of the reader is wholly Ono (fig. 1.2).

So futuristic so long ago, Yoko Ono has consistently appeared at the cutting edge of historic avant-garde movements. But she ultimately occupies an independent, even aristocratic, status that resists group identification. Although she was a progenitor and abiding member of Fluxus, classification within it alone is too hermetic and limiting: in the end, Ono was more concerned with high poetry and ritual than with Maciunas's love of "low gags and Vaudeville." Although she was the first to make concept literally the material of art with her exhibition of *Instructions for Paintings* in Tokyo in 1962—years ahead of those whose names would become associated with Conceptual Art, like Lawrence Weiner or Joseph Kosuth—she cannot be strictly categorized as a Conceptual artist. Unlike theirs, Ono's conceptualism is not engaged in a political critique of the institutions of art and their underlying structures of power and ideology. Indeed hers is not a critique at all, but rather an invitation to a magical unlocking of the mind. While the Conceptualists embrace an aesthetics of *negation* (critique) to arrive at art's radical dematerialization, Ono arrives at the same intangible, idea-based form of art by embracing an experience of *affirmation* (imagination). That she fabricated objects of nonart materials, such as Plexiglas, in a reductive form allows us to discuss her work in terms of Minimalist artists like Donald Judd or Robert Morris. But as her objects are imbued with more spirit than phenomenology, more poetry than monumentality, she defies the Minimalist title. Several of her film scripts, such as *Rape* (no. 45), and song lyrics, such as "Sisters O Sisters," offer a bold commentary on women that link her work to feminism. Yet her calls for women to "build a new world" are more about mental freedom than critical theory, leaving her status as a feminist artist ambiguous for the hard-liners. And finally, although she has been the object of popular culture since her association with John Lennon, popular culture has never been the object of her art. Even her events that reached mass audiences, such as *Bed-In for Peace* or the *War Is Over!* billboard campaigns, were more about using the media as a tool of social transformation than critiquing the media as a tool of commodity culture—what preoccupied Pop artists like Andy Warhol or Roy Lichtenstein. We can remain baffled, or we can try to fashion new art and cultural histories that navigate between fringe and rock, avant-gardism and celebrity, Japan and globalism, feminism and heroics.

Yoko Ono has created a world of objects and installations, films and music, instructions and texts, events and performances that continue to engage us on a remarkable level of metaphysical intelligence, formal innovation, and poetic beauty. She offers bits of time, perceptions, epiphanies that provoke an encounter with life's wit and wonder and make us, hopefully, a little sager and more humane. Guided by the suggestion of her 1966 instruction YES, this project examines the enduring creative force that has generated so legendary a figure in our time.

If consciousness in Zen Buddhism equals "creativity in every moment," then it is possible to see Ono's art as an ongoing practice of what she calls fabricating consciousness.[8] As for a true poet, no element of life is beyond her capacity to restructure its truth to serve her own reality. Yoko Ono occupies that fabricated world with steadfast belief, and her art consists often of a simple invitation to participate:

FLY PIECE

Fly.

1963 summer

ORIGINS

One of Yoko Ono's most powerful childhood memories dates to the final months of World War II in Japan. The U.S. firebombings of Tokyo in March 1945 that left tens of thousands dead and the city a vast charred ruin had forced Yoko's mother to evacuate her family to the countryside for safety. Yoko's father, Ono Yeisuke, had been stationed in Hanoi since 1942 as manager of Japan's leading wartime bank, and no word from him had been heard for the last year. Gathering her three children together with the last family servant who had not been pressed into military service, Mrs. Ono moved the family to a rural farm village where the threat of air raids was distant. For the next several months leading up to Japan's surrender, the national economy was devastated, starvation and suicide rampant, and the cities from north to south an accumulating ruin of war. Yoko, taunted by the local children for "smelling like butter" (*bata kusai*)—a reference to her being Americanized and a city girl—remembers spending the afternoons hiding with her brother Keisuke from the irate and unbalanced world outside. "Lying on our backs, looking up at the sky through an opening in the roof, we exchanged menus in the air and used our powers of visualization to survive."[9] The imaginary realm and the sky as a calling to vast, pale freedom would later become hallmarks of Ono's mind-centered art.

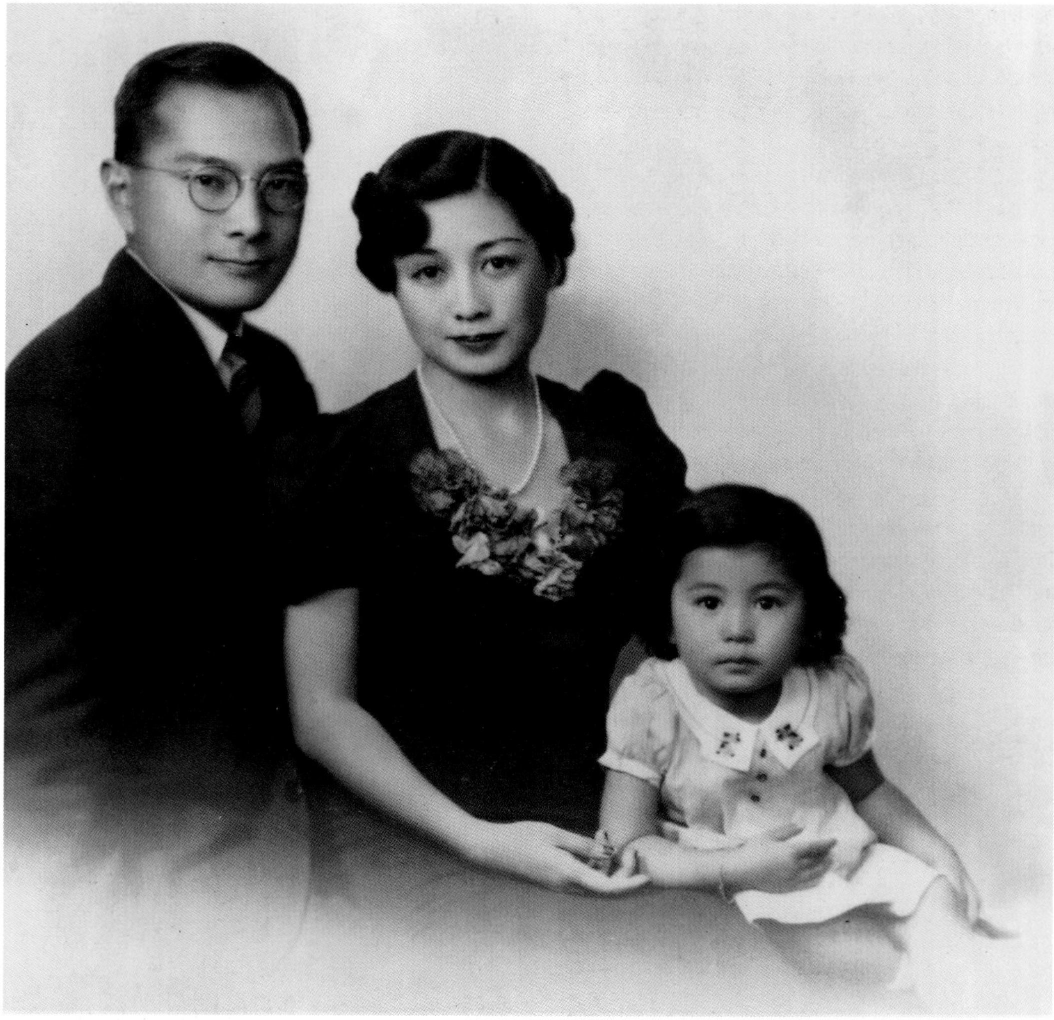

FIGURE 1.3
ONO WITH HER PARENTS
IN SAN FRANCISCO, 1935

By the time Yoko was twelve, when this story occurs, she had spent half of her childhood in America, following her father's banking business; painfully, her identity was often that of an outsider, isolated by others' projections of "otherness." As a child, Yoko used that space of difference to strengthen her independent resolve, and from an early age her teachers, friends, and family remarked on her precocious sense of free will. Ono's ability to imagine the unthinkable—and do it—would become the very content of her art. But the abiding image of being incomplete and hidden, of loss and absence, and the aspiration toward unity and connectedness that marked her childhood would also become recurring themes in her work.

Yoko Ono was born on February 18, 1933 in Tokyo. Her mother, Isoko, was the granddaughter of Yasuda Zenjirō, one of Japan's most famous merchant princes.[10] As founder of the Yasuda Bank, Zenjirō built one of the largest *zaibatsu*, or financial combines, in early modern Japan before he was assassinated by a right-wing ultranationalist in 1921. He was succeeded as head of the Yasuda Bank by Isoko's father, Zenzaburō. Inducted to the House of Peers in 1915, Zenzaburō retired early from his business career and, enjoying fabulous wealth, turned his attention to the arts. Yoko has described her mother as a quintessential *moga*, a term in vogue during the Japan's liberal twenties that conjures a chic and worldly "modern girl."[11] By 1945, Yasuda ranked as the fourth largest *zaibatsu* after Mitsui, Mitsubishi, and Sumitomo.

What celebrity the Yasuda clan gained through its formidable financial standing in Japanese society the Ono family matched in genuine nobility and educational pedigree. Yoko's great-grandfather, Saisho Atsushi, had been a viscount allied with the historic campaign against the Tokugawa shogunate that ushered in the Meiji Restoration of 1868. Saisho's progressive streak marked his daughter Tsuruko (Yoko's grandmother), who studied English and music at a Protestant college and was converted to Christianity. She married Ono Eijirō, the son of impoverished samurai, who eventually gave up academia for banking, becoming president of the powerful Japan Industrial Bank.[12] His son Yeisuke, who married Yoko's mother, earned degrees in both economics and mathematics from Tokyo Imperial University. At the time of Yoko's birth, he was a high-ranking executive at the Yokohama Specie Bank, a semigovernmental foreign-exchange bank that was one of the world's largest until 1947, when Occupation authorities reorganized it as a commercial bank and renamed it the Bank of Tokyo. Yoko's half-Buddhist, half-Protestant upbringing would influence her worldview as she matured.

Of all her family attributes on both the Yasuda and Ono sides,[13] Yoko feels the greatest connection to her father's passion for music. An aspiring pianist who forwent a concert career for banking, Yeisuke did all he could to encourage his eldest child to fulfill his own lost dream. At the prestigious Jiyū Gakuen (School of the Free Spirit), a progressive school for girls, as well as with home tutors, Yoko received rigorous musical training in German lieder singing, Italian opera, and classical piano. "My vocal training was like athletics," she recalls, "and I would fall asleep at night in terror that my hands were too small to meet my father's expectations."[14] Although she would later rebel against the formalism of her early education and reject her father's will, she regards these years as the foundation of her work as a composer and vocal artist. What Lennon called Yoko's "revolutionary...sixteen-track voice" is grounded in this foundation of classical training.[15]

Ono's aristocratic heritage may account for her natural ease in moving among all the arts—music, poetry, performance, and painting. Central to elite Japanese culture is the literati, or *bunjin,* ideal in which the practice of the "three perfections" of painting, poetry, and calligraphy and the "elegant pursuits" of music and the board game *go* are universally acknowledged as superior ways to refine the soul—life's loftiest goal. For Japanese literati, amateur delight was traditionally cultivated over professional gain, and spiritual content valued over technical proficiency. To move among and between art forms, seeking the higher self was the ideal. The close reach of that literati model combined with her later exposure to East Asian aesthetics in the context of Cagean thought and American conceptions of Zen may help explain the open range and essential poetics of Ono's art.

For most of Yoko's education while in Tokyo between the family's American sojourns (1933–37, 1941–42), she attended Keimei Gakuin, a Christian academy founded by the Mitsui family for children who had lived abroad, and later Gakushūin, or Peers' School. Gakushūin was exclusive to members and relatives of the imperial family and Japanese parliament until after the war, when the peerage and titles for all but the emperor and his immediate family were dissolved. When Ono entered in April 1946, her schoolmates included Hirohito's two sons, including the present emperor, Akihito; and Mishima Yukio, who later rose to international acclaim as a novelist and caused a sensation when he committed ritual *seppuku* in 1970 to protest Japan's aberrant Westernization.

In 1952, Ono was accepted as the first female student to enter the philosophy course at Gakushūin University. The euphoria of intellectual freedom that came with the collapse of Japan's totalitarian rule infused the high schools and universities across the country, as students felt themselves agents of the social and political reconstruction happening in their midst. Ono, who had been relatively sheltered from the ravages of World War II, was now affected by this postwar aftermath and the radical intellectual climate it fostered. While despair at the devastation of fifteen years of war created a postsurrender psyche of exhaustion, remorse, and despondency, an outpouring of relief, optimism, and liberation prevailed. Receptivity to new social, political, and cultural ideas created a spirit of freedom and openness unprecedented in modern Japanese society. As historian John W. Dower has written, "People were acutely conscious of the need to reinvent their own lives."[16]

As a student at Gakushūin during these heady years, Ono was affected by the dominant intellectual movements of Marxism and existentialism. Hundreds of new left-wing journals appeared that were at the forefront of cultural movements heralding change, denouncing militarists, landlords, *zaibatsu*, and the emperor-centered bureaucratic system. Pacifism replaced ultranationalism as the country's ideological faith. Leftists and progressive liberals, who had been active in prewar discourse but were later suppressed, reemerged to embrace the new ideals of democracy, respect for individuality, freedom of speech and religion, and the renunciation of war and the military. Modern selfhood and "autonomous subjectivity" were central to creating a new society where individuals could defend democracy and so prevent tyranny and dictatorship from arising ever again in Japan. Swept up by the fever, Ono was reading prerevolutionary Russian authors like Tolstoy, Gorky, Chekhov, and Dostoyevsky, and such modern philosophers as Gide, Malraux, Hegel, and Marx. Eventually, Ono too had to repudiate her past to participate in this postwar revolution—whose ideals surely influenced her leftist and antiwar politics of later years.

Besides Marxism, existentialism was the prevailing philosophy of Japan's postwar intelligentsia. The central philosophical problem in the writings of Kierkegaard, Heidegger, and Sartre that were so popular at the time was *being*—a state revealed by simple reflection on one's concrete existence in time and space. In the bleak wake of Hiroshima and Auschwitz, belief in the individual's power to affect the drastic scheme of history was slight. Existence—

FIGURE 1.4
ONO, CA. 1961

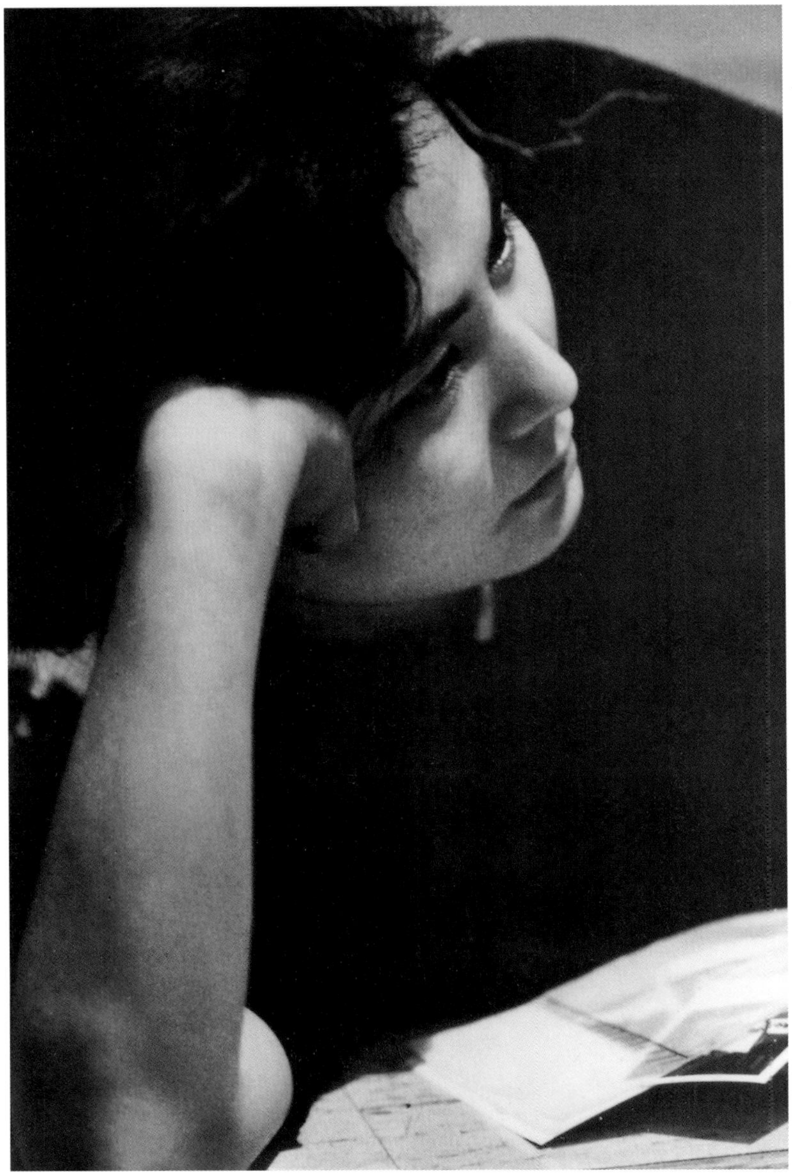

the basic facts of an individual's presence and participation in the world—was the sum of random choice, bracketed by vast nothingness on either side of birth and death. To writers like Dazai Osamu and Abe Kōbō who described Japan's postwar gestalt in such best-selling novels as *No Longer Human* and *The Woman in the Dunes*, existentialism provided a structure of both literary style and philosophical truth. Their ideas strongly appealed to the postwar Japanese avant-garde as it rose from the ashes of World War II, and provided the context for Ono as she began to distance herself from her family to articulate her own form of spiritual philosophy and creative activity. "My strength at that time was to separate myself from the Japanese pseudo-sophisticated bourgeoisie. I didn't want to be one of them. I was fiercely independent from an early age and created myself into an intellectual that gave me a separate position."[17]

Ono's choice of philosophy as a major at Gakushūin reveals what would become the artist's fundamental interest in the nature of reality, existence, and mind. So much of her work, as we shall see, engages these metaphysical questions on an immediate level—provoking, upending, mirroring our received notions so as to incite a new encounter with one's self and the nature of being. These encounters, which she called "events," are designed to break through banal reality to recover, in an often deceptively simple act, a moment of emptiness that she calls "wonderment." In her influential 1966 text, "To the Wesleyan People," Ono articulates her approach that draws on her early and abiding interest in both modern Western and Eastern metaphysical thought: "After unblocking one's mind, by dispensing with visual, auditory, and kinetic perceptions, what will come out of us? Would there be anything? I wonder. And my Events are mostly spent in wonderment."[18]

Ultimately, Yoko became disillusioned with academic philosophy at Gakushūin. In late 1952, after two semesters, she moved with her family to Scarsdale, New York, to join her father who had recently assumed the directorship of America's Bank of Tokyo's operations. She enrolled at Sarah Lawrence, a prestigious liberal arts college for women in nearby Bronxsville, where she focused on contemporary poetry and composition.

More and more at odds with her parents, whom she saw as artists who had failed to fulfill their talent in order to serve the cause of the "suffocating" Yasuda and Ono legacies, Yoko, either by resolve or impulse or both, determined to break away, to sunder her family's connection. The avant-garde, a world of ideas and possibilities, offered an escape at least to a conceptual freedom. In 1955, she dropped out of Sarah Lawrence, eloped with a young Japanese pianist and composer, Ichiyanagi Toshi, and moved to Manhattan. "The pressure of becoming a Yasuda/Ono was so tremendous—intellectual, social, academic, and bourgeois pressure. Unless I rebelled against it I wouldn't have survived."[19]

NEW YORK: ASIAN THOUGHT AND THE AVANT-GARDE

Yoko Ono arrived in New York when a convergence of East Asian aesthetics, poetry, and metaphysics and elements of Euro-American modernism were upending traditional art forms. Reacting against the heroics of Abstract Expressionism and the commercialism of high modernism, the new movements—Neo-Dada, Assemblage, Happenings, and Fluxus—championed anarcho-cultural sensibilities drawn from Dada, Western phenomenology and existen-

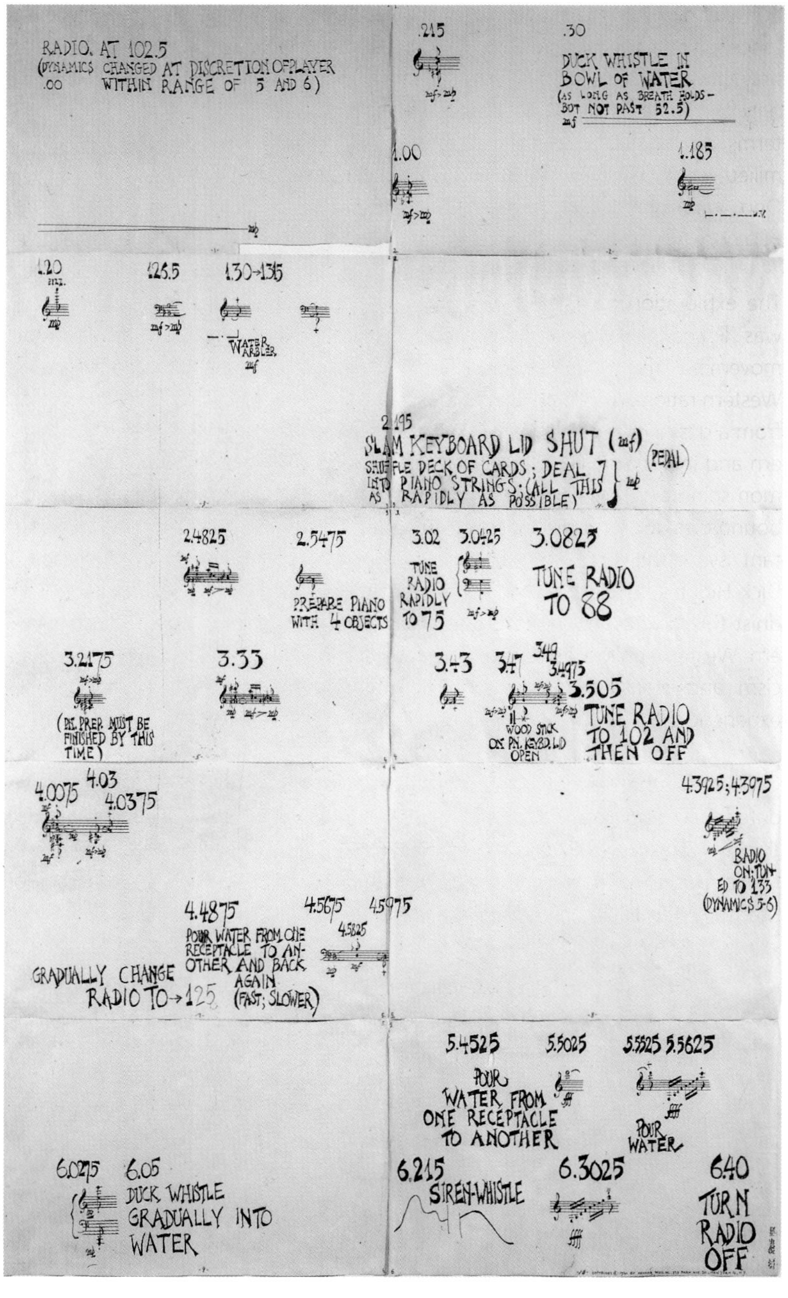

FIGURE 1.5
JOHN CAGE, *WATER MUSIC*, 1952. INK ON PAPER, 10 SHEETS, 11 X 17"; COLOPHON SHEET 9½ X 6". WHITNEY MUSEUM OF AMERICAN ART, NEW YORK; PURCHASE, WITH FUNDS FROM AN ANONYMOUS DONOR 82.38A-J. COURTESY OF THE JOHN CAGE TRUST

tialism, and notions of minimalism, indeterminacy, and everyday realism extracted from Buddhist thought. Loss of faith in "high modernism" and "progressive rationalism" spurred a subversive and philosophical interest in non-Western cultures—especially of China and Japan—to the extent that the 1963 *Fluxus Manifesto* summoned the vanguard to "Purge the World of 'Europanism'!"[20] They challenged the staid idealism of bourgeois (Western) culture and its corollary angst of subjective alienation. But the so-called "anti-art" movements were far from negative. Their affirmative subject was everyday life and its natural, often humorous, relation to art. Theirs was a cry to give art back to a social, rather than merely aesthetic, realm of meaning. Just as earlier manifestations of Dada and anti-art arose in Zürich in response to the cultural and moral blight wrought by World War I, when all that modernist progress had promised went severely wrong, so too the postwar avant-garde, emerging from the holocausts of World War II, renounced the abstractions of high art for the poetry of quotidian existence. Once again, concrete everyday being was the only universal a humanist could place any faith in—only this time, that universal was cast largely in terms of Asian philosophy and aesthetics. In this milieu, certain Japanese artists abroad, including Ono, were embraced and assimilated as mediums of a non-Western, antirationalist aesthetic.[21]

The exploration of Asian thought in American art was linked to a broad intellectual and cultural movement that sought alternatives to modern Western rationalism and utilitarianism. It also evolved from a desire to seek Jungian affinities among modern and indigenous cultures, to identify some common spirituality. "It's not simply the realization that boundaries don't count, but that in the most important issues there are no boundaries," Fluxus artist Dick Higgins later explained.[22] The aspects of Buddhist thought, especially Zen, that countered modern Western philosophies were its radical empiricism and embrace of spontaneous, unmediated experience.[23]

In America, the roots of this postwar engagement date to the early twentieth century, when the Asian thinkers Okakura Kakuzō (Tenshin), Ananda Coomaraswamy, and D. T. Suzuki first promoted an aesthetics of the East whose genius was—as Okakura wrote in *The Book of Tea* in 1906—"the adoration of the beautiful among the sordid facts of everyday existence."[24] The move in modern art, informed by Asian philosophy and championed by Vasily Kandinsky, from representation of the visible to an expression of "the inner spiritual side of nature," had an impact on American artists like Mark Tobey, John Graham, and Isamu Noguchi. In their articulation of spiritual content, these and other interwar and early postwar artists drew from contemporary writings on Daoism and Buddhism by such figures as Arthur Waley, R. H. Blyth, and Alan Watts. Several, including Tobey and Noguchi, traveled to Japan and China to study firsthand the distilled conceptual power of calligraphy, ink painting, rock gardens, *haiku*, and the art of tea. By the early 1950s, when D. T. Suzuki's lectures on Zen at Columbia University were the sensation of the New York art world, Asian art and thought was the preferred paradigm for much of the American avant-garde. The aspiration toward *satori*-like transcendence, which others found through drug experimentation, became central to the avant-garde imagination. From Happenings to the Beat generation and the San Francisco Renaissance poets, American Zen was ascendent. The Dao, Suzuki often explained, "is no more than one's everyday experience...when you begin to think, you miss the point."[25]

Suzuki's disciple John Cage was widely influential through creating and transmitting an alternative modernist aesthetic founded in Asian thought. His legendary 1952 composition of silence, *4'33"*, that tacitly turned the surrounding environmental sounds (of an increasingly restless audience) into music, demonstrated his revolutionary axiom, "let sounds be themselves." His experiments in chance and indeterminacy aspired to "imitate nature in her manner of operation" and reflected his interest in the *I Ching*, the Chinese book of divination.[26] Ambient, everyday, found sounds—such as those he scored for *Water Music*—made music of the ephemeral, accidental, and impersonal noises of modern life (fig. 1.5). Cage also dramatically privileged process and audience participation over the composer's "genius." These ideas resonated with Ono as she began to score her own work for music, events, and objects. "The essence of Zen that connected with Cage and all of us was a sense of laughter," Ono remarks. "Laughter is God's language."[27]

Ono first met Cage at one of Suzuki's lectures in the mid-1950s. Her friendship grew through her husband, Ichiyanagi Toshi, who was associated with Cage and would later emerge as one of Japan's preeminent electronic composers. Ichiyanagi had come to New York on a scholarship for the Juilliard School of Music. A precocious musician, he was trained in classical music but distinguished himself early as a composer of twelve-tone music in the tradition of Arnold Schönberg and Alban Berg. Electronic composition fascinated Ichiyanagi, who knew Edgard Varèse and was an early follower of Karlheinz Stockhausen. Ichiyanagi, an accomplished pianist and score-writer as well, was often commissioned to transcribe scores for an emerging group of avant-garde composers in New York and would occasionally perform in their concerts. By 1959, when Ichiyanagi attended John Cage's historic class in Experimental Composition at the New School for Social Research, he and Ono were regulars in the Cage circle, which included Morton Feldman, Richard Maxfield, David Tudor, Stefan Wolpe, and Merce Cunningham.

This early Fluxus period in New York saw artists developing a form of notation known as "event scores." Derived from Cage's codes of musical compositions, these terse instructions proposed mental and/or physical actions to be carried out by the reader/performer. These event scores were indebted as well to Marcel Duchamp, who in 1957 stated that the creative act could only be completed by the spectator. The early Fluxus scores were characterized by clarity and economy of language; to reinforce their status as art, artists often signed and dated them. They could be performed in the mind as a thought (their visualization being performative), or as a physical performance before an invited audience. The events described basic actions, such as George Brecht's score, "exit" (fig. 1.6), or could pose the reenactment of certain habits of daily life. Humor was an essential ingredient. Along with Brecht and the composer La Monte Young, Yoko Ono was among the first to experiment with the event score and its conceptual use of language as a form of art.

Ono's event scores evolved from a range of literary and metaphysical traditions that combined Duchampian poetics and irony with *haiku* and the Zen koan. Ono's instruction pieces, with their distilled conflation of image and word, epigrammatic structure, and frequent reference to nature (skies, clouds, water), recall *haiku*'s "quality of surreality" and "complex of multiple implications."[28] They convey wit, elegance, and profundity through irrational, often punning phrases intended to jolt the reader/viewer to a higher state of awareness. Contrary to the existentialist notions of nonsense and nothingness that reflect a subjectified, alienated, and pessimistic world of meaning, the Japanese literary and Duchampian views that Ono embraced share an affirmation of being and existence through a metaphysics of the everyday here and now.

The Zen koan offer another correspondence to Ono's event scores. These brief phrases—some a single character long and others such cryptic statements as "To turn a somersault on a needle's point"—are used as contemplative tools between master and disciple whose meaning, once grasped, leads to an experience of *satori* (enlightenment). In *Mystics and Zen Masters*, a classic American book on Zen well-known to the Fluxus circle, Thomas Merton writes: "The heart of the *kōan* is reached, its kernel is attained and tasted, when one breaks through into the heart of life as the ground of one's own consciousness."[29] His quote of the fourteenth-century master Bassui resonates with Ono's strategy:

> When your questioning goes deeper and deeper you will get no answer until finally you will reach a cul-de-sac, your thinking totally checked. You won't find anything within that can be called "I" or "Mind." But who is it that understands all this? Continue to probe more deeply yet and the mind that perceives there is nothing will vanish; you will no longer be aware of questioning but only of emptiness. When awareness of even emptiness disappears, you will realize that there is no Buddha outside Mind and no Mind outside Buddha. Now for the first time you will discover that when you do not hear with your ears you are truly hearing and when you do not see with your eyes you are really seeing Buddhas of the past, present and future. But don't cling to any of this, just experience it for yourself.

Some Fluxus scores feature banal and absurd elements of modern consumerism. Ono's work provokes contemplation on a different, even supernat-

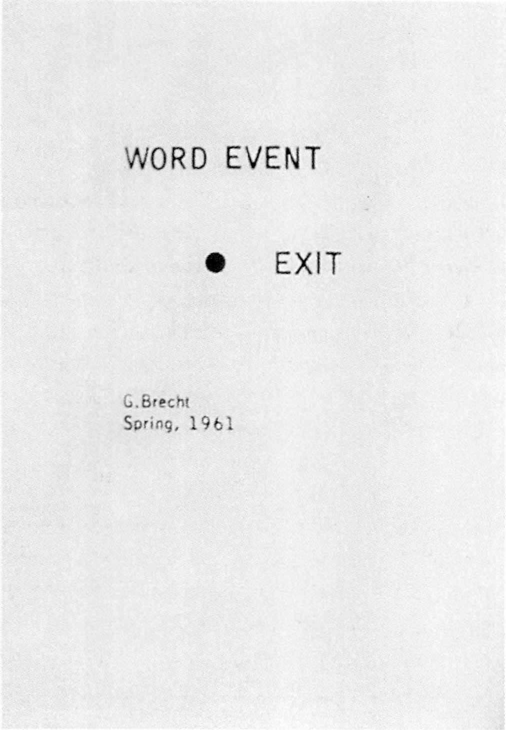

FIGURE 1.6
GEORGE BRECHT, ***WORD EVENT***, 1961. OFFSET ON PAPER

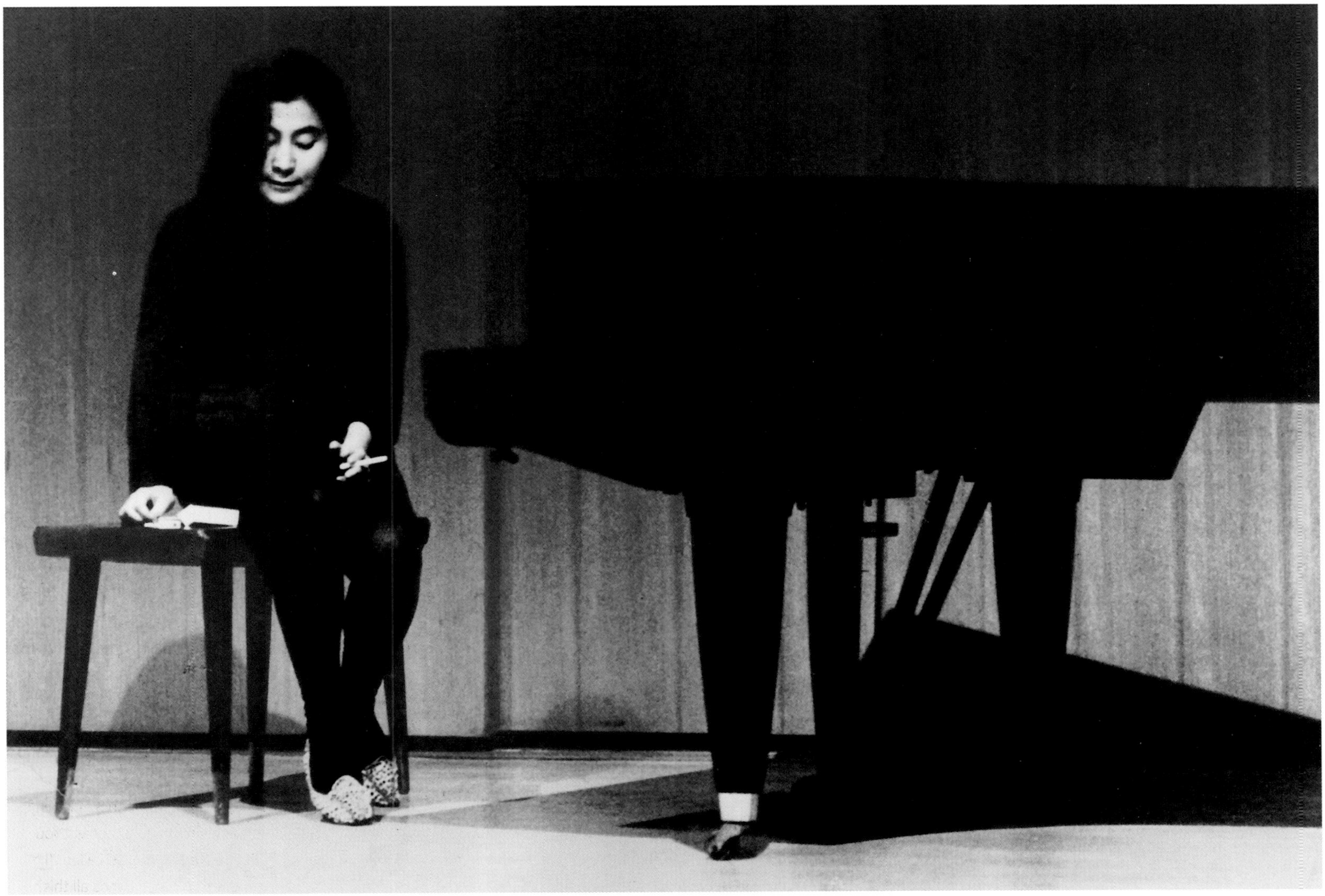

FIGURE 1.7
LIGHTING PIECE, 1955.
SŌGETSU ART CENTER,
TOKYO, 1962

ural, level of human existence. One of her earliest scores was composed in 1955 and performed in New York in 1961 and Tokyo in 1962 (fig. 1.7; no. 1):

> LIGHTING PIECE
>
> Light a match and watch till it goes out.
>
> 1955 autumn

In this and several of Ono's instruction pieces, she isolates a sensory act of everyday life to bring us in direct encounter with the self—what in Zen terms is "self-being." She calls events an "additional act," another dimension of art that provokes awareness of ourselves, our environment, our actions. In her 1966 work, *9 Concert Pieces for John Cage*, she scores *Breath Piece* with the simple instruction, "Breathe" and *Sweep Piece* with the instruction, "Sweep."[30] To Yoko, art is not a studio process but the process itself of living. It is experiental, sensual, and intuitive. In a critical definition of how her approach differs from Kaprow's Happenings, she wrote: "Art is not merely a duplication of life. To assimilate art in life, is different from art duplicating life."[31]

Unlike Brecht, who sometimes scored music for motor vehicles, train stations, and grocery deliveries, Ono's scores often suggest a realm of the wonderfully implausible and imaginary. At first glance, their conceptual aspect is less philosophical than wholeheartedly nonsensical in the tradition, say, of Lewis

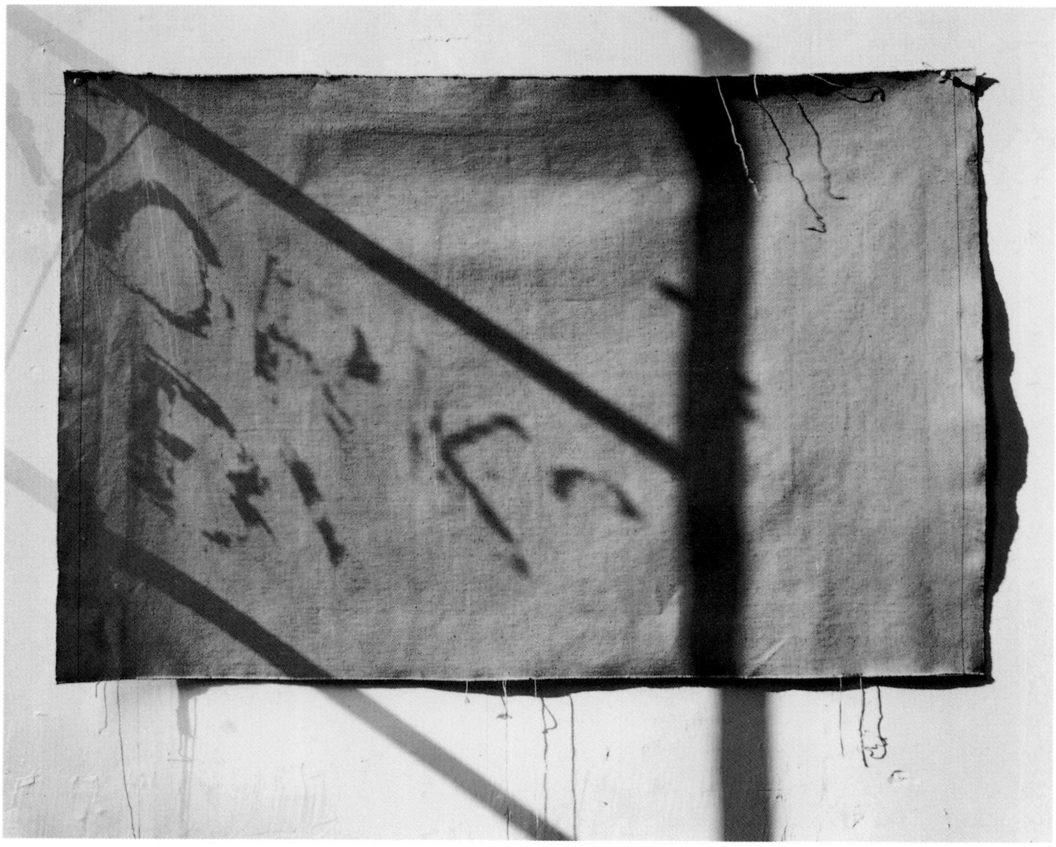

FIGURE 1.8
SHADOW PAINTING
(CANVAS VERSION),
1961. INSTALLATION
VIEW, AG GALLERY,
NEW YORK, 1961

Carroll. Yet Yoko uses humorous nonsense for serious intent. By tossing logic and all it represents away, she prompts us to create and experience a "mind-world."

> SUN PIECE
>
> Watch the sun until it becomes square.
>
> 1962 winter

To Ono, the mind-world is superior to the actual world that defines our "cluttered" lives because it goes "beyond time." Her more implausible instructions spring the reader/viewer from a state of complacency to a threshold of mental reflection:

> The mind is omnipresent, events in life never happen alone and history is forever increasing its volume. At this point, what art can offer (if it can at all—to me it seems) is an absence of complexity, a vacuum through which you are led to a state of complete relaxation of mind. After that you may return to the complexity of life again, it may not be the same, or it may be, or you may never return, but that is your problem.[32]

In *Grapefruit* (1964), Ono categorized her instruction pieces under sections marked Music, Painting, Event, Poetry, and Object (later editions included Dance and Film). Of these, the pieces for her Instruction Paintings are historically the most significant (nos. 2, 3). In 1960, Ono rented a cold-water loft at 112 Chambers Street and initiated a historic concert series that ran for seven months, through June 1961. Organized with La Monte Young, the "Chambers Street series" featured artists, musicians, dancers, and poets who were at the cutting edge of the new avant-gardism in American art. Together with Reuben Gallery where Kaprow's Happenings were first staged and the Judson Gallery, Ono's Chambers Street series is recognized as a historic forum for the development of the kind of radical new strategies and media that would define much of sixties art. The series attracted such legendary figures as Peggy Guggenheim and Marcel Duchamp, as well as George Maciunas, who soon drew many of the artists into his Fluxus collective. Ono presented some of the earliest versions of her pieces at Chambers Street. Later, in July 1961, she exhibited them under the title *Instruction Paintings* at Maciunas's AG Gallery on Madison Avenue.[33]

The radical element of Ono's Instruction Paintings is the concept that painting can be separated into two functions—instruction and realization. Unlike a finished Pollock or Johns, her *sumi*-ink canvases at AG Gallery required an action or an idea on the part of the viewer for their completion. Visitors were invited to walk on *Painting to Be Stepped On*, a torn piece of linen lying on the floor, and to drip water on *Waterdrop Painting* (figs. 6.3–4). *Shadow Painting*, a blank piece of linen hanging beside a window, was completed when shadows hit its surface in random and fleeting patterns (fig. 1.8). *Art News* critic Gene R. Swenson offered the following description of *Smoke Painting*, whose canvas viewers were asked to burn:

> Yoko Ono has made a "smoke painting." It consists of a grimy unstrung canvas with a hole in it. Into the hole she has stuck a burning candle, withdrawing it when the canvas began to smolder and smoke on its own. The painting's limited life was shortened by one minute for this report, its living presence snuffed out by a damp cloth as soon as the idea became clear.[34]

While Ono would soon renounce the canvas object, leaving the written instruction alone to stand in for "painting," her choice of *sumi* ink in these and related works shown at AG Gallery is significant (fig. 1.9). Revealing an abstract, calligraphic use of traditional ink on paper, these works are far from seductive exercises in Japanism. They relate instead to a move in modern East Asian calligraphy from a breakdown of the written character toward a total gestural abstraction—a metaphysics of the "dynamic movement of life."[35] Calligraphy's reductive form, minimal materiality, and essential expressionism appealed to Ono, who, like Korean-born artist Nam June Paik, injected action-based ink works into the Fluxus lexicon (fig 1.10).

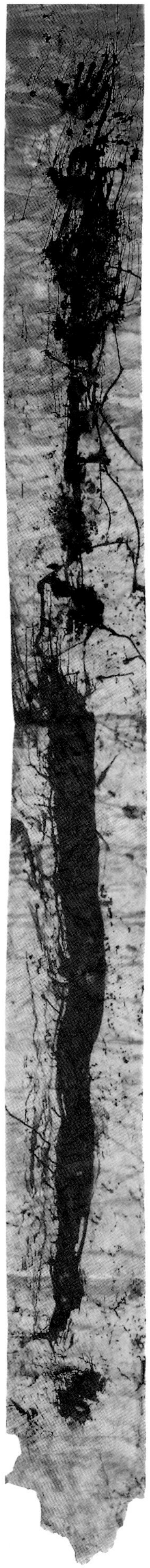

FIGURE 1.10
LA MONTE YOUNG, ***COMPOSITION 1960 #10***, OCTOBER 1960; REALIZED BY NAM JUNE PAIK AS ***ZEN FOR HEAD***, 1962. INK AND TOMATO JUICE ON TRANSPARENT PAPER. MUSEUM WIESBADEN

FIGURE 1.9
UNTITLED, CA. 1961.
SUMI INK ON CANVAS

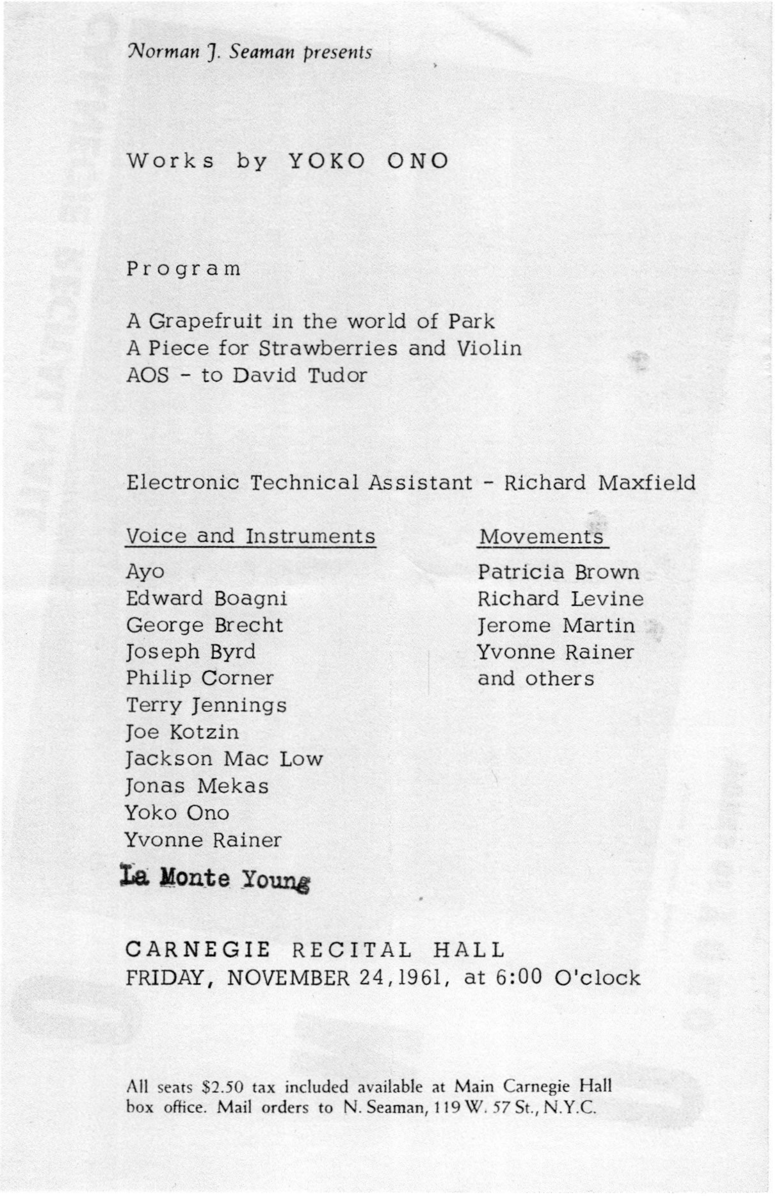

Norman J. Seaman presents

Works by YOKO ONO

Program

A Grapefruit in the world of Park
A Piece for Strawberries and Violin
AOS - to David Tudor

Electronic Technical Assistant - Richard Maxfield

Voice and Instruments	Movements
Ayo	Patricia Brown
Edward Boagni	Richard Levine
George Brecht	Jerome Martin
Joseph Byrd	Yvonne Rainer
Philip Corner	and others
Terry Jennings	
Joe Kotzin	
Jackson Mac Low	
Jonas Mekas	
Yoko Ono	
Yvonne Rainer	
La Monte Young	

CARNEGIE RECITAL HALL
FRIDAY, NOVEMBER 24, 1961, at 6:00 O'clock

All seats $2.50 tax included available at Main Carnegie Hall box office. Mail orders to N. Seaman, 119 W. 57 St., N.Y.C.

FIGURE 1.11
PROGRAM, ***WORKS BY YOKO ONO,*** CARNEGIE RECITAL HALL, NEW YORK, 1961

The significance of Ono's AG Gallery show in the history of Fluxus and Conceptual Art has only recently come to light. Along with her now-historic 1961 concerts at the Village Gate and Carnegie Recital Hall (fig. 1.11; no. 52), contemporary critics such as Jill Johnston of the *Village Voice* were "alternately stupefied and aroused"[36] by Ono's art. Nothing like it had ever existed before. Ono's radical strategies were at least five years ahead of the critical discourse on the "dematerialization of the art object" framed by Lucy Lippard, a discourse that defined "work in which the idea is paramount and the material form secondary, lightweight, ephemeral, cheap, unpretentious, and/or 'dematerialized.'"[37] In fact, Ono's early work in New York from 1960 until her departure for Tokyo in early 1962 gave realization to an aesthetic of "idea art" that became central to Maciunas's Fluxus movement, which he officially founded in the summer of 1961 and that opened the way for Conceptual Art practices of the mid-1960s.

Writing in 1966, Ono stated:

> "Idea" is what the artist gives, like a stone thrown into the water for ripples to be made. Idea is the air or sun, anybody can use it and fill themselves according to their own size and shape of his body.... Instruction painting makes it possible to explore the invisible, the world beyond the existing concept of time and space. And then sometimes later, the instructions themselves will disappear and be properly forgotten.[38]

TOKYO: "BLUE CHAOS" AND ONO'S CONCEPTUALISM

After a decade away, Yoko Ono returned to Japan in March 1962. Ichiyanagi, who had moved back to Tokyo in the fall, had arranged for her exhibition and concert at Sōgetsu Art Center, the center of avant-garde art and performance. Still separated from her family, Ono returned to Japan with her former privileges stripped. The city of wartime ruins she had left as a young college student had emerged, like a phoenix from ashes, as the world's first megalopolis—a sprawling industrial combine poised to host the summer Olympics of 1964. Politically, the idealism she remembered of her Gakushūin years had been sobered by the hardening cold war in Northeast Asia. Adoration of America as Japan's liberator and teacher of democracy had turned into mass protest against "Americanization"—encompassing the encroachments of Hollywood, nuclear threat, supermarkets, and prostitutes serving the American forces. Always working out the odds of her Japanese and American identity, Yoko personally found her years back "home" among her most isolated and difficult. But at age twenty-nine, in Tokyo, she saw her unique artistic vision come into full realization.

Ono arrived at an explosive moment in the Japanese avant-garde. Artists clamored to take art out of the art system, mixing genres and experimenting with language, street performance, and sound art to create an alternative expression rooted in the realities of everyday life rather than the conventions of high art. Anti-art collectives were staging events, concerts, and exhibitions that were euphoric in their abandonment of orthodox modernism and its reliance on traditional Western media and studio practices like oil painting.[39] Emerging like Fluxus in the cold aftermath of World War II, where the horrific consequences of modern rationalism were laid bare, the Japanese avant-garde reveled in anarchistic forms of art and performance to subvert, parody, and critique the political establishment. It took aim at Americanization, mass consumerism, and nuclear threat, and found solace in existentialism, absurdism, and the Buddhist void.

With assistance from Ichiyanagi, who was now a star in Tokyo's experimental music community, Ono's concerts and exhibitions gained attention among the underground mainstream of Tokyo's avant-garde. Music improvisationalists Kosugi Takehisa, Yasunao Tone, and Shigeko Kubota of Group Ongaku; experimental media artist Yamaguchi Katsuhiro; Hi Red Center's Akasegawa Genpei and Nakanishi Natsuyuki; the Butoh dancer Hijikata Tatsumi; and the influential critics Takiguchi Shūzō and Akiyama Kuniharu would all welcome Ono's activities. She participated in their events, including Hi Red Center's famous *Shelter Plan* (fig. 1.12) and Tone's conceptual jury and exhibition, *Tone-Prize Composition*, held in October 1964 (fig. 9.3).[40] Her work was reviewed in the leading art journals and discussed by top contemporary art critics like Tōno Yoshiaki. Together with her Fluxus friend, composer Nam June Paik, who was active in Tokyo around the same time, Ono introduced several members of Group Ongaku and Hi Red Center to the Fluxus collective, and so helped generate a critical exchange among the New York, Tokyo, and European avant-gardes all dedicated to forging a post-atomic art that found meaning in the essential irrationality of modern urban life.

Ono staged her first concert and exhibition, *Works of Yoko Ono*, at Tokyo's Sōgetsu Art Center in May 1962 (no. 27). The Events and Music sections presented sixteen individual pieces for the stage that featured recorded sounds of everyday noises like telephone rings, contact microphone sounds of people moving around on stage, and repetitive somatic actions like sweeping. Ono had performed some of the works previously in New York, such as *Of a Grapefruit in the World of Park* and *AOS—To David Tudor*—an opera of "blue chaos" (*ao* is Japanese for "blue," "os" is from "chaos") composed of a cacophony of recorded and live speeches in different languages. The Sōgetsu concert established Ono as among the most experimental composers and performers of the Fluxus/Cagean vanguard.

Concurrently on view at Sōgetsu were Ono's *Instructions for Paintings* (fig. 1.13; no. 3). This project, related to the AG Gallery exhibition, was based on a series of instructions for "paintings to be constructed in your head." Dismissing the tradition of art as an "original" expression by the hand of the artist, she asked Ichiyanagi to copy the instructions in his fine Japanese script on ordinary sheets of paper. For *Painting to Let the Evening Light Go Through*, the instructions required the viewer to hang a bottle behind a canvas "where the west light comes in. The painting will exist when the bottle creates a shadow on the canvas, or it does not have to exist" (no. 8). The idea that calligraphy made the written language into a visual object, like

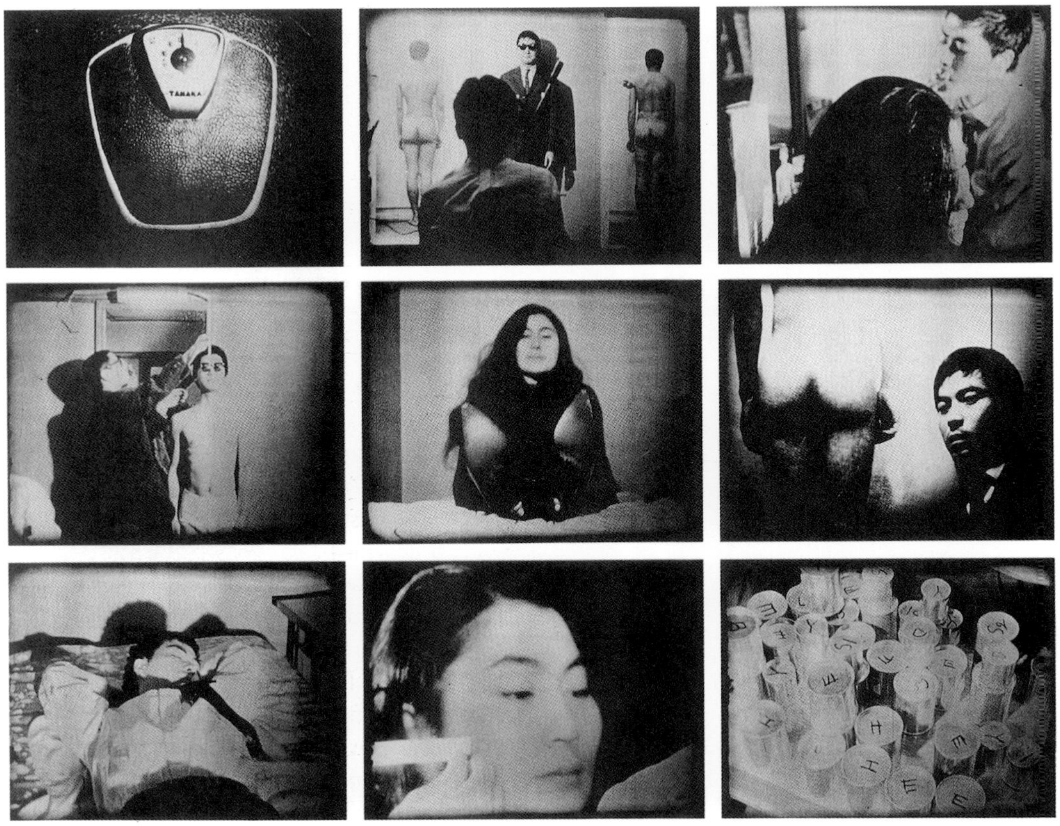

FIGURE 1.12
ONO PARTICIPATING IN HI RED CENTER'S ***SHELTER PLAN***. SELECTED FRAMES FROM JŌNOUCHI MOTOHARU, ***SHELTER PLAN***, VIDEO TRANSFERRED FROM 16MM FILM, 1964. MUSEUM OF CONTEMPORARY ART, TOKYO

a painting, may have reinforced the acceptance of Ono's instructions as objects of art. She then taped these sheets, some twenty-two, to the Sōgetsu gallery wall. With this gesture, Ono quietly overthrew the entire Western tradition of painting and its primacy of illusion and object over pure concept. As art historian Reiko Tomii has written:

> Yoko Ono revoked the self-sufficient body of the painting: not only was paint replaced by language, the structural syntax of the medium was also laid bare. Moreover, the role of the viewer was reconfigured as an active agent who completed the artwork either physically by her/his making it, or simply as a mental process.[41]

Although few critics recognized her innovation at the time, Ono's *Instructions for Paintings* are a watershed in the history of Conceptual Art. In Lucy Lippard and John Chandler's historic 1968 essay, "The Dematerialization of Art," the origins of Conceptualism are credited to those artists who had "almost entirely eliminated the visual-physical element" to forge an "ultra-conceptual or dematerialized art."[42] Although Ono is not mentioned, she was in fact among the first to do just that.

Instructions for Paintings share several formal elements of what later became canonized as "official" Conceptual Art. The acrylic-on-canvas paintings in New York–based Japanese artist On Kawara's *Today Series* (fig. 1.14), a serial accumulation of works that the artist has produced continuously since 1966, are significant for the elimination of all subject matter but the stark image of a stenciled date that corresponds to the day each was made. Like Ono, Kawara replaces visuality with language, creating a work that functions like a sign. Yet where Kawara's conceptualism lies in his reduction of art to an operation of infinite sameness—the dogged registration of time's relentless passing and the paradox of eternal time and relative existence—Ono's pen-on-paper instructions for "paintings to be constructed in your head" make all but the notation for a conceptual art vanish. In a move once again removed from the artist's hand, Ono made photocopies of the instructions Ichiyanagi had copied out and suggested they stand in for the "art" itself.[43]

Conceptualism, which gained recognition as an international movement in the mid-1960s, developed from a range of "art as idea" and "art as action" practices. Their common impulse was, as critic Benjamin Buchloh has termed it, a "withdrawal of visuality."[44] Rejecting expressionism and the hallowed aura of objecthood, it favored a philosophical, cog-

FIGURE 1.13
PAINTING TO SEE THE SKIES, 1962. INK ON PAPER. COLLECTION OF GILBERT AND LILA SILVERMAN, DETROIT

PAINTING TO SEE THE SKIES

Drill two holes into a canvas.
Hang it where you can see the sky.

(Change the place of hanging.
Try both the front and the rear
windows, to see if the skies are
different.)

1961 summer

—From *Grapefruit* (1964)

nitive process aimed at redefining the role of the object as a carrier of meaning. The proposal inherent in Conceptualism, as championed independently by Henry Flynt (a Fluxus artist who coined the term "concept art" in 1961), Sol LeWitt, and Joseph Kosuth, was to replace the traditional aesthetic experience with devices that reduced art to a linguistic definition or empirical structure. Spoken or written language, mathematics, numbering, documentary photography, and "analytic propositions" all entered the artistic realm. For example, Kosuth's *Meaning* from the series *Titled (Art as Idea as Idea)* presents a photostat of the dictionary definition of "meaning," making the material reality of the work the object of its pictorial depiction (fig. 1.15). "The absence of reality in art is exactly art's reality," Kosuth stated.[45]

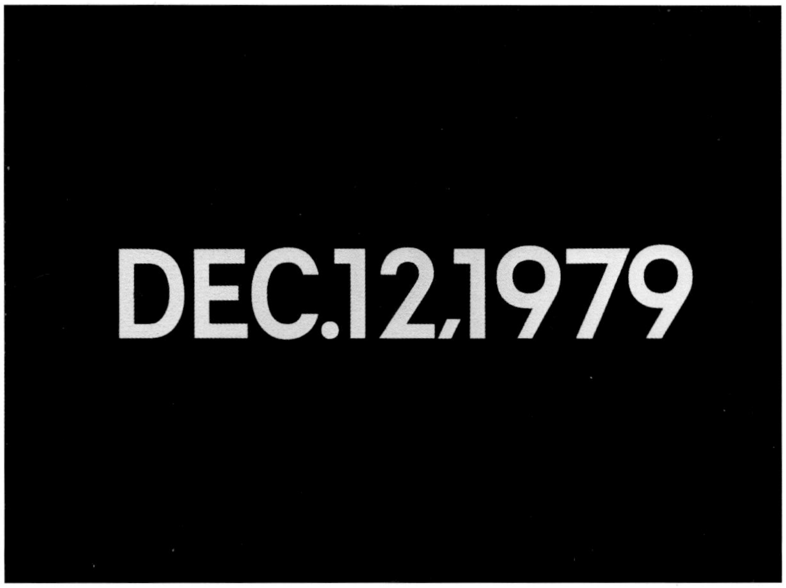

FIGURE 1.14
ON KAWARA, ***WEDNESDAY, DEC. 12, 1979***, 1979. SYNTHETIC POLYMER PAINT ON CANVAS, 18¼ X 24⅝" (46.4 X 62.5 CM). THE MUSEUM OF MODERN ART, NEW YORK. BLANCHETTE ROCKEFELLER FUND. PHOTOGRAPH © 2000 THE MUSEUM OF MODERN ART, NEW YORK

In North America, Conceptual artists commonly employed language, nonsense, participation, and minimalism to serve a theoretical end—to critique the art system and the definition of art itself. Yoko Ono used identical means to probe different, more metaphysical issues: the nature of being or, in the words of critic Miyakawa Atsushi, "to posit the mirror as a primary form of the imaginary...going beyond genres and categories to include all art and thought."[46] Where LeWitt and Kosuth presented philosophical discourse as art, often conflating the manifesto, the theoretical proposal, and the artwork into a single interlocking system, Ono's less-weighty philosophical theorems were structurally more provocative than didactic, more open than tautological. She used language but language itself was not her concern; experience was. While artists like Hans Haacke became increasingly devoted to the statistical collection of factual information and refused any transcendental dimension to their work, Ono sought the opposite: the imaginary *was* her empirical truth. Her proto-Conceptual work of the early 1960s expresses a growing commitment to art as a "ritual" for experiencing truth that resides only in a "fabricated" or conceptual realm of consciousness. In a remarkable essay published in a Japanese art journal in 1962, she writes:

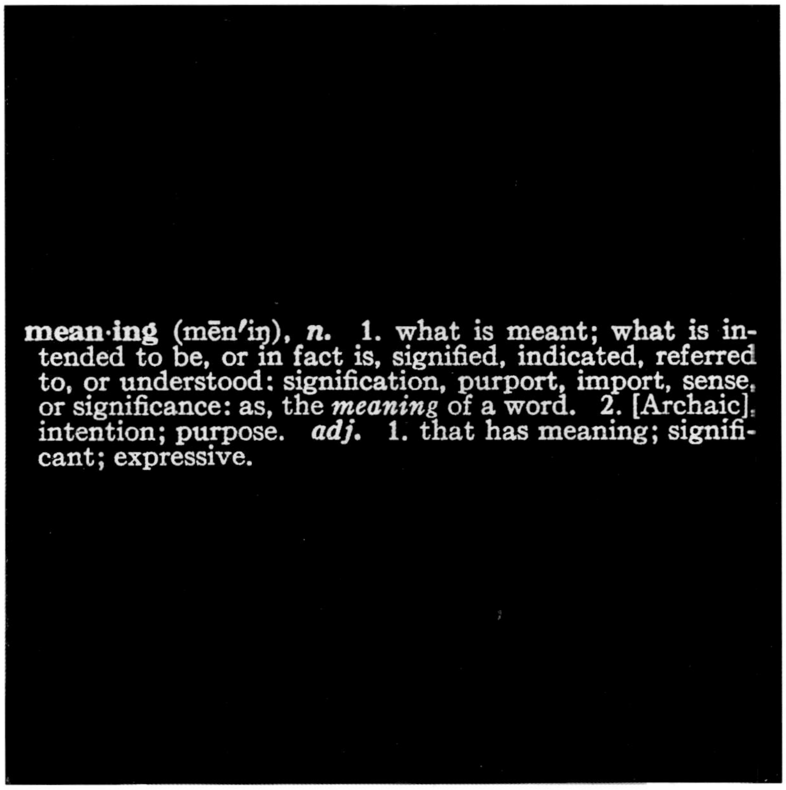

FIGURE 1.15
JOSEPH KOSUTH, ***MEANING***, CA. 1967. PHOTOSTAT ON PAPER MOUNTED ON WOOD. THE MENIL COLLECTION, HOUSTON

> I cannot stand the fact that everything is the accumulation of "distortion" owing to one's slanted view. I want the truth. I want to feel the truth by any possible means. I want someone or something to let me feel it. I can[not] trust the...manipulation of my consciousness. I know no other way but to present the structure of a drama which assumes fiction as fiction, that is, as fabricated truth.[47]

In October of 1962, Ichiyanagi arranged through Sōgestu Art Center for John Cage and David Tudor to visit Japan and perform several concerts. Ono participated in these programs, appearing in Cage's premiere performances of *Music Walk* and *Arias for*

Solo Piano with Fontana Mix. Increasingly, however, Ono felt limited by her associations with her famous husband and "Jesus Christ," as John Cage was known to his followers. "The whole avant-garde world seemed bourgeois to me," she reflected. "Who was I beyond Toshi's wife and John Cage's friend?"[48] The burden of once again being recognized as an Ono/Yasuda in Japanese society was also debilitating. Exhausted and depressed, she checked into a sanatorium in Tokyo. When she emerged several months later, her affections had shifted to a young American artist, Anthony Cox, whose daughter, Kyoko, she bore in 1963.

During this period, Ono compiled her instructions, scores, and poems for the publication of *Grapefruit* (no. 4). "*Grapefruit* was like a cure for myself without knowing it," Yoko reflected. "It was like saying, 'Please accept me. I am mad.' Those instructions are like that—a real need to do something to act out your madness. As long as you are behaving properly, you don't realize your madness and you go crazy."[49] But Ono's relationship to Conceptualism is hardly that of an Outsider artist. Like *An Anthology* (1963), edited by La Monte Young, *Grapefruit* is a seminal text in the history of Conceptual Art. As critic David Bourdon has stated,

> *Grapefruit* is one of the monuments of conceptual art of the early 1960s. She has a lyrical, poetic dimension that sets her apart from the other conceptual artists. Her approach to art was only made acceptable when white men like Kosuth and Weiner came in and did virtually the same things as Yoko, but made them respectable and collectible.[50]

Cox strongly believed in Yoko's art, and over the next four years helped produce and promote her activities in Tokyo, New York, and London. During their remaining time in Japan, Ono staged several events, including an all-night "touch" concert at the Zen temple Nanzenji in Kyoto (no. 29); her premiere performance of *Cut Piece* (no. 30); an exhibition at the vanguard Naiqua Gallery where she first presented *Fly* (no. 28); and a farewell concert at Sōgetsu in August 1964 entitled *Strip Tease Show*.

One of Ono's last events in Japan was *Morning Piece*. For this work, she assembled shards from broken milk bottles and tagged each with a random future morning date, like February 3, 1989 (fig. 1.16). In an amusing assault on the commercial art system, a strategy that would become central to formal Conceptualist politics, Yoko organized two events—one at Naiqua Gallery and the second on her Tokyo apartment rooftop—where she proposed to sell her collection of mornings. She composed a sales list and carefully documented her sales, all to luminaries of the Tokyo avant-garde (fig. 1.17). This event, which she restaged in New York the follow-

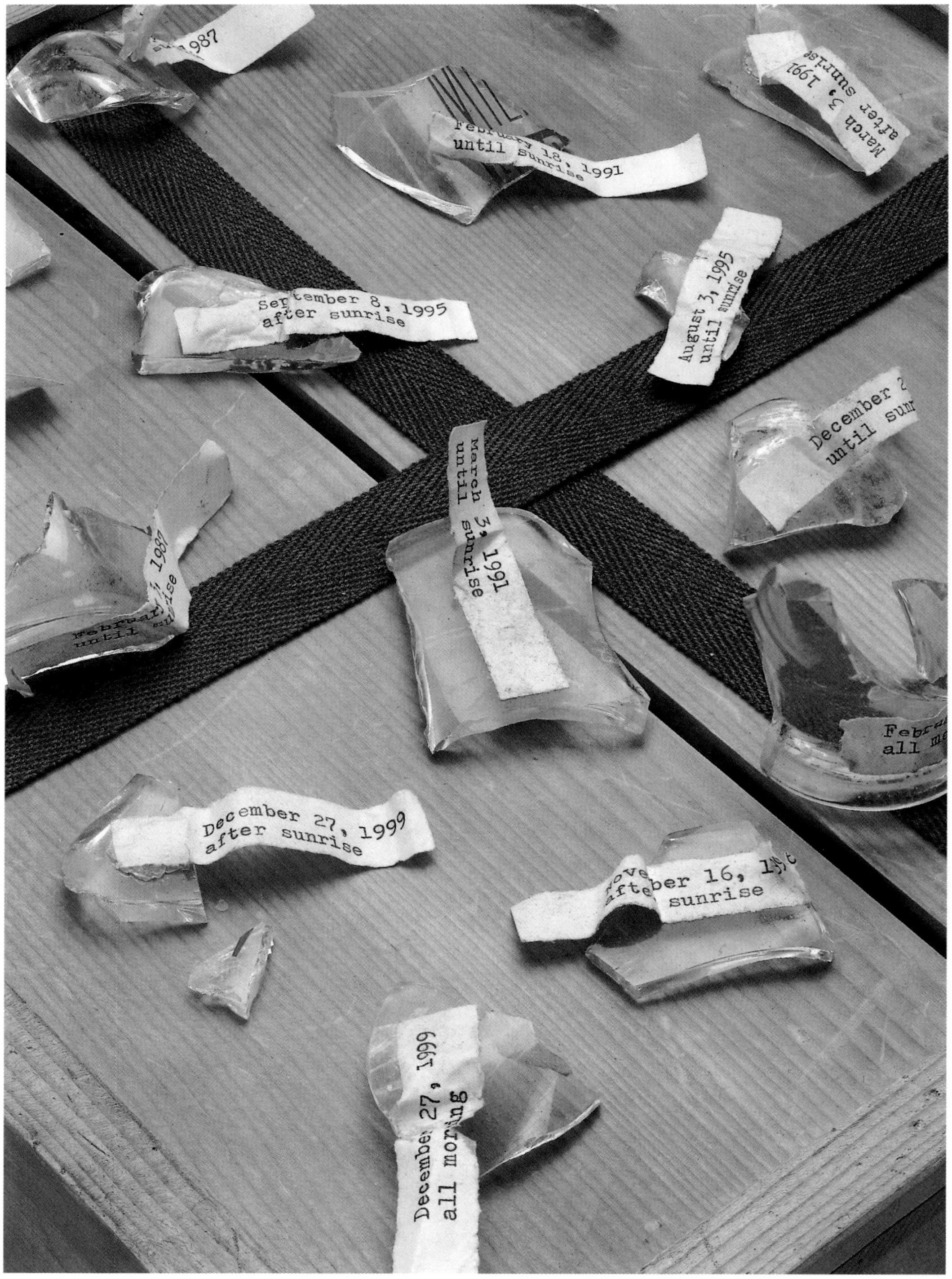

FIGURE 1.16
MORNING PIECE, 1964.
GLASS AND TYPESCRIPT
ON PAPER

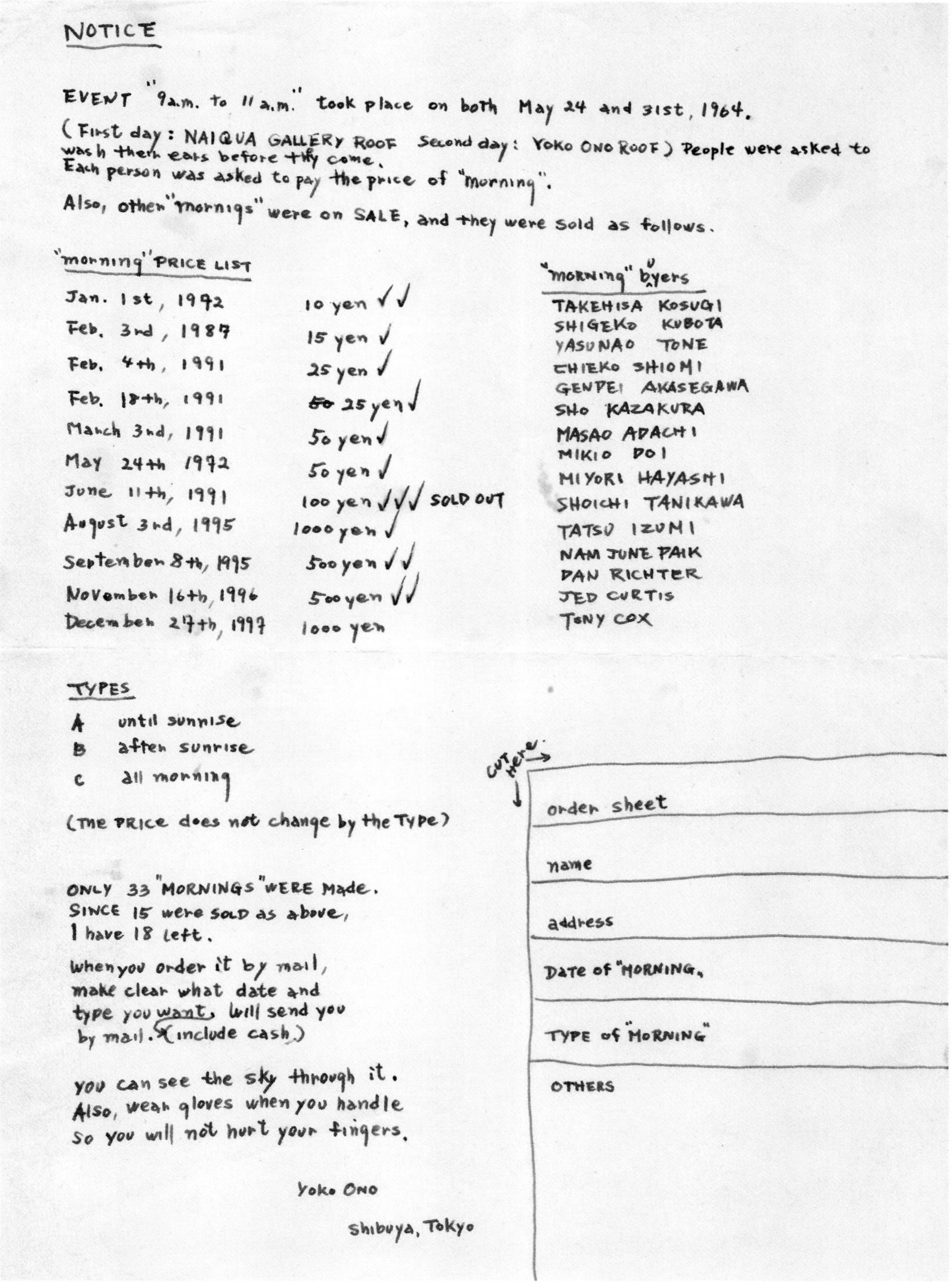
NOTICE

EVENT "9 a.m. to 11 a.m." took place on both May 24 and 31st, 1964.
(First day: NAIQUA GALLERY ROOF Second day: YOKO ONO ROOF) People were asked to wash their ears before they come.
Each person was asked to pay the price of "morning".
Also, other "mornings" were on SALE, and they were sold as follows.

"morning" PRICE LIST		"morning" byers
Jan. 1st, 1992	10 yen ✓✓	TAKEHISA KOSUGI
Feb. 3rd, 1987	15 yen ✓	SHIGEKO KUBOTA
Feb. 4th, 1991	25 yen ✓	YASUNAO TONE
Feb. 18th, 1991	~~50~~ 25 yen ✓	CHIEKO SHIOMI
March 3rd, 1991	50 yen ✓	GENPEI AKASEGAWA
May 24th 1992	50 yen ✓	SHO KAZAKURA
June 11th, 1991	100 yen ✓✓✓ SOLD OUT	MASAO ADACHI
August 3rd, 1995	1000 yen ✓	MIKIO DOI
September 8th, 1995	500 yen ✓✓	MIYORI HAYASHI
November 16th, 1996	500 yen ✓✓	SHOICHI TANIKAWA
December 27th, 1997	1000 yen	TATSU IZUMI
		NAM JUNE PAIK
		DAN RICHTER
		JED CURTIS
		TONY COX

TYPES
A until sunrise
B after sunrise
C all morning
(THE PRICE does not change by the TYPE)

ONLY 33 "MORNINGS" WERE Made.
SINCE 15 were SOLD as above,
I have 18 left.
When you order it by mail,
make clear what date and
type you want, will send you
by mail. (include cash)

You can see the sky through it.
Also, wear gloves when you handle
so you will not hurt your fingers.

Yoko Ono
Shibuya, Tokyo

cut here

order sheet
name
address
DATE of "MORNING"
TYPE of "MORNING"
OTHERS

FIGURE 1.17
"NOTICE" FOR
MORNING PIECE, 1964.
INK ON PAPER

ing year, fused a unique combination of elements that marked Ono's suprasensible, metaphysical conceptualism. *Morning Piece* functions like a flash of insight, bringing physical awareness of eternal time to the present moment of our existence, through a spontaneous exchange of art on a Tokyo rooftop. Yoko explained:

> Event, to me, is not an assimilation of all the other arts as Happening seems to be, but an extrication from the various sensory perceptions. It is not "a get togetherness" as most happenings are, but a dealing with oneself. Also, it has no script as happenings do, though it has something that starts it moving—the closest word for it may be a "wish" or "hope."[51]

LONDON: DOUBLE FANTASY

During Yoko's two-year stay in Japan, the Fluxus collective had become increasingly active in New York and Europe and was gaining a following among the international vanguard. Ono's Tokyo activities were known to the Fluxus group, and when she returned to Manhattan in fall 1964, impresarios George Maciunas, Norman Seaman, and Charlotte Moorman were quick to claim her for their Fluxus or Fluxus-like programs of concerts, festivals, and publication projects. Together with Cox, to whom she was now married, Ono presented several events, performances, and her first conceptual films at such legendary venues as the Judson Gallery and Judson Memorial Church, Carnegie Recital Hall, and Cinematheque at East End Theater from early 1965 until her departure for London in September 1966. During this period, the anarchist sensibility of Fluxus imposed by Maciunas became increasingly radical and absurdist as the celebrated "affluent society" erupted in political crises: the Bay of Pigs, the Cuban missile crisis, the assassination of John F. Kennedy, campus turmoil, racial unrest, and rising protests against the Vietnam War. This milieu, combined with the violent antinuclear turbulence she had witnessed in Japan, stimulated in Ono a deeper commitment to art as an agent of social and political change. From her notorious film *No. 4 (Bottoms)* (1966; no. 43), which she conceived in part as a "petition for peace," and throughout her years with John Lennon, with whom she collaborated on numerous public antiwar "happenings," Ono developed what performance historian Kristine Stiles has called "a utopian social program of love envisioned in the imagination and enacted before the world."[52] When she pronounced in 1969 that the "message is the medium," the message she implied was world pacifism realized through feminine thought and culture (Anthology 1).

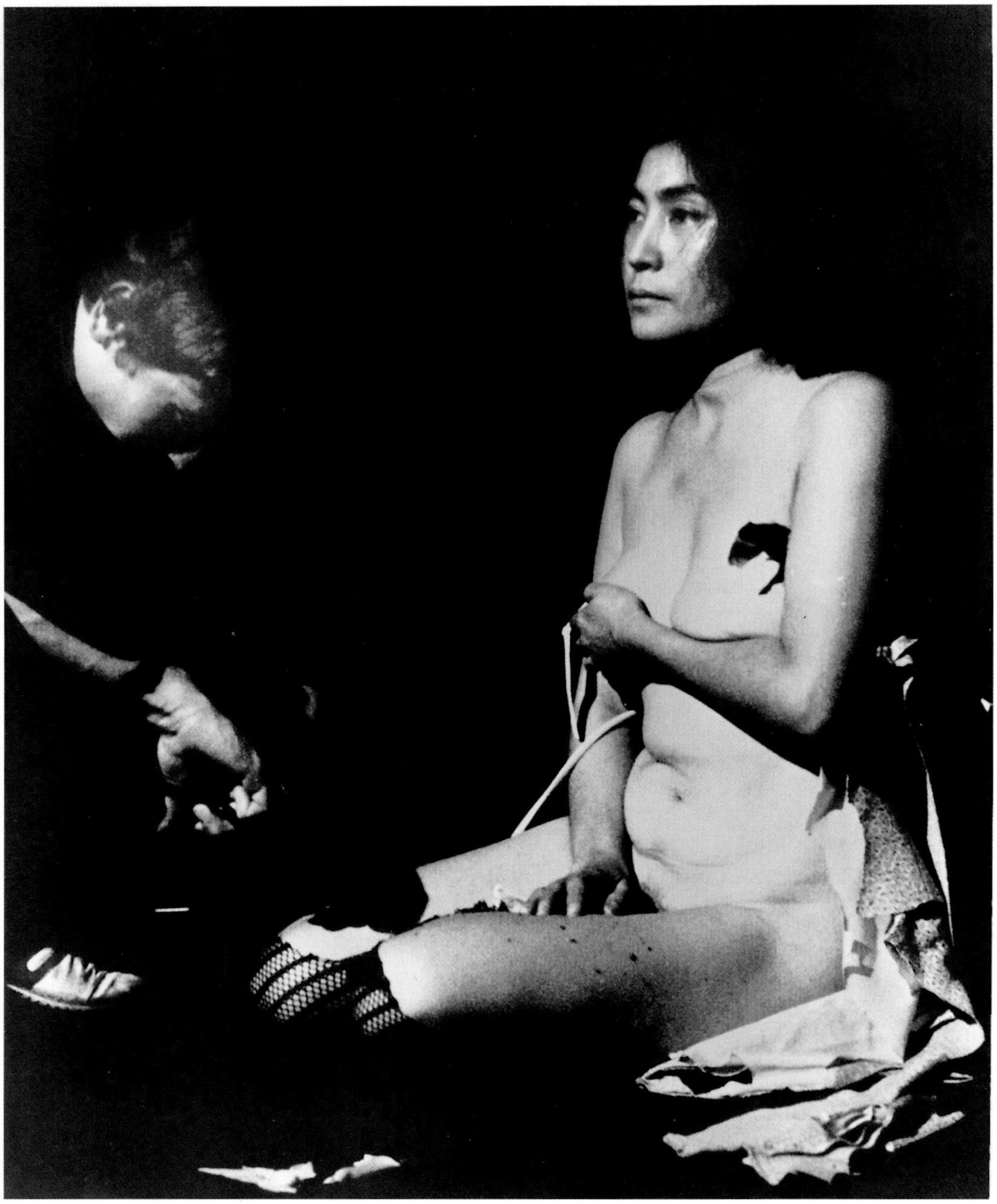

FIGURE 1.18
CUT PIECE, AFRICA
CENTER, LONDON, 1966

The site for Ono's new forms of social art was London. In what proved to be a prophetic trip, she and Cox traveled to London to take part in the *Destruction in Art Symposium (DIAS)*, an international gathering of artists whose work was linked by violent anti-art tendencies (no. 33). At *DIAS*, Ono performed *Cut Piece* (fig. 1.18), a work that has gained iconic stature in the history of performance art for its protofeminist conceptualism. In London, as in Kyoto, Tokyo, and New York, where she had previously presented this work, Ono sat motionless on stage in traditional Japanese feminine position—knees folded beneath her—and invited members of the audience to cut a piece of her clothing away until, nearly forty minutes later, she was left all but naked, her face masklike throughout. In her biographical statement of 1966, Yoko wrote:

> People went on cutting the parts they do not like of me finally there was only the stone remained of me that was in me but they were still not satisfied and wanted to know what it's like in the stone.[53]

Like many of her performances, *Cut Piece* is constructed around the phenomenological content of solitary actions, a concentration on the material of experience. What emerges in Ono's work through this piece, however, is a new level of psychological unveiling, an intimate and painful sensation of self that the public can encounter, watch, and feel. *Cut Piece* expresses an anguished interiority while offering a social commentary on the quiet violence that binds individuals and society, the self and gender, alienation and connectedness. The filmmaker Jonas Mekas, a longtime Fluxus friend, later commented that Yoko

> was very concentrated, very in herself, focused and intense. There was clearly something in her that had to come out, and in her performances she created explosions and moments of hysteria that were highly calculated and controlled.[54]

Invocations of the human body had for some time established Ono's language as essentially more sensuous and psychological than that of her Fluxus mates. References to touching, rubbing, hiding, sleeping, dreaming, and screaming sited her imagery in a protofeminist space defined by the terror, and the wish, to connect. She later commented that she wanted her participants to "start to see things beyond the shapes...[to] hear the kind of sounds that you hear in silence...to feel the environment and tension in people's vibrations...the sound of fear and of darkness...[and] of togetherness based on alienation."[55]

Ono's concentration on physicality, the concreteness of personal experience, shaped her ideas for film projects as well as her performances. She was part of the general revolt against film conventions that occurred during the 1960s, when independent filmmakers developed alternative aesthetics that directly acknowledged the material properties of film and the artifice of the production process. Cinematic time was also radically reconceptualized, as in Andy Warhol's *Eat* of 1963, a forty-minute narrative of Robert Indiana eating a single mushroom. Ono, who produced sixteen films between 1966 and 1982, shares several formal and stylistic issues with the independent film movement but is distinguished for her use of film to record, in real time, the very quality of physical being unattached to action, character, or even a face. Films such as *No. 4 (Bottoms)* (no. 43) and *Fly* (fig. 1.19; no. 46) present

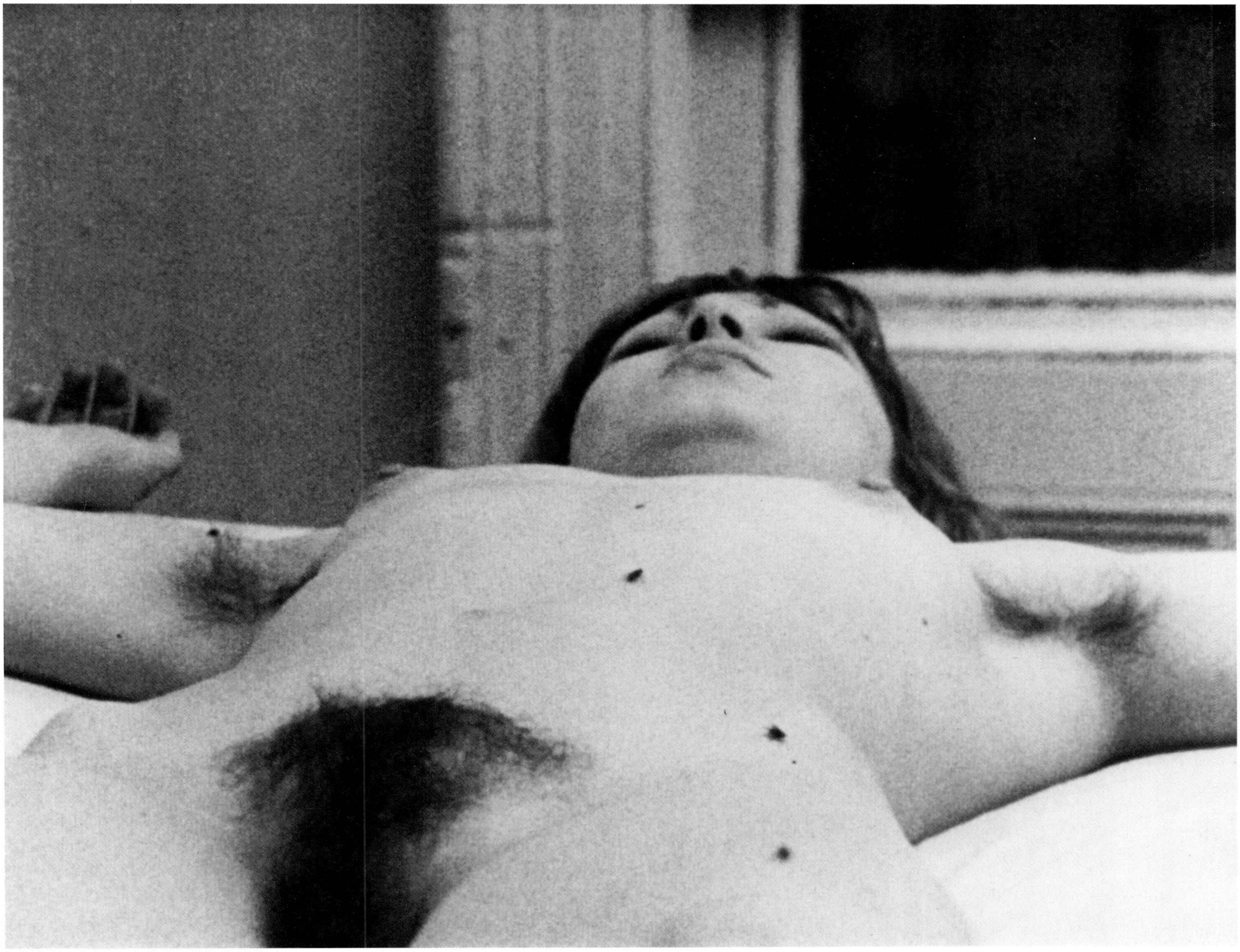

FIGURE 1.19
FRAME FROM ***FLY***,
FILM, 1970

cropped, single-image compositions of naked human forms, abstracted via cinematography into a realm of uncompromising—if strangely humorous and nonsexual—intimacy.

Fly, which magnifies the movements of houseflies as they traverse the naked body of a recumbent woman, is accompanied by a soundtrack (later issued on Ono's album of the same name). Yoko's voice suggests the unconscious, otherworldly life of the woman's knocked-out state, a life that is oblivious to yet omnipresent in the activities that occupy the flies in search of the sugared water that her flesh has been prepared with for their delectation. Ono's legendary vocal soundtrack is a continuous rhythm of the organic sounds of elemental womanhood—from the whimpers and groans of rapture to the cries of deep dread. Jonathan Cott wrote in *Rolling Stone* that Yoko's voice reminds "you of the screams, wails, laughter, groans, caterwauls of both a primordial, prebirth, premammalian past, as well as the fogged-over, pained immediacy of childhood." Her music evokes, he continues, "the feeling of being inside one's own body cavities."[56]

Yoko met John Lennon at her exhibition at the Indica Gallery in November 1966—while Beatlemania was still in force (fig. 1.20). The gallery, then in Mason's Yard near St. James's Piccadilly and housed in the same building as the British underground newspaper *International Times*, was a center of London's avant-garde art community. Lennon attended the opening and engaged Yoko, unaware and unimpressed by who he was, in her own game of

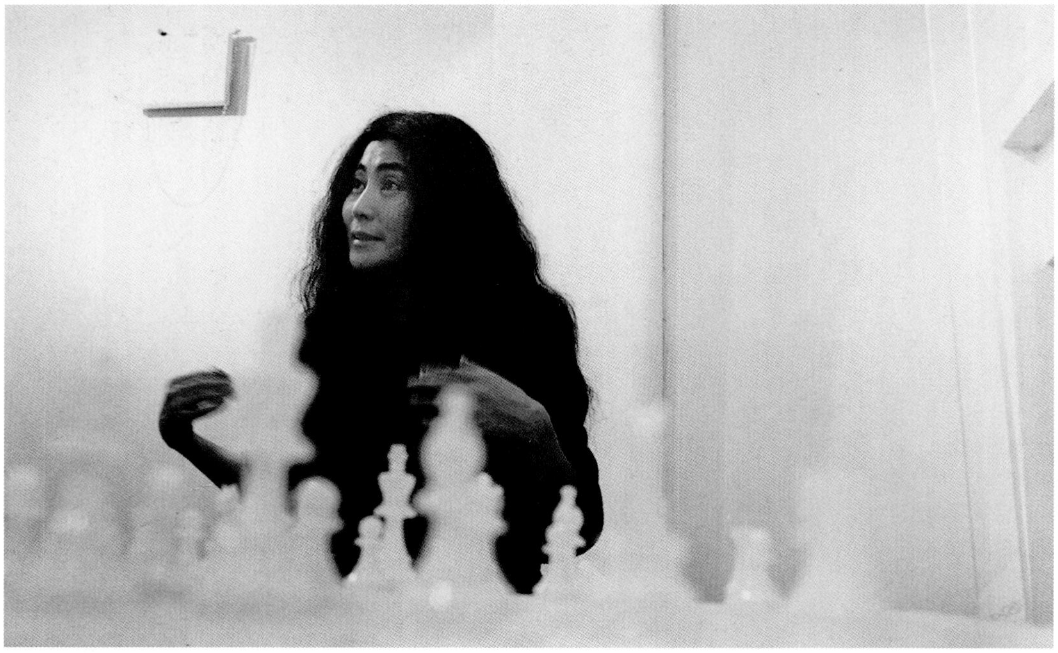

FIGURE 1.20
ONO WITH ***WHITE CHESS SET***, INDICA GALLERY, LONDON, 1966

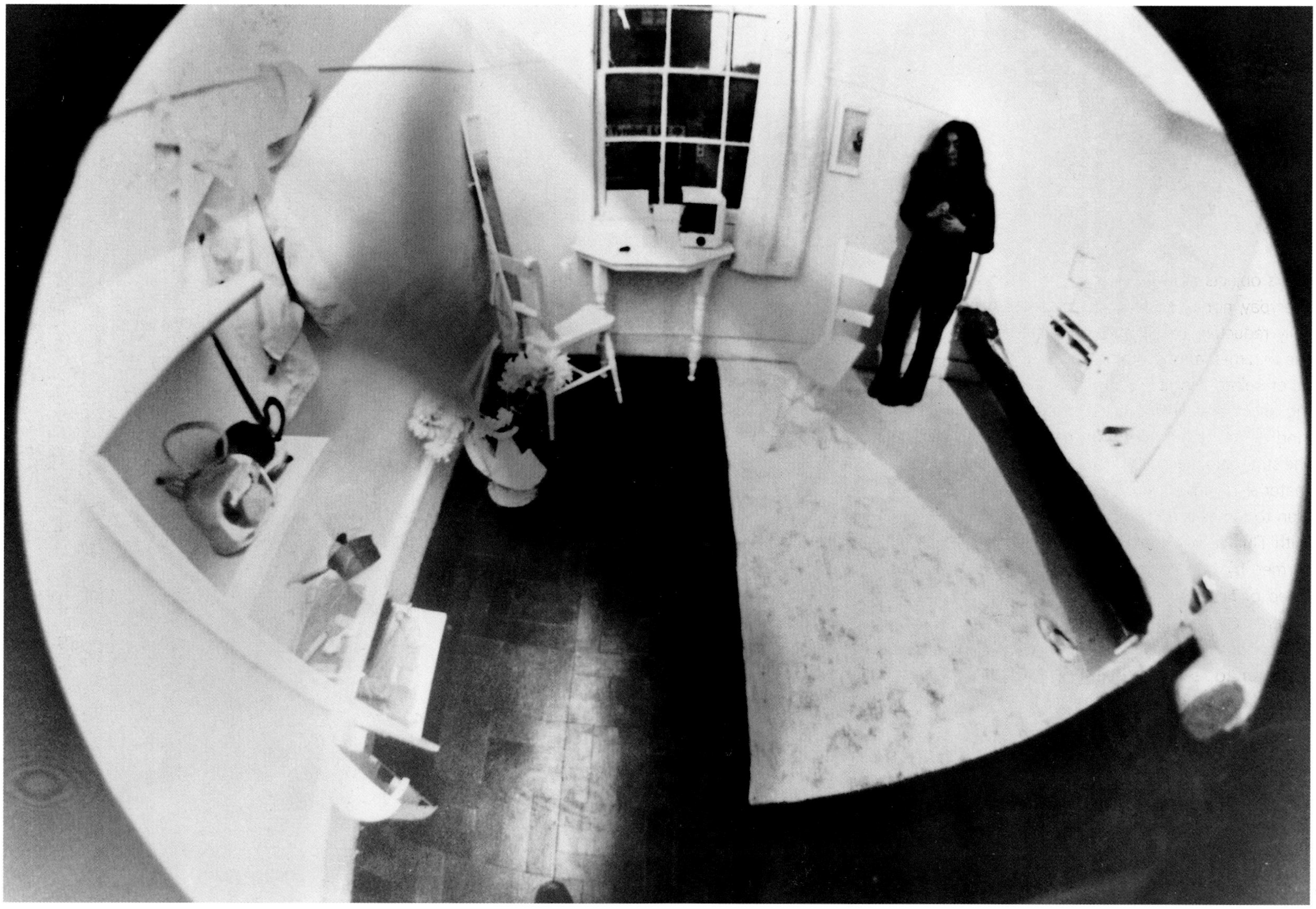

FIGURE 1.21
ONO IN ***HALF-A-ROOM***, LISSON GALLERY, LONDON, 1967

participation art by asking to follow the instruction for *Painting to Hammer a Nail* (no. 9). Yoko responded that he could hammer a nail in the painting for five shillings, and John quipped back, "I'll give you an imaginary five shillings and hammer an imaginary nail in." John often recounted, "And that's when we really met. That's when we locked eyes and she got it and I got it and, as they say in all the interviews we do, the rest is history."[57]

Yoko's exhibition at Indica was her most ambitious to date. It included versions or reenactments of her Instruction Paintings, and featured several objects that were realizations of earlier instruction pieces or new concepts altogether. Whereas her earlier Sōgetsu show of *Instructions for Paintings* was composed entirely of language, the Indica show with its all-white or transparent installation of fabricated Plexiglas and found or prepared objects presented Ono as a Minimalist sculptor. Works such as *Pointedness* (no. 12) and *Forget It* (no. 16) used readymade things—a white sphere and a sewing needle, respectively—attached on Plexiglas pedestals inscribed with their titles and instructions. *White Chess Set* (no. 25) presented Ono's first all-white chessboard and men. These objects established the visual form and style of Ono's objects and installations that she would present at London's Lisson Gallery in 1967 (fig. 1.21), the Everson Museum in 1971 (fig. 1.22), and the Whitney Museum of American Art in 1989 (pl. 59).

Ono's objects that are recycled and fabricated from everyday, nonart materials, and whose form is radically reductive, share certain formal elements with the Minimalism of sculptors Carl Andre, Mel Bochner, or Robert Morris. But her persistence in juxtaposing an idea against a visual situation to provoke a kind of telepathic poetry of irrational truths defies the strict Minimalist code of phenomenology, where material stands in for content. Her work is more akin to James Lee Byars, an artist loosely associated with Fluxus, who spent many years in Japan. Informed by a Zen poetics, Byars's work such as *The Head of Plato* (fig. 1.23), which presents a marble sphere in a glass vitrine, provokes a heightened focus on what is always potentially present if only we can learn to see it: thought. Like Byars's, Ono's minimalism does not reduce but rather increases the suggestive powers of her votivelike objects.

John and Yoko were married in March 1969 (fig. 1.24). They had already released a joint album, *Unfinished Music No. 1: Two Virgins* (no. 53), which caused a sensation over their nude double portrait on the jacket, and had collaborated as artistic partners in various peace events including *Bag Piece* at Royal Albert Hall (no. 31). In a gesture credited to Yoko, they exploited the media surrounding their marriage to campaign for peace. It was the height of the Vietnam War and America, Europe, and

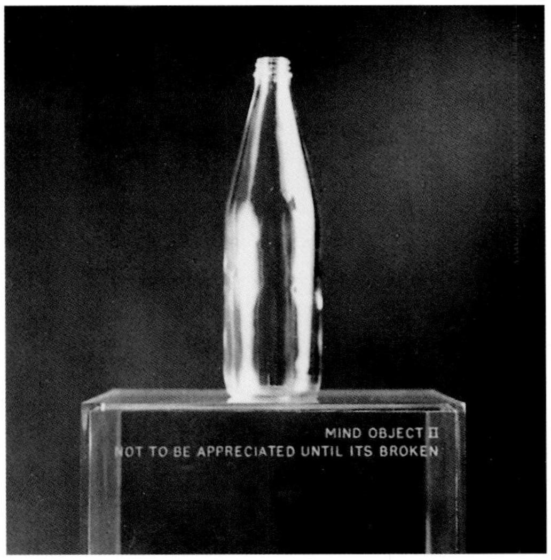

FIGURE 1.22
MIND OBJECT II WITH INSCRIPTION: NOT TO BE APPRECIATED UNTIL ITS BROKEN.

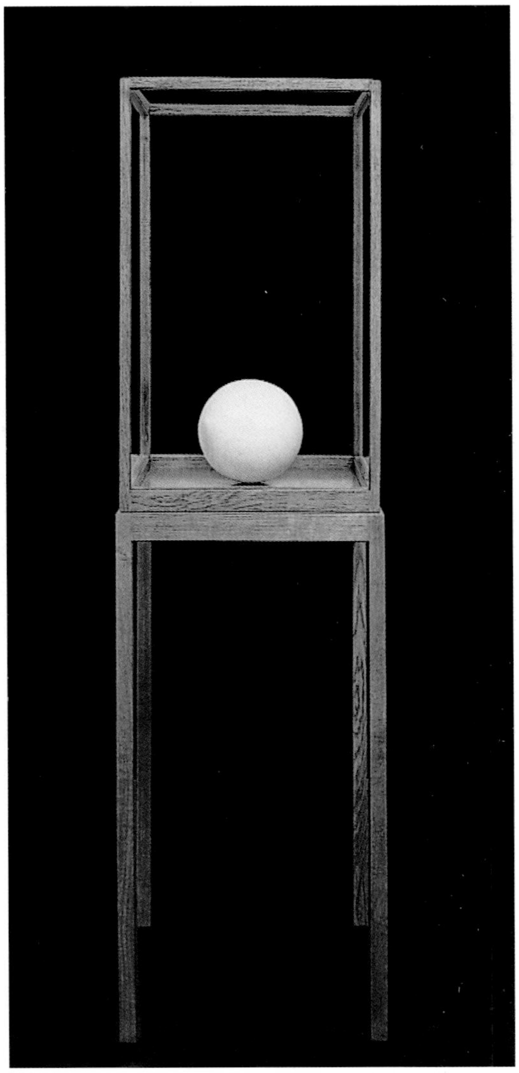

FIGURE 1.23
JAMES LEE BYARS, ***THE HEAD OF PLATO***, 1986. WHITE MARBLE SPHERE, WOOD, GLASS VITRINE. NEUES MUSEUM WESERBERG, BREMEN

Japan were rocked by massive student riots. In hotels in Amsterdam and later Montreal, Yoko and John staged a week-long *Bed-In for Peace* (fig. 1.25) where, dressed in pajamas, they invited the press into their bedroom to discuss their message of nonviolent opposition to the establishment—a message that culminated in the song that became the hymn of the peace movement: "All we are saying/Is give peace a chance." With this event and their billboard campaign that Christmas, *War is Over!* (fig. 1.26), the couple became the most popular icons of the international pacifist movement. Representing the union of East and West, she and John promoted their marriage as an act of universal love and racial equality at a time when (Euro-American) cold war polity still fostered suspicion of much of Asia as the "enemy."

Ono had pronounced at their wedding that she and John "would stage many happenings." With the *Bed-Ins*, they subverted the arcane worlds of radical politics and avant-garde performance art to propose for the mass media a private theater of love staged on the nuptial bed. The iconoclasm that had always marked Ono's crossover strategies in music, poetry, performance, and the visual arts now found another set of boundaries to transgress: the private and public. The numerous films, albums, performances, press conferences, and media appearances that Yoko and John produced together over the next eleven years, until Lennon's assassination in 1980, made their private physical and mental love the subject of their public art and life. Although John's marriage to Yoko was harshly criticized by his fans and the public at large, in fact, as *Rolling Stone* publisher Jann Wenner understood, "Yoko had liberated John, had freed him to become the person he always wanted to be. In her fearlessness, Yoko gave John the means to become himself."[58] What they strove to perform through the living art of their coexistence was authentic experience, an austerity of selfhood stripped of artifice including fame, magic, and rock 'n' róll. In his 1971 song "God" (from *John Lennon/Plastic Ono Band*), Lennon listed the *I Ching*, Tarot, Hitler, Jesus, Kennedy, Buddha, Elvis, and the Beatles as all that "I don't believe in."

> I just believe in me
> Yoko and me
> And that's reality

Ono's marriage to Lennon gave new dimension to her deeply philosophical art. She had always been engaged with transformation of consciousness via the medium of language and performance. Hers was a provocative art that reduced time, place, and self to the material feeling of experience, what she called the "world of stickiness."[59] Ono's achievement during her years with Lennon was an enlargement of that concept into a social and political message for peace, itself the logical outcome of a kind of meditative state of bodily awareness that her instructions help induce. Her message both connected to and helped construct the cultural history of the international peace movement around the globe from 1969 through the 1970s. Her work exemplifies what the Dadaist poet and critic Takiguchi Shūzō once wrote: "Poetry is not belief. It is not logic. It is action."[60]

FIGURE 1.24
LENNON AND ONO,
WEDDING ALBUM, LP,
1969. FRONT COVER

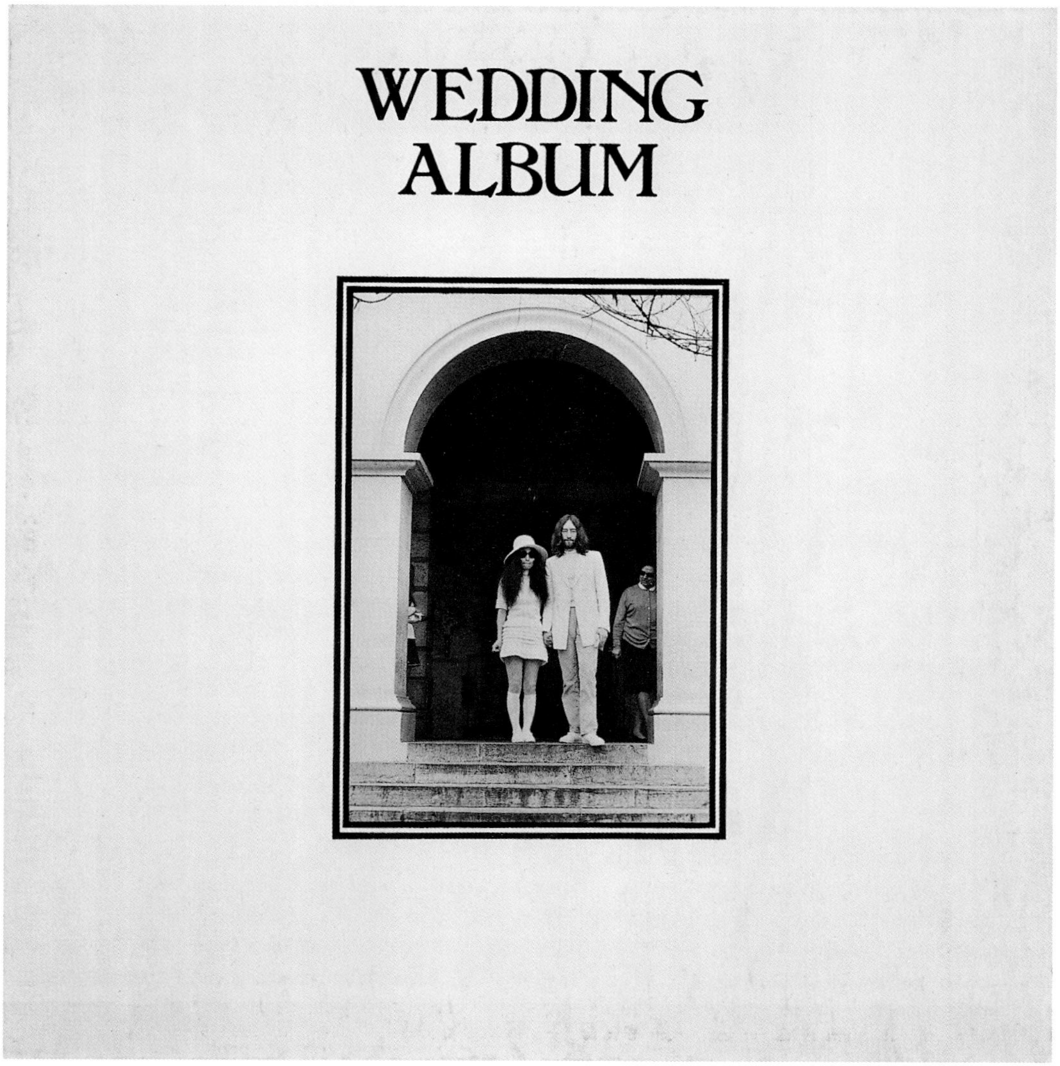

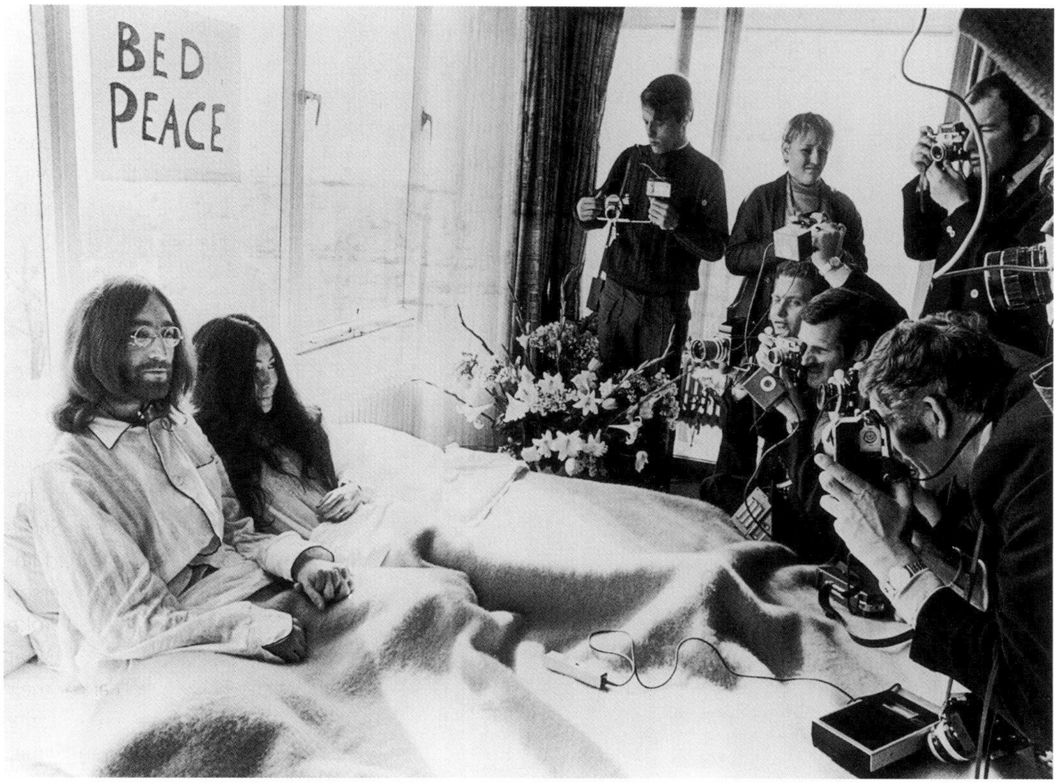

FIGURE 1.25
ONO AND LENNON,
BED-IN FOR PEACE,
AMSTERDAM, 1969

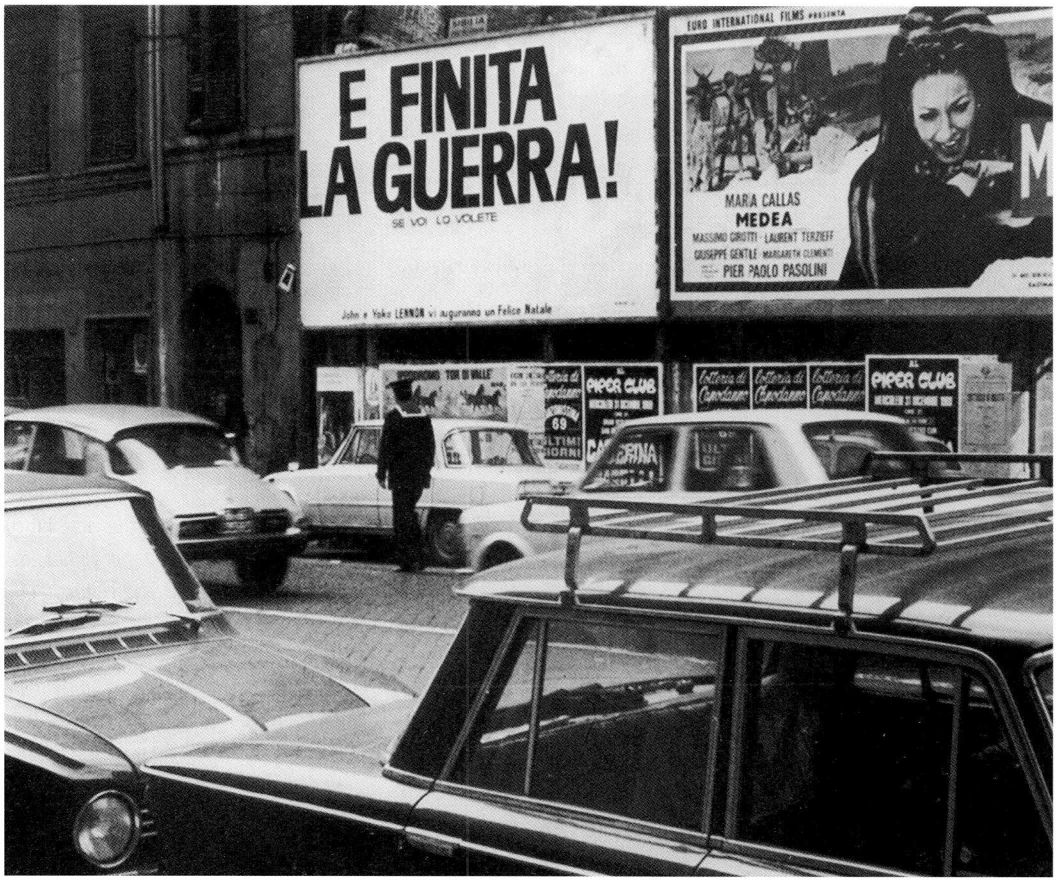

FIGURE 1.26
ONO AND LENNON,
WAR IS OVER! 1969.
BILLBOARD INSTALLED
IN ROME

RISING

John Lennon was murdered on December 8, 1980. Yoko's response to a world of mourners was to call for a silent ten-minute vigil on the following Sunday, December 14. Radio stations around the globe observed the silence while in New York 100,000 people gathered in Central Park outside the Lennons' Dakota residence and sang "Give Peace a Chance" before falling quiet en masse. Ono issued a statement signed with Sean, their five-year-old son, that was distributed to the worldwide media:

> Bless you for your tears and prayers.
> I saw John smiling in the sky.
> I saw sorrow changing into clarity.
> I saw all of us becoming one mind.
> Thank you.[61]

On the night of Lennon's death, Ono had finished recording what became widely recognized as her "pop masterpiece," "Walking on Thin Ice" (fig. 1.27; no. 57). Set to a striking rock rhythm, Yoko's lyrics describe a tale of a girl walking across a frozen lake as wide as the ocean. Terror at the unknown price of "throwing dice in the air" locks against a raw will to "play the game of life with all our hearts." Robert Palmer, among the first music critics to seriously promote Ono's work, wrote of "Thin Ice": "It begins with a pounding dance track, but the mood and lyric are hardly the stuff of disco dreams. This is a song of uncertainty, bristling with a sense of danger and foreboding that proved uncannily correct."[62]

Ono's art had always expressed an aspect of existential despair. From her earliest instruction pieces, spectral images of violence and death recur in her work. Stripped of narrative or literalism, these images are direct evocations of what she calls "white terror"—a peculiar, universal void that haunts all humanity.[63] Her focus on transcience and ephemerality constantly confront us with the other side of existence, trip us into a zone where our local bearings are lost. Ono fearlessly constructs much of her work on the site of this basic condition of life's desperation. Music, perhaps more than any other art form, offers her the expressive means to mine this realm of life's primal essence. Both Ono's lyrics and what critics call her "delirious wail"[64] push listeners beyond the edge to an experience whose only link to normalcy is the need to be saved by a human connection. "If you were drowning you wouldn't say: 'I'd like to be helped because I have a moment to live,'" Ono once said. "You'd say, 'Help!' but if you were more desperate you'd say, 'Eioghhh,' or something like that. And the desperation of life is really life itself, the core of life, what's really driving us forth."[65]

Ono released four solo albums between 1981 and 1995, including *Season of Glass* and *Rising*, a collection of songs marking the fiftieth anniversary of Hiroshima's atomic annihilation and a tribute to her friends who were suffering and dying of AIDS. "Have courage/Have rage/We're rising" she sang.[66] During this period, Ono's critical reception gradually began to shift, prompting a long-overdue reappraisal of her musical career that culminated in the 1992 production of *Onobox*, a multi-CD anthology of her recordings. After she spent two decades in the "strange, rare, invisible prison"[67] of the public's animosity toward the woman blamed for breaking up the Beatles, Ono's contribution to progressive music like punk and free jazz, and her creative influence on Lennon, finally came to be appreciated. "Listen to Patti Smith, P. J. Harvey, Courtney Love, and others and you can hear Yoko's inquisitive howl," a London critic wrote of Ono's historic collision of avant-garde and pop.[68] Rock historian Gillian Gaar proclaimed: "To anyone interested in tracing the development of rock 'n' roll, especially the punk movement of the 70s, listening to Onobox is like discovering a lost chapter in rock history, and one that clearly establishes Ono as a musical pioneer."[69]

Ono's recognition as a pioneer of progressive music paralleled a similar reassessment of her role in the history of Fluxus and Conceptualist art and film that began with her exhibition at the Whitney Museum of American Art in 1989. What had previously been dismissed as her "sentimental and frivolous uses of Conceptual art"[70] were gradually revealed as genuinely radical innovations in idea-based art. Her long neglect was credited to the elusive nature and multimedia experimentation of her work, and to the art world's latent recognition of Fluxus itself—a

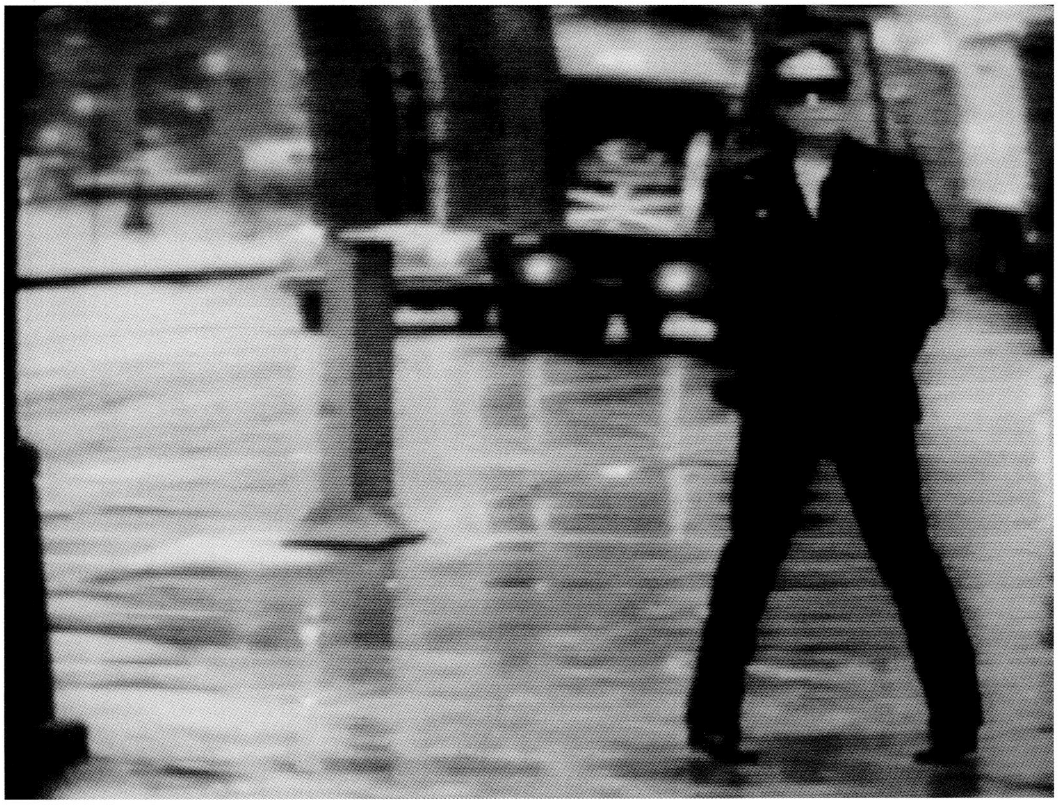

FIGURE 1.27
FROM *WALKING ON THIN ICE*, VIDEO, 1981

movement whose aesthetic politics that so resisted art's commodification assured its absence from the art market and museum. Ono's identity as an artist had also long been distorted by her sensational public status. "Romping, storming, and even reclining across the media's stage of magnified social consciousness, playing the martyr, the lover, the rabble-rouser, the wicked Oriental, the idiot savant, the shaman, expanding her whimsical improvisations in a marathon spectacle until they shattered, Ono left behind a potent legacy that has not been well tended," *Artforum* critic Carlo McCormick wrote in an article on the Whitney show:

> Her provocative, nonconformist career offers few handles to hold her by, and much of her work, notably the pop-performance events that used mass-media communications as a global canvas for her political activism and for an evolving scenario of "life as art," seems destined to fall into the cracks between museological and pop-cultural analysis.[71]

A reassessment and appreciation of Yoko Ono's art, McCormick argued, was long overdue. The Whitney show, together with a survey at The Cranbrook Academy of Art Museum curated by Jon Hendricks the same year, were among the first projects to recover an open, more positive reception for Ono in the international art world.

Taking off from the Everson Museum show of 1971, with all its playful pandemonium, Ono returned to object-making for the Whitney show with a series of austere bronze versions of her earlier AG Gallery and Indica sculptures (pl. 60b). Whereas Ono's earlier work not only accepted but cultivated a certain amateurism, an irreverant disregard for high-art standards, her *Bronze Age* posed as "finished" objects ready to serve the late-eighties boom in high-finance art. Nothing could be more deadening to the delicate remnants of her radical past. But Ono's real subject as she reentered the art world with this unexpected move was time. Inspired by a 1987 visit to Leningrad's Summer Palace, where sepia photographs of the original imperial rooms hung beside shots of them in ruins after Hitler's Russian invasion, she realized that she was walking through elaborate spaces that were completely new versions of the past. "It was a story of change and survival," Ono wrote. "It was a story of all of us."[72] By embracing bronze, symbol of all that the sixties were not, Ono relinquished her claim as icon of nostalgia and set forth with new material power to reinvent and expand her art.

The 1990s emerged as one of the most productive and creative periods in Ono's artistic career. As Neo-Conceptualism and art engaged with social issues came to dominate the international arena of contemporary art, Ono's objects, sculptures, and instal-

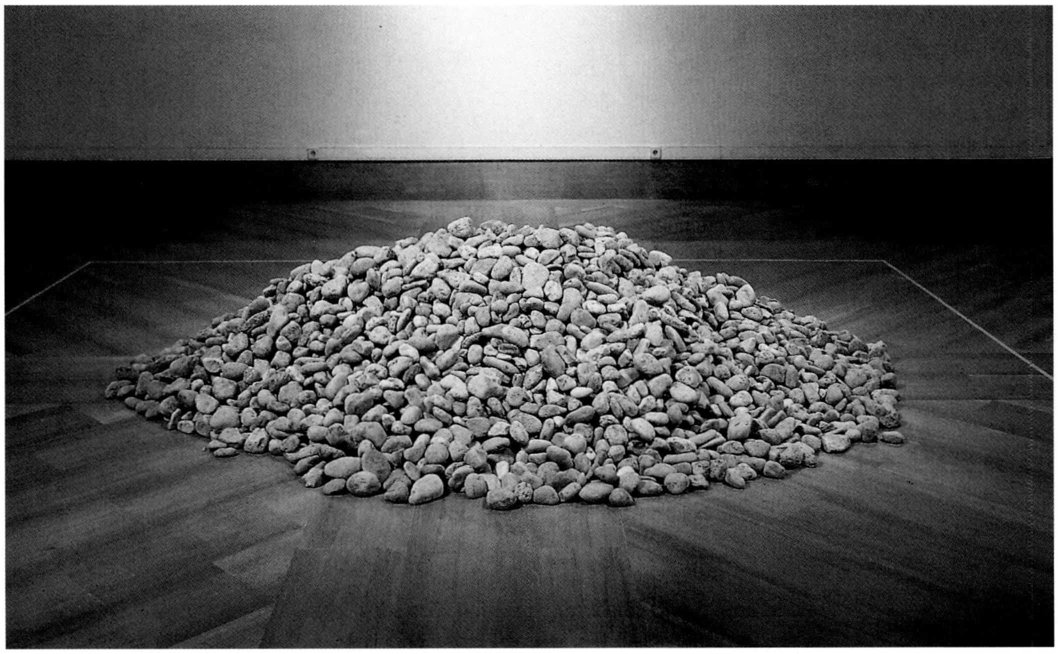

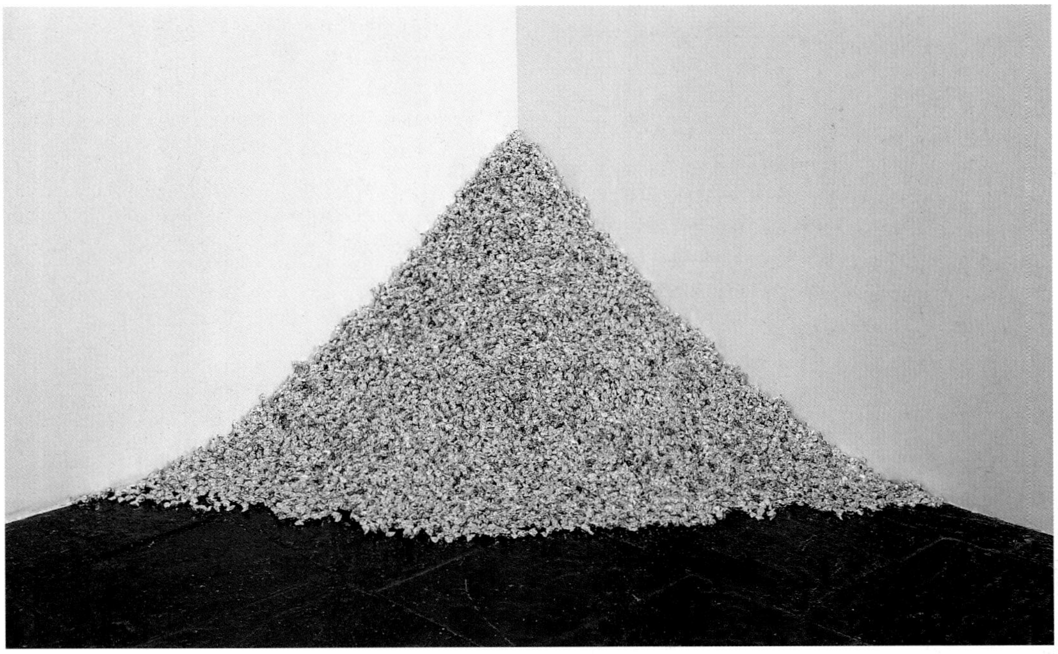

FIGURE 1.28
CLEANING PIECE, 1996. INSTALLATION VIEW, LONJA DEL PESCADO, ALICANTE, 1997

FIGURE 1.29
FELIX GONZÁLEZ-TORRES, ***UNTITLED (LOVER BOYS)***, 1991. CANDIES, INDIVIDUALLY WRAPPED IN SILVER CELLOPHANE. COLLECTION GOETZ, MUNICH

lations gradually assumed a wider position of influence. Her work, shown across Europe, America, and Japan with increasing activity, expressed affinities with the work of younger artists, making her a favorite of Kiki Smith, Cindy Sherman, Cornelia Parker, Donald Baechler, and others. *Cleaning Piece*, a mound of stones that people interact with to create their own piles of sorrows and joys, shares attributes with Felix González-Torres's *Untitled (Lover Boys)* (figs. 1.28–29). Both present works composed of readymades—river rocks and wrapped candies—in a form that is all about unfinished process. They invite viewer participation, offering parts of the work as votive gifts to wish for something unknown, upending the roles of artist and public, priestess and faithful. As the piles shift to the point of elimination, change becomes the vehicle and also the content of the works. With González-Torres, who died of AIDS at the age of thirty-nine, the idea of ephemeral art that can travel, be replenished, and take on transcendent humanitarian meaning has a poignant resonance with Ono's art.

The concept of "unfinished" runs through all of Ono's work. Her early instructions called for "paintings to be constructed in your head"; her Indica Gallery show was subtitled "Unfinished Paintings and Objects by Yoko Ono"; and the first album she released with John Lennon was called *Unfinished Music No. 1: Two Virgins*. Her recent work too challenges us to see the invisible, to make idea, imagination, and perception the content of art and the practice of life. Today, Ono continues to create with undiminished rigor an art that distills everyday things into pure, up-close experiences of contemplation. In this vacuum of heightened awareness, the unremarkable becomes extraordinary, revealing the power of art. Her long career in producing poetry and scores, films and music, objects and installations is linked by her profound intent to seek and provoke questions, and to engage us in that search. For Yoko Ono, being "unfinished" is a state of grace.

NOTES

1. John Lennon quoted in Jonathan Cott, "Yoko Ono and Her Sixteen-Track Voice" in *The Ballad of John and Yoko* (Garden City, N.Y.: Doubleday, 1982), 115.

2. Lennon quoted in Jann Wenner, "Lennon Remembers" in *The Ballad of John and Yoko*, 107.

3. Ono, "The Word of a Fabricator" (1962, translated by Yoko Ono 1999; Anthology 12).

4. Ibid.

5. Fluxus artist Dick Higgins coined the term "intermedia" to describe this new site of artistic activity that existed "between the media." See Higgins, "Statement on Intermedia" (1966) in *In the Spirit of Fluxus*, exh. cat. (1993), 172–73.

6. George Maciunas, "Neo-Dada in Music, Theater, Poetry, Art" (1962) in *Fluxus: Selections from the Gilbert and Lila Silverman Collection*, exh. cat. (1988), 26.

7. Ibid., 27.

8. Ono, "The Word of a Fabricator."

9. Ono, interview with author, August 1997.

10. Isoko's father, Zenzaburō, married Yasuda Teruko, the eldest of Zenjirō's five children, and adopted the family name. He succeeded his father-in-law as head of the Yasuda Bank for some time before his early retirement. For an excellent biographical essay on Ono, see Donald Kirk, "In Tokyo" in *The Ballad of John and Yoko*, 14–32.

11. Ono, interview with author, August 1997.

12. Ono Eijirō taught at Dōshisha University, a leading Protestant institution in Kyoto. He had acquired his doctorate at the University of Michigan with one of the best academic records ever achieved by a foreign student. See Kirk, "In Tokyo."

13. Yeisuke's brother (Yoko's uncle) went abroad to study in Moscow, where he eloped with an accomplished violinist who remained close to Yoko's family.

14. Ono, interview with author, August 1997.

15. Lennon quoted in Cott, "Sixteen-Track Voice," 114.

16. John W. Dower, *Embracing Defeat: Japan in the Wake of World War II* (New York: W. W. Norton/New Press, 1999), 121.

17. Ono, interview with author, October 1998.

18. Ono, "To the Wesleyan People" (1966; Anthology 14).

19. Ono, interview with author, August 1997.

20. For a reproduction of George Maciunas's *Manifesto* of 1963, see fig. 2.3. The opening lines read: "*Purge* the world of bourgeois sickness, 'intellectual,' professional & commercialized culture, PURGE the world of dead art, imitation, artificial, abstract art, illusionistic art, mathematical art,—PURGE THE WORLD OF 'EUROPANISM'!" This manifesto was distributed at *Festum Fluxorum Fluxus* in Düsseldorf at the suggestion of Joseph Beuys.

21. Other Japanese artists included Fluxus artist Ay-O and Conceptualist artists Shūsaku Arakawa and On Kawara.

22. Dick Higgins quoted in Ken Friedman's undated manuscript, "Fluxus & Co.," 4.

23. To certain Japanese intellectuals, existentialism corresponded with Zen Buddhism in its emphasis on personal enlightened insight into daily existence. The work of philosopher Nishida Kitarō was especially influential. Arriving at a position close to mysticism, which he termed "pure experience," Nishida articulated a new concept of *basho*, the "place" of "absolute Nothingness" wherein the full possibilities and dynamics of the self are revealed. The work of Nishida was central to twentieth-century Zen theology and influenced D. T. Suzuki.

24. Okakura Kakuzō, *The Book of Tea* (1906; reprint, Rutland, Vt.: Tuttle, 1956), 3.

25. D. T. Suzuki, *Zen and Japanese Culture*, 212. Zen philosopher Suzuki was a prolific author in both Japanese and English, and was widely translated into European languages as well. His most influential books in the West are *Essays in Zen Buddhism* (1933–49); *Zen Buddhism* (1956); and *Zen and Japanese Culture* (1959). For an excellent study on D. T. Suzuki's work, see Masao Abe, ed., *A Zen Life: D. T. Suzuki Remembered* (New York: Weatherhill, 1986).

26. Suzuki lectured at Columbia University from the late 1940s until at least 1957, and his classes were famous among the New York avant-garde. Cage attended from circa 1951 and thereafter considered Suzuki his spiritual mentor. For Cage's study with Suzuki and involvement with Zen, see David Revill, *The Roaring Silence. John Cage: A Life* (New York: Arcade, 1992), 107–25.

27. Ono, interview with author, September 1999.

28. Takiguchi Shūzō, "Toward Rrose Sélavy" in *Maruseru Dushan goroku/Selected Words of Marcel Duchamp: To and From Rrose Sélavy* (Tokyo: Bijutsu Shuppansha, 1982), 3. Takiguchi was Japan's foremost critic and translator of Duchamp.

29. Thomas Merton, *Mystics & Zen Masters* (New York: Dell, 1961), 236.

30. See *9 Concert Pieces for John Cage* (1966; Anthology 9).

31. Ono, "To the Wesleyan People."

32. Ibid.

33. For documentation of this show with photographs by George Maciunas, see Hendricks, *Paintings and Drawings by Yoko Ono,* exh. cat. (1993).

34. Gene R. Swenson, "Review and Previews: New Names This Month," *Art News* 60, no. 5 (September 1961): 14.

35. Groups like the Bokujin-kai, Japan's dominant avant-garde calligraphy movement in the 1950s and 1960s, worked with European artists such as Henri Michaux, Georges Mathieu, and Pierre Alechinsky as well as with native avant-garde groups like Gutai, to redefine calligraphy as a contemporary, international art. For more on Bokujin-kai and postwar avant-garde calligraphy, see Alexandra Munroe, *Japanese Art After 1945: Scream Against the Sky* (New York: Abrams, 1994), 129–32.

36. Jill Johnston's review of the Carnegie concert (no. 52) recounted the following: "I was alternately stupefied and aroused, with long stretches of stupor, as one might feel when relaxing into a doze induced by a persistent mumbling of low-toned voices" ("Life and Art," *Village Voice*, 7 December 1961, 10).

37. Lucy R. Lippard, "Escape Attempts" in *Reconsidering the Object of Art: 1965–1975*, exh. cat. (Los Angeles: The Museum of Contemporary Art, 1995), 17.

38. Ono quoted in "Yoko Ono: Instruction Painting" in *Yoko at Indica*, exh. cat. (1966), n.p.

39. For anti-art collectives, such as Group Ongaku, Neo-Dada Organizers, Hi Red Center, and Kyūshū-ha, see Munroe, *Scream Against the Sky*, 154–59 and Reiko Tomii's "Glossary" in the same volume.

40. For more on the Tone Prize, see Tomii, "Concerning the Institution of Art: Conceptualism in Japan" in *Global Conceptualism: Points of Origin, 1950s–1980s*, exh. cat. (New York: Queens Museum of Art, 1999), 20–21.

41. Ibid., 18.

42. Lucy R. Lippard and John Chandler, "The Dematerialization of Art," *Art International* 12, no. 2 (February 1968): 32–33.

43. A related instruction, *Painting to Exist Only When It's Copied or Photographed*, reads: "Let People copy or photograph/your/paintings./Destroy the originals." (1964 spring; published in *Grapefruit*, 1964).

44. See Benjamin Buchloh, "Conceptual Art, 1962–1969: From the Aesthetic of Administration to the Critique of Institutions," *October* 55 (winter 1990): 105–43.

45. Joseph Kosuth, *The Sixth Investigation 1969 Proposition 14* (Cologne: Gerd de Vries, 1971), n.p.

46. Miyakawa Atsushi, quoted in *Arakawa Shūsaku: Miyakawa Atsushi e-ten/The Exhibition of Shūsaku Arakawa: To Atsushi Miyakawa*, exh, cat. (Tokyo: Touko Museum of Contemporary Art, 1990), 59.

47. Ono, "The Word of a Fabricator."

48. Ono, interview with author, August 1997.

49. Ono quoted in Cott, "Sixteen-Track Voice," 117.

50. David Bourdon quoted in Paul Taylor, "Yoko Ono's New Bronze Age at the Whitney," *New York Times*, 5 February 1989.

51. Ono, "To the Wesleyan People."

52. Kristine Stiles, "Unbosoming Lennon: The Politics of Yoko Ono's Experience," *Art Criticism* 7, no. 2 (1992): 40. This is an excellent study of Ono's feminist politics and her related performance and film works, many realized in collaboration with Lennon.

53. Ono, "Biography/Statement" (1966; Anthology 26).

54. Jonas Mekas quoted in Kristine McKenna, "Yoko Reconsidered," *Los Angeles Times*, 11 April 1993.

55. Ono quoted in Jerry Hopkins, *Yoko Ono* (New York: Macmillan, 1986), 29.

56. Cott, "Sixteen-Track Voice," 123.

57. Lennon quoted in Ben Fong-Torres, "A Chronology" in *The Ballad of John and Yoko*, 32.

58. Wenner, "Remembering John Lennon" in *John Lennon: Drawings, Performances, Films*, exh. cat. (Stuttgart: Cantz, 1995), 19.

59. Ono, "The Word of a Fabricator."

60. Takiguchi (1931) quoted in Dore Ashton, *Isamu Noguchi East and West* (New York: Knopf, 1992), 89.

61. See, for example, "Vigil: Yoko Ono Sends Her Blessings," *Times* (London), 17 December 1980.

62. Robert Palmer, "On Thin Ice: The Music of Yoko Ono" in booklet in *Onobox* (1992), 74.

63. "White terror" appears in the lyrics of Ono's song, "Kiss Kiss Kiss" (1980).

64. Carlo McCormick, "Yoko Ono Solo," *Artforum* 27, no. 6 (February 1989): 120.

65. Palmer, "On Thin Ice," 46.

66. Ono, "Rising" in *Rising*, CD (1995).

67. Ono, interview with author, October 1998. She said, "Before meeting John, I was doing two concerts and lectures a month. I was in demand. I was able to express myself all the time. Suddenly, by becoming the wife of a Beatle, what was required of me was to shut up. Or if at all possible, to overdose and die. I took it as a challenge, like how can I create new works in jail? It was like a prison. A strange, rare, invisible prison."

68. Nick Hasted, "Starting Over," *Independent*, 24 June 1997.

69. Gillian Gaar, "ONO INA BOX," *The Rocket Magazine* (March 1992): 40. Gaar is author of *She's A Rebel: The History of Women in Rock & Roll* (Seattle: Seal Press, 1992), which features a preface by Ono.

70. Lawrence Alloway, "Art," *Nation* (8 November 1971): 48 (review of Ono's solo exhibition at the Everson Museum).

71. McCormick, "Yoko Ono Solo," 120.

72. Ono, "Bronze Age" (1988; Anthology 17).

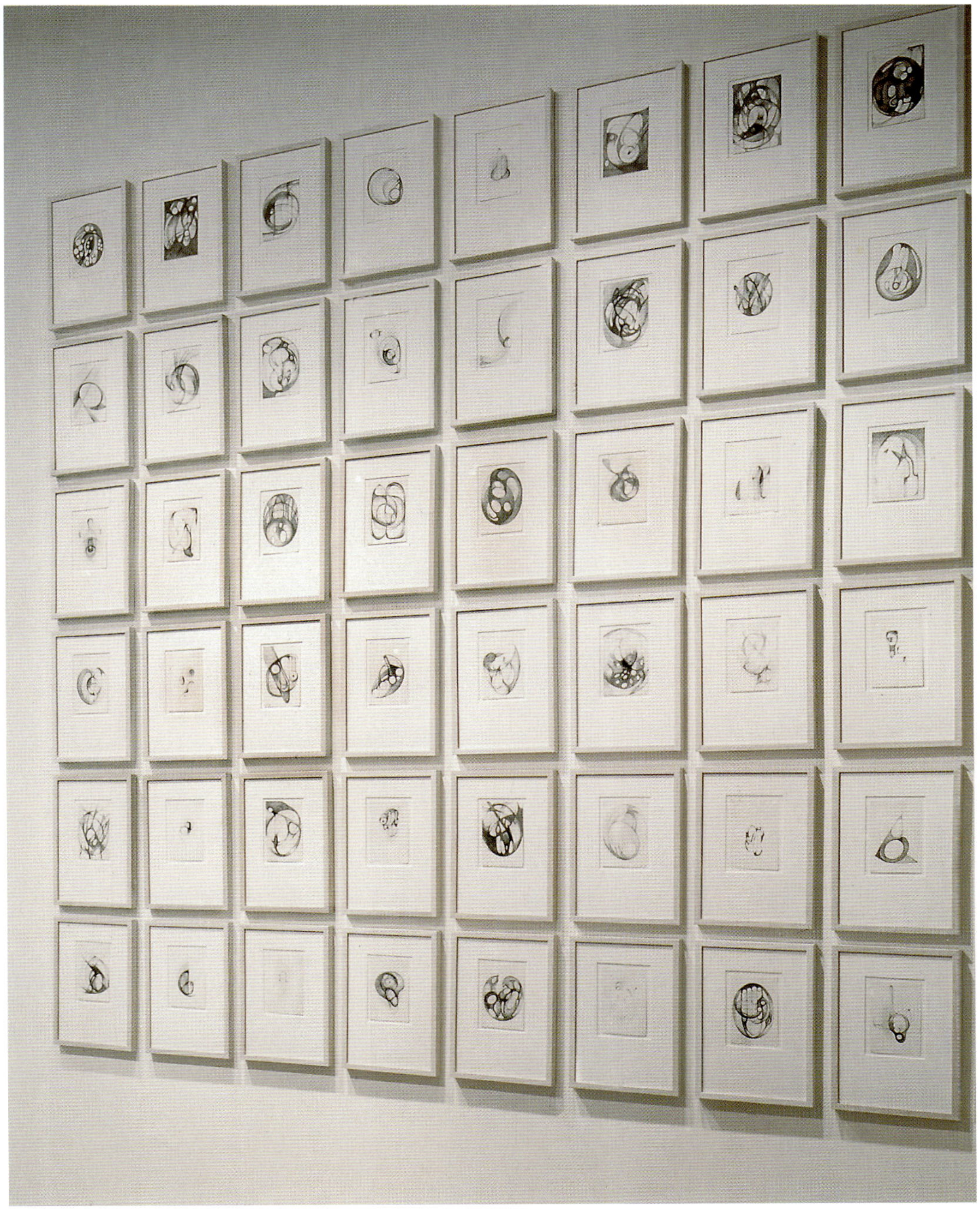

FIGURE 1.30
DRAWINGS FROM
FRANKLIN SUMMER,
1995–99. INSTALLATION
VIEW, NEW YORK, 2000

HOMAGE TO YOKO ONO *, by George Maciunas, Jan.11,1962

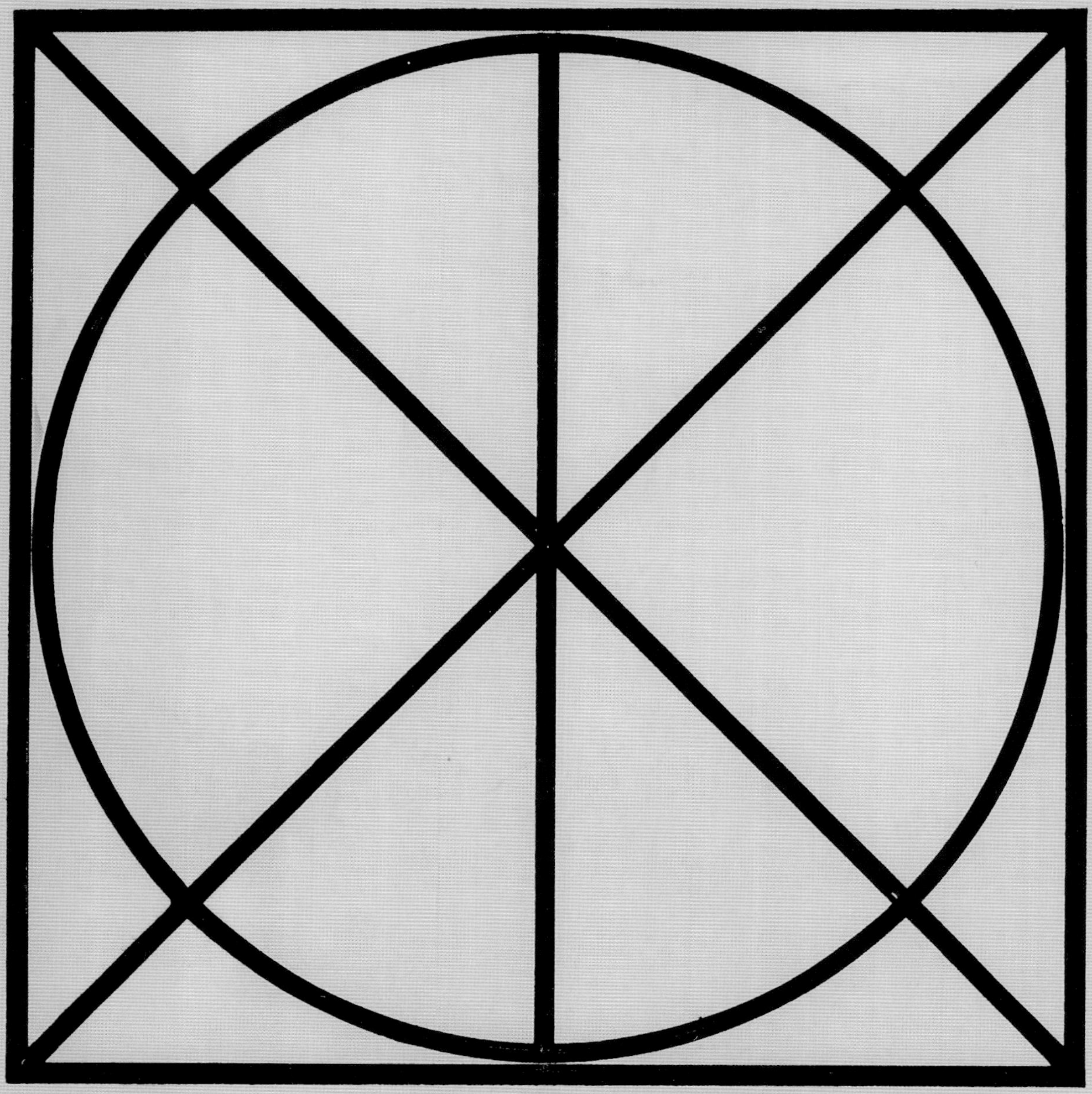

* the diagram says "YOKO ONO" in case you can not figure it out.

Yoko Ono and Fluxus

JON HENDRICKS

Fluxus is a complex art movement, with roots deep set into many springs. George Maciunas, the shaper and form-giver of Fluxus, reached back to such divergent sources as the Roman circus, Baroque mimicry, and Byzantine iconoclasm, and in the more recent past to Dada and Futurist sound poetry, abstract calligraphy, Futurist Brutalism, Luigi Russolo's "Art of Noise," Dada Theater, vaudeville, Marcel Duchamp and the idea of the Readymade, and the LEF and Novy LEF Constructivists of Russia. Maciunas has cited more immediate influences: Georges Mathieu's *Battle of Boudine* (1952), which he credits as an influence on Fluxus performance, and especially John Cage. Or, as he wrote of Fluxus in a 1965 Manifesto, "the fusion of Spike Jones, Vaudeville, gag, children's games and Duchamp" (fig. 2.6).

FIGURE 2.1 (LEFT)
GEORGE MACIUNAS,
HOMAGE TO YOKO ONO, DRAWING, 1962.
THE GILBERT AND LILA SILVERMAN FLUXUS COLLECTION, DETROIT

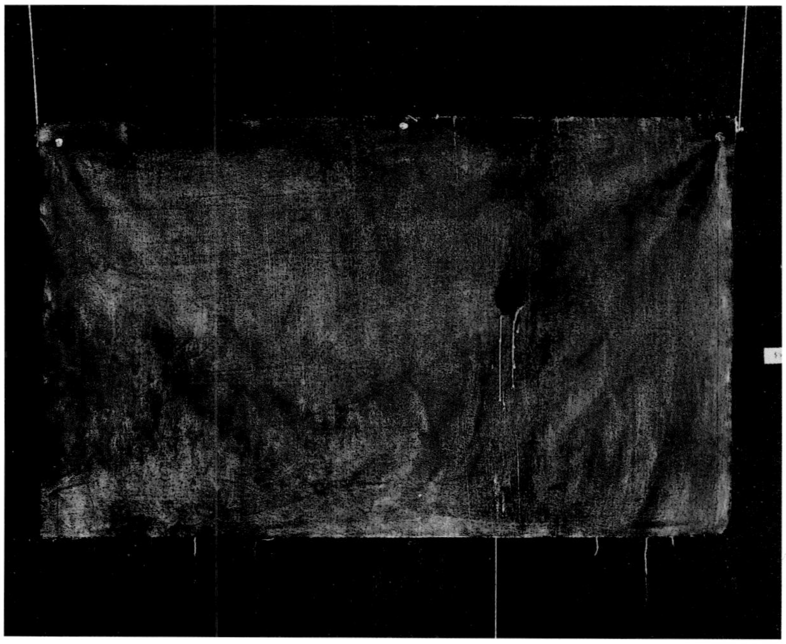

FIGURE 2.2 (RIGHT)
SMOKE PAINTING, 1961
(CANVAS VERSION).
INSTALLATION VIEW, AG GALLERY, 1961.
PHOTOGRAPH BY GEORGE MACIUNAS. THE GILBERT AND LILA SILVERMAN FLUXUS COLLECTION, DETROIT

George Maciunas envisaged a force of disparate artistic concerns, forms, and individuals: a global confluence of ideas. He had studied architecture at Carnegie Institute of Technology and Cooper Union and did postgraduate work on Siberian archaeology and the art of migrations. Through his studies he became well acquainted with modernist thought. Fluxus was about to be. Maciunas first came into contact with Yoko Ono in New York City during the series of events that she and La Monte Young had produced at her loft on Chambers Street in lower Manhattan during the winter of 1960–61. Although Ono did not present an evening of her own works during the Chambers Street series, she did perform in other artists' concerts there and had installed several of her own pieces in various situations in the loft. These included *Shadow Painting*, *Add Color Painting*, *Kitchen Piece*, *Smoke Painting* (fig. 2.2), and *Painting to Be Stepped On*, a work which she had placed on the floor and remembers having hoped that Marcel Duchamp would notice when he came to the loft for a concert, but he didn't. Maciunas was so impressed with the Chambers Street series that he decided to present a similar series at the uptown gallery that he and Almus Salcius ran at 925 Madison Avenue, called AG Gallery. Maciunas's series started in the spring of 1961 and continued through the end of July. The final exhibition, *Paintings & Drawings by Yoko Ono*, opened on the afternoon of Sunday, July 16, 1961. This extraordinary show consisted of ideas Ono had already presented at her Chambers Street loft with the addition of a number of new works also having to do with process, concepts, and license. The works themselves were for the most part crude canvases nailed to the gallery's bare brick walls or laid on the floor. The canvas surfaces had been altered with washes of *sumi* ink, and with accouterments, protrusions, and entrenchments. A commonality of this group of works was the attachment of a score, instruction, or script, provided in written or verbal form. There was another group of works in the show that George Maciunas had insisted upon showing, of abstract calligraphy that he thought he might be able to sell, thinking that the conceptual/process works had little chance of finding buyers. Maciunas photographed the exhibition, providing valuable documentation of these early works (fig. 2.2; see no. 2).

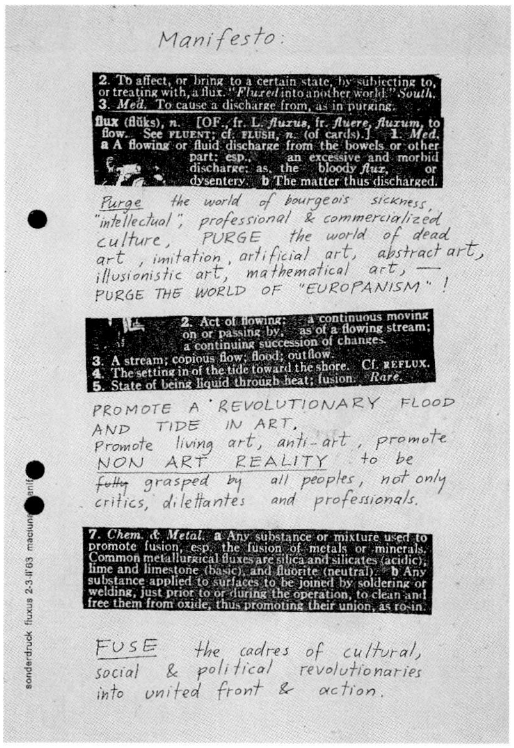

FIGURE 2.3 (LEFT)
FLUXUS COLLECTIVE, *FLUXUS MANIFESTO*, 1963. BY GEORGE MACIUNAS. THE GILBERT AND LILA SILVERMAN FLUXUS COLLECTION, DETROIT

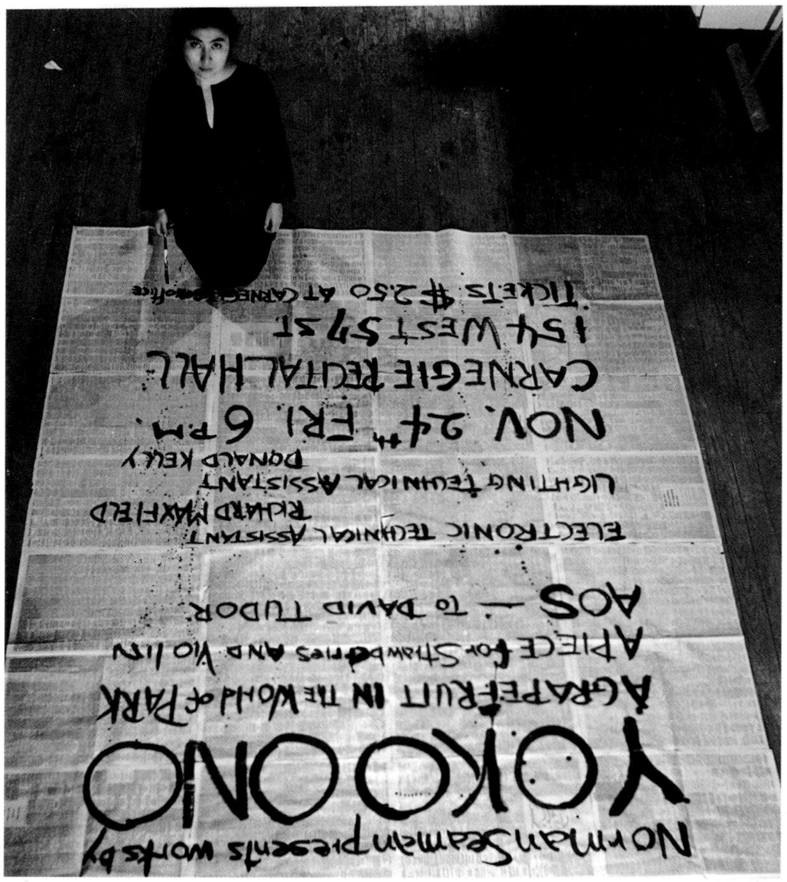

FIGURE 2.4 (RIGHT)
PHOTOGRAPH BY GEORGE MACIUNAS, INTENDED AS POSTER FOR *WORKS BY YOKO ONO* (CARNEGIE RECITAL HALL), 1961. THE GILBERT AND LILA SILVERMAN FLUXUS COLLECTION, DETROIT

During Ono's exhibition, the final three events in the Maciunas series were scheduled to take place at AG Gallery as well: on July 16 at 8 p.m., following Ono's 3 to 5 p.m. opening, *Works by Henry Flynt*; on July 23, *Works by Walter de Maria*; and on July 30, *Nothing by Ray Johnson*.

At this same time, Maciunas was actively trying to formulate his ideas for an international art movement and was searching for a name. One day he came to the gallery and discussed his vision with Ono, asking her if she could think of a name for the movement he envisioned. She couldn't, and told him that in any case she was not terribly interested in groups or in working as part of a group. The next day, Maciunas came into the gallery and was very excited. He had come up with the name for his movement: "Fluxus," a word that means change and fluidity, a flushing out of bodily waste, an element to solidify and harden metal (fig. 2.3).

The ideas that Yoko Ono was working with in her AG Gallery show were to have a profound effect on George Maciunas's evolving desire to start and shape Fluxus. These ideas were of conceptual painting and license, of letting someone else complete the process so that the artist did not have to do it by herself. These works would be completed in the viewer's mind. Works by license would be completed by the viewer, who would engage with the work—do-it-yourself things, which impressed Maciunas, because it meant that the artist was removing herself from the process. This became one of the underpinnings of Fluxus works, a strategy devised by Maciunas based on Ono's example: an artist

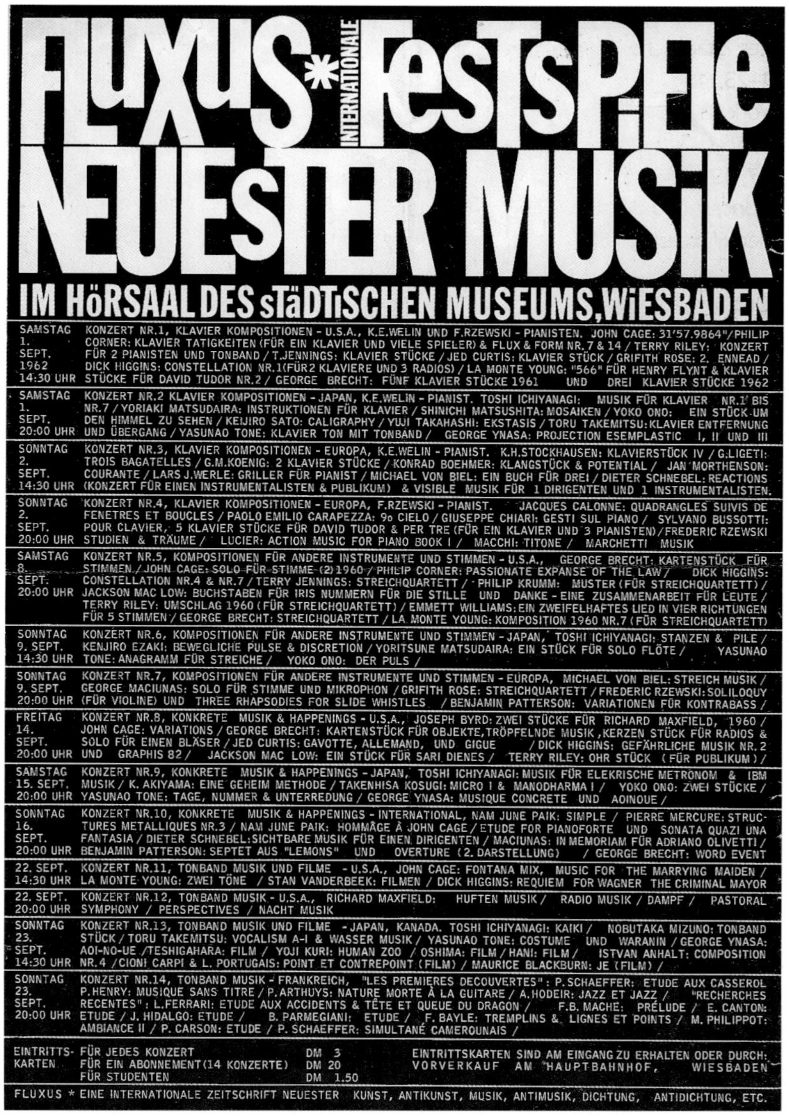

FIGURE 2.5
FLUXUS, ***FLUXUS INTERNATIONALE FESTSPIELE NEUESTER MUSIK***, POSTER, 1962. DESIGN BY GEORGE MACIUNAS. THE GILBERT AND LILA SILVERMAN FLUXUS COLLECTION, DETROIT

would give Maciunas an idea, he would interpret its contents, and produce an edition of the work as a cheap, repeatable, mass-producible art object, thus undermining, in his mind, the preciousness of art.

That autumn, Ono prepared for her next project, a concert at Carnegie Recital Hall on November 24, 1961, with a program featuring *A Grapefruit in the World of Park*, *A Piece for Strawberries and Violin*, and *AOS—To David Tudor* (see Anthology 4, 5). Ono and Maciunas devised an idea for a concert poster, which was to be a photograph, taken by Maciunas, of Ono interacting with a hand-lettered poster she had painted. Maciunas made a series of photographs of Ono with the poster, backlit, peering through it, and sitting on it (fig. 2.4; no. 52). None of these was used as the poster at the time of the concert; however, the idea of interaction and function reappeared in later Maciunas-designed posters in Fluxus newspapers.

Shortly after Ono's concert Maciunas departed for Wiesbaden, Germany, where he continued to expand his plans for Fluxus concerts and to promote Fluxus publications. Ono's use of Carnegie Recital Hall for a concert of new and radical music and performance gave Maciunas the idea of using established venues to stage Fluxus events. The first large series of Fluxus concerts in Europe, titled *Fluxus Internationale Festspiele Neuester Musik,* were staged in the Hörsaal des Städtischen Museum, Wiesbaden, September 1–23, 1962 (fig. 2.5). Later, on his return to New York George Maciunas staged two major Fluxus concerts at Carnegie Recital Hall, the first on June 27, 1964 titled *Fluxus Symphony Orchestra in Fluxus Concert* and the second on September 25, 1965 titled *Fluxorchestra at Carnegie Recital Hall* (fig. 2.6).

Ono remained in New York until early 1962. She took part in the January 8 benefit concert at the Living Theater, a fund-raiser to pay the printer of *An Anthology*, performing her piece *The Chair #1*. *An Anthology* was a proto-Fluxus publication edited by La Monte Young and designed by George Maciunas containing a collection of scores, notations, and writings characterized on its title page as "chance operations, concept art, anti art, indeterminacy, improvisation, meaningless work, natural disasters, plans of action, mathematics, dance constructions, compositions, music, poetry, essays, stories and diagrams" by Yoko Ono and other artists, many of whom became part of Fluxus.

After the Living Theater benefit, Ono traveled to Japan, where she exhibited her *Instructions for Paintings* at Sōgetsu Art Center and toured with John Cage. During this period from 1962 until her return to New York in late 1964, the first great burst of Fluxus activities occurred in Europe, and, surprisingly, Yoko Ono is only slightly represented in those early concerts. For instance, the September 1, 1962, Wiesbaden concert program lists her work *A Piece for Sky* and the September 9 concert lists a performance of her work *The Pulse* among the fourteen works presented. *The Pulse* is also listed on the November 25 program at the *Fluxus Musik og Anti-Musik det Instrumentale Teater* at Allé Scenen in Copenhagen, Denmark.

Ono is listed on the poster for *Festum Fluxorum Fluxus: Musik und Antimusik das Instrumentale Theater* at the Staatliche Kunstakademie, Düsseldorf, February 2 and 3, 1963 (fig. 14.8) and *Questionnaire* by Yoko Ono is listed on the program for the June 27, 1964, *Fluxus Symphony Orchestra in Fluxus Concert* at Carnegie Recital Hall.

The sphere of Fluxus encompassed a variety of activities, all coordinated to a greater or lesser extent by George Maciunas, as shaper of events, programmer of Fluxus concerts, producer of most Fluxus editions, editor and designer of Fluxus publications, and philosophical molder of the movement. In his early plans for Fluxus, besides a series of Fluxus concerts to be held in various countries around the world, Maciunas intended to produce Fluxus Yearboxes—anthologies of very new work being done around the world as well as compilations of precedent historical movements relevant to Fluxus. These anthologies were to come in two types: regular and "Luxus," which would contain additional inserts of original objects, films, records, etc. Eventually these Yearbox anthologies evolved into combined publications containing both two- and three-dimensional materials.

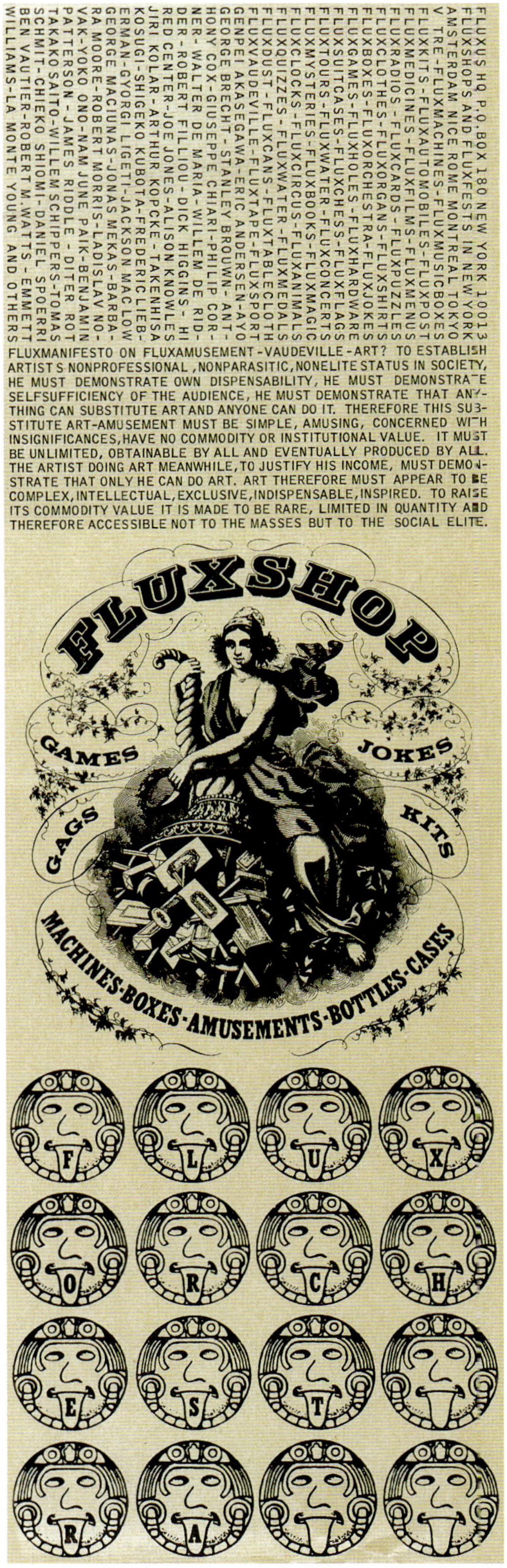

FIGURE 2.6
FLUXUS, ***FLUXSHOP / FLUXORCHESTRA*** INCLUDES ***FLUXMANIFESTO ON FLUXAMUSEMENT,*** 1965. DESIGN BY GEORGE MACIUNAS. THE GILBERT AND LILA SILVERMAN FLUXUS COLLECTION, DETROIT

Another early publishing idea for Fluxus was the distribution, as widely as possible, of scores by Fluxus artists, using a system pioneered by Peters Editions, publishers of John Cage's scores. This system was to have a master original and then a blueprint or ossolith copy could be made on demand from it. In an idea put forward in *Fluxus Newsletter No. 5*, January 1, 1963, the notion of production quickly evolved that year into a plan for publishing the complete works of a selected group of Fluxus artists, using a different format from the Peters Editions example.

The first work of Yoko Ono's that Maciunas planned to produce for Fluxus was her collected instructions, or scores. Fluxus Newspaper No. 2, February 1964, published an image of her baby Kyoko, her score *Instructions for Poem No. 86 (Fly)*, and the following notice: "Collection of works by Yoko Ono, $3.00 before $6.00 after publication. Subscribe to Grapefruit Apt. 1001 Kanna Bldg., 53 Kannomachi, Shibuya, Tokyo, Japan."

In an early note that Ono wrote to Maciunas from Japan, she characterized the works for the book in the following manner:

> Instructions for P. [Painting]
> Instructions for Po. [Poetry]
> Instructions for M. [Music]
> Instructions for E. [Events]
> Instructions for O. [Objects]
>
> The pieces here are works of 1952–64.
> There are more pieces of this period
> That I can send you by next mail which
> I intend to include in the book.
>
> On 1960 spring, I decided to instructionalized
> Poetry.
> On 1961 summer, I decided to instructionalized
> Painting.
> Also, time was given to Painting as in life.
>
> After 1960 fall, some of my music
> Pieces are meant to spread by word of
> mouth, therefore, do not have score
> or written instructions. This method
> is essential of the pieces since the
> gradual change which occurs in the
> piece by word-spreading is also
> part of the piece. If you want to
> know of these pieces, please ask
> people who already know of them.
> Some of my pieces were
> dedicated to the following people.
> Sometimes they were informed,
> but sometimes not.
>
> (Yoko Ono, notes for her letter to George Maciunas on publication of *Grapefruit*, n.d., late 1963–early 1964, collection of the artist)

Work progressed on this book slowly, due to the enormous number of projects that Maciunas had taken on during this period. At a certain point, Ono decided to publish the work herself in Japan and titled the compilation *Grapefruit* (no. 4). The book appeared on July 4 of that year. In a February 1, 1965 letter to Ben Vautier, George Maciunas wrote: "when I return I will mail you completed works of Yoko Ono. Many very good pieces. She is now in New York. One of the best composers. I will send you my own copy as soon as I microfilm it, ok?"

Following the publication of *Grapefruit*, Ono returned to New York in late 1964 and was immediately engaged in many projects both in and outside of Fluxus. These projects included *Draw Circle Event* (fig. 14.11), for which hundreds of cards were sent in the mail with an invitation to draw a circle and return it to Yoko Ono—a work certainly like those with Fluxus, but done independently. Another independent project, *Part Painting Series 5* (1965), typeset and printed by Maciunas, consisted of a white paper square glued onto a red sheet of paper, with a handwritten number and a printed text indicating that it was one of 10,000 similar parts, to be put together in the future. She also produced her own *Ono's Sales List* in 1965 (no. 37), which was the first conceptual sales list and differed greatly from the concrete Fluxus price lists published in Fluxus Newspapers.

Self Portrait, which would become a recurrent work of Ono's offered by Fluxus, appeared in 1965 both as an independent work and as a component of *Fluxus I*, the first great Fluxus Anthology produced by Maciunas. The version made by the artist consisted of a small mirror signed on the back and placed in a manila envelope that was rubber-stamped with the title and date and bore the handwritten notation "(framed) imaginary" and Ono's signature. The other version appeared from 1965 in some copies of *Fluxus I* as a small round mirror inserted in a rubber-stamped manila envelope and bound into the body of the anthology. Within Fluxus, *Self Portrait* metamorphosed into two or possibly three distinct works (figs. 2.9, 7.3). One was *Box of Smile* (no. 22). The second incarnation was *Flux Smile Machine*, produced by Maciunas and initially credited to Yoko Ono, then credited to George Maciunas with a dedication to Yoko Ono, and eventually credited to Maciunas only. The work consists of a plastic box containing a gadget that would physically force a smile when inserted into the mouth. Each label for the work was a unique cutout from a dental publication of people of different cultures showing their teeth, onto which Maciunas typed the title, artist's name, and sometimes a date. A third embodiment of *Self Portrait*, *Fluxfilm No. 4* (1966), entitled *Disappearing Music for Face*, is credited by Maciunas to Shiomi Mieko (Chieko) but considered by Ono at the time of the filming to be her work. The film was shot using a high-speed camera and depicted the "tran-

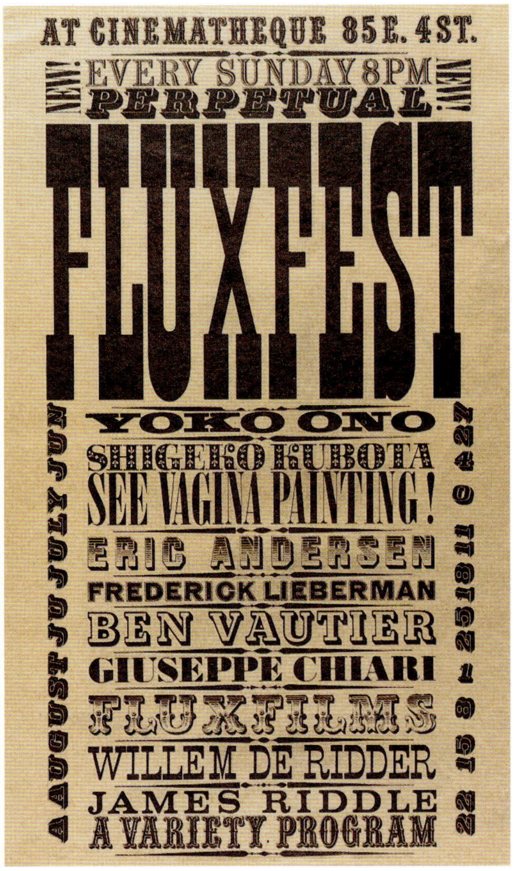

FIGURE 2.7
FLUXUS, ***PERPETUAL FLUXFEST***, INCLUDED IN *VACUUM TRAPEZOID* (FLUXUS NEWSPAPER NO. 5) 1965. DESIGN BY GEORGE MACIUNAS. THE GILBERT AND LILA SILVERMAN FLUXUS COLLECTION, DETROIT

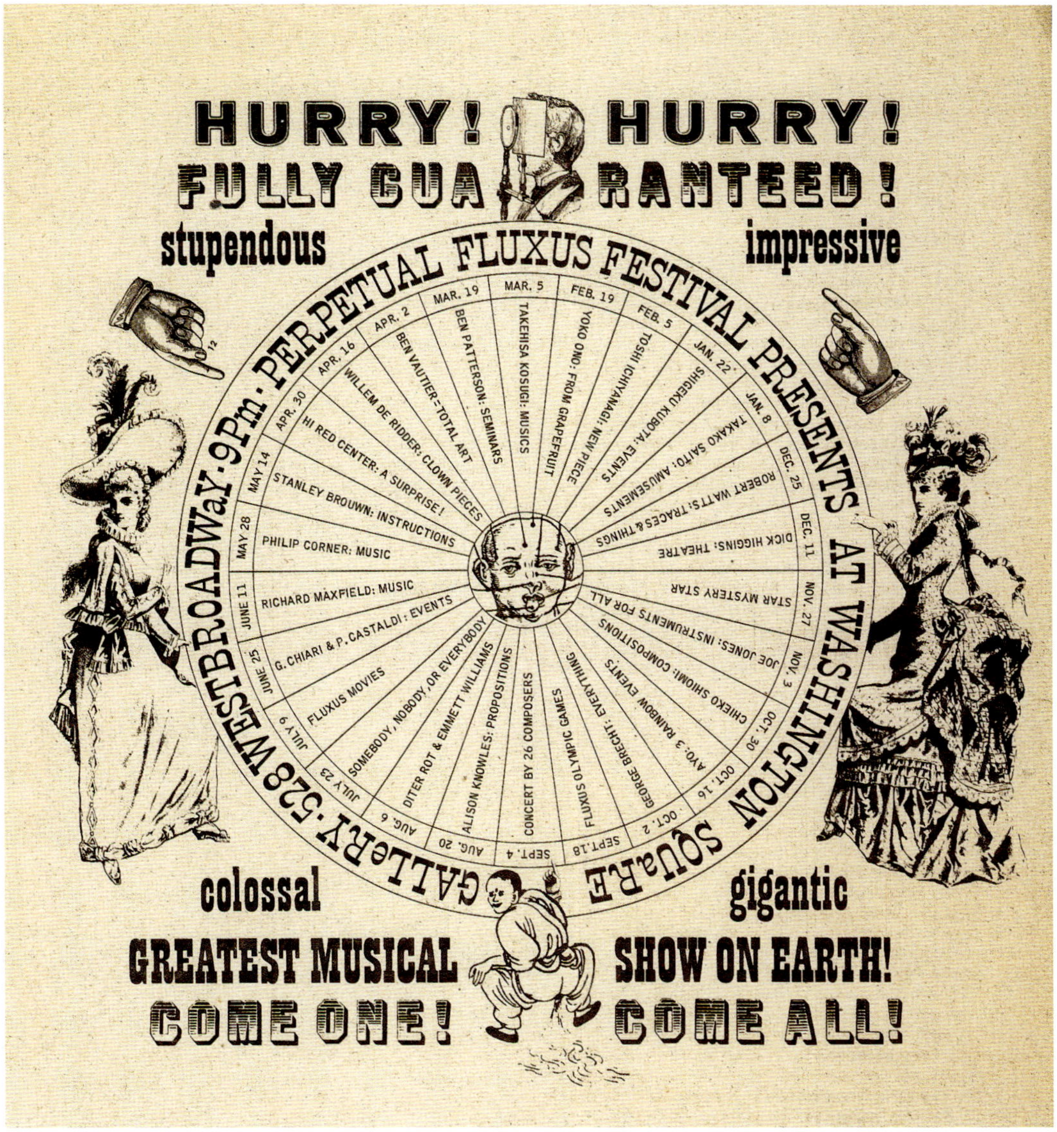

FIGURE 2.8

FLUXUS, ***PERPETUAL FLUXUS FESTIVAL,*** POSTER, 1964. DESIGN BY GEORGE MACIUNAS. THE GILBERT AND LILA SILVERMAN FLUXUS COLLECTION, DETROIT

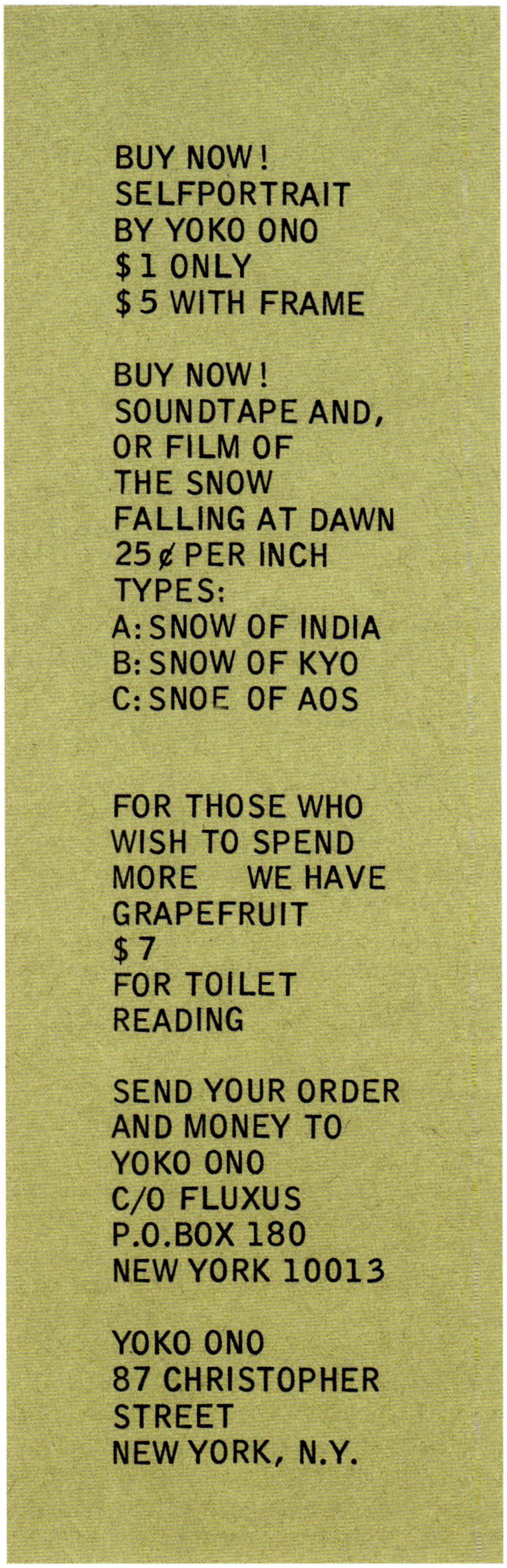
BUY NOW!
SELFPORTRAIT
BY YOKO ONO
$1 ONLY
$5 WITH FRAME

BUY NOW!
SOUNDTAPE AND,
OR FILM OF
THE SNOW
FALLING AT DAWN
25¢ PER INCH
TYPES:
A: SNOW OF INDIA
B: SNOW OF KYO
C: SNOE OF AOS

FOR THOSE WHO
WISH TO SPEND
MORE WE HAVE
GRAPEFRUIT
$7
FOR TOILET
READING

SEND YOUR ORDER
AND MONEY TO
YOKO ONO
C/O FLUXUS
P.O.BOX 180
NEW YORK 10013

YOKO ONO
87 CHRISTOPHER
STREET
NEW YORK, N.Y.

FIGURE 2.9

"BUY NOW! SELF PORTRAIT BY YOKO ONO...," FLYER, 1965. THE GILBERT AND LILA SILVERMAN FLUXUS COLLECTION, DETROIT

sition from smile to no-smile," performed by Ono. This simultaneous attribution, or confused attribution is not uncommon in Fluxus, where several artists could be credited for the same work in different situations. Two years later in 1968, Ono made a film titled *Film No. 5 (Smile)* (also known as *Portrait of John as a Young Cloud*) using high-speed cameras, showing John Lennon's face with a smile (no. 44).

In the summer of 1964 George Maciunas produced a poster for a *Perpetual Fluxus Festival* to be held at Washington Square Gallery, New York (fig. 2.8). Starting late that summer or early fall, and continuing two weeks "in perpetuity" (perhaps), George Maciunas planned to present concerts, events, and other activities of many of the artists connected with Fluxus at that time, as well as evenings of Fluxus Films, Fluxus Games, and collective concerts. *Yoko Ono: From Grapefruit* was scheduled for February 19. By the end of 1964, however, the *Perpetual Fluxus Festival* was dislodged from Washington Square Gallery and by the next summer, found a new home as *Perpetual Fluxfest* at Cinematheque in the East End Theater (fig. 2.7). The revised festival started June 27 with an evening of works by Yoko Ono. The program was very sparse: *Bag Piece* (no. 31), in which two performers onstage took off their shoes, climbed into a large black bag, took off their clothes, moving around a lot, perhaps taking a nap, then got dressed and reemerged from the bag; and *Beat Piece*, in which a group of performers including Nam June Paik, Shigeko Kubota, Ono, Anthony Cox, and others lay on top of one another on the stage and listened to each other's hearts beat. Ono remembers this took a long time to perform. She also remembers George Maciunas performing *Wall Piece for Orchestra* and nearly killing himself. The score reads:

> WALL PIECE FOR ORCHESTRA to Yoko Ono
>
> Hit a wall with your head.
>
> 1962 winter

On September 12, 19, and 26, Ono realized an event titled *Morning Piece (1964) to George Maciunas*, on the roof of her Christopher Street apartment building (figs. 1.16–17, 2.11–12). It had first been performed in Tokyo on May 24 and 31, 1964. In it, dates and times of "future mornings" were

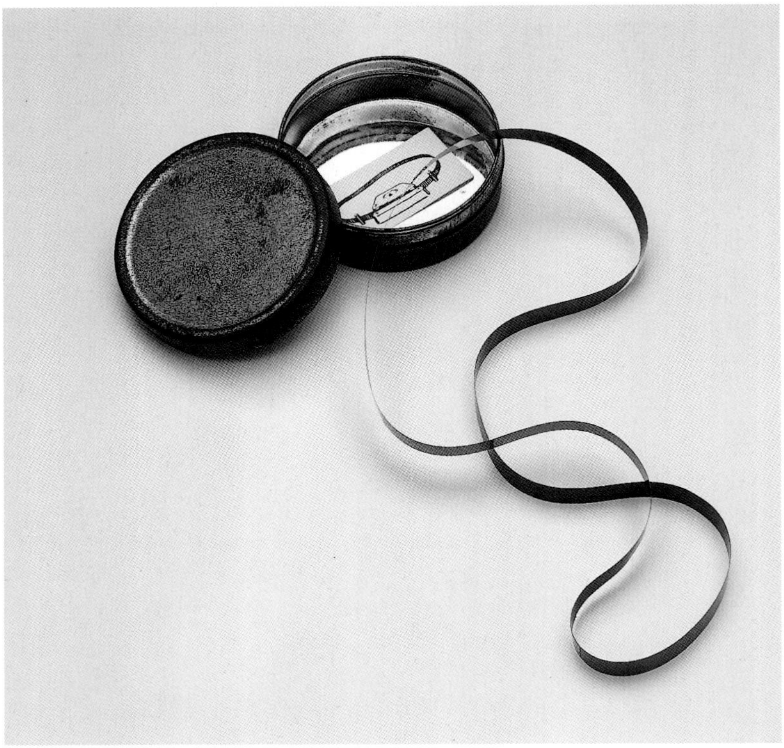

FIGURE 2.10
SNOW FALLING AT DAWN, SOUND TAPE, 1965. COLLECTION OF JON AND JOANNE HENDRICKS

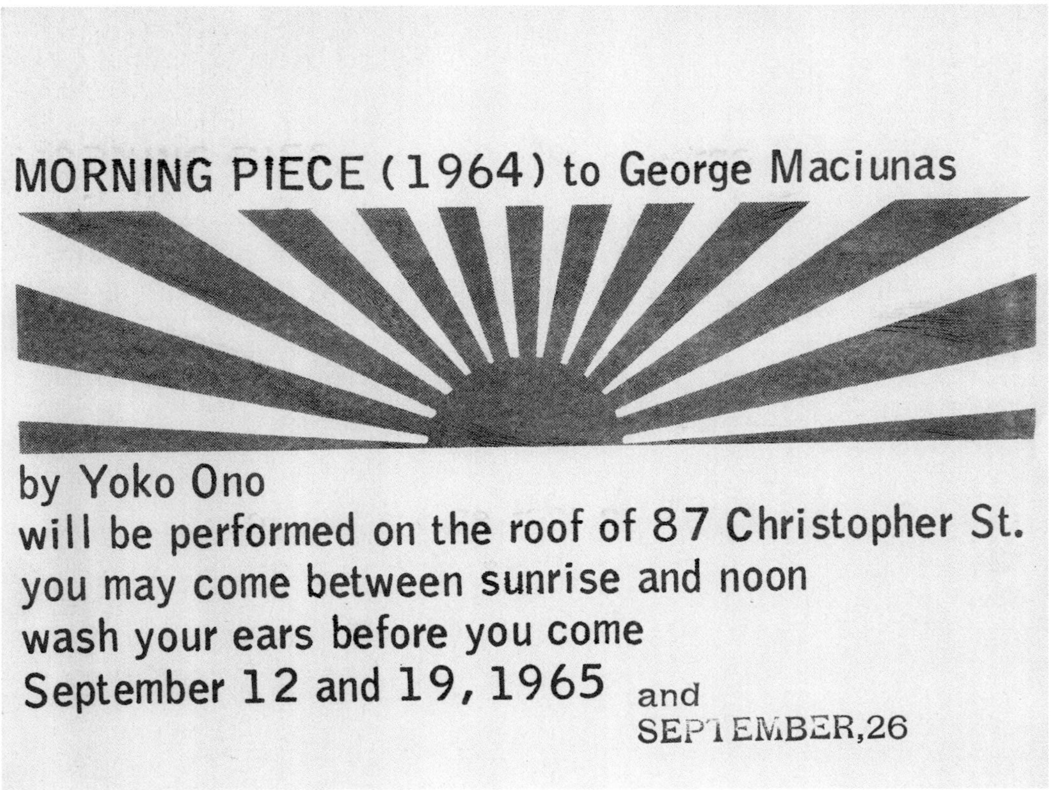

FIGURE 2.11
MORNING PIECE (1964) TO GEORGE MACIUNAS, FLYER, 1965. DESIGN BY GEORGE MACIUNAS. THE GILBERT AND LILA SILVERMAN FLUXUS COLLECTION, DETROIT

written on papers glued to thick shards of glass, offered for sale and priced according to date. In the New York event, Ono laid out bits of sea glass on a gridded tabletop labeled with a date and price for each "morning."

Less than two weeks later, the second historic Fluxus Concert at Carnegie Recital Hall took place (fig. 2.6). The admission tickets for the concert were imprinted balloons that had to be inflated and were popped for entry. The programs were folded into paper airplanes and sailed into the audience by the performers. Ono's *Touch Poems* (fig. 14.5) were exhibited in the Carnegie Recital Hall reception room, which was momentarily turned into a Fluxshop. The Fluxus Orchestra members wore T-shirts decorated with silkscreened images of hairy chests or bare breasts. The evening was conducted by La Monte Young. Ono's works performed that evening were described on the press release as "the most recent composition by this first counterpart in Japan of George Brecht and Ben Vautier." Ono and the orchestra performed *Sky Piece for Jesus Christ*. This piece calls for a chamber group to perform a piece by Mozart or other classical composer and to continue playing as long as they possibly can, while other performers wrap the musicians in gauze bandages, continuing to wrap the entire bodies of the musicians with their instruments until they cannot play (no. 32). They are then led off the stage.

Another 1965 work, *Soundtape and or Film of the Snow Falling at Dawn*, advertised as available through Fluxus, but almost certainly only produced by Yoko Ono, consisted of a small looped sound tape in a tiny metal canister (figs. 2.9–10). The sound produced was one of the purest Fluxus musical experiences imaginable.

Ono had been scoring films since publishing *Six Film Scripts by Yoko Ono* in Tokyo in June 1964. The winter of 1965–66 was a period of intense activity for both Ono and Fluxus. That winter, in late December or early January, she made *Film No. 4 (Fluxfilm No. 16)*, a radical film of naked, walking buttocks. This five minute and thirty second film was included in all versions of the collective *Fluxfilms* anthologies. *Film No. 4* was used in the following ways: in the short version of *Fluxfilms* (forty minutes); in the long version of one hour and forty minutes; packaged as an 8mm film loop with a handheld viewer as an individual Fluxus edition with a *Fluxfilms* label; as an

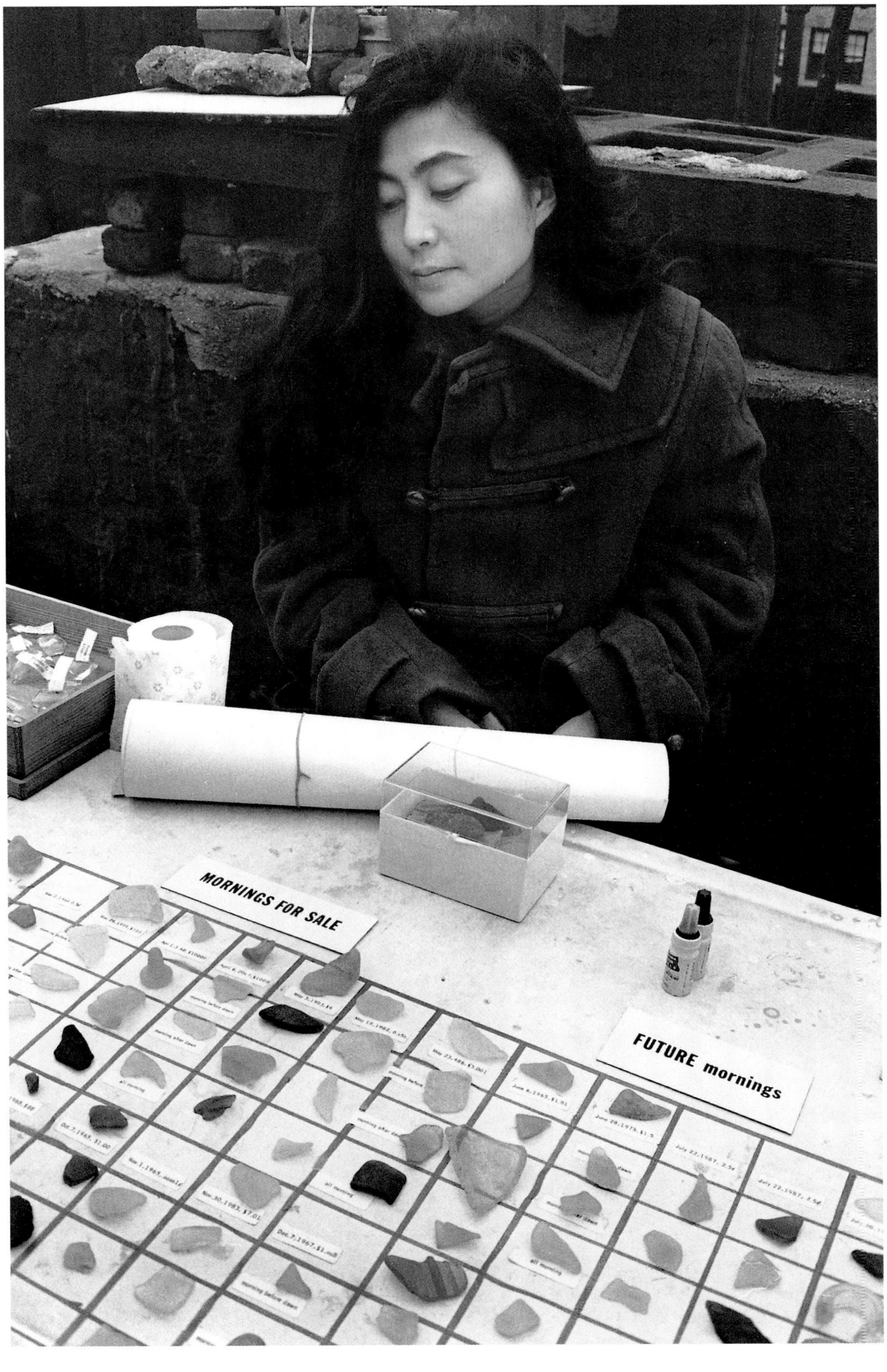

FIGURE 2.12
MORNING PIECE, ROOF OF 87 CHRISTOPHER STREET, NEW YORK, 1965. PHOTOGRAPH
© EST. PETER MOORE / VAGA, NY, NY

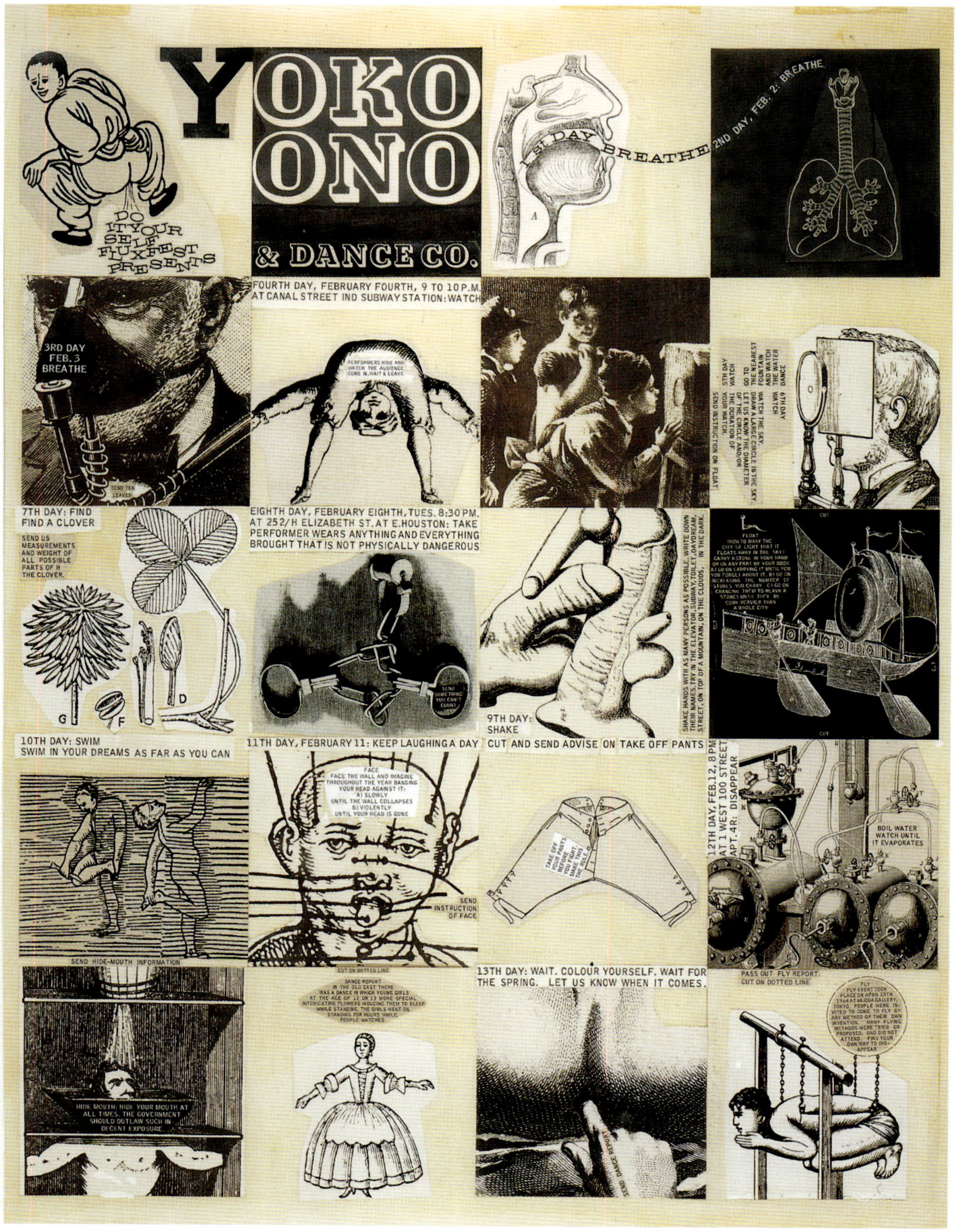

FIGURE 2.13
DO IT YOURSELF FLUXFEST PRESENTS YOKO ONO & DANCE CO., 1966. MECHANICAL FOR ARTIST'S PAGE IN *3 NEWSPAPER EVENTS FOR THE PRICE OF $1* (FLUXUS NEWSPAPER NO. 7), FEBRUARY 1966. DESIGN BY GEORGE MACIUNAS. THE GILBERT AND LILA SILVERMAN FLUXUS COLLECTION, DETROIT

8mm film loop included in all versions of *Flux Year Box 2* together with other Fluxus films; and additionally as a continuous projected loop in a film and sound environment scheduled in the *Fluxfest Presentation of John Lennon & Yoko Ono +*. In yet another incarnation, two stills from the film were used by George Maciunas for Fluxus wallpaper. Also included in the *Fluxfilms* anthology was Ono's *Eyeblink*, the image of a single eye blink performed by the artist and shot with a high-speed camera (the final film is nearly three minutes long). *Number 1* (Fluxfilm No. 14), based on Ono's *Match Piece*, was also filmed with a high-speed camera and is approximately three minutes long. It consists of a match being struck, its flame almost flickering out, and flaring up again. The film has a sexually charged quality.

The next ambitious project that Ono and Maciunas worked on was *Do It Yourself Fluxfest Presents Yoko Ono Dance Co.*, a thirteen-day dance festival published in *3 newspaper eVenTs for the pRicE of $1* (Fluxus Newspaper No. 7), February 1, 1966 (fig. 2.13). The newspaper featured photographs of recent Fluxus Concerts on the front page, and then devoted one page each to the artists Ben Vautier, Yoko Ono, and James Riddle. Ono's page, first titled *Do It Yourself Fluxfest Presents Yoko Ono & Dance Co.*, consisted of a page of images designed by Maciunas for her pieces, which were for performance in the mind, alone, or in public places at designated times and locations. The work is a graphic representation of the different works, divided into twenty sections, to be used as a full-page poster and/or to be cut up into individual cards. The multiple uses are both conceptual and functional.

Subsequently, Ono went on to use this work in a variety of ways. First, pieces found their way into *Art and Artists* as advertising art (no. 38). Then, Ono made her own graphics, revised the texts, and issued the work as *Yoko Ono's 13 Days Do-It-Yourself Dance Festival*, which, in a slightly altered form, was reprinted in the 1970 editions of *Grapefruit*.

In 1970 George Maciunas offered to produce a complex Yoko Ono and Fluxus festival in New York (fig. 2.14). This ambitious project was only partially realized. Many of the activities were recorded in *all photographs copyright nineteen seVenty by peTer mooRE* (Fluxus Newspaper No. 9) (fig. 2.15). The festival, *Fluxfest Presentation of John Lennon & Yoko Ono +*, took place at Joe Jones Tone Deaf Music Store on North Moore Street, on the cobblestone street in front of it, and at 80 Wooster Street, one of the original FluxHouse Co-Ops and home to the Anthology Film Archives at the time. Maciunas lived in the cellar of the building and some of the events took place in the labyrinth of hallways and corridors. More than half of Fluxus Newspaper No. 9 was devoted to photographs of the festival. Ono and Lennon did not attend.

Bag Productions Inc.
Tittenhurst Park,
Ascot, Berkshire.
Ascot 23022

Dear George,
The reason I want this to be Yoko & John and not YOKO ONO is because the whole thing is nicer if it is like a dialogue between Yoko and John with a chorus by Fluxus. . . .

Love,
John & Yoko

1. I am sending the original copy of "Fit to Die" poster we've made which is the second of our Peace Poster Event. (first was the "War Is Over")
I also send one without the "Fit to Die" red writing on so you can blow it up to a large size to maybe fill the shop window and then add the fit to die writing in red.

2. Also 4 photostat copies of A. B. drawing by John & Yoko which (you choose the one you like—large drawings or small drawings.) can be used as the cover of a catalogue for Yoko & John & Flux series in shop. The catalogue should have just three quotes from me re:

quotes from writings by Yoko Ono

1. It's sad that the air is the only thing we share. No matter how close we get to eachother, there is always air between us. It is also nice that we share the air. No matter how far apart we are, the air links us. (Re: Lisson Gallery catalogue)

and
2. Water Talk—(re: Grapefruit) Simon & Schuster copy

3. There's no two mouths alike in the world. Don't worry about being unique. The problem is how to be similar. (— Unit Magazine, London)

Also, our spoon pieces in the shop window should say

A. Three spoons by Yoko Ono
B. Four Spoons by John Lennon

So it is like A. B. works, you know.

MINIATURE PAINTING should be somewhere in "John Lennon as a Young Cloud" week and don't put anything under the microscope—let microscope have a title "John's smile". (you look in the microscope to see John's smile—imaginary, you know)

3. If you think it makes sense—Please print copies of Lisson Gallery catalogue and/or all the film catalogues, maybe, to sell or give them to people.

4. Also our "Making friends among Pigs" Poster (enlarge to shop window-size) which you can use for one of the week's shop window.

5. Also, Acorn Pieces catalogue of Coventry Sculpture Show—we have presented two Acorns in Coventry show—we planted them in one hole—one in the west of the hole and one in the east of the hole.

6. Also some week do you want to add Apple piece (fresh apple) re: Indica catalogue—which was for sale for 600 dollars (one apple) and it is now Collection of John Lennon (Just buy regular green apple from Grocery to use.

For George Maciunas

PROGRAM.

FLUXFEST PRESENTS Yoko Ono + John Lennon

1. Do-It-Yourself by Yoko & John & Everyone
2. Ticket by John & Everyboat
3. Measure by Yoko & John & Hi-Red-Center
4. Blue Room by Yoko & John & Fluxmasterliars
5. Weight & Water by Yoko & John & Fluxfiremen
6. CAPSULE by Yoko & John& Fluxstatecenter
7. Portrait of John Lennon as a Young Cloud by Yoko & Everycloud
8. The Store by Yoko & John & Fluxfactory
9. Examination by Yoko & John & Fluxschool

<u>1. Do-It-Yourself</u>

I will leave it to your judgement as to the selection of my pieces for this week. But try to read <u>Indica</u> & <u>Lisson</u> catalogues and select some from them, too. John's piece instruction "take two eggs—(1869, London Derry/John Lennon) and display two eggs if you want to.

<u>2. Ticket</u> ticket to anywhere (1970 London, John Lennon)

<u>3. Measure</u>
I want to give you my new piece <u>in addition</u> to my old one in Grapefruit.
Measure from the store to the nearest water (1970 London, Yoko Ono)
John's piece:
Measure from the nearest water to the store (1970 London, John Lennnon)
Add Hi-Red Centre to this.

<u>4. Blue Room</u>
The whole room should be completely white with maybe one chair, one table (also white)

Display 2 sets of 4 spoons in the shop window
One set should have a sign reading "3 spoons" by Yoko Ono London 1967 (It's in the Lisson Gallery catalogue)
The other set (Exactly the same set) should read "4 spoons" by John Lennon, London 1970

One soft rubber ball (white) somewhere in the room with a sign saying "This sphere will be a sharp point when it gets to the far side of the room in your mind" by Yoko Ono. 1964.

A standing needle somewhere in the room (re: Indica Gallery catalogue photo) with the sign saying "forget it" Yoko Ono 1966.
There should be another needle (exactly the same one next to it with a sign saying "needle" John Lennon 1970)

There should be a cup on a table with a sign saying "Not to be appreciated until it's broken" Yoko Ono 1966
"Mend" 1966 Y.O. (there should be broken pieces of a cup.

There should be a sign under the window saying
"This window is 2000 ft. long. Yoko Ono. 1967"
"This window is ———— ft. long <u>(the actual footage)</u> John Lennon 1970"

A big chest or box (also white) that occupies a large space and looks heavy with a sign saying "This is not here" Y.O. 1967

Other signs:
"A straight line exist only in your mind"
Y.O. 66 / Y.O. 70
This Line is a part of a large sphere" (long straight Line, of part of the structure of the room) Y.O. 70

Use Ashtray (don't leave any Ashtray around)
—Y.O. '66
NO SMOKING—J.L. '70
Do Not Disturb—J.L. '70
STAY UNTIL THE ROOM IS BLUE—Y.O. '66

Also, sign outside
Spring, rain, sky, wind, etc. (according to the weather of the day) by Yoko Ono '67.

5. <u>Weight & Water</u>
All the pieces should read Yoko & <u>(whoever brought the piece)</u>
John's pieces
Weight piece – A dry sponge (Yoko & John '70)
Water piece – A wet sponge (Yoko & John '70)

6. <u>CAPSULE</u>
Our contribution to this week will be a 8mm home movie by John & Yoko and we will make it and send it to you — it will be the world premiere of this piece. Also, please display our film catalogues and sell them or give them away (you must reprint them 1000 or 2000 copies each?)

7. instructions for this is "Open and Close" by Yoko Ono 1967 London (there is a open and close piece in Grapefruit, too if you can find it, but this 1967 version is a theatre piece and there is three versions. One is many, many, doors, cupboards, etc, to open. Other is despite the instruction, when people come, there is nothing for them to open and close, third is all the things are closed tight so they cannot be "opened and closed". I think 1st version is best for this shop.

8. <u>THE STORE</u>
Select any of my pieces you like
John's piece for this is tin money (with smooth surface) which you can put in vending machine instead of real money—to cheat, you know. (1970, John Lennon)

<u>Examination</u>
John's question is
"What time is it?" 1970, London
mine, you can select or make up. Or let people guess.
"guess what my question is " Y.O. 1970 London
and put many other questions by many other artists please.

FIGURE 2.14
LETTER BY YOKO ONO
TO GEORGE MACIUNAS,
EARLY 1970

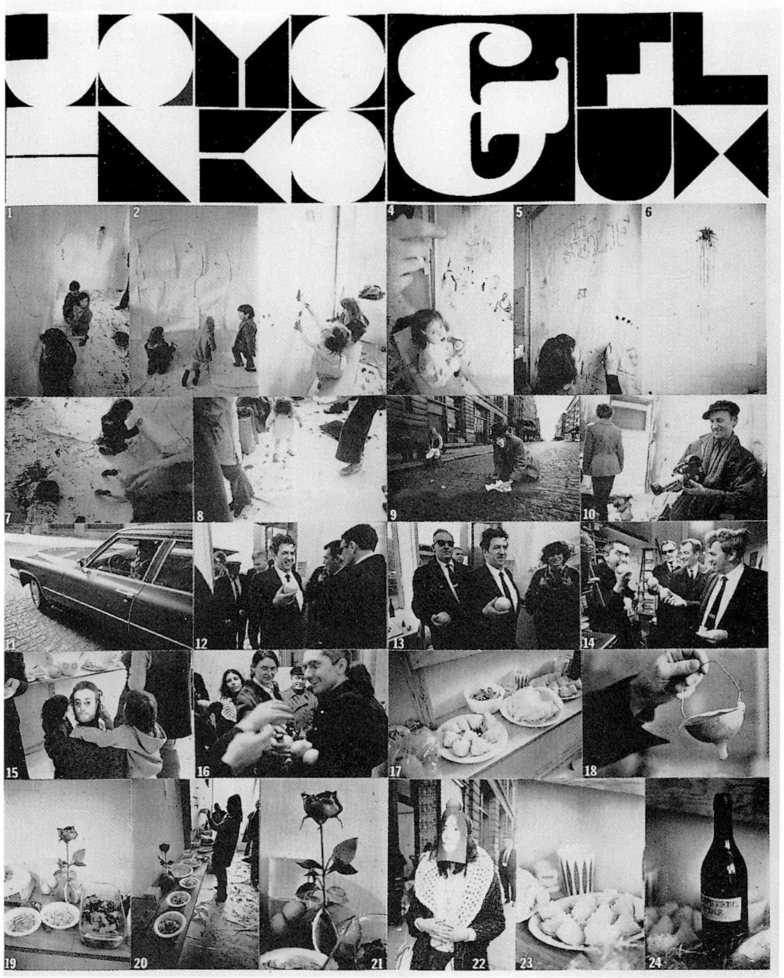

FIGURE 2.15
FLUXUS, PAGE 1, *ALL PHOTOGRAPHS COPYRIGHT NINETEEN SEVENTY BY PETER MOORE* (FLUXUS NEWSPAPER NO. 9), 1970

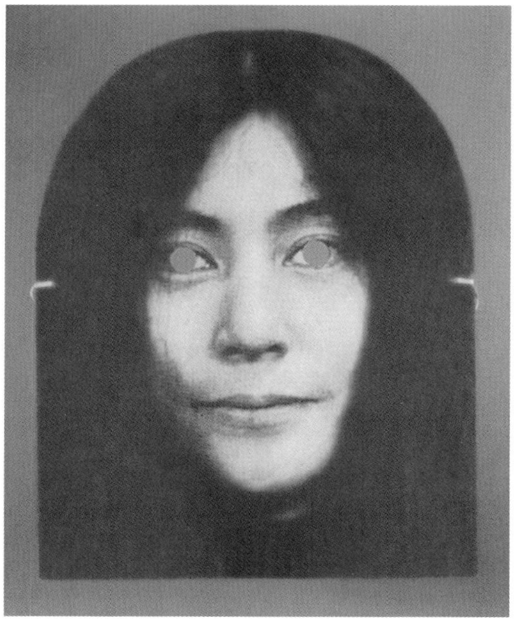

FIGURE 2.16
GEORGE MACIUNAS, ***YOKO ONO MASK***, FLUXUS EDITION, 1970. THE GILBERT AND LILA SILVERMAN FLUXUS COLLECTION, DETROIT

After the festival, Jim Harithas, Director of the Everson Museum in Syracuse, New York, invited Ono to have a retrospective of her work at his museum. Building on her concepts described in her letter to George Maciunas of an exhibition and series of events in dialogue with John Lennon, and realizing that Maciunas was unable to fully implement many of the ideas for the New York festival, she engaged him to actively help her produce work for the Everson show, titled *This Is Not Here*. That show in one sense is not a Fluxus event, and was never stated as such at the time. However, in certain ways, it became a fulfillment of what Maciunas had tried to do in certain Fluxus concerts and events of single Fluxus artists. *This Is Not Here* took over the entire museum, and contained a number of participatory and collaborative works (figs. 2.18, 14.24). Further, in making a deluxe edition of the catalogue, now called *Yoko Ono Everson Catalogue Box* (fig. 2.17), Maciunas was able to produce the kind of anthology of an artist's work that he had laid plans for as early as 1963.

Following the Everson retrospective was a period when Maciunas, busy with developing artist housing in SoHo called FluxHouse Cooperatives, was less intensely engaged in producing Fluxus concerts and events. Perhaps responding to what he viewed as a movement away from the ideals of Fluxus by a number of avant-garde artists, Maciunas organized an event at Anthology Film Archives, one of the earliest Fluxhouse Cooperatives: *Fluxfest presents: 12! Big Names!* on April 21, 1975. The event poster listed Acconci, Beuys, Phillip Glass, Kaprow, Levine, Manzoni, Nauman, Ono, Snow, Rinke, Vostel, and Warhol (fig. 2.19). In his May 3, 1975 *Flux Newsletter*, Maciunas described the event as follows:

> (very large names, about 20 ft wide were shown one at a time for about 5 minutes each, to the audience) Since many of the works of chosen big names are imitative of work by smaller names, the large audience attendance must be the cause of the names and not the works. We satisfied the audience therefore by omitting the works altogether and adding instead more big names.

Until his death in 1978, Maciunas continued to include Ono in collective Fluxus events, such as *Water Clock* (or *Kiss*) at the 1975/76 *Flux–New Year's Eve Event at Clock Tower*, New York (fig. 2.20), and *Invitation to Participate in Flux Summer Fest in South Berkshires* of March 4, 1977, which was unrealized. He also included her work *Shadow Box* in plans for one of his last anthologies of collective Fluxus work

FIGURE 2.17

GEORGE MACIUNAS, DRAWING FOR ***EVERSON CATALOGUE BOX***, 1971. INK ON PAPER. THE GILBERT AND LILA SILVERMAN FLUXUS COLLECTION, DETROIT

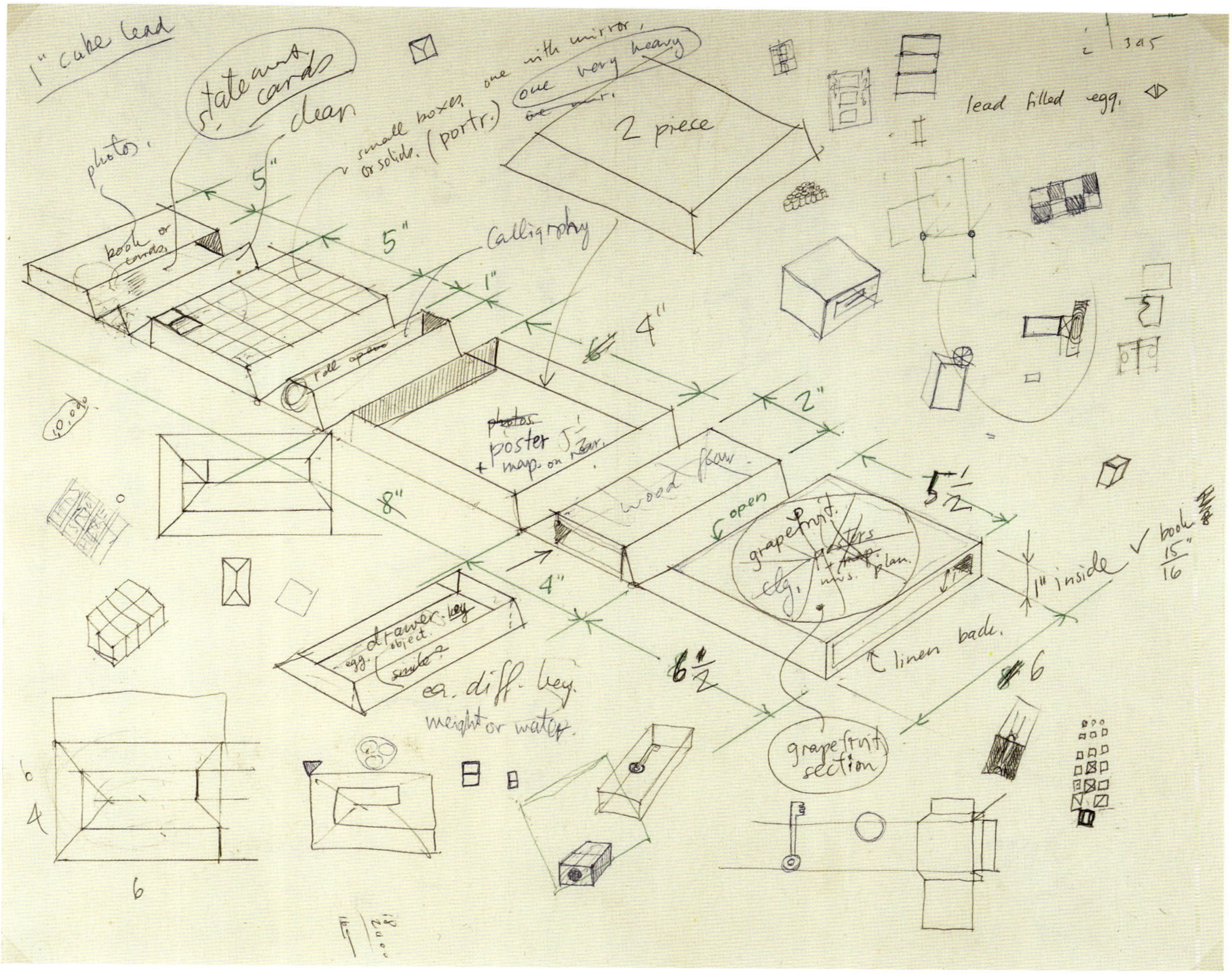

FIGURE 2.18

BLUE ROOM EVENT, RUBBER STAMPS, 1971. PRODUCED BY GEORGE MACIUNAS. THE GILBERT AND LILA SILVERMAN FLUXUS COLLECTION, DETROIT

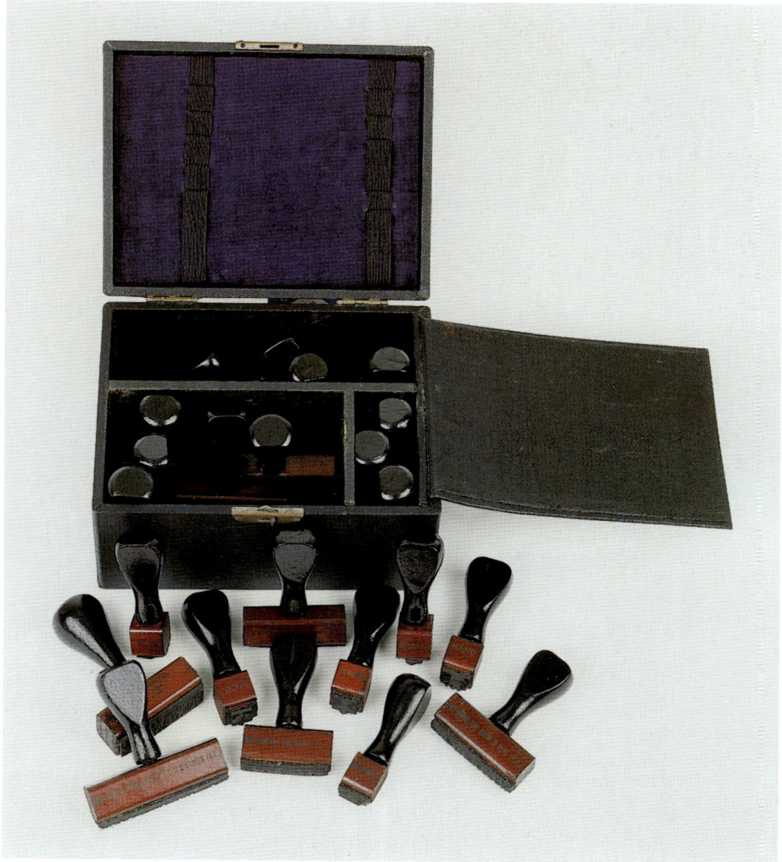

ca. 1976—a light and kinetic installation on the ceiling, floors, and walls of Jean Brown's Fluxus Room at the Shaker Seed House in Tyringham, Massachusetts.

Yoko Ono's contributions to Fluxus are only now beginning to be fully understood, but it is clear that she had a significant impact on the direction of Fluxus, and the impact of Fluxus on emerging movements from the sixties to the end of the century is now being felt. Fluxus never encompassed all of an artist's work, and much of Ono's work is outside Fluxus. Some is parallel to the movement and some harkens back to it. Ultimately, Yoko Ono must be considered both as a Fluxus artist and as an artist independent of Fluxus.

> On FLUXUS
>
> Fluxus is Flux: the act of continuous flow and change. During the exhibition, do not let the artists' statements about Fluxus stay on the wall like words carved on stone. Paint over the wall with the color you like. Keep painting. Y.O. 96
>
> (Written for *Prima fest di un altro mondo*, 1996, dedicated to Gino [Di Maggio])

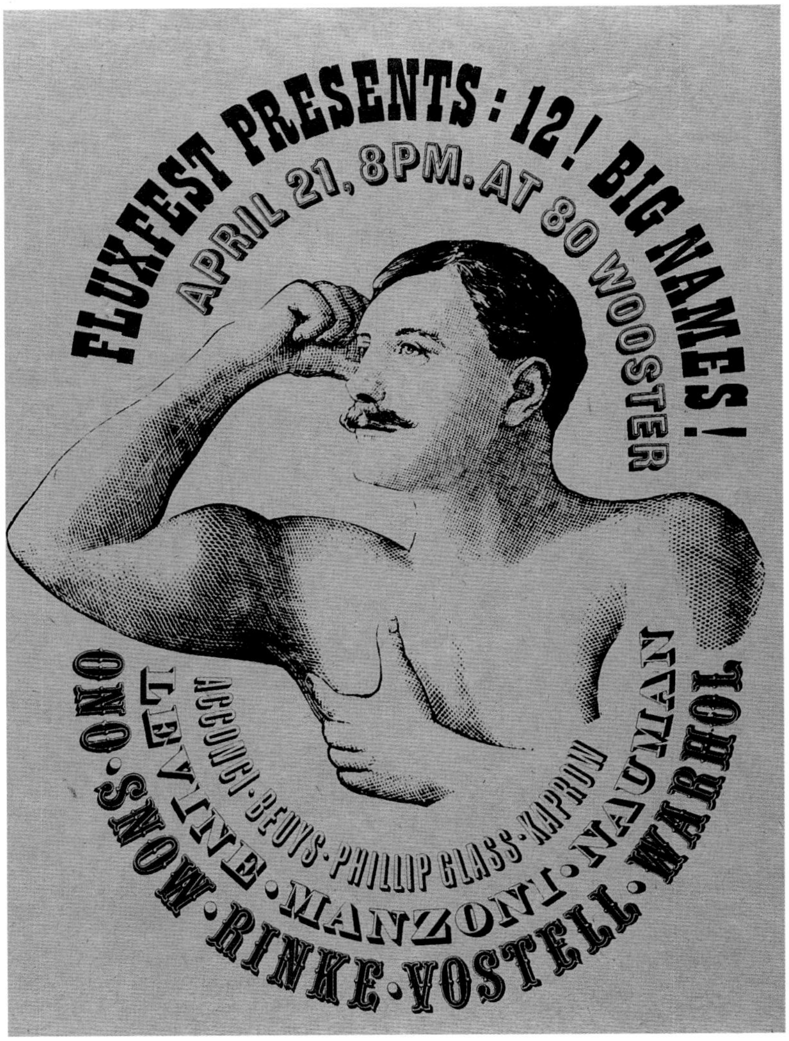

FIGURE 2.19
FLUXUS, ***FLUXFEST PRESENTS: 12! BIG NAMES!***, POSTER, 1975. DESIGN BY GEORGE MACIUNAS. THE GILBERT AND LILA SILVERMAN FLUXUS COLLECTION, DETROIT

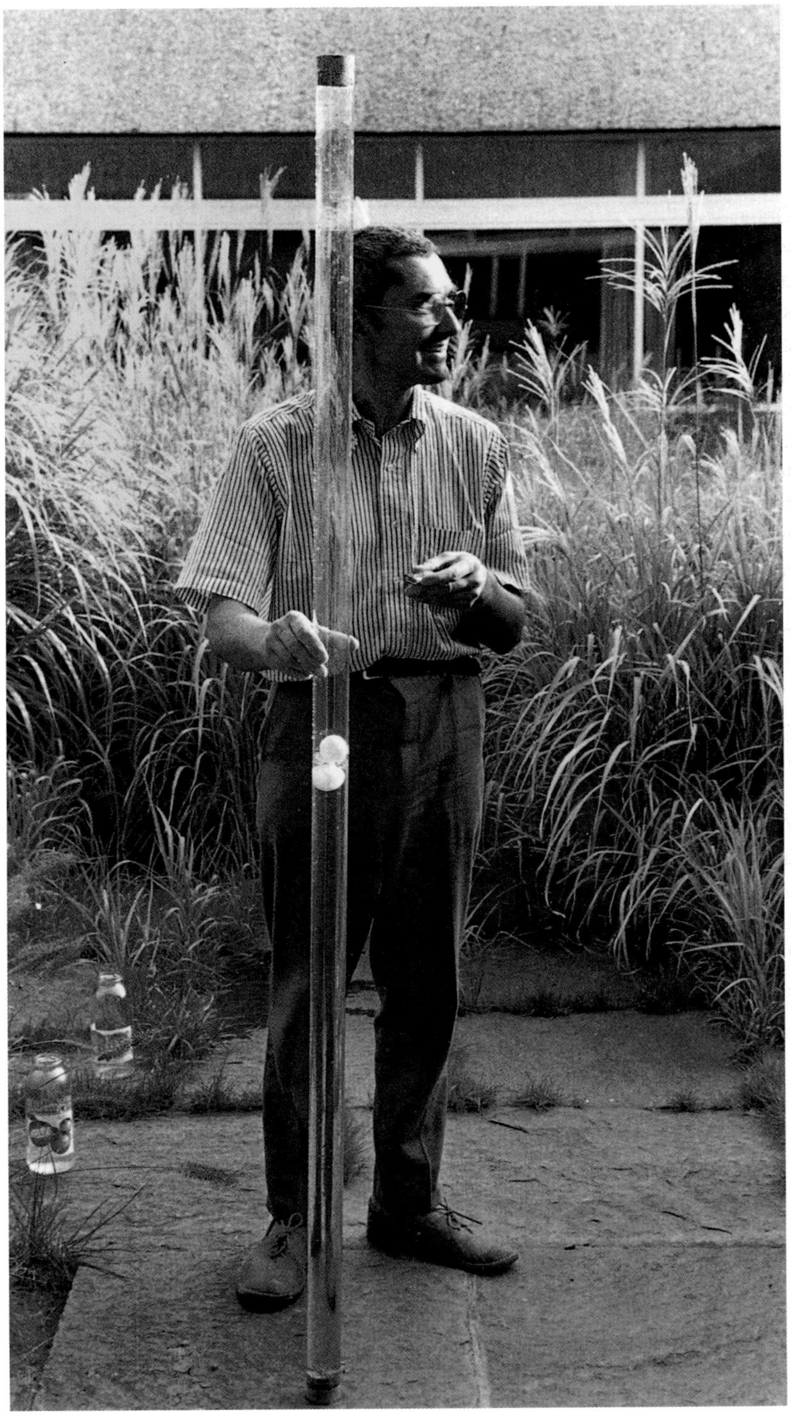

FIGURE 2.20
WATER CLOCK (KISS), 1976. HELD BY GEORGE MACIUNAS. PHOTOGRAPH © 1976 LARRY MILLER

The Making of Yoko Ono, Prophet of the 1960s

MURRAY SAYLE

Originality, it is said, means coming from somewhere else. "Somewhere else" can be many places: another time, another culture, the other gender, despair, madness—anywhere except familiar here and everyday now. John Lennon has told us of his first magical meeting with Yoko Ono, when he wandered into her one-woman show at Indica Gallery in London, on November 9, 1966, a pivotal date in the ferment immortalized as the Sixties, and was intrigued, as well as mystified, by what he saw. Invited by Ono to pay five shillings to hammer a nail into a piece of plain wood shown as artwork, Lennon made a counteroffer: "Well, I'll give you an imaginary five shillings and hammer an imaginary nail in." "That's when we really met," Lennon later recalled. "That's when we locked eyes, and she got it and I got it, and, as they say in all the interviews we do, the rest is history."

All lovers know the moment when complicity leaps like an electric spark, but in their case, founded on what? Outwardly, the two had nothing in common. Lennon had come from "genteel poverty" in a dysfunctional working-class family, via art school and sweaty teenage dance hangouts in England and Germany, to world fame and an honorable fortune as a rock 'n' roll musician, composer, and role model for the first generation of Western youth to recall nothing of World War II. Ono, seven years his senior, remembered all too well the apocalyptic end of Japan's Pacific War, the hunger and despair that followed the defeat and Occupation she had seen at first hand. But her own roots were in wealth and privilege: her mother, Isoko, came from the Yasuda banking family, and her father, Yeisuke, himself a banker by profession, descended from a long line of samurai warrior-scholars. Yoko had personally known little deprivation, and had been educated among Japan's business and intellectual elite. Just the same, like had recognized like at that mythic London meeting.

Like what? The explanation lies half-buried under decades of Japan's prosperity. By 1966 Lennon was becoming one of the gurus of the disillusioned, questing mood of the Sixties in the West. Yoko Ono had been there, at least spiritually, long before. Something very like the mood of the Sixties first took shape in Tokyo in the late 1940s; Japan's confused, hungry years were the "somewhere else" Yoko Ono came from. Even then, and there, it was the amalgam, rather than any of its elements, that was really new. Radical pacifism and politicized feminism had both bloomed in spiritually defeated Europe after the First World War, where they had found artistic expression in the instant arts of gesture and performance, made somewhat more durable by photographs.

By the late 1940s, after the Second World War, Japan was in a state of despair even deeper and longer-lasting than Europe had known after the first, and by the mid-fifties Japanese art had found a similar expression, this time not as an imported style, but with its own emotional authenticity. Japanese ingredients, notably the cerebral anti-intellectualism of Zen Buddhism, flavored a mixture which was original, distinctive, and more than the sum of its parts. Yoko Ono was the prophet who, with the help of John Lennon, brought the amalgam to a West at long last ready to reconsider its values. By different paths, Lennon and Western youth had arrived at a need, Ono with its fulfillment. More justifiably than most lovers, John and Yoko knew, in the flash of enlightenment at the Indica Gallery, that they were of one mind.

Ono's road to the rendezvous was the less obvious of the two. She was born in Tokyo on February 18, 1933, one year after Japan set up a puppet state in Manchuria, a long step toward the catastrophe of 1945. Two weeks earlier her father had been transferred to San Francisco with the Yokohama Specie Bank, the financial arm of Japan's expanding empire. His wife and daughter followed, and Yoko from infancy heard both English and Japanese, the foundation of her subsequent bilingualism. In the spring of 1937, as Japan began a full-scale war in China, Yoko, her mother, and younger brother Keisuke, born in December 1936, returned to Tokyo, where Yoko was enrolled in the kindergarten of the Peers' School (Gakushūin), a Tokyo institution then open only to relatives of the imperial family or of members of the parliament's House of Peers (her maternal grandfather, banker Yasuda Zenjirō, had been ennobled in 1915). In 1940 Yoko's mother, fearing that all Japanese might be interned if Japan and the United States went to war and that she might not see him for many years, bravely took her two children and rejoined her husband, by this time stationed in New York. The family finally sailed from San Francisco for Japan in the spring of 1941. At the time of Pearl Harbor Yoko's father was working at the Hanoi branch of his bank, while Yoko was enrolled in a Christian primary school in Tokyo, run by one of the Mitsui family for Japanese children returned from abroad.

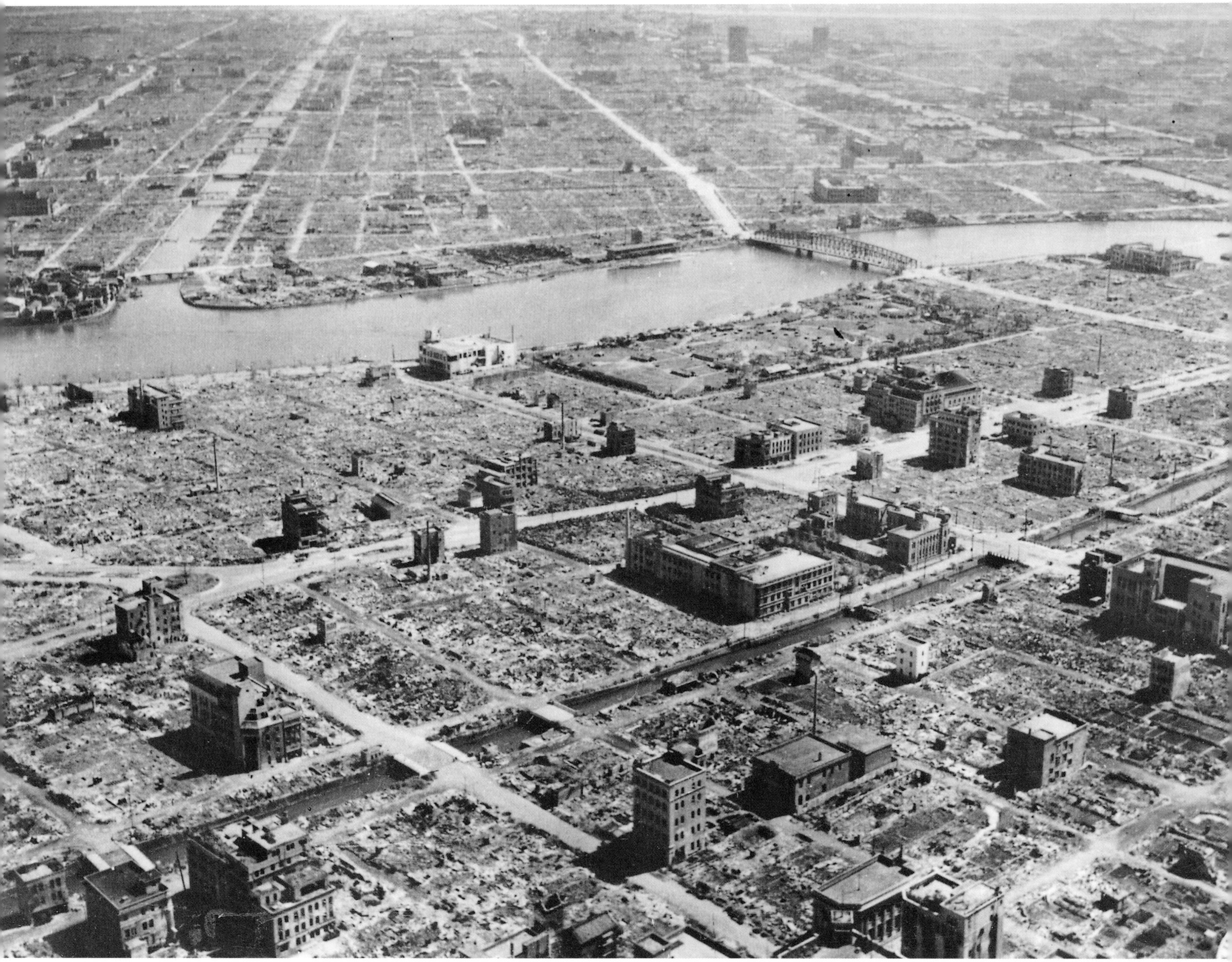

FIGURE 3.1
DOWNTOWN TOKYO
AFTER THE FIREBOMBING
OF MARCH 10, 1945

Mitsui Takasumi's school gave Yoko a safe and liberal refuge for most of the war. She continued studying English and was listed as a primary school student well after her twelfth birthday, when most boys and girls her age became liable for sometimes risky war work. She was still living in Tokyo and being privately tutored in the Bible, Buddhism, and the piano when a quarter of the city was burnt out in the great firebomb raid of March 9, 1945—an inferno she survived in the Ono family bunker in the affluent Azabu residential district, far from the incinerated downtown. Only then did her mother move her three children to a farming village near the still fashionable Karuizawa mountain resort. The choice of refuge proved fortunate, as Yoko and her brother and sister, in the desperate days of defeat and the collapse of the Japanese economy, were able to help their mother barter family treasures for food. At the end of the war the family returned to Tokyo, where Yoko rejoined the Peers' School in April 1946.

Founded in Tokyo in 1877, the Peers' School, like its near equivalents, Eton in England and Groton in the United States, has been more noted for social than for academic standing. Its campus near the Imperial Palace survived the great fire raids more or less intact, and its first postwar intake was very like the prewar ones. When the peerage was abolished in 1947 the school became theoretically open to anyone, including foreign exchange students (a classmate of the present Crown Prince Naruhito was the son of a plumber from Melbourne, Australia), but like Tokyo itself, the Peers' School has since recovered much of its high-society glitter.

The view from the school windows, however, has changed beyond recognition. When Yoko and her classmates looked over the school's walls in the spring of 1946 they saw a city all but returned, as General Curtis E. LeMay, Jr. had promised, to the Stone Age. Whole districts were sterile wastelands of twisted iron and blackened stone. People lived in holes clawed in the ground, roofed with stray sheets of iron. On every corner of what had once been shopping streets, famished men and women tried to sell trinkets, clothes, anything for food. Trains from the countryside brought farmers loaded with rice and vegetables for the black market. In makeshift bars in dank cellars workers formed lines to gulp industrial alcohol. To sharpen the misery, smartly dressed, well-fed American soldiers tootled around Tokyo's ruins in jeeps, driving on the side of the road they were accustomed to, the right—rare Japanese vehicles simply got out of the way. In a terminal degradation of Japanese martial values, American servicewomen smiled for souvenir snaps in rickshaws pulled by Japanese men still wearing the tattered remnants of military uniforms, eyes turned down in exhaustion, hunger, and shame. Few gazing over this desolate scene would have recognized the fertile seedbed of a great and original flowering of art and cinema—unless they happened to have seen Berlin in 1919, or Moscow after Russia's revolution and before Stalin.

Japan under Occupation was a paradox: democracy imposed by a conqueror, General Douglas MacArthur, "the Macarto," more autocratic than any shogun had been for centuries. Occupation supposedly freed the Japanese press, but two weeks after it began censorship was reimposed, and all mention of Hiroshima and Nagasaki, for instance, was bluepenciled. The predictable result was to turn the atomic bombs into monstrous symbols of evil, beyond all rational discourse, in which shape they haunt Japanese and the rest of us to this day. Some accused Japanese war criminals were arrested and leisurely trials began; but Emperor Hirohito, who (as all but a handful of Japanese believed) had directed Japan's war in person, was free to visit the conqueror—and the resulting photograph, of a stiffly correct Emperor and a showily casual general, was as ambiguous as the occasion. The trials were intended to show the Japanese their war crimes—but the Soviet judge was from the nation which held a half-million Japanese prisoner, many never to see their homes and families again.

Most Tokyo residents, as in any war-devastated city, were engrossed in searching for food and shelter. Even from an island of privilege like the Peers' School, the world outside no longer made sense. That America's war had been wholly just ("the justest war in history," U.S. propaganda claimed) and therefore Japan's totally unjust was by no means so clear to puzzled young people as it was to the victors. Yes, there had been crimes and cruelties, on both sides, and who could strike the balance? The best answer seemed to be that war itself was to blame. Pacifism has been Japan's most enduring legacy of those years: "Make love not war," the slogan of the Western Sixties, well expresses the mood of Tokyo in 1946, as of starving Berlin in 1918. Right up to this day, "Peace" (a brand of cigarette) and "Love" (with an arrow-pierced heart) are English words almost every Japanese knows.

Feminism was more prominent in Japan's early postwar years than ever since. Women were given the vote by the largely American-written 1946 constitution, and pressure from new woman members of parliament finally led in 1958 to the abolition of the licensed brothels. The law making adultery a crime for wives but not for husbands was repealed in 1947. Some professions, notably teaching, introduced equal pay. However, the feminism of Japan's postwar years was less ideological than situational, the feminism of hard times. War, especially in Japan, has always been a hypermasculine pursuit. The utter defeat of 1945 temporarily, perhaps permanently, discredited the warrior ethos. Strong, resourceful women like Yoko Ono's mother, who had kept homes and families afloat through eight years of war, saw Japan's surrender as simply another manmade crisis to be survived. Thousands of women, "pan pan girls," prostituted themselves to American soldiers, often for food for their families. Others hired out as the victors' maids, cooks, and nannies. In close to a millennium, only one part of the English-speaking world has known such total defeat. In Scarlett O'Hara, novelist Margaret Mitchell imagined a strong woman's response to the shipwreck of Southern male pretensions very like that of many Japanese women in 1945. In "Woman Is the Nigger of the World" by Ono and Lennon, we can hear, behind the offensive racial slur, the anger of a privileged girl at what her humbler sisters had once been driven to, just for survival.

One of the first arts to revive in Japan was cinema, by which a mass audience could be reached for the price of a seat in a battered hall. The great Akira Kurosawa had a script in shape for his enigmatic *Rashomon* as early as 1947, although it took until 1950 to find financing and finish it. Its theme, the impossibility of arriving at reliable truth about any event by way of the self-serving distortions of witnesses and participants, was a plain parable of Japan's situation. The first voice from within defeated Japan to be heard outside, *Rashomon* began the process, still incomplete, of explaining the pariah nation to a suspicious world. Kurosawa added an important aside to the bleak vision of Akutagawa Ryūnosuke, who wrote the two stories on which the film is partly based and killed himself, at thirty-five, in 1927. Kurosawa's addition has the woodcutter, one of the witnesses whose version of the rape of a samurai's wife and the murder of her husband by a bandit cannot be trusted, adopt a baby abandoned by the ruined city gate that gives the film its name. Life, says the film, goes on; there is always hope. A quarter century later, John Lennon climbed a ladder at the Indica Gallery and through a magnifying glass read the one word Ono had written on the gallery's ceiling: YES. "At least" Lennon later recalled, "her message was positive."

Kurosawa apart (*Rashomon* won the Grand Prix at the 1950 Venice film festival), all the outside world heard from Japan in the immediate postwar years came through the propaganda megaphone of the Occupation. MacArthur's headquarters censored not only what the Japanese media reported in Japan, but what the corps of foreign correspondents stationed in Tokyo could send abroad. The publication of John Hersey's searing "Hiroshima"

(1946), the century's most influential piece of journalism, was only possible because Hersey wrote in the offices of *The New Yorker*, far from the Occupation's censors. The year 1945, in fact, marked the sharpest discontinuity between generations in all Japanese history, but few outside Japan could distinguish this reality from the claims of MacArthur's personal publicity machine—and, as with all such breaks with the past, much continued unchanged, and a reverse current soon set in, guided by the same Occupation authority. What many Japanese still remember as the years of postwar democracy ended all too soon. The role assigned Japan in the world was changing. In 1949 the Soviets broke the U.S. nuclear monopoly, Chinese Communists won their civil war, and the Korean War broke out in June of 1950. The Occupation had already begun its "reverse course." No longer an enemy to be punished and reformed, Japan became a potential ally to be courted for the threatened new world war with Communism. Korean war spending, the opening of the huge U.S. market to Japanese products, the revival of Japan's wartime production system with its ties between banks, bureaucrats, and favored industrialists—the celebrated "Japan, Inc."—got Japan back on the dual road of economic recovery and social counter-revolution.

Good times are not necessarily propitious for the arts. By 1951, when Yoko Ono graduated from the Peers' School, the creative ferment of the postwar years was subsiding and mainstream Japan settled down to take advantage of the "reverse course" and its material payoffs. Feminism stalled and Japan's pacifism was entangled in the alliance with the nuclear-armed U.S. Early in 1952 Yoko entered the philosophy faculty of her school's associated Peers' University, its first female student of that most cerebral of disciplines, but after two semesters she dropped out. Approaching her twentieth birthday, her most impressionable years behind her, Ono rejoined her family in Scarsdale, New York, where her father was again a banker, and enrolled in nearby Sarah Lawrence College, strong in the visual arts. This led her to America's avant-garde, where she experimented with painting, music, film, and the various performance arts. By 1962 Yoko was back in Tokyo, exhibiting with some success as a member of the Japanese avant-garde. Leaving Japan again, she found her way to a small London gallery specializing in the avant-garde then finding a wider audience, as always in times of turmoil. It took the intellectual Ono a while to see what the untutored, instinctual Lennon offered her—the world, as audience.

How had John Lennon reached his side of the mysteriously fated rendezvous at the Indica Gallery in 1966? Born in 1940, he had no real memories of World War II. The years of his adolescence, the fifties, were a time of complacent self-satisfaction in the English-speaking world, of growing affluence, of interminable war movies presenting the victors as supermen (but not as superwomen—just as the war had deflated the male values of Japanese, it had inflated those of the Western winners, whose women were quickly ejected from the jobs they had held while the men were away fighting, and theoretically went back, for the last time, to being full-time housewives and mothers). The return of a prosperity not known since the 1920s, apparently permanently, did little for adult women, but a great deal economically for adolescents, now called "teenagers," who commanded real wages and competitively bigger allowances from ambitious parents, in economies finally freed of the threat of unemployment. Their purchasing power made a fresh market for recording companies and made the performers correspondingly rich—few richer than the Fab Four from Liverpool, the Beatles.

As much as anything, the Beatles owed their huge success to a creative tension between John Lennon and Paul McCartney, the duo who wrote most of their songs—Paul the sentimental and tuneful, John the tart realist. Such partnerships of opposites have often been wildly successful in popular music: Rodgers and Hart, Gilbert and Sullivan complemented each other creatively, but were drawn by temperament to very different lifestyles. Advised by their astute manager, Brian Epstein, to present a wholesome image unthreatening to British parents, the Beatles were made Members of the Order of the British Empire (a medal usually given to worthy civil servants like postmasters) in 1965, and they duly acquired wholesome girlfriends and/or wives to match. With a blonde English wife, Cynthia, and an infant son, Julian, Lennon later described feeling "trapped" in "a happily married state of boredom." Money and its rewards had never been his main motivation—rather, as the wordsmith and intellectual of the partnership, he sought self-expression. This inevitably meant expressing the feelings of his contemporaries, the very normal rebellion of any generation against the one before it, a rebellion delayed for Lennon and those who thought like him by the huge (and not unjustified) self-satisfaction of their elders who had won the war, and the peace, and then in their own minds the battle of life itself.

Aimless, shapeless discontent among young people who felt themselves overshadowed and marginalized by the war generation had already inspired James Dean's *Rebel Without a Cause* (1955), Allen Ginsberg's "Howl" (1956), John Osborne's *Look Back in Anger* (1956), and Jack Kerouac's *On the Road* (1957). These one-offs by unknown outsiders, meaningless to mainstream adults, could be ignored—whereas the Beatles were the Western establishment's lovable young rascals, with teenage followers in just about every English-speaking home. All that was needed to complete the radicalization of young people in the later sixties was a new war, a worldwide crisis that called for immediate public action. I happened to be in Vietnam covering the first big search-and-destroy operation by American regular troops in the very same week that Yoko met John. War was again front-page, news-dominating. After an on-again, off-again courtship, Lennon left his wife and their posh stockbroker-belt country mansion and set up house with Yoko in the London flat of Ringo Starr. Later, in 1968, they released *Unfinished Music No. 1: Two Virgins*, a sound collage they had recorded on their first night together, with a self-shot nude photograph of the couple on the cover. They married in March 1969, promising many "happenings." Their wedding was the first, followed by "Bed Peace" in an Amsterdam hotel, then a huge billboard in Times Square: "WAR IS OVER! / If you want it." The Lennons had become emblematic leaders of a universal cultural revolution. Long matured, the pre-occupations of Yoko Ono's vivid Tokyo adolescence had captured Lennon's energy, given his aimless life new direction, and at the same time brought her art to a world audience, Japan's own youth very much a part of it. Like the o's in Yoko Ono, the artistic wheel had finally come full circle.

Not Here

DAVID A. ROSS

t wasn't my idea. That was for certain. It had to be Yoko's, but then she never took much credit for ideas, one way or the other. It could have been Jim Harithas's, the director of the Everson Museum of Art in Syracuse. It was his idea to invite Yoko for her first career survey exhibition and to stage it in a city that was a bit outside of the art world as it was then known. Whosever it was, the idea was deceptively simple, like so many that at first seemed hardly an idea at all. "This is not here."

The question was how to provide an overview of Yoko Ono's work that would refocus the world's attention where it belonged—on the work, not the personalities surrounding it. For us, a side issue was how to get people to come to the grayest city in New York State, known by the charming nickname "Salt City." So, *This Is Not Here*, a simple and declarative exhibition title, told you something and negated it at the same time. Like the old New England saw, "You can't get there from here," Yoko's title for her 1971 Everson Museum survey seemed to pull the floor from under your feet, leaving the rug still mysteriously in place. But what was Yoko Ono really saying by framing her first retrospective in that manner?

The invitation to *This Is Not Here* was printed on a small square of unfixed photographic paper, corner-folded inward to make a square within a square, and mailed in a light-safe envelope. To the surprise and consternation of those opening the envelope and unfolding the corners in normal illumination, the text was a photographic image that began to disappear into an opaque golden surface within a minute of its exposure to light (fig. 4.2). It read:

You are invited
to the opening
of *THIS IS NOT*
HERE by yoko ono
john lennon as
guest artist at
everson museum
in Syracuse, n. y.
oct. 9 12 am–9 pm
this admits two

The reader was ultimately left with a telephone number and Yoko Ono's name with a request for a reply, printed lightly on the reverse. What was this thing you were invited to? Where was it?

The invitation, based on Yoko's idea, was designed by Yoko's Fluxus co-conspirator George Maciunas as a perfectly conceptual piece. Beyond that, it spoke to the underlying spirit of the exhibition: not a simple negation of being but, rather, the pure and completely open possibility of existential suspension. If not here, where? Syracuse? How apt.

The exhibition filled virtually the entire Everson Museum and, in a sense, was about the idea of the museum (or anti-museum). As an extension of her text-based performance and installation works, *This Is Not Here* consisted primarily of instruction works (both objects and installations); a film section; and an invitational section of works by Fluxus colleagues and other friends of Ono and Lennon's, ranging from Andy Warhol and Max Neuhaus to Julian Beck and Judith Malina, Nam June Paik and Bob Dylan. In a gesture typical of Yoko's participatory art, each "guest" artist was asked to deliver an object that Yoko (as host) would complete by conceptually filling with water. Warhol contributed his first-ever videotaped work: an audiovisual study of the surface of the Factory watercooler and the conversation that occurred in its immediate radius.

Ono's survey exhibition was a sociological phenomenon as much as a spectacular art world event. Although known as an artist in her own right among the international avant-garde community, by 1971 she had become world-famous as the wife of John Lennon, to many the most powerfully influential musician of the era. But at the time of the Everson show, Ono's full crossover identity as both a serious artist and a star in the world of popular culture was still emerging. Conceptual Art, though widely understood and appreciated today, was then generally misunderstood as a game, or worse, as an "emperor's new clothes" joke perpetrated by the heirs of Duchamp on an unwary world. Yoko's conceptual work was no exception. She was ridiculed by conservative critics in the popular press and by those

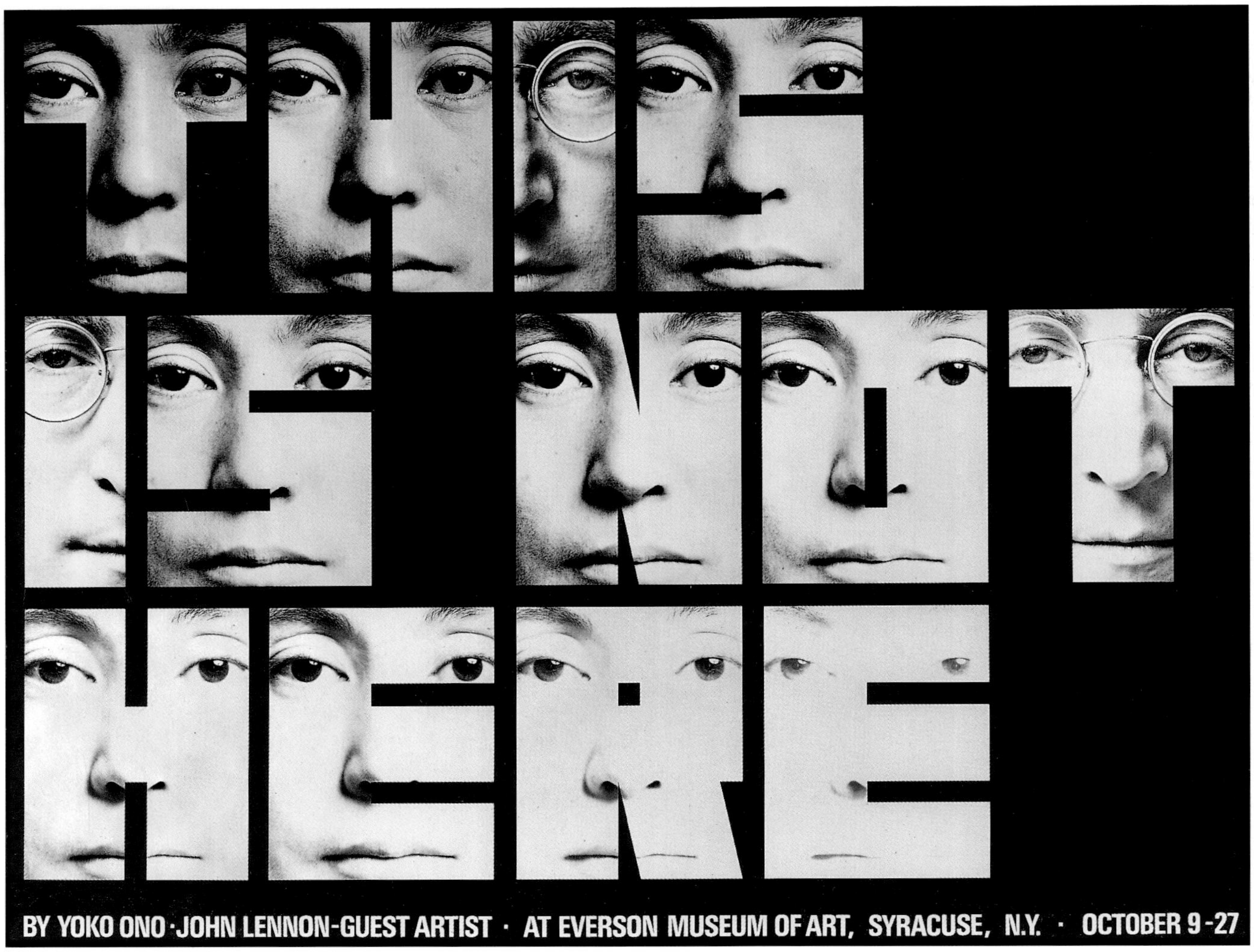

FIGURE 4.1
POSTER, *THIS IS NOT HERE*, 1971

who felt that her radical aesthetic stance had lured Lennon away from his pop music orientation and helped bring on the demise of the Beatles.

Yoko relished her complex status as an outsider as well as a consummate inside player—a Western Conceptualist working out of a fully Japanese set of philosophical and aesthetic traditions. Ironically, in both the worlds of art and pop music a powerful combination of artistic conservatism and unacknowledged racism allowed many to dismiss Yoko Ono as a poseur or mere dilettante. Within the art world of the late sixties and early seventies, her style of conceptual work, relying on poetic instructions infused with a Zen-like sensibility that mixed subtle humor with profound insight, was greeted with a predictable mix of critical responses ranging from supportive and admiring to hostile and indifferent.

Even though Yoko's serious work dated from the early sixties, it seems curious that a certain sector of the art world found it convenient to dismiss her contribution relative to that of her white male peers in Europe and the United States. And after her relationship to John Lennon became renowned, others sought to dismiss the work as only significant because of her reflected Beatle-world fame. Oddly enough, in the music world, the application of her hyperesoteric Fluxus sensibility to the production of mass-market rock 'n' roll resulted in the creation of a smaller, yet fiercely loyal, band of supporters. Yoko (both solo and with Lennon) worked the edges of pop and avant-garde music, bringing the intense emotional clarity of her art into an entirely new frame.

The combination of John and Yoko was far more than the sum of their parts. As a result, Yoko was loved and hated, revered and reviled, and though she bore her complex situation with graceful equanimity, it was nevertheless an enormously stressful period in her private and professional life. Her remarkable calm in the face of all this is even harder to comprehend if factored into the larger social and political milieu in which the couple worked.

As radical political activists, they were both committed to using their celebrity as a productive and positive social instrument. In the midst of widespread generational turmoil, as antiwar activists, as spokespersons for human rights at home and abroad, as proponents of the transformative power of love, and as artists who insisted that art (both their individual and increasingly collaborative works) be a tool for social change, Ono and Lennon made many influential friends and equally influential enemies. Both were targets, not only of continuous FBI harassment (including an ongoing attempt to deport Lennon as an undesirable alien), but also of those whose inner hatreds and reliance upon violence defined them as much as John and Yoko were defined by peace and love. And though they understood the price that they were paying and would continue to pay for their activist aesthetic, and had the same range of concerns and fears anyone else might, they managed to persevere.

Years later, I see that in this context, the title *This Is Not Here* seems far more than a clever linguistic allusion to Magritte or the tag line for some quasi-Buddhist sentiment. Rather than a statement of negation, it was an instruction. Not here, then where? If the work existed (and we knew it did), then it had to be somewhere—just not where we thought it would be. The inductive instruction was simple. Art resides in no physical place; not in a museum, not in any institutional framework. In fact, what Yoko was implying was that art exists only as a bridge between the human mind and soul.

When the exhibition opened on October 9, 1971, over 5,000 people were camped out in the cold Syracuse rain to ensure their place among the first to experience the show. On the eve of Lennon's thirtieth birthday, the exhibition was a gift from Yoko to John (whose active participation led to his listing as "Guest Artist") and an extension of their love for each other. As sentimental as this may sound, it was far from a corny show-business gesture. It was, and remains to this day, a primary example of how Yoko managed to use the simple concept of love as a universal social construction as the content for her own aesthetic and philosophical stance. This is not here, it is everywhere and eternal.

Yoko Ono.

Yes.

David A. Ross, director of the San Francisco Museum of Modern Art, was a member of the curatorial staff at the Everson Museum of Art at the time of the exhibition This Is Not Here.

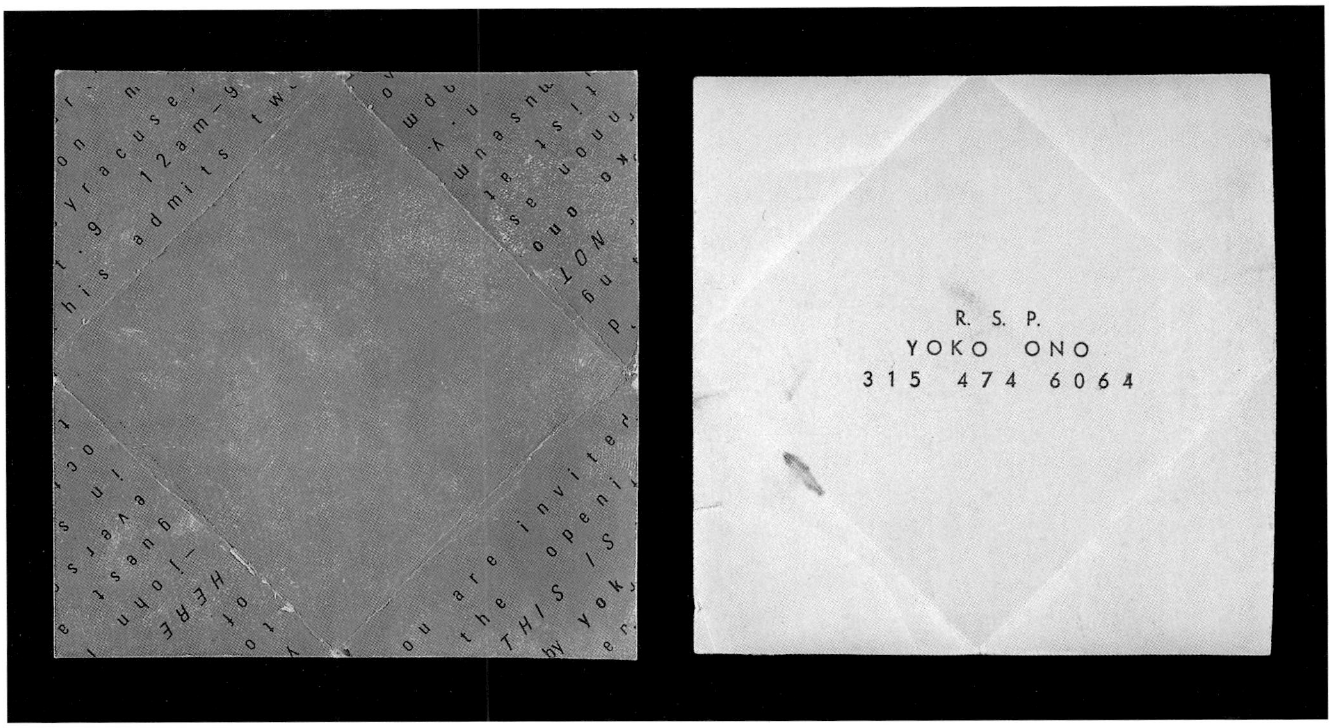

FIGURE 4.2
INVITATION, ***THIS IS NOT HERE***, 1971.
FRONT AND BACK

The Ballad of John and Yoko

JANN S. WENNER

On November 9, 1966, John Lennon climbed to the top of a ladder in the Indica Gallery in London and looked up at a framed paper attached to the ceiling. He peered at it, using a magnifying glass affixed to one side, and saw a single word inscribed in tiny letters: YES.

"I felt relieved," John said, recalling that moment during our December 1970 interviews, the historic first post-Beatles confessional memoirs published early the following year in *Rolling Stone*. "It's a great relief when you get up the ladder and you look through the spyglass and it doesn't say *no* or *fuck you*; it says *YES*."

The ladder, the spyglass, the paper, that word: these constituted John's first encounter with the art, and the heart, of his future companion and collaborator, Yoko Ono. The occasion was a preview of Yoko's one-person Indica show, *Unfinished Paintings and Objects*; the piece was called *Ceiling Painting (YES Painting)*. That evening, John and Yoko were introduced to each other for the first time by Indica co-owner John Dunbar. Lennon was a Beatle, and would be for another three and a half years. But he was already shedding layers of skin. He was anxious to take his words and music to new places, to seek fresh wisdom through his rock 'n' roll. YES was a door swinging open to the rest of his life, a perfect metaphor—everything is possible; nothing, and no one, is out of reach—for his personal and working relationship with Yoko, soon to go into high gear.

YES also defines, with Zen poise and sly humor, the essential character of Yoko's continuing body of work: the films, sculptures, and conceptual installations; her singing, songwriting, and record making; the Bed-Ins, *War Is Over!* billboards, and other public "peace" projects that she created, first with John, then in his memory.

They are expressions of art as community, as a sharing of pain, hope, and redemption. Yoko was born in a world (imperial Japan) and time (1933) far from the physical and sociocultural ground zero of rock 'n' roll; long before she entered the Beatles' orbit, she was a provocateur, a star in the catacombs of the New York avant-garde. But her art has always been a rock 'n' roll unto itself—an audience-participation experience in which she asks questions about life and love and celebrates individual freedom and common bonds. You don't merely look or listen to her work; you're in it, from the moment of conception.

"We are social beings. There is no such thing as a monologue," she says today. "I've only wanted to accentuate what is obvious: that life is a dialogue." So it was with John and Yoko, and ultimately between them and the rest of us. He showed her the wonders, liberties, and leverage of popular superstardom; she showed him—and through his faith and support, the world—the power of YES.

Yoko first appeared in the pages of *Rolling Stone* in 1968—not as John's new girlfriend, but as an artist in her own right. A series of news reports and reviews published in the magazine between August and December of that year covered the breadth and depth of her most recent projects, many of them initiated in a rush of combined energy with John. There was, most famously, the audio-collage album *Two Virgins*, recorded in a single night of passion and tape experiments and packaged between two self-portrait photos, front and back views of John and Yoko in the nude. In *"John" by Yoko Ono, "Yoko" by John Lennon*, a piece created at Coventry Cathedral in England, a pair of acorns was planted in a garden where people could sit on a white wrought-iron seat and literally watch the trees grow.

And two new films directed by Yoko and starring John created a split sensation—pro and con—at the Chicago International Film Festival. One movie, also titled *Two Virgins*, was a nineteen-minute short of John and Yoko's faces superimposed on each other, an ingenious visual rendering of their union. *Film No. 5* was a healing reel: three-minute footage of John's enigmatic grin, slowed down and manipulated by Yoko into fifty-one minutes of therapeutic impressionism, which also came to be known as just *Smile*.

"My ultimate goal was a long long film with everybody in the world smiling," she claimed at the time. "I needed the cooperation of world governments." But Yoko also drew rich meaning from her close-up portrait of the bemused John. "There wasn't any point in just making love, secretly and everything. We had to make a film which had the same vibrations as making love.... A smile for everyone." That

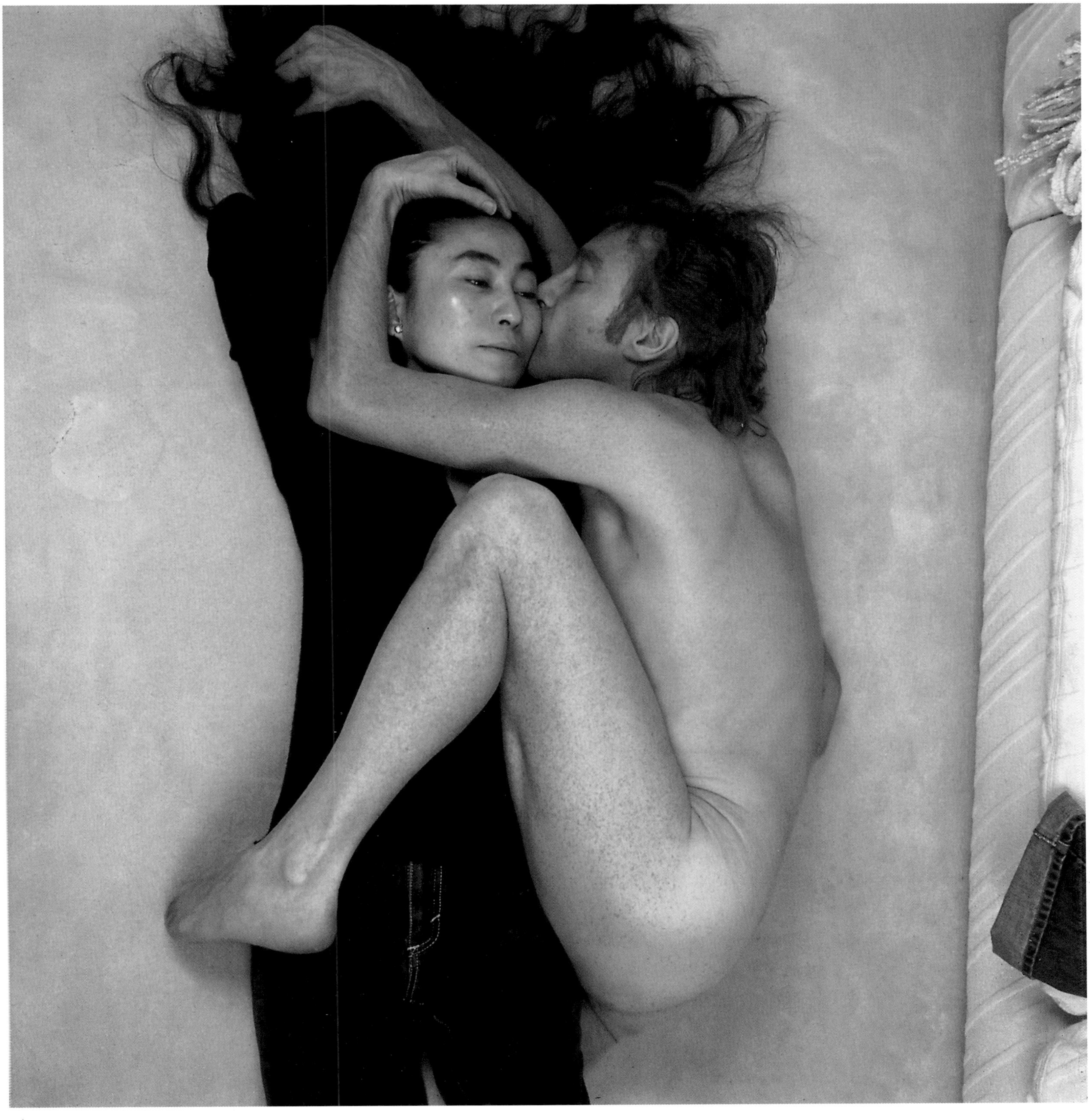

FIGURE 5.1
JOHN LENNON AND YOKO ONO AT HOME, THE DAKOTA, NEW YORK, DECEMBER 8, 1980. PHOTOGRAPH © 2000 ANNIE LEIBOVITZ / CONTACT PRESS IMAGES

included both academic and underground pundits, already pouncing on her for commercially exploiting her access to a Beatle, of using "world peace" as a thematic crutch for vacuous art.

"Some critic commented on us, John and I, as being lollipop artists, who are preoccupied with blowing soap bubbles forever," Yoko said in December of '68. "I thought that was beautiful. There's a lot you can do blowing soap bubbles."

You could see the proof, issue by issue, in *Rolling Stone*. In the late 1960s and throughout the 1970s, the magazine was, in a way, an extended print companion of the Beatles' 1969 single "The Ballad of John and Yoko," a tongue-in-cheek diary of the pair's love-and-peace escapades. John and Yoko's art, individually and together—the records and gallery shows; the cryptic Bagism events; the legendary concert debut of the Plastic Ono Band at the '69 *Toronto Rock 'n' Roll Revival*; even the 1970 "haircuts for charity"—was news, and we covered it with the same day-to-day immediacy with which they commanded the world's attention. (In 1970 I participated in the artist's work when I took my clothes off in New York for her film *Up Your Legs Forever*.)

In November 1968, *Rolling Stone* celebrated its first anniversary by publishing, uncensored, the nude photos of John and Yoko from *Two Virgins*. The LP had already caused a furor. Public opinion was against them. Copies were confiscated by police and record stores banned the album; where it was for sale, it was wrapped in brown paper. I wired John and Yoko in London from our San Francisco offices and offered to publish the photos. The *Two Virgins* issue, accompanied by an exclusive interview with John, was the first John and Yoko and *Rolling Stone* collaboration. It brought national recognition to the magazine and full attention to the poignancy, the honesty, and the politics of those photographs.

By today's standards, this might not seem remarkable, but in 1968, it was utterly astonishing. People did not pose naked, let alone famous people; and John was at the peak of his Beatles fame, a revered household icon around the world. Thus, these pictures were a revolutionary statement. Not only did John and Yoko strip themselves and say, "we are not different from any other man or woman, we are all naked underneath and we are all one," but they also said, "whoever you are, however ordinary your body, nothing to be ashamed of, be free." And when we published these pictures it was with a quote from Genesis 2, verse 25: "And they were both naked, the man and his wife, and were not ashamed."

It was one of their greatest and most important collaborations in art and politics.

John and Yoko's compelling 1969 film *Rape* was a brutal examination of their own lives. Seventy-seven minutes of a young woman being followed incessantly by the camera, a nonstop intrusion that appears to drive her to the precipice of psychosis, *Rape* captured the black side effects of John and Yoko's very public marriage and unity crusades: paranoia, rage, and theft of privacy. In its title and central distressed character, *Rape* also prefigured the bold, defiant feminism—"Woman Power," as Yoko called it in a song on her 1973 album *Feeling the Space*—that became a core theme of her own recordings.

"The mud of rock 'n' roll," as she puts it, was an ideal medium, and camouflage, for the playful sabotage and maternal fighting spirit running through every facet of Yoko's creative labor. "I did not think of rock 'n' roll as 'art' for the longest time," she admits now. When she first heard the Beatles' "Strawberry Fields Forever" (Mario Amaya, the editor of *Art and Artists*, played it for her in London right after its release), she was unimpressed with the group's dalliance with dissonance. Yoko's own experiments with the limits of tonality dated back to the early 1960s. Her astounding singing, a tremulous wordless wail, was an electrifying feature of her concerts at the Village Gate and Carnegie Recital Hall in 1961, and she had been hailed as a genuinely original voice by John Cage and Ornette Coleman.

When, early in their relationship, John showed Yoko some new Beatles lyrics, including "Yellow Submarine," she thought they were "a bit silly"—until she reconsidered them in terms of surrealist verse. "Yellow was the color of light," she explains, "and the yellow submarine—the unconscious mind—was moving under water, which was emotion. And we *all* live in that submarine. What a beautiful concept. This surrealist poetry was being played on radio and phonographs around the world to millions of people of all ages. Musically, the beat and chords of pop and rock felt too simplistic. I finally got it when I was sitting in on the Beatles' recording sessions. That simple beat was the heartbeat of the Universe."

It is strange to reread the polarized opinions in original *Rolling Stone* reviews of Yoko's first solo recordings: *Yoko Ono/Plastic Ono Band* (her visceral 1970 sister album to John's classic "primal scream" solo debut) and the double albums *Fly* (1971) and *Approximately Infinite Universe* (1973). There is stunned positive surprise, unpleasant disbelief, begrudging praise, and utter boredom, in equal measure, sometimes all in the same review. The advent of punk rock and the coming of age in the 1990s of a new outspoken breed of women in rock, many of them ardent students of those LPs, have since proven Yoko's rock 'n' roll—its open-heart honesty and abrasive fury; the way her voice soared in shivering arcs against John's whorls of guitar distortion and feedback—to be a powerful weapon of change and inspiration. She has worked on stage and in the studio with members of the New York avant-rock community, including Sonic Youth and the Beastie Boys. On her 1995 album *Rising*, Yoko bound together the principal ideals of her life and art—peace, family, the euphoric properties of unfettered electric guitar—in songs about holocaust and salvation, performed with the power trio IMA, led by her son, Sean.

"Being an incorrigible rebel, I literally fed on adversity," she told me recently. "Of course, it hurt. I won't say I liked it. In fact, it had gotten downright tiresome at one point. But in hindsight, it was better than having been totally adored. That's the worst killer, I think. Having been so severely attacked and laughed at by the whole world, I feel I became wiser, stronger, and more creative for it."

This exhibition is a long-overdue validation of Yoko's pioneering vision and multi-discipline gifts. It is sad and ironic that John is not here to revel in it with her. He was Yoko's most devoted fan; his very last recording session, the night of his death in 1980, was for what would prove to be her biggest and most memorable single, "Walking on Thin Ice." But his absence is, in a sense, further proof of the enduring force of her work. Just as her earliest achievements in the avant-garde predated her introduction to John that fateful night in the Indica Gallery, her art has outlived his loving patronage. I was particularly transfixed by *Ex It*, a 1998 installation in a SoHo garage consisting of 100 unpainted wooden coffins—adult- and child-size—punctuated by young, budding fruit trees and tape loops of chirping birds. It was a gripping meditation on the indivisibility of death and life and the natural order of coming and going; on man's unchecked capacity for cruelty to his own kind, the continued blessing of rebirth, and each generation's potential—and responsibility—for change.

Yet the word *art* is not big enough to describe the dimensions and lessons of two of Yoko's greatest works, both direct products of personal loss. At noon on December 14, 1980, six days after John's death, citizens of New York gathered in Central Park for ten minutes, at Yoko's request, in silent prayer. Similar ten-minute periods of silence were observed simultaneously in cities throughout the world. It was a truly universal memorial for John,

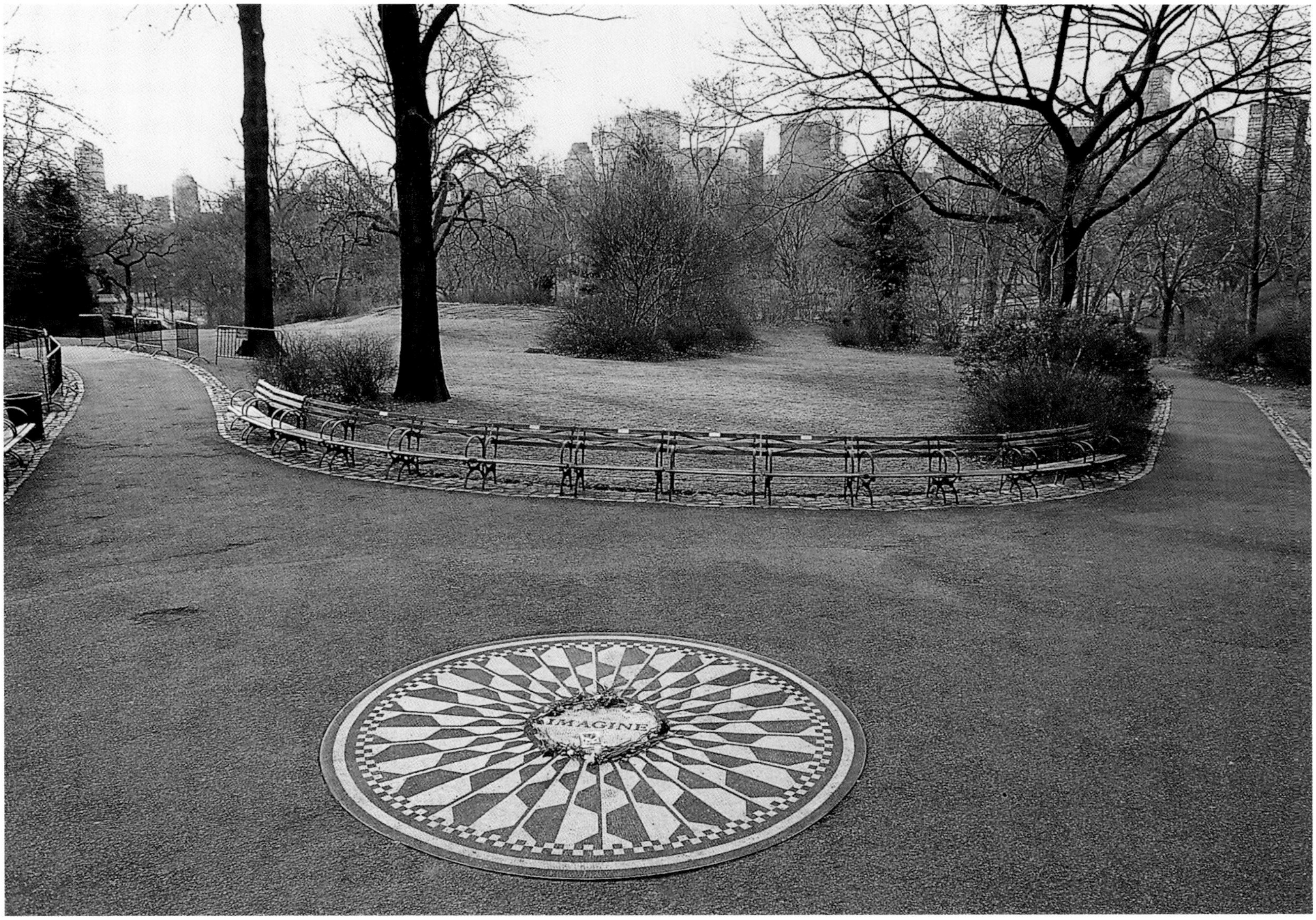

FIGURE 5.2
STRAWBERRY FIELDS, CENTRAL PARK, NEW YORK

simple in its ideals, breathtaking in its size and effect. In North America alone, 500 radio stations stopped broadcasting. I will never forget the quiet in Central Park that afternoon where I stood with more than 100,000 others in solemn contemplation, an exorcism of grief in which the entire city, and the globe, stood in suspended animation. There was, for those ten minutes, world peace.

Five years later, on October 9, 1985—what would have been John's forty-fifth birthday—Yoko officially opened Strawberry Fields, an "international garden of peace" honoring John, located in Central Park in an area that had been one of his, Sean, and Yoko's favorite walking spots. At the entrance, in a circle of benches and surrounded by trees contributed by more than 100 nations, is a black-and-white mosaic with a single word from one of John's most famous songs: *Imagine*. It is like a permanent outdoor version of the original YES piece in the Indica Gallery. When John came down that ladder, he was forever changed. When I walk through Strawberry Fields today, I can't help but sense the difference in the air: in the warmth of people's smiles, in the subtle electricity of introspection.

Strawberry Fields and the silent memorial are the most elaborate yet simple, quintessential, and expansive expressions of Yoko's work and ideas—art that calls for the participation of an individual, of several individuals, of *all* individuals, and asks viewers to think, to listen, to see the world that is in and around all of us. They are really living sculptures, global expressions of harmony and the call for peace.

All quotes are from *The Ballad of John and Yoko* (1982) and recent interviews by the author.

SCORES AND INSTRUCTIONS

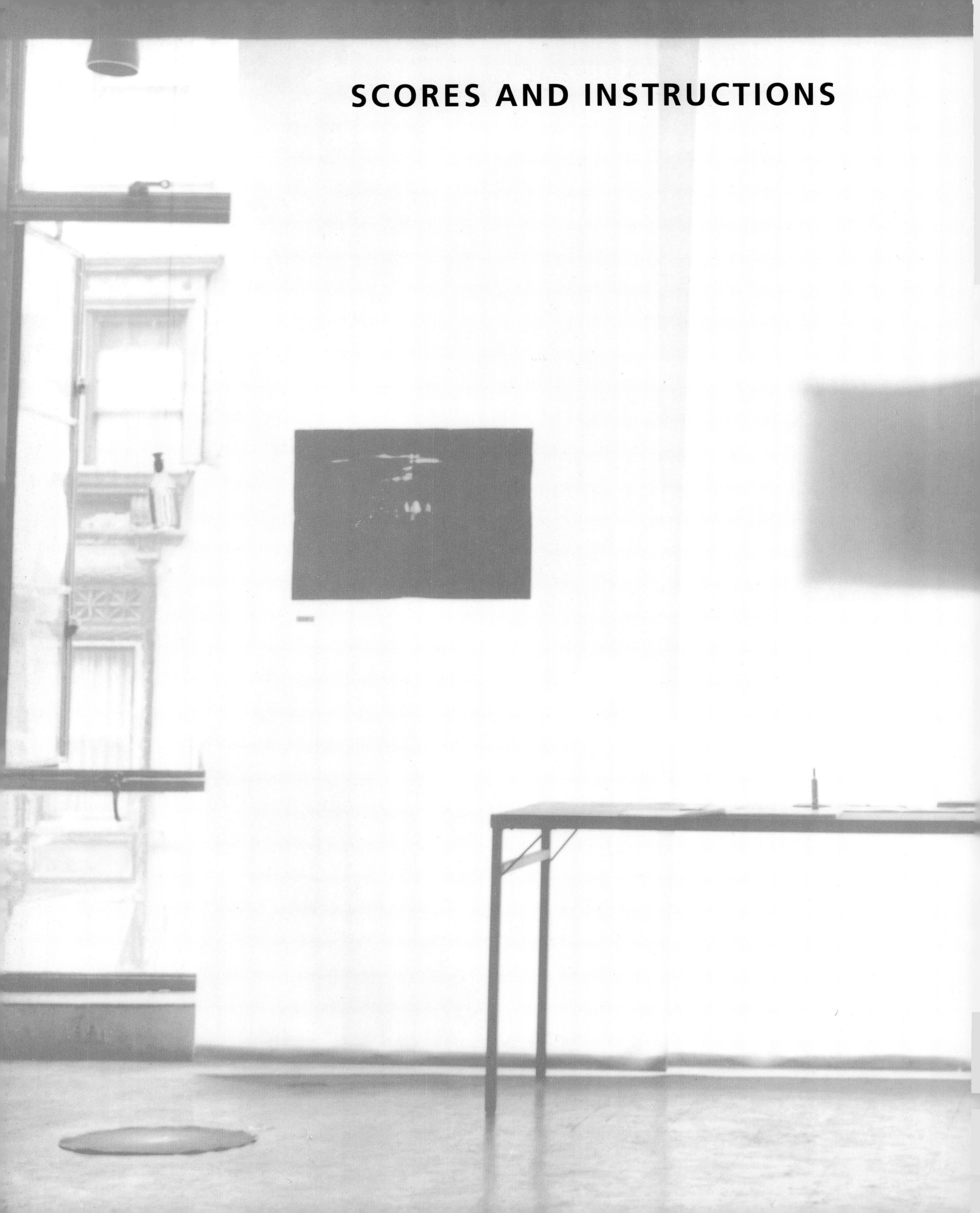

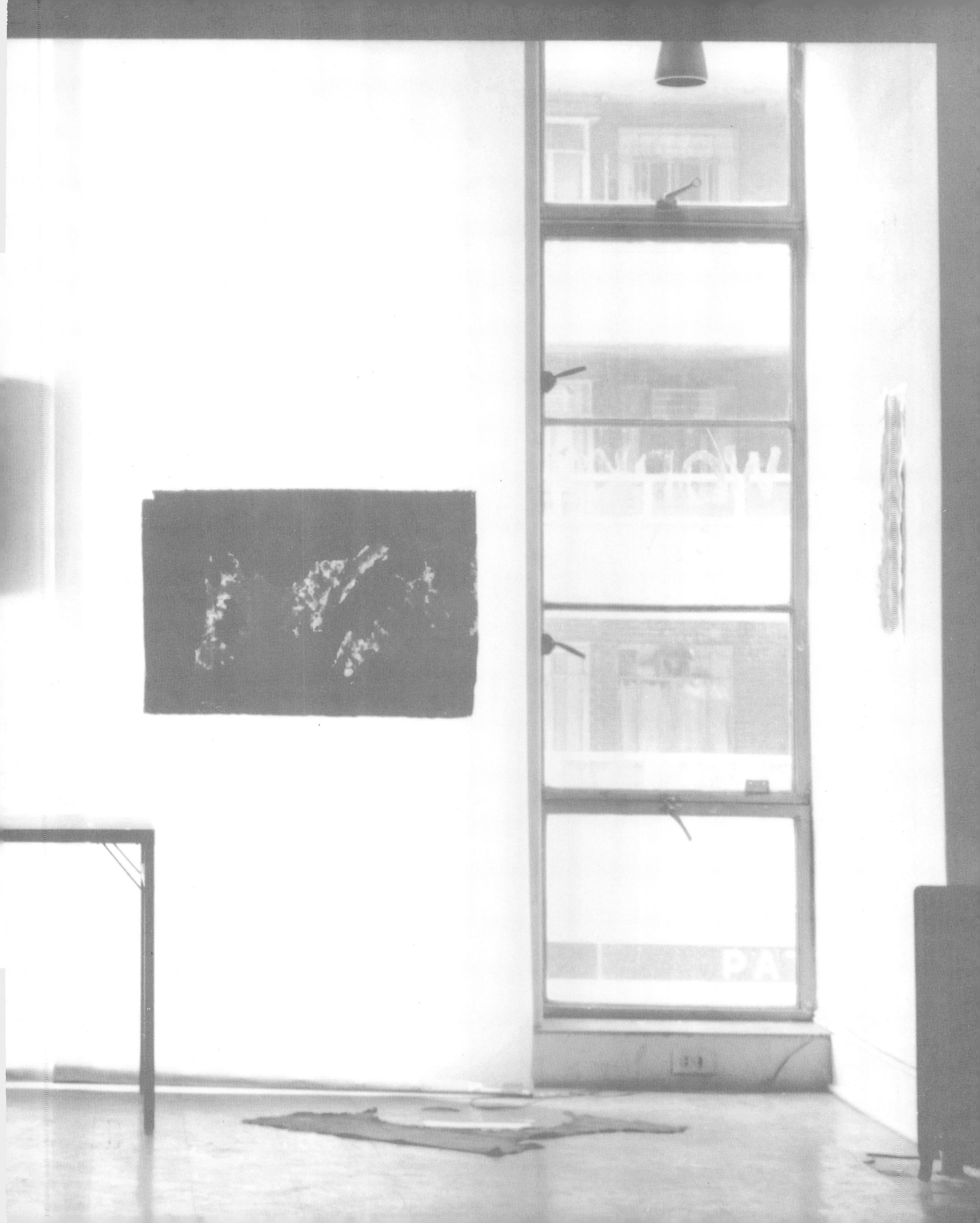
PAT

三楽章の絵

キャンバスに毎日水をやる。
一楽章
芽を出す迄
二楽章
つたがキャンバスをおほう迄
三楽章
つたが枯れる迄

Instructions for a World of Stickiness: The Early Conceptual Work of Yoko Ono

BRUCE ALTSHULER

Conceptual artists are mystics rather than rationalists. They leap to conclusions that logic cannot reach.

—Sol LeWitt, "Sentences on Conceptual Art," 1969

I am still groping in the world of stickiness.

—Yoko Ono, "The Word of a Fabricator," 1962

In 1961 Yoko Ono began to exhibit works of art that took the form of instructions. First in a show of paintings created according to specific directions, and later through the display and publication of written instructions themselves, Ono pioneered one of the central modes of Conceptualist art-making. Moving from objects to ideas as the center of her artistic practice, Ono anticipated the "dematerialization" that would characterize vanguard art from the mid-1960s into the early 1970s.[1]

Ono's Conceptualist work most often is viewed in relation to two influences, the reductive forms of traditional Japanese culture and the avant-garde compositions of the circle of John Cage. But the tone of Ono's early instruction pieces seems to issue from another source, the anguished cry of postwar existentialism. Working in New York, Tokyo, and later in London, Ono integrated these disparate influences, generating a body of work of unique texture and significance.

The most natural place to start is with John Cage, whose ideas were transmitted to the downtown avant-garde in part through his class in experimental composition taught at the New School for Social Research from the fall of 1956 to the summer of 1960.[2] In response to Cage's nonstandard assignments students created performance pieces employing chance procedures and everyday objects, developing interests that had drawn nonmusician participants like George Brecht, Allan Kaprow, and Jackson Mac Low to the class. But the course also attracted those with classical musical training. One of these individuals was Ichiyanagi Toshi, who had come to New York from Tokyo to study at Juilliard and was married at the time to Yoko Ono. Through Ichiyanagi, and by observing a class session, Ono learned of the innovative work being done in the class and saw the musical score transformed into a vehicle for broader art-making.

What we might call the metaphysics of the score is critical to the importance of this form. The use of the written score focuses attention on the openness of the work of art itself, both in its realization and in its interpretation. This openness is implicit in musical composition, in which many factors affecting performance and listener experience are unspecified and unspecifiable, but it comes to the fore in Conceptualist instruction pieces of the 1960s. Without reliance on a musical tradition, questions about how a score is to be executed and how the resulting object or performance is to be interpreted become central to the work. Citing the score of, say, George Brecht's *EGG* (January 1963) should make the point clear: "at least one egg." For such works, the fact of open-ended interpretation is both part of their content and a defining feature of their ontological status. Instruction works themselves are open-textured, admitting the world—through variations in execution and interpretation—into their very being.

Another significant figure within this context is the composer La Monte Young. In 1960, in California and New York, Young created a series of instruction pieces more minimal, and less theatrical, than most of those coming out of the Cage class, a reductive path that George Brecht also would pursue in the early 1960s. With such directions as "Draw a straight line and follow it." (*Composition 1960 #10, to Bob Morris*), and "The performer should prepare any composition and then perform it as well as he can." (*Composition 1960 #13, to Richard Huelsenbeck*), Young added a distinctive voice to a growing body of work that emphasized the open interpretation of ideas set down through performance instructions.

From December 1960 through May 1961, Young and Ono organized a series of events in Ono's loft on the top floor of 112 Chambers Street.[3] Here new music, poetry, performance, and instruction works met a small but sympathetic audience, which included Marcel Duchamp and the future impresario of Fluxus, George Maciunas. Although Ono had rented the loft as a place to hold performances and attempted to influence the program, Young monopolized the series and she found herself relegated to a subsidiary role. But it was during the loft concerts that Ono first displayed a number of her Instruction Paintings on the walls, and placed *Painting to Be Stepped On* on the floor.[4]

Maciunas, who had met Young in Richard Maxfield's electronic music class, became increasingly involved in the new art growing out of Cage's influence. Impressed by the performances at Ono's loft, in early 1961 he initiated a concert series at AG Gallery, which he owned with Almus Salcius. Later that year, before leaving New York for Europe (where in 1962–63 he would organize his seminal series of Fluxus festivals), Maciunas began collaborating with Young to publish *An Anthology*, the landmark compendium of avant-garde work that Young had as-

FIGURE 6.1
PAINTING IN THREE STANZAS FROM *GRAPEFRUIT* (1964)

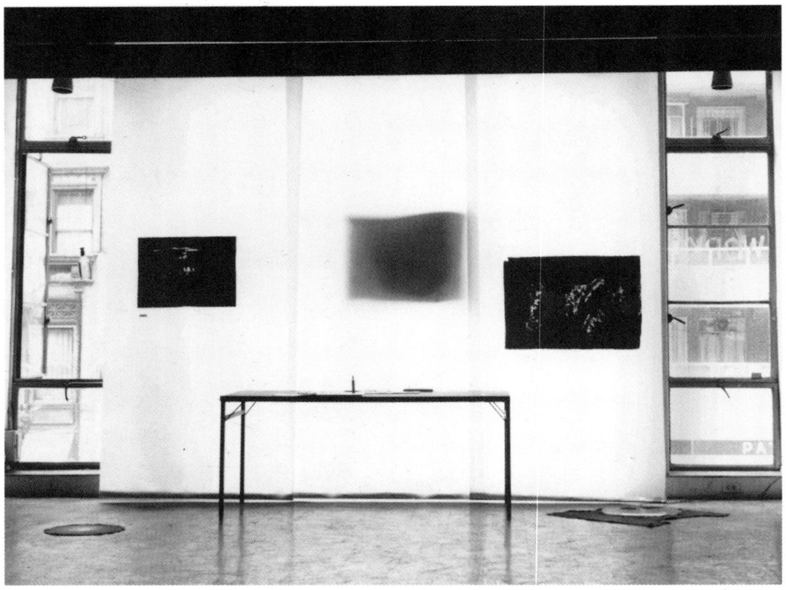

FIGURE 6.2
PAINTINGS AND DRAWINGS BY YOKO ONO**,** AG GALLERY, NEW YORK, 1961. INSTALLATION VIEW, WITH ***PAINTING TO BE STEPPED ON*** AND ***WATERDROP PAINTING*** ON FLOOR AND ***PAINTING UNTIL IT BECOMES MARBLE*** ON TABLE

sembled.[5] But most significantly for Yoko Ono, it was Maciunas who presented her first exhibition, *Paintings and Drawings by Yoko Ono*, in July 1961 at AG Gallery, 925 Madison Avenue (figs. 6.2–5; no. 2).[6]

There were only some twenty works in the AG Gallery exhibition, but these pieces formed two distinct groups. In the back part of the gallery were calligraphic images, some in the form of accordion-like books, demonstrating Ono's use of *sumi* ink on paper. Although she by no means was a master calligrapher, Ono earned money demonstrating calligraphy and other traditional Japanese arts—including *haiku*, flower arranging, and origami—for New York's Japan Society, and Maciunas thought, correctly, that such works would be salable. (Two of them were sold.) Calligraphic technique and the use of *sumi* ink, featured on the exhibition poster as well as in the gallery, also reinforced the natural association of Ono with Japan and, more important, with Zen Buddhism, much in vogue within the American avant-garde during the 1950s and 1960s. But while the calligraphic pieces looked toward her past, the second group of works looked toward the future: at least thirteen pieces (exhibited as *Instruction Paintings*) were based on ideas that could be stated as verbal directions, instructions that would be followed by the artist, and by viewers, to make the works.[7]

What were Yoko Ono's Instruction Paintings like? Most of the works required the viewer's participation, invited orally when she or Maciunas escorted the exhibition's few visitors around the gallery. *Waterdrop Painting*—of which there were two versions, one a round and the other an irregularly shaped piece of canvas—called for the visitor to drip water on the work, which lay on the floor (fig. 6.3). Another floor piece—*Painting to Be Stepped On*—asked the visitor to do just that, though in this case the artist's instruction, which also was the painting's title, could be read from a card on the floor (fig. 6.4).[8] *Smoke Painting* was to be completed by viewers burning the canvas and watching the smoke rise, the work being finished when there was no canvas left (fig. 6.5). Displayed on a table, *Painting Until It Becomes Marble* involved both addition and subtraction of materials: visitors were asked to remove and/or paint some of the elements of which it was composed (fig. 6.2). *Painting in Three Stanzas* consisted of a plant growing through a hole in the canvas, accompanied by a card written in English by Ichiyanagi that suggests three stages of the work: growth, decay, and rebirth (pls. 2a–b). Visitor participation was primarily cerebral, imagining these stages of the plant's—and the painting's—development. Similar mental effort was called for with the two versions of *Painting to See in the Dark*, in which the viewer was asked to imagine how these pieces would look without light. Projective imagination was also critical to the experience of *Shadow Painting*, which, in the manner of Robert Rauschenberg's *White Paintings* of 1951–52, takes its imagery from shadows cast on the canvas by objects in the environment (fig. 1.8).

In her 1965 self-published *Ono's Sales List*—which offered works directly to the public for prices ranging from 25¢ per inch for audio tape of snow falling to $3,000 for a machine that cries—Ono refers to these instruction pieces as "do-it-yourself paintings" (no. 37). Her phrase suggests a critical aspect of these works, the suggestion that art-making is available to anyone. Here Cage's democratization of music—in terms of both the sounds and the compositional strategies that count as musical—is moved toward Maciunas's view that art institutions would become obsolete as everyone becomes an artist. Although Ono did not focus on the political implications of this attitude in the manner of Maciunas, her AG Gallery exhibition applied to painting a perspective primarily manifested at this time in the context of performance.[9] Apart from the contemporary work of George Brecht, who employed the term "event" to conceptually unite performances and objects, this democratic—and anarchistic—attitude toward artistic production would not be directed to object-making until the mid-1960s. Eventually, entire exhibitions would consist of objects made by viewers following artists' instructions.[10]

It is interesting to compare Ono's *Instruction Paintings* with some of the objects George Brecht exhibited in autumn 1959 at Reuben Gallery in an exhibition entitled *Toward Events*. In four pieces that called for viewer participation, Brecht presented objects with which visitors could interact to create "events." Instruction texts for three of the works—*The Case*, *Dome*, and *Solitaire*—were printed on the invitation and displayed in the gallery, while instructions for engaging the fourth piece, *The Cabinet*, seem to have been understood as obviously similar to those for *The Case* and *Dome*. Instructions for *The Case* and *Dome* directed visitors to remove, manipulate, and replace objects enclosed in these containers, the event consisting of all "sensible occurrences" taking place during this activity. *Solitaire* consisted of a table, stool, and box of twenty-seven unique cards, with a set of instructions describing a complex solitairelike game to be played with the cards at the table. In these works Brecht seems primarily concerned with the events to be created through engagement with his objects, the objects themselves being something like props for these events. At AG Gallery, on the other hand, Ono would call for visitor participation in the creation of the objects themselves. But as both Brecht and Ono were looking for involvement by others in the creation of artworks—in his case "events," in her case "paintings"—these two exhibitions clearly were moving in the same direction, away from the artist's hand and out into the world. In May–June 1961, just before Ono's AG Gallery show, Brecht would employ this strategy again with his *Three Chair Events* at Martha Jackson Gallery, in the important group exhibition *Environments, Situations, Spaces*. By this time Brecht had begun to distribute event cards to friends, instructions for the kind of elaborate events that he had created in John Cage's New School class, and scores for works that could be realized as either events or objects.[11]

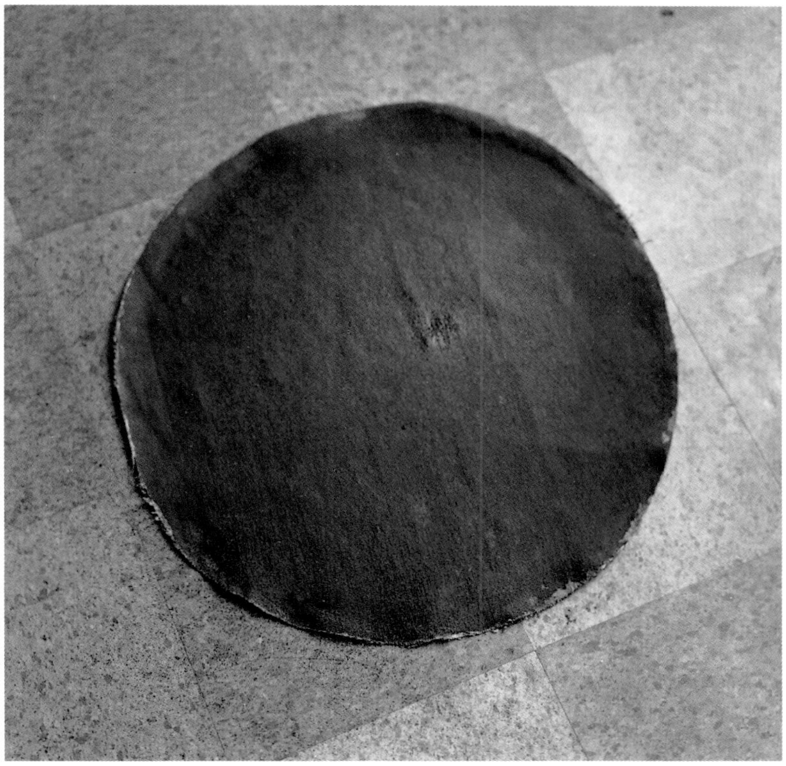

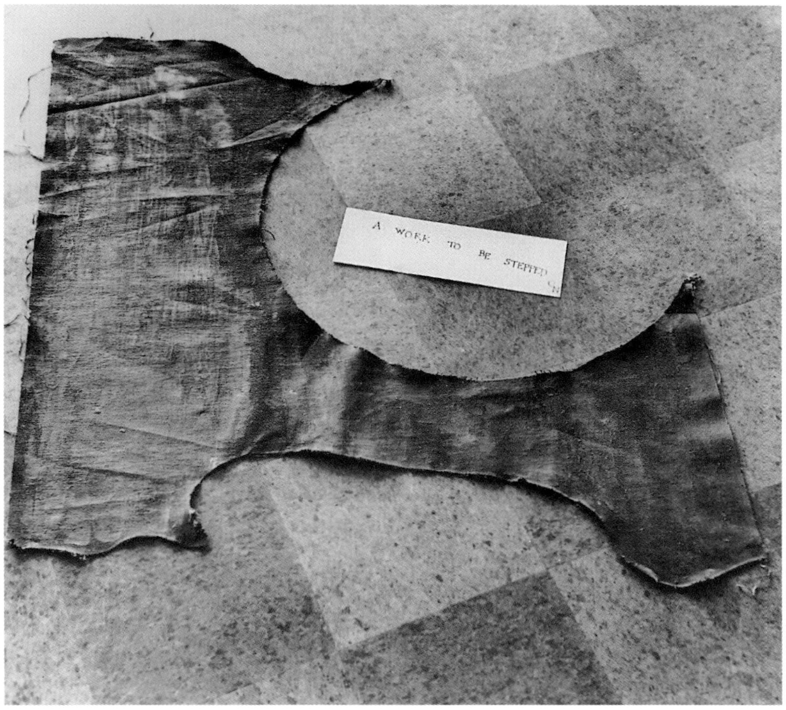

FIGURE 6.3 (LEFT)
WATERDROP PAINTING.
INSTALLATION VIEW,
AG GALLERY, NEW YORK,
1961

FIGURE 6.4 (RIGHT)
A PAINTING TO BE STEPPED ON.
INSTALLATION VIEW, AG GALLERY,
NEW YORK, 1961

It is tempting to read back onto the AG Gallery *Instruction Paintings* the verbal directions that Ono would publish for all but two of them in *Grapefruit* in 1964, but written instructions accompanied only three paintings in the exhibition. Although in the summer of 1961 it seems that Ono did not fully realize the radical implications of her use of instructions, her focus on viewer participation elicited by the artist's words soon led to an awareness of their conceptual significance. For if anyone can participate in the creation of an artwork by following directions for manipulating an object made by the artist, then the artist should be able to devise a set of instructions by which anyone alone can create an artwork. An artist's role then might consist only of formulating the instructions, and the idea of the work—as expressed through these instructions—would become central. Here thinking is more fundamental than making, or, perhaps more accurately, thinking is the most important kind of making. In 1962, on the walls of a Tokyo exhibition space, Yoko Ono presented this Conceptualist view of art and art-making.

In conjunction with her concert at Sōgetsu Art Center in Tokyo on May 24, 1962 (no. 27), Ono exhibited more than thirty *Instructions for Paintings* (no. 3), something very different from the *Instruction Paintings* shown at AG Gallery.[12] Sōgetsu Art Center was the premier avant-garde performance and exhibition venue in Japan, created and run by the artist and filmmaker Teshigahara Hiroshi as an extension of the nontraditional flower-arranging school established by his father, and this event conferred significant status within the world of advanced art.[13] But while Ono's performance of *Of a Grapefruit in the World of Park* and other pieces certainly presented works never before seen in Japan, her display of white sheets of paper taped to the lobby walls, with Japanese instructions neatly penned in blue and black ink, introduced something entirely new. By this time Ono understood and made clear the implication of her earlier Instruction Paintings: Given the conceptual primacy of idea over physical realization, verbal statements are all that one need exhibit. Seeing them on the same occasion as Ono's performance, the astute visitor might well identify with the artist as someone who could follow a set of instructions to create a work of vanguard art.

Ono's presentation of an exhibition consisting entirely of instruction sheets was a groundbreaking move in 1962, one that has only begun to receive recognition within the history of Conceptual Art. She was the first artist to develop an exhibition format that clearly presented the notion of ideas as constitutive of artworks, dramatically displaying the ascendancy of concept over material instantiation. It would take close to seven years for the next major innovation in this area, Seth Siegelaub's 1968–69 series of exhibitions in the form of printed catalogues.[14]

In order to emphasize the conceptual over the visual—as Ono put it in 1995, "To make the point that the instructions were not themselves graphic images"—she wanted the instruction cards to be typewritten.[15] But lacking a Japanese-language typewriter, she asked Ichiyanagi, experienced at copying musical scores, to write them in his careful lettering. Originally composed in English, the texts were translated by Ono into Japanese scores, which Ichiyanagi then copied onto ten-by-fifteen-inch white sheets of paper. The *Instructions for Paintings* displayed at Sōgetsu included scores for eight works that had been physically realized at AG Gallery, eleven more pieces with titles indicating the actions to be performed (e.g. *Painting to Hammer a Nail*), and additional works generically titled *An Imaginary Piece* on the exhibition announcement. (When such works were published in *Grapefruit*, this generic title became *Painting to Be Constructed in Your Head*.)

FIGURE 6.5
SMOKE PAINTING. INSTALLATION VIEW, AG GALLERY, NEW YORK, 1961

Ono's "imaginary pieces" broadened her pursuit of Conceptual art-making, expanding beyond the materials and activities associated with painting. Following the instructions required mental actions as well as physical ones—mixing the imagery of three paintings in one's mind and mentally reassembling the figures or, more elaborately, imaginatively transforming a square canvas into a circular one, identifying a shape arising in the process, and attaching to the canvas an object, smell, sound, or color associated in one's mind with that shape. This move to the imaginary continues the dematerializing trajectory from object-making to the composition and display of instructions, and it represents the future of Ono's interests.

The embrace of mental construction adds another layer of open interpretation to those implied by instruction works, and in a sense it brings the conceptual situation full circle. Beginning with an idea, the artist then formulates a verbal expression, spoken or written instructions for the creation of a work. But as is clear from the multiple written versions—in English and Japanese—of particular instruction works that Ono presented between her AG Gallery exhibition and the 1964 publication of *Grapefruit*, a single idea admits of many verbal statements.[16] Similar multiple possibilities exist at the next stage, where verbal instructions are followed to create physical objects or events. Here Ono's own practice is exemplary, as she has realized her works in quite diverse ways during the past four decades. And such openness of interpretation obviously is available to anyone following her instructions. Suggesting that this last stage be done mentally, in the imagination, radically extends the interpretative possibilities as well as allows instructions that cannot be realized physically. Thus, starting with ideas, Ono ends with ideas, with the power of the imagination.

Yoko Ono's instruction works, then, foretell a vast range of interpretative possibility, and this situation leads toward a renewed commitment to the social world. The existence of instruction works requires that they be realized—or realizable—by people other than the artist, implying an ongoing series of unforeseen interpretations. Instruction works thus project themselves into time, moving away from the artist into the indefinite future of possible realizations by others.[17] What began in the subjective consciousness of the artist comes to embrace the mental and physical activity of a community of interpreters, instruction works finding their significance in a world extending beyond that of their initial creators. In conversation Ono has marked the urge to communicate with others as essential to her work, and her instruction pieces satisfy this need in a fundamental way.[18]

Another sort of philosophical concern also pointed Ono in this direction. In the essay "The Word of a Fabricator," published in the Sōgetsu Art Center's journal in conjunction with her 1962 concert and exhibition, she grounds her work in an existentialist perspective.[19] Citing "an endless pessimism" as the root of artistic creation, Ono nonetheless wants to escape the subjective point of view. She marks the focus on chance operations as a self-delusive attempt to merge with nature—the attempt to "become a weed"—and instead opts to assign herself "rules," to create and follow sets of instructions. These instructions are conceptual, and become real by their enactment in the world. She seeks truth through the realization of her ideas in the actions of others, "attempting to make one's own fiction a reality by letting others cut off pieces of the romanticism that inevitably enwraps fiction." For Ono, Kierkegaardian anguish is to be mitigated by interpersonal imagination and embodied acts of interpretation. Unable to eliminate her distress through Buddhist or Cagean strategies, she is left "groping in the world of stickiness," directly confronting the messiness of life without preestablished solutions or definitions.

In "The Word of a Fabricator" Ono embraced a kind of Sartrean existentialism, a position encapsulated in the phrase "existence precedes essence." According to this view, people create what they are through what they do, by means of their actions and decisions. Pursuing art as a way of dealing with her subjective suffering, Ono enmeshes her work in the everyday world through instructions to be carried out by others in their own lives. She thus acknowledges the role of individual and interpersonal activity in the creation of personal identity, and she highlights our inability to escape "the world of stickiness."[20]

Although Ono repudiated meditation in favor of engagement with a public in her instruction works, her scores themselves have often been associated with *haiku* and Zen.[21] This is an illuminating connection, and it extends beyond such features as concise imagery and reductive form. In its aggressive aspects and bodily focus, much of Ono's work recalls us to physical being in as sharp a manner as the blow of the Zen master's *kyōsaku*. Equally important is the element of transience, a central aspect of traditional Japanese aesthetics and of Zen philosophy. The many disruptions of Ono's childhood and adolescence, with moves between countries and from house to house, instilled in her an acute sense of the transience of all things, something that she associates with her attraction to both

Zen and existentialism.[22] The existentialism to which she was exposed in the early and mid-1950s at Gakushūin University and Sarah Lawrence College combined with aspects of Japanese culture and found expression in the avant-garde art form of the instruction work.

While Ono's focus on ideas in the Sōgetsu exhibition clearly prefigures later Conceptual Art, the social dimension of her work distinguishes it from the Conceptualism that subsequently grew out of Minimalist sculpture practice in New York. Presented in classic form in the writings of Sol LeWitt, this position took the primacy of ideation to imply that once the artist had generated the idea for a piece there was no need for subsequent physical realization or interpretation.[23] But for Ono, connection with others was central. An ongoing process of interpreting, realizing, and imaginatively transforming ideas is an essential aspect of her work.

Ono remained in Japan for more than two years after her first Sōgetsu Art Center exhibition, and by the time she returned to the United States in August 1964, she had made her instruction pieces available to a broader public in her book *Grapefruit* (no. 4). One of the classic works of Conceptualism, *Grapefruit* was self-published in Tokyo in an edition of 500 under the mark of the Wunternaum Press. Symbolically associating Ono's work with freedom and liberation, and with the United States, the publication date of July 4, 1964, was printed on the copyright page (fig. 6.6).

Just after the publication of *Grapefruit* Ono presented another exhibition.[24] With her book in hand, and for sale, on July 20 Ono displayed a group of objects with accompanying instructions in Yamaichi Hall in Kyoto. The occasion—titled *Insound and Instructure*—involved a concert done with current husband Anthony Cox and friend Al Wonderlick (*Insound*), and an exhibition in the lobby (*Instructure*). The meaning of "instructure," a term derived by combining "instruction" and "structure," was explained in the program: "Something that emerged from instructions and yet is not quite emerged—not quite structured—never quite structured...like an unfinished church with a sky ceiling."[25] Displayed on about a dozen white pedestals, the *Instructures* consisted of instruction cards written by Ono in English and Japanese describing mental actions to be performed with the companion objects. Each set of actions involved the construction in the imagination of some sort of large-scale structure with the materials on that pedestal, which might be a pile of toothpicks, fingernails, or pubic hair.[26] Like quite a few of her instruction works and performance pieces, many of these materials were body-related and bordered on the taboo. The next day another event was held at the Zen temple Nanzenji, where, beginning at 6 p.m., thirty to forty attendees gathered in silence and together watched the moon and stars through the night (no. 29).

Occasioned by an invitation to perform in a much less meditative environment, Ono's move to London from New York two years later led to another display of instruction works, which would set the pattern for subsequent exhibitions. In September 1966 Ono went to London to participate in the *Destruction in Art Symposium (DIAS)*, presenting her ideas in conversation, lecture, and performance over the month-long event (no. 33).[27] Probably through Mario Amaya, editor of *Art and Artists* and an organizer of the Symposium, Ono met John Dunbar and arranged to have an exhibition at his Indica Gallery. *Yoko at Indica: Unfinished Paintings and Objects* opened on November 9. This was her most elaborate exhibition to date, consisting of at least eleven paintings and twenty-five objects, and it reinforced the notoriety she had received in her September performances.[28] The show also had a striking visual unity, with many works in the exhibition painted white. An important exception is *Add Color Painting*, a work inviting participation, which consisted of a canvas or board on the wall with colored paints and a brush on a chair next to it. Other works also asked for such viewer involvement, including *Apple* (an apple, sitting on a clear Plexiglas pedestal, that some visitors took as an invitation to eat; no. 15), *Rearrangement Piece* (needles on a white plexi box with a magnet underneath), *Painting to Hammer a Nail* (with attached hammer and available nails; no. 9), *Water Piece* (a sponge with a vial of water and a dropper on a clear plexi pedestal; no. 11), *Balance Piece* (on which visitors deposited their fingernails to bring a scale into balance), and a new version of *Painting to Be Stepped On*. Not surprisingly, visitor activity sometimes was imaginative instead of physical, as with *Pointedness*, a white ball on a pedestal bearing the suggestive words, "This sphere will be a sharp point when it gets to the far side of the room in your mind" (no. 12).[29] Mental participation could mix with physical action as well, as with *Mend Piece*, a broken cup alongside a tube of glue and a needle and thread, which could be put back together in your mind or right on its pedestal (fig. 6.7). Involving the mental and the physical in a different way was a reference to Marcel Duchamp, the progenitor of Conceptualism, who had given artists the freedom to designate as art any object or activity: a white chessboard and chess set, to be played with as long as one could remember where one's pieces were.[30]

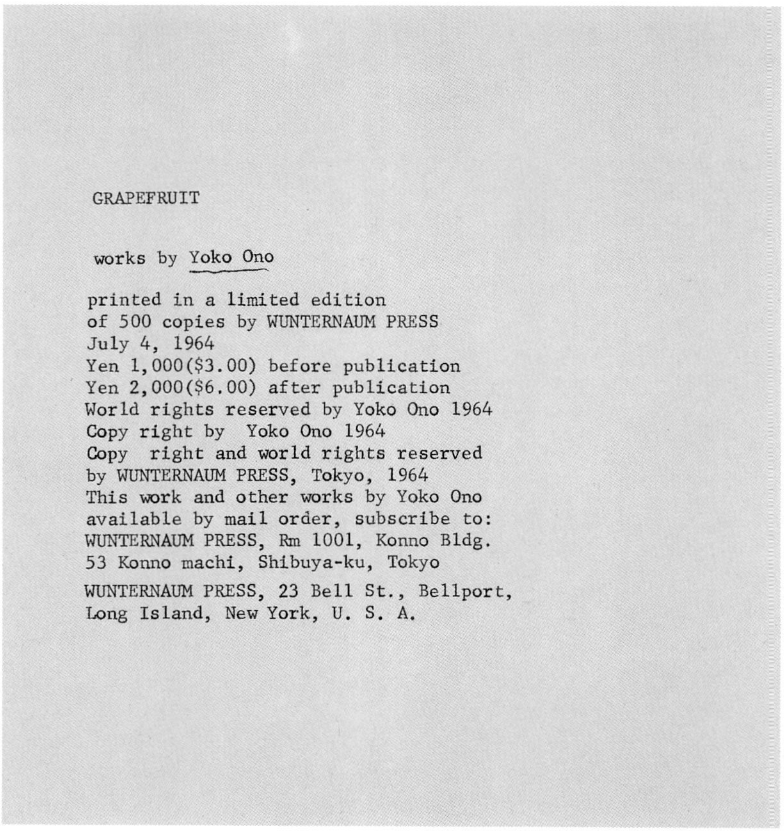

GRAPEFRUIT

works by Yoko Ono

printed in a limited edition
of 500 copies by WUNTERNAUM PRESS
July 4, 1964
Yen 1,000($3.00) before publication
Yen 2,000($6.00) after publication
World rights reserved by Yoko Ono 1964
Copy right by Yoko Ono 1964
Copy right and world rights reserved
by WUNTERNAUM PRESS, Tokyo, 1964
This work and other works by Yoko Ono
available by mail order, subscribe to:
WUNTERNAUM PRESS, Rm 1001, Konno Bldg.
53 Konno machi, Shibuya-ku, Tokyo
WUNTERNAUM PRESS, 23 Bell St., Bellport,
Long Island, New York, U. S. A.

FIGURE 6.6
GRAPEFRUIT, 1964.
COPYRIGHT PAGE

With an innovative catalogue prepared and financed by the artist, a notebook of preliminary drawings for the works and their installation, and the large number of pieces created for the show, this exhibition set the tone for Ono's future exhibitions, beginning with her group of installations and objects in *Half-A-Wind Show* at Lisson Gallery in London in November 1967. Ono's exhibitions would grow in complexity, but her orientation toward the conceptual and her focus on the imagination remained the same. Consider three of the many manifestations of *Blue Room Event*: the work originated as instructions attached to the walls of Ono's New York apartments in 1966 (no. 5). These instructions appeared at Lisson Gallery as one of the four environments, a white room that was to become blue through the imaginative acts of those sitting in it.[31] And for her 1971 exhibition at the Everson Museum of Art in Syracuse, where *Blue Room Event* comprised a section of the show, George Maciunas produced a set of rubber stamps that repeated such implicit instructions for mental gymnastics as "This room will be round when it gets to the center of your mind," "This window is 2,000 feet wide," and "Stay until the room is blue" (fig. 2.18). Visitors could leave the exhibition equipped to re-create *Blue Room Event* whenever and wherever they chose.

Yoko Ono's instruction works are critical contributions to the history of Conceptualism, both in their substantive content and in the form in which they were presented to the public. In particular, her 1962 Tokyo display of written instructions was the first exhibition whose form was based upon the primacy of idea over object. As Ono came to focus more on the activity of the imagination, the democratic and libertarian aspects of her work came to the fore, mining the political implications of Cage's practice, the social imperative that she found in existentialism, and a Zen-influenced interest in the operation of the mind. Her thoughts—communicated through instructions—were meant to be shared, and Ono's hope was for their development through interpretation by others. And in the end, the empowerment of others through imaginative activity forms the ongoing life of the instruction works of Yoko Ono.

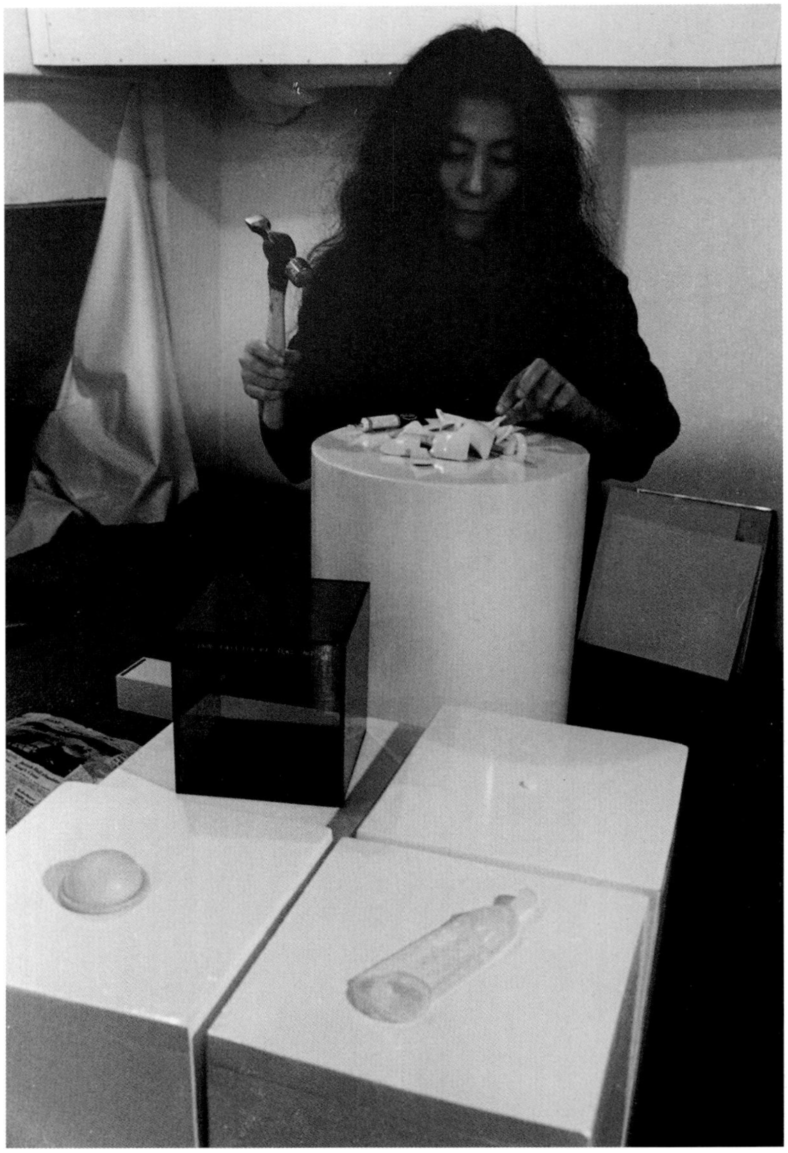

FIGURE 6.7
ONO PREPARING ***MEND PIECE***, INDICA GALLERY, LONDON, 1966

NOTES

1. The term was first used to characterize the new varieties of art-making in Lucy Lippard and John Chandler, "The Dematerialization of Art," *Art International* 12, no. 2 (February 1968). For documentation of the period, see Lucy Lippard, ed., *Six Years: The Dematerialization of the Art Object from 1966 to 1972* (New York: Praeger, 1973).

2. For an account of this class and its importance, see Bruce Altshuler, "The Cage Class" in *FluxAttitudes*, exh. cat. (Buffalo: Hallwalls Contemporary Arts Center, 1991), 17–23.

3. For a list of these performances, see Chronology, 1960–62. See also *Happening & Fluxus*, exh. cat. (1970); and Henry Flynt, "Mutations of the Vanguard: Pre-Fluxus, During Fluxus, Late Fluxus" in *Ubi Fluxus Ibi Motus: 1990–1962*, exh. cat. (1990), 104–5. Printed on the bottom of notices of performances at the loft was the following disclaimer: THE PURPOSE OF THIS SERIES IS NOT ENTERTAINMENT.

4. Ono, e-mail to author, 3 November 1999.

5. For an account of the history of this publication and of the period, see Jackson Mac Low, "Wie George Maciunas die New Yorker Avantgarde kennenlernte" in *1962 Wiesbaden Fluxus 1982: Eine kleine Geschichte von Fluxus in drei Teilen*, exh. cat. (Wiesbaden: Museum Wiesbaden, Nassuischer Kunstverein, and Harlekin Art, 1982), 110–25 (text in both German and English).

6. During the two-week run of Ono's exhibition the AG performance series included presentations by La Monte Young, Walter de Maria, Henry Flynt, and Ray Johnson. For an account of this exhibition, see Hendricks, *Paintings and Drawings by Yoko Ono* (1993).

7. Although only thirteen *Instruction Paintings* are documented, an unsigned typescript in the Silverman Collection mentions that fifteen instructions were shown at AG Gallery.

8. In addition to a swipe at high art in the manner of Dada, *Painting to Be Stepped On* also refers to *fumie*, Christian images used in Japan in the seventeenth century in the campaign to suppress Christianity. Purported Christians were tried by their willingness to step on these images of Christ or the Virgin. Ono's work likewise provides a test of the viewer's willingness to reject traditional ideas about art. See [Ono], *Yoko at Indica*, exh. cat. (1966), [P1].

9. While Ono did not emphasize the future obsolescence of professional art-making, she apparently agreed with Maciunas's view, writing to Ivan Karp in 1965: "Soon there will be no need of artists, since people will start to write their own instructions or exchange them and paint" (letter to Ivan Karp, 1965; Anthology 13).

10. On Brecht's use of the term "event," see Brecht, "The Origin of Events" (1970) in *Happening & Fluxus*, n.p. For the development of instruction works in the 1960s, see Altshuler, "Art by Instruction and the Pre-History of Do It" in *Do It* exh. cat. (1997), 22–28.

11. George Brecht conceived the works in *Toward Events* while taking Cage's class, and their development is documented in the notebooks in which he took his class notes, recently published in facsimile in *George Brecht—Notebooks I–V* (Cologne: Verlag der Buchhandlung Walter König, 1991, 1997). For an account of this exhibition see Joseph Jacobs, "Crashing New York à la John Cage" in *Off Limits: Rutgers University and the Avant-Garde, 1957–1963*, exh. cat. (Newark, N.J.: The Newark Museum, 1999), 90–92; see also plates 21 and 25 for color photographs of Brecht works in the exhibition. Brecht developed a complex view of the relation between objects and events, viewing all objects as events when considered in light of subatomic physics and Zen philosophy, a circumstance that merits further investigation in the evaluation of his work. On Brecht's work, in addition to the facsimile notebooks, the best sources are: Henry Martin, *An Introduction to George Brecht's Book of the Tumbler on Fire* (Milan: Multhipla, 1978); and Brecht's own *Water Yam*, boxed sets of his event cards published by Fluxus beginning in 1963. For the publication history of *Water Yam*, see Hendricks, *Fluxus Codex* (1988), 216–19. While it is not certain when Brecht began to send his event cards to friends, a notebook entry for 8 August 1959 asks whether "scores [should] be simply published in the newspaper, or available on printed cards or sheets of paper, to be sent to anyone" (Daniels, *George Brecht—Notebook III*, 135).

12. Without installation photographs or a checklist, it is difficult to verify the number of works in the Sōgetsu exhibition. The exhibition program (pl. 27a) lists ten pieces with unique titles and twenty-eight works generically titled (in English) *An Imaginary Piece*, suggesting that there were thirty-eight works in the exhibition. However, only twenty-two Japanese text sheets (and perhaps three in facsimile) survive.

13. For the history of Sōgetsu Art Center, see Dore Ashton, *The Delicate Thread: Teshigahara's Life in Art* (Tokyo: Kodansha International, 1997), 142–47.

14. For an account of Seth Siegelaub's exhibitions-as-catalogues, see Altshuler, *The Avant-Garde in Exhibition: New Art in the 20th Century* (New York: Abrams, 1994), 238–43.

15. Ono, "Painting to Be Constructed in Your Head" in *Instruction Paintings* (1995), 5.

16. See, for instance, the multiple versions of *Painting in Three Stanzas* in *Global Conceptualism: Points of Origin, 1950s–1980s*, exh. cat. (New York: Queens Museum of Art, 1999), 152–53. Whether each verbal expression represents a different idea rather than the development or interpretation of the same idea constitutes another question.

17. Here I reconstruct the line of reasoning of the last paragraph of a 1964 conversation among Ono, Tony Cox, and Al Wonderlick, published as "Yoko Ono: Instruction Painting" in *Yoko at Indica*, n.p.

18. Ono, conversation with author, 3 November 1999.

19. Ono, "The Word of a Fabricator" (1962, translated by Yoko Ono 1999; Anthology 12).

20. On existence preceding essence see Jean-Paul Sartre, "Existentialism Is a Humanism" (1946) in *Existentialism from Dostoevsky to Sartre*, ed. Walter Kaufmann (Cleveland and New York: World Publishing Company, 1956), 287–311, especially 289–91. Ono's reference to "the world of stickiness" resonates with Sartre's phenomenological investigation of the concept of *visqueux*, translated by Hazel Barnes as "slimy," but also meaning "sticky" or "gluey" (Sartre, *Being and Nothingness*, trans. Hazel E. Barnes [New York: Philosophical Library, 1956], 604–12).

21. See, for instance, Chrissie Iles, "Yoko Ono" in *Have You Seen the Horizon Lately?* exh. cat. (1997), 10–14. Much of Ono's press also has emphasized Japanese cultural connections, associations often used to promote her work. The press release for her performances at London's 1966 *Destruction in Art Symposium* quotes U.S. publications calling her "a new Zen type invention" (*New York Herald Tribune*) and "a fey Zen variant" (*Time*); and the Sphere Books press release for the 1971 edition of *Grapefruit* quotes *The Listener* referring to its content as "specimens of Oriental poetry," and as "haiku…divested of all its California disguises."

22. Ono, conversation with author, 3 November 1999.

23. See Sol LeWitt, "Paragraphs on Conceptual Art" (*Artforum*, June 1967) and "Sentences on Conceptual Art" (*0–9*, 1969 and *Art-Language*, May 1969), both reprinted in *Sol LeWitt*, exh. cat. (New York: The Museum of Modern Art, 1978), 166–68. The principle is most clearly seen operating in Lawrence Weiner's oft-repeated view that his work does not have to be "constructed," and that the decision whether or not to do so is that of the "receiver."

24. Just before the publication of *Grapefruit*, Naiqua Gallery in Tokyo presented *3 Old Paintings by Yoko Ono* in June 1964 (see Chronology, 1964, June 7, 14, 21). Ono does not remember actual paintings or instruction sheets being shown and believes the works in the exhibition were purely conceptual (e-mail to author, 3 November 1999).

25. Part of the *Insound and Instructure* program is printed in *Grapefruit* (1970); see also fig. 1.2; Anthology 2, 11.

26. No documentation of the content of the *Instructure* exhibition exists, and this description of the display is taken from a conversation with Al Wunderlich (formerly Wonderlick), 12 October 1999, which was confirmed by Ono (e-mail to author, 3 November 1999).

27. For a series of reminiscences of Yoko Ono's work in London in 1966–67, see "Is That an Apple? Yoko Ono in London," *Art Monthly*, no. 212 (December 1997–January 1998): 1–7.

28. The catalogue *Yoko at Indica* lists eleven paintings and twenty-five objects, illustrating all of the paintings and sixteen of the objects. However, it also includes an installation photograph showing a work that is not listed—*Help! Help! for R.B.*, a piece consisting of three small canvases (one thick, one thin, and one imaginary)—suggesting that there might have been more works than those mentioned or pictured.

29. This piece seems to refer to the Buddhist notion of mental concentration understood as a "state of one-pointedness." For this concept and its connection to artistic creation, see D. T. Suzuki, *Zen and Japanese Culture* (Princeton: Princeton University Press, 1959), 226.

30. Marcel Duchamp had attended a concert at Ono's loft in 1961 during which she waited with anticipation, and eventual disappointment, for him to notice and to step on her *Painting to Be Stepped On* (Ono, e-mail to author, 3 November 1999). Ono clearly embraced a Duchampian perspective on what constitutes art, remarking in a 1971 interview that "A work is something that has a value as a work of art to someone" ("Interview with Yoko Ono," Pacifica Radio Archive, Program Number BC0339).

31. See *Yoko Ono at Lisson*, exh. cat. (1967). *Blue Room Event* at the Lisson Gallery can be usefully compared to Yves Klein's exhibition of an empty gallery, *Le Vide* (*The Void*), presented at the Galerie Iris Clert in Paris in April–May 1958. Klein claimed that the white gallery actually was blue, but for him this blueness was the spiritual aura otherwise found before his blue monochrome paintings, with which he had filled the gallery by meditative exercises. Ono, in contrast, places the burden on the visitor, not on the artist, to perform the requisite mental act. For an account of *Le Vide* see Altshuler, *The Avant-Garde in Exhibition*, 192–97.

1 *Lighting Piece,* 1955

instruction/performance

LIGHTING PIECE

Light a match and watch till it goes out.

1955 autumn

The idea of *Lighting Piece* evolved between 1952 and 1957, while Ono was living in Scarsdale, New York, with her parents. Her early musical training in Japan had made her so sensitive to surrounding sounds that she was often compelled to stay in a dark room with her ears covered by sanitary pads tied in place with a strip of gauze. To cope with such isolation, Ono invented a ritual of lighting a match and watching it burn, repeating it until she became calm. Although this action was primarily visual, it also had something of an auditory effect on her: the sounds in her mind disappeared as the flame went out.[1] This experience made her keenly aware of the need for what she called the "additional act," that was "something more than painting, poetry, and music."[2] The artist recalls having also performed the ritual in front of her sister during those years.

Later, because of its private nature, Ono performed *Lighting Piece* "always as a part of another piece," or "slipped it in, so to speak." For example, a variation is incorporated in the script "AOS, the opera," which she first presented as *AOS—To David Tudor* at her Carnegie Recital Hall concert in 1961 (see Anthology 6). A version that reflects her 1955 score is documented from Ono's solo recital at Sōgetsu Art Center in 1962, when she used it as a finale to *A Piano Piece to See the Sky* (no. 27).[3] Other renditions of the piece include the film *No. 1 (Match)*, which presented a close-up view of the artist's hand striking a match and holding it until the flame burned down and the smoke vanished (no. 42). The high-speed camera (2,000 frames/second) captured the delicate movement of the flame and smoke, which unfolded in extreme slow motion when projected at normal speed. In Florence in 1992, the piece was realized as a projection of three slides, representing three stages of the burning match, onto church facades along the Arno River.

For Ono, the match flame symbolized the transience of human life. As her then husband Anthony Cox mentioned, Ono felt that watching burning matches made her life longer.[4] Through the various manifestations of *Lighting Piece*, Ono offers audience members an opportunity to step back and ponder their lives.
MY

NOTES

I would like to acknowledge the generous cooperation of the artist and her curator, Jon Hendricks, who was of great assistance in the location of material for my writing.

1. Accounts of Ono's first conception and performances of the piece are from Ono, e-mail to author, 13 September 1999 and 6 February 2000.

2. Ono quoted in Jonathan Cott, "Yoko Ono and Her Sixteen-Track Voice" in *The Ballad of John and Yoko* (Garden City, N.Y.: Doubleday, 1982), 116.

3. Fujimatsu Hiroshi mentions Ono lighting a cigarette, out of breath after playing the piano with her arms in "Kyokō no kurokami" (Fictitious black hair), *Bijutsu techō*, no. 206 (July 1962): 83.

4. Anthony Cox, "Instructive Auto-Destruction," *Art and Artists* 1, no. 5 (August 1966): 17.

OTHER VERSIONS
For film version, see no. 42

1993 handwritten text
First shown: 1994 *Outside the Frame*, Cleveland Center for Contemporary Art. Ink on paper, approx. 9 x 6"

1995 projection
Outdoor projection of three slides in Florence (pls. 67a–b)

1998 projection
Outdoor projection in Naples

PERFORMANCES: 1952–57 privately performed; 1961 (November 24) *Works by Yoko Ono*, Carnegie Recital Hall (variation); 1962 (May 24) *Works of Yoko Ono*, Sōgetsu Art Center; thereafter incorporated in different performances

VISUAL DOCUMENTATION: 1962, photo by Yoshioka Yasuhiro

LITERATURE: Linscott, *Liverpool Daily Post* (3 October 1967); Cott, *The Ballad of John and Yoko* (1982), 116; Hendricks, *Fluxus Codex* (1988), 420; Haskell and Hanhardt, *Arias and Objects* (1991), 8–9, 33; Jenkins, *In the Spirit of Fluxus*, exh. cat. (1993), 128; Iles, *Have You Seen the Horizon Lately?* exh. cat. (1997), 6–9, 119

PLATES 1A–B
LIGHTING PIECE,
1955. SŌGETSU ART
CENTER, TOKYO, 1962

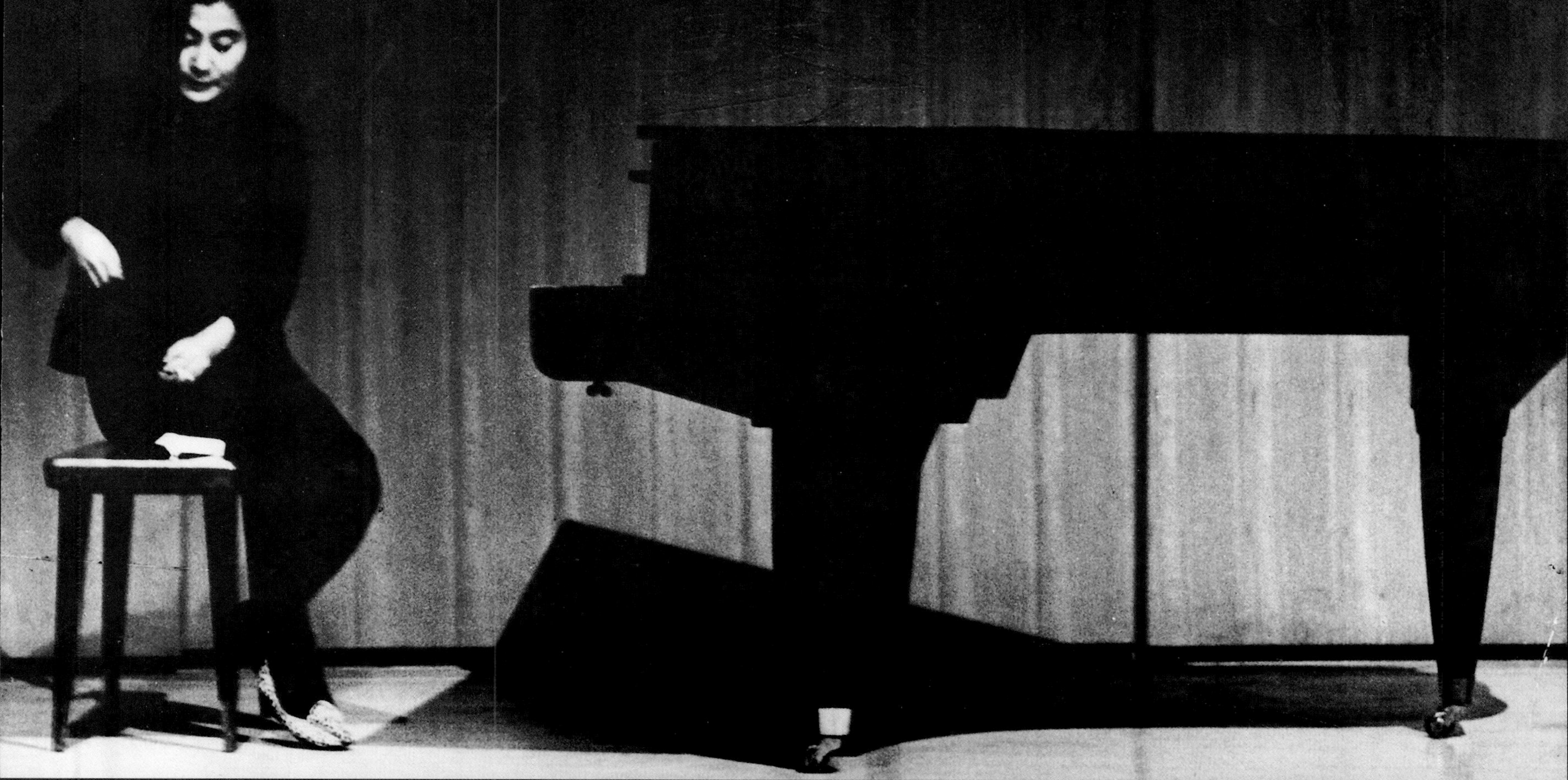

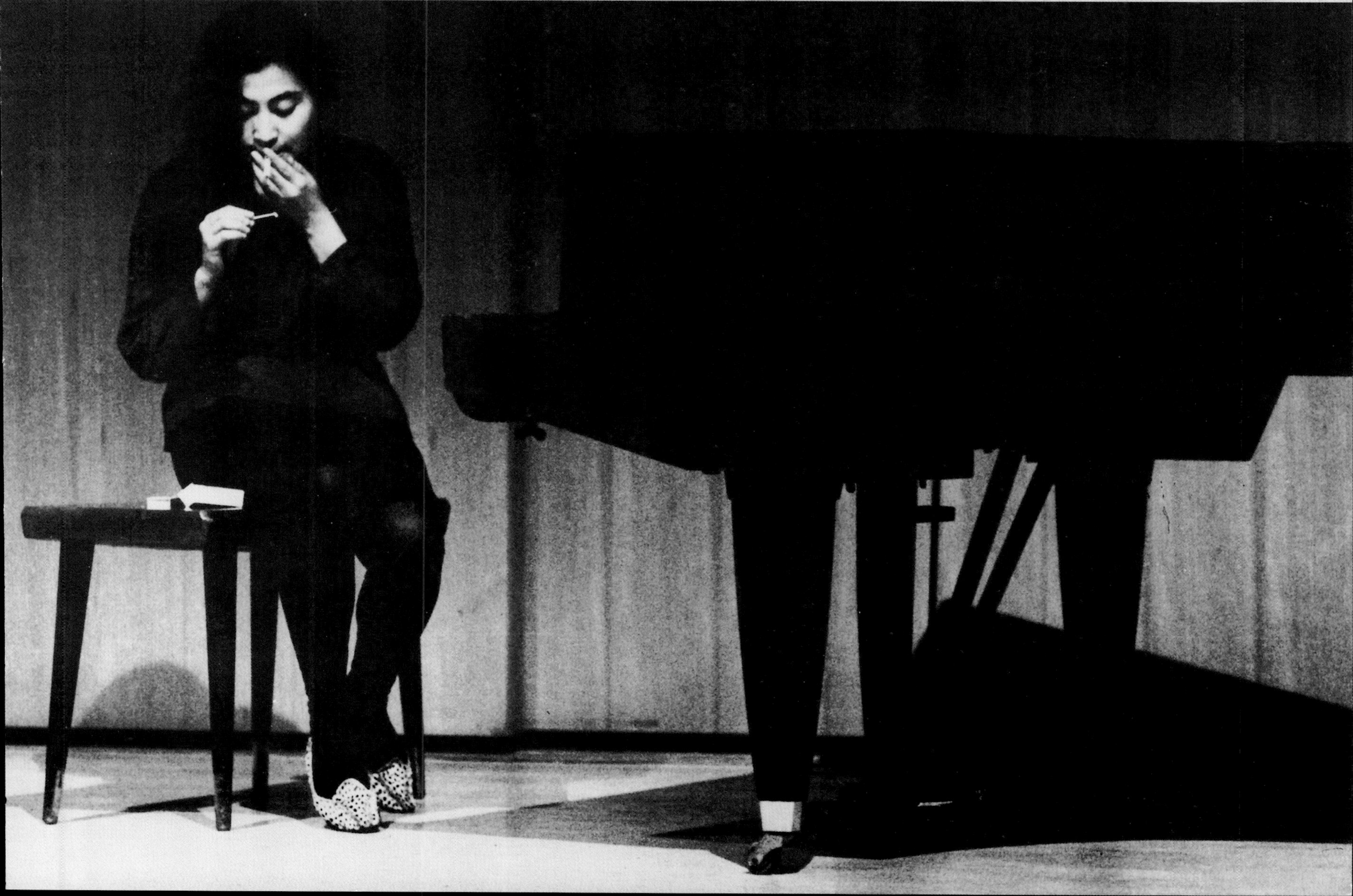

2 *Instruction Paintings,* 1961

13 documented paintings: ink on canvas (with some variations, as noted); dimensions variable; all lost
13 undocumented oral instructions
3 instruction cards (as noted)

PAINTINGS
Documented in photographs by George Maciunas; The Gilbert and Lila Silverman Fluxus Collection, Detroit (pls. 2a, 2c–d; figs. 1.8, 2.2, 6.2–5)

A Plus B Painting, 1961

Painting to Be Stepped On, 1960
instruction card: ink on paper; reads: A WORK TO BE STEPPED ON; lost

Painting to See in the Dark (Version 1), 1961
canvas: approx. 28 x 44" (71.1 x 111.8 cm)

Painting to See in the Dark (Version 2), 1961

Painting Until It Becomes Marble, 1961

Painting in Three Stanzas, 1961
ink on canvas with live plant: approx. 30 x 42" (76.2 x 106.7 cm)
instruction card: ink on paper, handwritten by Ichiyanagi Toshi; 3½ x 10⅝" (8.9 x 26.7 cm); collection of the artist

Painting to Let the Evening Light Go Through, 1961

Painting for the Wind, 1961
instruction card: ink on paper, handwritten by Ichiyanagi Toshi; lost

Shadow Painting, 1961

Smoke Painting, 1961

Time Painting, 1961
canvas: approx. 35 x 24" (88.9 x 61 cm)

Waterdrop Painting (Version 1), 1961

Waterdrop Painting (Version 2), 1961

Yoko Ono's first formal presentation of her *Instruction Paintings* was part of the exhibition *Paintings and Drawings by Yoko Ono*, mounted in July 1961 at George Maciunas and Almus Salcius's AG Gallery in New York. (Ono previously had displayed a few of these works during the concerts that she and La Monte Young had organized at her Chambers Street loft.) In addition to the thirteen instruction pieces, documented in a set of installation photographs taken by Maciunas, the exhibition included calligraphic works done in *sumi* ink on paper. Ono's instruction works also presented the gallery visitor with abstract imagery, but they differed radically in the ideas associated with their making. For most of these instruction pieces the artist specified particular directions whereby the work was to be completed, often inviting the viewer to participate in the act of creation. In defining the work by a set of instructions, Ono implicitly asserted the primacy of ideas over particular physical realizations and presented the concept of the piece as a verbal score generating the work as embodied performance.

Germinal at the time of the AG Gallery exhibition, this Conceptualist point of view would be made explicit when most of these works, with the addition of about twenty others, were exhibited solely as written instructions in 1962 at Sōgetsu Art Center in Tokyo (no. 3). With the apparent exception of three pieces, for which written instructions were exhibited alongside the works, it is not known whether Ono wrote texts for these paintings prior to the exhibition, where instructions were explained orally by the artist and the gallerist to exhibition visitors. The single surviving text of the three shown in the Maciunas photographs of the exhibition (*Painting in Three Stanzas*) suggests that the artist did not yet conceive of the works in terms of instructions that could be followed by another person to create the piece, a step that would be taken by the time of the Sōgetsu exhibition. When she published *Grapefruit* in 1964, Yoko Ono included in the "Painting" section texts for all but two of the instruction works that had appeared in the AG Gallery exhibition.
BA

NOTES
Where possible, measurements of canvases are given based on Maciunas's documentary photographs.

OTHER VERSIONS
For score and book versions, see nos. 3, 4. Individual paintings, such as *Painting to Be Stepped On* and *Painting to Let the Evening Light Go Through*, have separate histories of realization in various materials. Concept of *Painting in Three Stanzas* is in the collection of Bergen Kunstmuseum

EXHIBITIONS: 1961 *Paintings and Drawings by Yoko Ono*, AG Gallery; 1993 *Family Album*, Stiftung Starke (re-creation with stretched canvases); hereafter frequently re-created and exhibited

VISUAL DOCUMENTATION: 1961, photos by George Maciunas, pub. Hendricks, *Paintings and Drawings by Yoko Ono* (1993) and Ono, *Instruction Paintings* (1995)

LITERATURE: Swenson, *Art News* (September 1961); Haskell and Hanhardt, *Arias and Objects* (1991), 6–7, 14–16, 24–25; Hendricks, *Paintings and Drawings by Yoko Ono* (1993); Ono, *Instruction Paintings* (1995); Altshuler, *Do It*, exh. cat. (1997), 23–25; Iles, *Have You Seen the Horizon Lately?* exh. cat. (1997), 62, 64, 83, 128–31; Tomii, *Global Conceptualism*, exh. cat. (1999), 18–19

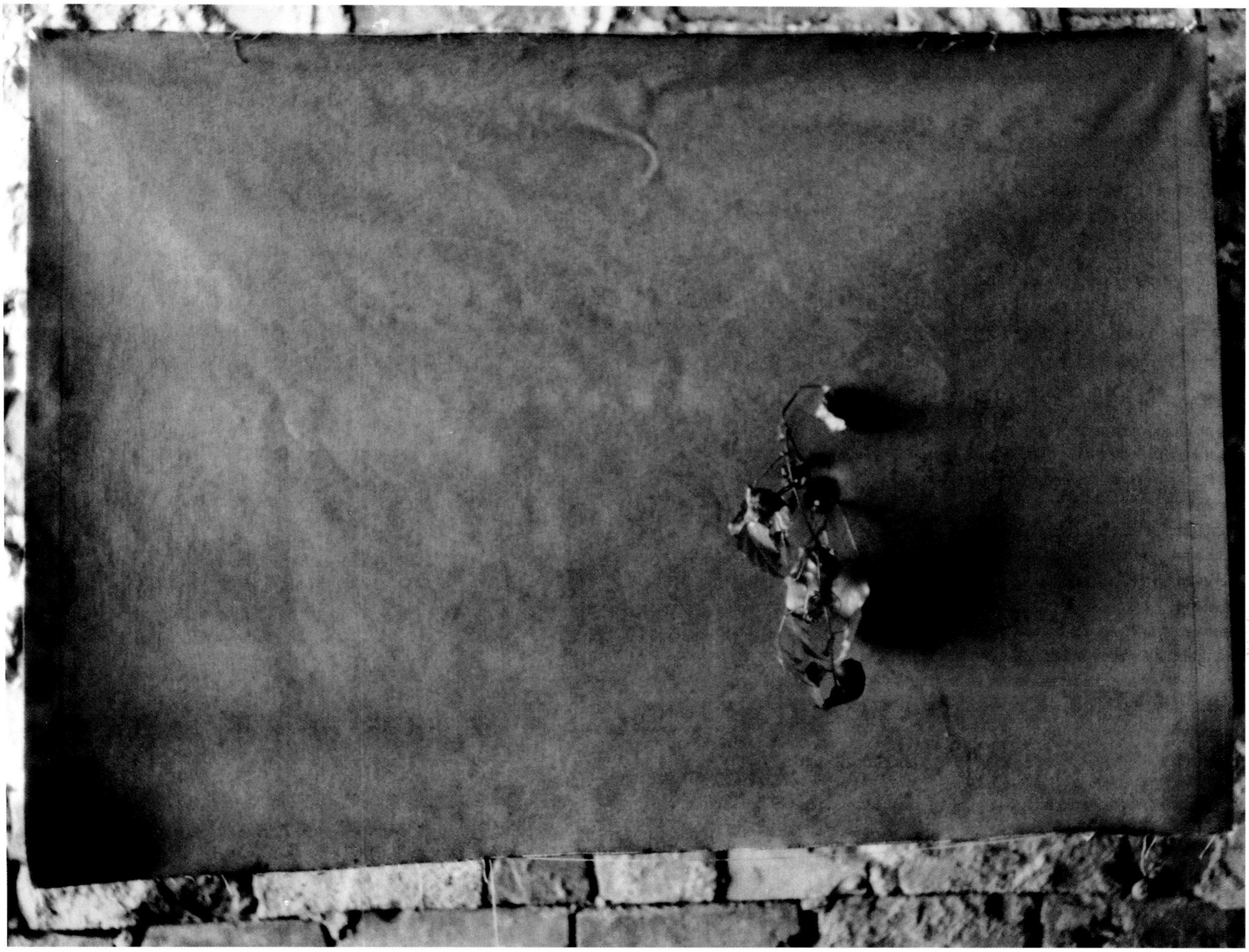

PLATE 2A (TOP)
PAINTING IN THREE STANZAS, 1961
(CANVAS VERSION)

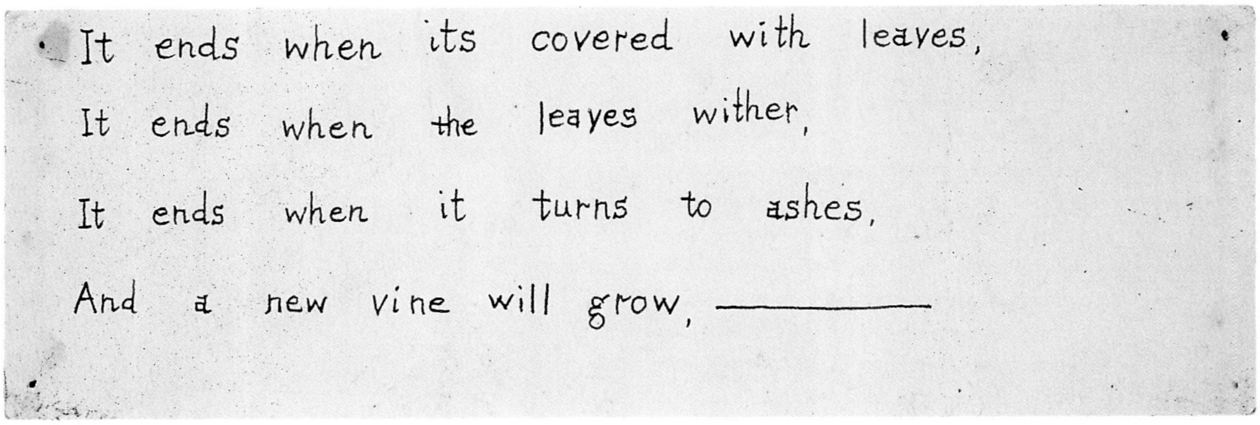
It ends when its covered with leaves,
It ends when the leaves wither,
It ends when it turns to ashes,
And a new vine will grow, ________

PLATE 2B (RIGHT)
INSTRUCTION CARD FOR *PAINTING IN THREE STANZAS*, 1961
(CANVAS VERSION)

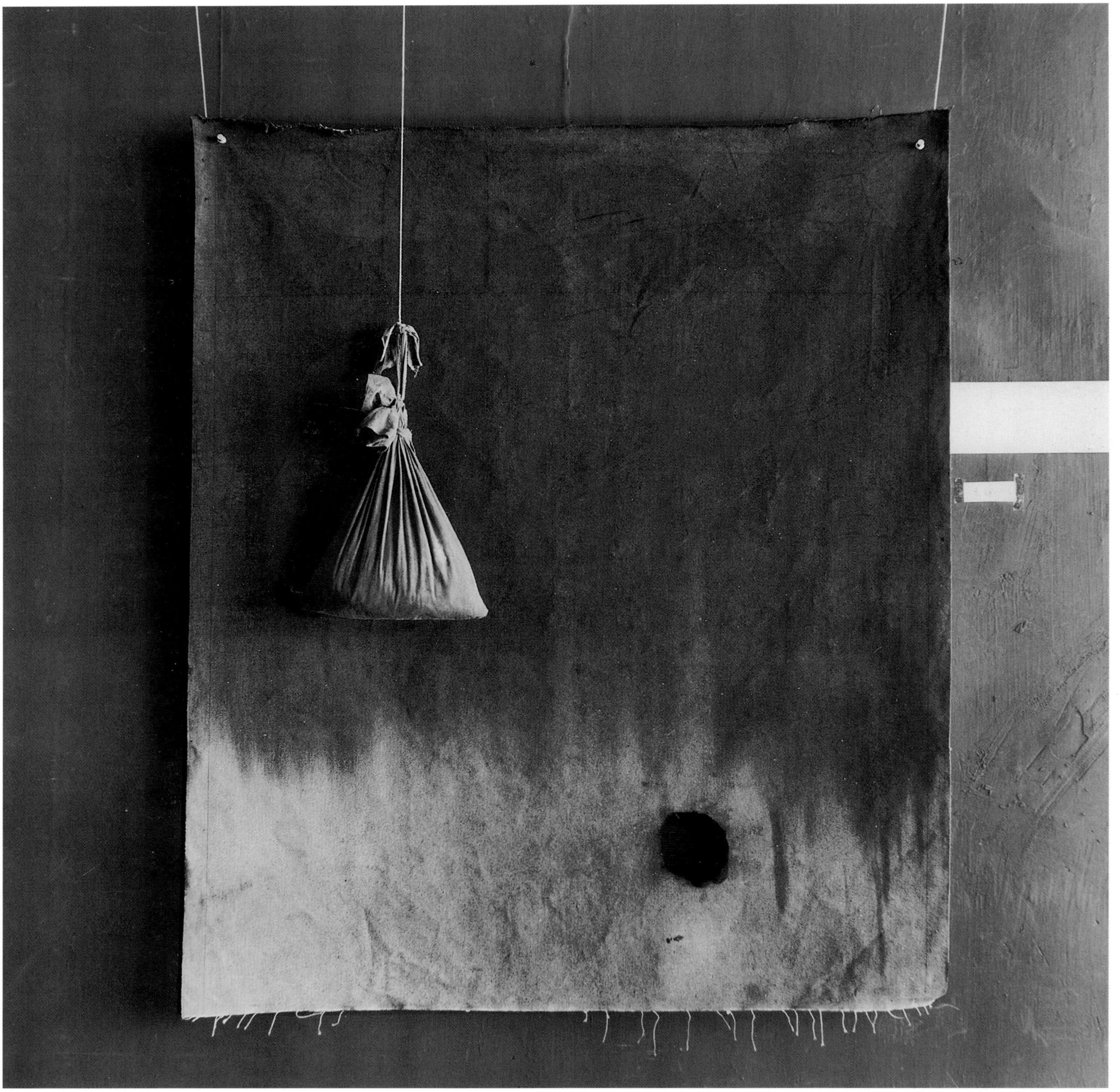

PLATE 2C
PAINTING FOR THE WIND, 1961 (CANVAS VERSION)

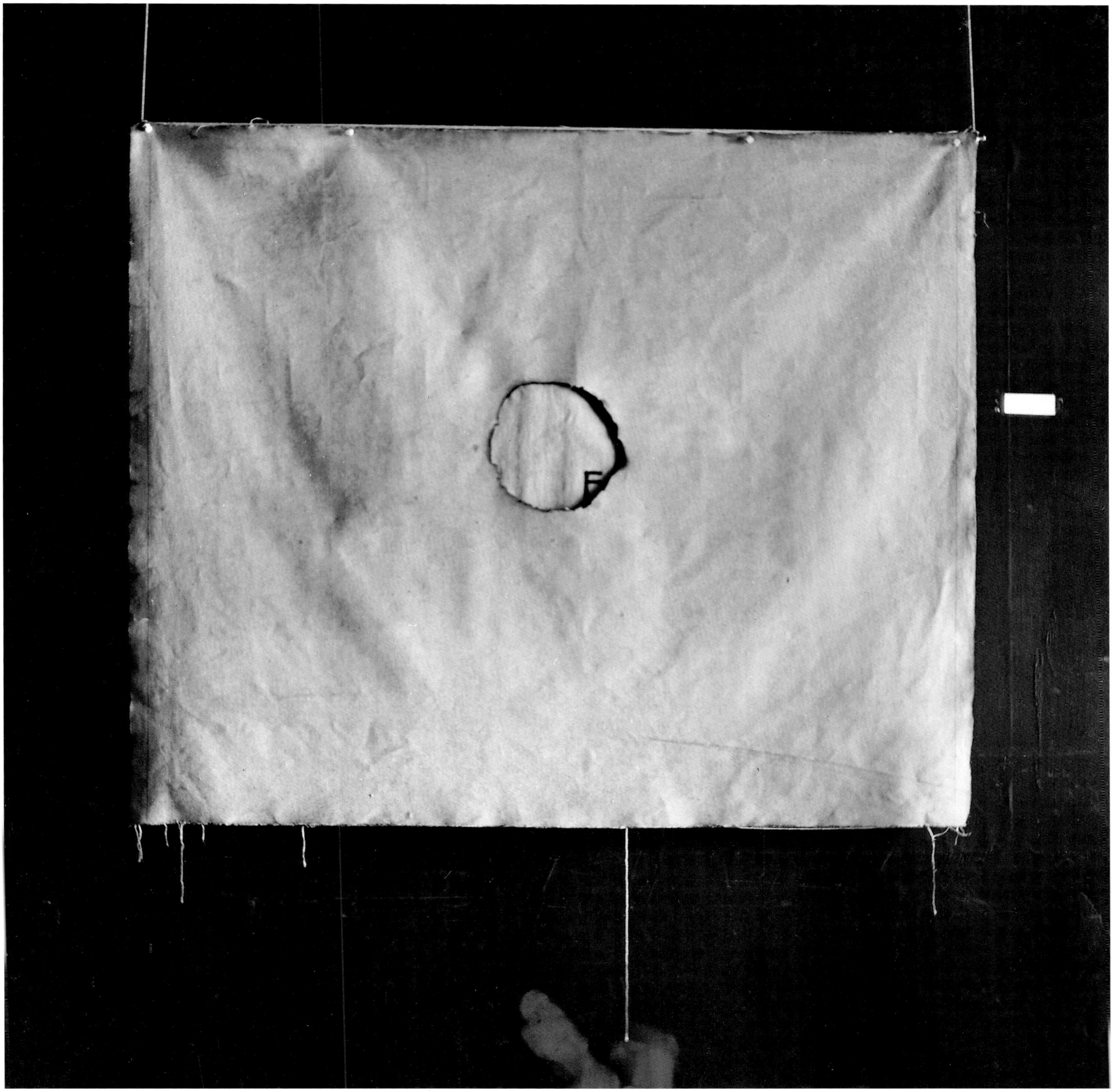

PLATE 2D

A PLUS B PAINTING,

'961 (CANVAS VERSION)

3 *Instructions for Paintings,* 1962

22 works; additional works lost
ink on paper, handwritten in Japanese by Ichiyanagi Toshi
approx. 10 x 15" (25.4 x 38.1 cm) each
Collection of Gilbert and Lila Silverman, Detroit

In conjunction with her performance on May 24, 1962, at Sōgetsu Art Center in Tokyo (no. 27), Yoko Ono exhibited the series of *Instructions for Paintings* on the lobby walls of Sōgetsu Kaikan Hall. In order to avoid the emotionality of her own handwriting the artist asked composer Ichiyanagi Toshi, to whom she was married at the time, to write the texts in Japanese in his more controlled hand. Ono had written these texts in English, translated them herself into Japanese, and then had her Japanese texts copied by Ichiyanagi.

This exhibition marks Yoko Ono's move to a fully Conceptualist orientation, advancing beyond her display of works created with the help of instructions at AG Gallery in New York in July 1961 (no. 2). By eliminating the object in favor of a text presenting directions for generating that object, the idea of the work assumed primary importance and the viewer became a potential participant in the process of creation. Juxtaposed with the artist's performance inside the hall, the lobby exhibition of *Instructions for Paintings* located the viewer as potentially in the same position as the artist on stage—following a score to create an avant-garde work of art.

The exhibition program lists ten pieces with specific titles, and twenty-eight works generically titled in English *An Imaginary Piece* (pl. 27a). It therefore appears that the exhibition included thirty-eight works. However, all but twenty-two instruction sheets have been lost.

In addition to foregrounding the notion of art as idea, the exhibition represents the further removal of her artwork from a reliance on Ono's hand. She had taken the first step by involving viewers in the creation of her work at AG Gallery in 1961; having the instructions written out for public presentation by Ichiyanagi moved the process to another stage. At the time of the Sōgetsu event Ono also had photostats of the instruction sheets made for possible magazine publication, thirty-six of which survive. Some of these were positive images and some were negatives (yet another transformation of the originals) and she came to see these photostats as further distancing the work from her personal touch. The final move in this direction took place with the 1964 publication of her instruction works in *Grapefruit* (no. 4). *Grapefruit* (1964) itself contains a reference to this conceptual trajectory:

> PAINTING TO EXIST ONLY WHEN IT'S
> COPIED OR PHOTOGRAPHED
>
> Let people copy or photograph your
> paintings.
> Destroy the originals.
>
> 1964 spring

BA

EXHIBITIONS: 1962 *Works of Yoko Ono*, Sōgetsu Art Center; 1993 *Glimpse*, Cranbrook Academy; 1994 *Japanese Art After 1945*, Yokohama Museum of Art/Guggenheim Museum SoHo; 1997 *Have You Seen the Horizon Lately?* MOMA, Oxford; 1999 *Global Art—Rheinland 2000*, Museum Ludwig

LITERATURE: Hendricks, *Instructions for Paintings by Yoko Ono* (1993); Munroe, *Japanese Art After 1945* (1994), 218; Ono, *Instruction Paintings* (1995); Tomii, *Global Conceptualism*, exh. cat. (1999), 18–19; *Global Art—Rheinland 2000*, exh. cat. (1999), 316

PLATE 3A

PAINTING IN THREE STANZAS, 1962 (SCORE VERSION)

PAINTING IN THREE STANZAS

Let a vine grow.
Water every day.

The first stanza—till the vine spreads.
The second stanza—till the vine withers.
The third stanza—till the wall vanishes.

1961 summer

—From *Grapefruit* (1964)

PLATE 3B
SMOKE PAINTING,
1962 (SCORE VERSION)

SMOKE PAINTING

Light canvas or any finished painting
with a cigarette at any time for any
length of time.
See the smoke movement.
The painting ends when the whole
canvas or painting is gone.

1961 summer

—From *Grapefruit* (1964)

PLATE 3C
PAINTING TO BE CONSTRUCTED IN YOUR HEAD, 1962
(SCORE VERSION)

PAINTING TO BE CONSTRUCTED IN YOUR HEAD

Go on transforming a square canvas in your head until it becomes a circle. Pick out any shape in the process and pin up or place on the canvas an object, a smell, a sound, or a colour that came to your mind in association with the shape.

1962 spring
Sogetsu

—From *Grapefruit* (1964)

4 *Grapefruit,* 1964

EDITIONS
1964
edition of 500
published by Wunternaum Press, Tokyo
5½ x 5½ x 1⅜" (14 x 14 x 3.8 cm)

1970 hardback
published by Simon and Schuster, New York
with introduction by John Lennon
5½ x 5½ x 1" (14 x 14 x 2.5 cm)

1970 hardback
published by Owen, London
with introduction by John Lennon
5½ x 5⅜ x ¾" (14 x 13.5 x 1.9 cm)

1971 paperback
published by Simon and Schuster, Touchstone Paperback, New York
with introduction by John Lennon
5¼ x 5¼ x ⅞" (13.3 x 13.3 x 2.2 cm)

1971 paperback
Sphere Books, London
with introduction by John Lennon
5¼ x 5¼ x ¾" (13.3 x 13.3 x 1.9 cm)

Also various editions in translation

A compendium of Yoko Ono's instruction works, *Grapefruit* is one of the seminal works of Conceptual Art. Ono published 500 copies of *Grapefruit* in Japan under her own imprint, Wunternaum Press of Tokyo and Bellport, Long Island. Associating her work with freedom, and with the United States, she printed July 4, 1964, as the date of publication (fig. 6.6).

Ono has stated that she chose the title because she liked grapefruit as a child and—believing this fruit to be a hybrid of an orange and a lemon—that it reflected her sense of herself as "a spiritual hybrid."[1] The book's title thus points toward the hybridization of Japanese and Western cultural sources in her instruction works, which unite the reductive forms of Zen-related aesthetics with the Conceptualist score developed by the circle of John Cage. But the notion of hybridization also has a psychological dimension, alluding to Ono's profound sense of never being at home in either Japan or the United States.

According to Ono, she was prompted by husband Anthony Cox to assemble and publish her instruction works while they were living in Tokyo in 1963.[2] Interestingly, at the same time, George Maciunas was planning to publish the collected works of a number of artists, including Ono. Although Maciunas's letters to Ono about this project seem not to have reached her in Japan, he eventually contacted her in Tokyo and she sent him some scores to publish in his Fluxus newspaper, which in February 1964 included a prepublication advertisement for *Grapefruit*.[3]

The first edition of *Grapefruit* presents more than 150 of Ono's instruction works, each dated by year and season, and organized into five sections: Music, Painting, Event, Poetry, and Object. Virtually all works in the book are in English; for about one-third of these pieces, Japanese translations appear somewhere in the volume.[4] In general, the Japanese translations are literal, although there are cases in which the English versions contain more explicit directions or more detail, Ono apparently feeling comfortable leaving things less clearly specified in Japanese.[5] Before the five sections of works there is a dedication to various figures to whom pieces were explicitly or imaginatively dedicated—including John Cage, La Monte Young, Nam June Paik, Peggy Guggenheim, George Maciunas, and Isamu Noguchi—followed by documentation relating to Ono's Japanese exhibitions and performances.

The second edition of *Grapefruit* appeared in 1970 under very different circumstances, no longer a self-published artist's book but a mainstream publication from Simon and Schuster. The reason for the interest of a commercial publisher in a volume of avant-garde instruction works was Ono's marriage to John Lennon, and the book appeared with an introduction and drawings by the pop star. (It literally is an introduction, reading, "Hi! My name is John Lennon. I'd like you to meet Yoko Ono.") Not surprisingly, there are no Japanese texts, but about eighty more pieces are presented than in the first edition, and there are two more sections of works, Film and Dance. The book ends with a selection of Ono's writings—including her important 1966 essay "To the Wesleyan People" (Anthology 14)—followed by letters from Ono to art dealers Ivan Karp (Anthology 13), Nicholas Longsdail, and Richard Bellamy.

The 1971 edition of *Grapefruit*, published in London by Sphere Books, presents the same works as the 1970 Simon and Schuster edition but has a striking new cover showing a bare female waist-to-thigh from the rear inserted into a giant grapefruit—an allusion to Ono's notorious film *No. 4*, generally referred to as "Bottoms" (no. 43). In 1971 a paperback edition was published by Simon and Schuster's Touchstone imprint, adding more than thirty works to existing sections plus a new nine-piece Architecture section.
BA

PLATE 4

GRAPEFRUIT, 1964. COLLECTION OF C. V. STARR LIBRARY, JAPAN SOCIETY, NEW YORK

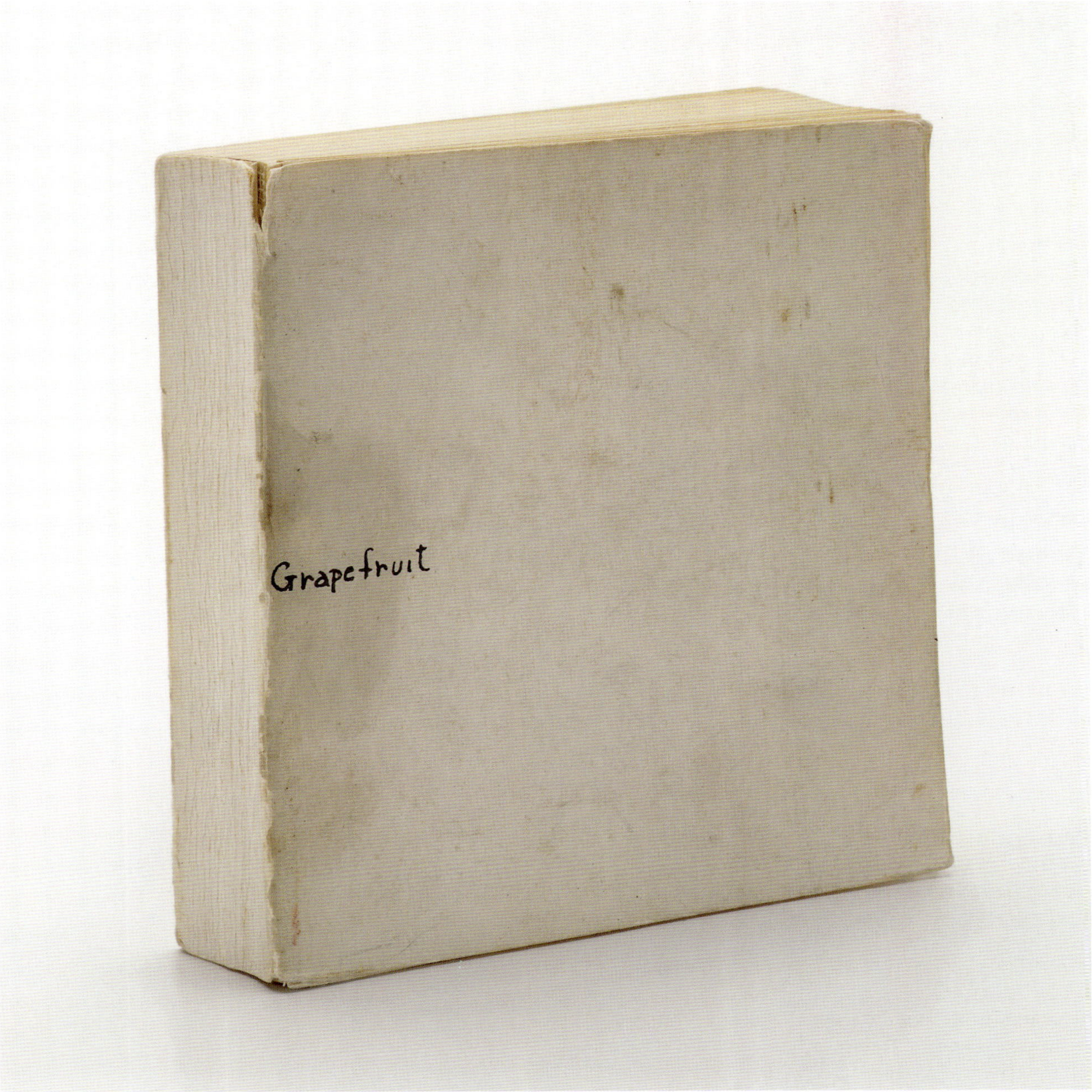

NOTES

1. Ono, e-mail to author, 8 November 1999. The symbolic importance of this fruit to Ono is also seen in the title of her first major performance piece, *Of a Grapefruit in the World of Park* (1961; Anthology 5).

2. Ono, e-mail to author, 8 and 22 November, 1999.

3. Other artists whose collected works Maciunas sought to publish included George Brecht, Daniel Spoerri, Allan Kaprow, Dick Higgins, and La Monte Young. For Maciunas's solicitation of artists, and announcements of his planned publication and distribution of *Grapefruit*, see "Fluxus News Leter [*sic*] No. 5 January 1, 1963" in Hendricks, *Fluxus etc./Addenda I* (1983), 155 and Hendricks, *Fluxus Codex*, 418–19. I thank Jon Hendricks and Yoko Ono for discussion of Maciunas and his connection to the early history of *Grapefruit*.

4. One work that is published only in Japanese is *Line Piece II (Dedicated to La Monte Young)* which reads: "Draw a line with your body./Continue drawing until your body vanishes" (translation Midori Yoshimoto).

5. For example, the end of the English text for *Smoke Painting* specifies that the painting is done when it has been completely burned up, whereas this statement is missing from the Japanese version. Similarly, the English text, but not the Japanese text, of *Clock Piece*, which directs the setting of all the clocks in a town to an irrational temporal system, at the end specifies that any system is acceptable except one in which the clocks are set to the correct time.

LITERATURE: DeMotte, *Villager* (18 March 1965); *Sunday Times* (8 February 1970); *Evening Standard* (18 February 1970); Sondheim, *Fusion* (20 February 1970); *Jersey Journal* (27 April 1970); Harvey, *Edmonton Journal* (29 May 1970); Foyle, *Daily Mail* (3 June 1970); Linscott, *Liverpool Daily Post* (10 June 1970); Cook, *Daily Mail* (18 June 1970); *Record Mirror* (27 June 1970); *Daily Express* (30 June 1970); Kaul, *Des Moines Register* (6 July 1970); Lyons, *New York Post* (9 July 1970); Barber, *Evening Post* (22 July 1970); See, *Miami News* (10 August 1970); Ireland, *Nichi Bei Times* (16 August 1970); *Evening Standard* (21 June 1971); *Sunday Express* (1 July 1971); *Daily Mirror* (3 July 1971); *Mail* (10 July 1971); Hanauer, *Detroit Free Press* (11 July 1971); Ezard, *Guardian* (16 July 1971); *Times* (20 July 1971); *Financial Times* (20 July 1971); Faulconbridge, *Liverpool Echo* (27 July 1971); Mandelkau and Bloom, *International Times* (12–26 August 1971); Drexler, *Village Voice* (7 October 1971); Iimura, *Yoko Ono* (1985), 61–94, 100, 117, 121; Taylor, *New York Times* (5 February 1989); Stiles, *In the Spirit of Fluxus*, exh. cat. (1993), 79

DATA BY KC

5 *Blue Room Event,* 1966

installation with handwritten texts
dimensions variable

This room is bright blue.
This room glows in the dark while we are asleep.
This room slowly evaporates every day.
This room moves at the same speed as the clouds.
Find other rooms which exist in this space.
This room gets as wide as an ocean at the other end.
This room gets very narrow like a point at the other end.
This window is 2000 ft. long.
This window is 2000 ft. wide.
Many rooms, many dreams, many countries in the same space...
This line is a part of a very large circle.
This is the ceiling.
This is the floor.
Stay until the room is blue.
This is not here.

—Instructions for *Blue Room Event*, 1966

Blue Room Event grew out of *Disappearing Piece*, first performed in 1966 at Ono's West 100th Street apartment in New York.[1] After painting the whole room white, Ono placed a "disappearing machine"—a still in the form of an elaborate contraption with glass pipes, created in collaboration with George Maciunas—in its center. As the water in the machine evaporated, the room was to conceptually turn upside down. Just before the audience came, Ono attached several statements to various surfaces. These included "This is the floor" on the ceiling; "This is the ceiling" on the floor; and "This window is 2000 ft. wide" on the windowsill.[2]

The idea of using words to subvert one's ordinary perception of a space became the core of *Blue Room Event*. The event adapted itself to the various architectural settings in which it was shown. The Lisson Gallery version in 1967, installed in a windowless back room like an alcove, consisted of the single text, "Stay until the room is blue." In *Half-A-Room*, installed in Lisson's front room, Ono placed several texts including "This window is 2000 ft. wide."[3] Although *Blue Room Event* sometimes incorporated objects with texts, such as *Ceiling Painting* (no. 7), these objects soon became independent pieces.[4] Returning to the economy of the Lisson Gallery version, recent installations of *Blue Room Event* concentrate on the texts alone, which are often written directly on the walls, floor, and ceiling of the gallery space.

Statements such as "This room gets as wide as an ocean at the other end" are at once humorous and wondrously childlike, and aphoristic as Zen koans. By contradicting almost everything the audience sees, *Blue Room Event* attempts to expand the viewer's limited perceptions through imagination. Like many other Ono

PLATES 5A–D
INSTRUCTIONS FOR
BLUE ROOM EVENT,
1966. AS EXECUTED AT
MUSEUM OF MODERN
ART, OXFORD, 1997

This room slowly evaporates everyday.

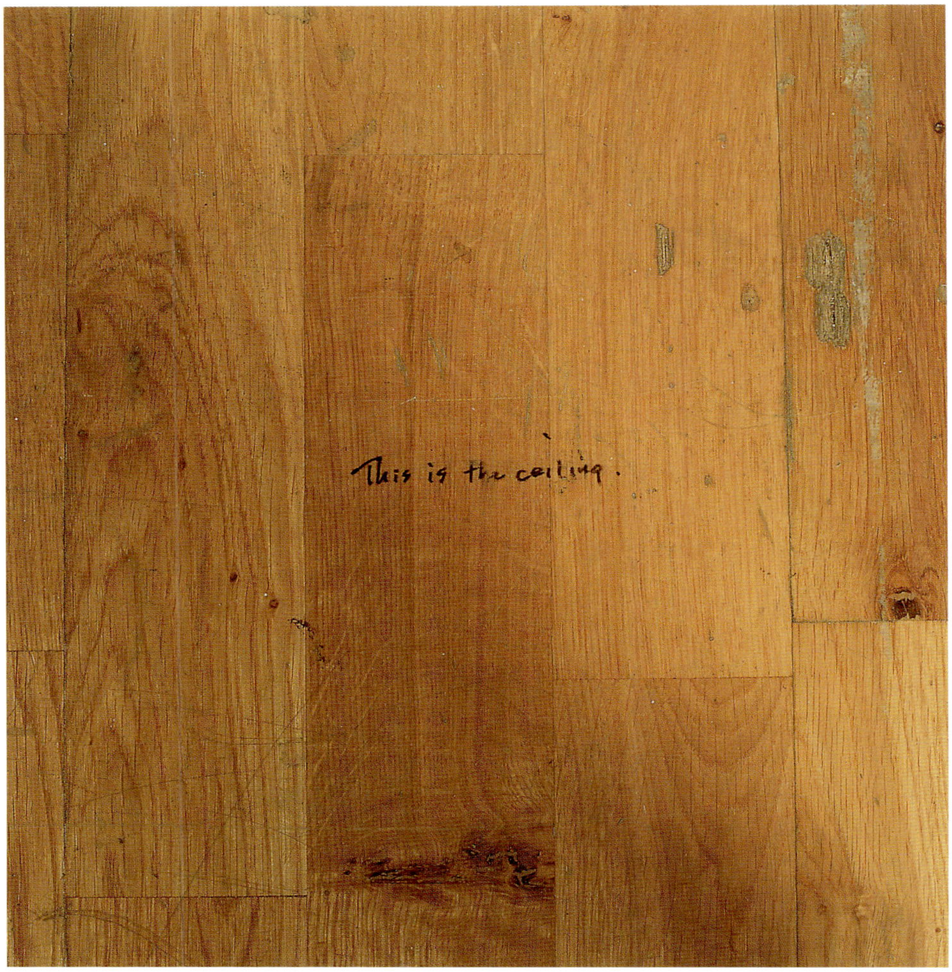
This is the ceiling.

works, *Blue Room Event* must be completed in the viewer's mind: in one's imagination, a white room can turn into a blue room as the title of this piece suggests.

MY

NOTES

Instructions and objects used in *Blue Room Event* varied from realization to realization. In 1990, Ono codified this set of instructions (p. 84), which has since been used in her exhibitions.

1. The score of *Disappearing Piece* reads: "Boil water. Watch until it evaporates." See "Yoko Ono & Dance Co." in *3 newspaper eVenTs for the pRicE of $1* (*VTRE*), or Fluxus Newspaper No. 7 (February 1966).

2. Accounts of the early phase of *Blue Room Event* are from Ono, e-mail to author, 13 September 1999 and 5 February 2000.

3. Ibid.

4. *Ceiling Painting* was included in *Blue Room Event* shown at Ono's apartment on Second Avenue in New York. In her exhibition at Indica Gallery in November 1966, it became a separate piece with a newly added ladder. See [Ono], *Yoko at Indica*, exh. cat. (1966), [P5].

OTHER VERSIONS

All realizations before 1990 (noted in Exhibitions below) considered different versions

1971 rubber stamp texts
4 from a set of 13 stamps with text by Ono and Lennon, produced by George Maciunas in conjunction with *This Is Not Here*

1990 framed texts
First shown: 1990 *Insound/Instructure*, Henie Onstad Arts Centre. A set of postcards with texts also produced

1996 framed Japanese texts
First shown: 1996 *The Blue Room Event*, Gallery 360°. 15 texts plus the work title, rendered in Japanese. A set of postcards with texts also produced

EXHIBITIONS: 1966 (early January) Ono's apartment at 1 West 100th Street, New York; 1966 (sometime in April–August) Ono's apartment at 99 Second Avenue, New York; 1967 *Yoko Ono at Lisson*, Lisson Gallery; 1970 *Fluxfest Presentation of John Lennon & Yoko Ono +*, New York; 1971 *This Is Not Here*, Everson Museum (with additional texts by John Lennon and George Brecht); 1990 *Insound/Instructure*, Henie Onstad Arts Centre (framed texts); hereafter frequently exhibited, either handwritten on the wall or as framed texts

LITERATURE: Concannon, *Fly*, exh. cat. (1996), 15–16

This line is a part of a very large circle.

This is not here.

6 *Water Event,* 1971

instruction and installation of water containers and concepts

Like "sky," water is a frequently occurring motif in Ono's oeuvre. In early Instruction Paintings such as *Waterdrop Painting* (1961) and *Water Piece (Painting to Be Watered)* (1962/1966; no. 11), water was used to make a hole in a stone or to wet objects. By 1967, Ono's water symbolism was developed and expressed in her text "Water Talk":

> you are water
> I'm water
> we're all water in different containers
> that's why it's so easy to meet
> someday we'll evaporate together
>
> but even after the water's gone
> we'll probably point out to the containers
> and say, "that's me there, that one."
> we're container minders[1]

The idea of water offers many layers of meaning and metaphor. Water is the greatest constituent of the human body. Buddhist philosophy compares human life to water and the human body to a container. Furthermore, in her 1972 song "We're All Water," Ono used water to address egalitarianism: "There may be not much difference between you and me."[2] When Ono invited friends and artists to participate in *Water Event* at the Everson Museum in 1971, her intention was to create collaborative works and unite with others through the medium of water.[3]

The work turned out to be a massive undertaking, with approximately 120 participants, ranging from artists and musicians to celebrities, art critics, and the artist's personal staff. Contributers included: David Bourdon, George Brecht, John Cage, Dick Cavett, Ornette Coleman, Joseph Cornell, Robert Filiou, David Frost, Richard Hamilton, Geoffrey Hendricks, Allan Kaprow, Per Kirkeby, Alison Knowles, Timothy Leary, Gordon Matta-Clark, Jonas Mekas, Nam June Paik, Sara Seagull, Shigeko Kubota, Michael Snow, Takahiko Iimura, and Andy Warhol. While participants provided containers such as a milk bottle (George Harrison, fig. 6.8), a salt carton (Jon Hendricks; fig. 6.8), and a Volkswagen (Robert Watts; fig. 6.9), Ono provided the content: "conceptual water."[4] Like the old Japanese proverb, "Water conforms to its container," Ono's concept accommodated itself to the containers prepared by others.[5]

MY

NOTES

1. Ono, "Water Talk" (1967; Anthology 27).
2. Included in the LP album by John & Yoko/Plastic Ono Band with Elephant's Memory, *Some Time in New York City* (1972).
3. Ono quoted in Takahiko Iimura, "Ono Yōko: Kachi o tenkan shi, kisei gainen kara no dakkyaku o/An Interview with Yoko Ono by Takahiko Iimura" (Let's change values and flee from stereotypical concepts), *Bijutsu techō*, no. 350 (January 1972): 206–7.
4. Ibid., 207.
5. Ibid., 206.

OTHER VERSIONS

1998, Belfast
For *Have You Seen the Horizon Lately?* Participants: Donald Baechler, George Condo, John Lathan, Carlos Leppi, Nam June Paik, Cornelia Parker, Kenny Sharf, Lawrence Weiner. Instruction reads: Imagine an empty bowl./Leave it in your room/to be filled with love./Leave many empty bowls/around the house.

VISUAL DOCUMENTATION: 1971, photos of objects by Iain Macmillan

LITERATURE: Iles, *Have You Seen the Horizon Lately?* exh. cat. (1997), 44–51, 138

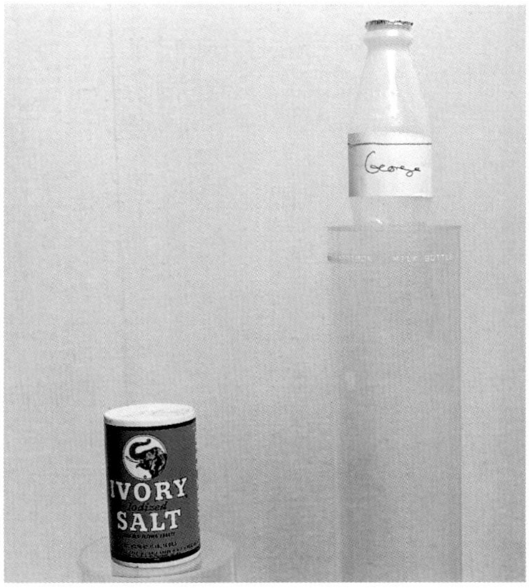

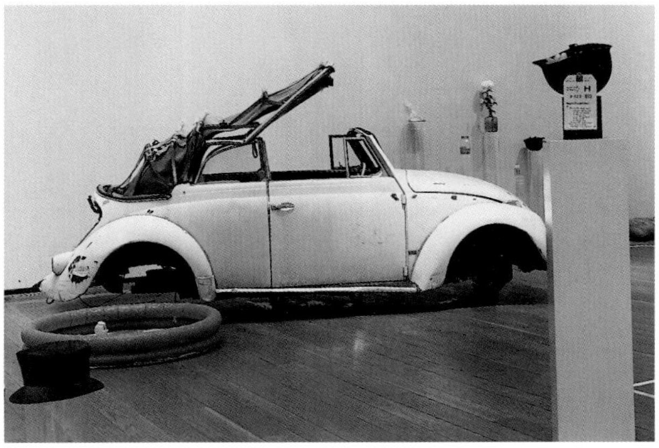

FIGURE 6.8 (LEFT)
SALT CARTON AND MILK BOTTLE FROM *WATER EVENT,* 1971

FIGURE 6.9 (RIGHT)
VW FROM *WATER EVENT,* 1971

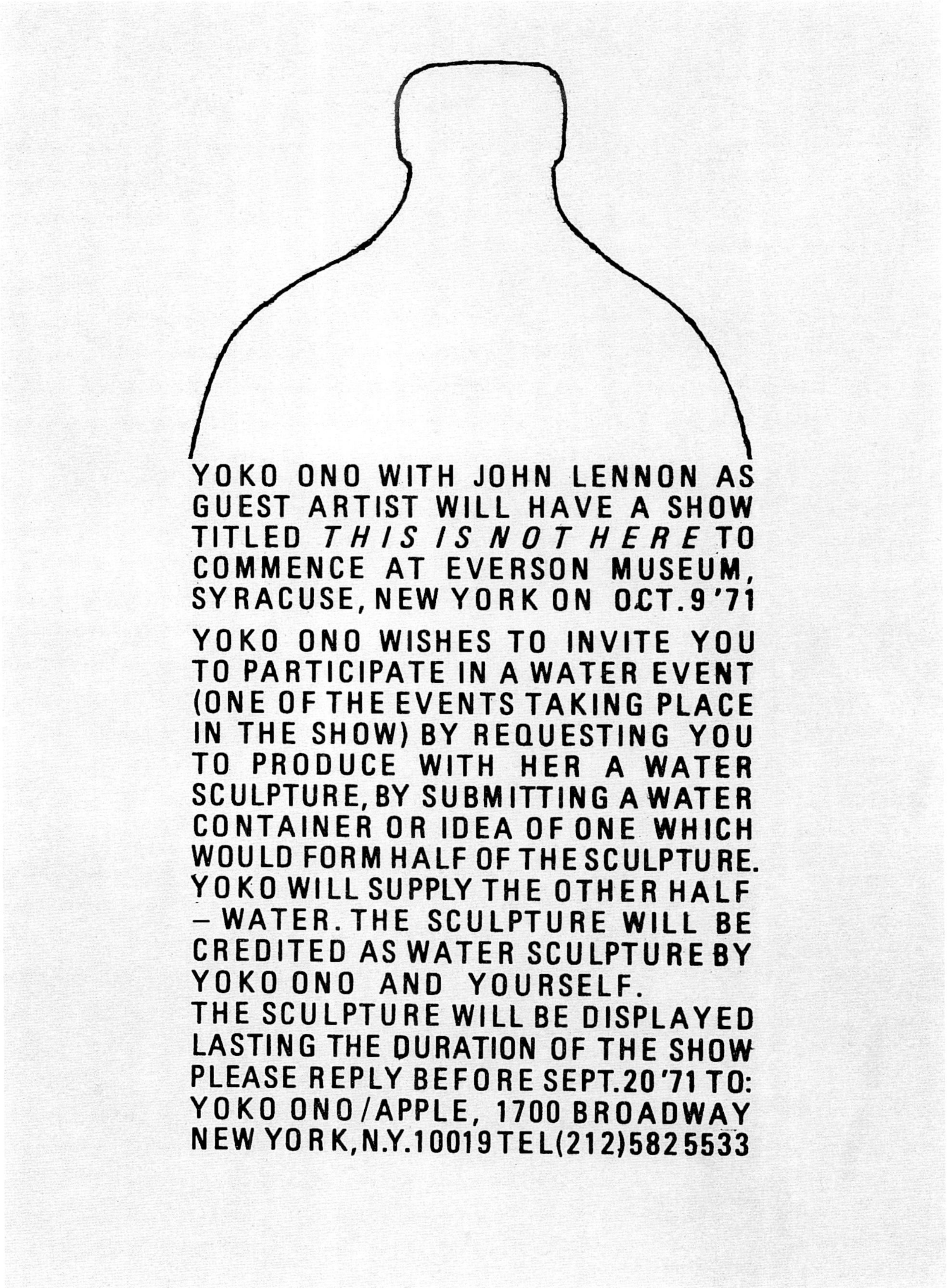
YOKO ONO WITH JOHN LENNON AS
GUEST ARTIST WILL HAVE A SHOW
TITLED *THIS IS NOT HERE* TO
COMMENCE AT EVERSON MUSEUM,
SYRACUSE, NEW YORK ON OCT. 9 '71

YOKO ONO WISHES TO INVITE YOU
TO PARTICIPATE IN A WATER EVENT
(ONE OF THE EVENTS TAKING PLACE
IN THE SHOW) BY REQUESTING YOU
TO PRODUCE WITH HER A WATER
SCULPTURE, BY SUBMITTING A WATER
CONTAINER OR IDEA OF ONE WHICH
WOULD FORM HALF OF THE SCULPTURE.
YOKO WILL SUPPLY THE OTHER HALF
– WATER. THE SCULPTURE WILL BE
CREDITED AS WATER SCULPTURE BY
YOKO ONO AND YOURSELF.
THE SCULPTURE WILL BE DISPLAYED
LASTING THE DURATION OF THE SHOW
PLEASE REPLY BEFORE SEPT. 20 '71 TO:
YOKO ONO / APPLE, 1700 BROADWAY
NEW YORK, N.Y. 10019 TEL (212) 582 5533

PLATE 6
INVITATION / INSTRUCTION
FOR *WATER EVENT*, 1971

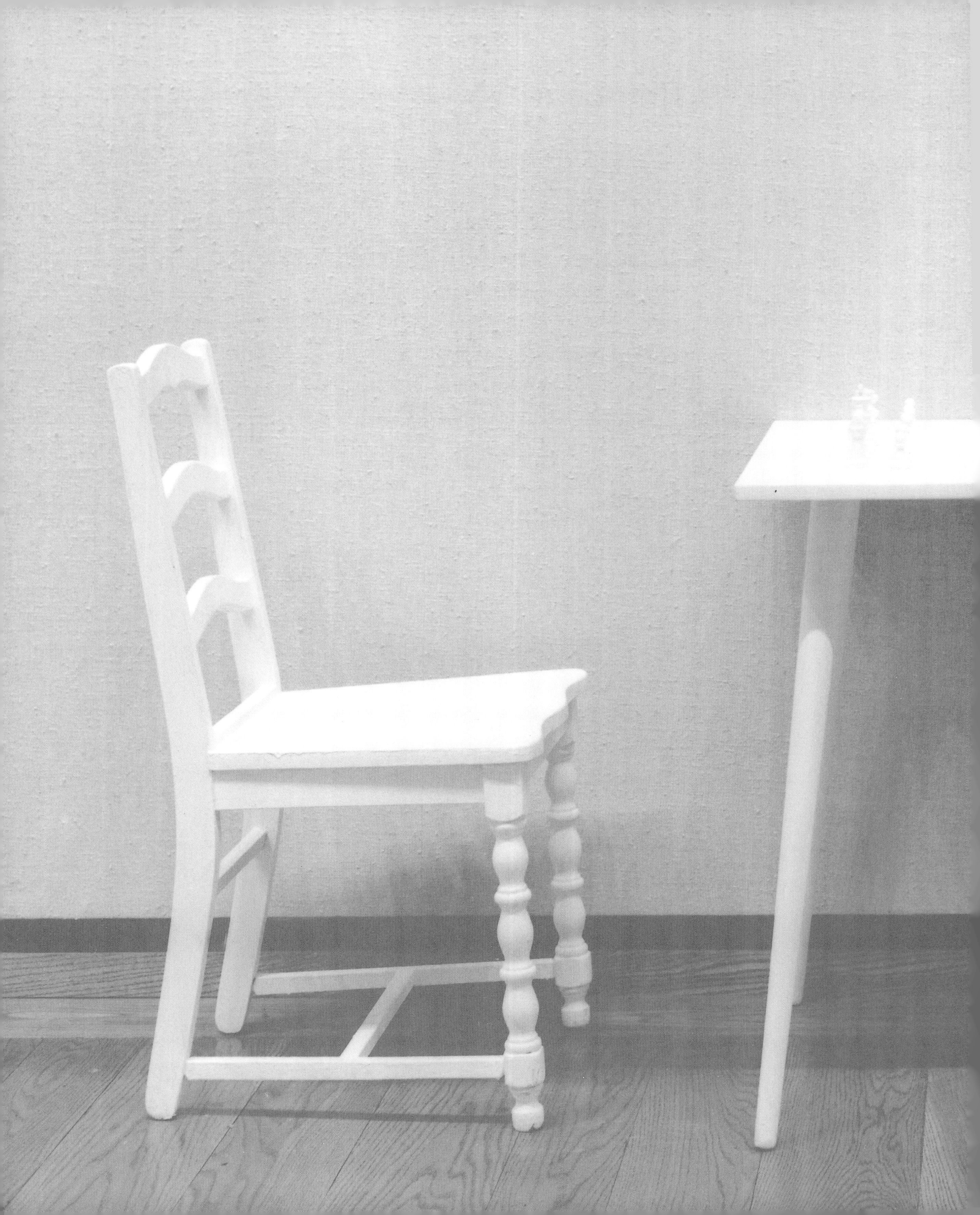

EARLY OBJECTS

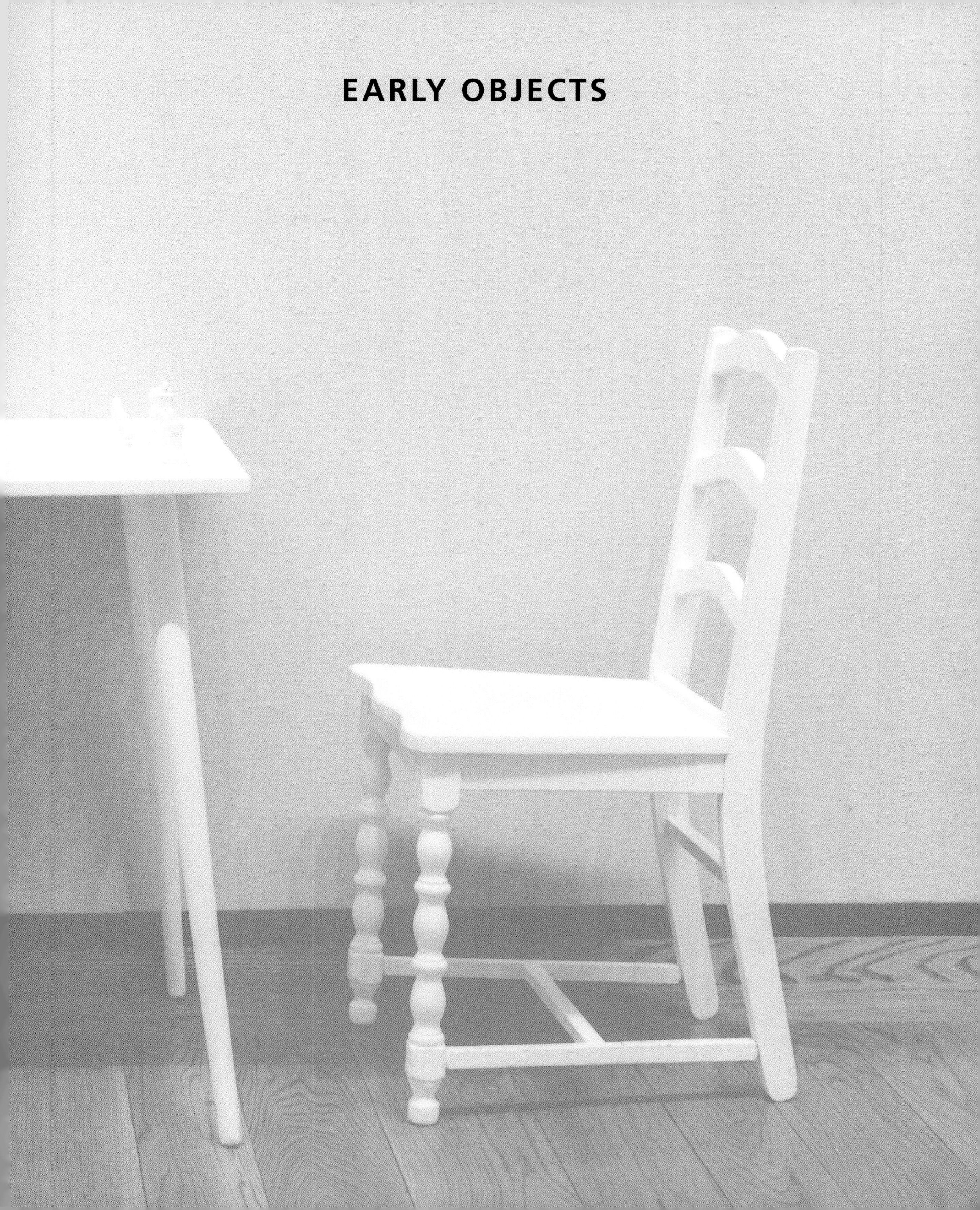

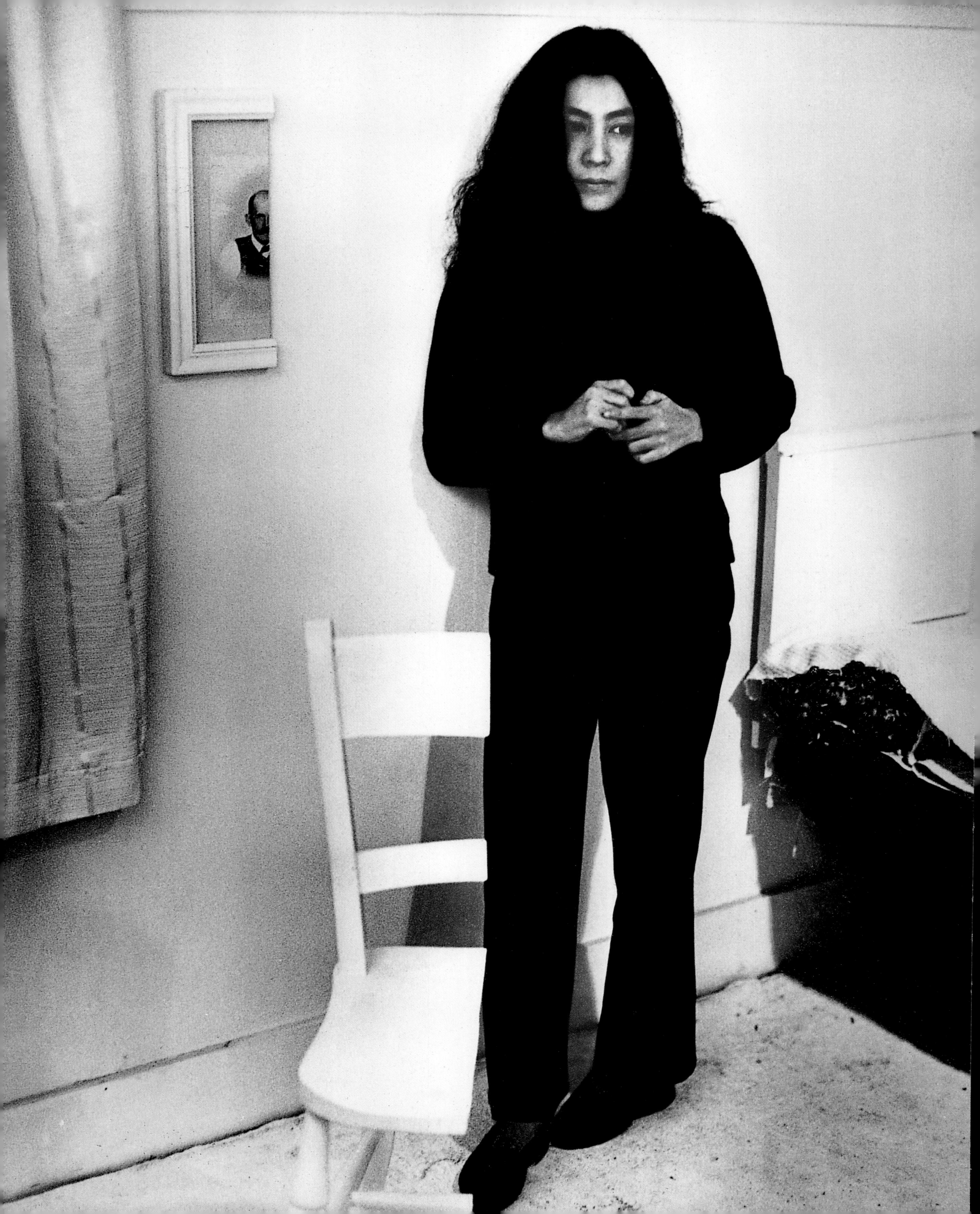

Somewhere for the Dust to Cling: Yoko Ono's Paintings and Early Objects

JOAN ROTHFUSS

During the early years of her career, the making of objects was not Yoko Ono's main preoccupation. In fact, her practice—like that of a handful of other artists of her moment—might even be characterized as an effort to reshape the artistic product into something more akin to a process, a performance, or an idea. Her alliance with the Cagean avant-garde and her role in shaping the international, multidisciplinary confederation known as Fluxus were consonant with her interest in such intangibles as temporality, duration, sound, illusion, silence, and idea. Until 1960, most of her creative energy was devoted to work in music and poetry rather than to the making of static objects. In fact, for most of her career Ono has not even had a conventional studio; and by her own account, she was much more comfortable during these early years working with ideas than objects.[1]

Ono nonetheless undeniably engaged in the production of *things* in the 1960s. One might wonder what purpose they served in a practice that was essentially conceptual and, as the decade progressed, increasingly performative. The question gets to the heart of what is most radical about Ono's work in all media: it pushes, gently but insistently, for realignment—of expectations, perception, position, action. It asks us to imagine that a poem could be a dance, that the sky could be locked (and then unlocked), that a painting could be a party or a handshake. It asks us to reorient ourselves physically and mentally in the hope that small-scale change, on an individual basis, might have a ripple effect and bring about dramatic change in the world at large.

Ono's objects of the 1960s advanced her agenda for change with their extraordinary ability to float from one arena to another without settling in any of them. Often they have a close relationship to her *haiku*-like texts. Some were used during her performances, and others were created while she performed; still others were meant to be completed in the course of someone else's activity. Some are unique, others have been made and remade in different materials, formats, and contexts, and many have had elements replaced or restored over the years. Occasionally they had to be destroyed in order to be complete. And while Ono certainly claims her objects as her own works, she rarely constructs them herself.

Under delicate pressure from these drifting objects, the once-stable triangle of artist, performer, and audience collapses. Artistic disciplines merge and then divide, reshaped; concept and realization are conflated; even the physical boundary between the actual and the imagined is tested. Ono's attitude toward this state of oscillation is illuminated in her 1966 essay "To the Wesleyan People" by her inclusion of an exchange between two Zen monks:

> The body is the Bodhi Tree
> The mind is like a bright mirror standing
> Take care to wipe it all the time
> And allow no dust to cling.
> —Shen-hsiu
>
> There never was a Bodhi Tree
> Nor bright mirror standing
> Fundamentally, not one thing exists
> So where is the dust to cling?
> —Hui-neng[2]

In a sense, Ono's object-making practice is based on this tension between matter and spirit. The things she makes are physically independent entities, but meaningless without some kind of concurrent mental or physical activity. Depending on the object in question, the balance between the two shifts, making it difficult to decide when the object is primarily an independent object and when it is the byproduct of a performance, for instance, or the demonstration of an idea.

FIGURE 7.1
ONO IN *HALF-A-ROOM*,
LISSON GALLERY,
LONDON, 1967

That, of course, is her point; but for the purposes of this essay, her "objects" will be defined as works with material presence that cannot be understood completely as something else (documentation, text, or film, for example). In our commodity-based culture, objects are more understandable when they can be possessed intact; perhaps for this reason it is easier to find a rhythm for Ono's object-making if one understands it as tied to her exhibitions, commissions, and private gift-giving. The things she made for these purposes were intended to circulate on their own, so she made them physically robust—in motion, but nevertheless places where the dust can cling.

WHEN IS A PAINTING NOT A PAINTING?: NEW YORK AND TOKYO, 1960–1962

Ono first approached object-making via the well-traveled road of painting, a medium that was undergoing extensive international reevaluation in the years after World War II. Since she came to painting as a poet, performer, and composer who had experimented with combining these disciplines, it was quite natural (if precocious) that her earliest paintings should be less objects than text-based performative ideas that depended upon an active viewer. Her first such work was conceived in New York between 1958 and 1961. Remarkably, it was essentially a request: participants would be asked to cut a painting into four parts and place each part in a corner of a room. Viewing the entire work would require physical and mental effort, and the goal was to conceptually mend the painting's severed parts.[3]

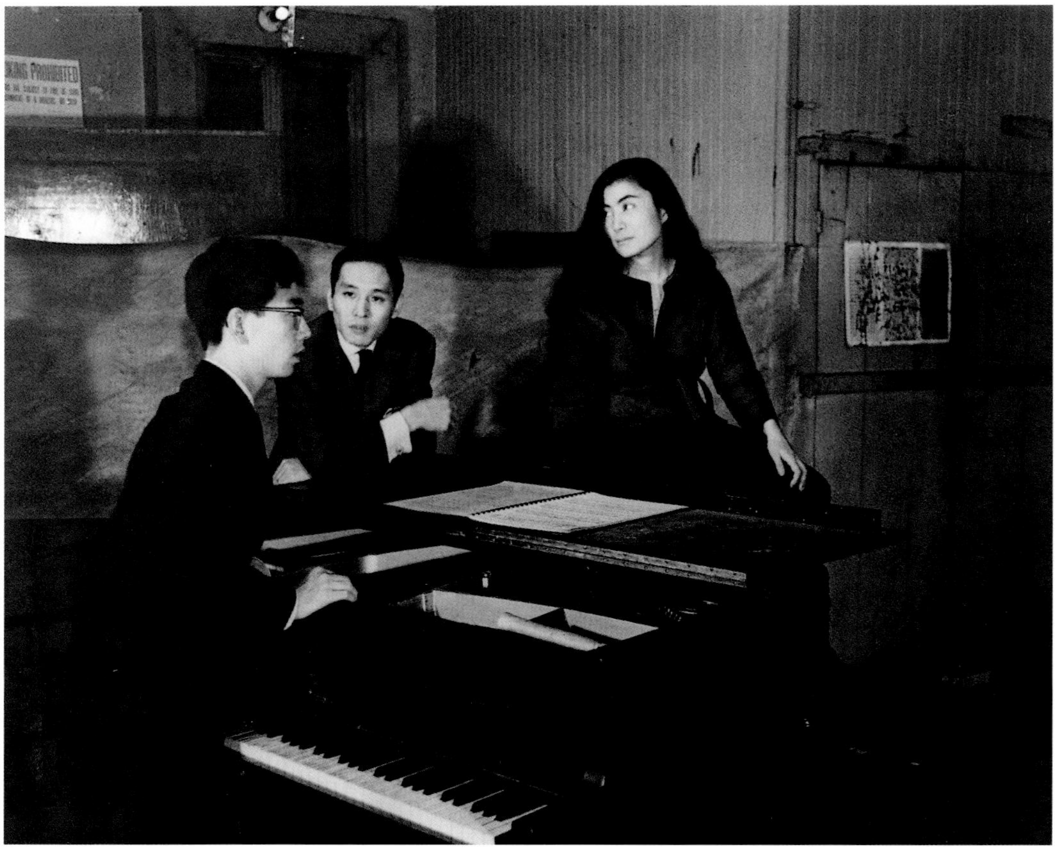

FIGURE 7.2
ONO AT CHAMBERS STREET LOFT, NEW YORK, CA. 1960

Many more concepts for such "performed paintings" (later called Instruction Paintings) were written between 1960 and 1962. Several of them were realized for the first time by Ono herself, probably in late 1960 or early 1961, on a large piece of canvas hung in her loft (fig. 7.2).[4] Some seem to have been created privately and others for the audiences at the so-called Chambers Street loft events. One audience member recalled Ono's performance of *Kitchen Piece*, which directed the painter to throw all of his or her leftover food onto the canvas, and *Smoke Painting*, in which the canvas was burned so the smoke might be observed:

> Yoko ran to the refrigerator, took out some eggs, ran to a wall covered with a huge piece of white paper [*sic*], and hurled the eggs onto the paper. Then she ran back and got some jello which she also threw at the wall. Then she splattered some sumi-ink on the paper and used her hands as paint brushes. When the painting was completed, she took a match and set fire to the paper.[5]

The energy, even violence, with which this work was created—as well as its public, performative dimension—links *Kitchen Piece* to Jackson Pollock's action paintings as well as the frenzied activities of Gutai artists Shimamoto Shōzō, Shiraga Kazuo, and Murakami Saburō, whose tools included paint-filled bottles and cannons as well as their feet and entire bodies.[6] However, these artists employed their revolutionary means toward the achievement of a conventional end: a static painting meant to hang on a wall. In contrast, Ono's use of the *Kitchen Piece* canvas for the destructive *Smoke Painting* placed her in the forefront of a younger generation of artists who, having grown impatient with the rigidity of painting's body, worked to assist its passage into what Allan Kaprow described in 1958 as "the space and objects of our everyday life."[7]

Ono recalls that she was very excited about her first gallery exhibition of *Instruction Paintings* (no. 2, figs. 6.2–5).[8] It opened in July 1961 at AG Gallery in New York, an adventurous but unprofitable enterprise operated by future Fluxus organizer George Maciunas and his friend Almus Salcius. The exhibition was a quiet presentation of modestly scaled objects: calligraphic works on paper and a group of variously shaped canvas fragments lyrically stained with *sumi* ink and dripped wax.[9] The latter's lush surfaces linked them to avant-garde painting styles of the day, including Abstract Expressionism, Color Field painting, and even Jasper Johns's work in encaustic. However, Ono's concept for their consumption marked them as something quite different.

First, the finished objects were the material traces of the artist's performances, which had themselves begun simply as concepts and were later published as textual scores. This hybrid activity was in itself a break from both the object-based practice of Pollock and Gutai and the performance-based practice of John Cage and the nascent Fluxus group. But Ono's further innovation was to present the paintings not as static objects but as ongoing temporal events. *Shadow Painting*, for example, "came to life" when a shadow was cast on it, which might or might not happen, depending on luck or the viewer's patience or both. *Painting to Be Stepped On*, an irregularly shaped scrap of canvas placed on the gallery floor, was created by the accrual of footprints (fig. 6.4); and *Painting Until It Becomes Marble*, through the action of visitors instructed to paint over their favorite parts with black ink.

Second, in a rather extraordinary move, Ono highlighted what she called the "Event bent" of these paintings by continuing to perform with them during the exhibition itself. One-on-one, she explained the genesis of each work to gallery visitors (Maciunas filled in for her when she was not present). The intent was not to provide interpretive closure but to make clear that anyone could make these paintings by following the artist's texts. Individual interpretation was encouraged, and Ono recalls that she enjoyed the subtle changes that took place when messages were passed on "by word of mouth."[10] This method made each painting less an object than an event; Ono's instructions were simply "something that starts it moving" and it was assumed that this movement would lead away from the artist.[11]

In this first exhibition, then, Ono's paintings were meant to be seen as demonstrations or ongoing events, each representing only one of the many possible realizations of a related text and by no means privileging the artist's own interpretation. In her second solo exhibition, which occurred in May 1962 at Tokyo's Sōgetsu Art Center, Ono exhibited only the texts (later known as *Instructions for Paintings*), meticulously copied out to ensure that they were not mistaken for a decorative or calligraphic display (no. 3). She remembers feeling that this was an exciting breakthrough that "pushed visual art to its optimum conceptualism."[12] In fact, it was a remarkable accomplishment: she had removed the physical body of the painting entirely, and then proposed that it be re-formed (or not), through language alone, as a kind of meditation aid toward the creation (or not) of an object. She insisted on calling the works paintings, perhaps to emphasize this gaping physical absence. "I like the old word painting because it immediately connects with 'wall painting' painting, and it is nice and funny."[13] This charming statement does not do justice to the profoundly innovative nature of this work, which managed to anticipate many of the developments of Conceptualism that occurred later in the decade.

THE INTENSITY OF A WINK: LONDON, 1966–1967

Although she went back to the production of objects after her Sōgetsu exhibition, Ono did not show a large group of them again until 1966. Instead, she focused her energies elsewhere, and some of her most important works in other media were realized during this time—the performances *Cut Piece* and *Bag Piece*, the infamous buttocks film *No. 4 (Bottoms)*, and the first edition of her book *Grapefruit* (nos. 30, 31, 43, 4).[14] Some objects were developed in conjunction with these other activities: *Eye Bag*, for example, was based on the cloth sack used in *Bag Piece*; *Self Portrait* (1965), a mirror in an envelope, was a contribution to Maciunas's anthological publication *Fluxus 1* (fig. 7.3); and *Eternal Time*, commissioned for a patron's birthday, was placed on stage during Ono's 1965 concert at Carnegie Hall (no. 13).[15] Others were listed in her whimsical *Ono's Sales List* (1965), a compilation of actual and projected works in several media, including "Underwear" (no. 37).

Ono moved to London in September of 1966. That November she brought a number of objects together for a solo exhibition at the avant-garde Indica Gallery. A stunning installation of mostly white and transparent objects, the Indica show was in many ways her most cohesive of the decade, both visually and conceptually. It primarily consisted of newly realized works (a mix of Instruction Paintings and objects, all made for the occasion) that looked strikingly different from those she had shown in 1961. The paintings were no longer suggestively stained, torn, burned, and saturated with the artist's touch, as they had been at AG Gallery. Instead, the new work was cool and nonemotive—empty white surfaces whose size and relationship to the wall marked them unmistakably as paintings. Or, more properly, paintings-to-be, since all the works at Indica were listed as "unfinished." Ono exhibited only the supplies necessary for (physical or conceptual) completion: *Painting to Hammer a Nail*, for example, consisted of a white wood panel, a hammer, and a jar of nails (no. 9); *Add Color Painting*, a wood panel, brushes, and paints. Blank, white, and waiting, these paintings were an open invitation rather than a finished thought.

An important structural shift had taken place in Ono's thinking about her objects: participation was now clearly emphasized over demonstration. The new works were "do-it-yourself kits" whose instruction and realization were distinct and separate functions. The artist's role was to provide the instruction and materials; "others" made the work a reality.[16] Direction was given in a variety of ways: verbally by the artist; implicitly through the title or materials furnished with the work (as in *Painting to Hammer a Nail*); or through a small caption on the object itself (the Plexiglas cube *Cleaning Piece for A.P.* was inscribed CLEAN IT). This left a great deal more of the work up to chance, and in at least one case—*Wrapping Piece for London*—viewers took the piece in an entirely different direction from that which Ono had intended (no. 19).

The notion that the object was unfinished and did not achieve full reality until it was completed by the viewer had been introduced at the AG Gallery show, but at Indica is an aspect of Ono's fully fleshed-out concept of "instructure." This conflation of the words "instruction" and "structure" indicates "something just about to emerge—not quite struc-

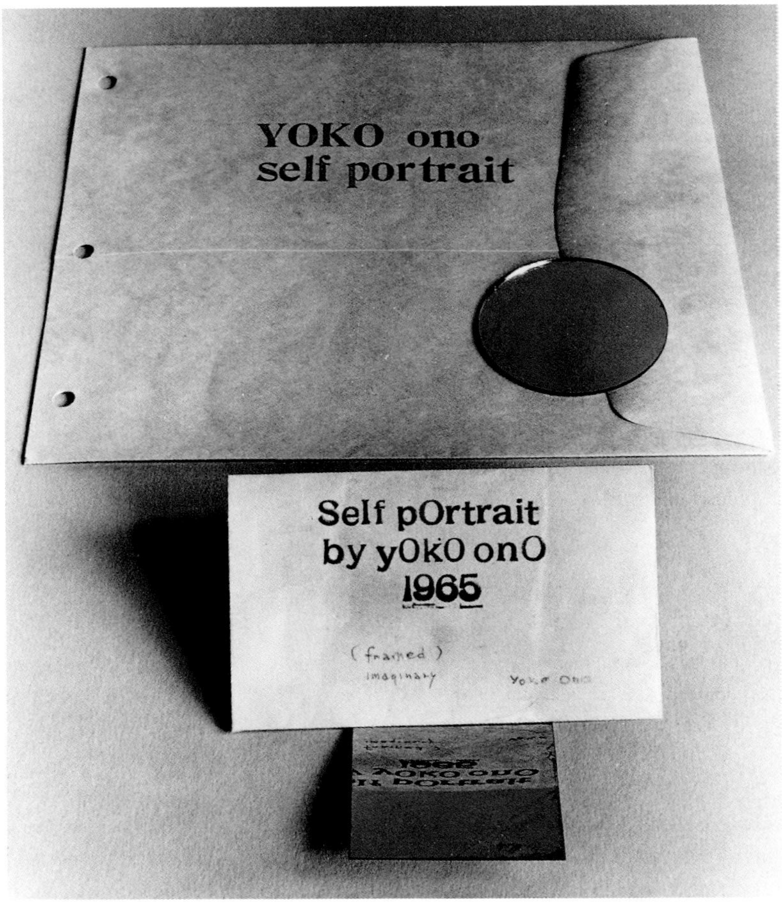

FIGURE 7.3
SELF PORTRAIT, 1965.
TWO VERSIONS: TOP, INCLUDED IN ***FLUXUS 1***; BOTTOM, DISTRIBUTED BY ONO AND FLUXUS

tured—never quite structured—like an unfinished church with a sky ceiling."[17] The image of a church with an ever-changing (and nonfunctional) "ceiling painting" is enlightening, as it suggests the continual oscillation of Ono's objects between the manmade and the natural, the tangible and the imaginary, the sublime and the absurd. As an exemplar, consider *Painting to Let the Evening Light Go Through*: it was realized at Indica as a clear Plexiglas panel with the work's title engraved across its lower edge (no. 8). Installed in front of a window, it was a redundancy that revealed everything and nothing. Ono has described it as "almost jarring in its senselessness, and therefore mysterious."[18]

Transparency is associated with both linguistic and physical disclosure, and it was an important theme for Ono's work at this time. For the Indica show, she consciously used clear materials such as glass, Plexiglas, and even daylight to indicate the conceptual nature of the works and the relationship between the hidden and the revealed. One work, *Parts of Light House*, was a mound of Plexiglas prisms to form a house constructed of light, "which exists in accordance with the changes of the day."[19] For the most part, those objects that were not transparent were painted opaque white, a noncolor that is at once concealing and neutral.[20] These white objects were mostly mute, with the notable exception of *Ceiling Painting*, which bore a message from the artist: a minuscule rendering of the word YES, legible only if the viewer climbed a stepladder (fig. 7.4; no. 7). An answer without a question—cryptic, to be sure, and reminiscent of those stories in which a man climbs a mountain to ask a monk the meaning of life, but for all his arduous effort receives an indecipherable reply. In this context, the artist's memorandum might be read as an affirmation of the value of art—both its creation and consumption.

Ono received significant attention in the press for her show at Indica, and less than a year later she had her next solo exhibition at London's more established Lisson Gallery. The show was a mixture of installations and objects that, according to the catalogue, included only one Instruction Painting (a glass-and-steel version of *Painting to Hammer a Nail In* that could only be used conceptually; no. 10). On the whole, it was less dependent on text and more performative than the exhibition at Indica. One reviewer found the Lisson show thematically unified around the idea of "the interdependability of men and things, one with another, in a constant process of change and interaction."[21]

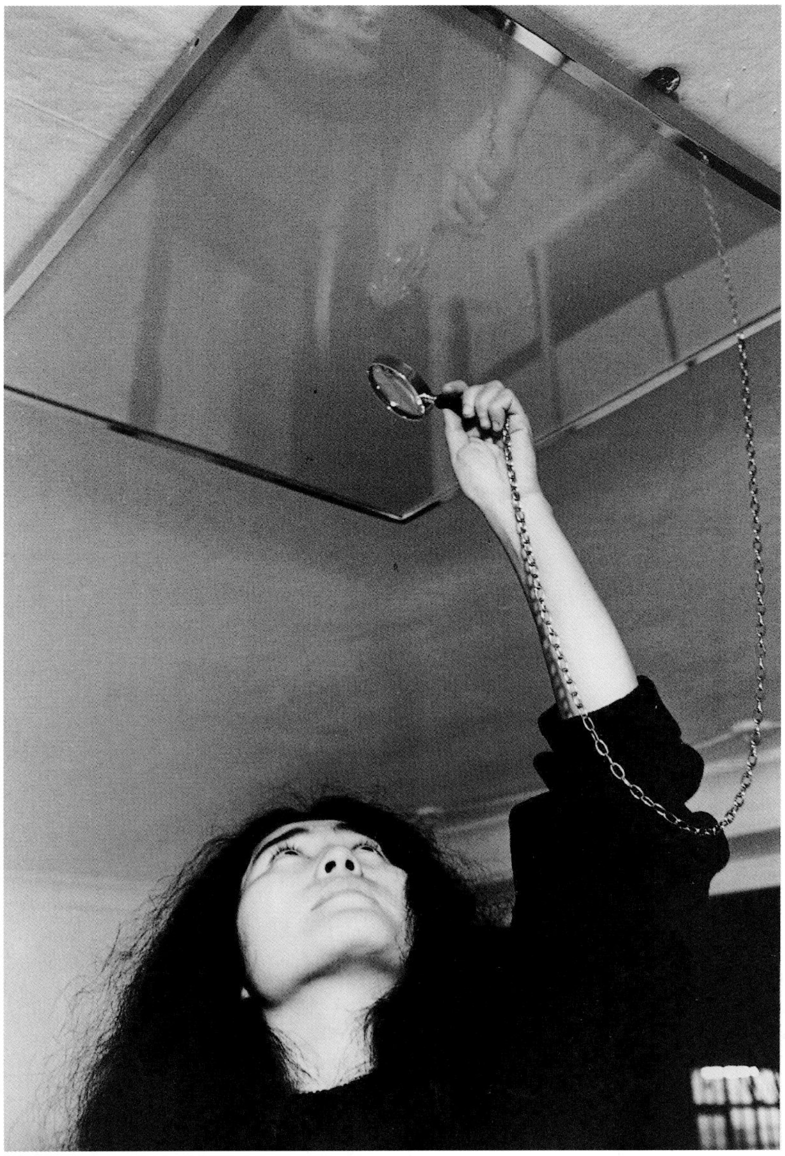

FIGURE 7.4
ONO LOOKING AT *CEILING PAINTING (YES PAINTING)*, INDICA GALLERY, LONDON, 1966

This is certainly suggested by its most ambitious work—an environment that appeared to be a studio apartment in which every object, from teapot to table lamp to twin bed, had been painted white and then halved (figs. 1.21, 7.1; no. 20). This installation, now known as *Half-A-Room*, presents a vignette of objects in flux that exemplifies her theory of "instructure," but also suggests the riddle of the glass that is both half empty and half full. There is something, but there is also nothing: *Half-A-Room* suggests both the hopefulness and the loss implicit in that statement. "Life is only half a game," Ono wrote in her notes for the exhibition catalogue. "Molecules are always at the verge of half disappearing and half emerging."[22] This theme was echoed in the exhibition's Zen koan of a title, *Half-A-Wind Show*.

At Lisson, this absence was captured and exhibited, specimenlike, in the quasi-scientific *Air Bottles* (fig. 7.5). A collaboration (the first) between Ono and John Lennon, *Air Bottles* were empty glass containers with hand-lettered labels that Ono said represented "the other half of my half-a-matter objects."[23] *Air Bottles*, like Marcel Duchamp's empty glass ampoule, *Paris Air* (1919), acknowledge the free-floating fiction of memory by using air—a material substance that cannot be tied to a specific place or time—to represent what is missing.

WITH A LITTLE HELP FROM HER FRIENDS: NEW YORK AND SYRACUSE, 1970–1971

After her London exhibitions, Ono's work veered back toward the performative and the collaborative. These methods of working accommodated her discomfort with the static—in 1966 she wrote, "The world of construction seems to me to be the most tangible, and therefore final. This made me nervous."[24] They also fit her belief that her art could function as a communication device and a way to bring people together. "When someone creates his own inner reality a little, my art becomes real. If one person has a dream, it is just a dream, but when two people dream it together, then it is real."[25]

Her interest in collaboration was connected to a broader issue that absorbed many artists during the 1960s: the search for alternatives to the old gallery-collector-museum system, which was perceived as

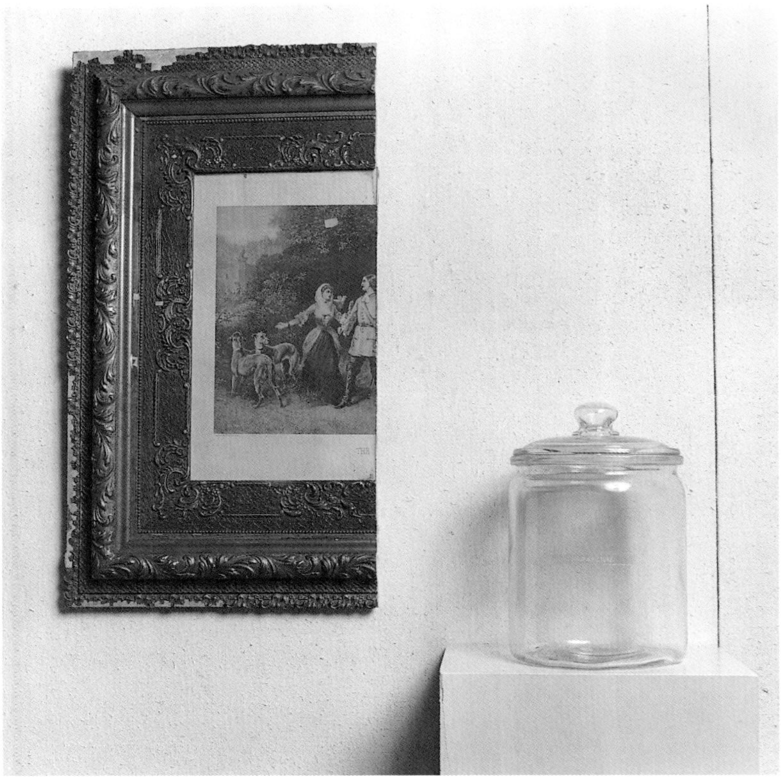

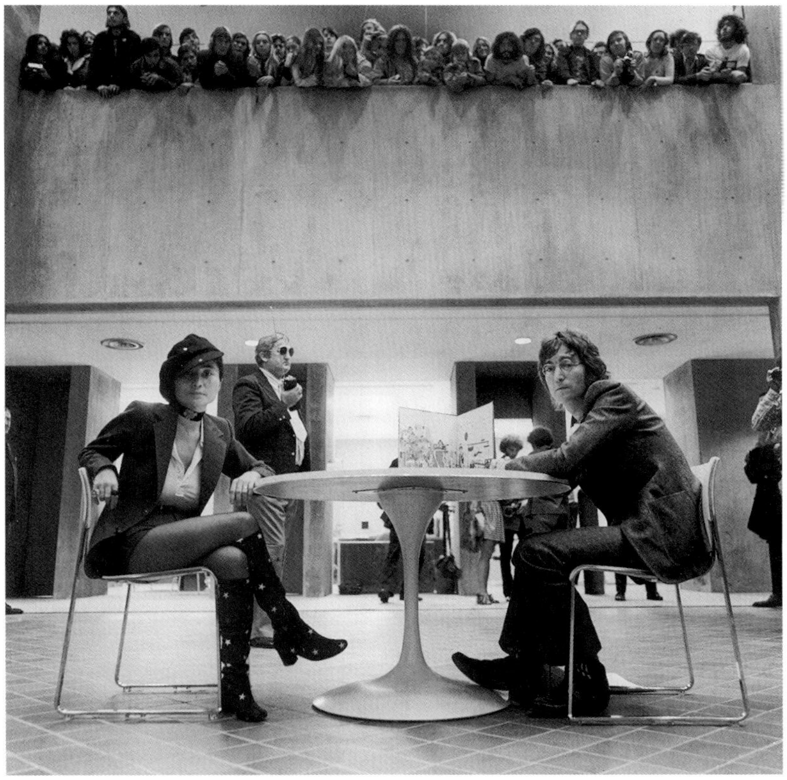

FIGURE 7.5 (LEFT)
HALF-A-PAINTING AND ***AIR BOTTLE***, 1967.
INSTALLATION VIEW,
EVERSON MUSEUM OF
ART, SYRACUSE, 1971

FIGURE 7.6 (RIGHT)
ONO AND LENNON AT
EVERSON MUSEUM OF
ART, SYRACUSE, 1971

elitist and object-oriented. Even in this climate, in which artists intentionally made work that was difficult to commodify, Ono's work stood out—along with that of Joseph Beuys—as obstinately democratic. Both declared that "everyone is an artist," and Ono's practice, at least, allowed for no other interpretation. By 1968 Ono counted herself an ex-member of the rarefied world of the avant-garde: "The art circle from which I came is very dead, so I am very thrilled to be in communication with world-wide people."[26] Her newfound access to "world-wide people" was the result of her association, beginning in late 1966, with pop icon John Lennon, and it was through his presence in her life that her aspirations for collaborative creative work came into full flower.

Ono's next exhibition project, the seven-week-long *Fluxfest Presentation of John Lennon & Yoko Ono +* (spring 1970), was organized by George Maciunas, her old friend and early collaborator. A miscellany of objects, environments, and events that Ono described as "a dialogue between Yoko and John with a chorus by Fluxus," the festival was the next step in the collectivization of her work. Some sections were planned in detail by Ono; others, left to Maciunas, bear the impish and unmistakable stamp of his sensibility. The opening week's presentation, titled *Do It Yourself, by John & Yoko + Everybody*, included *Painting to Be Stepped On*, interpreted by Maciunas as an inked doormat, and *Kitchen Piece*, presented as a "painting to wipe floor and street with."[27] For her part, Ono planned the fourth week's exhibition of object-based riddles entitled *Blue Room* (see Ono's letter to Maciunas, fig. 2.14). *Three Spoons* (four spoons on a pedestal) was conceived as a window display of spoons and sign, like a perverse shopkeeper's joke; *Pointedness* would be transformed from a marble sphere to a rubber ball; and two coffee cups (one broken) would carry labels reading "mend" and "not to be appreciated until it's broken." In addition to the collaborative planning process, the festival depended as usual on a large measure of viewer participation, and in retrospect it almost looks like a trial run for Ono's exhibition *This Is Not Here*, which would take place the following year at the Everson Museum.

In 1970 Ono was also included in an exhibition exploring "new multiple art" at London's Whitechapel Art Gallery. All the works in the exhibition were multiples, and all were available for purchase with price and distributor listed in the catalogue. Ono offered five multiples based on older works—*Apple* (with or without stand), *Glass Key*, two versions of *All White Chess Set*, and *Bag Piece* (nos. 15, 23, 25, 31); she also listed the book *Grapefruit*.[29] She had experimented with mail-order sales of her work in

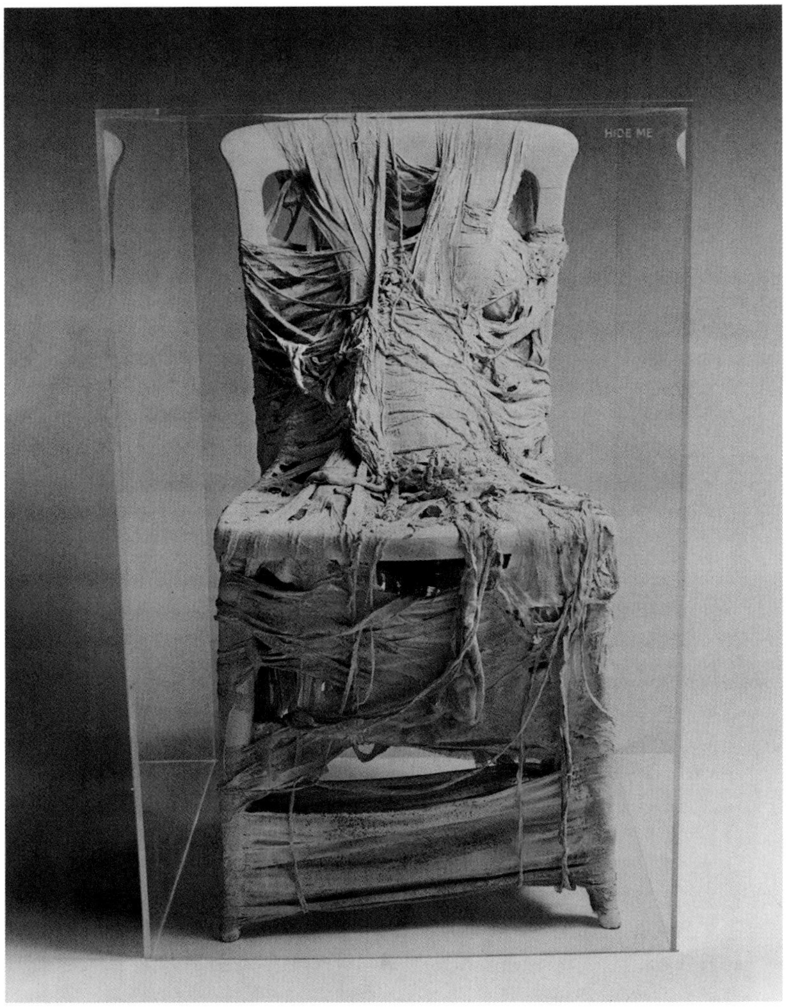

FIGURE 7.7
HIDE ME, 1971, OVER
WRAPPED CHAIR, 1966

the self-published *Ono's Sales List*, but that text tends to have a poetic distance from material reality—and a corresponding idiosyncratic, personal feel—that the Whitechapel list lacks. The new multiples seem to have hardened into objects of commerce, perhaps due to the intermediaries of museum and distribution agency (in this case, Ono and Lennon's own company, Bag Productions).

Ono's last major exhibition of this period—*This Is Not Here*, presented in late 1971 at the Everson Museum in Syracuse, New York—evolved naturally out of her participation in the *Fluxfest* and Whitechapel projects and could be seen as a summa of her work. Although it was billed as a "10-year retrospective," it was intensely collaborative: John Lennon was listed as an "assisting guest artist" and was represented by many works of his own (fig. 7.6); a good deal of the gallery space was given over to the dozens of artists who responded to Ono's invitation to collaborate with her on "water sculptures" (no. 6); and, perhaps most notably, George Maciunas played a major role in the exhibition's design and execution.[30]

Like the 1970 *Fluxfest*, *This Is Not Here* was a mixture of objects, film screenings, performance events, and participatory environments. Traditional museum practice was accommodated by the presentation of a dozen or so previously made objects (many of them shown at the Indica and Lisson galleries), but most of the works on view were newly realized and interactive, including a gallery of "Do It Yourself Paintings," a "Vending Arcade" featuring a number of Ono's dispensers (nos. 17–18), and two large installations conceived by Ono and executed by Maciunas: the Plexiglas labyrinth *AMAZE* (no. 26) and the bank of modular cabinets called *Portrait of John Lennon as a Young Cloud*. The work encouraged participation but apparently suffered because of extremely heavy use due to record-breaking attendance (Ono was after all the famous wife of a beloved pop star). Writing just a month after the exhibition's opening, Lawrence Alloway noted that "the exhibits have been ripped off and broken at great speed" and that "the original museum-wide show had been contracted to three galleries." He goes on to lament that while Conceptual Art is all well and good, Ono "has had difficulty in structuring the uses of her work after the initiatory move.... Dumb physical sharing means the loss of suspense and of wit and the works were blunted by it."[31]

Alloway was probably not alone in feeling that the exhibition had failed in some basic way, but he also missed the point, because what Ono had attempted was a complete revision of the paradigms that governed museum exhibitions. This was not here, after all. If her enterprise was compromised, it was due to the huge audience she commanded because of her new status as a celebrity—ironically, the very factor that made that enterprise an exciting possibility. She realized this paradox and responded to it with a new work that was one of the most poignant and funny objects in the exhibition: a clear Plexiglas vitrine engraved with the pleading phrase HIDE ME, which she placed over one of her earlier works, an empty chair swathed in gauze (fig. 7.7). Ono has said that this work equated the futility and comedy of trying to hide inside a transparent box with "the stupidity of the situation I put myself in."[32] Because of her celebrity she had become like the chair: objectified, silenced, and no longer able to move freely.

Ono's objects function best when they are in constant motion between the worlds of matter and idea. This oscillation is not a weakness but a strength: if one follows their lead, the boundary can be breached and one gains a view from the other side. Ono has compared the seesaw action of her work to her own movement from Japan to America, which she has said necessitated "drawing a somersault in my mind just to think, speak, move around, and observe." She did not seek a place to rest, however, because she realized that experiencing things "with two minds" gave her strength. Motion was power. "I wanted to inspire people to experience that power."[33] Her objects attempt to teach us how to turn our own mental somersaults, and encourage us to keep moving—like her *Eternal Time*, a clock with only a second hand that marks the passage of time without measuring it. Ono described her position in 1962 by saying, "I am still groping in the world of stickiness."[34] This seems a wonderfully apt metaphor for her understanding of the artist's task: the fabrication of material things upon which the dust of ideas can settle and, for a moment, cling.

NOTES

I would like to express my gratitude to Jon Hendricks and Karla Merrifield for their assistance in my research for this essay, and my very special thanks to Yoko Ono, who generously participated in an extended conversation about her work that was for me both enlightening and pleasurable.

1. Ono, e-mail to author, November 1999.

2. Ono used these poems as the conclusion to the essay (Anthology 14). The famous exchange occurred between Hui-neng (Huineng; 638–713), the Sixth Patriarch of Chinese Zen Buddhism, and renowned proponent of Northern Zen teachings, Shen-hsiu (Shenxiu; 605?–706), when both were monks in training.

3. Ono, e-mail to author, November 1999. This piece was apparently never published, but it is related to *Mend Painting*, dated summer 1962 in *Grapefruit* (1964).

4. Although specific documentation has not been located, the artist has confirmed that she realized several works in her loft using this stretch of canvas, including *Kitchen Piece*, *Smoke Painting*, and *Shadow Painting* (adding, "The works were not on the canvas at the same time."). The remnant of this canvas was finally used for *AOS—To David Tudor* performed at Carnegie Recital Hall (November 1961) and discarded after the concert (Ono, e-mail to author, December 1999).

5. Beate Sirota Gordon, *The Only Woman in the Room: A Memoir* (Tokyo: Kodansha International, 1998), 175–76. The quote is from the manuscript for this book rather than the published version, which omitted some information of interest. I thank Kevin Concannon for providing this material.

6. See for example Alexandra Munroe, ed., *Japanese Art After 1945: Scream Against the Sky* (New York: Abrams, 1994); and *Out of Actions: Between Performance and the Object, 1949–1979*, exh. cat. (Los Angeles: The Museum of Contemporary Art, 1998). Ono has said that her knowledge of art history was spotty; she first heard about Gutai in early 1960, but didn't see any of their works until about thirty years later (e-mail to author, October 1999).

7. Allan Kaprow, "The Legacy of Jackson Pollock," *Art News* 57, no. 6 (October 1958): 57.

8. Ono, e-mail to author, November 1999.

9. The AG Gallery paintings were cut from "another rolled up funkier looking canvas of a smaller size" than the large canvas she had used in performance (see note 4). These *Instruction Paintings* made from the smaller canvas hung in her Chambers Street loft for a time before the exhibition (all information from Ono, e-mail to author, December 1999). None of these seems to be extant; for photographic documentation see Hendricks, *Paintings and Drawings by Yoko Ono* (1993).

10. Ono, e-mail to author, September 1999.

11. Ono, "To the Wesleyan People" (1966; Anthology 14).

12. Ono, "Painting to Be Constructed in Your Head" in *Instruction Paintings* (1995), 5–10. In the essay she relates that she would have preferred to have the instructions typewritten for a completely neutral look, but was unable to get access to a typewriter with Japanese characters. Instead, because her handwriting was "too emotional," she asked her husband Ichiyanagi Toshi to copy them out.

13. Ono, "To the Wesleyan People."

14. During these years, Ono did have several "conceptual exhibitions" of ideas, performances, and/or texts, including *3 Old Paintings* (Naiqua Gallery, Tokyo, 1964) and *Blue Room Event* (New York, 1966). She operated a conceptual exhibition venue, the IsReal Gallery, and considered presenting some objects during *The Stone* (Judson Gallery, 1966). She also approached Leo Castelli Gallery in 1965 with an exhibition proposal, which was not accepted. See Concannon, "Nothing IsReal" (pp. 177–82).

15. Sheldon Williams, "Patterns in Today's Art: 1. Miniature Philosopher—the Trials of Yoko Ono," *Contemporary Review* 212 (May 1968): 264.

16. Ono's reference to her paintings as "kits" is contained in her letter to Ivan Karp (1965; Anthology 13). See also "Yoko Ono: Instruction Painting" in *Yoko at Indica*, exh. cat. (1966), n.p.

17. Ono, "To the Wesleyan People." See also Anthony Cox, "Instructive Auto-Destruction," *Art and Artists* (London) 1, no. 5 (August 1966): 17–20.

18. Ono, e-mail to author, October 1999.

19. [Ono], *Yoko at Indica*, exh. cat. (1966), [O8].

20. One exception was *Cleaning Piece for A.P.*, whose smoked Plexiglas cube was, according to Ono, a playful reference to Larry Bell's Minimalist boxes (e-mail to author, October 1999).

21. Eddie Wolfram, "Well, Whatever *Did*?," *Art and Artists* (London) 2, no. 7 (October 1967): 39.

22. Ono, "Some Notes on the Lisson Gallery Show" (1967; Anthology 15).

23. Ibid., 2.

24. Ono, "To the Wesleyan People."

25. Ono, quoted in Donald Singleton, "Princess of Pop! The Head for This Story Is in the Bag," *Daily News* (London), 23 November 1971, 42.

26. Ono, quoted in "Yoko Ono Speaks," *Observer* (London), 21 July 1968.

27. This piece is described as such in issue no. 9 of the Fluxus newspaper *VTRE* (*all photographs copyright nineteen seVenty peTer mooRE*, 1970), insert, photo no. 9.

28. It is unclear whether this part of the festival ever took place. Maciunas's plans were published in *VTRE* (ibid.), along with photographs of some of the events; there are no photographs, however, of *Blue Room Event*.

29. See the catalogue *3 → ∞ : New Multiple Art*, exh. cat. (London: Arts Council of Great Britain, 1970), 48, 59–60. John Lennon was also included in the exhibition, and Ono is acknowledged as a contributor to two of his works: *Acorn Piece* and the album cover for *Unfinished Music No. 1: Two Virgins*.

30. Because of Maciunas's involvement, Jon Hendricks has referred to this exhibition as a "clear extension of Fluxus." See Hendricks, *Fluxus Codex* (1988), 397.

31. Lawrence Alloway, "Art," *Nation* (8 November 1971): 477.

32. Ono, e-mail to author, September 1999.

33. All quotes from Ono, e-mail to author, October 1999.

34. Ono, "The Word of a Fabricator" (1962, translated by Yoko Ono 1999; Anthology 12).

7 *Ceiling Painting (YES Painting),* 1966

text on paper, glass, metal frame, metal chain,
magnifying glass, painted ladder
framed text: 25½ x 22$\frac{3}{16}$" (64.8 x 56.4 cm);
chain and magnifying glass: 28½ x 3 x ¾" (72.3 x 7.6 x 1.9 cm);
ladder: 72 x 19¼ x 47½" (182.8 x 48.9 x 120.6 cm)
Collection of the artist

In the catalogue for her exhibition at Indica Gallery, Ono wrote a note about this work: "From *Blue Room Event* in NYC, in which one entire room was white with a few furnishings on the walls, on the ceiling was a painting, this is it, ladder which comes with painting is a new addition for London Show."[1] The reference is to an installation in her New York apartment in which she had posted statements on furniture, ceiling, and windows that encouraged viewers to effect an imaginary transformation of the space (no. 5). One of the texts was the single word YES installed on the ceiling. *Ceiling Painting* is a work in Ono's series of Position Paintings, which seek to alter the viewing experience by requiring an unorthodox relationship between the body and the work of art.[2]

When Ono prepared for her exhibition at Indica in late 1966, she made a framed version of this text, rendered in tiny letters on a large sheet of paper. The text was nearly impossible to read from the floor; the addition of the ladder was an invitation for viewers to ascend and complete the piece by reading it with the magnifying glass hanging from the frame. When this was done, the open-ended affirmation of the word YES became the viewer's reward for making the climb. At least one viewer—John Lennon—remembered feeling relieved to find that the text was not an example of the "negative…smash-the-piano-with-a-hammer, break-the-sculpture boring, negative crap" that he associated with avant-garde art of the period. "That 'YES' made me stay…."[3]
JR

NOTES

1. [Ono], *Yoko at Indica*, exh. cat. (1966), [P5]. Ono notes that the ladder is a new component added for the London installation, but it is unclear whether the other elements of the work (framed text and magnifying glass) were also new for London, or whether they were the same objects that had been used in *Blue Room Event*.

2. For Position Paintings, see no. 21.

3. Lennon, *The Playboy Interviews* (1981), 92.

OTHER VERSIONS

1996 ***Yes Painting***
India ink on primed canvas with magnifying glass and painted stepladder. Two replicas made for: 1998 *En Trance*, Andre Emmerich Gallery; and 1999 *At the Threshold of the Visible*, ICI

1999 ***Yes***
First shown: 1999 *Open Window*, Umm El-Fachem Art Gallery. From Instruction Paintings series. Acrylic on linen, hung on the wall

1999 ***Yes Painting***
Drawing. Ink on paper

EXHIBITIONS: 1966 *Blue Room Event*, Ono's apartments, New York (possibly different version); 1966 *Yoko at Indica*, Indica Gallery; 1971 *This Is Not Here*, Everson Museum; 1989 *Happenings & Fluxus*, Galerie 1900–2000; 1989 *The Bronze Age*, Cranbrook Academy; 1990 *In Facing*, Riverside Studios; 1990 *Insound/Instructure*, Henie Onstad Arts Centre; 1990 *Fumie*, Sōgetsu Art Museum; 1990 *To See the Skies*, Fondazione Mudima; 1991 *Birch Monologue*, Porin Taidemuseo; 1991 *Peace! Friður!* Reykjavík Municipal Art Museum; 1997 *Have You Seen the Horizon Lately?* MOMA, Oxford

VISUAL DOCUMENTATION: 1966, photo by Iain Macmillan, pub. *Yoko at Indica*, exh. cat. (1966); 1966, photo by Graham Keen, pub. *The Bronze Age*, exh. cat. (Cranbrook 1989) and elsewhere; 1971, photo by Iain Macmillan (Everson installation)

LITERATURE: [Ono], *Yoko at Indica*, exh. cat. (1966) [P5]; Haskell, *Arias and Objects* (1991), 41

PLATE 7
CEILING PAINTING (YES PAINTING), 1966.
INSTALLATION VIEW,
THE ISRAEL MUSEUM,
JERUSALEM, 2000

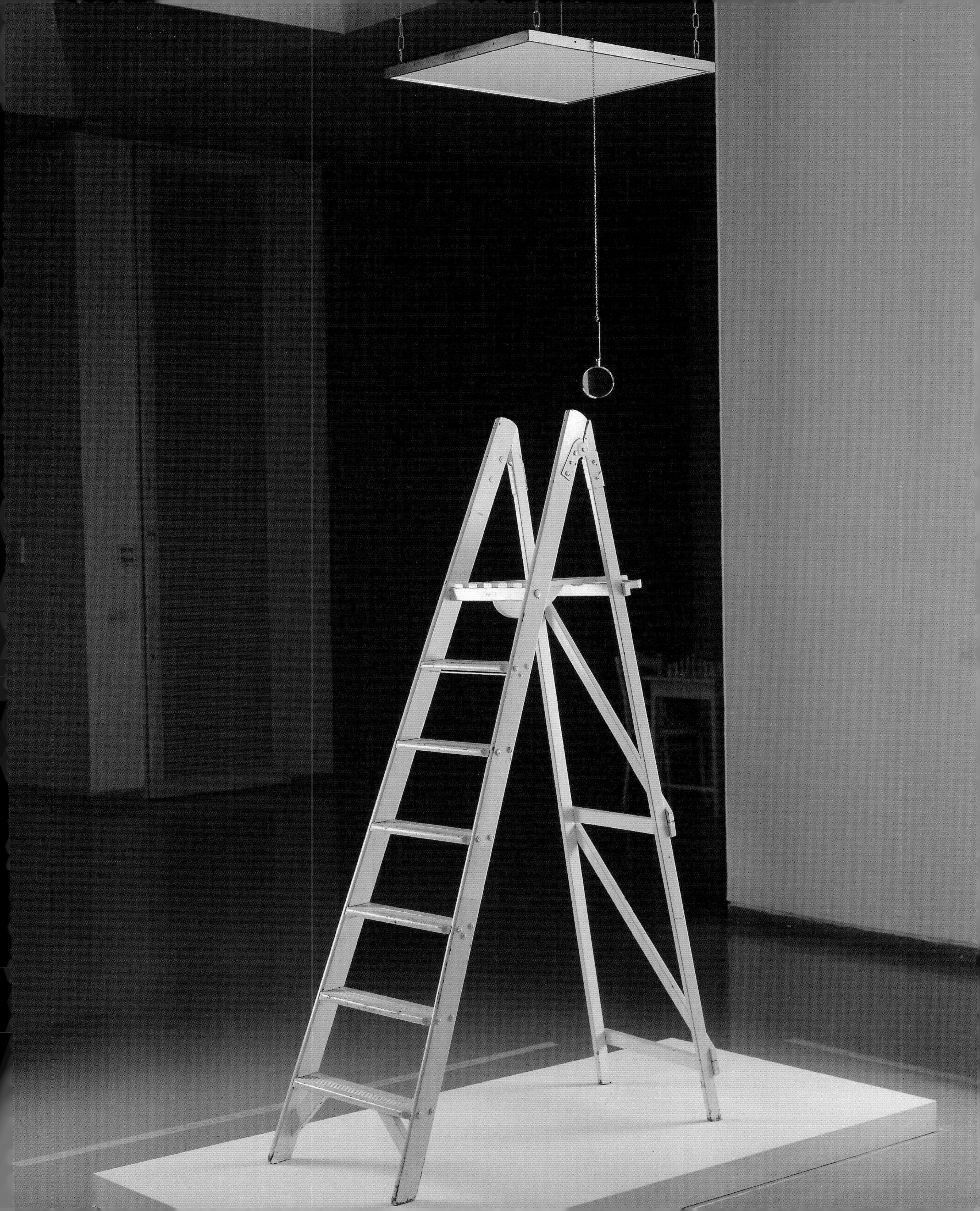

8 *Painting to Let the Evening Light Go Through,* 1961/1966

Plexiglas
engraved: PAINTING TO LET THE EVENING LIGHT GO THROUGH
YOKO ONO 1961
32⅞ x 27 x ½" (83.5 x 68.6 x 1.3 cm)
Collection of the artist

In a number of texts and objects of the early and mid-1960s, Ono referred to "evening light" as a means of evoking the intangible, the temporal, and the transformative.[1] Among these was a concept for an Instruction Painting, later published in *Grapefruit* (1964):

> PAINTING TO LET THE EVENING LIGHT GO THROUGH
>
> Hang a bottle behind a canvas.
> Place the canvas where the west light comes in.
> The painting will exist when the bottle creates a shadow on the canvas, or it does not have to exist.
> The bottle may contain liquor, water, grasshoppers, ants or singing insects, or it does not have to contain.
>
> 1961 summer

In 1961 Ono included a physical manifestation of this concept in her exhibition at George Maciunas's AG Gallery. She prepared a rectangle of canvas stained with *sumi* ink and hung it in front of a glass bottle in the gallery's window, intending that it be seen from the street (where it would have functioned as a kind of inverse of another work in the exhibition, *Shadow Painting*). However, the concept did not work as planned, partly because the gallery's electricity had been cut off. "We realized that unless a very strong light would hit the canvas [from behind], we could not see the bottle from the street.... I left the bottle dangling, anyway, because I thought it looked interesting, like a bottled soul."[2] The canvas was ultimately installed alone, on an interior brick wall. The following spring she included a text-only version of the piece in her exhibition of *Instructions for Paintings* at the Sōgetsu Art Center (no. 3).

Four years later Ono returned to the concept for her exhibition at Indica Gallery. This time she realized the piece as a rectangle of clear Plexiglas and installed it hanging in a gallery window. "It was so obvious and redundant to place a transparent Plexiglas painting over a transparent glass window. It was like showing a cup and calling it 'This Is A Cup.' It was almost jarring in its senselessness, and therefore mysterious.... Nothing was showing through the transparency except transparency itself. It was only waiting for the evening light to go through."[3]

JR

NOTES

1. See also Ono's later text, "On Ownership II" (undated) in *Museum of Modern [F]art* (1971). For further discussion of the concept, see *AMAZE* (no. 26).

2. Ono, e-mail to author, October 1999.

3. Ibid. *Yoko at Indica*, exh. cat. (1966) lists this work as *Painting to Let the Evening Light Go Through 1961 summer no. 3*. Ono says that the numbering referred to the three installation options she had imagined for her loft: one for the window, another for the back window, and one for the skylight. The work was also installed in the window at the Everson Museum in 1971 (pl. 8).

OTHER VERSIONS
For score and canvas versions, see nos. 2, 3

1988 bronze
First shown: 1989 *Objects, Films*, Whitney Museum. Edition of 9.
Engraved: PAINTING TO LET THE EVENING LIGHT GO THROUGH YOKO ONO 1988

EXHIBITIONS: 1966 *Yoko at Indica*, Indica Gallery; 1971 *This Is Not Here*, Everson Museum; 1972 *Documenta 5*; 1989 *Objects, Films*, Whitney Museum; 1989 *The Bronze Age*, Cranbrook Academy; 1990 *In Facing*, Riverside Studios; 1990 *Insound/Instructure*, Henie Onstad Arts Centre; 1990 *Fumie*, Sōgetsu Art Museum; 1990 *To See the Skies*, Fondazione Mudima; 1991 *Birch Monologue*, Porin Taidemuseo; 1991 *Peace! Friður!* Reykjavík Municipal Art Museum; 1993 *In the Spirit of Fluxus*, Walker Art Center; 1997 *Have You Seen the Horizon Lately?* MOMA, Oxford

VISUAL DOCUMENTATION: 1971, photo by Iain Macmillan (Everson installation); 1971, photo by Takahiko Iimura (Everson installation), pub. *In Facing*, exh. cat. (1990); 1968–69, photo by John Reader (installation at Weybridge, U.K.), pub. Haskell and Hanhardt, *Arias and Objects* (1991)

LITERATURE: Glueck, *New York Times* (11 October 1971); Wasserman, *Artforum* (January 1972); Hendricks, *The Bronze Age*, exh. cat. (Cranbrook 1989), n.p.; Kent, *In Facing*, exh. cat. (1990), n.p.; Blom, *Insound/Instructure*, exh. cat. (1990), 36; Haskell, *Arias and Objects* (1991), 22–23; Iles, *Have You Seen the Horizon Lately?* exh. cat. (1997), 56

PLATE 8
PAINTING TO LET THE EVENING LIGHT GO THROUGH, 1961/1966.
INSTALLATION VIEW, EVERSON MUSEUM OF ART, SYRACUSE, 1971

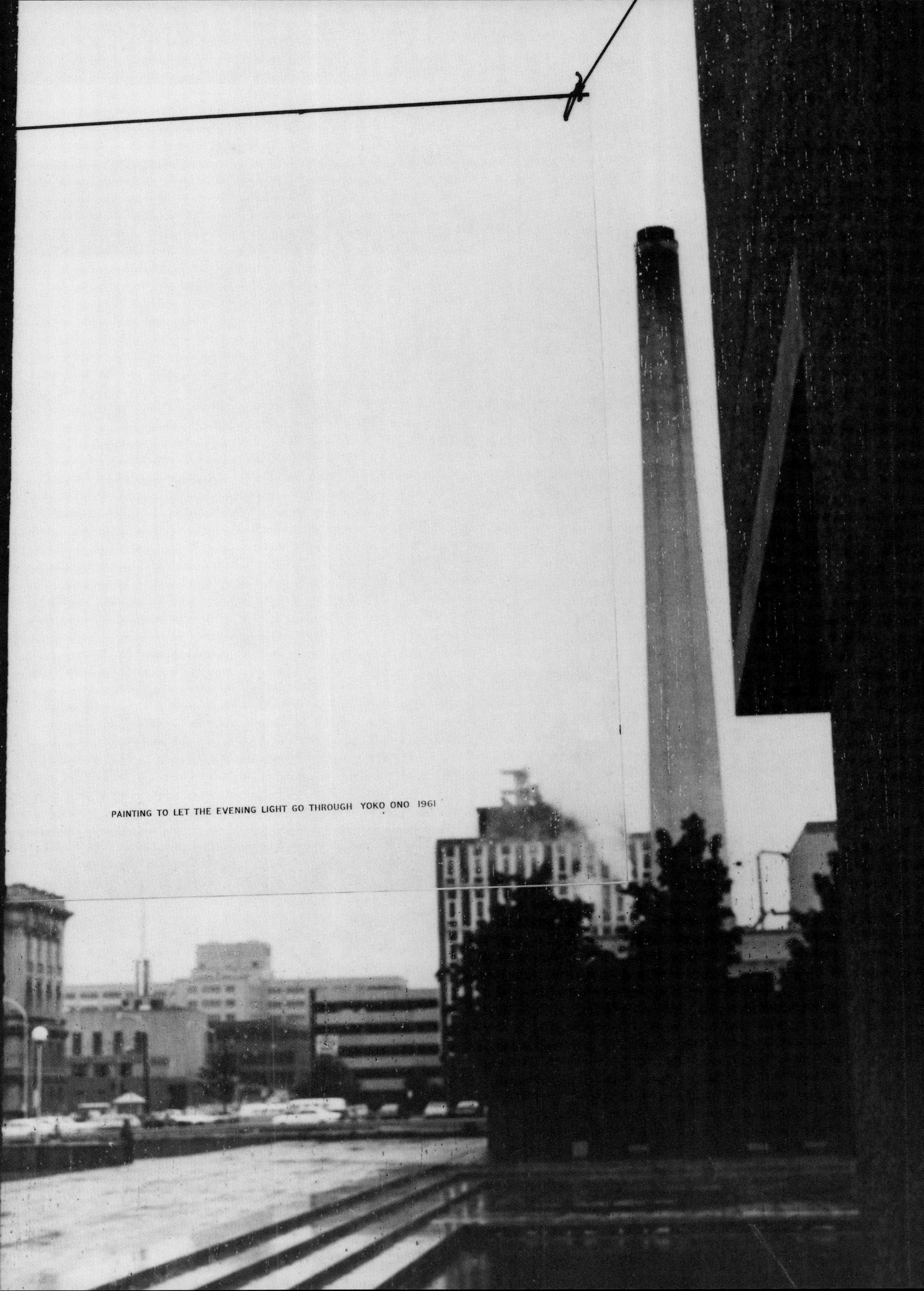
PAINTING TO LET THE EVENING LIGHT GO THROUGH YOKO ONO 1961

9 *Painting to Hammer a Nail,* 1961/1966

(also known as *Painting to Hammer a Nail In*)
painted wood panel, nails, painted hammer, chain
panel: 13¾ x 10½ x 4½" (34.9 x 26.6 x 11.4 cm);
hammer and chain: 36¼" (92 cm) long
Collection of the artist

10 *Painting to Hammer a Nail In,* 1961/1967

stainless steel, glass
inscribed on base: Hammer a nail in for John. '67 London
Yoko Ono.
panel: 13¾ x 1½ x 9½" (34.9 x 3.9 x 24.1 cm);
hammer and chain: 49" (125 cm) long
Collection of the artist

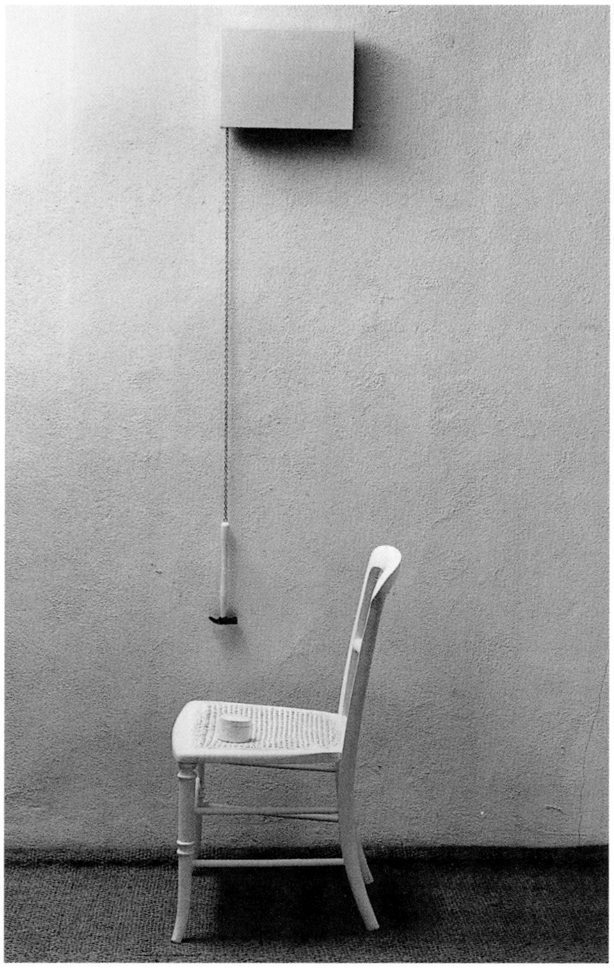

FIGURE 7.8
PAINTING TO HAMMER A NAIL, 1961/1966 (INITIAL STATE). INSTALLATION VIEW, INDICA GALLERY, LONDON, 1966

Both of these objects are manifestations of one of Ono's most familiar Instruction Paintings, a 1961 concept later published in *Grapefruit* (1964):

> PAINTING TO HAMMER A NAIL
>
> Hammer a nail into a mirror, a piece of glass, a canvas, wood or metal every morning. Also, pick up a hair that came off when you combed in the morning and tie it around the hammered nail. The painting ends when the surface is covered with nails.
>
> 1961 winter[1]

The 1966 version was created for her Indica Gallery exhibition and consisted of a pristine, white-painted wood panel from which a hammer dangled on a chain and a jar of nails on a white-painted chair (fig. 7.8). Visitors to the show hammered a nail into the panel if they wished; at the exhibition's end, the object was considered finished.

Although the text calls for the addition of hair as well as nails, no hair has survived on the extant object. Ono has said that when visitors hammered a nail into the panel she "let them know that the next step was to put your hair around it. But because of the method of explanation, which was verbal, [this step] was gradually forgotten."[2] The importance of the hair is underscored by Ono's note on the work in the exhibition catalogue: "Japanese Temples have a place for you to tie wish knots, in the case of this painting the wish knot is tied with your hair."[3] The combination of the wood, nails, and hair suggests that the piece could be seen as a fetish, but this reading is negated by the work's straightforward functionality and visual neutrality.

One year later, Ono made a second version of the piece, inscribed to John Lennon, whom she had met at a preview of the Indica Gallery exhibition. She recalled, "When 'Hammer a Nail' painting was exhibited at Indica Gallery, a person came and asked if it was alright to hammer a nail in the painting. I said it was alright if he pays 5 shillings. Instead of paying the 5 shillings, he asked if it was alright for him to hammer an imaginary nail in. That was John Lennon. I thought, so I met a guy who plays the same game I played."[4]

Responding to Lennon's suggestion that participation be conceptual, Ono's reworking is in some ways a reversal of the earlier piece. The nail and hammer provided are useful only if the piece is realized in the mind, and this purely conceptual nature allows for an infinite number of participants. Using the object's physical components would result in the work's destruction rather than its completion.

JR

PLATE 9
PAINTING TO HAMMER A NAIL, 1961/1966

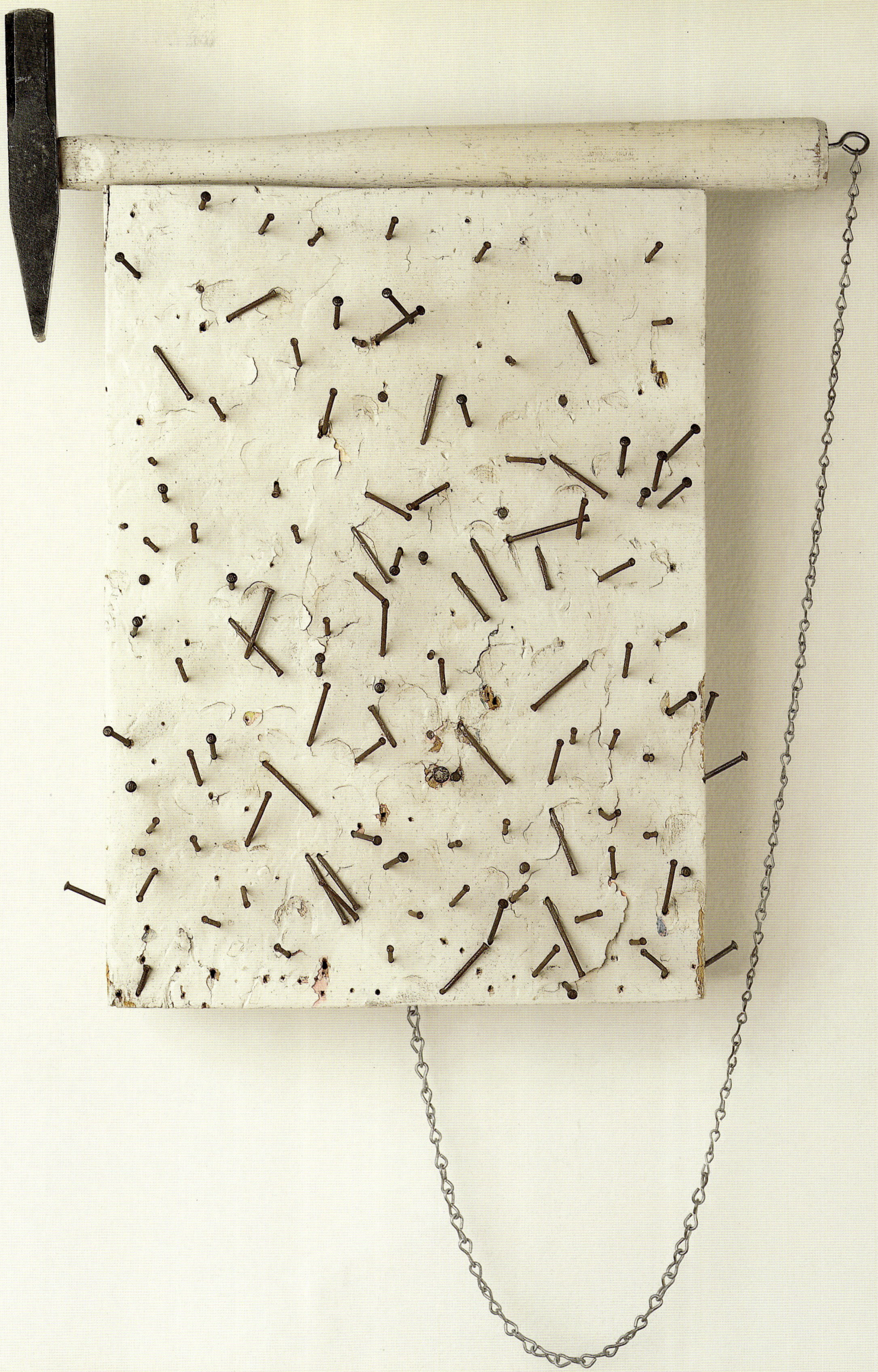

NOTES

1. One of several versions of this concept reads: PAINTING TO HAMMER A NAIL // Hammer a nail in the center of a piece/of glass. Send each fragment to an/arbitrary address. // 1962 spring. In this text, the collective creative activity is not in the hammering but rather in the implied possibility that the recipients of the fragments will come together to mend the glass. In *Painting to Be Constructed in Your Head*, the action is the same but the distribution of fragments is done conceptually (both published in *Grapefruit*, 1964).

2. Ono, e-mail to author, October 1999.

3. [Ono], *Yoko at Indica* (1966), [P7].

4. Ono, "Some Notes on the Lisson Gallery Show" (1967; Anthology 15). As a way of recouping part of her expenditure for materials, Ono had planned to charge a small fee to visitors who wished to participate in *Painting to Hammer a Nail* at Indica Gallery. However, it wasn't until Lennon's visit to Lisson Gallery that she implemented the idea (e-mail to author, January 2000).

OTHER VERSIONS

For score version, see no. 3

1967 mahogany
First shown: 1967 *Yoko Ono at Lisson*, Lisson Gallery

1967–71 ivory
Inscribed on panel: Painting to hammer a nail in Yoko Ono

1970–
Beginning with 1970 *Fluxfest Presentation of John Lennon & Yoko Ono +: Do It Yourself*, New York, numerous participatory versions in different materials (e.g., bed, cross, toilet, table) produced, especially in the 1990s (fig. 7.9)

1988 bronze
First shown: 1989 *Objects, Films*, Whitney Museum. Edition of 9.
Inscribed on hammer: PAINTING TO HAMMER A NAIL IN

EXHIBITIONS (1966 VERSION): 1966 *Yoko at Indica*, Indica Gallery; 1972 *Documenta 5*; 1989 *Objects, Films*, Whitney Museum; 1989 *The Bronze Age*, Cranbrook Academy; 1990 *In Facing*, Riverside Studios; 1990 *Insound/Instructure*, Henie Onstad Arts Centre; 1990 *Fumie*, Sōgetsu Art Museum; 1990 *To See the Skies*, Fondazione Mudima; 1991 *Birch Monologue*, Porin Taidemuseo; 1991 *Peace! Friður!* Reykjavík Municipal Art Museum; 1993 *In the Spirit of Fluxus*, Walker Art Center

EXHIBITIONS (1967 VERSION): 1967 *Yoko Ono at Lisson*, Lisson Gallery; 1971 *This Is Not Here*, Everson Museum; 1997 *Have You Seen the Horizon Lately?* MOMA, Oxford

VISUAL DOCUMENTATION: 1966, photo by Iain Macmillan (unfinished state), pub. *Yoko at Indica*, exh. cat. (1966)

LITERATURE: [Ono], *Yoko at Indica*, exh. cat. (1966), [P7]; Wasserman, *Artforum* (January 1972); Ono, "Some Notes...," *Yoko Ono at Lisson*, exh. cat. (1967); Haskell, *Objects, Films* (1989), exh. brochure, 4; Watanabe, *Fumie*, exh. cat. (1990), 46; Kent, *In Facing*, exh. cat. (1990), n.p.; Haskell, *Arias and Objects* (1991), 21; Iles, *Have You Seen the Horizon Lately?* exh. cat. (1997), 98; Rico Lacasa, *Wish Trees for Brazil,* exh. cat. (1998), 20

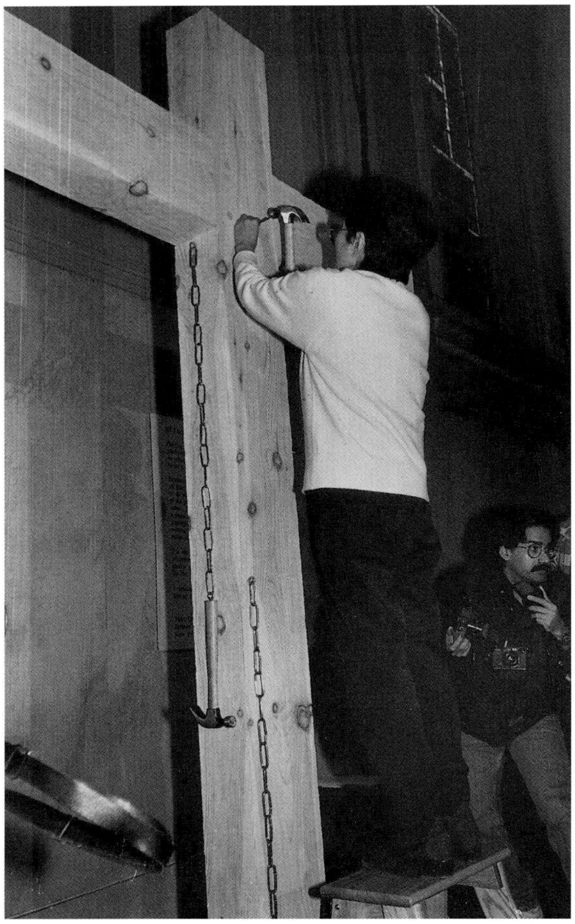

FIGURE 7.9
ONO INSTALLING
PAINTING TO HAMMER A NAIL IN NO. 4,
JUDSON MEMORIAL CHURCH, NEW YORK, 1990. COPYRIGHT © FRED W. MCDARRAH

IN FACING

Painting To Hammer A Nail In has been presented in several different shapes since its conception in 1961. This time I decided to do it in this form: a shape of a cross.

Immediately after my decision, I recognized an immense fear in me which had nothing to do with my concern for the artistic merit of the piece but with my warped sense of value. I was afraid of hammering a nail in a piece of recycled wood while I shared and participated in a society which allowed men, women, children and other species on earth to be on the cross.

For me, this piece has worked as a kind of atonement, to start a new decade with a clearer vision, and to replace my reverence for the abstract with that of life.

I dedicate this piece to all martyrs in the history of the earth.

Yoko Ono
January 5, 1990
New York City

PLATE 10
PAINTING TO HAMMER A NAIL IN, 1961/1967

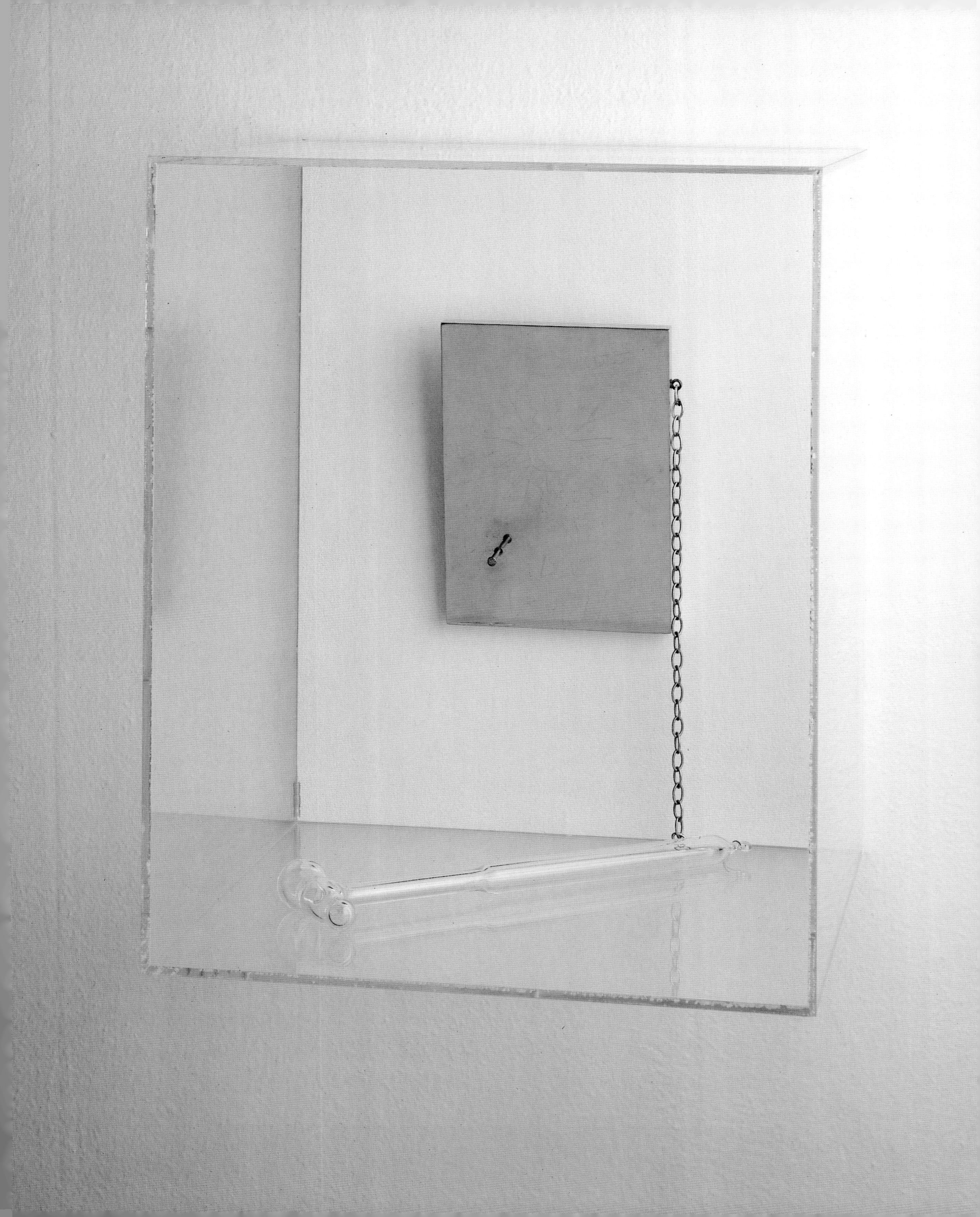

11 *Water Piece (Painting to Be Watered),* 1962/1966

sponge, eyedropper, water in glass vial on Plexiglas pedestal
engraved on pedestal: WATER PIECE YOKO ONO 1962 / WATER EVERY DAY
sponge: dimensions variable; eyedropper: dimensions variable;
pedestal: 23½ x 23½ x 23½" (59.6 x 59.6 x 59.6 cm)
Collection of the artist

Water was important as both motif and material in Ono's work and appears in many of her songs, events, texts, and objects. A basic and essential nourishment for all living beings, water is also a significant part of our physical makeup and is common to all humans. "We're all water in different containers," Ono wrote, "that's why it's so easy to meet/someday we'll evaporate together."[1] The continual, cyclical passage of water from liquid to vapor to liquid has a metaphysical corollary in the theory of reincarnation; in both physical and metaphysical cases, material seems to alternate between states of being and not-being. Ono explored these ideas in numerous works, including the performance *Disappearing Piece*, during which she boiled a pan of water until it completely evaporated,[2] and a collaborative project with John Lennon that comprised a dry sponge suspended over a wet sponge.[3]

This object, a realization of one of Ono's Instruction Paintings, was presented in her 1966 exhibition at Indica Gallery and is directly related to a text published in *Grapefruit* (1964):

> PAINTING TO BE WATERED
>
> Water every day.
>
> 1962 summer

A portion of this text was engraved on the work's Plexiglas pedestal, functioning as both invitation and instruction for anyone who wished to make a contribution to the piece. Paint, brush, and canvas have been reconfigured as water, dropper, and sponge, and art-making is presented as a collective activity linked to nourishment, growth, and the circular nature of life's processes. However, since no image appears and nothing grows, *Water Piece* has to be understood as a conceptual work that is infinitely repeatable—and never complete.

JR

NOTES

The sponge, eyedropper, and bottle have been replaced over the life of the piece due to loss, breakage, etc.

1. Ono, "Water Talk" (1967; Anthology 27).

2. Performed in both New York and London during 1966. See Ono, "Disappearing Piece" (Anthology 9).

3. Produced for the *Fluxfest Presentation of John Lennon & Yoko Ono +* (1970). For another water-related work, also collaborative, see *Water Event* (no. 6).

EXHIBITIONS: 1966 *Yoko at Indica*, Indica Gallery; 1971 *This Is Not Here*, Everson Museum; 1990 *En Trance*, Randers Kunstmuseum; 1991 *Birch Monologue*, Porin Taidemuseo; 1991 *Peace! Friður!* Reykjavík Municipal Art Museum

VISUAL DOCUMENTATION: 1966, photo by Iain Macmillan, pub. *Yoko at Indica*, exh. cat. (1966)

LITERATURE: Glueck, *New York Times* (11 October 1971); Iles, *Have You Seen the Horizon Lately?* exh. cat. (1997), 50

PLATE 11
WATER PIECE (PAINTING TO BE WATERED), 1962/1966

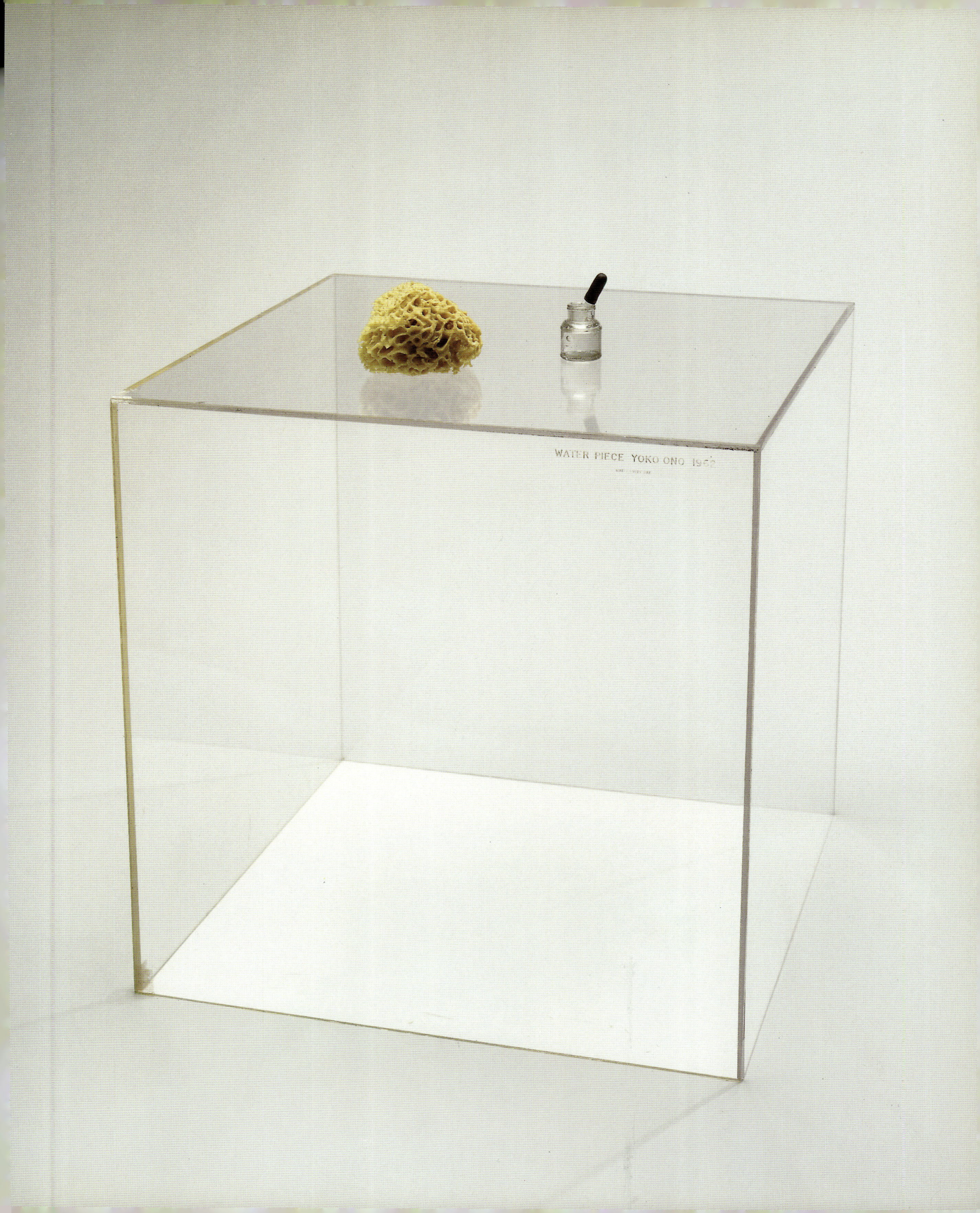
WATER PIECE YOKO ONO 1962

12 *Pointedness,* 1964/1966

crystal sphere on Plexiglas pedestal
engraved on pedestal: POINTEDNESS YOKO ONO 1964 / THIS SPHERE WILL BE A SHARP POINT WHEN IT GETS / TO THE FAR CORNERS OF THE ROOM IN YOUR MIND
sphere: diam. 2⅝" (6.6 cm); pedestal: 58⅛ x 10½ x 10" (147.6 x 26.6 x 25.4 cm)
Collection of the artist

This piece developed out of an experience Ono had during her event *Evening till Dawn*, held in 1964 at a Kyoto temple (no. 29). As the event concluded at dawn under a full moon, Ono recalls that "the monks served us breakfast, consisting of barley-rice, pickles, and miso soup. The moonlight, which had lit the garden as if it was daylight, now became a pointedness in my heart. It seemed that we were a billion miles away from the moonlight."[1]

This impression became the basis, in early 1966, for one of a group of objects that Ono imagined could be used as stimuli for meditations on the fluctuating nature of matter. Her proposal read: "A marble sphere (actually existing) which, in your head, gradually becomes a sharp cone by the time it is extended to the far end of the room."[2] Later that year, for her exhibition at Indica Gallery, Ono actually constructed the object by placing a white marble sphere on a pedestal engraved with the instructional text. She called it *Pointedness* in reference to her Kyoto experience.[3]

The work's genesis in the garden of a moonlit Buddhist temple suggests that it refers not only to Zen meditation practices but also to the dramatic (but illusory) shift in scale that occurs when bodies are separated by a great physical distance. From Earth, the moon may look like a small, inert sphere; in *Pointedness*, Ono gives the viewer a chance to restore its distance, power, and mystery.

JR

NOTES

1. Ono, e-mail to author, September 1999.
2. Ono, "To the Wesleyan People" (1966; Anthology 14).
3. In its present form, *Pointedness* includes a crystal sphere, but photographs and reviews of its first presentation reveal that it was first realized with a white marble sphere. Ono changed it when she could afford to do so, feeling that the clarity of crystal better suited the conceptual nature of the exercise.

OTHER VERSIONS

1970 soft rubber ball
First shown: 1970 *Fluxfest Presentation of John Lennon & Yoko Ono +: Blue Room*, New York. With sign: This sphere will be a sharp point when it gets to the far side of the room in your mind.

1971 rubber stamp text
2 editions known. From a set of 13 stamps with texts by Ono and Lennon, produced by George Maciunas in conjunction with *This Is Not Here*. Text reads: THIS SPHERE WILL BE A SHARP POINT / WHEN IT GETS TO THE FAR SIDE OF / THE ROOM IN YOUR MIND (Y.O.)

1988 bronze (pl. 60b)
First shown: 1989 *Objects, Films*, Whitney Museum. Edition of 9. With Corian pedestal. Engraved on pedestal: POINTEDNESS YOKO ONO 1988 / THIS SPHERE WILL BE A SHARP POINT WHEN IT GETS / TO THE FAR CORNER OF THE ROOM IN YOUR MIND

1997 crystal
Created for the collection of Fine Arts Museum of Valencia. With Plexiglas pedestal. Based on 1964/66 version, dimensions based on 1988 bronze version

EXHIBITIONS: 1966 *Yoko at Indica*, Indica Gallery; 1971 *This Is Not Here*, Everson Museum; 1989 *Objects, Films*, Whitney Museum; 1989 *The Bronze Age*, Cranbrook Academy; 1990 *In Facing*, Riverside Studios; 1990 *Insound/Instructure*, Henie Onstad Arts Centre; 1990 *Fumie*, Sōgetsu Art Museum; 1990 *To See the Skies*, Fondazione Mudima; 1991 *Birch Monologue*, Porin Taidemuseo; 1991 *Peace! Friður!* Reykjavík Municipal Art Museum; 1994 *Japanese Art After 1945*, Yokohama Museum of Art/Guggenheim Museum Soho; 1996 *L'art du plastique*, Ecole Nationale Supérieure des Beaux-Arts

VISUAL DOCUMENTATION: 1966, photo by Iain Macmillan, pub. *Yoko at Indica*, exh. cat. (1966) and Wasserman, *Artforum* (January 1972)

LITERATURE: Overy, *Artscanada* (January 1967), supplement; Wasserman, *Artforum* (January 1972); Hendricks, *Fluxus Codex* (1988); Haskell, *Objects, Films*, exh. brochure (1989), 4; Blom, *Insound/Instructure*, exh. cat. (1990), 35; Watanabe, *Fumie*, exh. cat. (1990), 46; Haskell, *Arias and Objects* (1991), 54

FLATE 12

POINTEDNESS,

1964/1966

13 *Eternal Time,* 1965

(originally known as *Eternal Time Clock*)
battery-run, gilded clock with second hand only, Plexiglas box, stethoscope, Plexiglas pedestal
inscribed on clock front: Happy Birthday Julius Love Sylvia / ETERNAL TIME / by Yoko Ono 3/15/65
box: 3 x 6 x 6.5" (7.6 x 15.2 x 16.5 cm); pedestal: 40 x 8 x 9" (101.6 x 20.3 x 22.8 cm)
Collection of the artist

Time is a vital element in Ono's art. When performed and actualized, her scores and instructions acquire a temporal dimension. The clock, a literal index of time, is a recurrent motif in her works: as many as six works entitled *Clock Piece* appear in *Grapefruit* (1964). While one piece instructs the reader to

> Steal all the clocks and watches
> in the world.
> Destroy them.

another urges,

> Make all the clocks in the world fast by
> two seconds without letting anyone know
> about it.

By destroying or changing the time of clocks, Ono means to free the self from the establishment or the absolute systems of the world.

Eternal Time gives form to Ono's longing for freedom. Although its second hand moves, the clock cannot indicate the time without its minute and hour hands.[1] By listening to the clock's continuous beat through a stethoscope, one has a sense of eternity. At the same time, the beat of the clock brings to mind the pulsing of the human heart. Through such analogies, human life is made eternal like the timeless clock. Cast in bronze, the 1988 version is truly frozen in time.
MY

NOTES

1. The artist included a performance called *Clock Piece* in her concerts at Yamaichi Hall, Kyoto (1964); Sōgetsu Kaikan Hall, Tokyo (1964); and Carnegie Recital Hall (1965). According to her script "Strip Tease Show," which records the program presented at these venues, an alarm clock was placed on the stage to announce the end of her concerts (1966; Anthology 8). She notes that the clock's face and hands were removed "so that it was impossible to know what time the clock had been set to." See Anthology 8. *Eternal Time* was also used (without pedestal, box, or stethoscope) in the 1965 Carnegie concert.

OTHER VERSIONS
1965 ***Eternal Time*** (presently known as *Sky Clock*)
Clock with painted face. Realized by Geoffrey Hendricks

1988 bronze
First shown: 1989 *The Bronze Age*, Cranbrook Academy. Edition of 9. With Plexiglas case, Corian pedestal, and bronze stethoscope. Inscribed on base: ETERNAL TIME / by Yoko Ono 3/15/65

EXHIBITIONS: 1965 *New Works of Yoko Ono*, Carnegie Recital Hall; 1966 *Yoko at Indica*, Indica Gallery; 1971 *This Is Not Here*, Everson Museum; 1989 *The Bronze Age*, Cranbrook Academy; 1990 *In Facing*, Riverside Studios; 1990 *Insound/Instructure*, Henie Onstad Arts Centre; 1990 *Fumie*, Sōgetsu Art Museum; 1990 *To See the Skies*, Fondazione Mudima; 1991 *Birch Monologue*, Porin Taidemuseo; 1991 *Peace! Friður!* Reykjavík Municipal Art Museum

VISUAL DOCUMENTATION: 1965, photo by Peter Moore; 1966, photo by Iain Macmillan, pub. *Yoko at Indica*, exh. cat. (1966)

LITERATURE: Sturt-Penrose, *The Art Scene* (1969), 46; Haskell, *Arias and Objects* (1991), 37, 56

PLATE 13
ETERNAL TIME, 1965

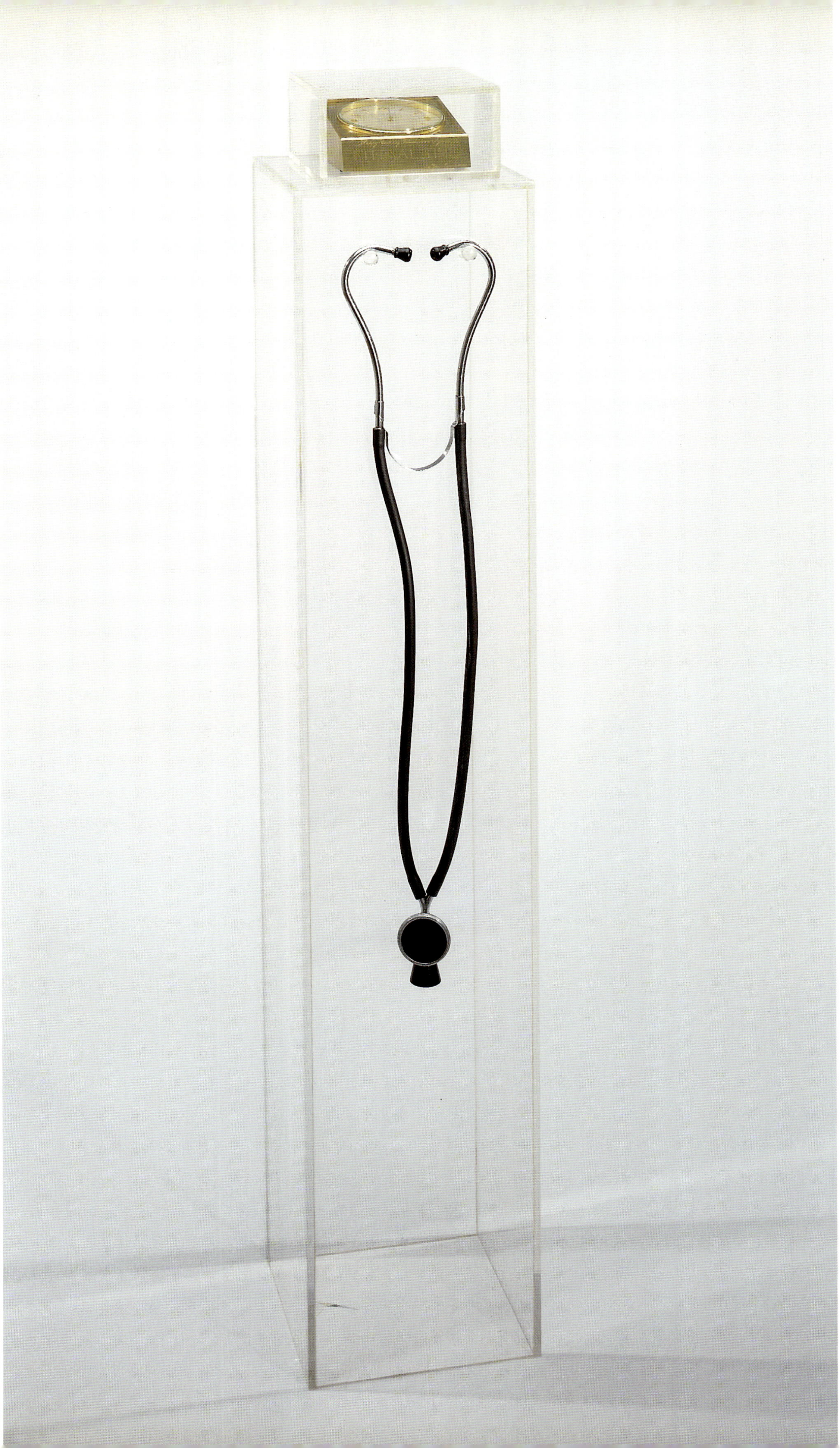

14 *Object in Three Parts,* 1966

condom, diaphragm, birth control pill, each placed on a pedestal
each pedestal: 39 x 11¾ x 11¾" (99 x 28.7 x 28.7 cm)
original, lost; 1989 reconstruction: collection of the artist

Ono has been associated in the public mind with the women's liberation movement through several songs she composed after 1971, most notably "Woman Is the Nigger of the World," which she coauthored with Lennon.[1] But some artworks of the 1960s had already revealed her acute sensibility of the imbalance in sexual dynamics. When *Object in Three Parts* was first presented at Indica Gallery in 1966, contraception, while a hotly debated issue, had not yet served as a subject for works of art. Breaking this unwritten taboo on utilizing objects of everyday sexual life, Ono made the contraceptives into art objects by placing them carefully on white pedestals.[2]

As in other works by Ono, the three-part composition of this work may suggest three different stages in time.[3] It may represent the evolution of the contraceptive from the condom to the pill: large to small; male control to female control. *Revolution*, the title given to the 1988 bronze version, may refer to the women's revolution and contraception as a revolution in human history (fig. 7.10).

MY

NOTES

For the 1989 reconstruction, a new condom is used for each exhibition.

1. "Woman Is the Nigger of the World" as well as "Sisters O Sisters" and "Men, Men, Men" are in the LP album by John & Yoko/Plastic Ono Band with Elephant's Memory, *Some Time in New York City* (1972). Other songs addressing women's issues include "Angry Young Woman," "She Hits Back," and "Woman Power" in Ono, *Feeling the Space* (1973); and "What a Bastard the World Is" and "What a Mess" in Ono, *Approximately Infinite Universe* (1973). Also, Ono created a theme song in 1973 for the women's liberation movement in Japan, entitled "Josei jōi banzai" (Cheers to women on top), upon request from the group Chūpiren, whose full name may be translated as "Women's liberation union that objects to the Abortion Prohibition Law and demands free access to contraceptive pills." Coverage in the Japanese press included "Yarō-domo yoku kikeyo!: Datō dansei mokuromu ribu sanka" (Guys, listen up!: A tribute to women's lib, aiming to overthrow men), *Hōchi shinbun*, 7 May 1973.

2. *You and Me*, shown at Indica Gallery, is also composed of contraceptives: two water-filled condoms suspended by strings against a white-painted board or canvas (original lost).

3. Three-part composition is also used in such works as *Painting in Three Stanzas* (1961), *Shadows* (1961/1971), and the slide-projection version of *Lighting Event* (1995; pls. 67a–b).

OTHER VERSIONS

1988 ***Revolution: Objects in Three Parts*** (bronze)
First shown: 1989 *The Bronze Age*, Cranbrook Academy.
Edition of 9. With Plexiglas case

1989 reconstruction
First shown: 1989 *The Bronze Age*, Cranbrook Academy.
Based on 1966 original

EXHIBITIONS: 1966 *Yoko at Indica*, Indica Gallery

VISUAL DOCUMENTATION: 1966, photo by Iain Macmillan, pub. *Yoko at Indica*, exh. cat. (1966)

LITERATURE: Amaya, *Financial Times* (12 November 1966); Haskell, *Arias and Objects* (1991), 98

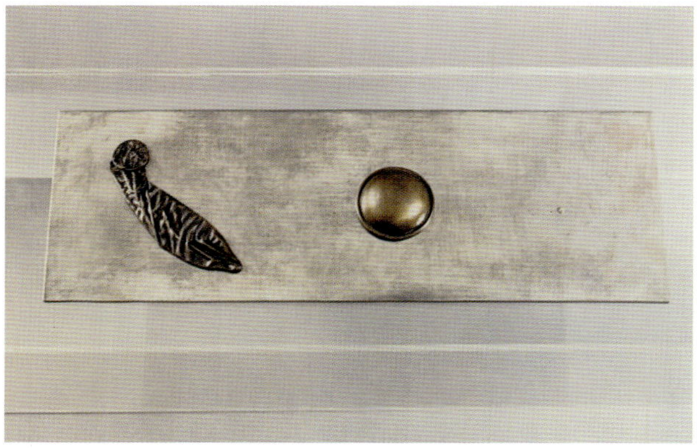

FIGURE 7.10
REVOLUTION: OBJECT IN THREE PARTS,
1966/1988 (BRONZE VERSION)

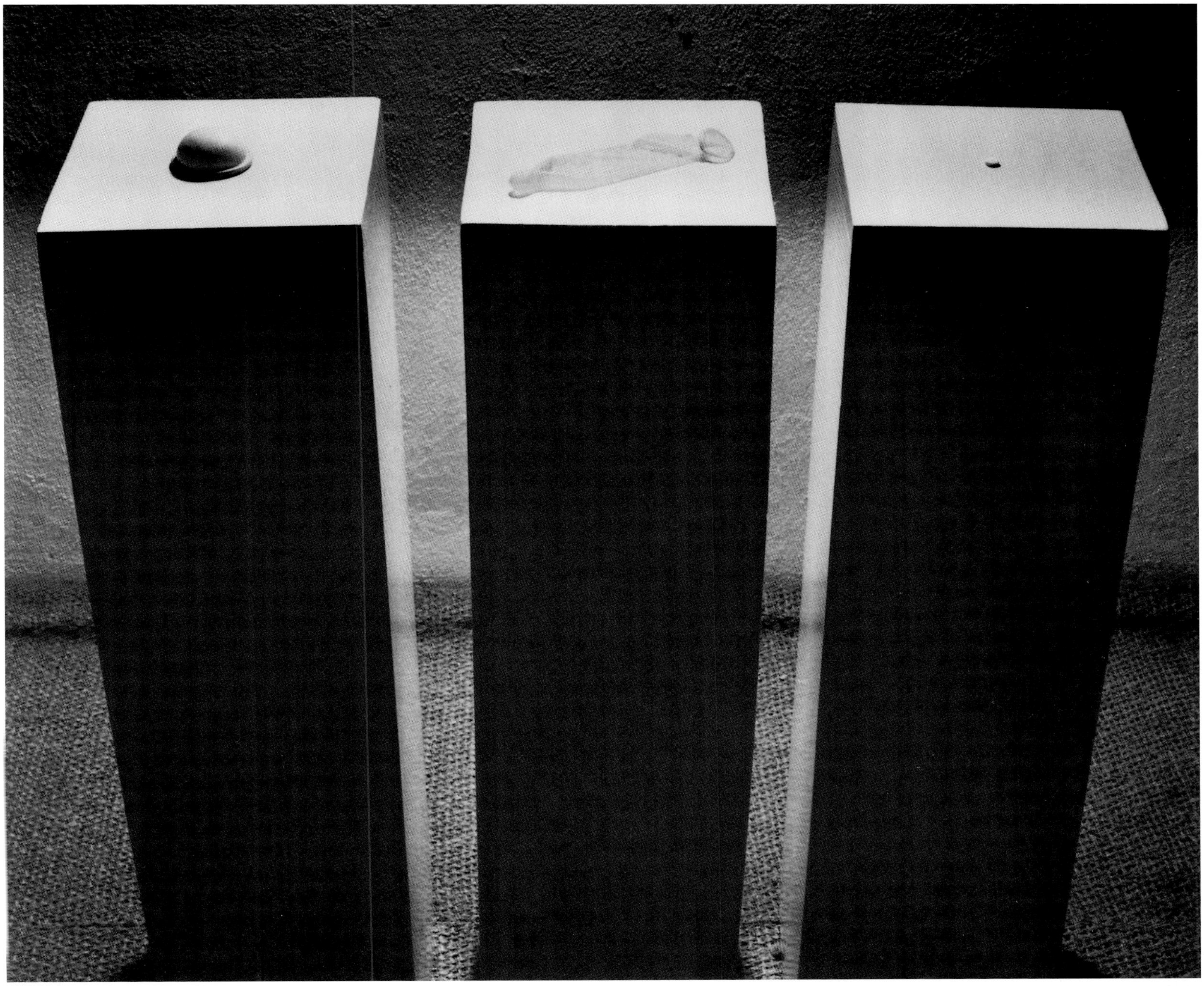

PLATE 14
OBJECT IN THREE PARTS, 1966.
INSTALLATION VIEW,
INDICA GALLERY,
LONDON, 1966

15 *Apple,* 1966

apple, Plexiglas pedestal with brass plaque
engraved on plaque: APPLE
pedestal: 36 x 10 x 10" (91.5 x 25.4 x 25.4 cm)
Collection of the artist

One of the "unfinished objects" presented at Indica Gallery in 1966, *Apple* embodies the life cycle of birth, decay, death, and rebirth. Placing the apple on a pedestal in a gallery foregrounded the beauty of that cycle and encouraged viewers to imagine the fruit's inevitable decomposition and its potential, through its seeds, for regeneration. The label APPLE on the pedestal functions as a reminder of what was—and would be again—after the fruit deteriorates beyond recognition (fig. 7.11).

In Christian iconography the apple is equated with Eve, the archetypal female, and the ruinous effects of succumbing to her/its temptation. This history was in Ono's mind when she made the piece, but she thought of the apple as the fruit of "wisdom" rather than evil.[1] Nevertheless, her apple frequently proved irresistible to visitors, who saw it as an offer (or perhaps a dare) to take a bite. After the Indica show, Ono said this interaction "was an interruption of the piece that I had not planned. I was very upset at the time. But now I think it was a very interesting thing that happened: the cycle of organic change was interrupted by human action."[2] Her 1988 bronze version of the work, in which the apple is depicted with a bite taken out of it, embodies this intervention and the resulting stasis.

Ono's deadpan presentation of an apple on a pedestal is also a witty and incisive revision of that hoary artistic subject, the still life. However, instead of serving up a traditional *nature morte*, a representation of life that she would have considered dead or frozen, Ono here presented viewers with a little bit of life itself.
JR

NOTES

1. Ono, e-mail to author, September 1999.
2. Haskell, *Arias and Objects* (1991), 42. John Lennon was the viewer who took a bite. When the piece was shown at the Everson Museum in 1971, the apple was also bitten. See Michael Benedikt, "Yoko Notes," *Art and Artists* 6, no. 10 (January 1972): 26–27.

OTHER VERSIONS
1988 bronze
First shown: 1989 *Objects, Films*, Whitney Museum. Edition of 9. With brass plaque on Corian pedestal. Inscribed on brass plaque: APPLE

EXHIBITIONS: 1966 *Yoko at Indica*, Indica Gallery; 1971 *This Is Not Here*, Everson Museum; 1989 *Objects, Films*, Whitney Museum; 1989 *The Bronze Age*, Cranbrook Academy; 1990 *In Facing*, Riverside Studios; 1990 *Insound/Instructure*, Henie Onstad Arts Centre; 1990 *Fumie*, Sōgetsu Art Museum; 1990 *To See the Skies*, Fondazione Mudima; 1991 *Birch Monologue*, Porin Taidemuseo; 1991 *Peace! Friður!* Reykjavík Municipal Art Museum; 1993 *In the Spirit of Fluxus*, Walker Art Center; 1997 *Have You Seen the Horizon Lately?* MOMA, Oxford

VISUAL DOCUMENTATION: 1966, photo by Iain Macmillan, pub. *Yoko at Indica*, exh. cat. (1966)

LITERATURE: *Daily Sketch* (15 November 1966); Benedikt, *Art and Artists* (January 1972); Wasserman, *Artforum* (January 1972); Haskell, *Objects, Films*, exh. brochure (1989), 4; Haskell, *Arias and Objects* (1991), 42

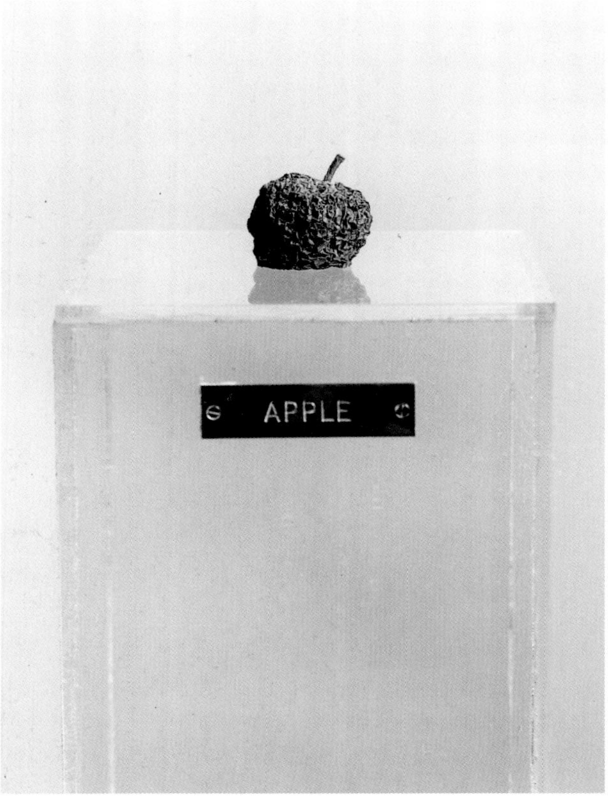

FIGURE 7.11
APPLE, 1966 (WITHERED STATE)

PLATE 15
APPLE, 1966

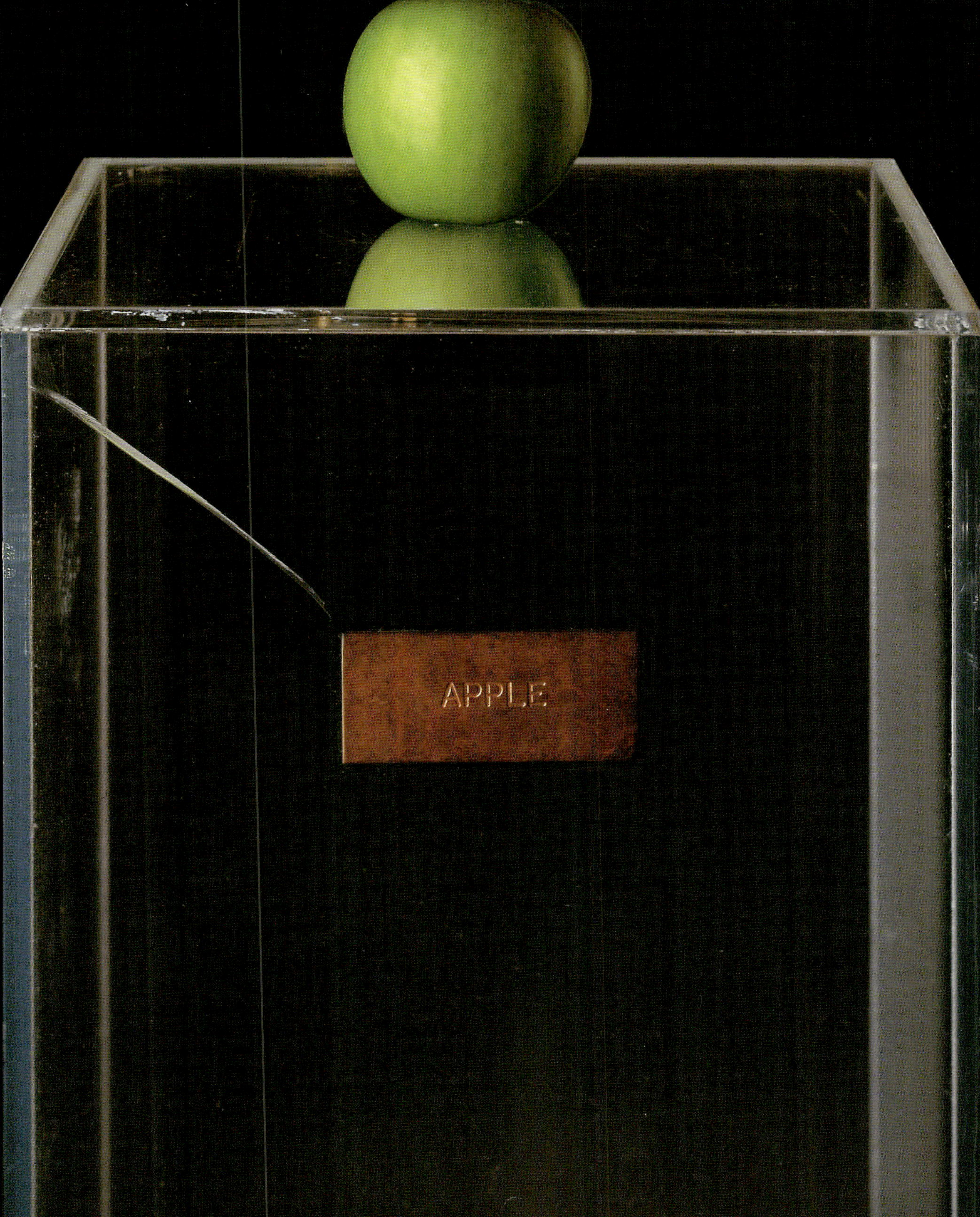
APPLE

16 *Forget It,* 1966

stainless steel needle on Plexiglas pedestal
engraved on pedestal: FORGET IT YOKO ONO 1966
needle: 3¼" (8.2 cm) long; pedestal: 58⅛ x 10½ x 10"
(147.6 x 26.6 x 25.4 cm)
Collection of the artist

Like *Pointedness* (no. 12), this work consists of a single object placed on a Plexiglas pedestal that is engraved with a text. In both works the text instructs the viewer to engage in an intellectual rather than a physical activity—here, an ambiguous command to "forget it." The numerous connotations of this phrase—to dismiss, forgive, cleanse, move on, and so forth—ensure that its meaning will be dependent on the context of the individual viewer's life.

Ono's use of a needle to represent the activity of forgetting is illuminated in an excerpt from a 1966 essay:

> Didn't Christ say that it was like a camel trying to pass through a needle hole, for John Cage to go to heaven? I think it is nice to abandon what you have as much as possible, as many mental possessions as the physical ones, as they clutter your mind.... It is nice to keep oneself small, like a grain of rice, instead of expanding.[1]

In this witty paraphrasing of the well-known biblical adage, Ono casts John Cage as the "rich man" and suggests that intellectual baggage can be just as burdensome as material possessions. The needle itself, presented point up, might even be seen as a tool with which to correct such a situation of overexpansion.

But Ono also thinks of this work as a "peace [*sic*] of healing" that acknowledges the tragicomedy of human existence. She has likened the upward orientation of the needle to our desperate need to attain unity with the infinite. The text signals the possibility of release from that need. "By saying 'forget it,'" she has written, "we free ourselves from that impossible journey. We can go forward, then, hopefully, without looking back."[2]
JR

NOTES
1. Ono, "To the Wesleyan People" (1966; Anthology 14).
2. Ono, e-mail to author, September 1999.

OTHER VERSIONS
1970 upright needle
First shown: 1970 *Fluxfest Presentation of John Lennon & Yoko Ono +: Blue Room*, New York. With sign: Forget it. (Yoko Ono)

1971 rubber stamp text
2 known editions. From a set of 13 stamps with texts by Ono and Lennon, produced by George Maciunas in conjunction with *This Is Not Here*. Text reads: FORGET IT (Y.O.)

1988 bronze
First shown: 1989 *Objects, Films*, Whitney Museum. Edition of 9. With Corian pedestal. Engraved on pedestal: FORGET IT YOKO ONO 1988

1997 steel needle
Created for the collection of Fine Art Museum of Valencia. With Plexiglas pedestal. Based on 1966 version, dimensions based on 1988 bronze version

EXHIBITIONS: 1966 *Yoko at Indica*, Indica Gallery; 1971 *This Is Not Here*, Everson Museum; 1972 *Documenta 5*; 1989 *Objects, Films*, Whitney Museum; 1989 *The Bronze Age*, Cranbrook Academy; 1990 *In Facing*, Riverside Studios; 1990 *Insound/Instructure*, Henie Onstad Arts Centre; 1990 *Fumie*, Sōgetsu Art Museum; 1990 *To See the Skies*, Fondazione Mudima; 1991 *Birch Monologue*, Porin Taidemuseo; 1991 *Peace! Friður!* Reykjavík Municipal Art Museum; 1994 *Japanese Art After 1945*, Yokohama Museum of Art/Guggenheim Museum Soho; 1996 *L'art du plastique*, Ecole Nationale Supérieure des Beaux-Arts

VISUAL DOCUMENTATION: 1966, photo by Iain Macmillan, pub. *Yoko at Indica*, exh. cat. (1966)

LITERATURE: Hendricks, *Fluxus Codex* (1988), 418; Haskell, *Arias and Objects* (1991), 55

PLATE 16
FORGET IT, 1966

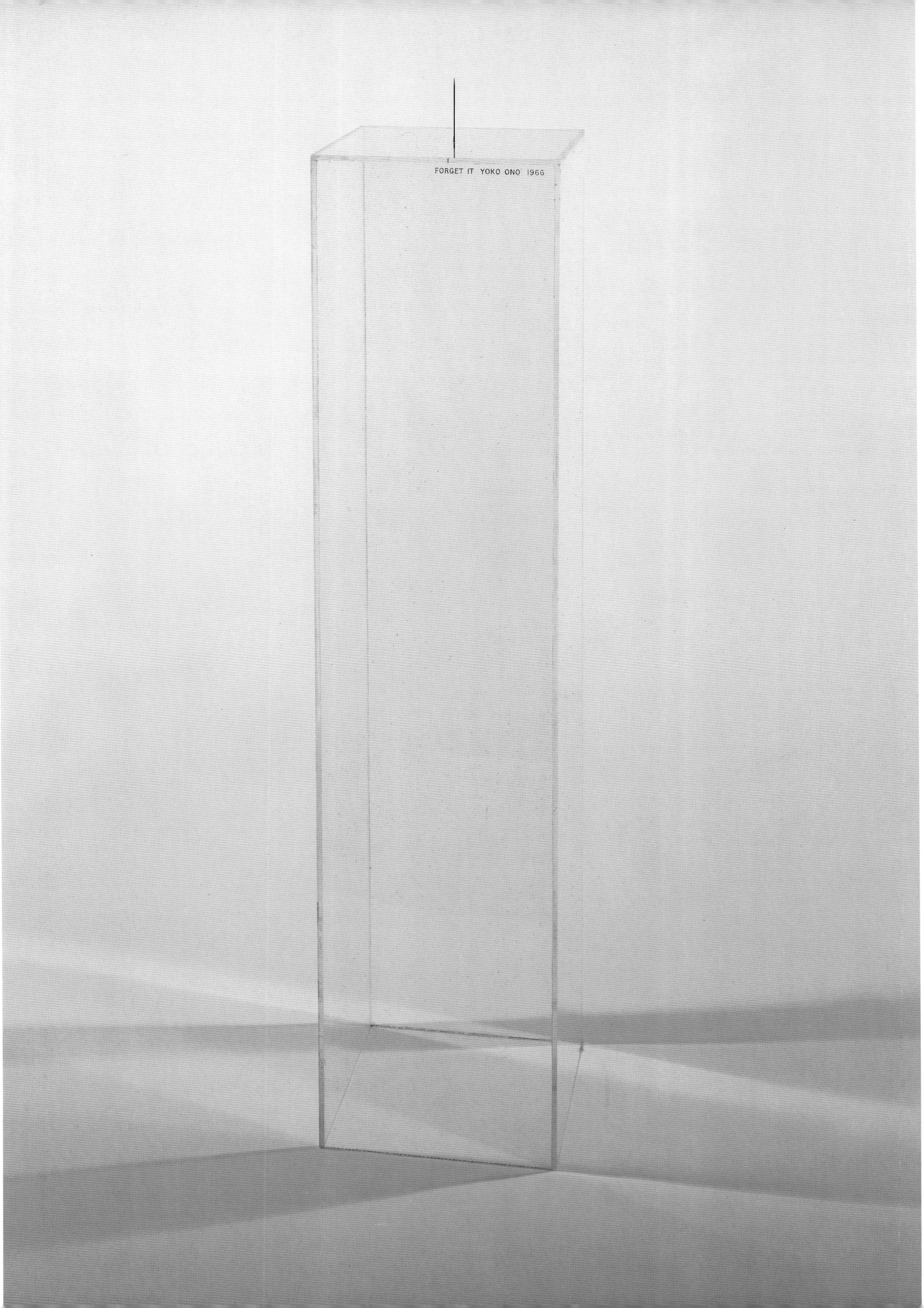
FORGET IT YOKO ONO 1966

17 *Sky Machine,* 1966

(originally known as *Sky Dispenser*)
stainless steel ticket dispenser, paper cards, pedestal
dispenser: 51 x 16 x 16" (129.5 x 40.6 x 40.6 cm);
card: approx. 1 x 1¾" (2.5 x 4.4 cm)
inscribed at bottom: WORD MACHINE PIECE #1 'SKY MACHINE' BY YOKO ONO 1961, REALIZED BY ANTHONY COX 1966
handwritten on cards, recto: sky; verso: 1966 y.o.
The Gilbert and Lila Silverman Collection, Detroit

18 *Air Dispenser,* 1971

stainless steel and glass candy dispenser, empty plastic capsules
inscribed on top cover: AIR CAPSULES BY YOKO ONO 10¢
whereabouts unknown

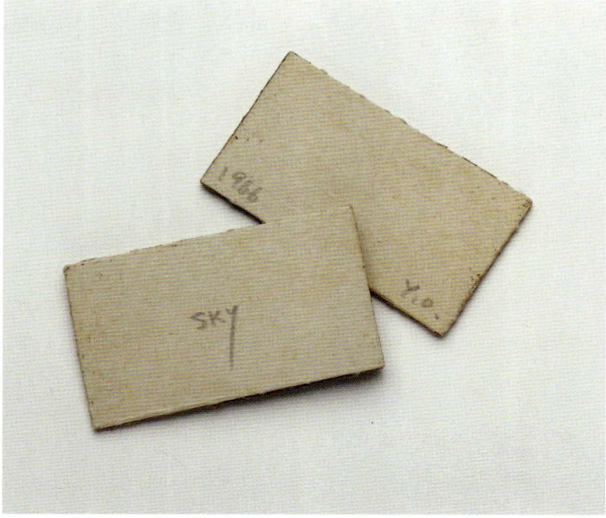

FIGURE 7.12
CARDS FOR ***SKY MACHINE,*** 1966

Like Ono's other dispenser machines,[1] *Sky Machine* and *Air Dispenser* evolved from her instruction published in *Grapefruit* (1964):

> CHEWING GUM MACHINE PIECE
>
> Place Chewing Gum Machines with
> many different word cards in them
> next to Coca-Cola Machines on
> every street corner.
>
> Put more auxiliary words than nouns.
> More verbs than adjectives.
>
> 1961 winter

When *Sky Machine* was sold in 1966, the buyer was required to agree to "a contract in which he only received the right to possess the machine but had to agree that servicing of the machine would remain the right of the maker and that the maker would receive 60% on the proceeds of the sale of 'sky' cards."[2] By having her work take on the format of a commercial vending machine, the artist commented on art and consumerism.[3]

What Ono sold through these machines, however, was not a consumable product but conceptual "sky" or "air" (via a card or empty capsule; fig. 7.12). Stating that "We need more skies than coke,"[4] she meant to propagate imagination in an era of mass production. The artist considers "air" as "the only thing we share" and the only link between people.[5] Similarly, her favorite

PLATE 17
SKY DISPENSER, 1966

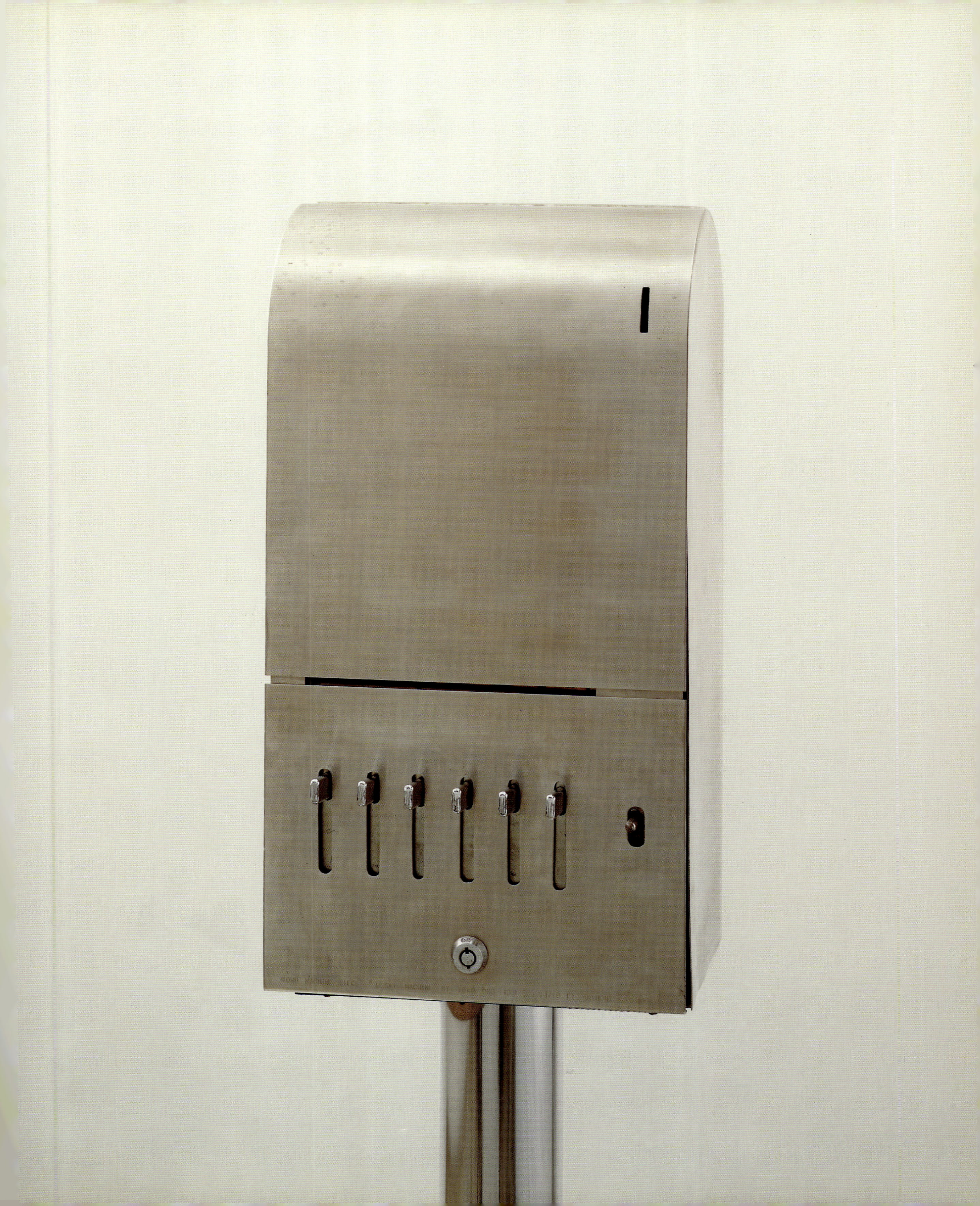

motif, "sky," has been "always there" for her and "the only constant factor" of her life.[6] Through her humor and imagination, Ono transformed the intangible "air" and "sky" into something that everyone can easily afford.

MY

NOTES

Documentary photographs suggest that the inscription and pedestal for *Sky Machine* were later additions.

1. Many dispensers, including a capsule dispenser of tears, were made and presented at the Everson Museum exhibition in 1971 (fig. 7.13). See the installation diagram of the exhibition in *This Is Not Here*, exh. cat. (1971), n.p.

2. Anthony Cox, "Instructive Auto-Destruction," *Art and Artists* 1, no. 5 (August 1966): 19.

3. Robert Watts, an early associate of Fluxus, used a commercial stamp dispenser to sell artists' stamps in 1961. See Joan Marter, "Happenings, Pop Art, and Fluxus at Rutgers University" in *Off Limits: Rutgers University and the Avant-Garde, 1957–1963*, exh. cat. (Newark: The Newark Museum, 1999), 30.

4. Ono, "To the Wesleyan People" (1966; Anthology 14).

5. Ono, "Some Notes on the Lisson Gallery Show" (1967; Anthology 15).

6. Ono, "SKYTALK with love to Denmark" in *Color, Fly, Sky*, exh. cat. (1992), 5.

Sky Machine

EXHIBITIONS: 1966 *Works by Behrman…*, Judson Memorial Church; 1989 *The Bronze Age*, Cranbrook Academy; 1991 *Colors of Money*, Musée de la Poste; 1997 *Have You Seen the Horizon Lately?* MOMA, Oxford

VISUAL DOCUMENTATION: 1966, photo by Peter Moore; 1966, photo by Iain Macmillan, pub. *The Bronze Age*, exh. cat. (Cranbrook 1989); n.d., photo by Brad Iverson, pub. *Fluxus Codex* (1988)

LITERATURE: Cox, *Art and Artists* (August 1966); Hendricks, *Fluxus Codex* (1988), 423

Air Dispenser

EXHIBITIONS: 1971 *This Is Not Here*, Everson Museum

VISUAL DOCUMENTATION: 1971, photo by Iain Macmillan, pub. Hendricks, *Fluxus Codex* (1988)

LITERATURE: Hendricks, *Fluxus Codex* (1988), 415

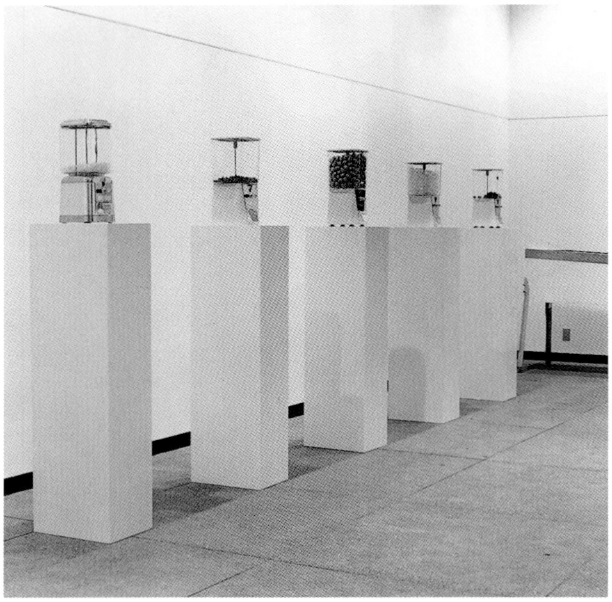

FIGURE 7.13
VARIOUS DISPENSERS IN VENDING ARCADE. INSTALLATION VIEW, EVERSON MUSEUM OF ART, SYRACUSE, 1971

PLATE 18
AIR DISPENSER, 1971. INSTALLATION VIEW, EVERSON MUSEUM OF ART, SYRACUSE, 1971

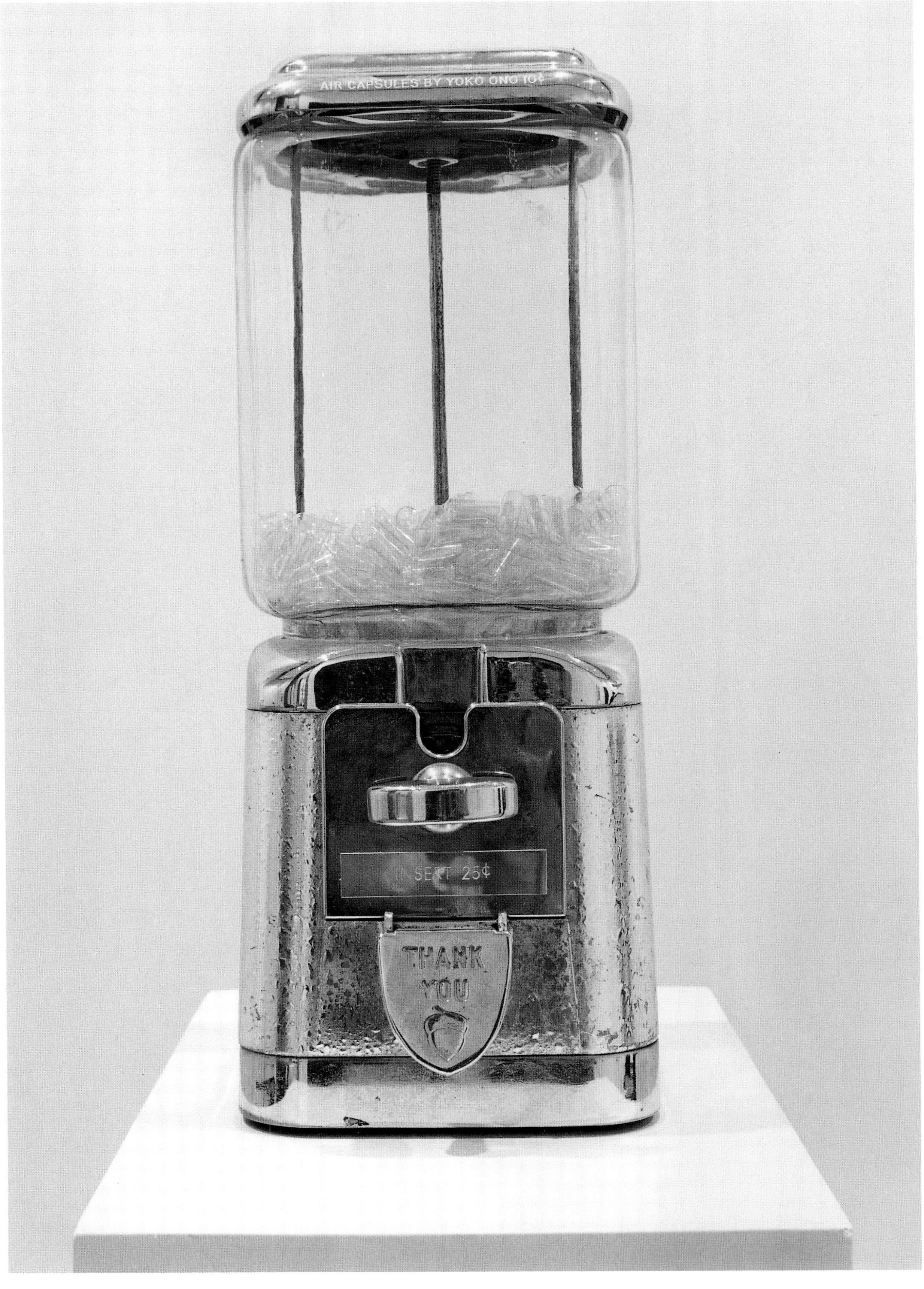
AIR CAPSULES BY YOKO ONO 10¢
INSERT 25¢
THANK YOU

19 *Wrapping Piece for London,* 1966

(also known as *Wrapped Chair*)
wood chair, gauze, white paint
32¾ x 16 x 15½" (83.2 x 40.6 x 39.4 cm)
Collection of the artist

This work began as a simple presentation of two rolls of gauze and a white-painted cane-seat chair—one of the "unfinished objects" in Ono's Indica Gallery exhibition of 1966. As the artist describes it, she had

> placed a ball of gauze on a chair for people to keep making the ball larger [fig. 7.14]. A pack of gauze was placed next to the chair as an indication. People kept wrapping the chair instead [of the ball]. My idea was to see the ball become so large that it would fill the whole room, thereby changing the relationship between the audience and the ball in size, rather like in *Alice in Wonderland.*[1]

The intended shift in scale would have been a literal transformation of the work that mirrored the conceptual shift proposed in *Pointedness*, also on view in the Indica show (no. 12). However, the viewers' unplanned response to the work transformed what was to have been an ephemeral event into an indexical object that included, unintentionally, the chair.[2] Ono later painted the whole thing white, preserving it and acknowledging its stasis in a way that anticipates her later reinterpretation, in bronze, of other early objects, such as *Apple* (no. 15).

Wrapping Piece for London (Wrapped Chair) is part of Ono's extended exploration, beginning in 1961, of the activity of wrapping. The metaphor is a rich one, suggesting traditional women's activities like binding wounds and swaddling infants, and alluding more generally to preservation, hiding, muffling, and shrouding. In this object, the figurative associations of the chair were for Ono accentuated by the layers of gauze: she recalls that

> the chair showed glimpses of itself through the wrapped gauze, like a woman who yearned to cover herself, or a scarred soul which hid its pain unsuccessfully.... The wrapping itself sometimes dangled like memories of disappointment, disillusion, and tears, sometimes as weblike nerves crisscrossing with incredible complexity and going nowhere.[3]

JR

NOTES

1. Ono, e-mail to author, September 1999.

2. The wrapping event performed by viewers at Ono's exhibition *This Is Not Here* (1971) was closer to her original intention for Indica. She presented a ball of gauze, and the audience, this time, used it to drape the room. At the end of the exhibition the work was destroyed (ibid.). In response to Indica viewers' intervention, Ono conceived *Lion Wrapping Event*, in which she had one of the famous lions of London's Trafalgar Square wrapped and unwrapped (see Chronology, 1967, August 3).

3. Ibid.

EXHIBITIONS: 1966 *Yoko at Indica*, Indica Gallery; 1989 *The Bronze Age*, Cranbrook Academy; 1990 *In Facing*, Riverside Studios; 1990 *Insound/Instructure*, Henie Onstad Arts Centre; 1990 *To See the Skies*, Fondazione Mudima; 1991 *Birch Monologue*, Porin Taidemuseo; 1991 *Peace! Friður!* Reykjavík Municipal Art Museum; 1993 *In the Spirit of Fluxus*, Walker Art Center; 1997 *Have You Seen the Horizon Lately?* MOMA, Oxford

VISUAL DOCUMENTATION: 1966, photo by Iain Macmillan (unfinished state), pub. *Yoko at Indica*, exh. cat. (1966); 1971, photo by Iain Macmillan (*Wrapped Chair/Hide Me* variation), pub. *Have You Seen the Horizon Lately?* exh. cat. (1997)

LITERATURE: [Ono], *Yoko at Indica*, exh. cat. (1966), [O23]; Haskell, *Arias and Objects* (1991), 76; Iles, *Have You Seen the Horizon Lately?* exh. cat. (1997), 67–74

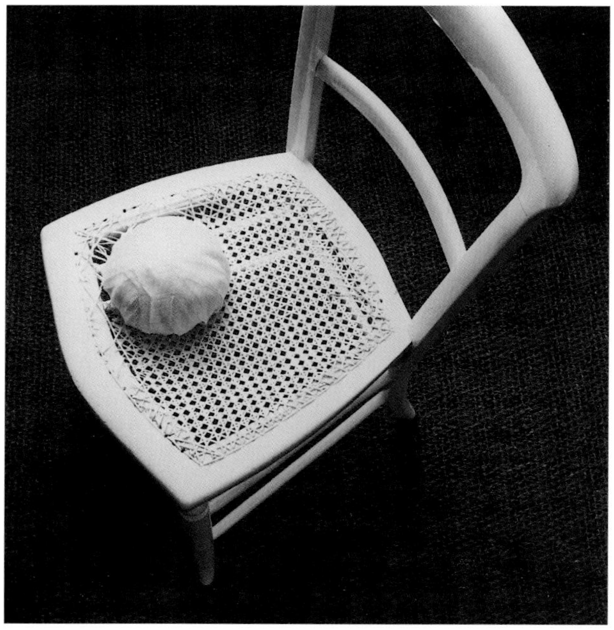

FIGURE 7.14
WRAPPING PIECE FOR LONDON, 1966 (INITIAL STATE). INSTALLATION VIEW, INDICA GALLERY, LONDON, 1966

PLATE 19
WRAPPING PIECE FOR LONDON, 1966. INSTALLATION VIEW, THE ISRAEL MUSEUM, JERUSALEM, 2000

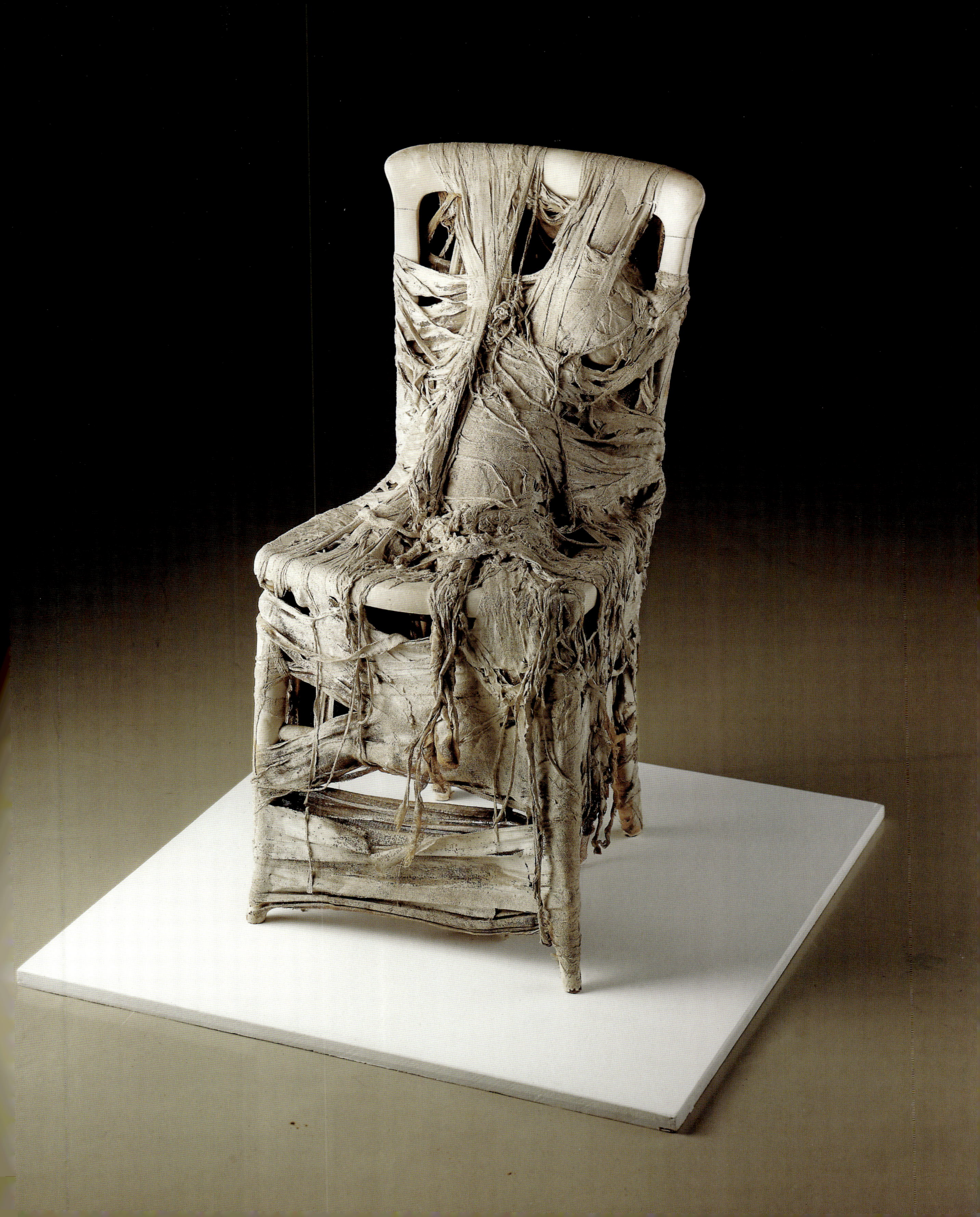

20 *Half-A-Room,* 1967

altered readymades
dimensions variable
Collection of the artist

Photographs of this installation at the Lisson Gallery show the artist standing in what appears to be a modestly furnished one-room apartment in which everything—from the rug on the floor to the picture on the wall—has been cut in half and painted white (figs. 1.21, 7.1, 7.15).[1] The installation was part of Ono's *Half-A-Wind Show*, an exploration of bisection—both psychic and physical—as a condition of human existence.[2] "Life is only half a game," she wrote. "Molecules are always at the verge of half disappearing and half emerging."[3] Looking at the neatly halved objects, our tendency may be to understand them as incomplete, but Ono insists that the room is both half empty and half full, like the glass of water in the familiar riddle. The confrontation with this kind of fragmented absence/presence may stimulate us to imagine a whole that is far more vividly drawn than any physical representation of it could be.

Ono's decision to present these ideas in the form of a truncated domestic environment suggests an additional narrative involving personal loss or existential loneliness (a reading that is underscored by the extant photographs, which show the artist standing alone, eyes downcast, inside the room). However, her statements indicate instead a focus on her understanding that incompleteness is a fact of life. "Somebody said I should also put half-a-person in the show. But we are halves already."[4]

The related *Air Bottles*, a collaboration between Ono and John Lennon, also appeared in the Lisson Gallery exhibition. "John suggested how about selling the other half of my half-a-matter objects in bottles. It was such a beautiful idea I decided to use it even though it was not mine."[5] These took the form of small glass bottles with paper labels inscribed, for example, with "half-a-life," "half-a-hat," or "half-a-sky" (fig. 7.5).

JR

NOTES

1. Not all of the original elements have survived, and various combinations of them have been shown during the 1990s. Additional elements continue to turn up and are being added to the piece as they are discovered.

2. In the exhibition catalogue the work is entitled *Half-A-Spring Room*, but since then it has been exhibited under the title *Half-A-Room*.

3. Ono, "Some Notes on the Lisson Gallery Show" (1967; Anthology 15).

4. Ibid.

5. Ibid.

OTHER VERSIONS

1998 ***Half-A-Hospital Room***

First shown: 1998 *Wish Trees for Brazil*, Teatro Nacional, Brasília. With bisected accoutrements of a hospital room, including bed, chair, mirror, towels, etc.

EXHIBITIONS: 1967 *Yoko Ono at Lisson*, Lisson Gallery; 1989 *The Bronze Age*, Cranbrook Academy; 1990 *In Facing*, Riverside Studios; 1991 *Birch Monologue*, Porin Taidemuseo; 1991 *Peace! Friður!* Reykjavík Municipal Art Museum; 1995 *Revolution*, Museum of Contemporary Art, Tokyo; 1997 *Have You Seen the Horizon Lately?* MOMA, Oxford

VISUAL DOCUMENTATION: 1967, photo by Anthony Cox

LITERATURE: Ono, "Some Notes…," *Yoko Ono at Lisson*, exh. cat. (1967); Wolfram, *Art and Artists* (October 1967); Williams, *Contemporary Review* (May 1968); Haskell, *Arias and Objects* (1991), 40; Iles, *Have You Seen the Horizon Lately?* exh. cat. (1997), 51–56; Rico Lacasa, *Wish Trees for Brazil*, exh. cat. (1998), 18

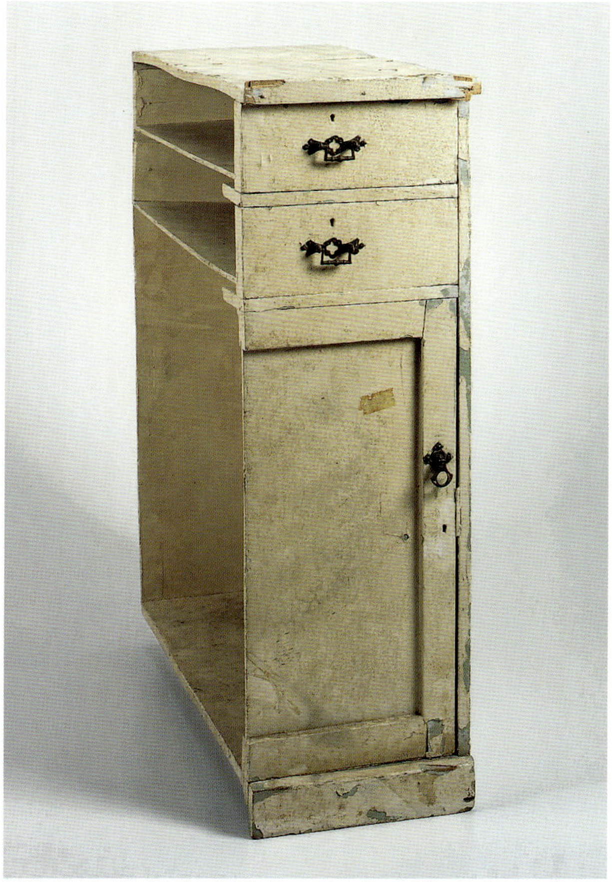

FIGURE 7.15
HALF-A-CABINET FROM
HALF-A-ROOM, 1967

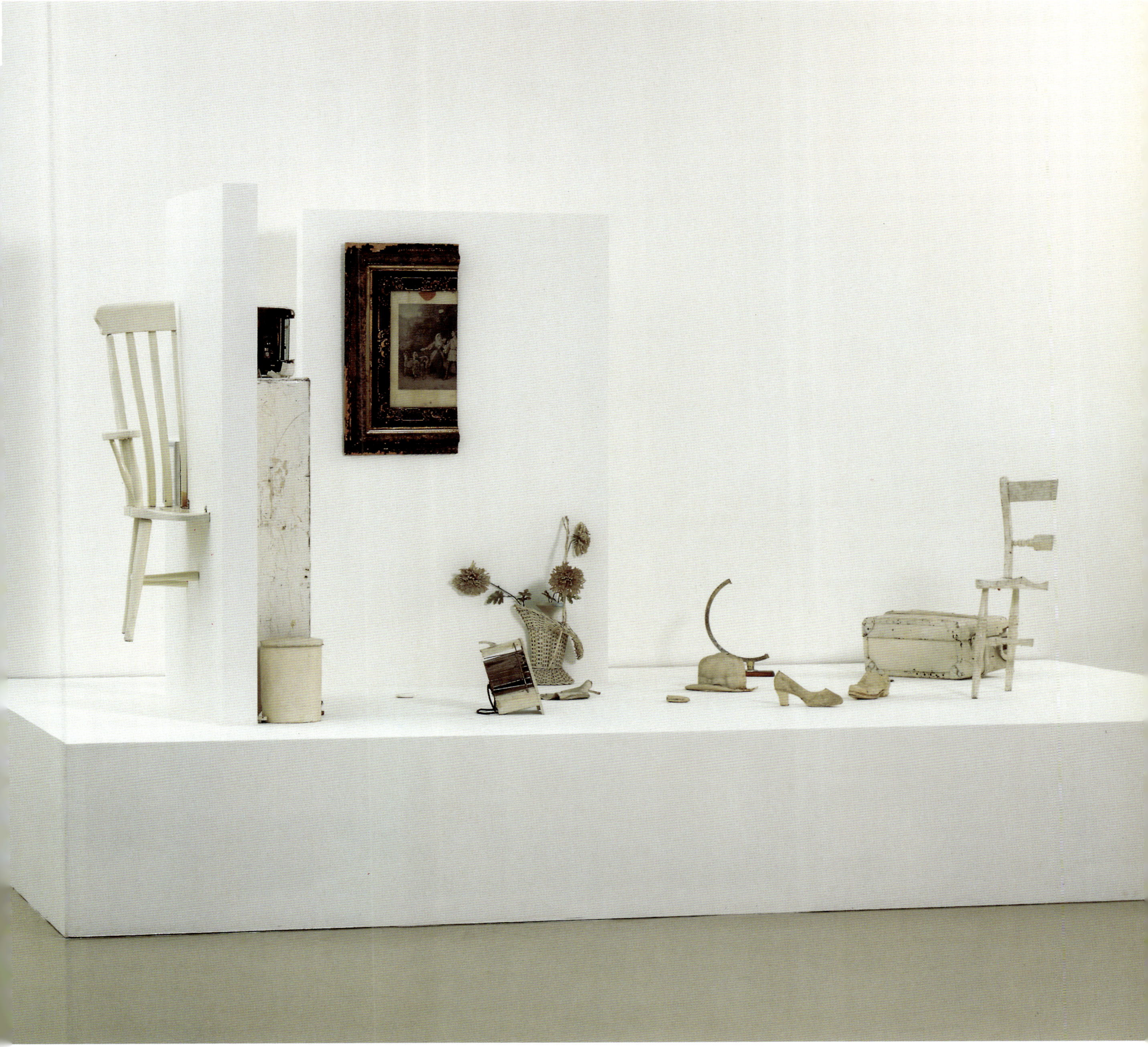

PLATE 20
HALF-A-ROOM, 1967.
INSTALLATION VIEW,
THE ISRAEL MUSEUM,
JERUSALEM, 2000

21 *Corner Painting*, ca. 1966–71

canvas over wood with gilded frame
each side: 16⅜ x 9⅞ x 3¾" (41.9 x 24.9 x 9.5 cm)
Collection of the artist

Ono's published ideas for paintings include a number that she refers to as Position Paintings, which involve unorthodox physical orientations for both viewer and object. In *Painting to Be Stepped On*, for example, one steps on a piece of canvas lying on the floor; *Painting to Shake Hands* requires two people to shake hands through a hole in the canvas. In each case, viewers interact physically with the canvas in unconventional ways that Ono says "bring life experiences into the world of paintings [and] change the classical two-dimensional viewing experience to [one] of more complex dimensions."[1]

Painting's physical and conceptual conventions alike are abandoned in *Corner Painting* and the closely related *Chair Painting* (fig. 7.16). Both examples of Position Paintings, they are canvas-covered, shaped wood panels with elaborate gilt frames. The right angle of *Corner Painting* is architecturally oriented, while the U-shaped *Chair Painting* is meant to fit over the back of a chair. Each object, by virtue of its shape, relates only to a specific kind of space, one not traditionally associated with the display of paintings; viewing either work straight-on would be impossible without significant movement of one's body. Moreover, these "paintings" are blank and unidentifiable as such without their signal gold frames. This absence, along with the emphasis on the position of the viewer's body, connects these works to *Position Piece*, a 1963 text in *Grapefruit* (1964) in which Ono instructs the participant to assume a yoga position, imagine a painting (any painting) for two days, and then destroy it. "In the East," Ono has said, "position is a way of changing life—not by changing life itself, but by changing how you view it."[2]

JR

NOTES

The artist dates this work to one of two periods: either in New York after 1965, or in London before 1971. The object was certainly in the planning stages by the time of her exhibition at the Everson Museum, when George Maciunas included "corner and wrap around paintings with gold leaf frame" in a list of "new objects" he was preparing for Ono for that exhibition (Ono, e-mail to author, October 1999).

1. Other examples cited by the artist include *Painting for the Burial* and *Painting to See the Room* (Ono, e-mail to author, October 1999).

2. Ibid.

OTHER VERSIONS

1971 unstretched canvas
First produced: 1971 *This Is Not Here*, Everson Museum. Without frame

1996 canvas on wood
Edition of 3, with 2 a.p. Wood frame painted in silver leaf

EXHIBITIONS: 1971 *This Is Not Here*, Everson Museum; 1994 *Not Knowing*, Gallery Schlesinger

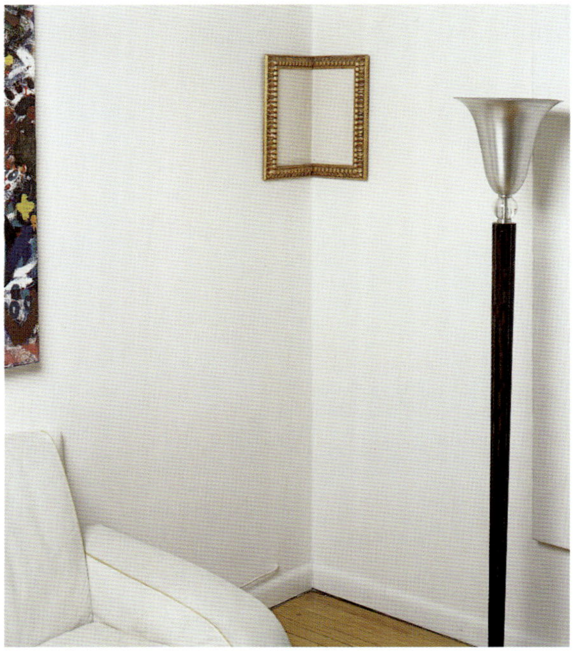

PLATE 21B
CORNER PAINTING, CA. 1966–71. INSTALLATION VIEW, NEW YORK, 2000

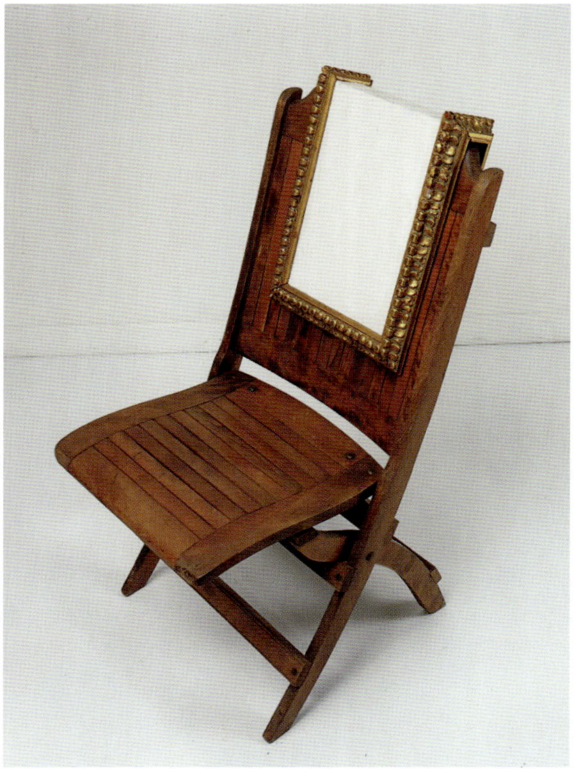

FIGURE 7.16
CHAIR PAINTING, CA. 1966–71. COLLECTION OF BARBARA GOLDFARB, NEW YORK

PLATE 21A
CORNER PAINTING, CA. 1966–71

22 *A Box of Smile,* 1967

sterling silver box, mirror
engraved on front: A BOX OF SMILE Y.O. '67
closed: 2⅝ x 2½ x 2½" (6.8 x 6.4 x 6.4 cm)
Collection of the artist

A Box of Smile is a small, handheld box with a hinged lid that opens to reveal a mirror on the bottom surface of the box. The title of the work functions as a kind of instruction or score, and is usually inscribed on the top or front of the box; the work is performed by any viewer who smiles in surprise upon discovering the mirror inside. For Ono, the box sometimes functioned as a kind of "collection box," or even a means by which to transport a smile from one person to another; in this way, it could be seen as a positive inversion of the mythical Pandora's box, the source of all humankind's sorrows and misfortunes.[1]

The work, which was produced in numerous materials and for various occasions both public and private (fig. 7.17), is one of a number of objects, texts, and films (no. 44) addressing a favorite theme of Ono's—the act of smiling. It is very closely related to *Self Portrait* (1965), a manila envelope containing a mirror, which she assembled and distributed on her own and through Fluxus (fig. 7.3).[2] In this prototypical work, Ono redefined the traditional genre of self-portraiture, letting "self" stand for the viewer rather than the maker, and thus reiterating her belief that everyone is an artist.

JR

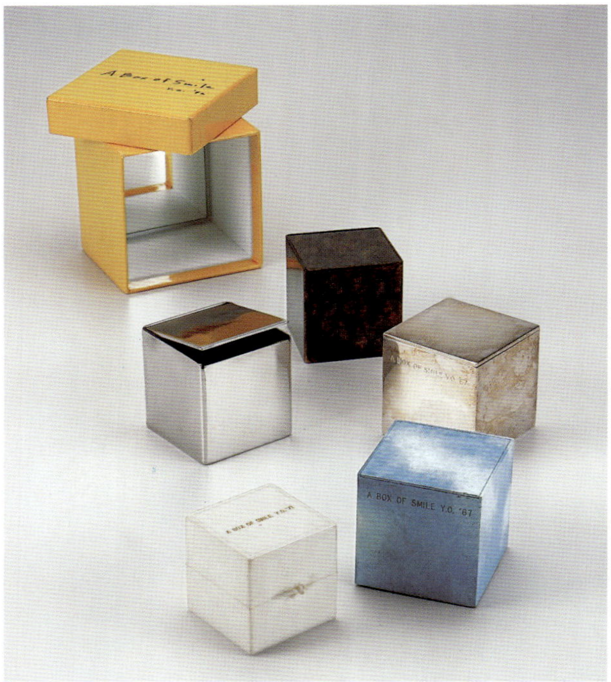

FIGURE 7.17
A BOX OF SMILE,
VARIOUS VERSIONS

NOTES

1. Ono performed *A Box of Smile* with John Lennon and Mike Douglas during the couple's week-long appearance on Douglas's talk show in February 1972.

2. In her self-published *Ono's Sales List* of 1965, she advertised a work called "self portrait," available framed or unframed (see no. 37). The piece was also included in some copies of the Maciunas-edited anthology *Fluxus 1*. See Hendricks, *Fluxus Codex* (1988), 422.

OTHER VERSIONS

1968 platinum
Made as a gift for John Lennon. With sliding lid. Engraved on lid: A BOX OF SMILE / FOR JOHN / YOKO ONO '68

1971 antique wood boxes
Produced by George Maciunas in conjunction with *This Is Not Here*. Approximately six prepared, some with keys. With text: A BOX OF SMILE YOKO ONO '71

1971 plastic
Produced by George Maciunas in conjunction with *This Is Not Here*. Edition unlimited. In two color variations: white with gold inscription and black with gold inscription. Another, possibly unique, variation with transparent top, white bottom, and gold inscription was made by Maciunas around the same time. Engraved on top of lid: A BOX OF SMILE Y.O. '71

1971 stainless steel
Edition of approx. 150. Engraved on front, some with personalized dedication: A BOX OF SMILE / Y.O. '71

1989 bronze
First shown: 1989 *The Bronze Age*, Cranbrook Academy. Edition of 25, each with a different patina. Stamped and numbered on back; engraved on front: A BOX OF SMILE Y.O. '67

1992 cardboard
With fitted, lift-off lid, made in four colors: red, yellow, black, and white. Inscribed on front: A BOX OF SMILE Y.O. '92

1997 bronze
Produced for private distribution as holiday gift. Edition of 35. With blue and white patina in sky pattern. Engraved on front: A BOX OF SMILE Y.O. '67; on back: XMAS '97 YOKO ONO

EXHIBITIONS: Beginning with 1971 *This Is Not Here*, Everson Museum, various versions shown in many of Ono's solo and group exhibitions

LITERATURE: Hendricks, *Fluxus Codex* (1988), 422; McCormick, *Artforum* (February 1989); Haskell, *Arias and Objects* (1991), 57; Iles, *Have You Seen the Horizon Lately?* exh. cat. (1997), 119–21

PLATE 22
A BOX OF SMILE, 1967

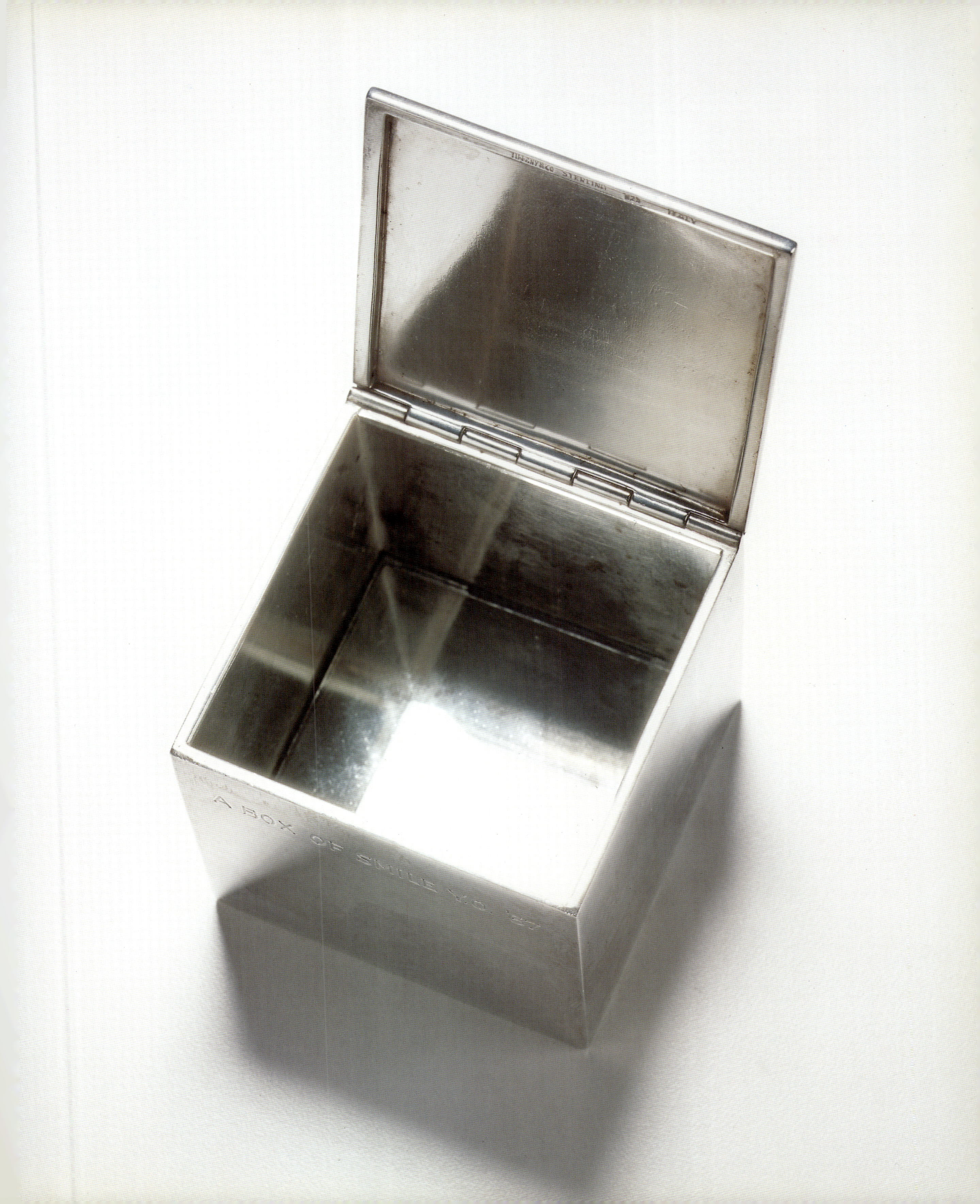
A BOX OF SMILE Y.O. '67

23 *Glass Keys to Open the Skies*, 1967

four glass keys in Plexiglas box with brass hinges
box: 7½ x 10 x 1½" (19.1 x 25.4 x 3.8 cm); keys: l. 5" (12.7 cm)
Collection of the artist

Glass Keys to Open the Skies brings together two leitmotifs in Ono's work: the sky and the key. The former was a comforting presence for Ono during her family's exile from wartime Tokyo:

> I started to love just lying down on the tatami and watching the sky.... It was so high and bright that you felt faint and exhilarated at the same time. Since then, all my life, I have been in love with the sky. Even when everything was falling apart around me, the sky was always there for me.... As I told myself then,...I can never give up on life as long as the sky is there.[1]

The sky came to represent timelessness, constancy, and unlimited space in her work; the key has served as a metaphor for knowledge, as well as desire.

Glass Keys to Open the Skies brings these themes together as a box of keys designated for a job that is both unnecessary and impossible: to unlock that which is already open but will always remain out of reach. Our (and Ono's) desire to possess that eternal, constant, and infinite space is intense, but these keys—made of fragile glass—are unsuitable for any but a conceptual, or magical, unlocking.

JR

NOTES

1. Ono, "SKYTALK with love to Denmark" (1992) in *Color, Fly, Sky*, exh. cat. (1992), 5.

OTHER VERSIONS

1964/1967 single key
With twine, tag. Inscription handwritten on tag: SKY No. 1

ca. 1967 eight glass keys
In Plexiglas box with brass hinges

1967–68 (winter) five single glass keys, each in knitted case
One in yellow knit case given to each member of the Beatles. One additional, in white knit case, given to John Lennon

1971 single glass key
Designed and constructed by George Maciunas in conjunction with *This Is Not Here* and included in *Everson Catalogue Box*

1985 ***Seasons Boxes***
First shown: 1985 *Rain Dance*, 292 Lafayette Street, New York. Four Plexiglas boxes with single glass key inside. Inscribed on front: A GLASS KEY / FOR WINTER [SPRING, SUMMER, FALL] / y.o. '85. Shown with flashlight and handwritten instructions

1988 ***Keys to Open the Skies***
First shown: 1989 *Objects, Films*, Whitney Museum. Edition of 9. Four bronze keys, bronze plate

1992 ***A Key to Open a Faded Memory***
Edition of 40, with 5 a.p. Foam heart with single glass key in paper box

1992 ***A Key to Open a Universe***
Planned edition of 350 (250 produced), part of *Onobox*. Glass key, string, white paper tag with printed text: A key to open a universe. / Yoko Ono '92

1993 ***A Key to Open a Faded Memory***
Three unique versions produced. Gold Murano glass key suspended in two-part block of clear Murano glass. Engraved on back: A Key To Open A Faded Memory Y.O. 93

EXHIBITIONS: 1971 *This Is Not Here*, Everson Museum; 1989 *Objects, Films*, Whitney Museum; 1989 *The Bronze Age*, Cranbrook Academy; 1990 *In Facing*, Riverside Studios; 1990 *Insound/Instructure*, Henie Onstad Arts Centre; 1990 *Fumie*, Sōgetsu Art Museum; 1990 *To See the Skies*, Fondazione Mudima; 1991 *Birch Monologue*, Porin Taidemuseo; 1991 *Peace! Friður!* Reykjavík Municipal Art Museum; 1997 *Have You Seen the Horizon Lately?* MOMA, Oxford

LITERATURE: Iles, *Have You Seen the Horizon Lately?* exh. cat. (1997), 56–57

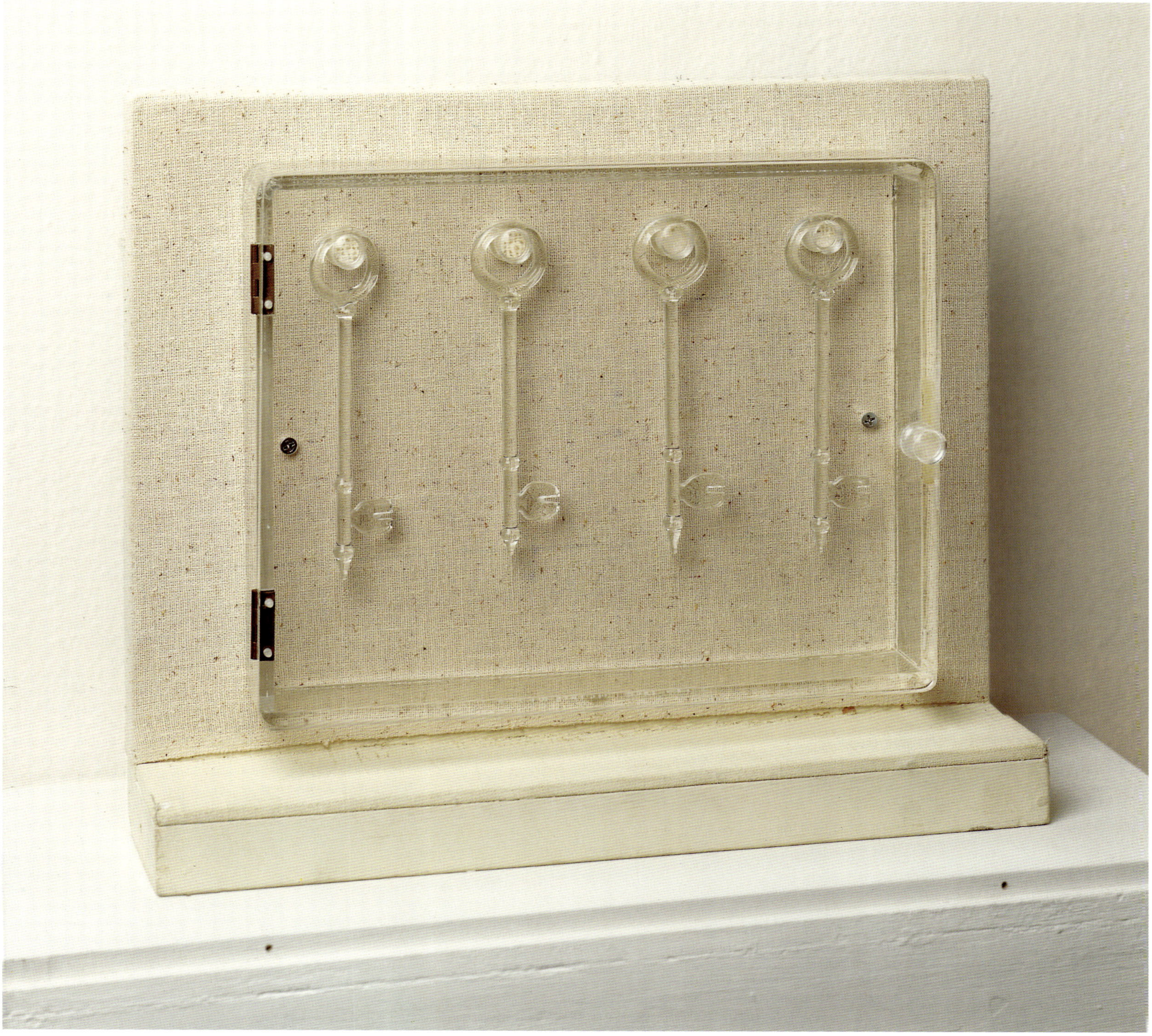

PLATE 23
GLASS KEYS TO OPEN THE SKIES, 1967

24 *Three Spoons,* 1967

four silver spoons, Plexiglas pedestal with brass plaque
engraved on plaque: THREE SPOONS / Y.O.'67
spoons: approx. 6" (15.2 cm) long (dimensions vary);
pedestal: 55 x 11¼ x 11¼" (139.7 x 28.5 x 28.5 cm)
The Gilbert and Lila Silverman Fluxus Collection, Detroit

Ono's presentation of four spoons with the contradictory caption "three spoons" poses a Zen-like riddle about the relationship between language, object, image, illusion, and reality. The artist herself has said that the work is about "illusional beliefs, illusional situations, illusional relationships. I've realized that the maps in our minds have very little to do with reality."[1] The paradox she presents in this work recalls Magritte's famous painting of a pipe with the inscription "this is not a pipe," which pointed out the obvious truth that neither the image nor the name of a thing is the thing itself. *Three Spoons* pushes this idea further by suggesting that even the thing itself cannot necessarily be assumed to be the thing itself. At a time when Minimalist and Conceptualist artists were looking to both phenomenology and semiology as methods through which to explore objects, Ono developed a view that embraced both. "I think it is possible to see a chair as it is," she wrote in 1966. "But when you burn the chair, you suddenly realize that the chair in your head did not burn or disappear."[2] On a more personal level, Ono has said the work was for her "the flushing out of a painful memory" and that the fourth, unnamed spoon represents the extraneous, the unnoticed, and the missing—all positions of emotional isolation.[3]

Though Ono has made several versions of this work, the format is always the same: four matching spoons lying unfixed on a Plexiglas pedestal with a brass label. Since its first presentation in 1967, the spoons have been replaced at least once, probably due to loss or damage. As with Duchamp's Readymades, which also were reconstructed and replicated many times, our inability to freeze the work in time or space only underlines its conceptual basis.
JR

NOTES

1. Ono, e-mail to author, September 1999.
2. Ono, "To the Wesleyan People" (1966; Anthology 14).
3. Ono, e-mail to author, September 1999. The loss implicit in *Three Spoons* is made poignantly explicit in the 1988 bronze *Four Spoons*: three spoons alongside an empty, spoon-shaped depression.

OTHER VERSIONS
1970
First shown: 1970 *Fluxfest Presentation John Lennon & Yoko Ono +: Blue Room*, New York. Sign reads: 3 spoons

1988 bronze (fig. 7.18)
First shown: 1989 *Objects, Films*, Whitney Museum. Edition of 9. Entitled: *Four Spoons*. Engraved: FOUR SPOONS Y.O. 88

EXHIBITIONS: 1967 *Yoko Ono at Lisson*, Lisson Gallery; 1971 *This Is Not Here*, Everson Museum; 1989 *Objects, Films*, Whitney Museum; 1989 *The Bronze Age*, Cranbrook Academy; 1990 *In Facing*, Riverside Studios; 1990 *Insound/Instructure*, Henie Onstad Arts Centre; 1990 *Fumie*, Sōgetsu Art Museum; 1990 *To See the Skies*, Fondazione Mudima; 1991 *Birch Monologue*, Porin Taidemuseo; 1991 *Peace! Friður!* Reykjavík Municipal Art Museum

VISUAL DOCUMENTATION: probably 1967, photo by unknown photographer, pub. Hendricks, *Fluxus Codex* (1988)

LITERATURE: Benedikt, *Art and Artists* (January 1972); Hendricks, *Fluxus Codex* (1988), 424–25; Haskell, *Objects, Films*, exh. brochure (1989), 4; Haskell, *Arias and Objects* (1991), 58

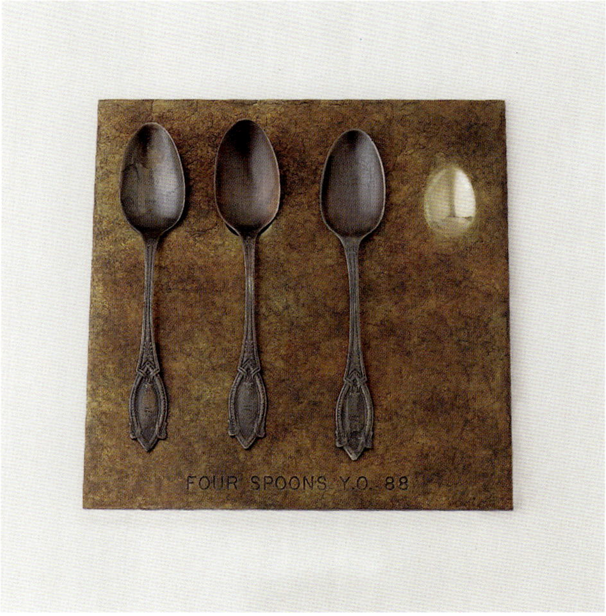

FIGURE 7.18
FOUR SPOONS, 1988

PLATE 24
THREE SPOONS, 1967

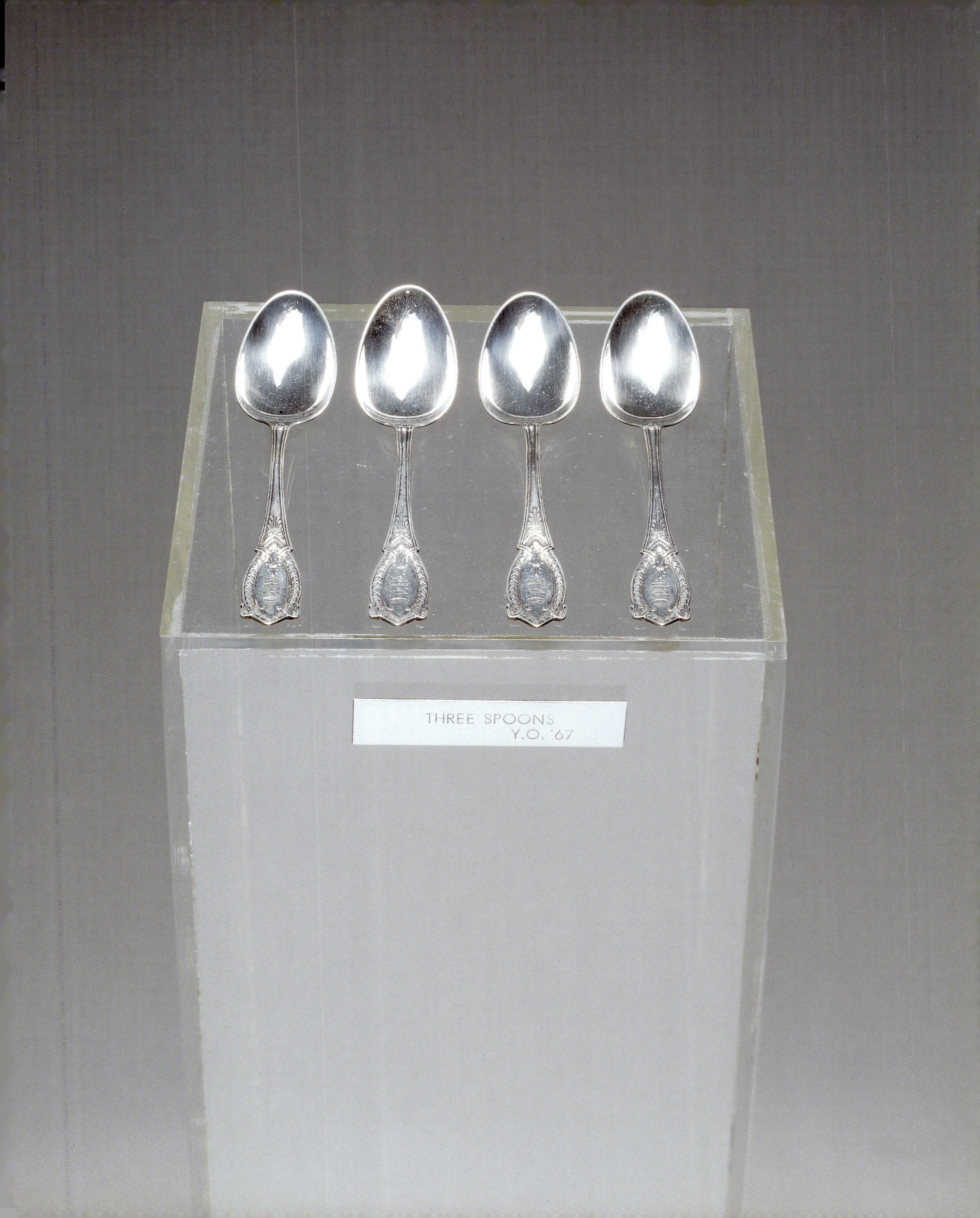
THREE SPOONS
Y.O. '67

25 *White Chess Set,* 1966

(originally known as *Chess Set*)
wood chess table, two wood chairs, wood chess set, all painted white
engraved on brass plate on table underside: CHESS SET FOR PLAYING AS LONG AS YOU CAN REMEMBER WHERE ALL YOUR PIECES ARE YOKO ONO 1966
table: 28½ x 24 x 24" (72 x 61 x 61 cm)
Hahn Collection Museum Moderner Kunst, Vienna

An avid chess player, Ono has made numerous objects based on a 1966 concept for an all-white chess set. Her simple alteration—painting the board and pieces a uniform white—derails any ordinary play of the game according to traditional rules. Instead, the players lose track of their pieces as the game progresses; ideally this leads to a shared understanding of their mutual concerns and a new relationship based on empathy rather than opposition. Peace is then attained on a small scale; perhaps the rules will even be revised so that the game can continue. While *White Chess Set* is of course closely related to Ono's consistent and varied activities toward the attainment of world peace, its one-on-one scenario is consistent with her wish that her work encourage each of us first to "deal with oneself."[1]

The first version of this piece was made for Ono's 1966 Indica Gallery exhibition and titled simply *Chess Set*. It consisted of a table whose surface was a chessboard made of alternating raised squares, a set of chess pieces, and two chairs, everything painted white. An accompanying sign attached to the table instructed viewers to play. Subsequent realizations of the concept, beginning with the 1987 bronze version made as a tribute to John Cage on his seventy-fifth birthday, were entitled *Play It By Trust*, a phrase that points toward the benefits (and difficulty) of recognizing our mutual interdependence.

Ono's interest in chess is contextually linked to that of Fluxus mentor Marcel Duchamp, who in the 1920s announced his withdrawal from art-making to pursue his passion for chess. Some Fluxus artists dealt with the game in their works; Ono herself conceived several variant objects, including a "game of *go*, all transparent," a "game of chess with no queen—that must be imagined,"[2] and a chess set in which the pieces were hidden inside identical individual containers.[3] None of these appear to have been realized.
JR

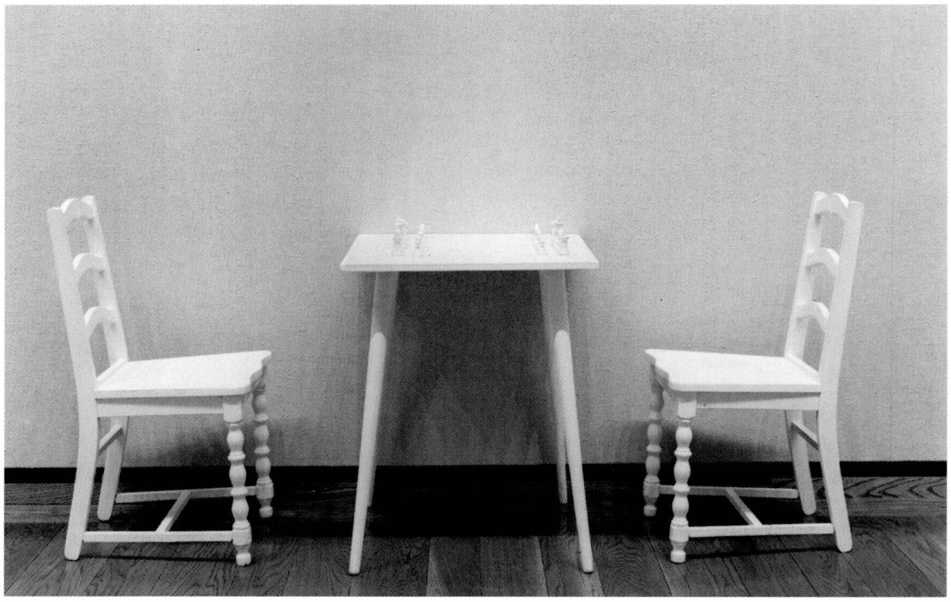

FIGURE 7.19
WHITE CHESS SET,
1966. INSTALLATION VIEW, EVERSON MUSEUM OF ART, SYRACUSE, 1971

NOTES

Plate 25 documents *White Chess Set* as it appeared in 1966. Sometime between then and 1978, when it entered the collection of the Museum Moderner Kunst, Vienna, many of the chess pieces were lost. In its current state, the work includes only pawns and rooks.

1. Ono, "To the Wesleyan People" (1966; Anthology 14).

2. See Ono, unpublished notes for Indica exhibition, collection of the artist. Ono dates her idea for the transparent game of *go* (Japanese board game with black and white stones) to 1962, just after her return to Japan (e-mail to author, October 1999).

3. Hendricks, *Fluxus Codex* (1988), 421.

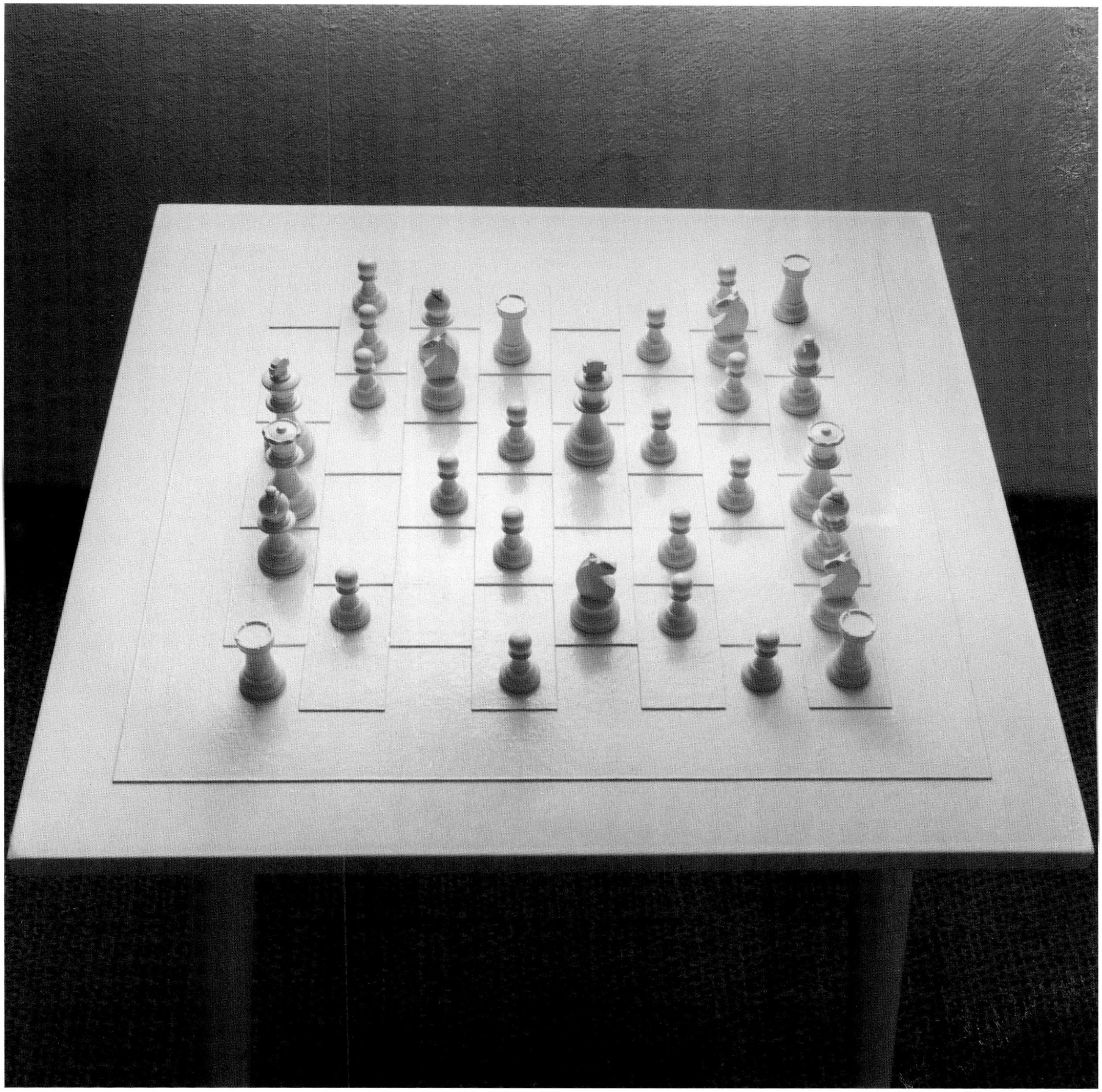

PLATE 25
WHITE CHESS SET, 1966.
DETAIL: INSTALLATION
VIEW, INDICA GALLERY,
LONDON, 1966

OTHER VERSIONS

1970 ***All White Chess Set***
Proposed edition of 20. Acrylic on wood. Published by Bag Productions, Ascot, England. Pocket version in proposed unlimited edition also produced

1987 ***Play It By Trust*** (bronze)
First shown: *Tribute to John Cage*, Carl Solway Gallery. Edition of 8. Engraved on chessboard: PLAY IT BY TRUST YOKO ONO

1990 ***Play It By Trust*** (floor version)
First shown: 1990 *En Trance*, Randers Kunstmuseum. Plywood board with plastic pieces

1991 ***Play It By Trust*** (fig. 7.20)
First shown: 1991 *Social Sculpture*, Vrej Baghoomian Gallery. Ten chess sets, one table, twenty chairs, framed text. Inscribed on silver plaques: PLAY IT BY TRUST YO '66–'91

1992 ***Play It By Trust***
First shown: 1992 *Excellent*, Malmö Kunsthalle. Made of cardboard

1994 ***Play It By Trust*** (garden version)
Installed at the artist's country home. Cast concrete and marble dust. Variation dated 1999 installed at Longhouse Reserve, Easthampton, New York

1997 ***Play It By Trust*** (fig. 7.21)
First shown: 1997 *En Trance—Ex It*, Lonja del Pescado, Alicante. Six chess sets, six tables, twelve Hoffman-style chairs. Variation dated 1996 in the artist's collection, chess set with antique table; also a few other variations with old furniture

1997 ***Play It By Trust***
First shown: 1997 *Have You Seen the Horizon Lately?* MOMA, Oxford. Chess set, table, two chairs, painted wood

1998 ***Play It By Trust***
First shown: 1998 *Crickets*, Serge Ziegler Galerie. Chess set, table with built-in board, two chairs, painted wood

1998 ***Play It By Trust***
First shown: 1998 *Wish Trees for Brazil*, Teatro Nacional, Brasília. Six chess sets, six oval tables, twelve chairs, painted wood

1999 ***Play It By Trust***
First shown: 1999 *Codex*, Roskilde Museum. Chess set, table, two chairs, painted wood. Inscribed on silver plaques: PLAY IT BY TRUST YO '66–'99

EXHIBITIONS: 1966 *Yoko at Indica*, Indica Gallery; 1971 *This Is Not Here*, Everson Museum; 1972 *Documenta 5*

VISUAL DOCUMENTATION: 1966, photo by Iain Macmillan, pub. *Yoko at Indica*, exh. cat. (1972)

LITERATURE: *Museum Moderner Kunst: Sammlung Hahn* (1979), n.p.; Hendricks, *Fluxus Codex* (1988), 421; McCormick, *Artforum* (February 1989); Haskell, *Arias and Objects* (1991), 138; Concannon, *Fly*, exh. cat. (1996), 15; Rico Lacasa, *En Trance—Ex It*, exh. cat. (1997), 40, 42; Iles, *Have You Seen the Horizon Lately?* exh. cat. (1997), 96–98; Rico Lacasa, *Wish Trees for Brazil*, exh. cat (1998), 18, 20

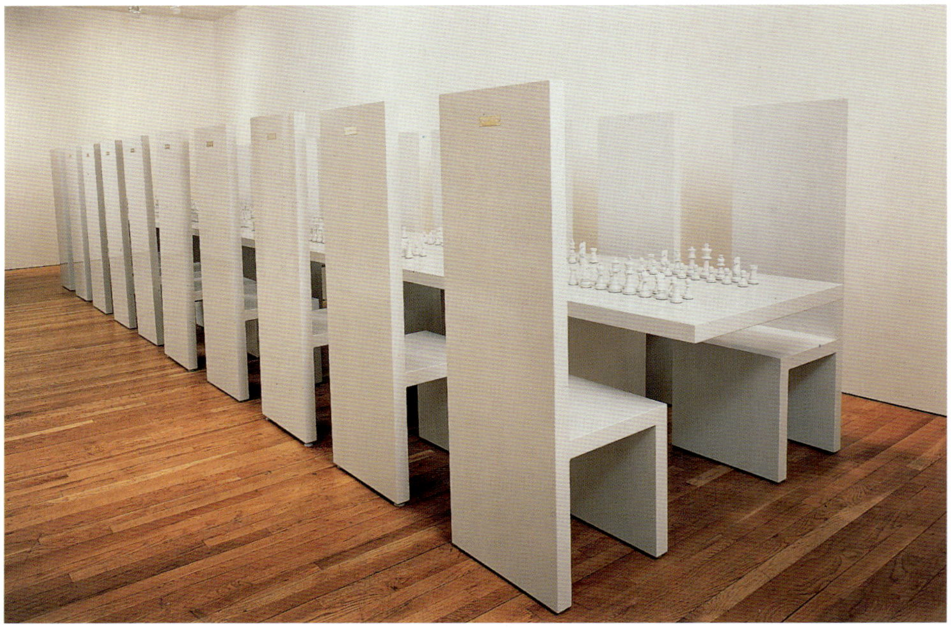

FIGURE 7.20
PLAY IT BY TRUST, 1991, INSTALLATION VIEW, VREJ BAGHOOMIAN GALLERY, NEW YORK, 1991

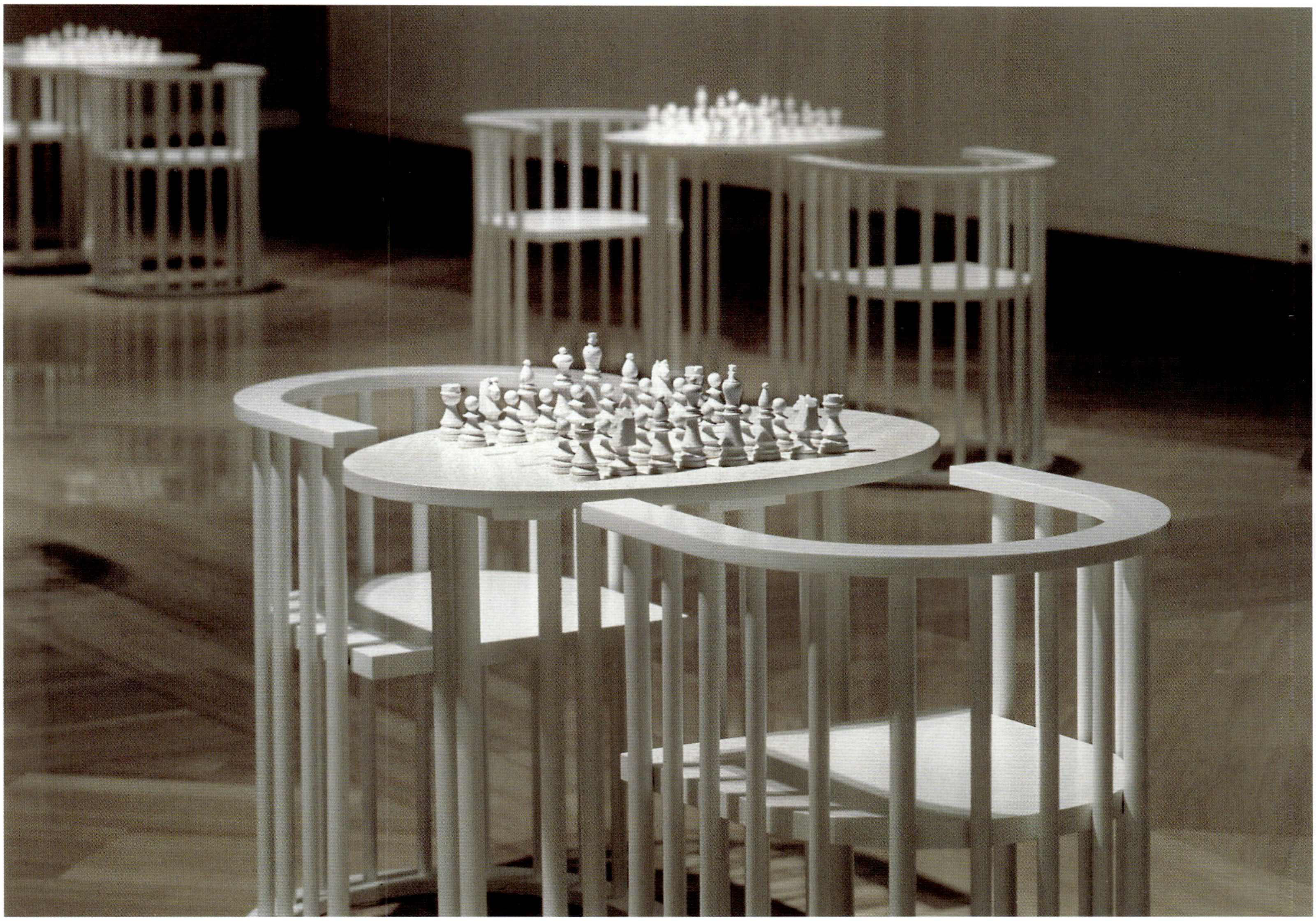

FIGURE 7.21
PLAY IT BY TRUST,
1997. INSTALLATION VIEW, LONJA DEL PESCADO, ALICANTE, 1997

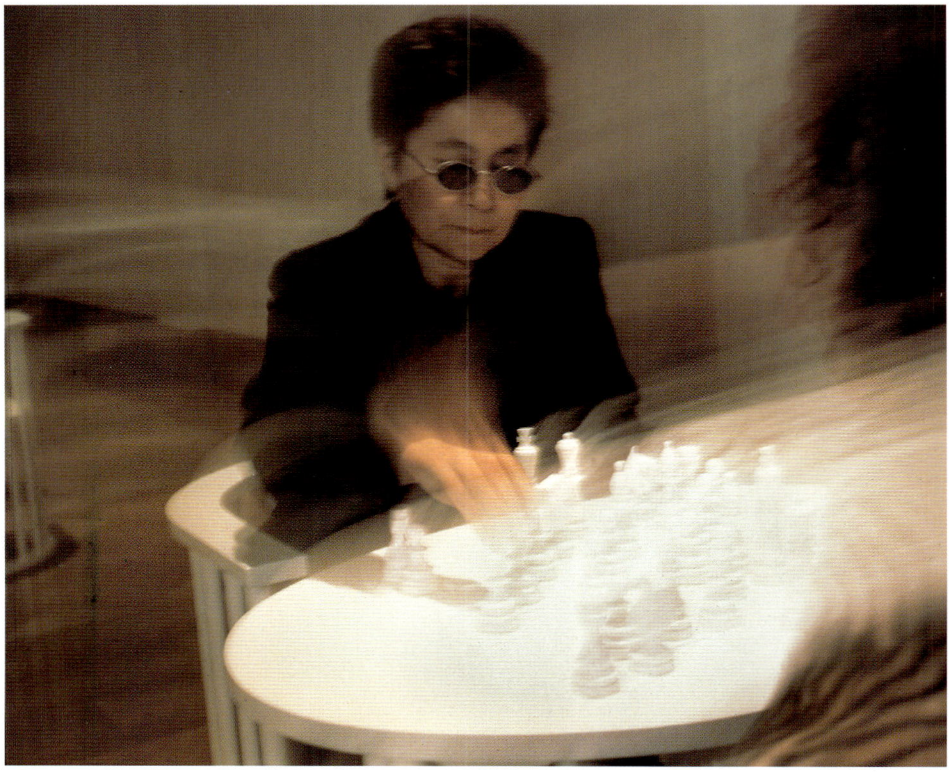

FIGURE 7.22
ONO PLAYING CHESS ON
PLAY IT BY TRUST,
1997

26 *AMAZE,* 1971

Plexiglas, toilet, wood
8 x 16 x 16' (243.8 x 487.6 x 487.6 cm)
original disassembled

AMAZE was designed and built for Ono's 1971 retrospective at the Everson Museum. Her old friend, Fluxus "chairman" George Maciunas, collaborated with Ono on this and other works in the show.[1] It was a 16-foot-square structure made of clear Plexiglas. The center cubicle—where a visitor arrived if he or she "solved" the maze—was constructed of one-way-mirror-finish Plexiglas. Occupants of the cubical could see out in all directions, but were mostly invisible to viewers on the outside. This central cubicle contained a toilet.[2]

To date, *AMAZE* is the physical culmination of Ono's long-standing interest in light as a sculptural material that is intangible, temporal, and colorless. The first published ideas date to 1965 and include a group of architectural ideas dedicated to Maciunas, who had studied architecture at Carnegie Institute of Technology, Pittsburgh. One of them reads, in part:

> Build a house
> with walls which come into existence
> only with the particular prism effect
> created by the sunset
>
> If necessary, some walls or parts of
> the walls can be made of material other
> than light[3]

The first physical manifestation related to these ideas appeared in 1966. *Parts of Light House*, comprising small prismlike pieces of Plexiglas displayed in a mound on a Plexiglas pedestal, was shown at Indica Gallery along with the related work *Painting to Let the Evening Light Go Through* (no. 8). *AMAZE* adds a layer of meaning with its partially enclosed, but not private, space of the toilet. The predicament of being simultaneously hidden and utterly exposed links *AMAZE* with the 1971 Plexiglas box *Hide Me* (fig. 7.7), as well as with Ono's infamous performance event *Bag Piece* (no. 31).

In addition to its connection to Fluxus environments by Maciunas, Ay-O, and others, *AMAZE* must be seen in the context of a more generalized interest among artists during the 1960s in labyrinths, corridors, and other (often disorienting) architectural structures.[4] However, the pun in this work's title (along with its undeniable resemblance to a funhouse) signals a certain lightheartedness on the artist's part, and suggests that she was less interested in exploring the mechanics of perception and physical orientation than in provoking a transformative psychological experience.

JR

NOTES

1. Maciunas also constructed two other environment works for Ono, both titled *Portrait of John Lennon as a Young Cloud*. The first, made for the 1970 event *Fluxfest Presentation of John Lennon & Yoko Ono +*, was a maze consisting of a series of "trick" doors that visitors made their way through. The second, built for the Everson exhibition, was a wall of drawers and cupboards, all empty save one that contained a microscope labeled "John's smile." See Hendricks, *Fluxus Codex* (1988), 129, 422.

2. The toilet was used as a motif by Ono in performances of the early 1960s, including her 1961 concert at Carnegie Recital Hall in which the curtain rose on Ono seated on a toilet, with her back to the audience; during the concert, amplified flushing sounds could be heard from offstage.

3. Dated spring 1965, PIECES DEDICATED / TO / GEORGE MACIUNAS /, / THE PHANTOM ARCHITECT was first self-published. Pieces from this work, later called *8 Architecture Pieces Dedicated to a Phantom Architect*, appear in *Grapefruit* (1971). See also Ono, "Some Notes on the Lisson Gallery Show" (1967; Anthology 15), in which she describes a similar "light house" under the heading, "Some practical and tangible future plans."

4. For example, works by Robert Smithson, Bruce Nauman, Robert Morris, Dan Graham, Kusama Yayoi, and Lucas Samaras. See Iles, *Have You Seen the Horizon Lately?* exh. cat. (1997), 89–90.

EXHIBITIONS: 1971 *This Is Not Here*, Everson Museum; 1997 *Have You Seen the Horizon Lately?* MOMA, Oxford (reconstruction)

VISUAL DOCUMENTATION: 1971, photo by Iain Macmillan, pub. *Have You Seen the Horizon Lately?* exh. cat. (1997)

LITERATURE: Wasserman, *Artforum* (January 1972); Hendricks, *Fluxus Codex* (1988), 82, 129, 421–22; Iles, *Have You Seen the Horizon Lately?* exh. cat. (1997), 84–90

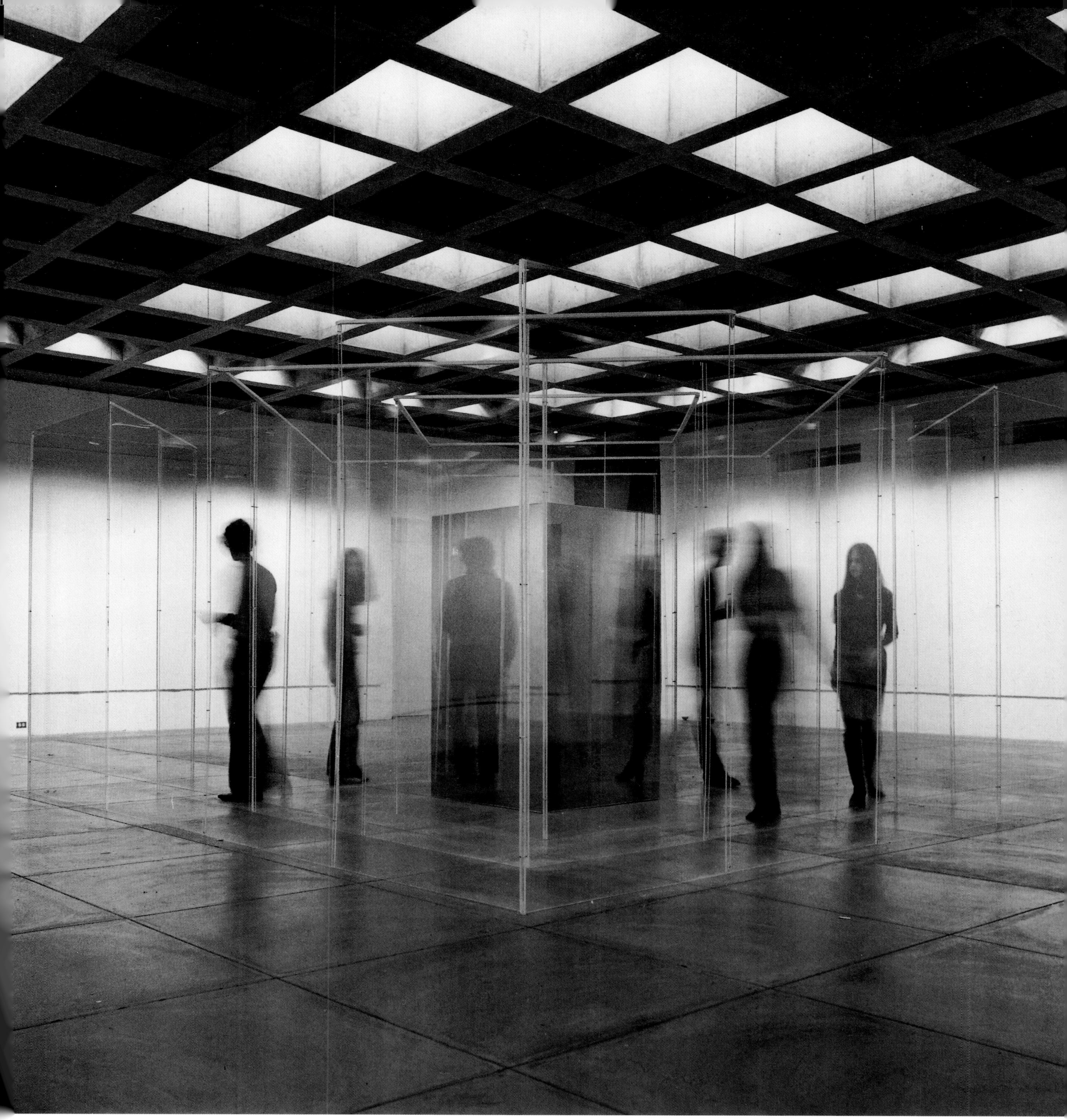

PLATE 26
AMAZE, 1971.
INSTALLATION VIEW,
EVERSON MUSEUM OF
ART, SYRACUSE, 1971

EVENTS AND PERFORMANCES

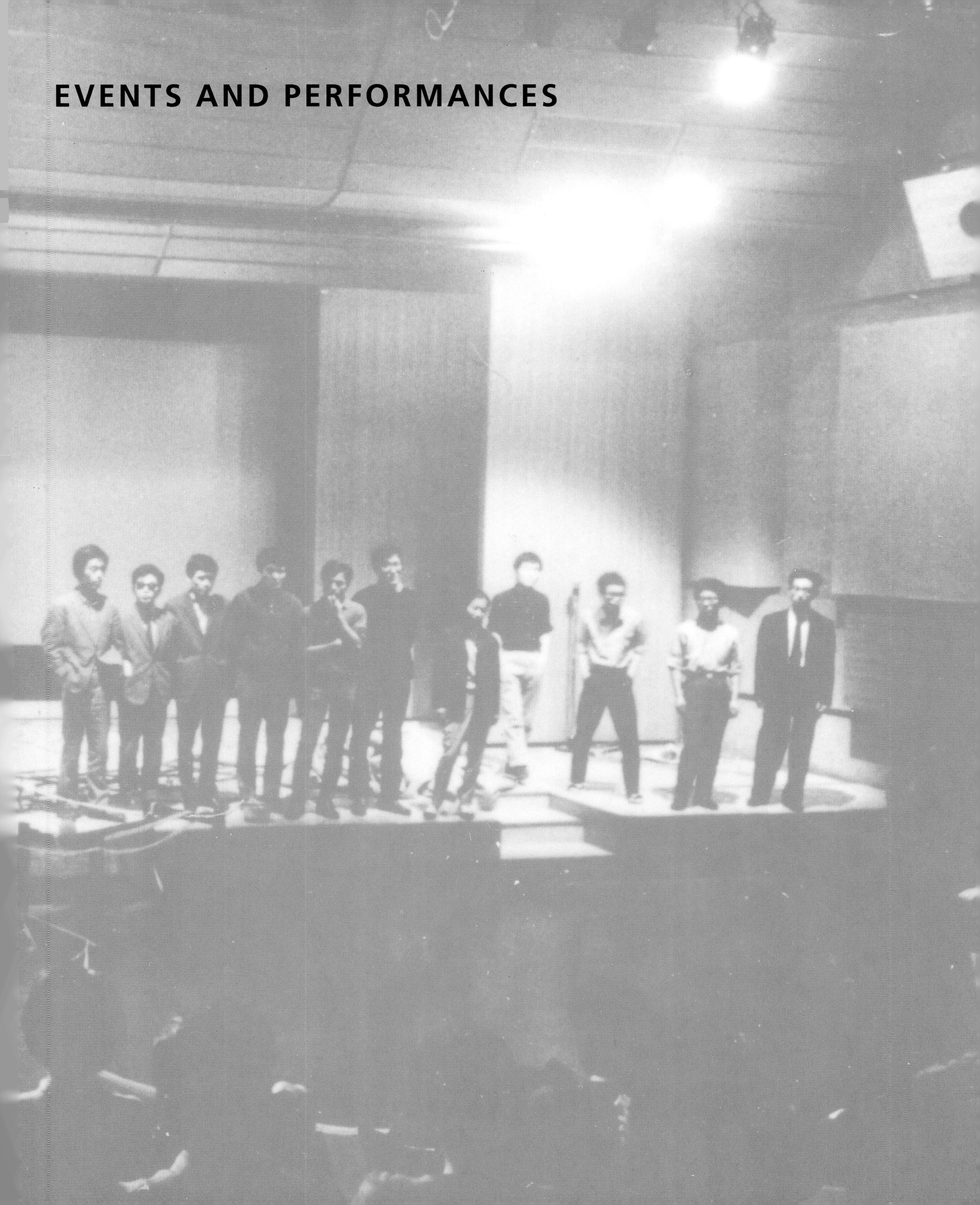

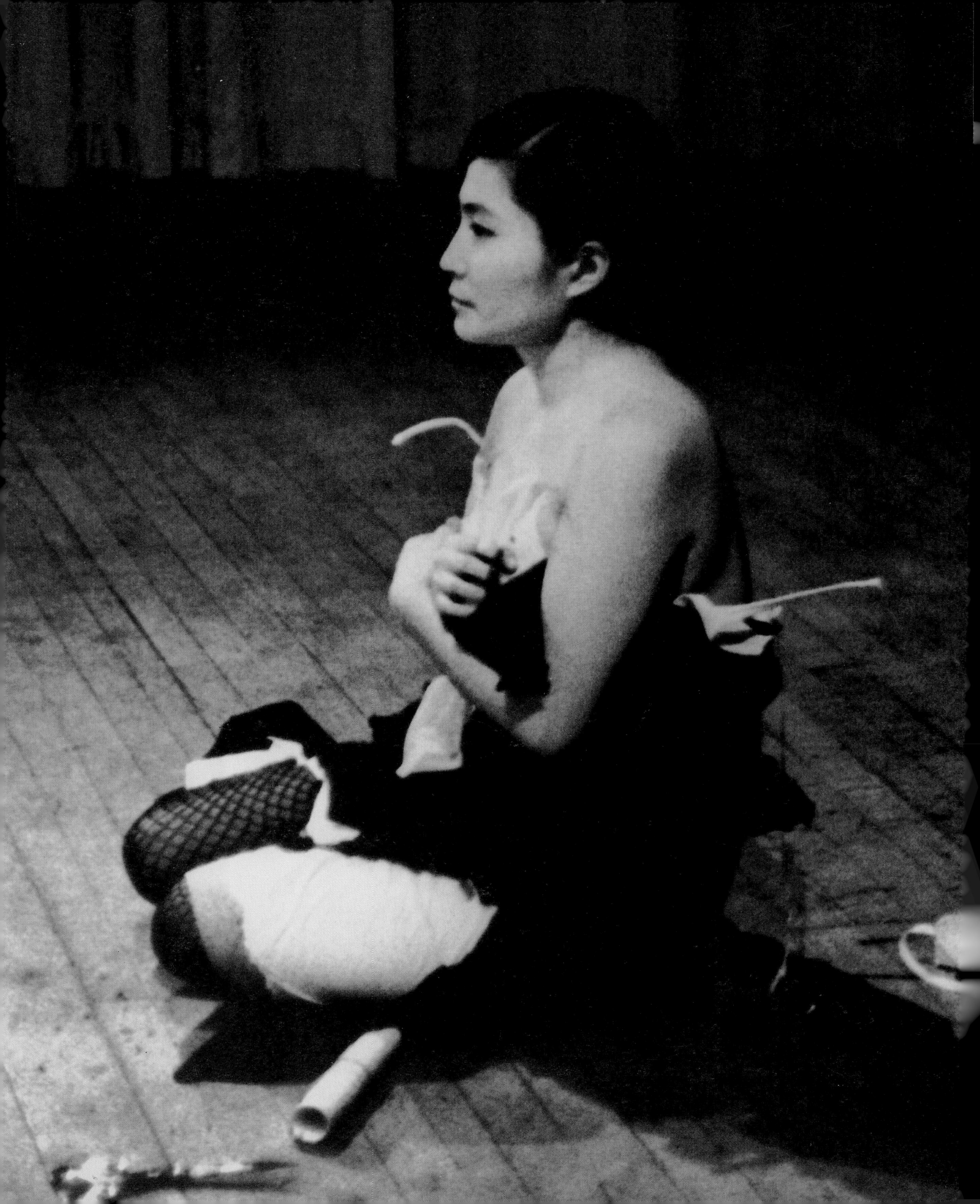

Being Undyed: The Meeting of Mind and Matter in Yoko Ono's Events

KRISTINE STILES

Yoko Ono's ideas for events are often found in her "instructions" for actions. These brief, poetic texts offer direction for an encounter with a particular idea, which may be performed physically or mentally, envisioning the circumstances of a prospective perceptual event. At the same time, they are the foundation of an art that sets in motion a directed interplay between internal concepts (manifest in words) and external actions (the actual events of perceptual apprehension). Ono's performances represent an aesthetic deliberation on and enactment of the precarious meeting of mind and matter. They may be defined as a conjunction of idea and objective world in the event of an act carried out by the body.[1]

The bridge from idea to act that links mind and world in an event may be approached through the German word *Weltinnenraum*, which names the inner ambient space (*innenraum*) of self-contained consciousness (*Welt*).[2] *Weltinnenraum* describes those aspects of the self, knowable through language, and is also a name for the boundary of mind between that which can and cannot be accessed through logos, but nevertheless pervades the body at the level of cellular knowledge. The term stands for and creates a visual representation of the architectonics of the mind's imaginative interplay with itself. Ono adopted this word for seven self-contained sets of sequentially numbered instructions, each titled *Card Piece* (figs. 8.1–2). In each of these instructions, Ono created the scene for the event of the opposition between objective things and consciousness. She constructed a conceptual card game that explores the existentialist duality of knowing and doing, being and becoming, nature and freedom.

CARD PIECE I

Walk to the center of your Weltinnenraum.
Leave a card.

CARD PIECE II

Cut a hole in the center of your
Weltinnenraum.
Exchange.

CARD PIECE III

Shuffle your Weltinnenraums.
Hand one to a person on the street.
Ask him to forget about it.

CARD PIECE IV

Place a stone on each one of the
Weltinnenraums in the world.
Number them.

FIGURE 8.1
CARD PIECE I–IV FROM *GRAPEFRUIT* (1964)

PLATE 30C
CUT PIECE, CARNEGIE RECITAL HALL, NEW YORK, 1964

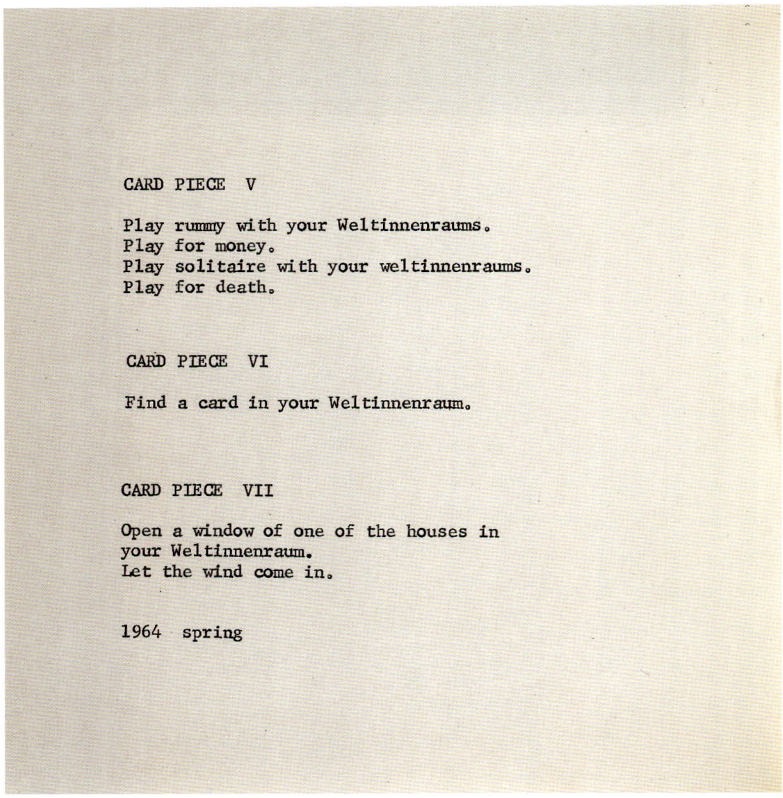

CARD PIECE V

Play rummy with your Weltinnenraums.
Play for money.
Play solitaire with your weltinnenraums.
Play for death.

CARD PIECE VI

Find a card in your Weltinnenraum.

CARD PIECE VII

Open a window of one of the houses in
your Weltinnenraum.
Let the wind come in.

1964 spring

FIGURE 8.2
CARD PIECE V–VII FROM *GRAPEFRUIT* (1964)

Imagine Ono as a player in each of these *Card Pieces* grappling with performing an action in relation to herself, an action wherein she becomes self-conscious for the purpose of self-observation. It is a conceptual game between consciousness and the self as an object of self-perception.[3] The series begins in *Card Piece I* when she leaves a mark of her presence—"Leave a card." It progresses to the act of separation from self when she "cuts a hole in the center" of her *Weltinnenraum* in *Card Piece II* and then conceptually exchanges the hole with the dissociated aspect of her self, with whom she engages in the event. Next, in *Card Piece III*, Ono hands out a part of her inner worlds to a person on the street, who is instructed to forget the gift. By asking the recipient to forget this gift, the artist anticipates that her *Weltinnenraum* will merge (by being forgotten) with the core of another person's self (that is unknowable as *Weltinnenraum*). The ensuing *Card Piece IV* requires the placement of numbered stones in all the interior mental spaces in the world. A "stone" has multiple implications, particularly in the iconography of Ono's work. But the stones may also refer to the previous *Card Piece III*, like an act of burdened mourning, an event that creates monuments for the forgotten gift of self. In *Card Piece V* the game with the self is no longer the earnest spiritual and philosophical exploration of the prior sequence. It deteriorates into a game of chance—first for money, then for death. *Card Piece VI* reengages the player in the game itself through the task of finding "a card in your Weltinnenraum." Finally, the game concludes in *Card Piece VII* when the player opens a window of her *Weltinnenraum* to let the wind in.

The concept of *Weltinnenraum* can be found in the romantic poetry of Rainer Maria Rilke. His analysis of the existential melancholic condition of modernity, particularly in relation to Christianity and death, was, in part, gleaned through his contemplation (as a traveler) of the *Weltinnenraum*—"the soul, culture, and speech"—of strangers in foreign lands.[4] Moreover, it is a concept that connotes the passing of Orpheus (in Rilke's poem "Sonette an Orpheus," 1922) between the exterior and interior worlds, "clear[ing] the way for the moment of epiphany."[5]

Rilke's usage of *Weltinnenraum* parallels aspects of Yoko Ono's childhood that are related to her self-identification with grapefruit. She first tasted this fruit in about 1935 (at the age of two) when she visited the United States. This encounter led her to associate both the grapefruit and the German language with her often absent father, who worked in the United States, spoke German, and was an accomplished pianist, and who shared his strong interest in German music with his daughter. During her college years, the artist adopted her memory of this hybrid fruit as a metaphor for her own hybrid experience between East and West. This self-identification with the grapefruit culminated in "Of a Grapefruit in the World of Park," a story she modified for her event *A Grapefruit in the World of Park*, performed at the Village Gate and Carnegie Recital Hall in 1961 (no. 52).

Together, the *Weltinnenraum* (a mental space) and the grapefruit (a material object) comprise the semiotics of Ono's multicultural, intellectual, and emotional experience. Her circumstances demanded that she be simultaneously inside and outside both Eastern and Western culture, much in the way in which she experienced the dichotomy of body and mind. Her instructions create "events" as analogs for passing from one experiential sphere to another, from one conceptual plane to another. In them, she sought aesthetic melding as a process and means for perceptually transcending the boundaries of material phenomena in order to gain an epiphany, thereby transforming conditions of Being. In her notes on her Wesleyan College lecture, Ono spoke about the "Event bent" in her work.[6] Differentiating Events from Happenings, she maintained that Events were not "an assimilation of all the other arts…but an extrication from the various sensory perceptions." Unlike the "get togetherness" of the Happening, an Event was a place for "dealing with oneself," she explained, and added that her Events were "something" like a "'wish' or 'hope.'"

Ono's events, culled from her own private experiences, always draw the spectator into an act of self-reflection, either through the mechanism of textual instructions or by actual engagement in the work of art. In this regard, Ono's instructions are distinctive in their imperative grammatical structure (fig. 8.3). They are calls to action demanding imaginative and decisive behavioral responses. Sometimes these works direct readers to take very specific actions, typified by those she performed at the 1966 *Destruction in Art Symposium (DIAS)* (no. 33): *Hide Piece*: "Hide." *Question Piece*: "Question." *Sweep Piece*: "Sweep." *Cut Piece*: "Cut." *Touch Piece*: "Touch." *Fly Piece*: "Fly." *Promise Piece*: "Promise." In contrast, "decide" is the first word of the first instruction in *Grapefruit*: it not only explicitly requires the ability for abstract, critical thought that comes to a resolution but indicates its conclusion in certainty.[7]

Derived from the Latin *decidere*, meaning "to cut," this sense of "decide" is integral to Ono's most famous action, *Cut Piece*, and is one of the most frequently used verbs in her instructions written between 1962 and 1964. To cut presupposes a material thing into which one might cleave or make an incision, or trim something off, away, or from the real, and is therefore often associated with pain. In addition to "decide," "imagine" is another one of the handful of verbal imperatives that reoccur in these early instructions. "Imagine" is a more ethereal notion, a conceptual action of the mind, insinuating the creation of a mental image, dissociating (if not distracting) one from suffering. In Ono's published instructions for events, these two verbs establish a system of meaning across which other frequently used verbs indicating creativity negotiate the action of decision: verbs like "let," "do," "make," "place," "use," "send," "leave," and "take."

It was through the imperative tense of verbs that Ono translated her abstract philosophical meditations into concrete materiality. But action (and its connection to perception) is also rendered accessible through the simplicity of her means. In *Bag Piece* (no. 31), the body is surrounded by the mediating tissue of a material membrane, in the same way that the complex multidimensionality of a human personality is hidden behind the enclosure of skin. "You can only see the outline of the bag," Ono explained. "That's all we see of each other."[8] In *Bed-In for Peace* (no. 34), she and Lennon inverted and opened the bag as a bed, attempting to visualize the physical site of love as an agent powerful enough to end the Vietnam War "if you want it." In these simple and direct ways, Ono's events move perception beyond the visible and auditory in order to explore a corporeal means for communicating intangible emotive states.

The intersection between intellect and emotion in her own personal iconography may be approached through the noun "stone" and the verb "hide." For example, she joined these two states of mind in her song "Dogtown."[9] There stone becomes a physical response to pain and its hidden dimension: "One day I'll be just a little stone/Nobody'll know that the stone had such emotions…." She performed *Hide Piece* in various explicit ways, ranging from hiding in a large canvas sheet on an unlit stage (1961) to hiding behind a three-foot pole for thirty minutes (1966). A key to her life's work may be represented in the metaphor of hiding (which she, her brother, her sister, and her mother did in the Japanese mountains during World War II), with the resulting experience of feeling like stone. Certainly there are many veiled references to the hydrogen bomb in her work. Perhaps the most vivid is a section of *AOS—To David Tudor*, performed at Carnegie Recital Hall in 1961. There in utter darkness she created "a mountain of human bodies," a pile of flesh

FLY PIECE

Fly.

1963 summer

FIGURE 8.3
FLY PIECE FROM *GRAPEFRUIT* (1964)

that a performer would "illuminate dimly by holding a match or a lighter near a leg or a face or a hand, re-creating a situation of blindness."[10] Her aim was to create an environment for the event in which one's whole being strained for understanding. Indeed, from the bombing of Hiroshima and Nagasaki to the murder of John Lennon, Yoko Ono's world has been steeped in a violence and desperation that one has to strain to understand.[11]

By making her internal suffering present in physical events that reconstituted ideas and emotions in bodily presentations, Ono's aesthetic translations of mind into matter assisted her own and others' survival. The physical manifestation of psychological conditions that are key to the relationship between her instructions and her events corresponds to Ono's strong interest in the theories of psychiatrist Wilhelm Reich, who theorized the role of physical therapy in resolving anxieties and neuroses. His concepts of primal forms of "life energy," the function of sexual energy, and his combination of psychoanalysis and physical therapy appealed to Ono and to many artists interested in visualizing aesthetic concepts in bodily presentations. As she honed her concepts of events in the late 1950s, Reich's work drew international attention after his persecution by the U.S. government.[12] In this regard, the evolution of Happenings, Fluxus, Body Art, Action Art, and Performance Art, to which Ono's work uniquely contributed, enabled art to express and viewers to feel "the process of history...passing from potentiality into act."[13]

Ono's particular contribution to this process of rendering history as a bodily act was to comprehend that the reservoirs of psychological experience that are manifest in the physical body can be extended into the visual domain by corporeal traces that visualize aspects of consciousness. Given this insight, a further interpretation of *Cut Piece* might suggest that the artist created a confrontational language of interaction in order to emphasize the process of cleaving through to a knowledge of interior substance, the world of the "Weltinnenraums." In this way, perhaps she augmented participants' ability to cut through to the hidden sources of Being where questions of human will, purpose, destiny, and teleology coincide with considerations of God. No wonder a British woman who witnessed Ono perform *Cut Piece* at *DIAS* could state that before seeing Ono's performance she thought the artist was "ugly," but after witnessing her event she found her "beautiful."[14]

Ono's thoughts about God may be approached through her probing essay "The Word of a Fabricator" (1962) and her January 1966 address "To the Wesleyan People." In the latter, she described dance as "once the way people communicated with God and godliness in people." This association draws one back to *Cut Piece* as a ritualized event, a kind of conceptual dance communicating with God. Therein the rent of a cut in the performance might stand for the empty gash in the world left by the absence of godliness in human behavior.[15] In this sense, *Cut Piece* acquires an even more tragic and metaphysical tone and implication as it becomes a representation of the translation of mental concepts into corporeal and spiritual deliberations on the problem of ethical human interaction. Ono had already pursued these ideas four years earlier in "The Word of a Fabricator," an essay that suggests ways in which the artist thought about God and offers insight into her meditations on the body and its use in art. It also bears directly on her study of existential philosophy and her attempts to address the role of false consciousness in both ideas and acts.

Ono began her essay by expressing an "attraction to the first man in human history who lied...when he said he saw God." The first lie was a form of "stylization" tied to "the human desire to free oneself from the irrational rationality of life."[16] She argued that "an endless pessimism" resides at the foundation of such eternal lies and "that nothing but a fictional order could rescue us from death." She then recited the convoluted manner in which false consciousness occurs. First, humanity holds in contempt "any fictional act in the realm of consciousness." Then, failing to understand that human laws are artificial constructs, it naturalizes its own fictions in order to dominate nature. Finally, humanity imitates nature, regarding its chance operations as superior to the lies of its fictional order, and hypocritically "succumbing to and adopting random operation" of nature as its own.[17] Given this false consciousness, the twenty-nine-year-old artist asked, "Is a human body worthy of such trust?" She answered:

> We are talking about a body of a betrayer/l'étranger to the natural world, who carries the misfortune of being capable of even controlling the length of his life by will.[18]

Ono's solution to contemporary man who is "soaked to the bones with a fabricator called consciousness" was to create rituals to "rationalize the irrationality in us, humans," by exploring the "world of fictional rules: the laws of the fabricator." She concluded:

> I cannot stand the fact that everything is the accumulation of "distortion" owing to one's slanted view. I want the truth. I want to feel the truth by any possible means. I want someone or something to let me feel it.... I know no other way but to present the structure of a drama which assumes fiction as fiction, that is, as fabricated truth.

In this last remarkable statement, Ono anticipated by fifteen years the semiotic analysis of theatrical performance proposed by the distinguished Italian linguist and novelist, Umberto Eco, who wrote in 1977:

> An object, first recognized as a real object, is then assumed as a sign in order to refer back to another object (or to a class of objects) whose constitutive stuff is the same as that of the representing object.... The very moment the audience accepts the convention of the *mise en scène*, every element of that portion of the world that has been framed becomes significant. And as soon as the performer (or image) makes a performative statement—I am acting—by this implicit statement the actor tells the truth since he announces that from that moment on he will lie.[19]

Ono, the self-confessed "Fabricator," offers a truth in her events through the presentational format which is, itself, a lie insofar as the act cannot attain truth through its own means. This conundrum represents the operation of what Ono identified as the "irrational rationality" that is nature.

To unlock this aspect of nature means to become what I shall call "being undyed," namely, to receive in consciousness through the event of the unity of mind and matter that which is already immanent. Being undyed may be related to Ono's use of white in many of her works. As she noted:

> In Japan when you get married, women wear white and men wear black. The reason for that is man has to stick to his principles and black can't be changed; whereas white is able to be any colour. In other words the woman has to be willing to be dyed any colour.[20]

White is nothing and everything, the absence of presence and its fullness. White also embodies the conceptual, an ideal associated with purity, beauty of form, or grace. "Grace," according to the *I Ching*, the Chinese Book of Changes, relates directly to an aesthetic approach to life, and means being undyed, a state that "consists not in external ornamentation but in allowing the original material to stand forth, beautified by being given form."[21] Ono learned the value of form *in* itself, in part, through her study of and skill in writing *haiku*. Bashō, the ancient teacher and reformer of *haiku*, advised his students to learn from the thing itself. "To submerge oneself into the object until its intrinsic nature becomes apparent, stimulating poetic impulse," he wrote, and added that "every form of insentient existence—plants, stones, or utensils—has its individual feelings similar to those of men."[22] Being undyed means becoming open to things in themselves and equally to becoming attentive to the infinite dimensionality of one's "Weltinnenraums" as they intersect in acts that create world events. Ono's work presents instructions for following such a path. As Renato Poggioli wrote in his monumental study and theory of the avant-garde and its poetics:

> in the poetics of the Word, it is not God who is made Word, but Word made God.... In other words, for modern poetry the word is not sound-sense, but idea-thing; in its vision the Word is not spirit which became flesh, but flesh which became spirit.[23]

Poetic parallels may be drawn between Ono's meditations on chance and truth and those of the French Symbolist poet Stéphane Mallarmé, who considered the relationship between chance and the infinite. Moreover, both artists undertook such contemplation during periods of severe emotional crises, when thoughts of suicide were paramount. Although Ono criticized the imitation of chance operations of nature, she did not deny the role of chance in modeling all experience, and shaping the interstice between consciousness and the objective world through the conditions of acts. But since perception is always mediated by the incidental, fortuitous, and random, it is the "irrational rationality," or chance, that reconciles ideas with matter, creating the conditions that give fleeting meaning and structure to the encounter between imagination and world.

Mallarmé analyzed these paradoxical aspects of chance in his poem "Igitur" (1869). The poet, like his hero Igitur (meaning "meanwhile"—the suspended state between two acts), pondered the nothingness of consciousness in relationship to considerations of his own death.[24] Mallarmé wrote:

> Briefly, in an act where chance is in play, chance always accomplishes its own Idea in affirming or negating itself. Confronting its existence, negation and affirmation fail. [Chance] contains the Absurd—implies it, but in the latent state and prevents it from existing: which permits the Infinite to be.[25]

Mallarmé overcame his suicidal thoughts when he realized that the very act of recognizing both the existence and the absurdity of chance defeats either its negation or affirmation, thus opening up a space for the infinite. In this way, chance challenges the instrumental reason of philosophy, religion, and history, all of which fail to account for how chance inevitably, absurdly, and profoundly forms existence. Only an art that dissects, plays with, and meditates on this paradox may approach the ways chance reconciles existential nothingness (death) and the infinite on the stage of Being.

Ono has sought her truth in carefully constructed acts of chance correspondence between idea and the objective world. By opening experience to unexpected insights and perceptions of the invisible, yet material, order of things, her events offer the possibility for others to find their own truths. Is this not the lesson of *Beat Piece*? "Listen to a heartbeat."[26]

NOTES

1. Fluxus artists used texts for scoring behavior, reflecting their debt to John Cage's experiments with the codes of musical composition. George Brecht introduced the term "event score" to describe his brief texts in the fall of 1959, writing that the word "event" described "the total, multi-sensory experience" that could emerge from a "situation," the "event" being the smallest unit of a "situation." See George Brecht, "The Origin of Events" (1970) in *Happening & Fluxus*, exh. cat. (1970), n.p.

2. The "s" at the end of the word in Ono's *Card Piece III–V* indicates the multiplicity of these inner states of mind and consciousness, grammatically attaching the English language plural to the German term.

3. In college, Ono was particularly interested in the philosophers Friedrich Nietzsche, Jean-Paul Sartre, Albert Camus, Alan Watts, C. G. Jung, Franz Kafka, and especially Wilhelm Reich.

4. Kay-Volker Koschel, *Biographisch-Bibliographisches Kirchenlexikon*, vol. 8 (Herzberg: Verlag Traugott Bautz, 1994), 361–68; published on the Internet at http://www.bautz.de/bbkl/r/rilke_r_m.shtml. See also Werner Günther, *Weltinnenraum, Die Dichtung Rainer Maria Rilkes* (Berlin-Bielefeld: Erick Schmidt Verlag, 1952); and Vera Hauschild, ed., *Rilke Heute der Ort des Dichters in der Moderne* (Frankfurt Am Main: Suhrkamp, 1997).

5. Fatima Naqui Peters, "Bookreview of Annette Gerok-Reiter's *Wink und Wandlung: Komposition und Poetik in Rilke's 'Sonette an Orpheus'* (Tübingen: Niemeyer, 1996)," *The Germanic Review* 72–73 (summer 1997): 242–45.

6. Ono, "To the Wesleyan People" (1966; Anthology 14).

7. The instruction is *Secret Piece* (*Grapefruit*, 1964). See fig. 11.1.

8. Ono, conversation with author, 23 August 1999.

9. Ono, "Dogtown," in *Season of Glass*, LP (1981).

10. Ono explained that what she performed at Carnegie Recital Hall was her most original work. Yet when pressed to discuss these events, she demurred, preferring to wait until other artists comment on them or documents can be discovered pertaining to them (Ono, conversation with author, 23 August 1999).

11. "The Word of a Fabricator" (see note 16), for example, was written in a moment of "sheer loneliness and the punishment I received for being fiercely independent, [and] a few months after I had written the essay, I voluntarily entered a 'rest home,' the one Yayoi Kusama would make famous a decade later. I felt a strong need to 'hide'" (Ono, e-mail to author, 29 August 1999).

12. Much of his work was destroyed by the Pure Food and Drug Administration, and he was imprisoned in the Federal Penitentiary at Lewisburg, Pennsylvania, where he died in 1957.

13. Renato Poggioli, *The Theory of the Avant-Garde*, trans. Gerald Fitzgerald (Cambridge: Harvard University Press, 1968), 154–55. This is the phrase Poggioli used to describe how one might approach the historical reconstruction of the "historicity of artistic experience in our day" in order to grasp art not as a "monument or document, but as a drama and action, as a work in process."

14. Unidentified woman interviewed by Tom Lopez in an unpublished tape, "Yoko Ono at Africa Center" (1966), collection of the artist.

15. Ono's father and mother were, respectively, a nonpracticing Christian and a nonpracticing Buddhist. More important, her mother had Ono tutored in world religions beginning at the age of five.

16. Ono, "The Word of a Fabricator" (1962, translated by Yoko Ono 1999; Anthology 12). All further quotes from this essay come from this translation.

17. Ono's criticism of chance operations established her own philosophical and aesthetic identity apart from that of John Cage and his many followers. This is a noteworthy position for a young female artist, who was then traveling and performing in Japan with her husband Ichiyanagi and their friend Cage.

18. The reference to "l'étranger" summons Albert Camus's book *The Stranger* (1946).

19. Umberto Eco, "Semiotics of Theatrical Performance," *The Drama Review* 21, no. 1 (March 1977): 115.

20. Robert Enright, "Instructions in the Marital Arts: A Conversation with Yoko Ono," *Border Crossings* 13, no. 1 (January 1994): 33.

21. *The I Ching*, trans. Richard Wilhelm, foreword by C. G. Jung (Princeton: Princeton University Press, 1950), 494–95.

22. R. H. Blyth, *A History of Haiku*, vol. 1, *From the Beginning Up to Issa* (Tokyo: The Hokuseido Press, 1963), 13.

23. Poggioli, 199.

24. Leo Bersani has argued that in "Igitur," Mallarmé staged a "radical temptation: that of suppressing any consciousness *of* (the world or the self) as the precondition for a suicidal, non-articulated 'gathering-in' of the mind—or in other terms, for a divorce of consciousness from all existential circumstance" (Leo Bersani, *The Death of Stéphane Mallarmé* [Cambridge: Cambridge University Press, 1982], 61).

25. *Stéphane Mallarmé: Selected Poetry and Prose*, ed. Mary Ann Caws (New York: A New Directions Book, 1982), 99.

26. Score for *Beat Piece* from "Record of 13 Concert Piece Performances" in *Grapefruit* (1970), n.p.

27 *Works of Yoko Ono,* 1962

concert and exhibition at Sōgetsu Art Center, Tokyo, May 24

Ono made her debut in the world of the Japanese avant-garde through Sōgetsu Art Center, a project of Sōgetsu Kaikan, the headquarters of an established flower arrangement school. From 1959, the Art Center had actively introduced programs of experimental music and art by Japanese and Western artists to Tokyo audiences.[1] Several press previews treated Ono as a novelty, a young female avant-garde composer who had come back from New York after ten years. For example, the influential Japanese art critic Takiguchi Shūzō said:

> What a strange artist has come. What she is doing, however, is natural and logical. I consider it as a natural "action" against contemporary art, which has corrupted and has been standardized and confused.[2]

The multimedia program consisted of four sections: Events, Music, Poems (fig. 14.5), and *Instructions for Paintings* (no. 3); the last two were exhibited in the Kaikan's hallway for a longer time. The Events and Music sections were performed onstage by Ono and more than thirty vanguard luminaries, including Akasegawa Genpei (artist), Akiyama Kuniharu (music critic), Hijikata Tatsumi (dancer), Ichiyanagi Toshi (composer), Kobayashi Kenji (violinist), Kosugi Takehisa (composer), Nakahara Yūsuke (art critic), Takahashi Yūji (pianist), Yasunao Tone (musician), and Yoshimura Masunobu (artist).

In addition to works listed in the program, many small works such as *Lighting Piece*, *Hide Piece*, *Wind Piece*, *Question Piece*, and *Audience Piece* were incorporated into or performed simultaneously with larger pieces.[3] For *Sweep Piece*, for example, musician Mizuno Shūkō kept sweeping the stage throughout the entire program.[4] The evening began with Ono's solo *A Piano Piece to See the Skies*, in three stages: repetitions of "inaudible sounds," "sounds that reached the sky," and "breaths."[5] In the last phase, still out of breath, Ono lit a match and smoked a cigarette in slow motion, an action which was called *Lighting Piece*.[6]

In *Of a Grapefruit in the World of Park*, fourteen participants repeated acts of their choice for twenty-five minutes in reaction to Ono's recitation of her poem in English. While lighting each other by flashlights, the participants performed such actions as writing on a blackboard, making sounds with toy instruments, and throwing soapy water onto others.[7] *A Piece for Strawberries and Violin* experimented with sounds as byproducts of actions such as eating fruit and breaking things. Contact microphones, the most advanced audio technology of the time, were attached to the performers, whose movements produced various sounds.

For *The Pulse*, seven performers sitting in front of microphones at a table made different sounds each time they solved a mathematical question.[8] Ono's handwritten questions, lettered from A to K,

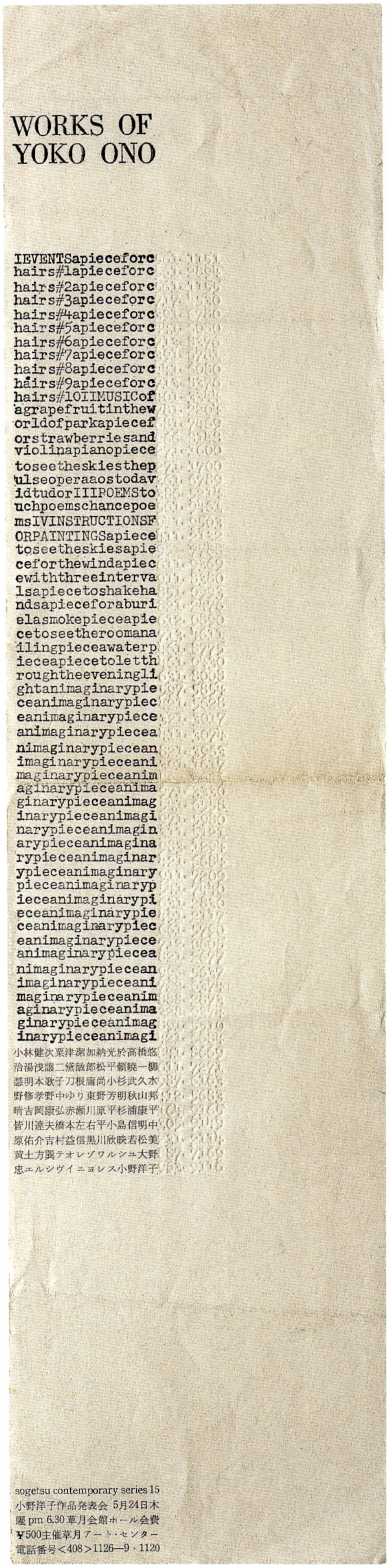
WORKS OF
YOKO ONO

IEVENTSapieceforc
hairs#1apieceforc
hairs#2apieceforc
hairs#3apieceforc
hairs#4apieceforc
hairs#5apieceforc
hairs#6apieceforc
hairs#7apieceforc
hairs#8apieceforc
hairs#9apieceforc
hairs#10IIMUSICof
agrapefruitinthew
orldofparkapiecef
orstrawberriesand
violinapianopiece
toseetheskiesthep
ulseoperaaostodav
idtudorIIIPOEMSto
uchpoemschancepoe
msIVINSTRUCTIONSF
ORPAINTINGSapiece
toseetheskiesapie
ceforthewindapiec
ewiththreeinterva
lsapiecetoshakeha
ndsapieceforaburi
elasmokepieceapie
cetoseetheroomana
ilingpieceawaterp
ieceapiecetoletth
roughtheeveningli
ghtanimaginarypie
ceanimaginarypiec
eanimaginarypiece
animaginarypiecea
nimaginarypiecean
imaginarypieceani
maginarypieceanim
aginarypieceanima
ginarypieceanimag
inarypieceanimagi
narypieceanimagin
arypieceanimagina
rypieceanimaginar
ypieceanimaginary
pieceanimaginaryp
ieceanimaginarypi
eceanimaginarypie
ceanimaginarypiec
eanimaginarypiece
animaginarypiecea
nimaginarypiecean
imaginarypieceani
maginarypieceanim
aginarypieceanima
ginarypieceanimag
inarypieceanimagi
小林健次粟津潔加納光於高橋悠
治湯浅譲二篠敏郎松平頼暁一柳
慧明本歌子刀根康尚小杉武久水
野修孝野中ゆり東野芳明秋山邦
晴吉岡康弘赤瀬川原平杉浦康平
皆川達夫橋本左右平小島信明中
原佑介吉村益信黒川欣映若松美
黄土方巽テオレゾワルシユ大野
忠エルシヴイニヨレス小野洋子

sogetsu contemporary series 15
小野洋子作品発表会 5月24日木
曜 pm 6.30 草月会館ホール会費
¥500主催草月アート・センター
電話番号＜408＞1126—9・1120

PLATE 27A
PROGRAM, ***WORKS OF YOKO ONO,*** 1962

most likely had their source in a middle-school math textbook.[9] Although the score (entitled *The Pulse for Chamber Music* and included in *Grapefruit*, 1964) did not specify what sounds performers should make, the length of each pause was determined by the difficulty each performer had in solving the question. One of the performers, composer Mayuzumi Toshirō, played a *tsuzumi*, a small Japanese drum. Accompaniment was also provided by bird songs from a tape recorder and the sound of a telephone being dialed.

A series of ten events, *A Piece for Chairs I–X*, were also performed. In one, several people sat in chairs reading newspapers, and then cut the chair legs with a saw. In *A Piece for Chairs VI*, several participants dragged around chairs bound to their bodies. One reviewer noted that in her pieces Ono "treated humans as objects" by "creating a strange drama between a chair and a human, that is, a wondrous interaction between minds and objects."[10]

The last piece, *AOS—To David Tudor*, was "an opera without any sound of instruments."[11] Its five acts included a number of participants reading newspapers in different languages by the light of a flashlight or a match flame; several men bound by rope to different objects proceeding from one side of the stage to the other and back;[12] speeches of historic figures such as Hitler and the Japanese emperor played on a tape recorder; and a twenty-minute French lesson by art critic Tōno Yoshiaki and pantomimist Thèo Lèsoualch, while women's hands and legs moved through openings in the back curtain.[13] For the finale of *AOS*, later called *Audience Piece*, "all the participants lined up on the stage and watched members of the audience, becoming [themselves] the 'audience.'"[14] Each watched a different member of the audience until that person averted his or her eyes, and then repeated this with a different target. It was past 1 a.m. when the event finally ended by the hall administrator's order.[15]

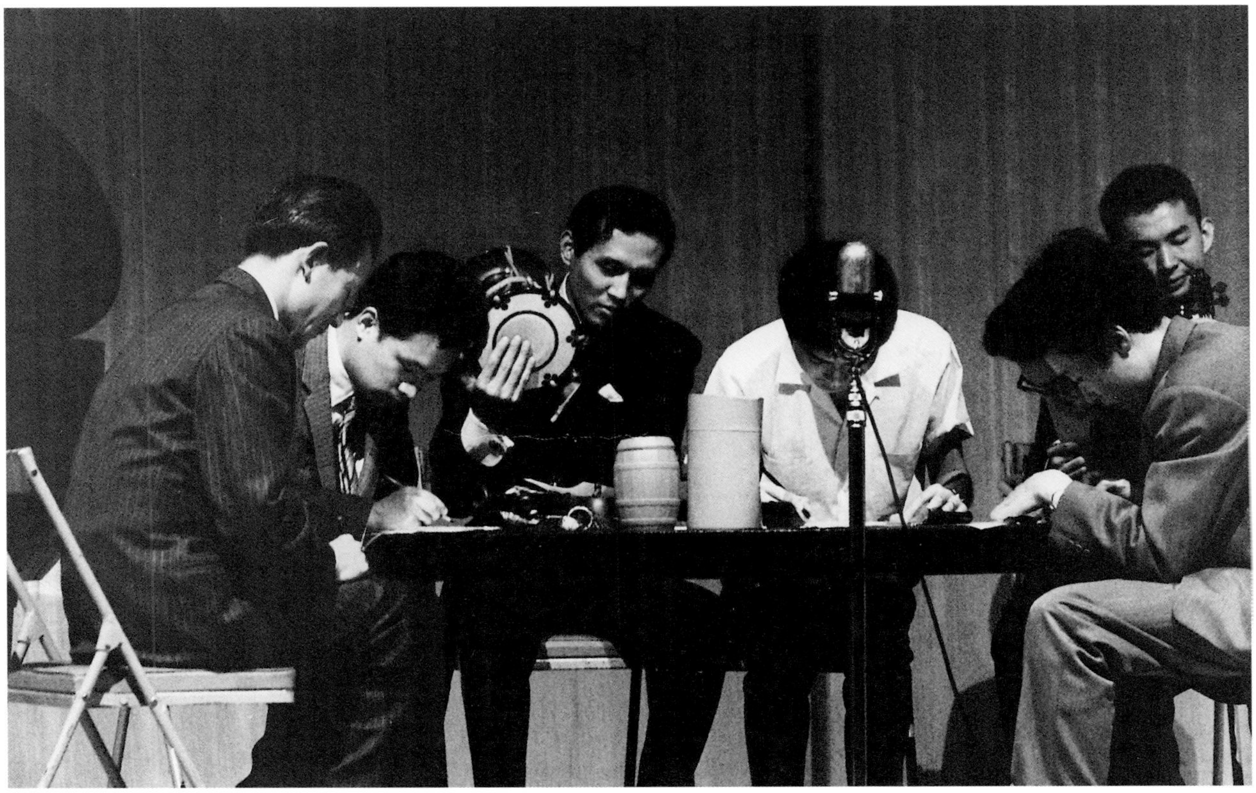

PLATE 27B
THE PULSE, SŌGETSU ART CENTER, TOKYO, 1962. PERFORMERS SOLVING MATHEMATICAL QUESTIONS (MAYUZUMI WITH A *TSUZUMI* DRUM)

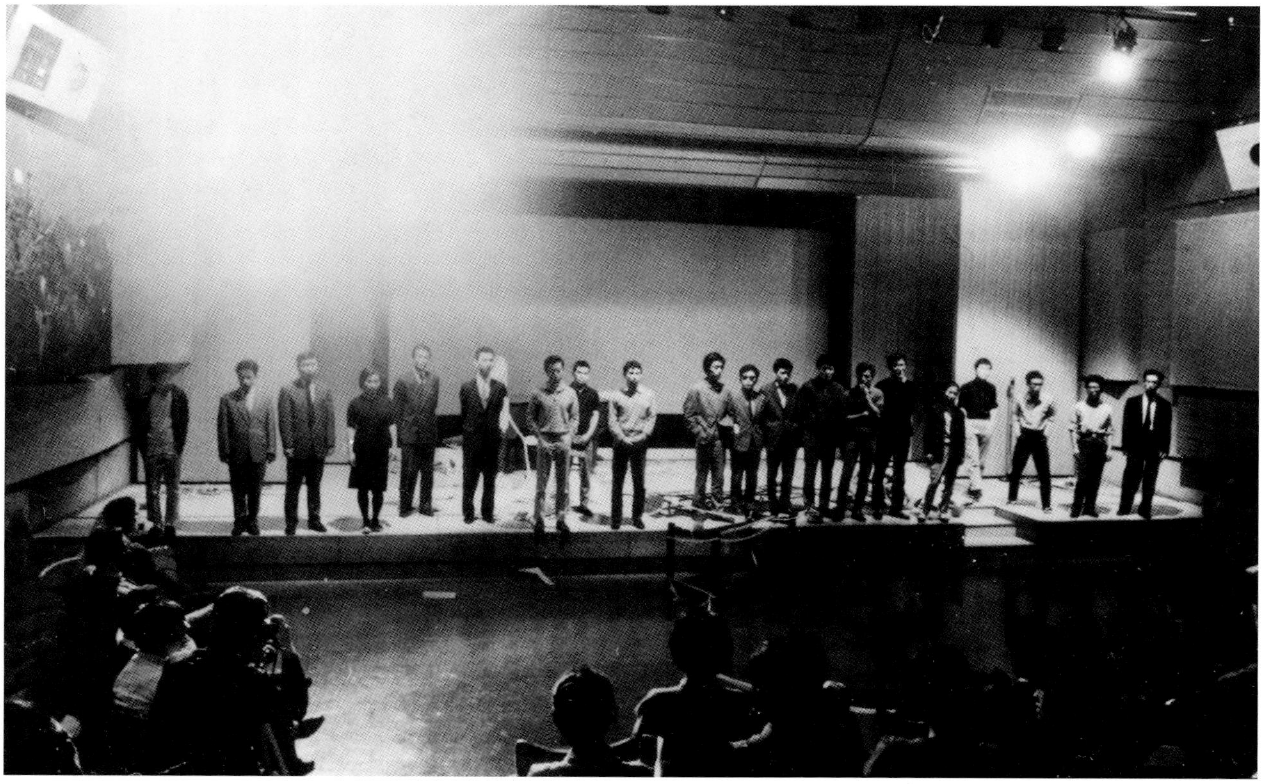

PLATE 27C
AUDIENCE PIECE,
SŌGETSU ART CENTER, TOKYO, 1962. PERFORMERS STARING AT AUDIENCE MEMBERS. ONO, FOURTH FROM LEFT

The entire concert was conducted in darkness, only partially lit by flashlights or spotlights, or even a match, and the sounds were often very subtle. Although most of the reviews criticized this aspect, an unidentified reviewer commented:

> The audience seems to have had unusual experiences... seeing the sequence of these apparently senseless mundane acts. It is not an art that has already been completed, but an art from which the audience can receive something by witnessing the unfolding of nonsense acts, experiencing the process together with the performers.[16]

Indeed, throughout the evening, Ono attempted to challenge the traditional one-way relationship between performer and audience. To appreciate Ono's work, the audience had to take an active role, filling in the invisible or inaudible parts though their own imagination, or participating in performances. As the artist put it, "the work is not something for me to present but for them [the audience] to seek out."[17]

MY

NOTES

All translations from Japanese material are by the author.

1. Sōgetsu Art Center was in operation from April 1959 until April 1971. In addition to art exhibitions, the Center hosted performances of avant-garde music, dance, film, and events at a 400-seat auditorium on the underground level of the Kaikan. In connection with these activities, the Center published *SAC Journal*, in which Ono's "The Word of a Fabricator" appeared in 1962 (Anthology 12).

2. Takiguchi, quoted in [Higashi], "Konnichi no kao: Ono Yōko, kisei geijutsu eno teikō" (Today's face: Yoko Ono resists conventional art), *Yomiuri shinbun*, evening edition, 6 April 1962.

3. Ono noted which pieces were performed at Sōgetsu in her *9 Concert Pieces for John Cage*, manuscript (1966; Anthology 9), John Cage *Notation* Collection, Northwestern University Music Library. In her e-mail to the author (25 September 1999), she explained how small pieces were used as parts of larger pieces.

4. E-mail to author, 25 September 1999.

5. Ichiyanagi Toshi, "Saizen'ei no koe: Donarudo Richī eno hanron" (Voice of the most avant-garde: Objection to Donald Richie), *Geijutsu Shinchō* 13, no. 8 (August 1962): 138.

6. Fujimatsu Hiroshi, "Kyokō no kurokami" (Fictitious black hair), *Bijutsu techō*, no. 206 (July 1962): 83.

7. Tōno Yoshiaki, "Chansu operēshon (gūzen sōsa)" (Chance operation), *Kamera geijutsu* 9, no. 7 (July 1962): 126.

8. "Daitanna kokoromi: Ono Yōko no ivento" (Bold experiment: Yoko Ono's event), *Asahi jānaru/Asahi Journal* ([?] June 1962): 45.

9. Mathematical questions prepared by Ono remain in her collection.

10. "Daitanna kokoromi."

11. Ibid.

12. Ibid.

13. Tōno, 126.

14. Ibid.

15. While Tōno and Thèo Lèsoualch noted that the event lasted beyond 1 a.m., Akiyama Kuniharu noted that it was over by midnight. See Tōno, 128; Lèsoualch, "Sakusha no inai kūhaku no go-jikan: Ono Yōko risaitaru no koto" (Five hours of void without the creator: On Yoko Ono's recital), *Nihon dokusho shinbun*, 8; Akiyama, "Sōgetsu āto sentā" (Sōgetsu Art Center) in *Bunka no shikakenin: Gendai bunka no jiba to tōshizu* (Entrepreneurs of culture: Fields and perspectives of contemporary culture), ed. Akiyama (Tokyo: Seidosha, 1985), 486.

16. "Daitanna kokoromi."

17. Ono, quoted in Ichiyanagi, 138.

LITERATURE: *Shūkan Yomiuri* (6 April 1962); *Asahi jānaru/Asahi Journal* ([?] June 1962); Fujimatsu, *Bijutsu techō* (July 1962); Lèsoualch, *Nihon dokusho shinbun* (9 July 1962); Richie, *Geijutsu Shinchō* (July 1962); Tōno, *Kamera geijutsu* (July 1962); Ichiyanagi, *Geijutsu Shinchō* (August 1962); Akiyama, *Bunka no shikakenin* (1985), 485–86; Iimura, *Yoko Ono* (1985), 79–83; *Sōgetsu to sono jidai, 1945–1970*, exh. cat. (1998), 218–19, 271

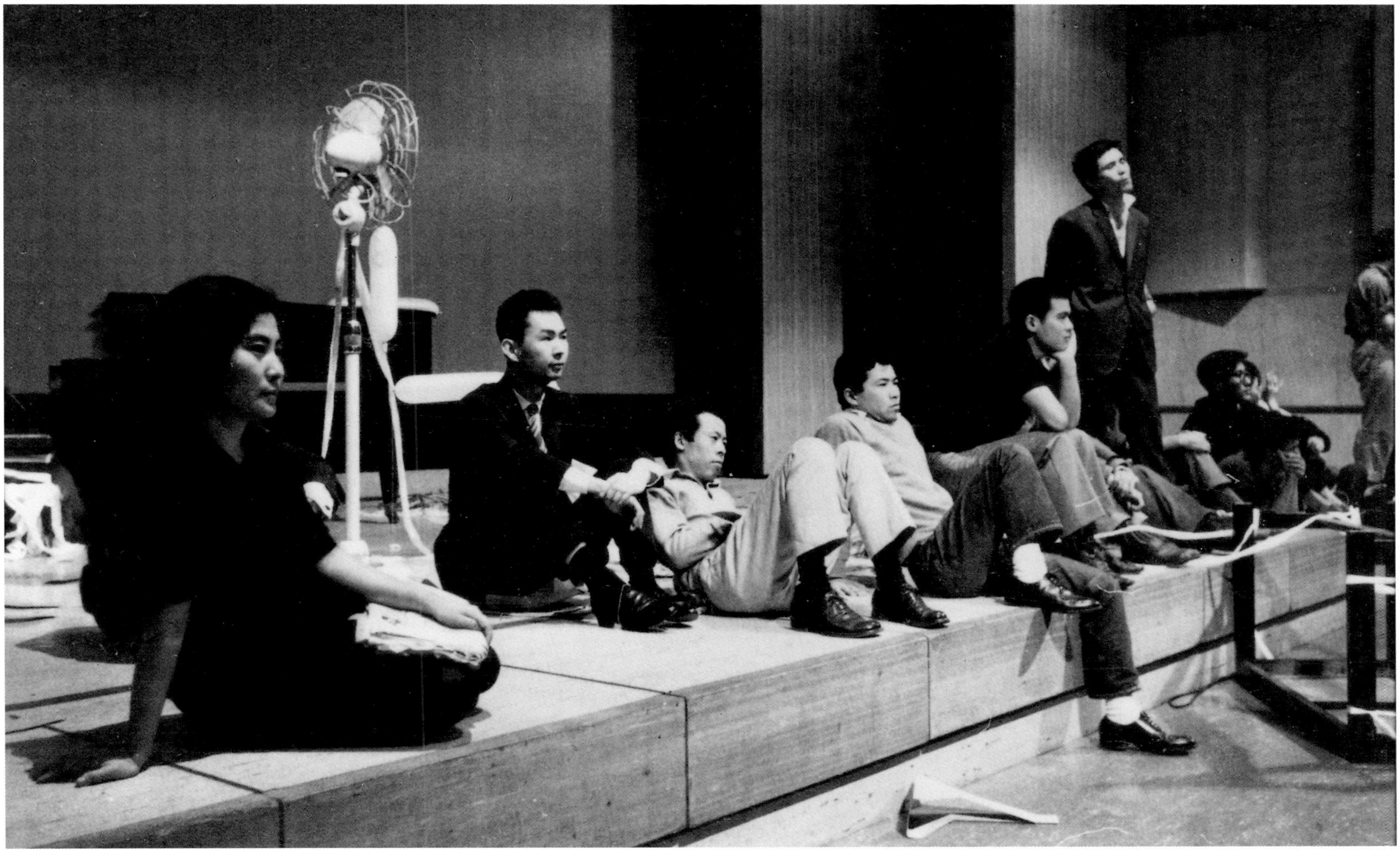

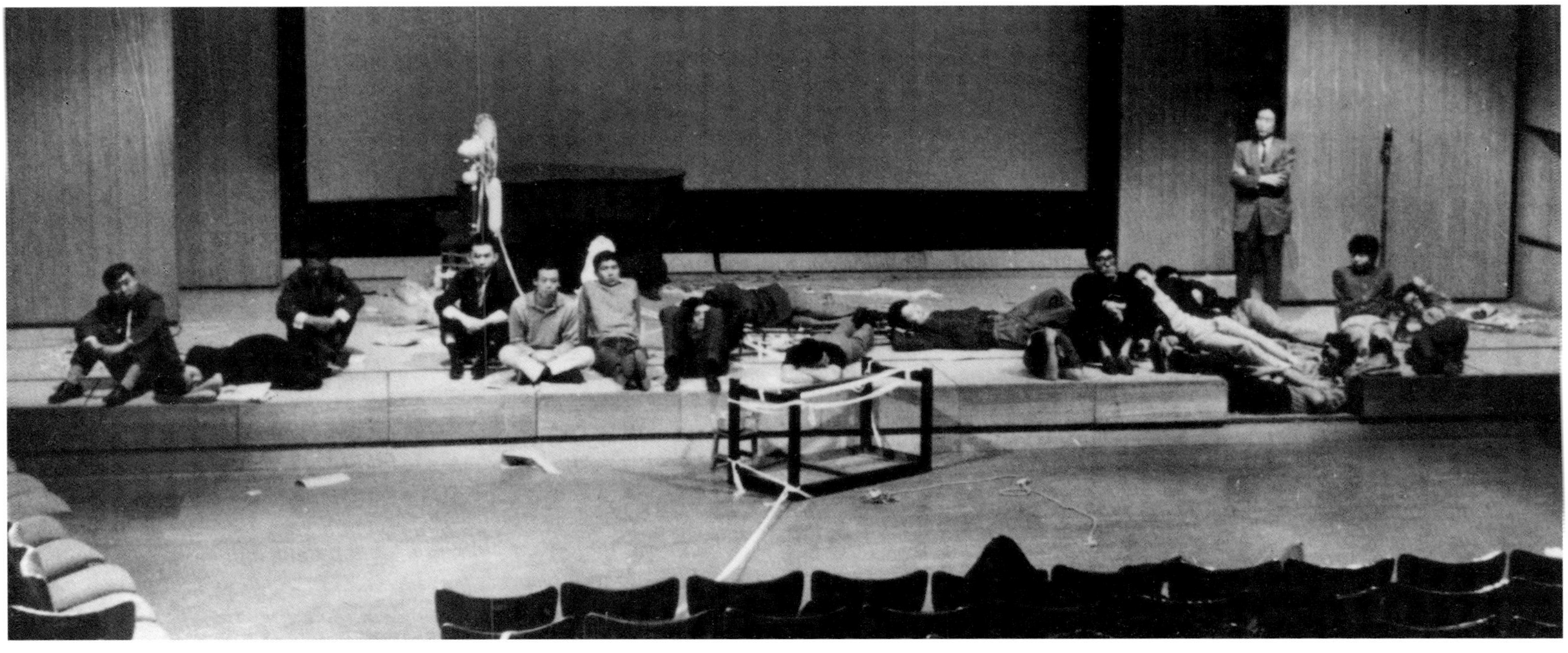

PLATES 27D–E
AUDIENCE PIECE,
SŌGETSU ART CENTER,
TOKYO, 1962. PERFORMERS STARING AT AUDIENCE MEMBERS. ONO,
FAR LEFT (TOP); SECOND
FROM LEFT (BOTTOM)

28 *Fly,* 1964

event at Naiqua Gallery, Tokyo, April 25

A key concept in Ono's creative output, *Fly* originated as an instruction, later published in *Grapefruit* (1964):

> FLY PIECE
>
> Fly.
>
> 1963 summer

By early 1964, the single-word instruction "Fly," under the title *Instructions for Poem No. 86*, was included in the leaflet *Untitled (Birth Announcement)* (fig. 14.7), which Ono mailed to a select number of friends.

For the first performance of *Fly* in Tokyo, Ono sent a postcard:

> FLY
> Yoko Ono
> Place: Naiqua Gallery
> Time: April 25, Saturday, 8 P.M.
> Come prepared to fly.

On the day of the performance she was absent, but her artist friends—Anthony Cox, Nam June Paik, Shigeko Kubota, Akasegawa Genpei, and Kosugi Takehisa, among others—assembled at the gallery and "flew" from a ladder, each in his or her own way.[1] Ono's absence reified *Fly* as a piece that was both participatory and possible to effect in one's imagination. Recently asked why she was absent at Naiqua, Ono replied:

> I always tried to stress what I had wished to communicate by how I presented the piece. It was very important that I was not there. Not only that it made the piece more conceptual, but it did make a point that I did not have to be there physically. The piece had its own life, and the participation of others, in fact, made the piece.[2]

In later performances or installations, ladders of varied heights, sometimes with a stool, were provided, inviting audience members to jump from different heights.

Despite its simplicity, *Fly* evokes an infinite range of meaning. From the beginning, the question of what it means to "fly" incited sober reactions from the audience. At the time of the Naiqua performance, participants were said to have seriously discussed whether flying was the same as falling or dying.[3] At Ono's Kyoto symposium in July 1964 (no. 29), one audience member who was requested to "fly" retorted, "I can fly only once in my lifetime. So, I cannot fly *now*, definitely when I die I fly, I think."[4]

But by overcoming such fears, Ono wishes, people can disengage themselves from various obstacles in their lives. As she poetically explains in her 1971 essay "How to Fly," in order to fly, we have to be light both psychologically and physically, not clogged by "resentment, anger, secrets, and the past" and "excess fat and excrements." Moreover, in order for our "wings" to be free, the world itself has to be free. To achieve this condition, it must "be unclogged and have good circulation." She then declares with conviction, "When the whole world is in good circulation we will all fly together."[5] *Fly*, then, in its essence, embraces an implicitly political motive—to free not only individuals but also the entire world.
MY

NOTES

All translations from Japanese material are by the author.

1. Ono, notes on *Fly Piece* in *9 Concert Pieces for John Cage* (1966; Anthology 9).
2. Ono, e-mail to author, 13 September 1999.
3. Ono, in tape recording of *Symposium: !* (1964), collection of the artist.
4. Ibid.
5. Ono, "How to Fly," *Museum of Modern [F]art* (1971), n.p.

OTHER VERSIONS
See no. 40 (1971 *Museum of Modern [F]art*); no. 41 (1996 billboards); no. 46 (1970 film); no. 56 (1971 LP album). See Exhibitions for canvas, ladder(s), and combination versions

PERFORMANCES: 1964 (April 25) *Fly*, Naiqua Gallery; 1964 (July 20) *Insound/Instructure*, Yamaichi Hall; 1964 (July 22) *Symposium: !* French Cancan Coffee House; 1966 (September 28) *DIAS/Two Evenings with Yoko Ono*, Africa Center; 1966 (November 17) *Music of the Mind*, Jeanetta Cochrane Theatre; 1967 (September 26) *Music of the Mind*, Bluecoat Society of Arts; 1971 (broadcast October 14) *Free Time*, WNET TV (performed by John Lennon and Jonas Mekas); performed several times in the 1990s

EXHIBITIONS: 1989 *The Bronze Age*, Cranbrook Academy (stepladders); 1990 *In Facing*, Riverside Studios (silkscreened canvas); 1990 *En Trance*, Randers Kunstmuseum (silkscreened canvas and white ladder); 1992 *Color, Fly, Sky*, Museet for Samitidkunst, Roskilde (stepladders); 1993 *Color, Fly, Sky*, Stiftung Starke (stepladders); 1993 *Color, Fly, Sky*, Frauen Museum (stepladders); 1996 *Fly*, Anderson Gallery (canvas and stepladders); 1998 *En Trance*, Andre Emmerich Gallery (handwriting on canvas and white ladder)

LITERATURE: Linscott, *Liverpool Daily Post* (3 October 1967); Concannon, *Fly*, exh. cat. (1996), 9–13; Leigh, *Beatles Unlimited Magazine* (January/February 1998)

FLY
小 野　洋 子
場所：内 科 画 廊
時：4月25日（土）8. P.M.
飛ぶ用意をして来る事。

PLATE 28A
POSTCARD ANNOUNCEMENT, *FLY* AT NAIQUA GALLERY, TOKYO, 1964

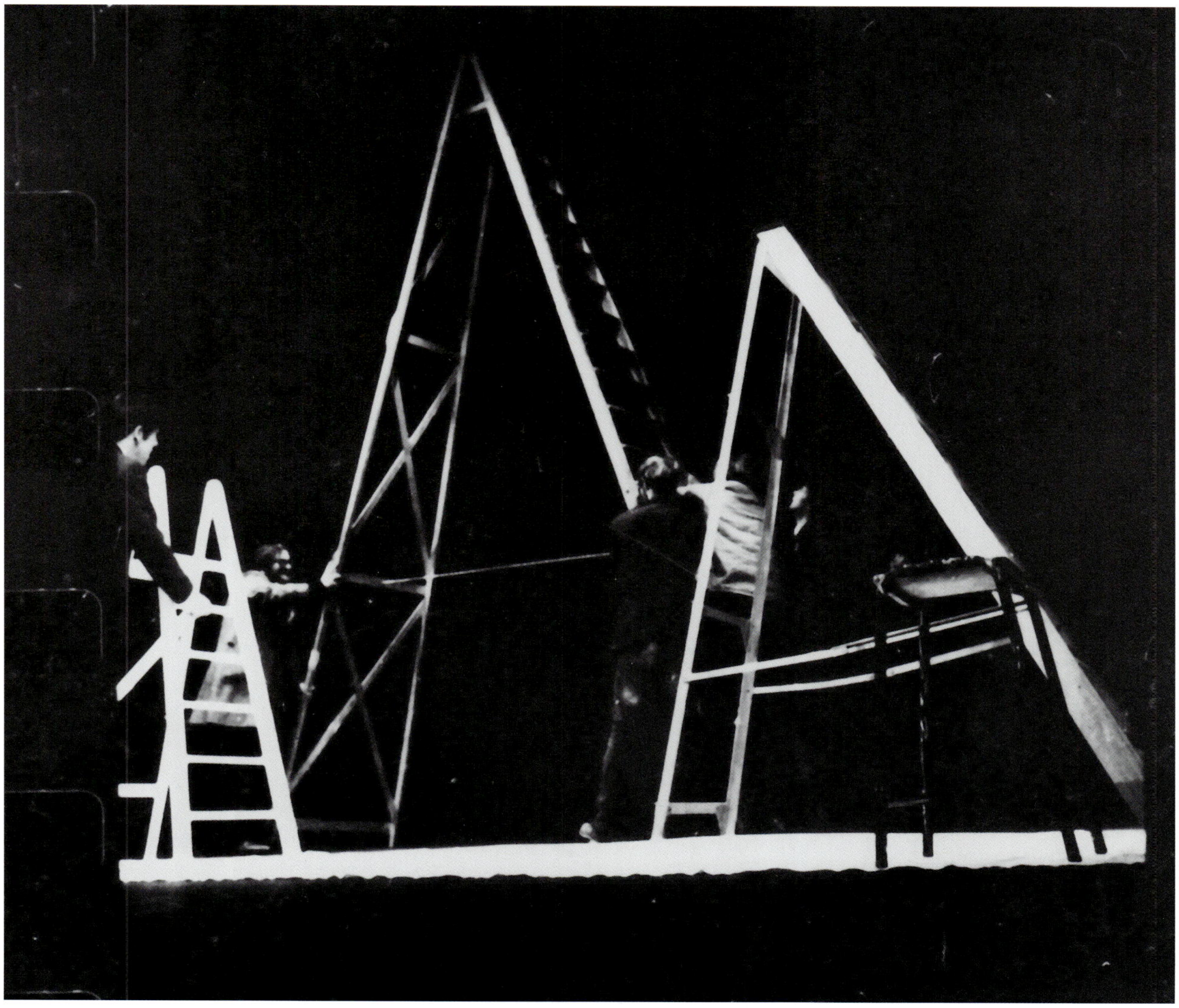

PLATE 28B
FLY, JEANETTA COCHRANE THEATRE, LONDON, 1966

29 *Evening till Dawn*, 1964

event at Nanzenji, July 21

! 1964

symposium at French Cancan Coffee House, July 22

In July 1964, in collaboration with Anthony Cox and Al Wonderlick (currently Wunderlich), Ono realized a three-day program comprising a concert, an event, and a symposium at three different venues in Kyoto. The event, *Evening till Dawn*, was held the day after *Contemporary American Avant-Garde Music Concert: Insound and Instructure* was held at Yamaichi Hall, presenting performances of *Fly Piece*, *Bag Piece*, *Strip Tease for Three*, *Word of Mouth Piece*, and *Cut Piece*.[1]

An unprecedented offer by the senior monk of one of Kyoto's leading Zen monasteries, Nanzenji, allowed Ono use of a temple and garden (with the exception of the monks' private rooms) for her event. On the night of a full moon, approximately fifty people—mostly Kyoto residents, but also some American and French participants—gathered at the temple gate, where each was given a card with the instruction, "silence."[2] Walking quietly to a garden behind the temple, they received another instruction card, "touch," and spread themselves throughout the garden, the verandah, the corridor, and the *tatami*-mat rooms. Interpretation of the instruction was left to the participants, although Ono explained to them that objects to touch were not limited to physical things.[3] While some literally touched other participants' bodies, others watched the moon or sky, wishing to touch. This *Touch Piece*[4] peacefully ended after dawn with a hot bath, a breakfast, and a voluntary cleaning of the temple.[5] The meditative and imaginative character of the event was partially influenced by the environment of Kyoto and the Zen temple. Ono recalls:

> The monks accepted and greeted my work with a very Zen attitude themselves, without being on guard. The evening went so well because of this symbiotic vibration.[6]

On the following day, Ono, Cox, and Wunderlich hosted a symposium at the French Cancan Coffee House.[7] It began with *Fly Piece* (no. 28) in which audience members were asked to "fly" from the ladder or present alternative ways to "fly." Being shy or reluctant, however, most people declined to participate physically, excusing themselves for various reasons.[8] Interspersed with performance of *Fly Piece* were questions asked by the audience about Ono's intention behind her art, the reception of Zen in New York, John Cage's chance operation, and Pop Art. Although the Kyoto audience generally maintained a conservative but argumentative attitude, this may have been their way of expressing curiosity toward something new.

MY

NOTES

All translations from Japanese material are by the author.

1. Al Wunderlich confirms that these five pieces were actually performed, although they did not necessarily correspond to the titles given in the program (conversation with author, 13 September 1999). I thank him for his generous cooperation.

2. Al Wunderlich recalls that a card was given to participants at the gate (ibid.); Ono recalls that "silence" was the instruction (e-mail to author, 14 September 1999). Ono also documents the event in "To the Wesleyan People" (1966; Anthology 14).

3. Ono, conversation with author, 5 October 1999.

4. *Touch Piece* was also performed at Naiqua Gallery in Tokyo in June 1964.

5. Ono, "To the Wesleyan People."

6. Ono, e-mail to author, 14 September 1999.

7. The exclamation mark "!" used in the symposium title may have derived from the signature mark of Hi Red Center, a Japanese avant-garde group that was active in Tokyo in 1963–64. Ono concurs that "'!' was used because Hi-Red was so known for it, and people, organizers, or whoever liked it so much" (e-mail to author, 13 September 1999).

8. See tape recording of *Symposium: !*

AUDIO DOCUMENTATION: 1964, tape recording of *Symposium: !* collection of the artist

LITERATURE: Ono, "To the Wesleyan People" (1966); Iimura, *Yoko Ono* (1985), 84–85

PLATE 29
TICKETS FOR THREE
KYOTO EVENTS, 1964

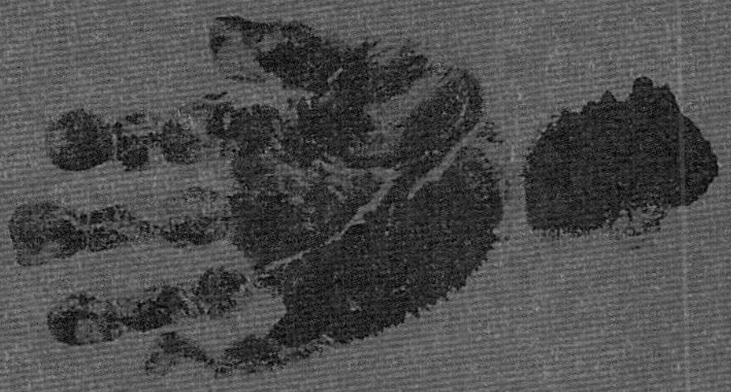

CONTEMPORARY AMERICAN AVANT-GARDE MUSIC CONCERT
- Insound and Instructure -

Yoko Ono Tony Cox Al Wonderlick
YAMAICHI HALL KYOTO JULY 20, 1964 from 6 P.M.

¥35

現代アメリカ前衛音楽演奏会
—インサウンドとインストラクチュアー

小 野 洋 子

トニー・コックス

アル・ワンダリック

京都山一ホール 7月20日, 6 P.M.

1

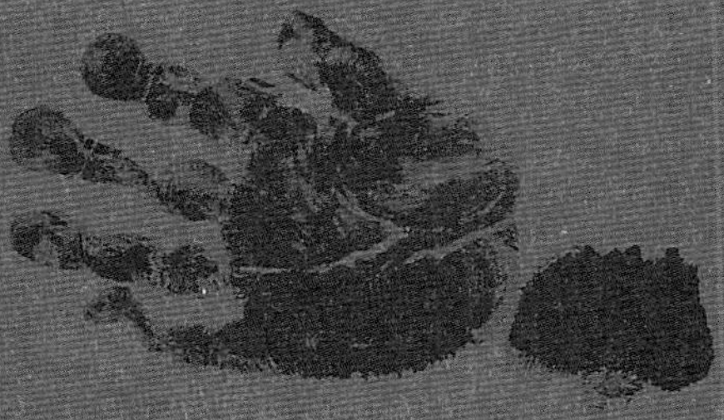

EVENT - EVENING TILL DAWN -

Yoko Ono Tony Cox Al Wonderlick
NANZENJI, KYOTO JULY 21, 1964 6 P.M.

¥500

イヴェント —夕方から夜明迄—

小 野 洋 子

トニー・コックス

アル・ワンダリック

京都南禅寺 7月21日 6 P.M.

¥500

2

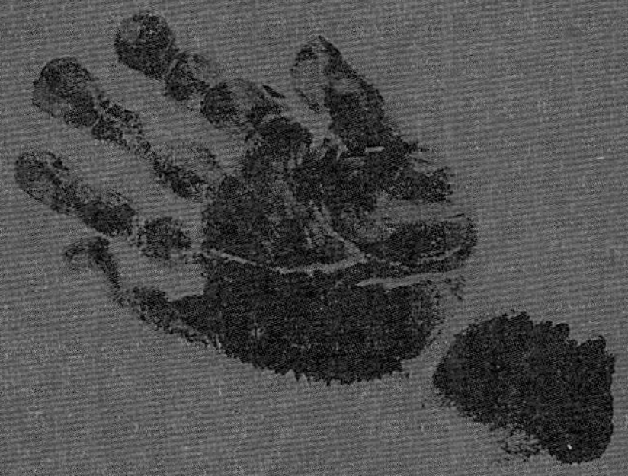

SYMPOSIUM - ! -

Yoko Ono Tony Cox Al Wonderlick
FRENCH CANCAN COFFEE HOUSE, KYOTO
July 22, 1964 8 P.M.

シンポジユウム —！—

小 野 洋 子

トニー・コックス

アル・ワンダリック

フレンチカンカン喫茶店
7月22日 8 P.M.

3

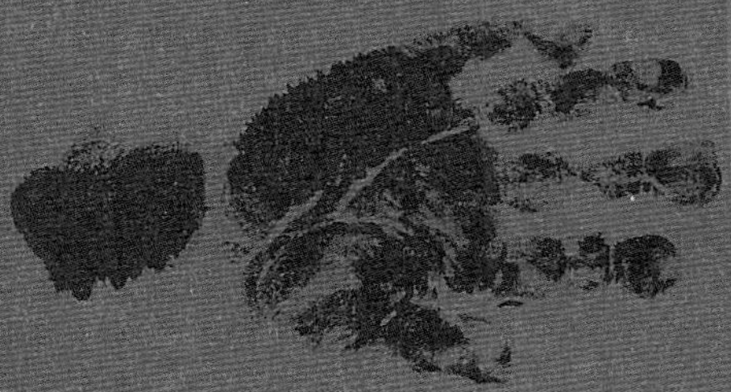

CONTEMPORARY AMERICAN AVANT-GARDE MUSIC CONCERT
EVENT - EVENING TILL DAWN -
SYMPOSIUM - ! -
July 20, 21, 22, 1964 KYOTO
Yoko Ono Tony Cox Al Wonderlick

¥750

現代アメリカ前衛音楽演奏会
京都山一ホール 7月20日 6 P.M.
イヴェント —夕方から夜明迄—
京都南禅寺 7月21日 6 P.M.
シンポジユウム —！—
フレンチカンカン喫茶店
7月22日 8 P.M.

小 野 洋 子

トニー・コックス

アル・ワンダリック

¥750

4

30 *Cut Piece,* 1964

performance

Ono entered the stage carrying scissors. Moving to the center, she invited the audience to cut off her clothing. Then she sat down, legs tucked under her, placed the scissors on the floor, and remained motionless, silent and waiting. She always assumed a similar physical position, followed her score strictly, and wore her best clothes. But the audience, the context, and the environment varied in each performance of *Cut Piece*.

In Kyoto, a man came on stage and raised the scissors over Ono's head, threatening her for a long time as if ready to stab her. Ono's response was dismay rather than fear, for his gesture made her action more theatrical than she intended, a theatricality she avoided by suppressing her emotions and not reacting. Ono remembered that in Japan the audience was more discreet about cutting away her clothing than in New York.[1] In London, her performance was highly publicized as part of the international *Destruction in Art Symposium* (no. 33). There a wild scene ensued, exacerbated by the presence of cameras and the press, and the audience cut off all her clothing.

Cut Piece entails a disrobing and a denouement of the reciprocity between exhibitionism and scopic desires, victim and assailant, sadist and masochist. It unveils the interpersonal alienation that characterizes social relationships between subjects, dismantling the disinterested Kantian aesthetic model. *Cut Piece* moves beyond the psychological interaction of artist and participants to uncover the latent subject/object condition behind the edifice of art and the presumed opaque neutrality of objects. Instead of offering objects to be contemplated by respectful observers, Ono delivers art as an immediate social event, eliminating the reserve of aesthetic distance. *Cut Piece* is an aesthetic commentary on the complicit relationship between individuals and the social body as a whole in its collectivized behavior. It demonstrates the reciprocity between artists, objects, and viewers and the responsibility beholders have to the reception and preservation of art.

Cut Piece exposed the voluntary and incisive potential of the gaze to puncture and wound, to cut away at that which is observed. This theme permeates Ono's work and is vivid in many scores that call for variations of penetration, truncation, destruction, incineration, dismemberment, disappearance, breakage, and laceration. An equally destructive score from the summer of 1962, also entitled *Cut Piece*, reads: "Throw it off a high building" (*Grapefruit*, 1964). *Cut Piece* anticipates the gendered themes of invasion, especially of woman, that Ono explored in such works as *Rape* (1969; no. 45), *Fly* (1970; no. 46), *Horizontal Memory* (1997; pl. 70), *Vertical Memory* (1997; pl. 69), and *Portrait of Nora* (1992; pl. 71). It also reveals an aspect of Ono's psychological state, which she expressed in *The Stone*: "People went on cutting the parts they do not like of me," she wrote, "finally there was only the stone remained of me that was in me but they were still not satisfied and wanted to know what it's like in the stone."[2]

Cut Piece is as much a vehicle for the visible languages of art as it is for the invisible expression of anguish.

KS

NOTES

1. Ono, quoted in Robert Enright, "Instructions in the Marital Arts: A Conversation with Yoko Ono," *Border Crossings* 13, no. 1 (January 1994): 37.

2. *Statement* in *The Stone*, exh. cat. (1966; Anthology 26).

PERFORMANCES: 1964 (July 20) *Insound and Instructure*, Yamaichi Hall; 1964 (August 11) *Yoko Ono Farewell Concert*, Sōgetsu Art Center; 1965 (March 21) *New Works of Yoko Ono*, Carnegie Recital Hall; 1966 (September 28, 29) *DIAS/Two Evenings with Yoko Ono*, Africa Center; 1967 (September 29) *14-Hour Technicolour Dream*, Alexandra Palace (with hired model). Performances by other artists include: 1966 (September 9) *4th Annual New York Avant Garde Festival*, Central Park, by two men in black bags, under Charlotte Moorman's direction; thereafter, by various performers including Moorman and Jon Hendricks

VISUAL DOCUMENTATION: 1964, photos by unknown photographers (Yamaichi Hall and Sōgetsu Art Center); 1965, photos by Minoru Niizuma (Carnegie Recital Hall); 1965, film by Albert and David Maysles (Carnegie Recital Hall); 1966, photos by John Prosser (Africa Center); 1966, film by unknown filmmaker (possibly press conference, Africa Center), collection The WPA Film Library, Orland Park, Ill. (Job #97846)

LITERATURE: *Shūkan Shinchō* (August 1964); *Tokyo shinbun*, evening (8 August 1964); DeMotte, *Villager* (25 March 1965); Cox, *Art and Artists* (August 1966); McDarrah, *Village Voice* (15 September 1966); Cardew, *Financial Times* (29 September 1966); Day-Lewis, *Daily Telegraph/Morning Post* (29 September 1966); Greville, *Daily Mail* (29 September 1966); Jordan, *Resurgence* (November/December 1966); Ryan, *Punch* (29 March 1967); Turnbull, *Look* (18 March 1967); Perry and Elliott, *Unit* (December 1967); Williams, *The Contemporary Review*

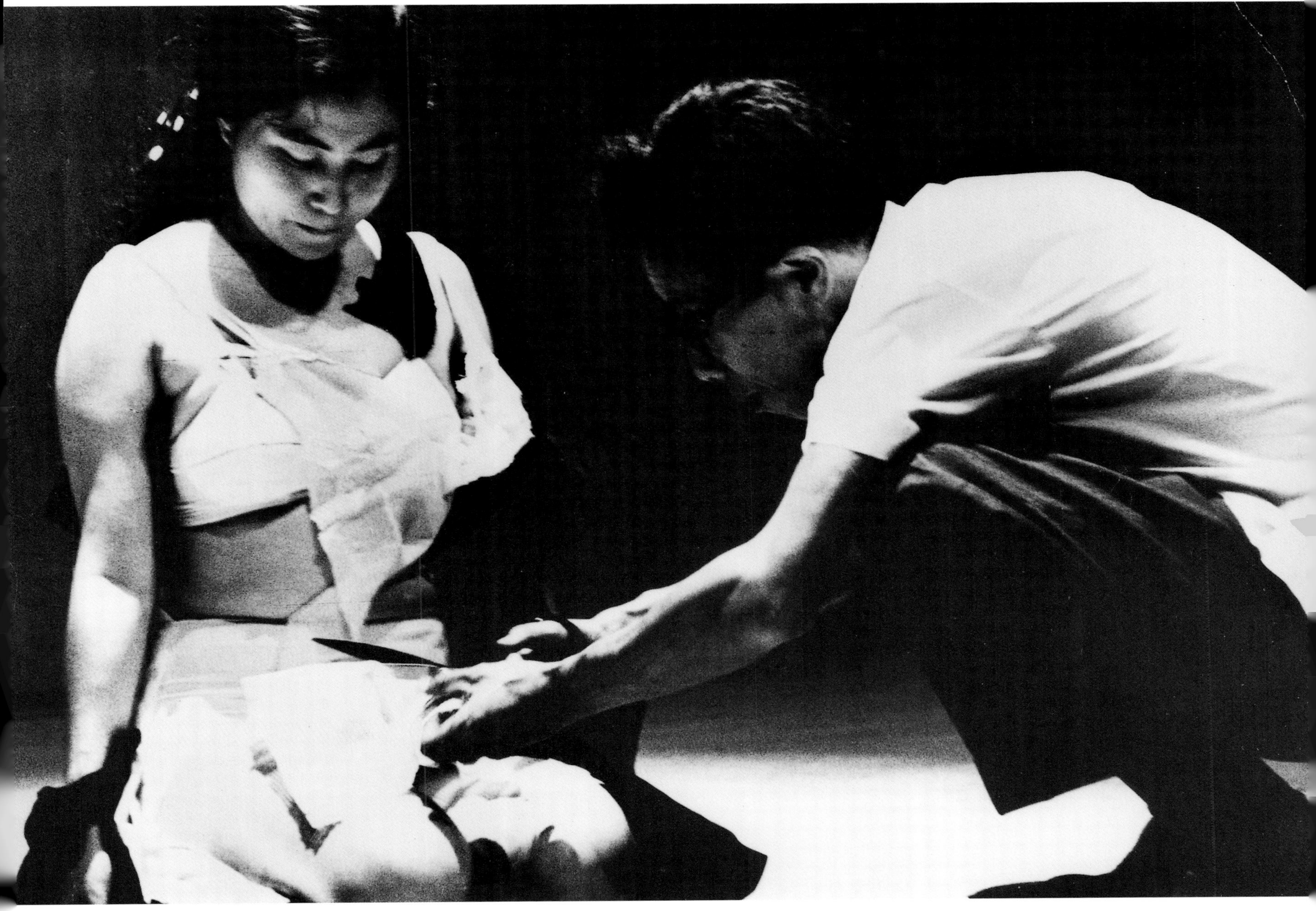

PLATE 30A
CUT PIECE, YAMAICHI
HALL, KYOTO, 1964

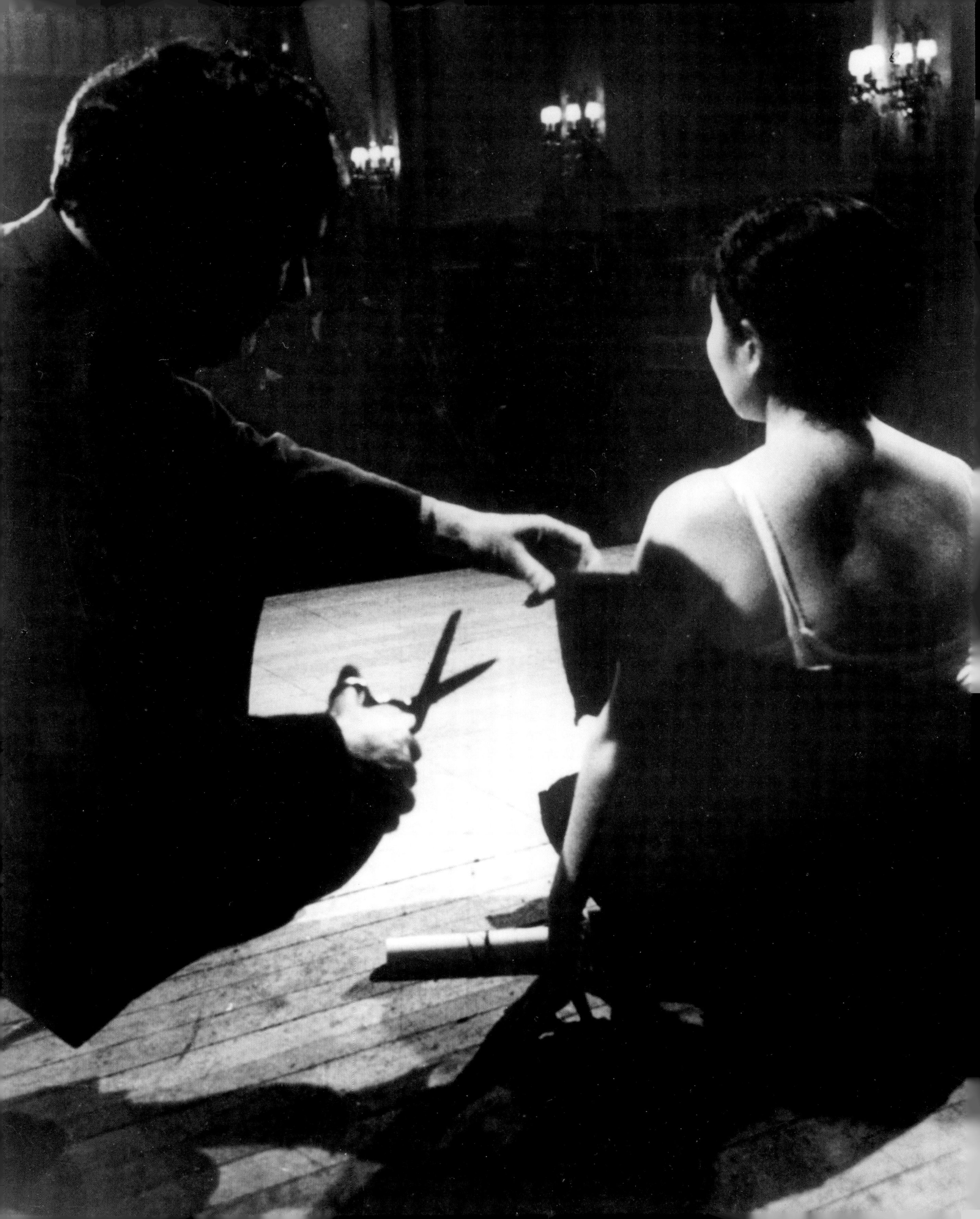

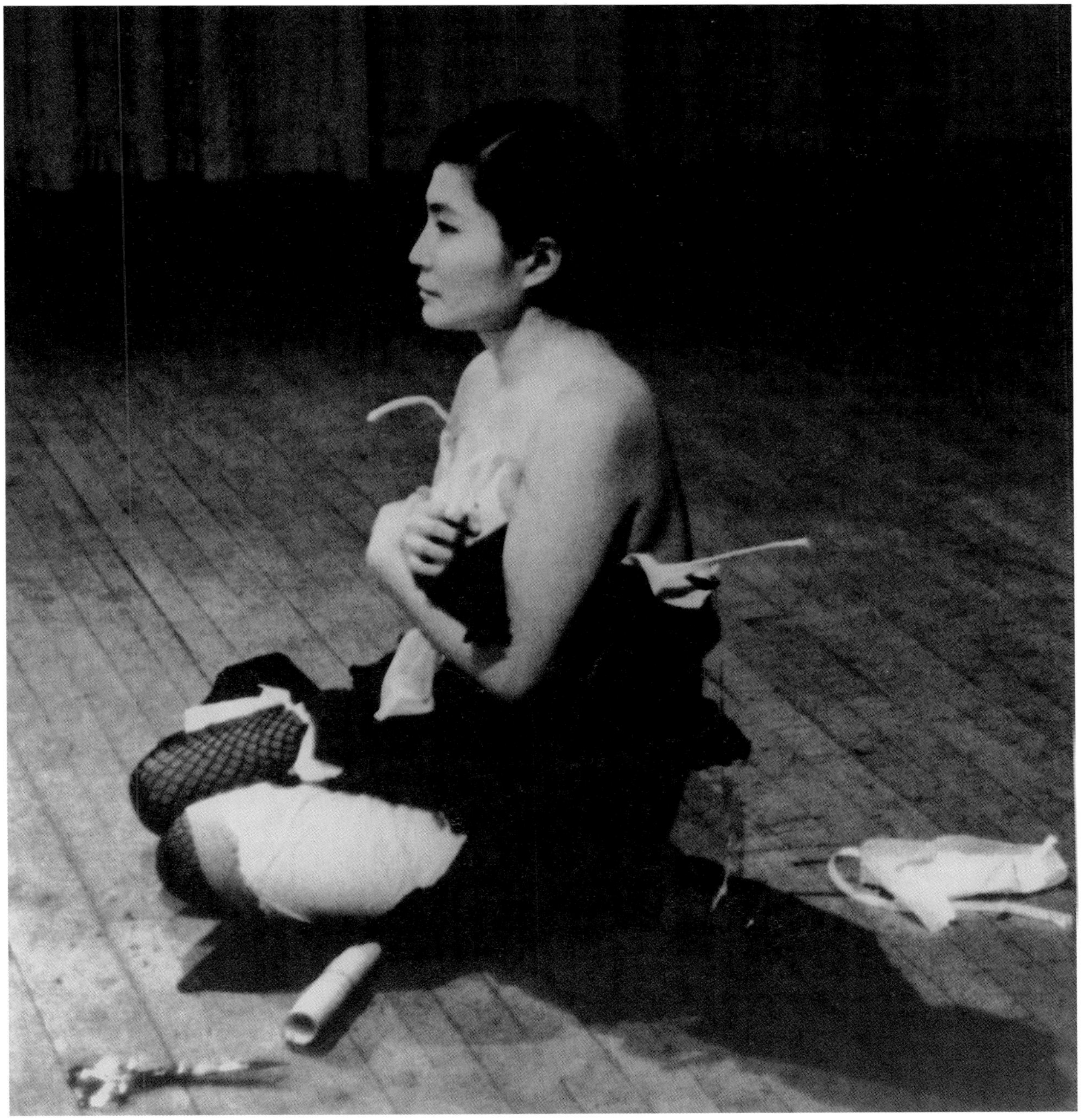

PLATES 30B–C
CUT PIECE, CARNEGIE RECITAL HALL, NEW YORK, 1965

(May 1968); *TAB* (June 1968); Sturt-Penrose, *The Art Scene* (1969), 42–43, 46; *Dapper* (March 1969); Rollin, *Look* (18 March 1969); Mandelkau and Bloom, *International Times* (12–26 August 1971); Ono, *Just Me!* (1986), 34–36; Stiles, "The Destruction in Art Symposium (DIAS)," dissertation (1987); Haskell, *Objects, Films*, exh. brochure (1989), 2; Perreault, *Village Voice* (7 February 1989); Haskell, *Arias and Objects* (1991), 90–92; Watson and Rob, *Performance* (March 1991); Blom, *Homage to Nora*, exh. cat. (1992), 23–25; Stiles, *Art Criticism* (1992); ———, *In the Spirit of Fluxus*, exh. cat. (1993), 81; Tanner, *Bad Girls*, exh. cat. (1994), 59–65; Enright, *Border Crossings* (winter 1994); Crow, *Rise of the Sixties* (1996), 133; Press, *The Wire* (April 1996); Iles, *Have You Seen the Horizon Lately?* exh. cat. (1997), 124–27; O'Dell, *The Drama Review* (spring 1997); Concannon, "Yoko Ono's *Cut Piece* (1964)," thesis (1998); Stiles, *Out of Actions*, exh. cat. (1998), 278; Phillips, *The American Century*, exh. cat. (1999), 242–43; Reed, *Daily Yomiuri* (18 March 1999); Hoffberg, *Umbrella* (April 1999)

DATA BY KC/MY

31 *Bag Piece,* 1964

performance

Bag Piece called for one or two people to get into a large black muslin bag, take off clothing, and carry out activities, including possibly taking a nap. This work was prefigured in actions that took place in *AOS—To David Tudor* (1961), where a canvas on the stage floor was used to create the same effect as the bag. Namely, the lines and the shape created by the person underneath the canvas were the event. In 1964, Ono performed the piece in Japan using a bag. As the documentary photographs indicate, when someone sat still in the bag, its shape resembled a stone.

The Stone was the title of a multimedia environmental-performance created by Ono and others, presented March 10–27, 1966, at the Judson Gallery. Within this environment, *Bag Piece* was a performative element to be enacted by the public and "bagwear" was available for purchase.[1] Several months later, Ono and Anthony Cox advertised related events to take place at the Paradox restaurant where Ono worked:

> Let the others go to Fire Island, the Berkshires, Provincetown...(spending lots of money), you can beat them to the cocktail hour conversation draw by dropping down to the Paradox...to participate in the Stone—art form of the future. Is it psychedelic? Is it avant-garde? Is it Zen? Whatever you think about it, you will have something to talk about. Everybody else is. Stop in any day 1–11PM and spend an hour cooling out....[2]

Participants were invited to perform *Bag Piece* at the Paradox just as they had done in *The Stone.* In this way, *Bag Piece* could be an individual event performed by the artist alone or with someone else, or it could become a hybrid, interactive performance-installation-environment.

Ono and Cox performed *Bag Piece* themselves at the *Destruction in Art Symposium* that September in London (no. 33). As a witness to this performance explained:

> There is a lot of moving about, very slow sort of movements.... They can see out [of the bag], but you can't see what's happening in it. It's sitting on this small stage. You see an arm sort of push and a foot, and it goes on like that for about twenty minutes. Every now and then another article of clothes will come out of the hole in the bag, until finally the movements become slower and slower, and oddly enough it really holds your attention, and you can assume that all the clothes are gone. I think another assistant comes and hands them robes.... So you don't get to see any skin, at least then.[3]

Elements of *Bag Piece* anticipated many developing artistic tendencies. These include the increasing attention paid by many

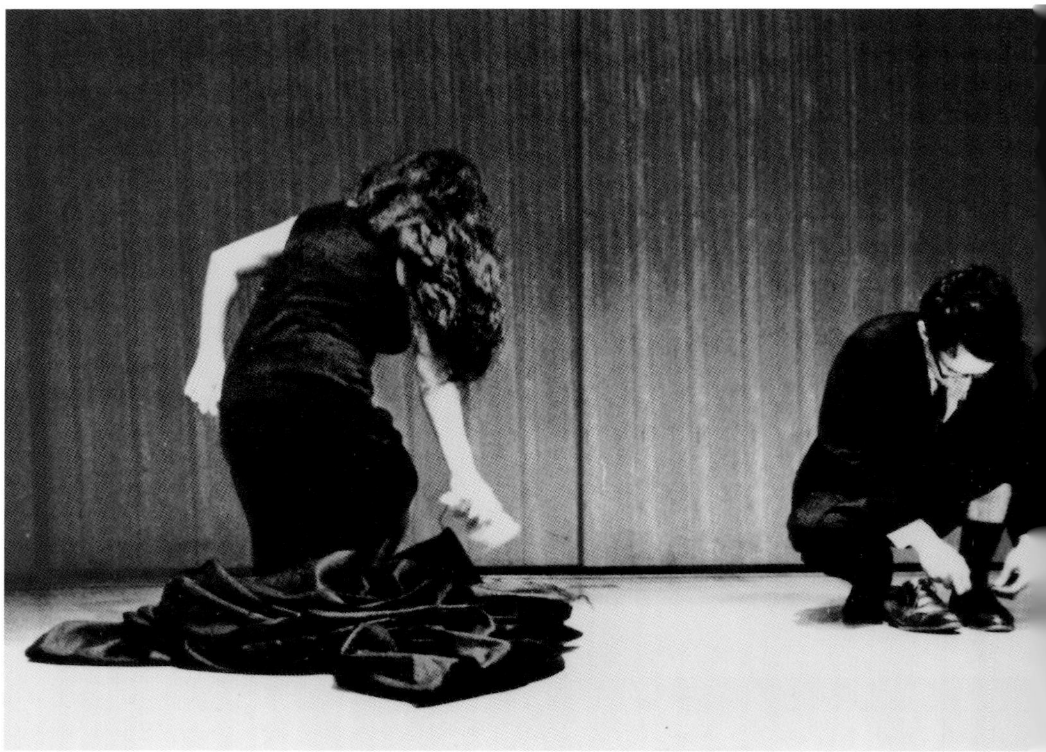

PLATES 31A–C
BAG PIECE, PERFORMED BY YOKO ONO AND ANTHONY COX, SŌGETSU ART CENTER, TOKYO, 1964

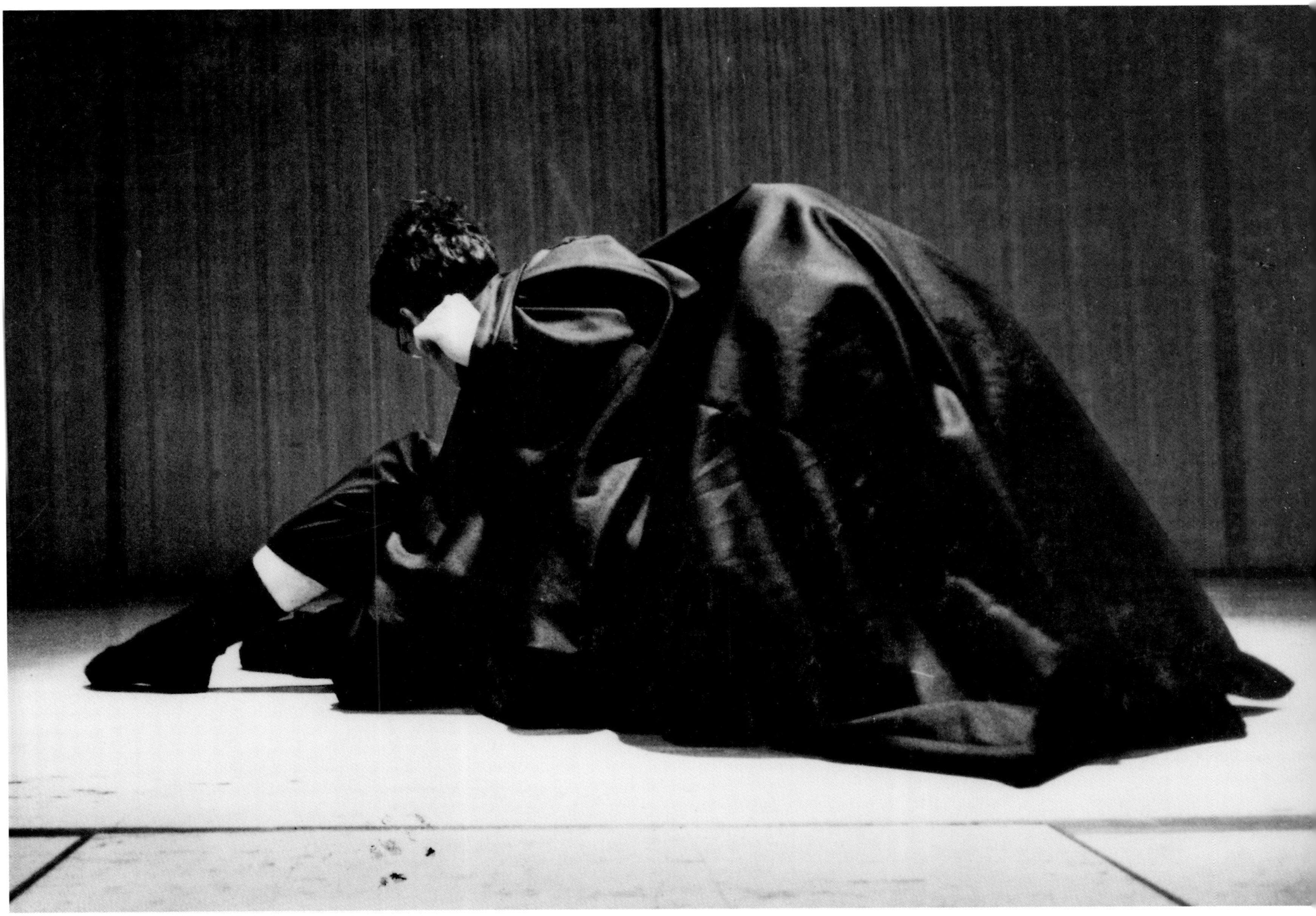

sculptors, beginning in the late 1960s, to the behavior of materials and the processes by which materials assume different forms; the interpersonal negotiation of intimate interaction characteristic of Allan Kaprow's "Activities" in the early 1970s; and the interactivity prevalent in art in the 1990s. An ephemeral event, *Bag Piece* equally visualized the enigmatic relationship between interior and exterior space and forms, suggesting philosophical and psychological considerations. Since viewers were alerted to the hidden qualities behind the veil of appearances, Ono seemed to invoke the *haiku* principle which holds that a thing "is," not "has," infinite value.[4]

When Ono and Lennon began performing *Bag Piece* together, they playfully attached the term "bagism" to their performances and activities related to peace. In 1969, they adopted the "bag of laughs" as a motif symbolic of a peaceful and joyful attitude of resistance to the Vietnam War. Finally, Lennon himself "loved the idea of the Bag Piece," as Ono has pointed out:

> So he wanted to name our first company together "Bag Production." He also wanted to call his first lithograph series "Bag One." At the time, he might have been thinking that he could one day do a "Bag Two," and so on. That never happened. John simply loved the idea of the word "Bag," in the context of my artwork.[5]

KS

NOTES

1. Ono, "Ads for Bagwear" and "Forms to Be Filled...," *The Stone*, exh. cat. (1966).

2. "New York Is a Stone Summer Festival," ad in "Village Bulletin Board," *Village Voice*, 14 July 1966, 2.

3. Unknown individual in Tom Lopez's tape recording of Ono's *DIAS* events at Africa Center, London, 1966.

4. R. H. Blyth, *A History of Haiku*, vol. 1, *From the Beginning up to Issa* (Tokyo: The Hokuseido Press, 1963), 13.

5. Ono, e-mail to author, November 1999.

PERFORMANCES: 1962 (May 24) *Works of Yoko Ono*, Sōgetsu Art Center (by male performer during Ono's *Hide Piece*); 1964 (July 20) *Insound and Instructure*, Yamaichi Hall; 1964 (August 11) *Yoko Ono Farewell Concert*, Sōgetsu Art Center; 1965 (March 21) *New Works of Yoko Ono*, Carnegie Recital Hall; 1965 (June 27) *Perpetual Flux Fest Presents Yoko Ono*; 1966 (March 10–27) *The Stone*, Judson Gallery; 1966 (July 15–August) *The Stone*, The Paradox; 1966 (September 28 and 29) *DIAS/Two Evenings with Yoko Ono*, Africa Center; 1967 (spring) Leeds College of Art; 1967 (September 26), *Music of the Mind*, Bluecoat Chambers; 1967 (mid-December), *Evening with Yoko Ono*, University of Keele; 1967 (late December) Casino; 1968 (early January) La Contrescarpe; 1968 (December 18) *Alchemical Wedding*, Albert Hall (with Lennon); 1969 (March 31) press conference, Sacher Hotel (with Lennon); 1969 (April 3) *The Eamonn Andrews Show*, ITV (with Lennon); 1969 (September 13) *Toronto Rock 'n' Roll Revival*, College Stadium

VISUAL DOCUMENTATION: 1966, film by unknown filmmaker, WPI Film Library, Orland Park, Ill. (Job #97846)

LITERATURE: *Tokyo shinbun*, evening (8 August 1964); DeMotte, *Villager* (25 March 1965); Gustaitis, *New York Herald Tribune* (20 March 1966); Bourdon, *Village Voice* (24 March 1966); Smith, *Village Voice* (14 July 1966); Cox, *Art and Artists* (August 1966); *Daily Mail* (29 September 1966); Cardew, *Financial Times* (29 September 1966); Day-Lewis, *Daily Telegraph* and *Morning Post* (29 September 1966); *International Times* (14–27 October 1966); Jordan, *Resurgence* (November/December 1966); Amaya, *Financial Times* (12 November 1966); *Sunday Telegraph* (1 January 1967); Campbell, *Sunday Times* (8 January 1967); Turnbull, *London Look* (18 March 1967); Linscott, *Liverpool Daily Post* (3 October 1967); Perry and Elliott, *Unit* (December 1967); *Evening Sentinel* (15 December 1967); Williams, *The Contemporary Review* (May 1968); Chowen, *Daily Mail* (19 December 1968); *Guardian* (20 December 1968); Frischauer, *Evening Standard/ Evening Citizen* (1 April 1969); McEwen, *Times* (2 April 1969); Yalkut, *East Village Other* (25 June 1969); *Herald Examiner* (16 September 1969); Baker, *Chicago Tribune* (16 September 1969); Gelmis, *Newsday* (4 October 1969); Hansen, *John Lennon*, exh. cat. (1995), 176–78; Giuliano and Giuliano, *The Lost Lennon Interviews* (1996), 120–31; Leigh, *Beatles Unlimited Magazine* (January/February 1998)

DATA BY KC

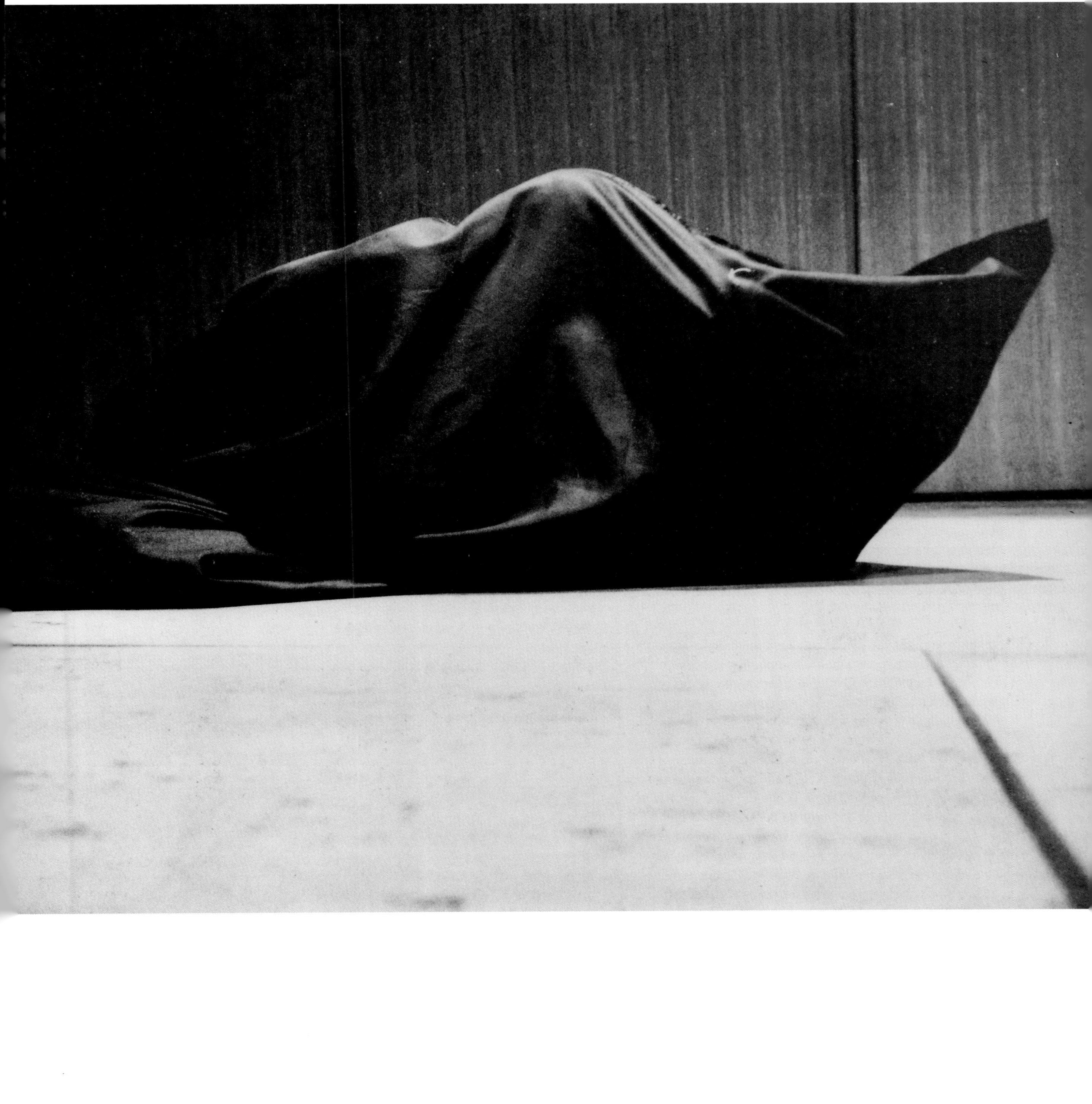

32 *Sky Piece for Jesus Christ,* 1965

(also known as *Sky Piece to Jesus Christ*)
performance at *Fluxorchestra at Carnegie Recital Hall*, New York

Ono and assistants methodically wrapped each member of the orchestra for *Sky Piece for Jesus Christ* in white gauze until they were wound into a continuous, uninterrupted web. Just as the orchestra played in unison, so their bodies gradually became attached into a single, albeit awkward, form. While she progressively enveloped them, the musicians struggled to continue playing their instruments, which were also swathed in gauze.[1] The more difficult it became to play, the more fragmented and contorted the sound became, as the group made its way collectively down the stairs from the stage.

Sky Piece for Jesus Christ highlighted conditions of the unity of a social body (the orchestra). At the same time, it destroyed the group's associated function and ability to play together, all the while maintaining the integrity of the whole, and requiring it to continue to move together even though constrained in its function to do so. In these ways, Ono alluded to phenomena greater than the mere making and unmaking of the affiliated motion of the musicians in their progressively more conceptualized musical performance. For while the clumsy movement of the once-graceful orchestra presented a ludicrous image, it also represented a visual analogue to blind faith as the blind led the blind in a gradually more dissonant movement.

Far from being what has been described as a lighthearted Fluxus or "neo-Dada" performance, the analogies invoked in this work may be found in the relationships among her title, the gauze she used to envelop the performers, and the progress of the event that eventually silenced the players. *Sky Piece for Jesus Christ* required the audience to contemplate the sky *for* Jesus Christ, at the same time as it considered the progressively immobilized and heavily bandaged human beings struggling to do their work. The same Christian sky of the glorified risen Christ could become the heaven that rained damage and death on a principally Buddhist East. Many similar and only slightly veiled references to the effects and impact of the atomic bombs dropped on Japan are suggested in the artist's work in such phrases as "Roaches are moving forms of flowers" and "Teeth and bones are solid forms of clouds."[2]

Commenting on the Christian theme of the work, Ono admitted:

> *Sky Piece for Jesus Christ* is not respectful. When you see them come off the stage, you either have to laugh or feel terrible; and you don't want to laugh. It's tragic/comic. It's black humor. Instead of being created in the image of God, it's just the opposite of what we consider beautiful.... It's very similar to the hypocrisy of Christianity. I say look at it. This is what we are.[3]

While Ono is critical of the sanctimony of Christianity, her reference to "we," and her evocation of a bandaged and fumbling humanity, is a deeply empathic effort to draw "us" into humanitarian sympathy.

KS

NOTES

1. Ono's use of gauze, a medical or surgical material, as a sculptural medium anticipated the celebrated performance photographs of the Austrian artist Rudolf Schwarzkogler (1940–1969) who between 1965 and 1966 used gauze to wrap his own and his model's (Heiz Chibulka) bodies as a dual metaphor for pain and healing. Ono had used bandages as sculptural material in her events as early as 1961.

2. Phrases from Ono's work quoted in Robert Enright, "Instructions in the Marital Arts: A Conversation with Yoko Ono," *Border Crossings* 13, no. 1 (January 1994): 33.

3. All quotes from Ono, unless otherwise cited, are from conversation with author, 23 August 1999.

PERFORMANCES: 1965 (September 25) *Fluxorchestra at Carnegie Recital Hall*, New York; 1990 *Ubi Fluxus Ibi Motus* at Venice Biennale; 1993 (March 5) *Fluxus: East of Moscow*, Willow Place Auditorium (performed by S.E.M. Ensemble); 1994 (March 4) *Outside the Frame*, Severance Hall (by Larry Miller)

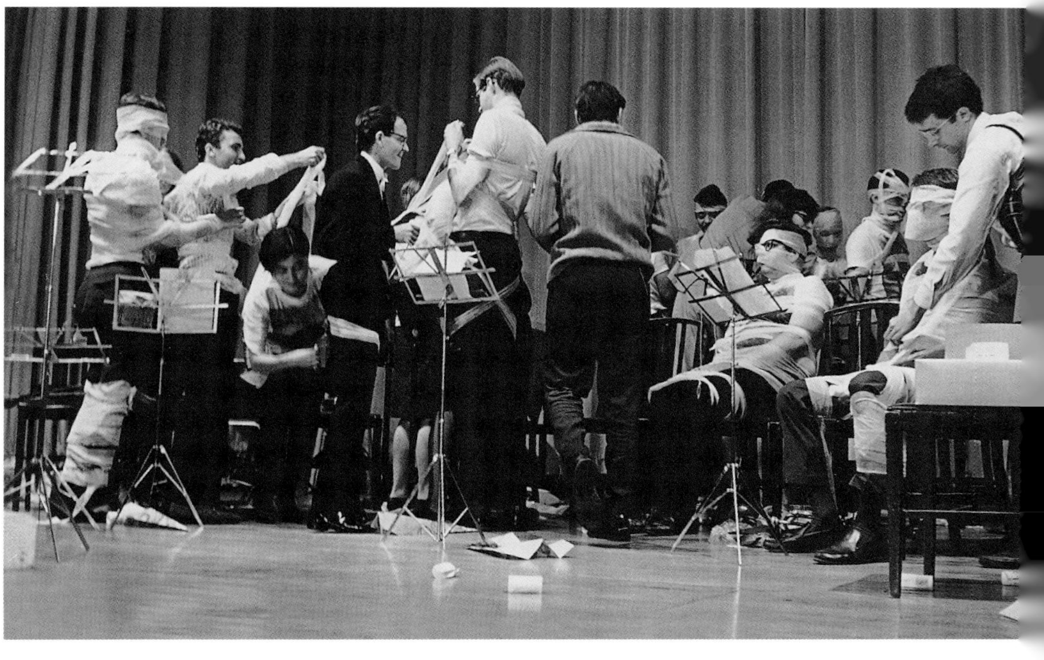

PLATE 32A
SKY PIECE TO JESUS CHRIST, CARNEGIE RECITAL HALL, NEW YORK, 1965. ONO ON LEFT, WRAPPING ORCHESTRA MEMBERS. PHOTO BY PETER MOORE © EST. PETER MOORE / VAGA, NY, NY

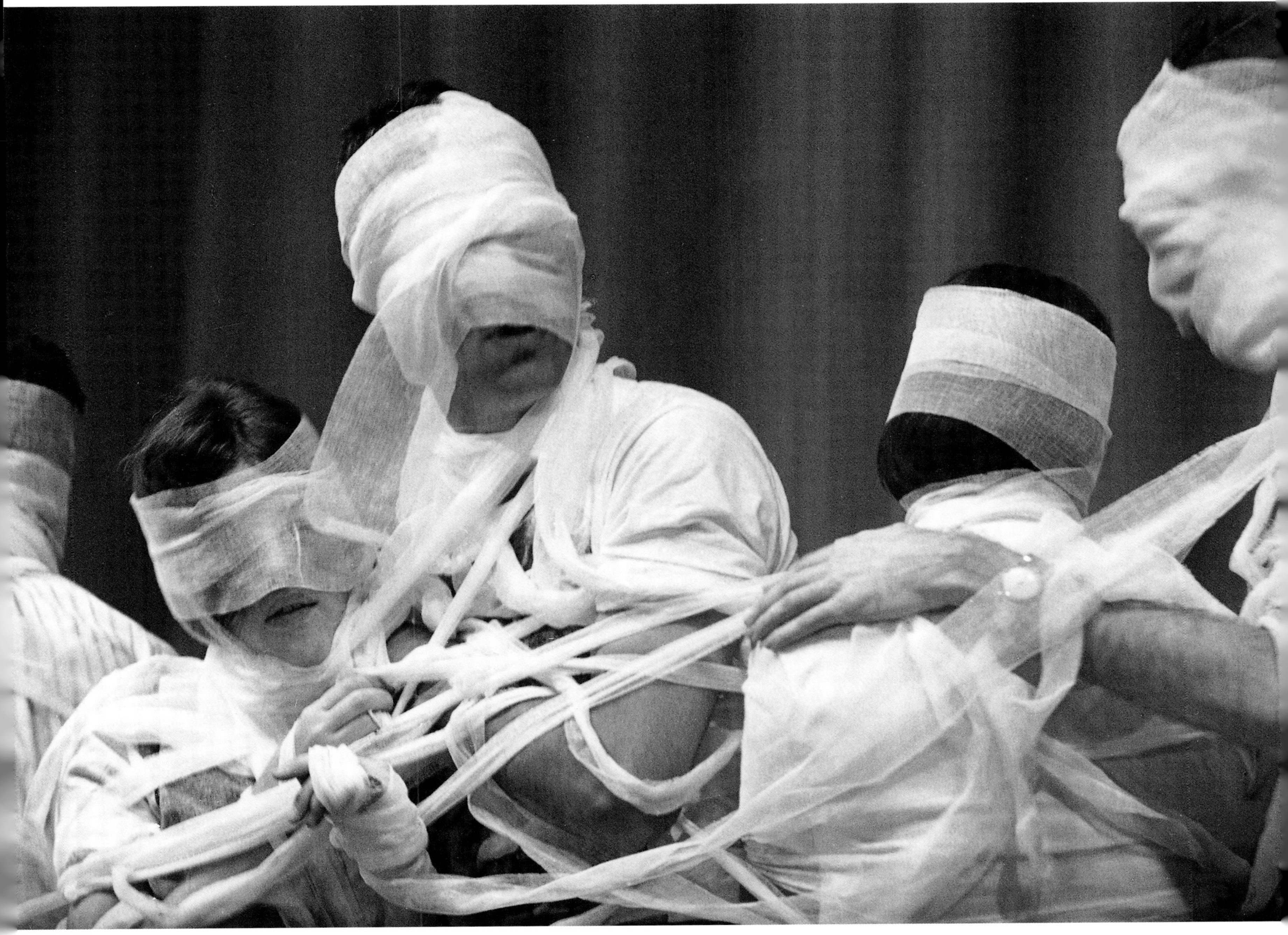

PLATE 32B
SKY PIECE TO JESUS CHRIST,
CARNEGIE RECITAL HALL,
NEW YORK, 1965. PHOTO BY
PETER MOORE © EST. PETER
MOORE / VAGA, NY, NY

33 *Destruction in Art Symposium (DIAS)*, 1966

symposium and performance events in London, September 9–30

CHRONOLOGY

September 11
talk, Africa Center

September 12
performance of *Whisper Piece*, "Concert at Conway Hall"

September 13
performance of *Shadow Piece*, "Afternoon Events at London Free School Playground"

September 15
performance of *Shadow Piece*, "Afternoon Concert at Africa Center"

September 28–29
Two Evenings with Yoko Ono, Africa Center
Programs A (28) and B (29)

September 30
performance of *Disappearing Piece (Boil Water)*, "Final Event," Mercury Theatre

Ono was particularly active at the *Destruction in Art Symposium (DIAS)*, a multinational, multidisciplinary event organized by artist Gustav Metzger that included a month of performances and a three-day symposium.[1] A diverse group of artists and poets from fifteen countries in Eastern and Western Europe, the United States, South America, and Japan was invited, chosen for their interest in the relation between destruction in art and society. The participants, all associated with the counterculture of the mid-1960s, included pioneers of Happenings, Fluxus, Viennese Action Art, Concrete Poetry, and the "anti-psychiatry" movement of Irish psychiatrist R. D. Laing. Ono was one of two women to give a talk at the symposium, and the only woman to perform her own events.[2]

Ono's symposium talk focused on subtle, unexpected poetic relations between, and even whimsical instances of, destruction and creation. She noted that Japanese monks burned their temples in order to prevent them from deteriorating, and sometimes take off their pants before they fight. She also observed that Happenings had become part of the establishment and that her work was "a rehearsal and not an ultimate state of mind."[3] Her poetic and philosophical approach to destruction was especially expressed in *Whisper Piece*, an event based on a child's game that called for players to whisper to each other a phrase that would become successively eroded and reconstructed by its sequential transmission and repetition. While her male colleagues were burning books, destroying pianos and furniture, blowing up buildings, and creating similar physically and emotionally challenging actions, her work was seen by some as not destructive enough. Perhaps they did not know that she had "cut her finger and let the blood drip onto a blank canvas,"[4] and had written the instruction (published in *Grapefruit*, 1964):

> BLOOD PIECE
>
> Use your blood to paint.
> Keep painting until you faint. (a)
> Keep painting until you die. (b)
>
> 1960 spring

Regardless, Ono's *Shadow Piece* could not have been more poignant in its evocation of violence and genocide. She traced the bodies of twenty participants on a long continuous cloth on the Free School Playground, a strip of land bombed during World War II and still littered by debris. Her event offered a mute analogue to the imprints of bodies left on the sidewalks of Hiroshima after the bomb. Given the *terrain vague* of the "playground," she seems to have summoned the shadow as the symbol Carl Jung associated with the primitive and instinctive, or negative "double" of the body, or the base side of humanity.[5]

PLATE 33A
POSTER, ***DIAS PRESENTS TWO EVENINGS WITH YOKO ONO***, 1966

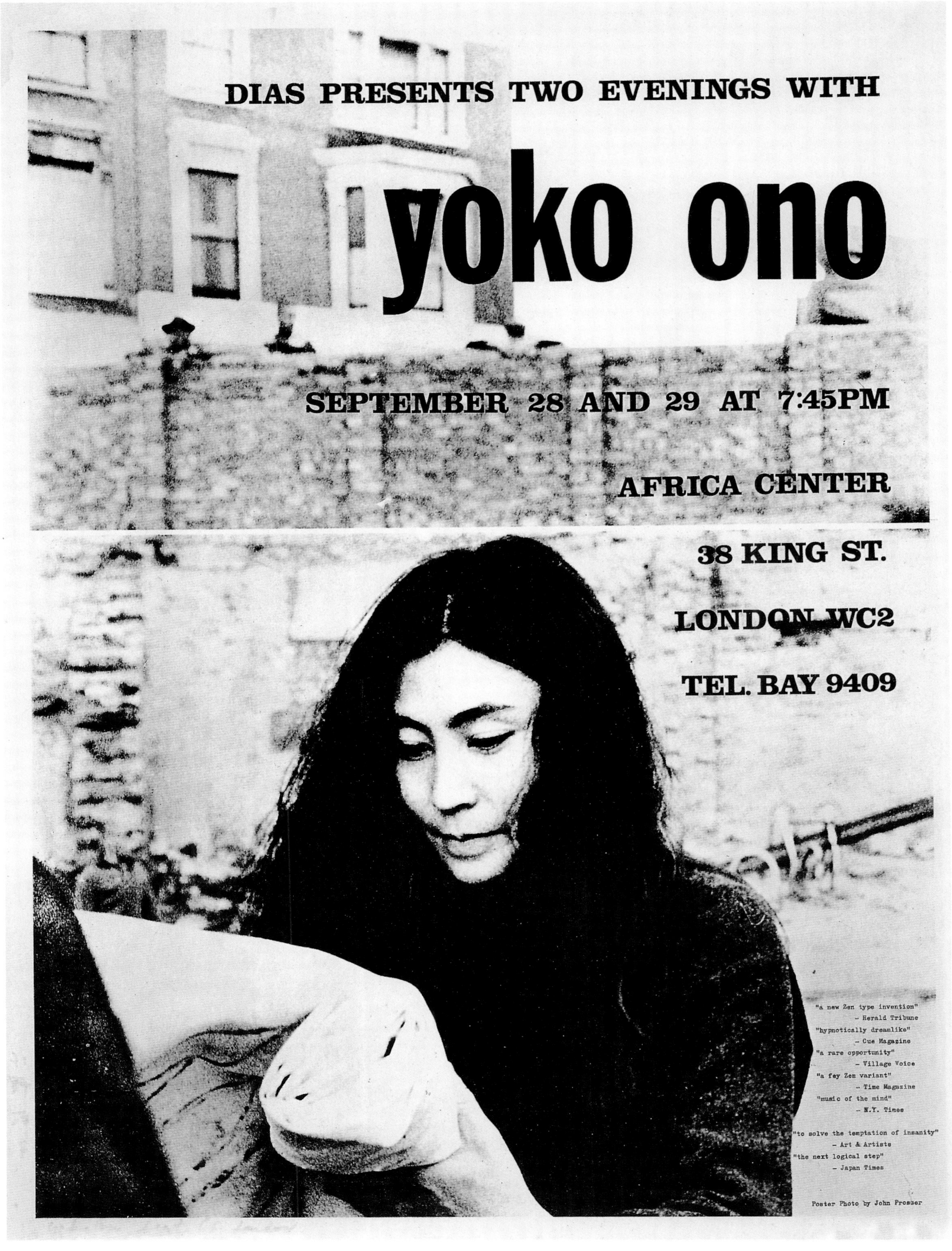
DIAS PRESENTS TWO EVENINGS WITH
yoko ono
SEPTEMBER 28 AND 29 AT 7:45PM
AFRICA CENTER
38 KING ST.
LONDON WC2
TEL. BAY 9409
"a new Zen type invention"
- Herald Tribune
"hypnotically dreamlike"
- Cue Magazine
"a rare opportunity"
- Village Voice
"a fey Zen variant"
- Time Magazine
"music of the mind"
- N.Y. Times
"to solve the temptation of insanity"
- Art & Artists
"the next logical step"
- Japan Times
Poster Photo by John Prosser

Ono also offered two evenings of events at the Africa Center. On September 28, she presented *Line Piece*, *Bag Piece* (simultaneously with *Bicycle Piece for Orchestra*), and *Cut Piece*, followed by an intermission during which *Add-Red Painting* was offered for auction. After the intermission, she performed *Sky Piece*, *Dawn Piece*, *Touch Poem*, and *Fly Piece*. Many of these works, like *Line Piece* (which consisted of a line of white chairs on the stage that the audience watched for about half an hour), were either conceptual or sculptural sound pieces rather than actual performances by Ono. The following evening, September 29, she performed *Bag Piece*, *Striptease for Three*, and *Cut Piece*, before the intermission during which her *Circle Painting* was auctioned. Next she performed *Question Piece*, *Wall Piece*, *Clock Piece*, and *Wind Piece*. The program also announced that *Toilet Pieces* would be on "display in the lavatory," a wry reference to Marcel Duchamp's 1917 Readymade, *Fountain*, and to the intermittent activities of the audience. Her program further noted that works such as *Wind Piece* "would be performed sometime throughout the two evenings." There were also strangely poetic, spontaneous events that occurred as well, such as when the audience broke into whistling the "Colonel Bogey March" from *The Bridge on the River Kwai* during *Touch Piece*.

On September 30, the final evening of performances at the Mercury Theatre, Ono announced that her piece had already occurred at some other place.

KS

NOTES

1. Metzger worked with a group of artists, poets, and writers to organize *DIAS*. They included the Irish concrete poet John Sharkey and the English concrete poet Bob Cobbing (then manager of Better Books, a London bookshop that functioned in the mid-1960s as a gathering place for poetry readings and performances of the international literary and artistic underground). Other members of the committee included: Wolf Vostell, Happenings and Fluxus practitioner in Germany; Roy Ascott, British artist, theorist, and educator interested in cybernetics; Mario Amaya, the first editor of *Art and Artists*; and "Miles" (Miles Burrows), a regular contributor to the *East Village Other* and editor of the *International Times* (*IT*), the organ of the international underground, located in London. Jim Haynes was also on the *DIAS* organizing committee and the editorial board of *IT*. He had formerly been with the Traverse Theatre in Edinburgh, and in 1966 founded the Jeanetta Cochrane Theatre in London, which served experimental artists in all disciplines.

2. The American dancer Barbara Gladstone (who would later became a psychologist) gave a talk at the symposium. Carolee Schneemann was invited, but was unable to attend; Anna Lockwood participated in various actions with Raphael Montañez Ortiz; and Susan Cohen, an artist, performed in an action by Günter Brus and Otto Mühl. Barbara Stevini performed with Ono in *Shadow Piece*.

3. Ivor Davies, "Notes" from *DIAS*, personal archive of Ivor Davies, Penarth, Wales.

4. Alexandra Munroe, "A Box of Smile: Tokyo Fluxus, Conceptual Art, and the School of Metaphysics" in *Japanese Art After 1945: Scream Against the Sky* (New York: Abrams, 1994), 218.

5. Ono said she read Jung closely during her college years (conversation with author, August 1999). Chrissie Iles has pointed out that an eighteenth-century German physiognomist, Johann Caspar Lavater, mechanically reproduced human shadows in the belief that in their tracing he might "capture a precise image of the soul." Such an event might draw "out of the inner soul" as a curative. See Iles, *Have You Seen the Horizon Lately?* exh. cat. (1997), 82.

VISUAL DOCUMENTATION: 1966, film by unknown filmmaker, WPI Film Library, Orland Park, Ill. (Job #97846)

AUDIO DOCUMENTATION: tape recording by Tom Lopez, "Yoko Ono at Africa Center" (1966), collection of the artist

LITERATURE: special issue on "Auto-Destructive," *Art and Artists* (August 1966); *Time* (23 September 1966); Amaya, *London Life* (8 October 1966); special feature on *DIAS*, *International Times* (14–27 October 1966); Hansen, *Arts Magazine* (November 1966); Durgnat, *Studio International* (December 1966); Reichardt, *The Architectural Review* (December 1966); Farrell, *Life* (February 1967); special issue on *DIAS*, *Dé-coll/age* (July 1967); Stiles, *The Act* (spring 1987); ———, "The Destruction in Art Symposium (DIAS)," dissertation (1987)

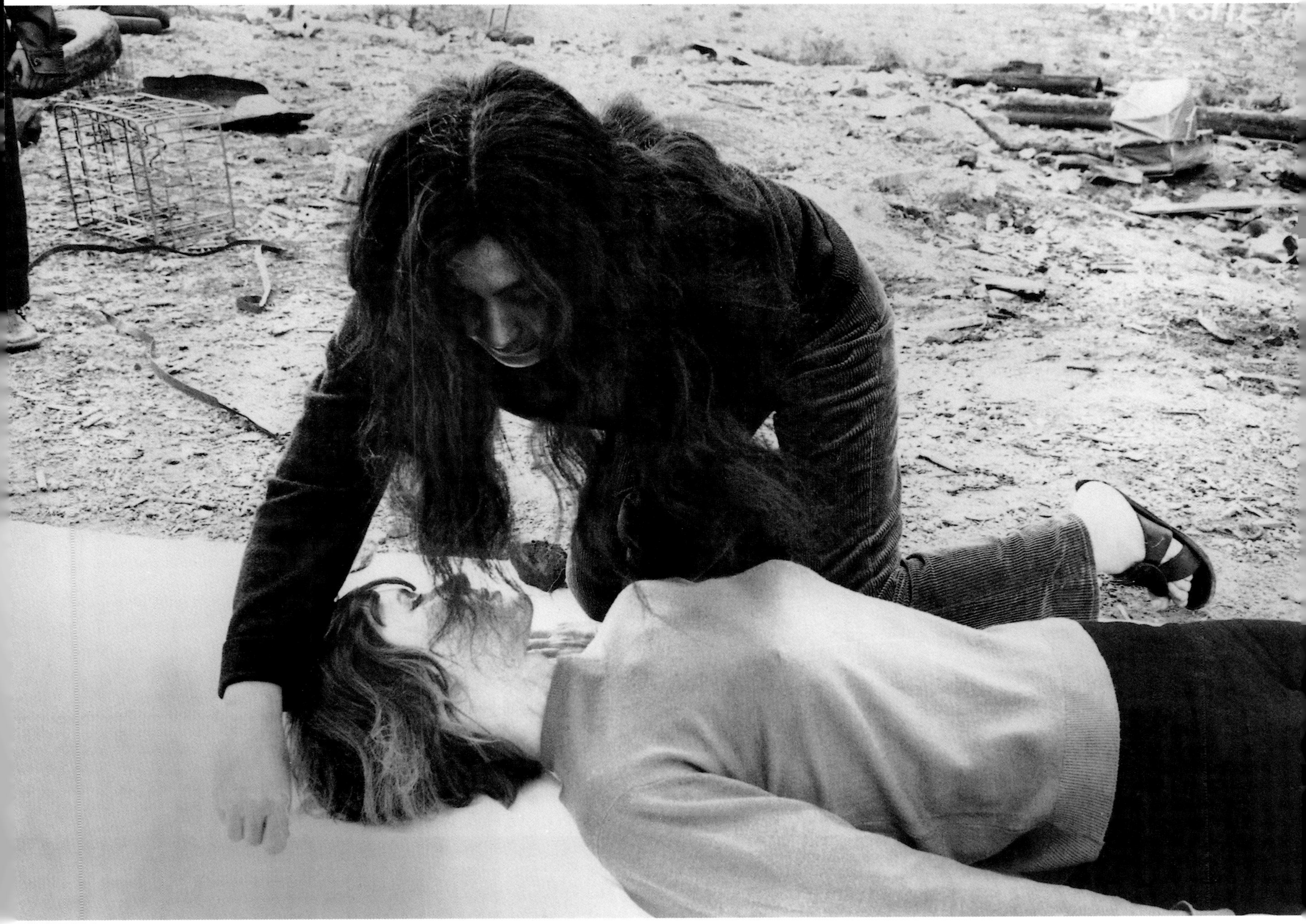

PLATE 33B
SHADOW PIECE,
PERFORMED BY YOKO
ONO AND BARBARA
STEVINI, FREE SCHOOL
PLAYGROUND, LONDON,
1966

34 *Bed-In for Peace,* 1969

event at Amsterdam Hilton Hotel, March 25–31

Bed In, 1969

event at Queen Elizabeth Hotel, Montreal, May 26–June 2

Once Ono and Lennon became a couple, they expanded the aesthetic and philosophical import of *Bag Piece* (no. 31) to include larger political concerns. In *Bed-In for Peace*, for example, they converted the ubiquitous 1960s psychedelic gathering-of-the-tribe, the "Be-In," into a week-long international media event. Signs over the couple's marital bed that read "Hair Peace" and "Bed Peace" were clear references to Ono's earlier instruction "pieces," transformed into the global language of the countercultural social movement to end the war in Vietnam, to which Ono and Lennon belonged. In this way, Ono's aesthetic practice reached an international audience and transformed the artistic event into a broad cultural and political statement.

In addition, Ono and Lennon inverted the viewing conditions of *Bag Piece* from the intimate situation involved in witnessing an enigmatic cultural event, utilizing the mass media to create a mass cultural representation for involvement in a political movement by an international social body. Drawing upon the philosophical and phenomenological aspects of Ono's *Bag Piece*, they publicized the intimacy of the nuptial bed as a metaphor for cultural transformation, demonstrating the essential relation between private beliefs and public behavior. In this way, *Bed-In for Peace* wedded erotic love and an intellectual desire for world peace with the ideological goal of ending the Vietnam War.

Following *Bed-In for Peace*, at the height of the war, Ono and Lennon launched a Christmas peace campaign, "War Is Over!/ If You Want It" (no. 39). They strategically installed billboards with this phrase in urban settings, locating them in the entertainment centers of the world: Times Square (the theater district), Sunset Boulevard in Hollywood (the film industry), Shaftsbury in London (the theater, literary, and art district), and so forth. On several occasions involving the press, they held up a small bag designated the "bag of laughs." This permutation of Ono's *Bag Piece* was a playful gesture simultaneously signaling the folly of war and the joy of peace. Laughing in the face of "states of war," they insisted that responsibility for change and peace resides in the individual "if you want it."

As with the *Bed-In for Peace*, they generated publicity for billboards and posters as static works of art that linked the installation sites to their highly publicized events, joining art as entertainment to entertainment as spectacle, and spectacle to the theater of war. This chain of signifiers visualized how individuals might intervene in the process of ending war, through concrete visual representations, physical actions, intellectual decisions, and a commitment they described as "love." Such a dense semiotics provided an international stage for the conjunction of art and politics, an arena that artists like Hans Haacke, Suzanne Lacy, Jenny Holzer, and others mined increasingly in the 1970s and 1980s.

KS

VISUAL DOCUMENTATIONS: film by Lennon and Ono, *Bed-In* (1969); video, Lennon and Ono, *The Bed-In* (1990)

LITERATURE: *Dayton Daily News* (25 May 1969); *Pembroke Observer* (26 May 1969); *Staten Island Advance* (26 May 1969); Winslow, *Montreal Star* (28 May 1969); Vincent, *La Presse* (29 May 1969); *Montreal Star* (2 June 1969); *Calgary Alberton* (4 June 1969); *St. John's News* (4 June 1969); Cochnar, *NEA Lively Arts Special* (10 June 1969); *Toronto Daily Star* (12 June 1969); Bott, *Boston Herald Traveler* (15 June 1969); Gleason, *San Francisco Chronicle* (18 June 1969); Yorke, *Rolling Stone* (28 June 1969); *Philadelphia Enquirer* (8 July 1969); Sanders, *Saturday Review* (11 July 1969); Bott, *Houston Chronicle* (13 July 1969); C.P., *Toronto Star* (25 May 1986); Kearney, *Houston Chronicle* (19 September 1993); *Ottowa Citizen* (15 January 1994); *Daily Telegraph* (5 February 1994); Dannatt, *Daily Telegraph* (2 March 1994); Magee, *Herald* (29 July 1995); Hansen, *John Lennon*, exh. cat. (1995), 168–71; Fox, *Ottowa Citizen* (23 November 1996); ———, *Toronto Star* (30 November 1996); *New York Times* (10 August 1997); Kearney, *Houston Chronicle* (10 August 1997); *Los Angeles Times* (17 August 1997); Gaar, *Goldmine* (7 November 1997); *Toronto Star* (29 September 1998); *Financial Times* (2 October 1998); Carter and Marks, *Independent* (7 December 1998); Carpenter, *Los Angeles Times* (15 December 1998); Laurence, *La Presse* (22 May 1999); *Gazette* (27 May 1999); Bist, *Gazette* (30 May 1999)

DATA BY KC

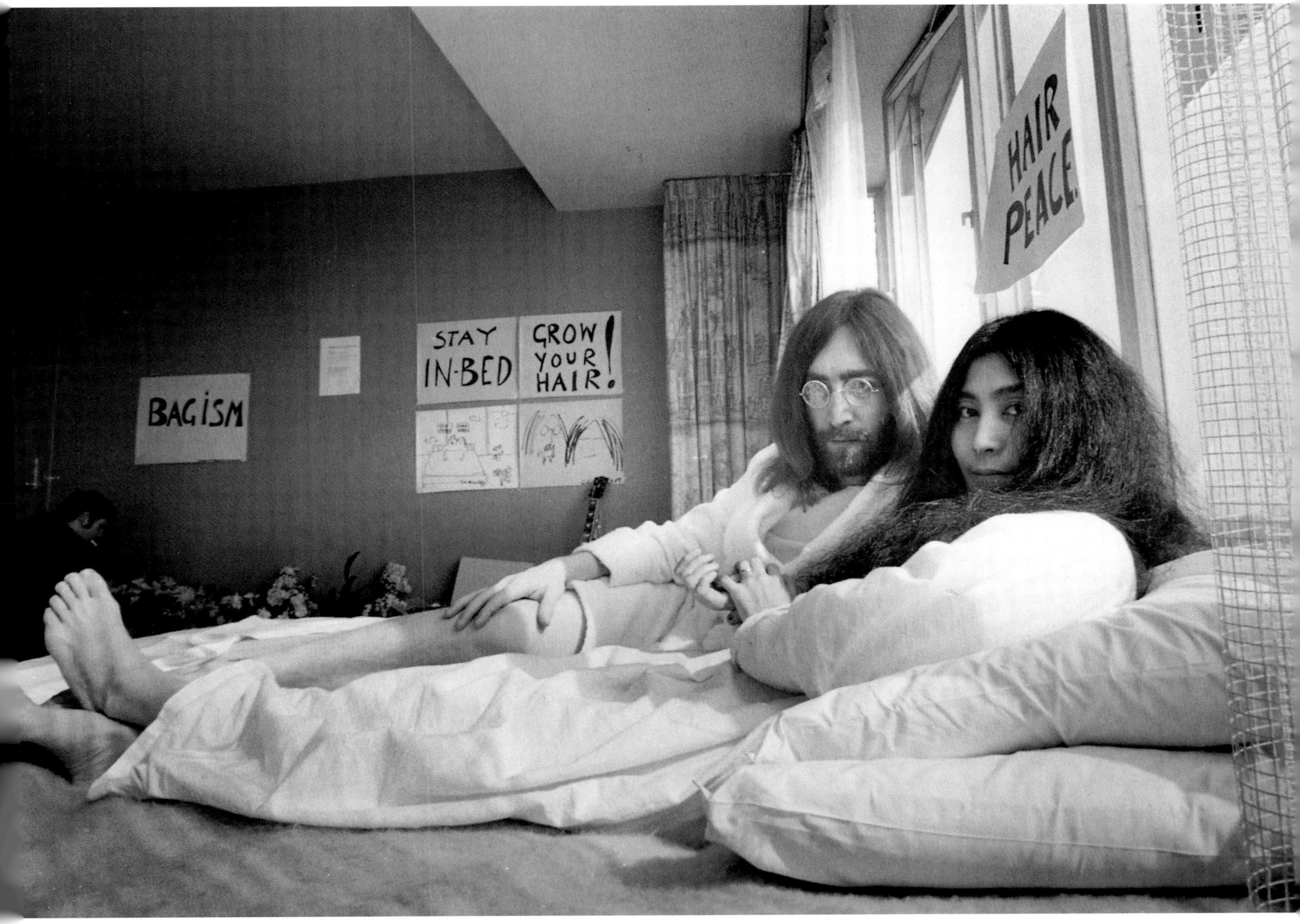

PLATE 34
BED-IN FOR PEACE,
AMSTERDAM HILTON
HOTEL, 1969

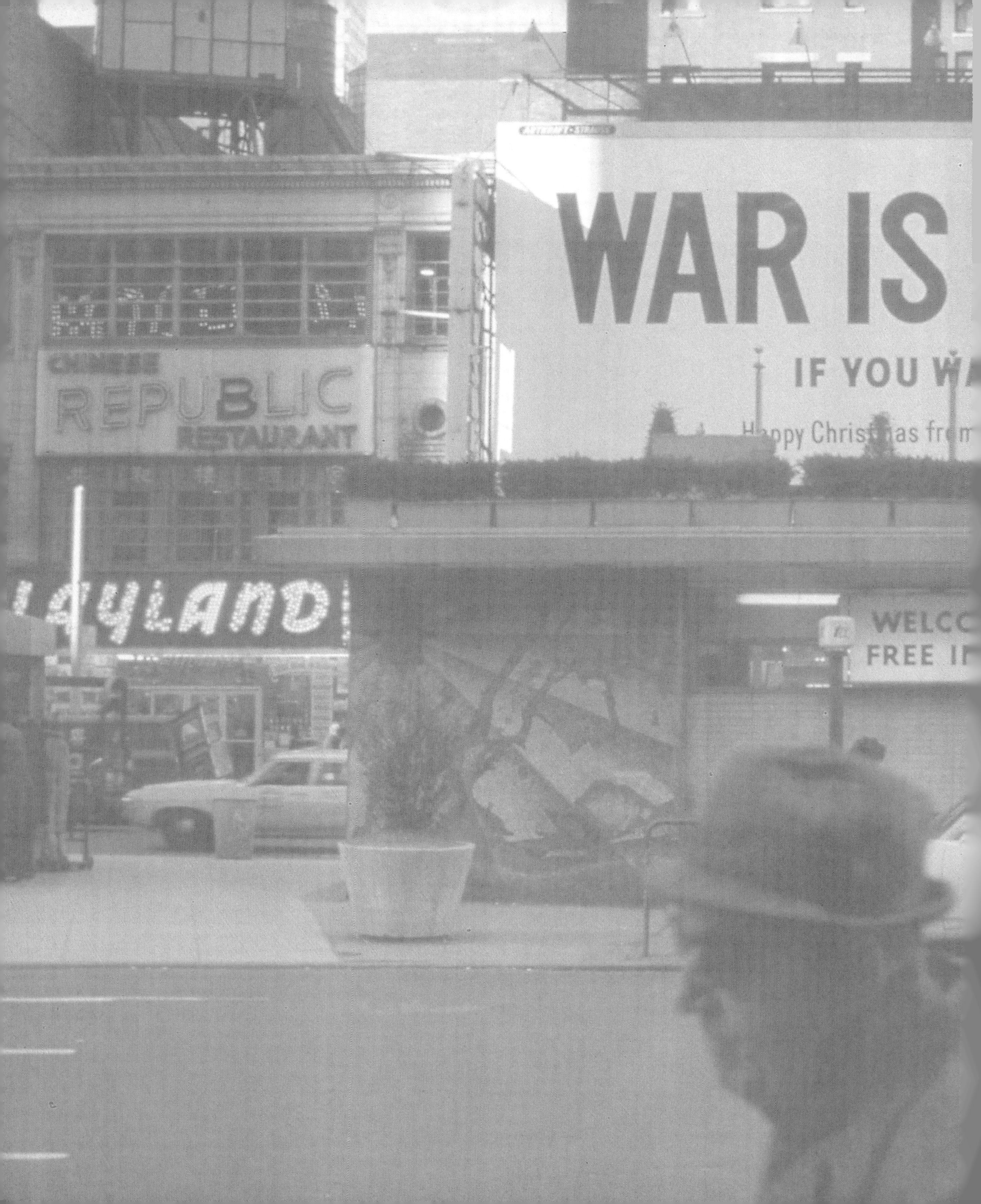
WAR IS
IF YOU W
Happy Christmas from
CHINESE
REPUBLIC
RESTAURANT
AYLAND
WELC
FREE I

ADVERTISEMENTS

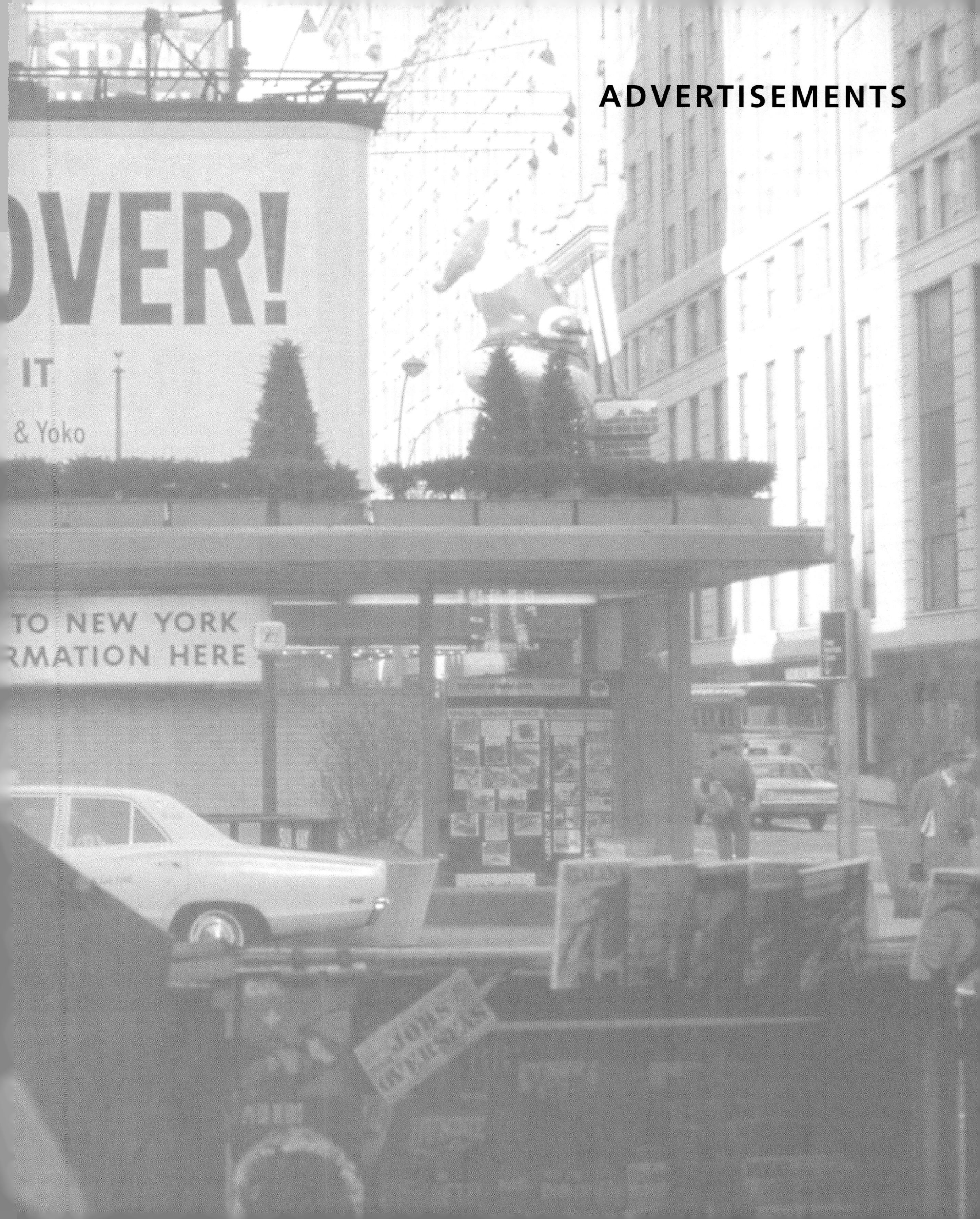

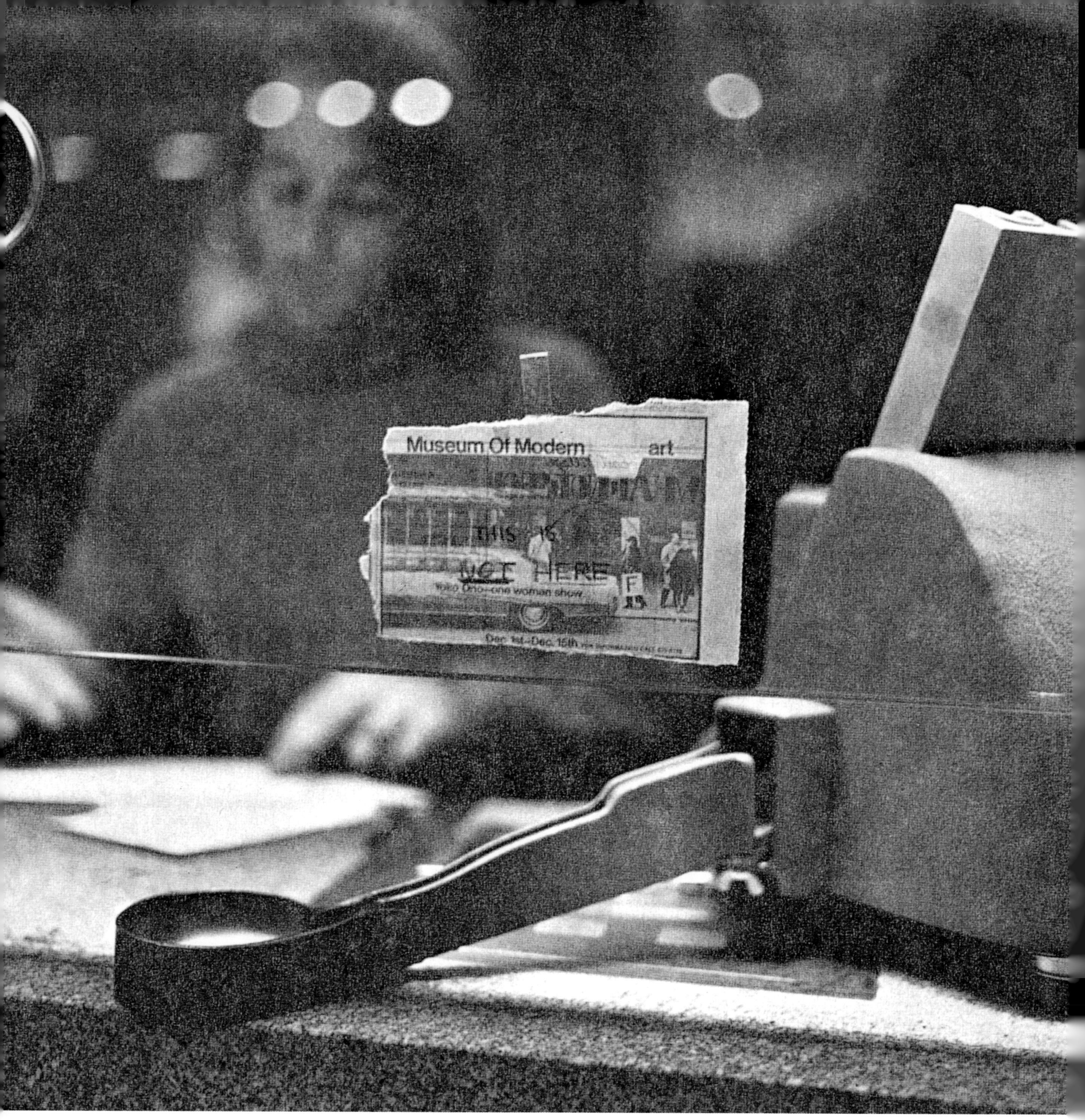

FIGURE 9.1
ADVERTISEMENT FOR
MUSEUM OF MODERN
[F]ART IN MOMA TICKET
WINDOW. FROM
ARTIST'S BOOK / EXHIBI-
TION CATALOGUE, 1971

Nothing IsReal: Yoko Ono's Advertising Art

KEVIN CONCANNON

Among Yoko Ono's artistic accomplishments, possibly the least recognized are her various series and works for advertising media (created as early as 1964), which clearly manifest the strategy of institutional critique that would in later years be considered a hallmark of Conceptual Art. From *IsReal Gallery* (1965) through *War Is Over!* (1969) and beyond, these works in many ways prefigure the trajectory of Conceptual Art's development through the 1960s and into the 1970s.

Although a number of authors have noted the importance of Ono's advertising works in passing, it is only very recently that they have been considered in any depth.[1] Even such a widely publicized project as *War Is Over!* (billboards, posters, and ads created with John Lennon) has received little art historical or critical attention.[2] This scholarly oversight can be explained in part by the fact that "ad art" is yet to be recognized as a separate category of artmaking. Artists' billboards are often understood as "installation art,"[3] postcards as "mail art," and print ads as a type of "artist's page." And some of Ono's advertising works have also been categorized simply as "scores."

The sphere of advertising allowed Ono to reach far wider audiences with her characteristic participation works than would otherwise have been possible. For works that are explicitly intended to be completed in the viewer's mind, advertising is an especially potent medium. Whereas the conventional objective of advertising is to encourage consumption, Ono's ads encourage creation. Draw a circle; drill a hole; swim in your sleep. Hovering between the real and the imaginary, Ono's art offers a virtual reality that the viewer must help construct, tangibly or conceptually. The aim of this chapter is to introduce Ono's advertising works and to prepare a foundation for understanding their significance in the history of Conceptualism.

The first advertisements as such that Ono placed in a magazine or newspaper were two *IsReal Gallery* ads in *The New York Arts Calendar* (no. 36). One was a full-page display in the March 1965 issue, which advertised "Circle Events" at *IsReal Gallery*.[4] According to the ad, "circle events" could be ordered on different materials (leather, silk, glass, canvas, or others), in varying sizes (from 3¼ x 2" to 40 x 24"), for the price of "about $250."[5] The exhibition dates were given in the listings page as March 3–31, and the gallery described as open twenty-four hours a day. No address was offered, but a telephone number was listed. The magazine's next issue featured another ad for *IsReal Gallery*, this one offering "Hole Events," also on "leather, silk, glass, canvas, or other material to order."[6] *IsReal Gallery*, however, existed only in the pages of *The New York Arts Calendar* and in the minds of the artist and her readers.

The *IsReal* advertisements are among the earliest examples of Conceptual Art in an advertising medium, coming three years before Dan Graham's *Figurative* (fig. 9.2) in the March 1968 issue of *Harper's Bazaar*, a work that is generally cited in this regard.[7]

Graham's ad, a cash-register tape with the title *Figurative by Dan Graham*, appeared sandwiched between advertisements for Warner bras and Tampax tampons.[8] The coincidence of *Figurative*'s place-

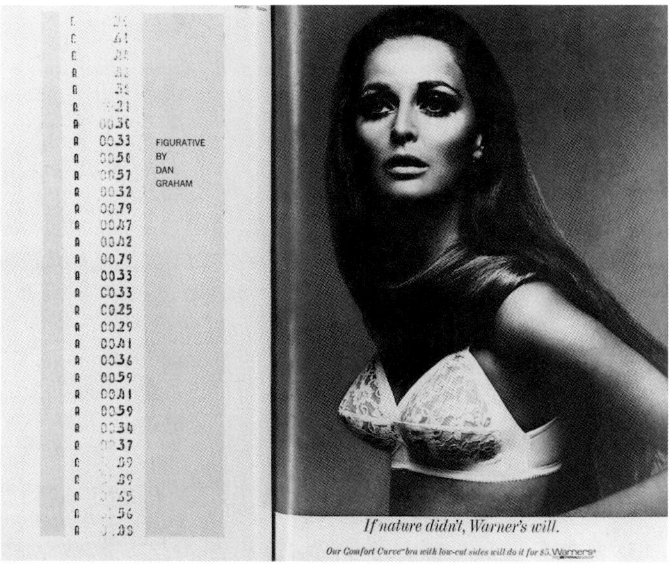

FIGURE 9.2
DAN GRAHAM,
FIGURATIVE, 1968.
ADVERTISEMENT IN
HARPER'S BAZAAR,
MARCH 1968

ment adjacent to an ad for bras extends the pun inherent in the work, which—to an art-savvy reader—already suggests a play between "figurative art" and the column of "figures" on the tape. In an essay titled "My Works for Magazine Pages: 'A History of Conceptual Art'" (1985), Graham offers this explanation of the work:

> I became involved with the art system accidentally when friends of mine suggested that we open a gallery.... At our gallery, John Daniels, we gave Sol Lewitt a one-man show, and presented several group shows that included all the proto-Minimalist artists.... However, the gallery was forced to close at the end of the first season due to bankruptcy.... Through the actual experience of running a gallery, I learned that if a work of art were not written about and reproduced in a magazine, it would have difficulty attaining the status of "art." It seemed that to be defined as having value (that is, value as "art"), a work had only to be exhibited in a gallery and then to be written about and reproduced as a photograph in an art magazine. It was this record of the no-longer-extant installation, along with more accretions of information after the fact, that became the basis for the art work's fame and, to a large extent, its economic value.[9]

Ono's *IsReal Gallery* was constructed of little more than these "accretions of information": in it, she effectively conflated the exhibition and its documentation. The *Draw Circle* and *Drill Hole* works—actually blank rectangles—were "reproduced" in *The New York Arts Calendar* as illustrations, "documenting" works available at an immaterial gallery. (Curiously, in the same March 1965 magazine in which the first *IsReal Gallery* ad appeared, Graham had an advertisement as well—for his very real, soon-to-be-bankrupt gallery, John Daniels.[10])

As with much Conceptual Art, language and geometry are both implicated in the *IsReal Gallery* works. (Indeed, the ads prominently feature the phrase "concept art.") The name itself suggests the nation of Israel (enough to confuse the typesetter who gave it as such on a listings page of *The New York Arts Calendar*) and was in fact inspired by the name of prospective patron Sylvia Israel, for whom the artist created *Eternal Time* in 1965 (no. 13). And as Ono had pointed out in her 1962 article "The Word of a Fabricator," circles and lines are abstract concepts—"a perfect circle and a perfect line which we have not encountered except in our conceptual world."[11] The ads, moving from "Circle Events" to "Hole Events," even showed a progression in dematerialization: a circle might be rendered in one material or another, whereas a hole is defined by the lack of a given material; it is immaterial by definition.

In a short 1966 essay titled "On Circle Event," in the publication for the collaborative environment *The Stone*, Ono explains the origins of *IsReal Gallery*, as well as her related "Draw Circle" postcard (fig. 14.11):

> The circle painting idea was taken to a gallery for a possible presentation. They did not like the idea. They did not know exactly what was going to be shown.
>
> "Are we going to show circles?"
> "No, we are going to ask people to come and draw circles."
> "But what will be on the canvas before that?"
> "A blank canvas will be alright."
> "Are we going to show blank canvases?"
> "We are not going to show, we are going to prepare."
> "But what then is the point of the show? Can't you draw a few circles before they draw?"
> "Is that necessary?"
> "Don't you think your circles will be better than theirs, that is, your being an artist and all that?"
> "Do you think so?"
> "But if somebody wants to buy the painting, for instance, what are they going to buy?"
> "They can buy blank canvases, or they can buy the unfinished painting and take it home and ask circles to be added on each time they have a guest. They can go on adding circles that way and it will be an endless painting."
>
> But the gallery did not like the idea. So Tony Cox and I opened a gallery called "IsReal" and put the circle painting on sale. This gallery was even listed in one of the art magazines under the "gallery index" but the only physical thing that existed was the phone number.[12]

The gallery referred to is Leo Castelli. An exchange of letters in January 1965 between Ono and Castelli director Ivan Karp documents her proposal and its rejection. In her letter to Karp, dated January 4, 1965, Ono refers to a meeting between Karp and Anthony Cox (presumably described above) and counters with a proposal that Castelli invite a group of well-known artists to contribute a circle to the proposed painting, thus making it more salable.[13] Among the artists she cites are Robert Rauschenberg, Jasper Johns, Max Ernst, Marcel Duchamp, and Isamu Noguchi. Karp's reply reads, in part,

> Thank you so much for your urgent missive. It is indeed laden with pungent metaphysics and adventurous aesthetics. It seems now, however, after your clarified and detailed exposition that the kind of show you have in mind fails to suit our temperament which is essentially restless, driven, aggressive, fiercely Western and concrete—not materialistic mind you—perish the thought—but terribly concrete.[14]

It would be a few years still before Conceptual Art became part of the program at Castelli.

The *IsReal Gallery* ads clearly fit Graham's conception of his own advertisement as institutional critique. Although Graham's *Figurative* has been highlighted in previous studies of Conceptualism, several interventional uses of advertising and other print media have recently been brought to light. For example, in 1966, a year after Ono's *IsReal*, Latin American artists Eduardo Costa, Raúl Escari, and Roberto Jacoby proposed, as Alexander Alberro explains, "to 'derealize' objects by presenting accounts to newspapers and magazines of artistic exhibitions and events that did not in fact take place."[15] Again, the resemblance to Ono's work is remarkable.

A few notable earlier examples of this strategy exist. One is Ray Johnson's ad for *his* imaginary gallery, Robin Gallery, in the pages of the *Village Voice* in the summer of 1964. Critic David Bourdon explains that "Robin" was a pun on the former Reuben Gallery, "the birthplace of happenings."[16] "[The Robin Gallery] never held an exhibition though it was always advertising an 8-man show of George

Brecht, George Herms, and Ray Johnson. The eight (two threes make an eight) was usually on its side signifying infinity."[17] Bourdon's story documents the "closing" of this imaginary gallery a month after the "opening" of *IsReal*. He also notes that Johnson "detests commercial art galleries," which might allow an inference of the Robin Gallery ads as institutional critique as well. But although Johnson's ad for the July 30 issue of the *Village Voice* announces one such eight-man show with no address, phone number, or dates,[18] it is not immediately clear to the reader that the Robin Gallery is not "real." Another ad on the same page, for example, simply states "Paintings by Beaudreau at Stanley's," also lacking location or contact details. And another Robin Gallery ad from the September 17 issue of the *Village Voice* further confuses the question of real vs. imaginary. It states (in its entirety): "Ray Johnson & other Living Americans in 38-man show at Robin Gallery, Section B2, 1st Ave & 27th St./Hours: 7–8, Mon., Wed., Fri.; 2:30–4, Tues., Thurs., weekends & holidays."[19] The Robin Gallery, then, seems to exist as something between an art world in-joke and a conceptual artwork, and it certainly warrants further study. Ono was apparently unaware of Johnson's gallery at the time, recalling, "After I did the IsReal Gallery, somebody told me that George Brecht did it before me, or something to that effect.... However, I think it's nice that so many of us were thinking in the same direction, if that was the case."[20]

Another example is a work by Ono's fellow Tokyo Fluxus artist Yasunao Tone, *Tone-Prize Composition* advertisement, unearthed by art historian Reiko Tomii and included in the 1999 exhibition *Global Conceptualism*. Tone's ad pokes fun at the independent exhibition system and award exhibition programs then common in Japan. The ad, which appeared in the September 1964 issue of *Ongaku geijutsu* (Music art), begins:

> Call for Entries: 1st Tone-Prize Composition
> Tone Prizes are given to all entries.
> Deadline: October 1st
> Certificates will be mailed in lieu of official announcement: in early October.
> There is no restriction on form or content. However, phenomena will not be accepted for they are impossible to present; instead, please submit texts, etc.[21]

Contact information and other details are followed by the announcement that all winners automatically qualify for a series of other awards, each named after an artist or composer—one of whom is Yoko Ono. A request for further information would have yielded a Tone-Prize application (fig. 9.3), which included the following special note regarding qualification for the Ono Award: "Ono Award, given by Yoko Ono, will be open to works by male composers only. [Entrants] are required to present 'face and forms,' i.e., a photograph and data for weight, height, bust size, etc."[22]

Whereas Tone's competition event did in fact take place, Ono's *IsReal Gallery* had no physical incarnation at the time the ads appeared. Although there was an effort to incorporate *IsReal Gallery* as a legal entity,[23] the shift and slide between the real and the virtual—and perhaps the propensity for the latter—characterizes Ono's humorous appropriations of advertising media in the mid-1960s. In a sense, unlike conventional advertising, Ono's ads implicitly acknowledge that the goods or services on offer are often better imagined than actually had.

This play between real and imaginary is demonstrated by at least two works before *IsReal* in which the artist used direct mail advertising. In a postcard from early 1964, she invites recipients to her *Touch Poem No. 3* in Nigeria, Africa, on March 33, 1964 (no. 35). The date of March 33 makes it clear that this event takes place only in the reader's mind. Ono

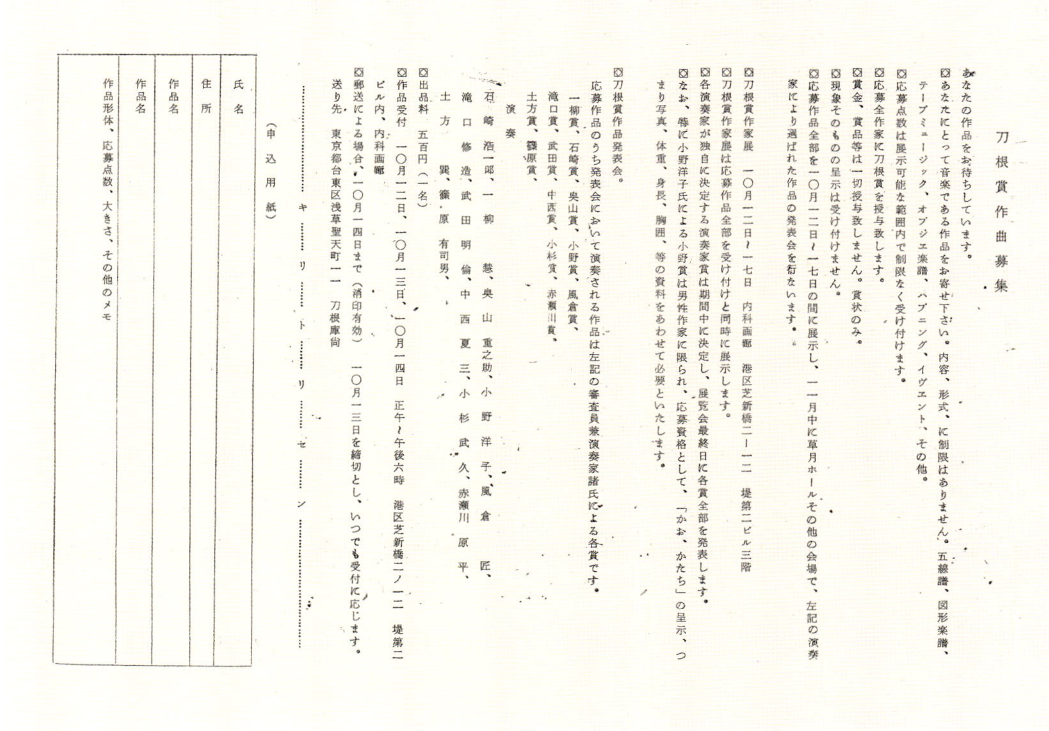
刀根賞作曲募集

あなたの作品をお待ちしています。
☒あなたにとって音楽である作品をお寄せ下さい。内容、形式、に制限はありません。五線譜、図形楽譜、テープミュージック、オブジエ楽譜、ハプニング、イヴエント、その他。
☒応募点数は展示可能な範囲内で制限なく受け付けます。
☒応募全作家に刀根賞を授与致します。
☒賞金、賞品等は一切授与致しません。賞状のみ。
☒現象そのものの呈示は受け付けません。
☒応募作品全部を一〇月一二日〜一七日の間に展示し、一一月中に草月ホールその他の会場で、左記の演奏家により選ばれた作品の発表会を行ないます。
☒刀根賞作家展　一〇月一二日〜一七日　内科画廊　港区芝新橋二ー一二　堤第二ビル三階
☒刀根賞作家展は応募作品全部を受け付けと同時に展示します。
☒各演奏家が独自に決定する演奏家賞は期間中に決定し、展覧会最終日に各賞全部を発表します。
☒なお、特に小野洋子氏による小野賞は男性作家に限られ、応募資格として、「かお、かたち」の呈示、つまり写真、体重、身長、胸囲、等の資料をあわせて必要といたします。
☒刀根賞作品発表会。
応募作品のうち発表会において演奏される作品は左記の審査員兼演奏家諸氏による各賞です。
一柳賞、石崎賞、奥山賞、小野賞、風倉賞、
滝口賞、武田賞、中西賞、小杉賞、赤瀬川賞、
土方賞、篠原賞、
演奏
石崎浩一郎、一柳　慧、奥山重之助、小野洋子、風倉　匠、
滝口修造、武田明倫、中西夏三、小杉武久、赤瀬川原平、
土方　巽、篠原有司男、
☒出品料　五百円（一名）
☒作品受付　一〇月一二日、一〇月一三日、一〇月一四日　正午〜午後六時　港区芝新橋二ノ一二　堤第二ビル内、内科画廊
☒郵送による場合、一〇月一四日まで（消印有効）　一〇月一三日を締切とし、いつでも受付に応じます。
送り先　東京都台東区浅草聖天町一一　刀根康尚
…………キ……リ……ト……リ……セ……ン…………
（申込用紙）

氏名
住所
作品名
作品名
作品形体、応募点数、大きさ、その他のメモ

FIGURE 9.3
YASUNAO TONE, APPLICATION FOR ***TONE-PRIZE COMPOSITION***, 1964

used this same strategy in her postcard *Miss Ono's Tea Party*, probably from early 1966 (fig. 9.4; see no. 35). Professionally printed postcards were at that time (as today) commonly used in Japan for personal holiday greetings and were thus relatively easy to produce.[24]

After *IsReal*, Ono's deployment of advertising media became more interventional. A case in point is the three ads—*Fountain Piece*, *Mouthpiece*, and *Do It Yourself Dance Piece (Swim in Your Sleep)*—Ono placed in the fall of 1966 in the London-based magazine *Art and Artists* (no. 38).[25] These works are varyingly related to Ono's dance instructions published in her *Do It Yourself Fluxfest* (designed by Fluxus founder George Maciunas) as part of *VTRE*, or *3 newspaper eVenTs for the pRicE of $1* (Fluxus Newspaper No. 7), in February 1966 (fig 2.16). This festival actually began as an ad for *"Do It Yourself" Dance Festival* in the *Village Voice* that announced it as a subscription event (fig. 9.5).[26]

Although the dance instructions in *VTRE* could be more properly thought of as an "artist's page" (one of three in the newspaper) than an advertising work, the *Art and Artists* realizations are clearly advertising interventions, contextualized as such by their placement within the magazine's pages among other ads and listings. The works thus began as a dance festival of the mind, the participants for which were solicited through an ad in the *Village Voice*, and ended up as instructions realized within advertising spaces. With the *Art and Artists* realizations, Ono conflates the solicitation of participation and the product offered. Whereas *Village Voice* readers were required to send money for instructions to be delivered by mail, *Art and Artists* readers were offered instructions outright.

Perhaps the best known of Ono's published print advertising pieces is *Museum of Modern [F]art* of 1971 (no. 40; fig. 9.1). No longer the "starving artist," Ono placed a paid display advertisement in the *Village Voice* announcing her (again, purely conceptual) "one-woman show" at the Museum of Modern Art. The works associated with *Museum of Modern [F]art* as a whole extend the implicit institutional critique evident in the earlier *IsReal Gallery* works. *IsReal Gallery* mainly existed for the comparatively small readership of *The New York Arts Calendar*, but Ono's putative MoMA show was presented to the much wider audience of the *Village Voice*. Further complicating the boundary of the real and the virtual, Ono published a "catalogue" as an artist's book and also documented it in a film, *The Museum of Modern Art Show*.

Ono's advertising work gained a worldwide audience with the *War Is Over!* campaign, created in collaboration with John Lennon (no. 39). For this event, launched on December 15, 1969, the couple commissioned billboards and posters in twelve cities: Athens, Berlin, Hong Kong, London, Los Angeles, Montreal, New York, Paris, Port-of-Spain (Trinidad), Rome, Tokyo, and Toronto.[27] In the language of the city where they were sited, the billboards and posters declared: "WAR IS OVER! / IF YOU WANT IT / Happy Christmas from John & Yoko." As Ono had appropriated the medium of the professionally printed postcard popular for Japanese holiday greetings for her *Touch Poem No. 3* and several other works, *War Is Over!* similarly echoes the British practice of placing advertisements with holiday greetings in lieu of sending cards.[28] *War Is Over!* extended its impact through other media as well, including newspaper ads, postcards, and The Peace Station Network.[29]

In 1989, Ono began creating advertising works again on a significant scale, at first re-creating her signature *War Is Over!* works as postcards, banners, and wall paintings in conjunction with her museum exhibitions. Indeed, one could argue that the *War Is Over!* campaign was renewed in earnest in January of 1983 with Ono's placement of a full-page ad, "Surrender to Peace," in the *New York Times* (fig. 14.31), proposing a Nationwide Peace Poll:

> The Poll should be authorized and organized by the Congress as a national undertaking for the sake of expedience alone, with the balloting through the media to minimize administrative expense.[30]

The *IsReal Gallery* ads literally provided a space in which readers could contribute circles or holes; "Surrender to Peace" offers an opportunity for col-

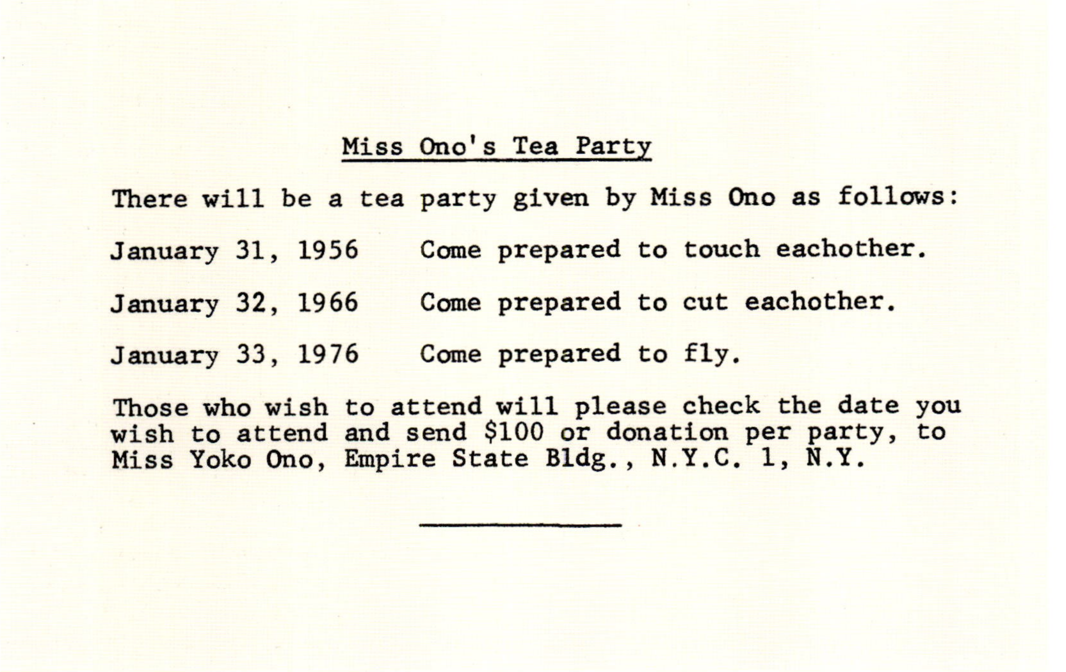

Miss Ono's Tea Party

There will be a tea party given by Miss Ono as follows:

January 31, 1956 Come prepared to touch eachother.

January 32, 1966 Come prepared to cut eachother.

January 33, 1976 Come prepared to fly.

Those who wish to attend will please check the date you wish to attend and send $100 or donation per party, to Miss Yoko Ono, Empire State Bldg., N.Y.C. 1, N.Y.

FIGURE 9.4
MISS ONO'S TEA PARTY,
POSTCARD, 1966

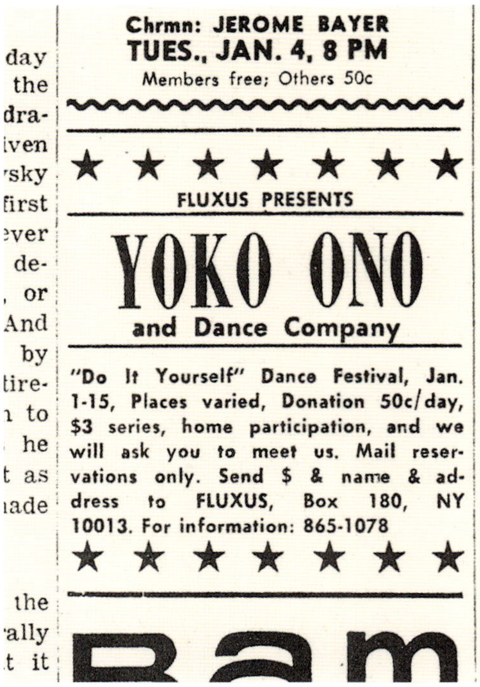

FIGURE 9.5
ADVERTISEMENT FOR
"DO IT YOURSELF" DANCE FESTIVAL IN
VILLAGE VOICE,
DECEMBER 1965

lective action through the mass media.[31] Since then, the explicit mixing of art and life has become a hallmark of Ono's advertising projects, as exemplified by, among others, the 1994 project *A Celebration of Being Human*, in Langenhagen, Germany (pls. 65a–e), and the 1996 *Fly* billboards in Richmond, Virginia (no. 41). Ono's remark in response to a journalist's query at the time of the Langenhagen event perhaps best sums up her philosophy in advertising works—that they are "designed to make viewers wonder about the subject and to prompt thoughts of peace. Art, as a part of peace, is beautiful."[32]

Over the course of a career that has evolved from the confines of the international avant-garde to the headlines of popular magazines and other mass media, Ono developed a Conceptualist practice that parallels her personal circumstances. As the *IsReal Gallery* works critique the market realities and other politics of the art world, later works such as *War Is Over!* offer an implicit critique of the art of politics. Specifically, as the *IsReal Gallery* works exploit the centrality of marketing to the art world, *War Is Over!* operates from the precept that politics is largely conducted through the media as well. As Ono told *Penthouse*, "We're using our money to advertise our ideas so that peace has equal power with the meanies who spend their money to promote war."[33] And as the developing culture of celebrity in which Ono found herself cast with increasing regularity became more and more engaged with the world of politics proper, Ono and Lennon seized the moment for positive change.[34] Although Ono's advertising works can rightly be seen as institutional critique, the critique is offered in positive and empowering terms. With their blank rectangles as the central illustrations, the *IsReal Gallery* ads literally valorize "nothing," while at the same time empowering the reader with the potential for the creative act. Likewise, the *War Is Over!* campaign does not denounce war or those who wage it, but rather suggests that the power to create peace is *ours*: *War Is Over! If You Want It*.

Ono has stated that all her work is a form of wishing,[35] and this might be what lends her advertising works their special power. For advertising, too, works from the premise of desire. The difference, of course, is that conventional advertising operates by provoking desires that can be fulfilled by their clients' products, whereas Ono's faith in the power of wishing to create positive vibrations is freely shared.

NOTES

1. References to Ono's advertising works are, for example, found in Emily Wasserman, "Yoko Ono at Syracuse: 'This Is Not Here,'" *Artforum* 10, no. 5 (1972): 73, n. 6; and Carlo McCormick, "Yoko Ono Solo," *Artforum* 27, no. 6 (1989): 120–21. More recently, her advertising works have been discussed in Concannon, "Yoko Ono's *Cut Piece* (1964): A Reconsideration," thesis (1998); Jon Hendricks, "Terrain Vague" in *Wish Trees for Basil*, exh. cat. (1998); and Concannon, "Not for Sale: Yoko Ono's Discounted Advertising Art," *Athanor* 17 (1999): 77–85.

2. For example, *Billboard: Art on the Road* (1999), an exhibition and catalogue by the Massachusetts Museum of Contemporary Art, makes no mention at all of *War Is Over!* in its history of artists' billboards.

3. See, for example, *Blurring the Boundaries* (San Diego: Museum of Contemporary Art, 1997), which discusses the museum's billboard projects within the context of "installation art" (136–37).

4. Thanks to Janis Ekdahl of the Museum of Modern Art Library in New York for assistance in locating this citation.

5. An error in the paste-up of the ad resulted in the transposition of the first and second lines, so that the ad actually reads: MATERIAL TO ORDER 3¼" X 2" TO 40 X 24 ABOUT $250/CIRCLE EVENTS ON LEATHER SILK GLASS CANVAS OR OTHER. This error was corrected in the next month's ad.

6. Thanks to Barbara Moore of Bound and Unbound in New York for bringing this ad to my attention.

7. Graham's *Figurative* has often been cited with an incorrect date. For example, it is reproduced in the catalogue for the 1995 exhibition *Reconsidering the Object of Art* with a date of 1965. This confusion may stem from the fact that Graham has dated to 1965 a related work, *Scheme for Magazine Page "Advertisement"*, in the same 1995 exhibition. The latter work shows a cash register tape "framed" in a drawn box with the title, date, and signature at the bottom. Although the cash register tapes are clearly not identical, both works are presented under a single listing (dated 1965) as "original source materials and publication documentation" in the exhibition checklist. See *Reconsidering the Object of Art: 1965–1975*, exh. cat. (Los Angeles: The Museum of Contemporary Art, 1995), 325. In both works, store name and date are lacking on the register tape (ibid., 124–25).

8. *Harper's Bazaar* (March 1968): 90–91.

9. Dan Graham, "My Works for Magazine Pages: 'A History of Conceptual Art,'" originally written in 1985; published in *Dan Graham*, exh. cat. (Perth: Art Gallery of Western Australia, 1985); reprinted in *Rock My Religion* (Cambridge: MIT Press, 1993), xviii–xx.

10. Graham does not recall having seen Ono's *IsReal* ad, one of only a handful of full-page ads, in the same issue in which his Daniels show was advertised (telephone conversation with author, 1 March 1999).

11. Ono, "The Word of a Fabricator" (1962, translated by Yoko Ono 1999; Anthology 12).

12. Ono, "On Circle Event" in *The Stone*, exh. cat. (1966), n.p.

13. See Ono, letter to Ivan Karp (1965; Anthology 13).

14. Ivan Karp, letter to Ono (1965; Anthology 13).

15. Alexander Alberro, "Reconsidering Conceptual Art, 1966–1977" in *Conceptual Art: A Critical Anthology*, ed. Alexander Alberro and Blake Stimson, (Cambridge: MIT Press, 1999), xxvi. See also Eduardo Costa, Raúl Escari, and Roberto Jacoby's "A Media Art (Manifesto)" (1966), made available in an English translation for the first time, in Alberro and Stimson, 2–4. Mari Carmen Ramírez discusses their media interventions in her essay "Tactics for Thriving on Adversity: Conceptualism in Latin America, 1960–1980" in *Global Conceptualism: Points of Origin, 1950s–1980s*, exh. cat. (New York: Queens Museum of Art, 1999), 66.

16. David Bourdon, "Art: The Robin Gallery," *Village Voice*, 8 April 1965, 14.

17. Ibid.

18. *Village Voice*, 30 July 1964, 9.

19. *Village Voice*, 17 September 1964, 13. The gallery address corresponds to that of Bellevue Hospital. This ad most likely was placed by Andy Warhol: in "Art: The Robin Gallery," Bourdon states that Warhol, Johnson's friend, had advertised Johnson's hospitalization for hepatitis at Bellevue as a Robin Gallery Event.

20. Ono, e-mail to author, 21 January 2000.

21. Cited in Reiko Tomii, "Concerning the Institution of Art: Conceptualism in Japan" in *Global Conceptualism*, 21. Also of note in Tomii's essay is Matsuzawa Yutaka's ad in another art magazine, advertising an exhibition of conceptually imagined works titled *Independent '64 Exhibition in the Wilderness*. The magazine's publication date is not clear, but the advertised exhibition dates of 3–9 December suggest the ad appeared following Ono's return from Japan to New York in September 1964. Curiously, Matsuzawa's ad notes "installation/deinstallation date: past, present, future," recalling Ono's earlier *Touch Poem III* (1964; no. 35).

22. Ibid. Tone has confirmed that Ono did indeed provide this information for the ad (telephone conversation with author, 23 February 1998). The requested information is quite similar to information appearing in the liner notes for Ono's 1973 LP album, *Feeling the Space*. Along with each musician's name and instrument, the band credits list birthdates, telephone numbers, height, weight, and chest, waist, and hip measurements for the all-male ensemble.

23. In 1966 Anthony Cox (then Ono's husband) distributed a "Prospectus" for the "Is-Real Gallery Incorporated" with a budget for the rental and operation of an actual gallery in which the installation of *The Stone*, first presented at the Judson Gallery in March 1966, was to have a "permanent home." The prospectus promised an early June opening but the project was never fully realized. Ono stated that Cox simply used the name for an unrelated venture (conversation with author, 28 April 1999). The document's past-tense reference to the Judson Gallery installation and promise of an early June opening place it within a two-month period between the end of March and the end of May 1966—at least one year after the Is-Real ads were placed. A copy of this document is held in Jean Brown Archives, Getty Research Institute, Los Angeles.

24. Thanks to Reiko Tomii for this information.

25. I am grateful to Jon Hendricks for bringing these works to my attention.

26. "Fluxus Presents Yoko Ono and Dance Company," advertisement, *Village Voice*, 23 December 1965, 17; and 30 December 1965, 11. A phone number was added to the second week's ad.

27. Dorothee Hansen, "War Is Over!" in *John Lennon: Drawings, Performances, Films*, ed. Wulf Herzogenrath and Dorothee Hansen (Stuttgart: Cantz Verlag, 1995), 172.

28. The practicality of such a strategy was noticed at the time by some writers. See, for example, Robert J. Herguth's column, "Herguth's People: John and Yoko Find an Easy Way to Stamp Out Christmas Card Woes," *Chicago Daily News*, 15 December 1969. For information about the British practice of using ads in lieu of cards, see Gloria Emerson, "Ads Act as Yule Cards for Some Britons," *New York Times*, 25 December 1969, 4.

29. See "War Is Over!" *Billboard* (24 January 1970): 49. "Radio Peace," an example of the "free John and Yoko station breaks and IDs" offered to participating media in this ad, can be heard on the CD accompanying *Let's Have a Dream: Omaggio a John Lennon*, exh. cat. (Rome: Promotore Gini O Graphics, 1990).

30. Ono, "Surrender to Peace," advertisement, *New York Times* 24 January 1983, B10. This opinion ad provokes the question of whether her op-ed pieces and paid opinion ads (some of which were jointly written with Lennon) should be considered in the context of her advertising works in particular and artmaking in general. These "opinion pieces" include, among others, the following works placed in the *New York Times*: "The Feminization of Society," 23 February 1972 (see Anthology 24); "Feeling the Space," 24 August 1973; Ono and Lennon, "A Love Letter from John and Yoko to People Who Ask Us What, When, and Why" (advertisement), 27 May 1979; "In Gratitude" (advertisement), 18 January 1981; and "Strawberry Fields Forever" (advertisement), 28 August 1981.

31. This use of polling can be traced back to "Draw Circle" postcard (1965), a work related to *IsReal Gallery*. See Chronology, 1965, spring.

32. Ono, in Maryann Bird, "People: Artful Yoko's Piece of Cheek," *Independent*, 28 October 1994, 15.

33. Ono, quoted in Charles Childs, "Penthouse Interview: John and Yoko Lennon," *Penthouse* (October 1969): 29, 34.

34. Ono, of course, had been actively promoting peace with her art before her famous partnership with Lennon. Well-known examples include *White Chess Set* (1966; no. 25); and the film *No. 4 (Bottoms)* (1966; no. 43), characterized by Ono as a "petition for peace."

35. Ono, "All My Work Is a Form of Wishing" (n.d.) in *In Facing*, exh. cat. (1990).

35 *Touch Poem No. 3,* 1964

Postcards in English and Japanese
each 3⅝ x 5⅞" (9.1 x 14.7 cm)
Collection of the artist

Ono created and distributed *Touch Poem No. 3* during early 1964 in the form of a postcard, in English and Japanese versions. The English version is in three parts: a nonsensical phonetic phrase credited to Nam June Paik;[1] date and location information for the event performance; and an instruction to "Wash your hair well before attending." The Japanese version lacks Paik's epigraph. The location given for the performance is "Nigeria, Africa," and the obviously fictional date is "March 33rd, 1964."

Touch Poem No. 3 is a realization of an instruction piece first published in *Grapefruit* (1964):

> TOUCH POEM III
>
> Hold a touch poem meeting at somewhere
> in the distance or a fictitious address
> on a fictitious day.
>
> 1964 spring

An earlier, related work in the same publication is:

> TOUCH POEM FOR GROUP OF PEOPLE
>
> Touch each other.
>
> 1963 winter

Ono performed the latter version with audiences on numerous occasions. In a program-flyer presumably distributed at her performance of *Touch Poem* [for Group of People] at the *3rd Annual New York Avant Garde Festival* in September 1965, Ono offered a history of the work:

> touch poem was first exhibited in the lobby of the Living Theater in New York City on January 8 '62 in the evening of AN ANTHOLOGY.
> it was then exhibited at the Sogetsu Art Center in Tokyo for the evening of WORKS BY YOKO ONO.
>
> touch poem, the audience participation piece, was first performed in NAIQUA GALLERY, february, 1964. since then it was performed in Kyoto, Nigeria, Berlin, Florence, Aachen and New York.

Here, Ono describes two types of *Touch Poem*—objects (fig. 14.5)[2] and performances—and treats "real" and "imaginary" performances without distinction. The Kyoto and New York references most likely are to actual performances she gave in these cities. The references to Berlin, Florence, and Aachen correspond to performances by Charlotte Moorman and Paik on their European tour in June 1965. And the Nigerian performance refers, no doubt, to the work under discussion. The conflation of real and imaginary performances underlines the work's conceptual nature.

Another postcard work, *Miss Ono's Tea Party* (fig. 9.3), extends the idea of the imaginary performance as defined in *Touch Poem III* and first realized in *Touch Poem No. 3*. Probably dating from January 1966, it invites recipients to one of three tea parties to take place on January 31, 1956; January 32, 1966; and January 33, 1976. For each date, a different instruction is offered: the first advises, "Come prepared to touch each other."

KC

NOTES

1. Paik's nonsense phrase is a string of Japanese *katakana* syllables (*ma, mi, mu, me, mo*), with accent marks that in conventional use suggest "hard" pronunciations (e.g., "g" would be the hard pronunciation of "k"). In this case, however, since "m" lacks a hard sound, the phrase is unpronounceable.

2. The object version of *Touch Poem* is a booklet of "poem to touch," which consists of strips of paper as text and strands of hair as illustration.

LITERATURE: Concannon, *Athanor* (1999)

マ″ミ″ム″メ″モ″——Nam June Paik

touch poem no. 3
yoko ono
place : Nigeria, Africa
time : March 33rd, 1964

wash your hair well before
attending

タッチ・ポエム 第三回
小野 洋子
場所 : ナイジエリア・アフリカ
時 : 3月33日・1964

髪をよく洗つて来る事。

PLATE 35A
TOUCH POEM NO. 3,
1964 (ENGLISH VERSION)

PLATE 35B
TOUCH POEM NO. 3,
1964 (JAPANESE VERSION)

36 *IsReal Gallery,* 1965–66

full-page advertisements published in *The New York Arts Calendar* 2, no. 6 (March 1965) and no. 7 (April/May 1965)
magazine: 5¼ x 7" (13.3 x 17.8 cm)

In spring of 1965, Ono placed advertisements for her conceptual gallery IsReal in two issues of *The New York Arts Calendar*, a magazine of gallery listings. The *IsReal Gallery* ads offered two "events" by the artist: *Circle Event* and *Hole Event*.[1] Space for the ads was donated by the magazine's publisher, Marshall Matusow.[2]

Ono conceived the idea of *IsReal Gallery* when Ivan Karp, director of Leo Castelli Gallery, declined to exhibit Ono's *Circle Painting* on the grounds that his gallery was interested in work that was "fiercely Western and concrete—not materialistic mind you—perish the thought—but terribly concrete."[3] The gallery's name was inspired by a patron, Sylvia Israel, to whom Anthony Cox had negotiated the sale of Ono's *Eternal Time* (no. 13).[4]

Ono's *IsReal Gallery* advertisements are among the earliest manifestations of Conceptual Art as advertising, as well as institutional critique. With *IsReal*, Ono mocks the gallery system by attempting to sell work that challenges the notion of artistic authorship: a blank canvas to be completed by the purchaser, offered by a gallery that exists only as documentation in an art magazine.

While the physical gallery did not exist, Ono did use the name to sell her art. A flyer from 1965, for example, offers a "beautifully framed portrait of Mona Lisa by Yoko Ono" for five dollars. Interested parties are advised to make out and mail checks for that amount to *IsReal Gallery* at 87 Christopher Street (actually Ono's apartment). This request suggests that the conceptual gallery actually had a bank account as well.[5]

Ono also designed stationery for the gallery, which spread the *IsReal* logo from the very top to the very bottom of the page. To use the stationery in any conventional manner would result in the obliteration of any part of the writer's text that ran across the black lettering of the logo. The stationery in this respect may be compared to Ono's *A Plus B Painting* of 1961, in which text or a picture on one layer of canvas can only be partially seen through a hole on a second layer that covers it (pl. 2d).

KC

NOTES

1. As its ad had been placed in the magazine, IsReal Gallery was mentioned in that month's listings section and was given a reproduction (of *Circle Event*) in the March issue.

2. Marshall Matusow is Harvey Matusow, best known for his controversial role in the McCarthy hearings, which he described in the book *False Witness* (1955). The magazine folded after the April/May 1965 issue.

3. Ivan Karp, letter to Ono (1965; Anthology 13).

4. Ono, e-mail to author, 10 August 1999.

5. In a document titled "Prospectus for Presenting 'The Stone,'" issued by Anthony Cox probably in April 1966, a bank account number for IsReal Gallery is listed, along with a claim that the account held assets of $2,250. According to Cox, *IsReal Gallery* was legally incorporated (conversation with author, July 1999).

LITERATURE: Ono, "On Circle Event," *The Stone*, exh. cat. (1966), n.p.; Wasserman, *Artforum* (January 1972); McCormick, *Artforum* (February 1989); Concannon, *Fly*, exh. cat. (1996), 12; Hendricks, *Wish Trees for Brazil*, exh. cat. (1998), 28; Concannon, *Artforum* (January 1999); ———, *Athanor* (1999)

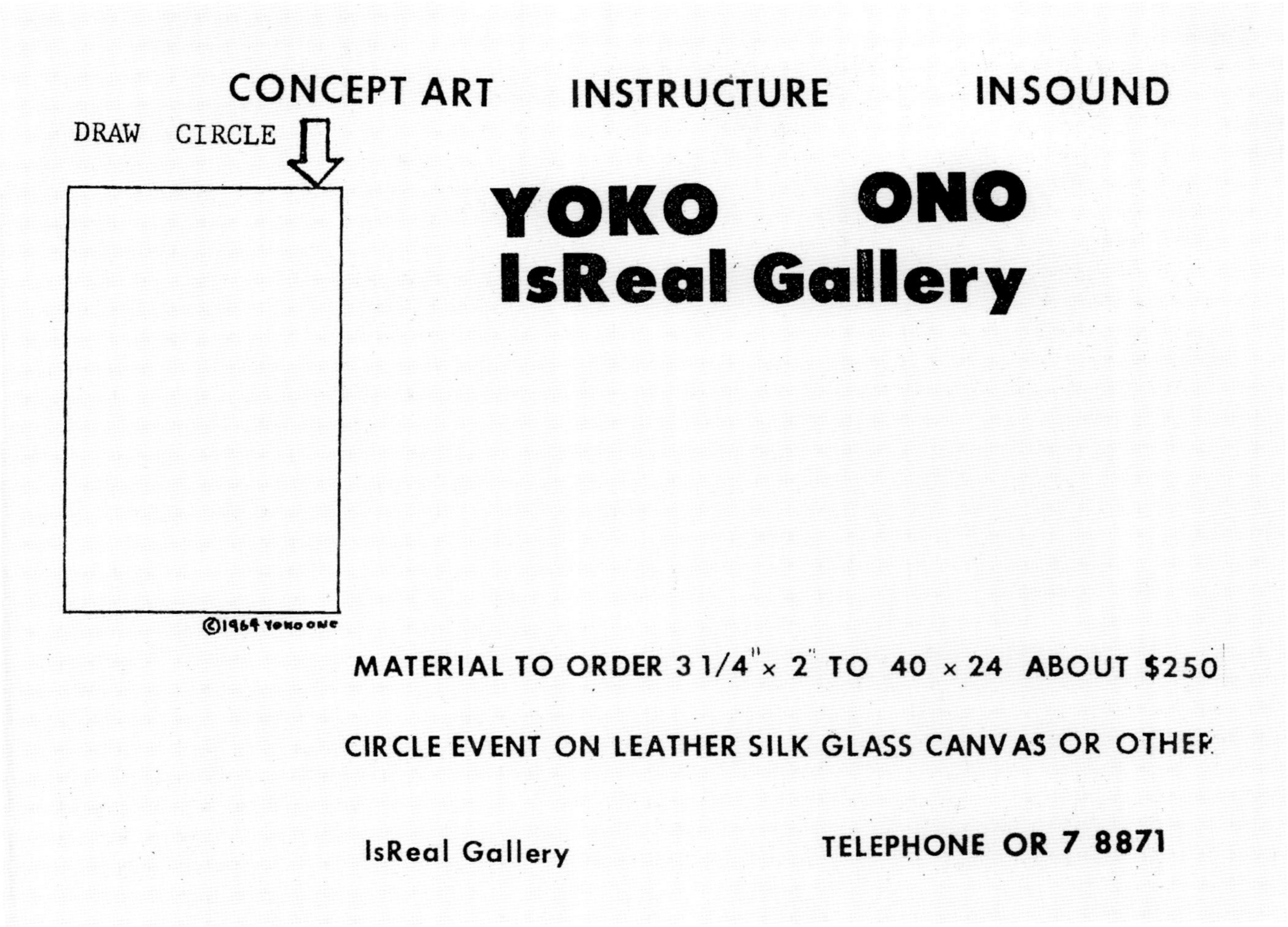

PLATE 36A
ADVERTISEMENT FOR *ISREAL GALLERY: CIRCLE EVENT*, MARCH 1965

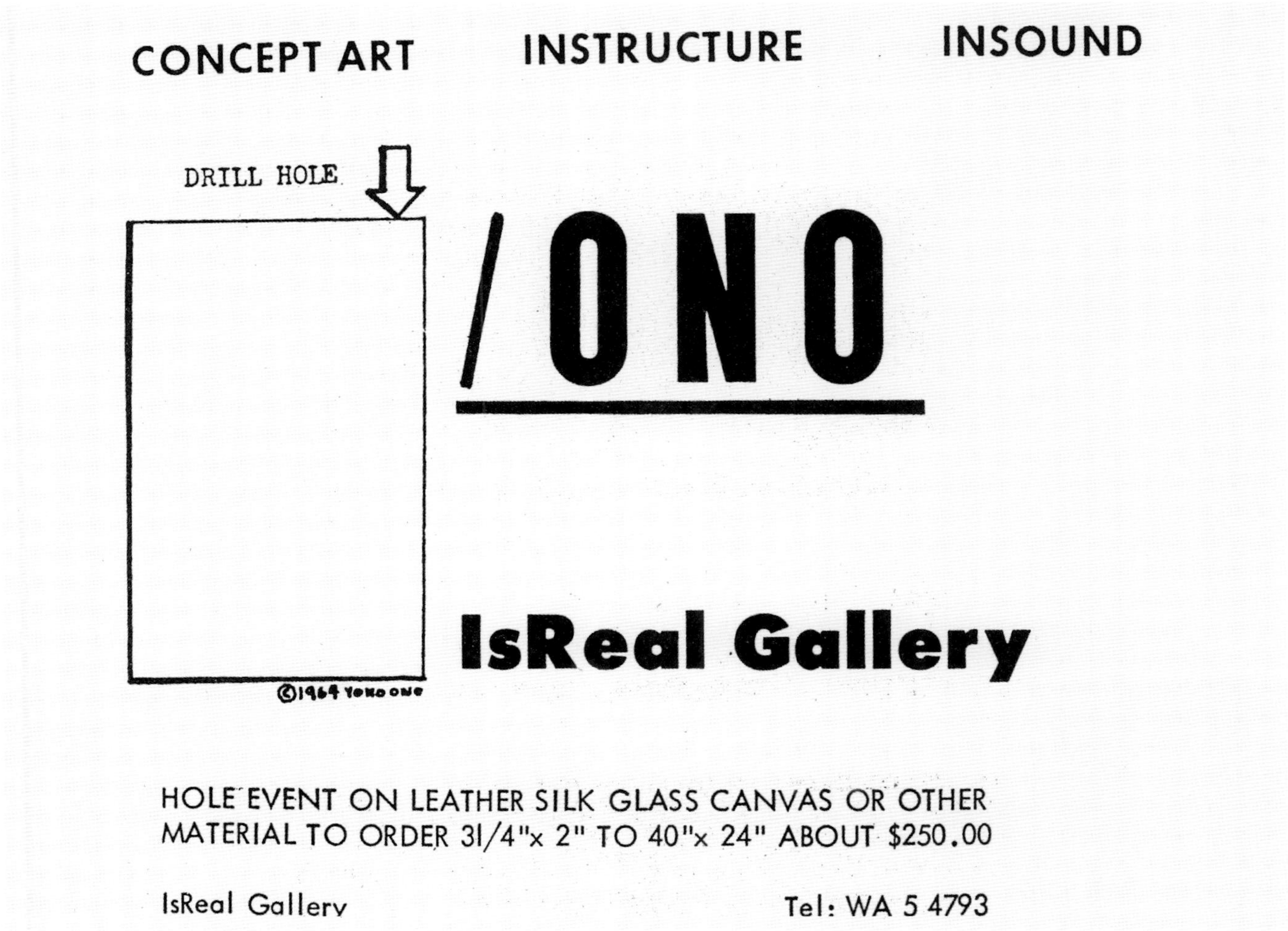

PLATE 36B
ADVERTISEMENT FOR *ISREAL GALLERY: HOLE EVENT*, APRIL/MAY 1965

37 *Ono's Sales List,* 1965

mimeographed typed sheet
14⅛ x 8⅝" (35.8 x 22 cm)
Collection of the artist

Ono's Sales List catalogues a broad variety of works by the artist in the form of a price list printed on a legal-size sheet of paper. Many items on the list, such as *Sky Machine* and *Self Portrait*, were apparently sold to paying customers. Some of the offered items clearly did not exist. *Grapefruit II*, for example, is offered at a pre-publication price of five dollars, but was never produced. Of the "events" offered, *Circle Event* and *Hole Event* were realized as advertisements for *IsReal Gallery* (no. 36). The first event, however, "to let pink snow fall and cover your town—guaranteed not to be artificial," offered as both a score and a performance, was unlikely to be performed, even at the $2,000 asking price.

Ono has described her *Sales List* as a "Walking out of the ivory tower and getting down to business kind of feeling. It's a list of what's sold in a conceptual market, if you will!"[1]

Apparently distributed in the autumn of 1965, the list was featured by writer John Wilcock in his column for the *Village Voice*.[2] Inquiries were directed to Ono at a New York address that was, in fact, the office of Norman Seaman, her friend who presented her 1961 and 1965 Carnegie Recital Hall concerts. Wilcock's column (which presumably generated requests for the list, if not sales) concluded, "you won't be able to afford many of the items but the sales list is free."

A related work from the previous year, *Notice*, offered "mornings" for sale. This handwritten sheet complete with order form itemized mornings that had been previously sold at events in Tokyo on May 24 and 31, 1964, along with a list of previous purchasers and mornings still available.

KC

NOTES

1. Ono, e-mail to author, 21 January 2000.

2. John Wilcock, "The Village Square," *Village Voice*, 4 November 1965, and *Los Angeles Free Press*, 12 November 1965, 5.

PUBLICATION HISTORY: self-published, 1965; *The Stone*, exh. cat. (1966); *Yoko at Indica*, exh. cat. (1966); Ono, *Grapefruit* (1970 and later editions); *The Bronze Age*, exh. cat. (Cranbrook 1989); *In Facing*, exh. cat. (1990); *To See the Skies*, exh. cat. (1990); *Wish Trees for Brazil*, exh. cat. (1998)

LITERATURE: Wilcock, *Village Voice* (4 November 1965) and *Los Angeles Free Press* (12 November 1965)

PLATE 37
ONO'S SALES LIST,
1965

ONO'S SALES LIST   These Works (c)copyright 1965 by Yoko Ono

orders & inquiries to Yoko Ono, rm711, 119w57th st, nyc 10019 usa

A. SELF PORTRAIT...........$1-
types: with frame.......$5-

B. SOUNDTAPE of the SNOW FALLING at DAWN........25¢ per inch
types: a. snow of India
b. snow of Kyo
c. snow of AOS

C. TOUCH POEMS*............priced according to material...$150-to $10,000-
types: a. paper set   d. hair set
b. flower set   e. cloud set
c. water set   f. wind set

D. Machines*
types: a. CRYING MACHINE-machine drops tears and cries for you when coin is deposited-......................$3,000-
b. WORD MACHINE-machine produces a word when coin is deposited-....................................$1,500-
c. DISAPPEARING MACHINE-machine that allows an object to disappear when button is pressed..........$1,600-
d. DANGER BOX-machine that you will never come back the same from if you get in(we can not guarantee your safety in its use)-..........................$1,100-
e. SKY MACHINE-machine produces nothing when coin is deposited-....................................$1,500-
f. ETERNAL TIME-a beautiful ETERNAL TIME CLOCK that keeps eternal time-.........................$800-

E. Architectural Works*(priced according to contractors' arrangements and cost of property)
types: a. LIGHT HOUSE-a house constructed of light from prisms, which exists in accordance with the changes of the day.
b. WIND HOUSE-a house of many rooms designed so that the wind may blow through creating a different sound for each room.
c. TRANSPARENT HOUSE-a house intended so that the people inside can not see out, and so that the people outside can see in.

F. Paintings
types: a. NAIL PAINTING......FLOWER PAINTING.....SHADOW PAINTING, and many other great do it your self paintings....$50-
b. PART PAINTING-details upon request, contains ten thousand parts-..............................$100-per 3sq inches
c. INSTRUCTURE-scores-...............50¢ a piece
d. PAINTINGS TO BE CONSTRUCTED IN YOUR HEAD-...scores 50¢ a piece

G. GARDEN SETS(priced according to contractors' costs, stones, pebbles, etc.)
types: a. a shallow hole for the moonlight to make a pond
b. a deep hole for the clouds to drip in
c. elongated hole for fog ways
e. stone settings for the snow to cover
f. stones & pebbles set like a dry river bed

H. Letters
types: a. letter to Ivan Karp...........original...$300-
copies.........50¢
b. reply from Ivan Karp..........original........2¢
copies.........50¢

I. EVENTS
types: a. to let pink snow fall and cover your town-guaranteed not to be artificial-score........$1-
performance....$2,000-
b. circle event.....2"x3" free upon request
40"x24"......................$150-
c. hole event.......2"x3" free upon request
40"x24"......................$150-

J. Record of Events-a complete record of all Events by Yoko Ono since 1951 with photographs and illustrations...........$7-

K. Dance Scores-twentyfive scores.........................$3-

L. Music Scores
types: a. actual sound scores..............................50¢
b. IMAGINERY MUSIC-scores............................75¢
c. opera scores.....................................$1-
d. INSOUND MUSIC-scores..............................$1.50

M. Underwear(custom made to order)
types: a. special defects underwear for men-designed toaccent your special defects-in cotton..................$10-
in Vicuna..................$175-
b. UNDERWEAR TO MAKE YOU HIGH-for women, discription upon request-............................about $10-to $35-

N. Books
types: a. GRAPEFRUIT-published in Tokyo, July 4, 1964, a limited edition of 500 copies, in English & Japanese, over 200 compositions in Music, Painting, Event, Poetry, and Objéct, since 1951....................................$10-
b. GRAPEFRUIT II-over 200 compositions not published in GRAPEFRUIT, in Music, Painting, Event, Poetry, and Objéct,(including TOUCH POEMS), to be published in 1966-pre publication price..........................$5-
post publication price.........................$10-

O. SIX FILM SCRIPTS-includes WALK TO THE TAJ MAHAL-.........$3-

*patents applied for, machines,and models for Architectural Works, may be viewed by appointment, only written requests accepted

38 Advertisements in *Art and Artists,* 1966

Fountain Piece
published in *Art and Artists* 1, no. 7 (October 1966): 44
image: approx. 2½ x 2½" (6.3 x 6.3 cm)

Mouthpiece
published in *Art and Artists* 1, no. 8 (November 1966): 39
image: approx. 4¾ x 3¼" (12 x 8.2 cm)

Do It Yourself Dance Piece (Swim in Your Sleep)
published in *Art and Artists* 1, no. 9 (December 1966): 73
image: approx. 4¾ x 3¼" (12 x 8.2 cm)

Ono continued her advertising works after she moved to London in September 1966. Mario Amaya, the editor of the British art magazine *Art and Artists*, who had invited her to participate in the *Destruction in Art Symposium (DIAS)* in London (no. 33), provided her with free advertising space in the October, November, and December issues.

The three works—*Fountain Piece*, *Mouthpiece*, and *Do It Yourself Dance Piece (Swim in Your Sleep)*—have their distinct histories in Ono's oeuvre. *Fountain Piece* can be traced to the instruction *Central Park Pond Piece*, dated 1956 autumn, first published in *Grapefruit* (1964). *Mouthpiece*, which instructs "Hide Mouth," was concurrently realized on the catalogue cover of *Yoko at Indica*, for Ono's exhibition that November in London (fig. 14.14).

Most significantly, all three relate in differing degrees to *"Do It Yourself" Dance Festival*, a work originally advertised in the *Village Voice* in December 1965. Presented by Fluxus, the "Yoko Ono and Dance Company" event was to take place, according to the ads, during January 1–15, 1966 (fig. 9.5).[1] Although it is unclear whether the festival actually occurred on these dates, her dance instructions, with illustrations designed by George Maciunas, were published in several formats shortly thereafter.

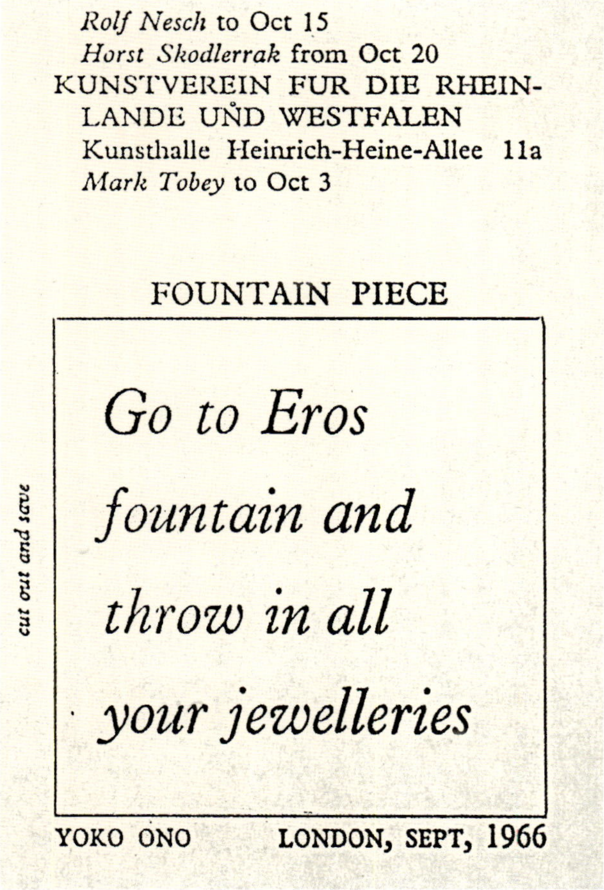

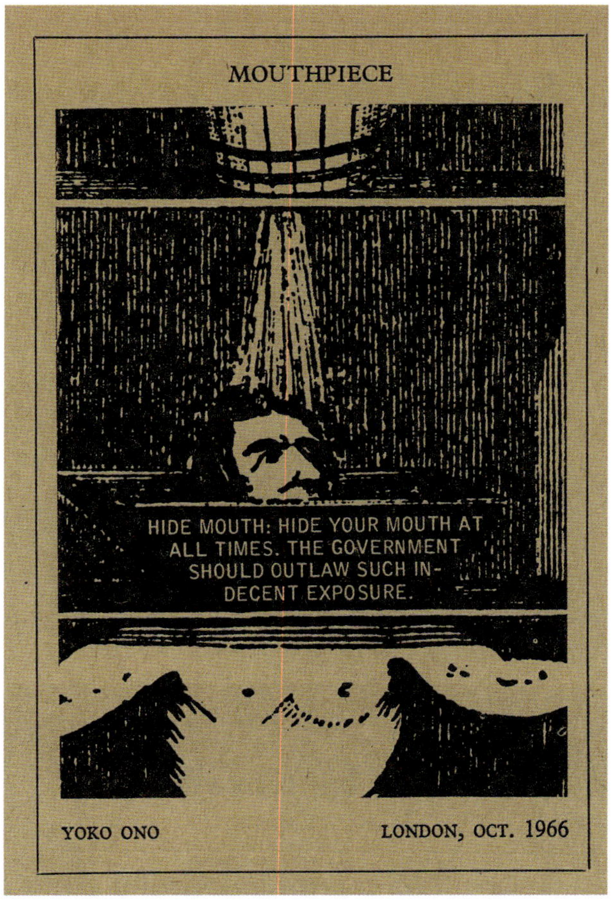

PLATE 38A (FAR LEFT)
ADVERTISEMENT IN *ART AND ARTISTS:* ***FOUNTAIN PIECE,*** OCTOBER 1966

PLATE 38B
ADVERTISEMENT IN *ART AND ARTISTS:* ***MOUTHPIECE,*** NOVEMBER 1966

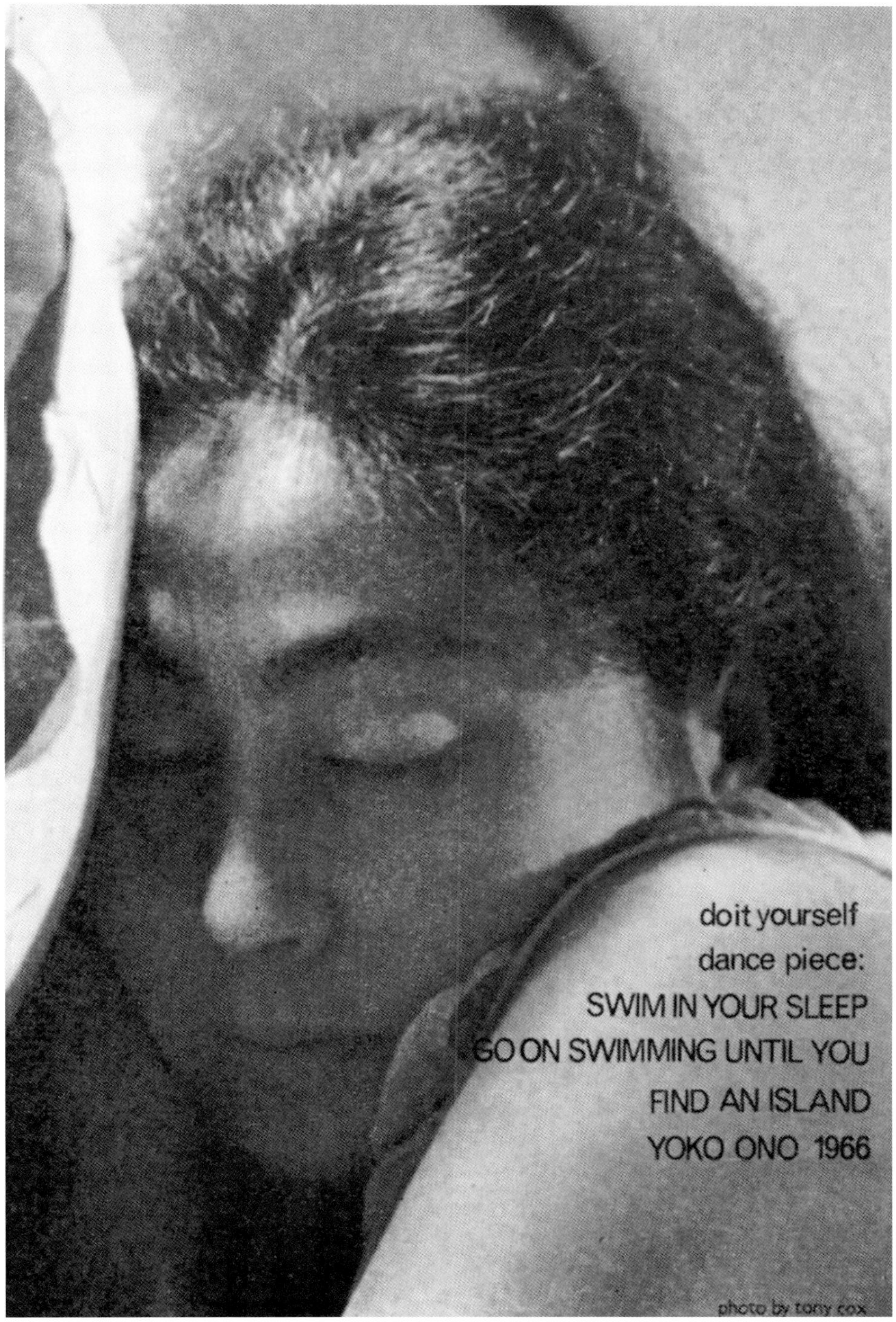

PLATE 38C
ADVERTISEMENT IN *ART AND ARTISTS*: ***DO IT YOURSELF DANCE PIECE (SWIM IN YOUR SLEEP)***, DECEMBER 1966

Among them is a full page of thirteen daily "dance" instructions in *3 newspaper eVenTs for the pRicE of $1* (Fluxus Newspaper No. 7), February 1966, under the title "Do It Yourself Fluxfest" (fig. 2.16). In this version, three instructions varyingly anticipate the *Art and Artists* ads:

> 5th Day. Watch. Go to the nearest fountain and watch the water dance.
>
> 10th Day. Swim. Swim in your dreams as far as you can.
>
> [no day given] Hide Mouth. Hide your mouth at all times. The government should outlaw such indecent exposure.

Although Ono adopted Maciunas's graphics for the *Mouthpiece* ad, she substituted a photograph (by Anthony Cox) of herself asleep on a pillow in the *Swim in Your Sleep* ad.[2]

Ono offered a subscription version of the dance festival in London as well in 1967. The instruction cards prepared for the London festival were illustrated with her own drawings and subsequently reprinted in *Grapefruit* (1970 and later). The work was transformed back into a newspaper ad in May 1999, when Ono's solo exhibition *Impressions* was held in Bergen, Norway.[3]
KC

NOTES

1. "Fluxus Presents Yoko Ono and Dance Company," *Village Voice*, 23 December 1965, 17; and 30 December 1965, 11.
2. In January 1968, the *VTRE* version of "Swim in Your Dreams as Far as You Can" was published, without Ono's knowledge, in *Promethean* (a magazine published in Boston by the group Liberal Religious Youth), edited by Ken Friedman, who was chief organizer of Fluxus West at the time.
3. "Do It Yourself Dance Festival," *Bergens Tidende*, 21 May–4 June 1999.

LITERATURE: Concannon, *Fly*, exh cat. (1996), 12; Hendricks, *Wish Trees for Brazil*, exh. cat. (1998), 30; Concannon, *Athanor* (1999)

39 *War Is Over!* 1969

Yoko Ono and John Lennon

Multimedia advertising campaign, including billboards, posters, handbills, newspaper advertisements, radio spots, and postcards

CHRONOLOGY

December 15 billboards and posters
Put up in twelve cities: Athens, Berlin, Hong Kong, London, Los Angeles, Montreal, New York, Paris, Port-of-Spain (Trinidad), Rome, Tokyo, and Toronto. Text reads, in each city's language: WAR IS OVER! / IF YOU WANT IT / Happy Christmas from John & Yoko

December 15 *Peace for Christmas*
Lyceum Ballroom, London. Benefit concert for UNICEF. *War Is Over!* posters and handbills displayed on stage

December 17 skywriting event
Toronto, upon Lennon and Ono's arrival. Message in smoke; handbills also distributed on the ground

December 17 press conference
Ono and Lennon announce their campaign in Toronto

December 21 newspaper ad
Full-page advertisement placed in *New York Times*, sec. 4, 16

1969–70 Worldwide Peace Campaign
Ronnie Hawkins and Ritchie Yorke travel worldwide with *War Is Over!* posters

1970 *The Peace Station Network* ad
Placed in *Billboard* (January 24)

1970 postcard
Text identical to billboard

1971 "Happy Xmas (War Is Over)"
Single record by John & Yoko/The Plastic Ono Band with the Harlem Community Choir (released December 1)

The best known of Ono's advertising works, *War Is Over!* was created in collaboration with John Lennon as part of the couple's Peace Campaign of 1969–70, launched immediately after their March 20, 1969, wedding during a very public honeymoon in Amsterdam: the first of two *Bed-Ins for Peace* (no. 34). It was at the *Bed-Ins* that the seeds of the *War Is Over!* campaign were sown. Interviewed during the second *Bed-In* in Montreal (May 26–June 1) by *Penthouse* magazine, Ono explained:

> Many other people who are rich are using their money for something they want. They promote soap, use advertising propaganda, what have you. We intend to do the same.... We're using our money to advertise our ideas so that peace has equal power with the meanies who spend their money to promote war.[1]

Ono, of course, had at this point been using advertising in her art for several years. And Lennon, leader of the world's most popular recording group, certainly knew about publicity; but as he later stated, "The poster idea was Yoko's."[2]

On December 15, 1969, Ono and Lennon performed with other musicians as the Plastic Ono Band (also called the Plastic Ono Supergroup) at the *Peace for Christmas* concert at the Lyceum Ballroom in London. *War Is Over!* banners and posters were prominently displayed on and around the stage.[3] This UNICEF charity concert effectively launched the *War Is Over!* campaign in public. That same day, billboards and posters appeared around the world, from London to Hong Kong, Tokyo to New York, in each city's language.[4] When questioned about the cost of this campaign, Lennon told the press that he would send the $72,000 printing bill to President Richard Nixon.[5]

To further propagate their peace message, Ono and Lennon placed full-page ads in print media. The *New York Times* ad on December 21, 1969 replicated the billboards;[6] but an ad in the music-industry magazine *Billboard* on January 24, 1970, went

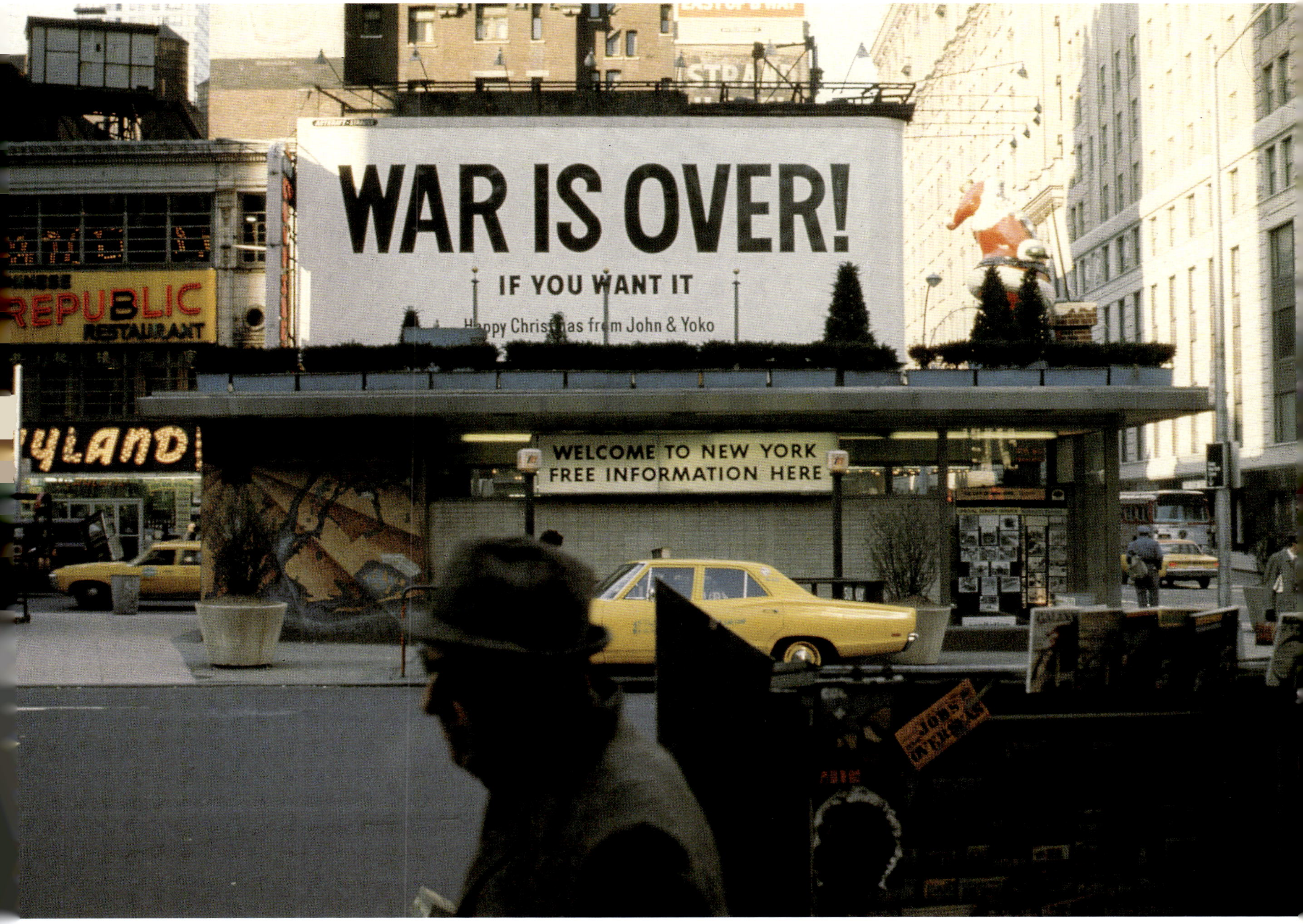

PLATE 39A
ONO AND LENNON,
WAR IS OVER! 1969.
BILLBOARD INSTALLED
IN TIMES SQUARE,
NEW YORK

a step further, promoting their "Peace Station Network." In it, the two extended an invitation to radio and television stations to join their network, offering as special incentives "free John and Yoko station breaks and ID's, plus the regular John and Yoko Peace Report."

The campaign continued in earnest throughout 1970 with the help of friends Ronnie Hawkins and Ritchie Yorke, who traveled the globe, carrying *War Is Over!* placards and otherwise spreading the peace message.[7] Lennon and Ono also continued their press promotion, telling a Liverpool paper in February, for example, about their "new, improved" product: "We are calling it new blue peace like they do with washing powders."[8] In December 1971, the couple released a single with the song "Happy Xmas (War Is Over)," which incorporated the "War Is Over/If You Want It" slogan as its chorus.

Ono resurrected the campaign in 1989, periodically installing *War Is Over!* billboards and banners in conjunction with her exhibitions. During the 1998 Christmas season, she re-created the original 1969 billboard in Times Square, New York. At this time, Rykodisc (publishers of the *Onobox* CD set and her reissued album series) offered Internet users a live Webcam view of the billboard and an opportunity to submit their photos in front of the billboard for posting on Rykodisc's Web site.

KC

NOTES

1. Charles Childs, "Penthouse Interview: John and Yoko Lennon," *Penthouse* (October 1969), 29, 34.

2. "Cities Get the Lennon Message," *West Lancashire Evening Gazette* (Blackpool, Lancashire, U.K.), 15 December 1969.

3. Ray Connolly described the use of "huge placard WAR IS OVER, on to which coloured slides were repeatedly and quickly flashed" in "Connolly's Discs," *Evening Standard* (London), 17 December 1968. Other photographs show the band members waving *War Is Over!* handbills.

4. At the press conference in Toronto on December 17, 1969, Lennon noted that a billboard in Port-of-Spain, Trinidad, was being arranged by a friend, insinuating that it may or may not have been placed.

5. See, for example, Robert J. Herguth, "Herguth's People," *Chicago Daily News*, 17 December 1969.

6. During this period, Capitol Records of Canada paid for the ads in Canadian newspapers.

7. Bryan Hayter, "Ritchie Yorke Led 69–70 Peace Campaign," *Erin (Ontario) Advocate*, 17 December 1980. They traveled as far as the border of the People's Republic of China and Hong Kong, as documented by, among other news accounts, "Peter Cole's Beat: Peace—The Five-Letter Word Chairman Mao's Men Don't Like," *Evening News* (London), 18 February 1970.

8. James Brewer, "Now John and Yoko Plan a Peace Campaign That's Bluer Than Blue," *Liverpool Daily Post*, 5 February 1970.

RECENT VERSIONS

Banners installed on museum exteriors, unless otherwise noted

1989 postcard
Facsimile postcard included in *The Bronze Age*, exh. cat. (Cranbrook 1989)

1991 banners/postcard
For *Birch Monologue*, Porin Taidemuseo. Banners in English and Finnish; also Finnish banner installed at Helsinki's railroad station. Postcard facsimiled as part of invitation to Ono's performance (February 22)

1991 banner
For *Peace! Friður!*, Reykjavík Municipal Art Museum. English banner from *Birth Monologue* installed

1993 wall painting
For *Color, Fly, Sky*, Stiftung Starke, Berlin. In German. Painted at the exhibition's entrance

1995 newspaper ad
For *Vital Use II*, org. Museum in Progress, Vienna. Full-page ad placed in *Der Standard* (September 13)

1998 billboard/Webcast/postcard
Re-creation of the original 1969 billboard at Times Square (December 1, 1998–January 3, 1999). Live camera shot posted on Rykodisc's Web site. Monochrome postcard subsequently produced by Ono

1999 banner
Installed at Cinematheque, in conjunction with garden installation of Ono's *Ex It*, The Israel Museum, Jerusalem (May). On view as of January 2000

1999 poster event
Kunstbiblioteket og Byens Billede exhibits framed poster on easel at Nikolaj Plads, Copenhagen (June 4–18)

1999 billboard/postcard
For *War Zones*, Presentation House Gallery, North Vancouver (July–August)

2000 billboard
For *Live in Your Head: Concept and Experiment in Britain, 1965–75*, Whitechapel Art Gallery, London. Installed inside (February 4–April 2)

LITERATURE: *Miami News* (15 December 1969); *Philadelphia Daily News* (15 December 1969); *West Lancashire Evening Gazette* (15 December 1969); *New York Times* (16 December 1969); Herguth, *Chicago Daily News* (17 December 1969); *Cincinnati Enquirer* (18 December 1969); Begley, *Los Angeles Tribune* (21 December 1969); Emerson, *New York Times* (25 December 1969); *Framingham News* (7 January 1970); *Champaign-Urbana Courier* (10 January 1970); King, *Los Angeles Times* (18 January 1970); *Rolling Stone* (21 January 1970); Brewer, *Liverpool Daily Post* (5 February 1970); Wenner, *Rolling Stone* (7 February 1970); Cole, *Evening News* (18 February 1970); Sondheim, *Fusion* (20 February 1970); *Sun* (22 May 1970); Hayter, *Erin Advocate* (17 December 1980); Hansen, *John Lennon: Drawings, Performances, Films*, exh. cat. (1995), 172–75; Concannon, *Fly*, exh. cat. (1996), 11–12; Vetrocq, *Art in America* (July 1999); Concannon, *Athanor* (1999)

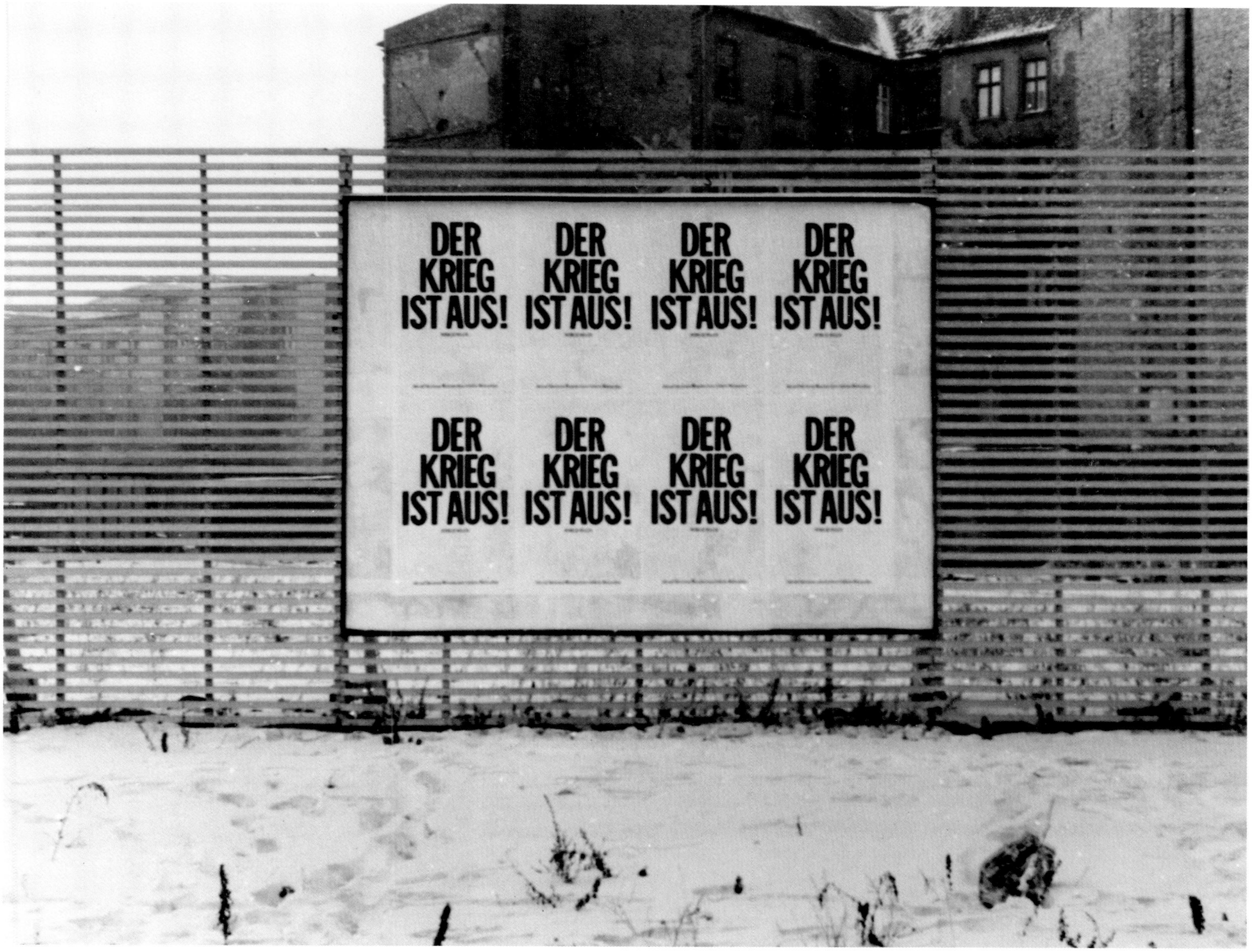

PLATE 39B
ONO AND LENNON,
WAR IS OVER! 1969.
POSTERS INSTALLED IN
BERLIN

40 *Museum of Modern [F]art,* 1971

advertisement published in *Village Voice*, 2 December 1971, p. 25
image: 11⅞ x 12 x ⅜" (30 x 30.5 x 1.1 cm)
Collection of the artist

In its weekly issue of December 2, 1971, the *Village Voice* in New York carried a strange ad in the form of a photograph accompanied by a mail-in book order form. The sign on the edifice in the photo prominently reads, "Museum Of Modern art." The informed reader would notice the irregularity—shouldn't that be "Museum Of Modern Art," and isn't that indeed the revered institution on 53rd Street? Also in the photo is a woman walking under the sign in front of the museum entrance. She is carrying a white paper bag conspicuously marked with the letter "F"! If the "F" is placed in the gap above (in the viewer's mind), the sign now reads Museum Of Modern Fart.

The advertisement was placed by Ono, who was, according to the ad, having a "one woman show" from December 1 through 15...where? The altered photograph, with added sign, recognizably showed the museum entrance. But given the parodic nature of this ad, the question naturally arises.

One answer would be that the exhibition was a purely conceptual incident, although the exhibition catalogue *did* exist.[1] Or, according to the *New Yorker*, "the 'show' consisted of a sandwich man who walked to and fro on the sidewalk in front of the Museum."[2] His sign explained that flies had been put in a glass container having the same volume as Yoko's body, and then placed in the middle of MoMA's Sculpture Garden (fig. 9.6). The flies were released, and a photographer was dispatched to follow them around the city, documenting their travels. The flies could be identified, the sign explained, by their odor, acquired from the artist's favorite perfume also put in the container with the flies. Handbills with the identical text were distributed to bystanders, who were invited to join in the search.

The catalogue, which interested parties could purchase using the ad's order form, "documented" the flight of the flies throughout the city with photographs of the locations where they had been seen, complete with arrows indicating the exact spots. Toward the end of the catalogue is a photograph of the MoMA box office showing on its window the *Village Voice* ad, with the words "THIS IS / NOT HERE" written across it (fig. 9.1). This sign placed on the window may have confused Ono's fans, since only a few months earlier her major retrospective called *This Is Not Here* had taken place in Syracuse. Not only did Ono offer a catalogue for the "one woman show," she also documented it in her seven-minute film *The Museum of Modern Art Show* (1971), through interviews with viewers as they left the museum.

In 1996, the *Museum of Modern [F]art* flies reemerged, after twenty-five years, at the Los Angeles Museum of Contemporary Art, and their subsequent travels have been documented on the World Wide Web, expanding further Ono's use of advertising media to document this conceptual event.[3] A "virtual" exhibition from the outset, its current digital incarnation seems entirely appropriate.

KC

NOTES

1. Ono, *Museum of Modern [F]art* (New York, 1971).

2. Hendrick Hertzberg, "A Reporter at Large: Poetic Larks Bid Bald Eagle Welcome Swan of Liverpool," *New Yorker* (9 December 1972), 140. See also *Museum of Modern [F]art*, n.p., for the placard text.

3. *Yoko Ono: One Woman Show*, 16 September 1996–2 January 1997. While the official exhibition dates would suggest otherwise, as of April 2000 the work still existed on the Internet through the Web site http://www.artcommotion.com.

LITERATURE: Hertzberg, *New Yorker* (9 December 1972); Concannon, *Fly*, exh. cat. (1996), 12; ———, *Athanor* (1999)

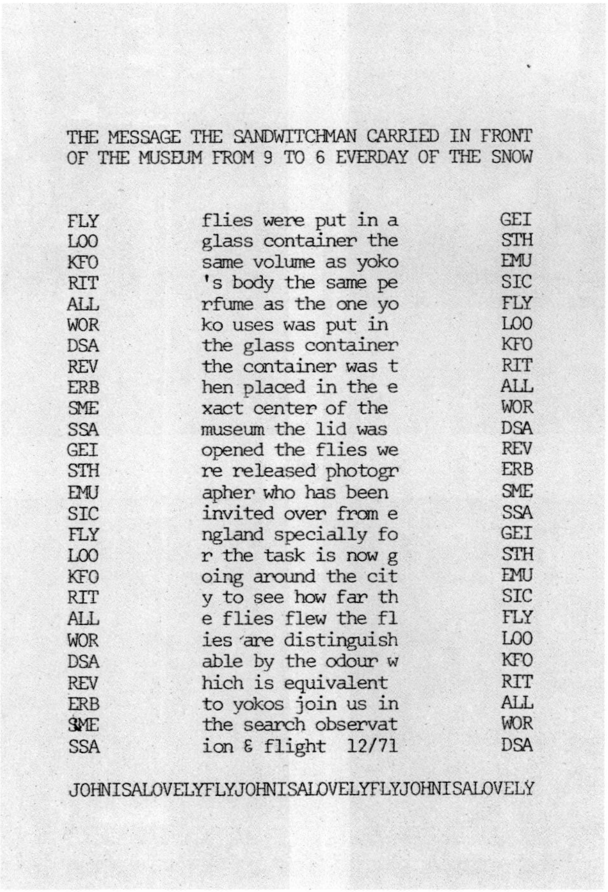

THE MESSAGE THE SANDWITCHMAN CARRIED IN FRONT
OF THE MUSEUM FROM 9 TO 6 EVERDAY OF THE SNOW

FLY	flies were put in a	GEI
LOO	glass container the	STH
KFO	same volume as yoko	EMU
RIT	's body the same pe	SIC
ALL	rfume as the one yo	FLY
WOR	ko uses was put in	LOO
DSA	the glass container	KFO
REV	the container was t	RIT
ERB	hen placed in the e	ALL
SME	xact center of the	WOR
SSA	museum the lid was	DSA
GEI	opened the flies we	REV
STH	re released photogr	ERB
EMU	apher who has been	SME
SIC	invited over from e	SSA
FLY	ngland specially fo	GEI
LOO	r the task is now g	STH
KFO	oing around the cit	EMU
RIT	y to see how far th	SIC
ALL	e flies flew the fl	FLY
WOR	ies are distinguish	LOO
DSA	able by the odour w	KFO
REV	hich is equivalent	RIT
ERB	to yokos join us in	ALL
SME	the search observat	WOR
SSA	ion & flight 12/71	DSA

JOHNISALOVELYFLYJOHNISALOVELYFLYJOHNISALOVELY

FIGURE 9.6
"THE MESSAGE THE SANDWITCH MAN CARRIED..." FROM ***MUSEUM OF MODERN [F]ART,*** ARTIST'S BOOK / EXHIBITION CATALOGUE, 1971

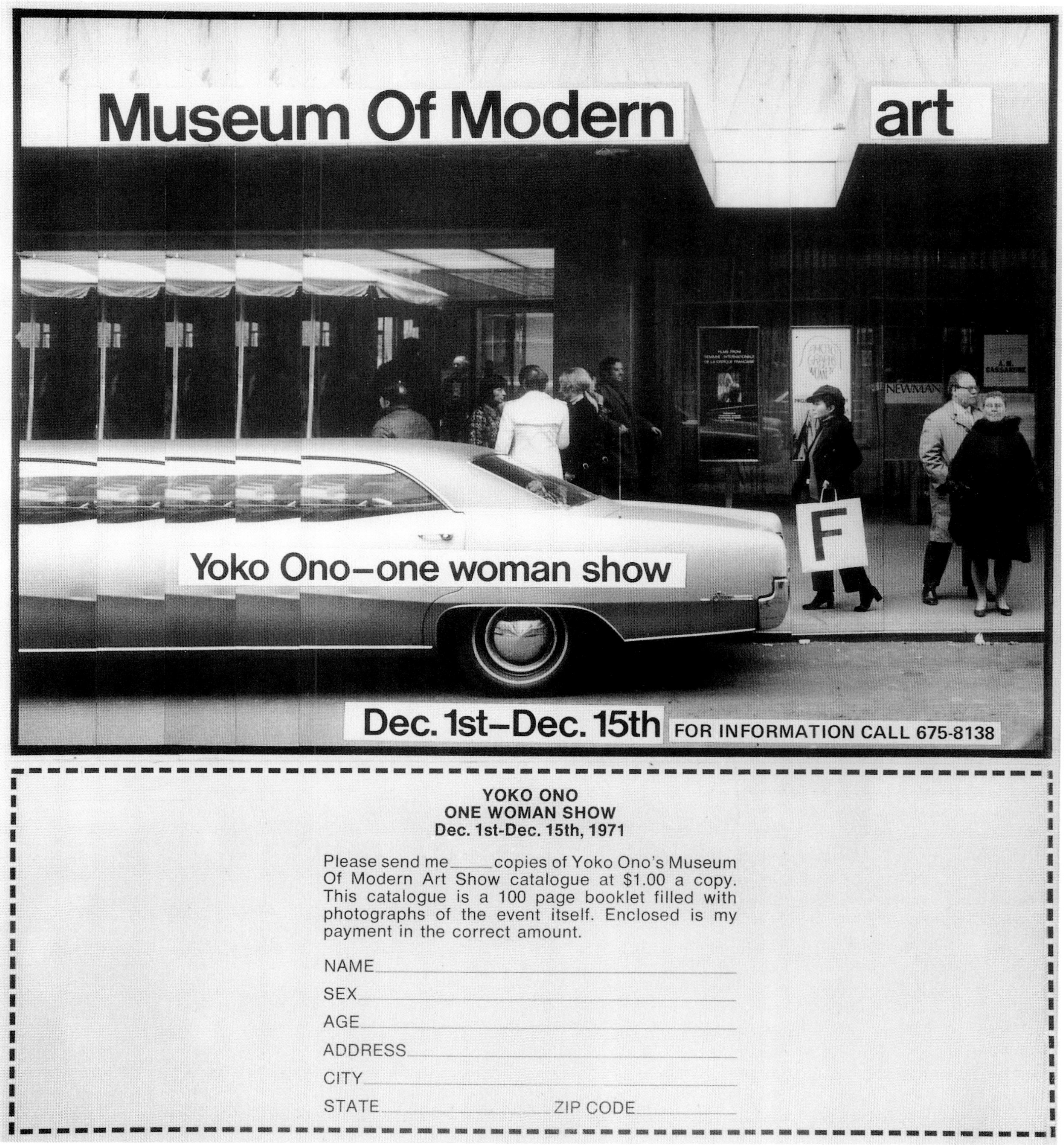

PLATE 40
ADVERTISEMENT FOR *MUSEUM OF MODERN [F]ART* IN *VILLAGE VOICE*, DECEMBER 2, 1971

41 *Fly,* 1996

billboards at five locations in Richmond, Virginia
dimensions variable

Realized in various forms—score, performance, film, music—*Fly* is one of Ono's favorite concepts and themes (nos. 28, 46, 56). In October 1996, Anderson Gallery at Virginia Commonwealth University in Richmond presented *Fly*, a solo exhibition that borrowed its title from her 1963 instruction piece (fig. 8.3). As part of the exhibition, Ono created a series of public works sited around Anderson Gallery and throughout the city. They included five billboards at various locations, a banner at the gallery's entrance, and posters and T-shirts for sale in the gallery shop. The catalogue, which was produced in two versions, also featured the text on its cover.[1] In each case, the word FLY appears alone in capital letters, without grammatical context.

The billboards quite naturally attracted journalistic and popular attention. On the opening day of the exhibition, Richmond's daily newspaper, the *Richmond Times-Dispatch*, thoughtfully advised readers: "It's not subliminal play from the airlines; it's art."[2] Indeed, people seemed puzzled. The *Times-Dispatch* critic began her brief interview with Ono by asking the artist to explain:

> Q: What should people make of the *Fly* billboard?
> A: This particular billboard, it's a message. It's an artwork that's taking the form of a billboard.
> Q: And there are T-shirts and posters with the word on it, too, all for sale.
> A: I'm sure the gallery wanted to make the T-shirts and posters.
> Q: What separates the billboards and T-shirts from advertising?
> A: It's the fact that it's not selling anything.
> Q: Some might argue it's selling your art.
> A: Well. But. It's not. The T-shirts you have to buy anyway. You might buy a blank T-shirt. It's not saying "Buy Coca-Cola." It's just a communication of the idea of flying. The spiritual flight or whatever.[3]

And certainly, the billboards sold nothing in any traditional sense. The only other information on the billboards was a line in small type, in the bottom right corner: "y.o. 1963–1996"; no indication of Ono's name or the details of her exhibition at the Anderson Gallery were included.[4]

The 1996 billboard version of *Fly* finds a particular resonance with its earliest public manifestation: *Untitled (Birth Announcement)* (1963; fig. 14.7). The leaflet, which includes *Instructions for Poem No. 86*, reading simply "Fly," is an advertising work of sorts. It announces the birth of Ono's daughter Kyoko, with a baby picture, and carries an ad for Ono's yet-to-be-published book, *Grapefruit*.

KC

NOTES

1. The catalogue was a box that contained a booklet along with various objects, including stones, acorns, postcards, and a bookmark. It was also produced as an unnumbered signed edition of 100. An overrun of the booklet was also available separately.

2. Sibella C. Giorello, "Yoko Ono's Work No Fly-by-Night Effort," *Richmond Times-Dispatch*, 18 October 1996, C1.

3. Ibid.

4. The Gallery placed a magazine ad to publicize the exhibition, mimicking the artist's style by "virtually" installing a FLY billboard on the VCU sculpture department building which had been demolished recently. See "Yoko Ono: Fly," *Artforum* 35, no. 2 (October 1996), 64.

LITERATURE: Concannon, *Fly*, exh cat. (1996), 9–11; Giorello, *Richmond Times-Dispatch*, 18 October 1996; Concannon, *Athanor* (1999)

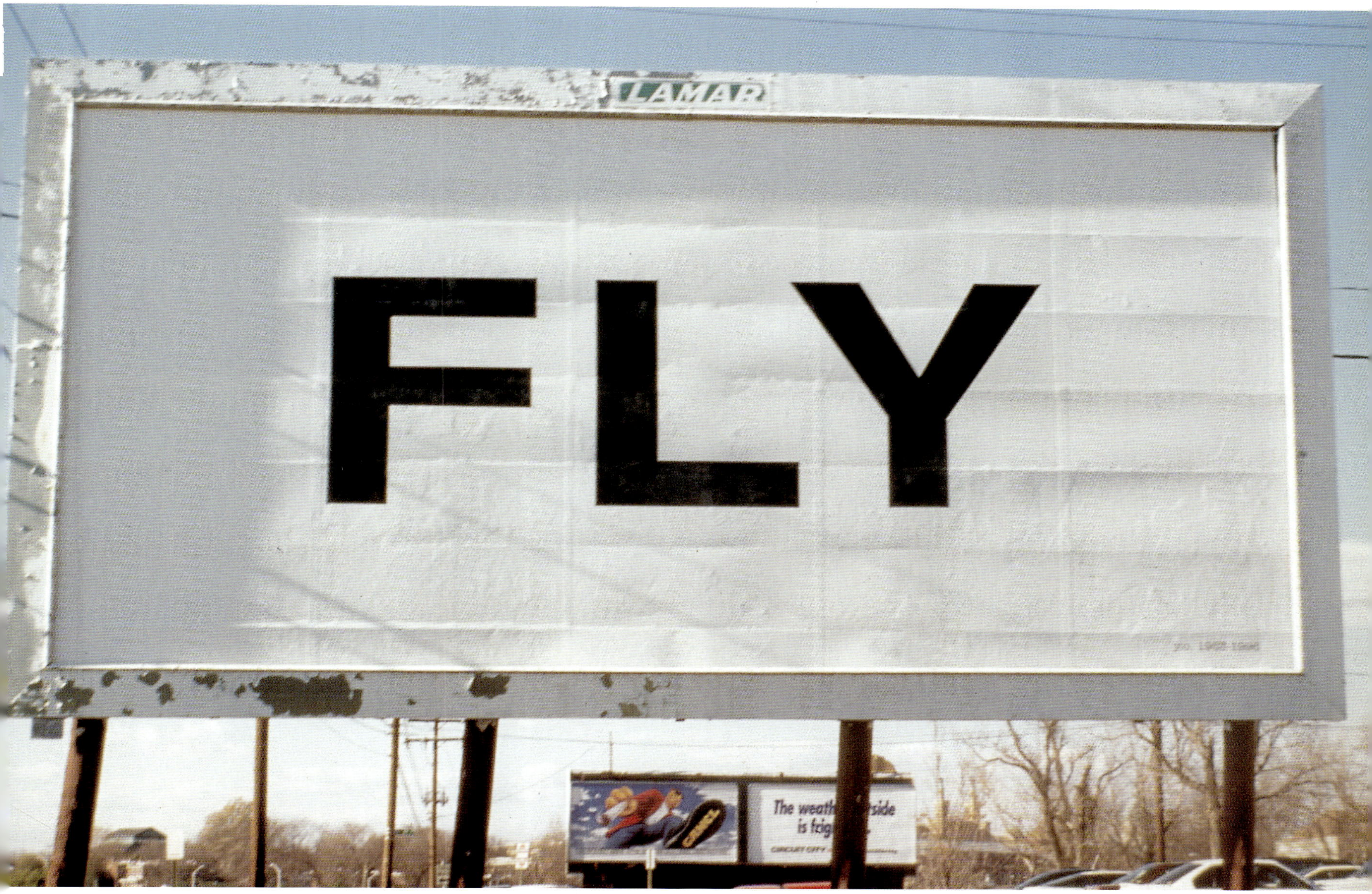

PLATE 41

FLY, 1996. BILLBOARD

INSTALLED IN

RICHMOND, VIRGINIA

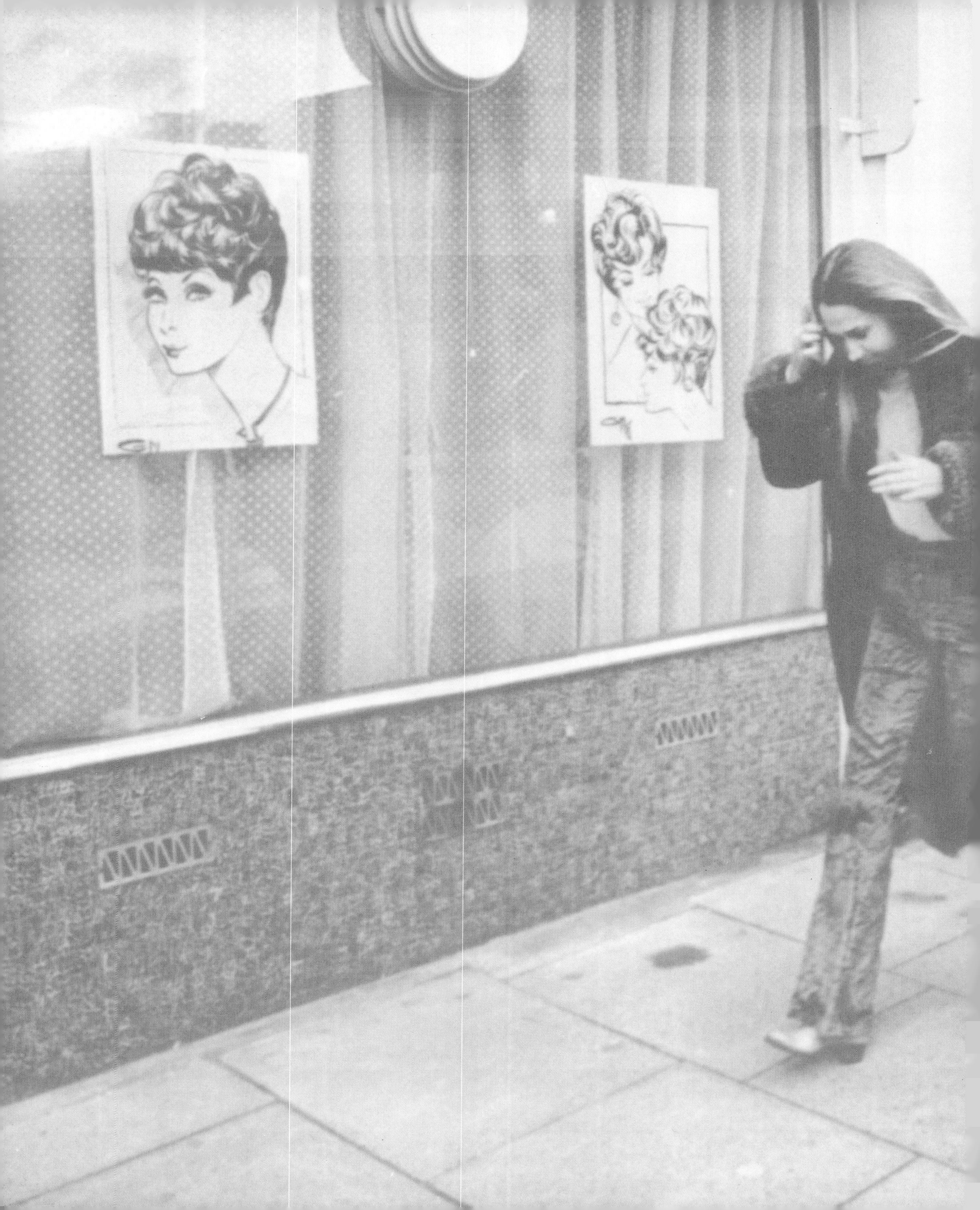

FILMS AND VIDEO

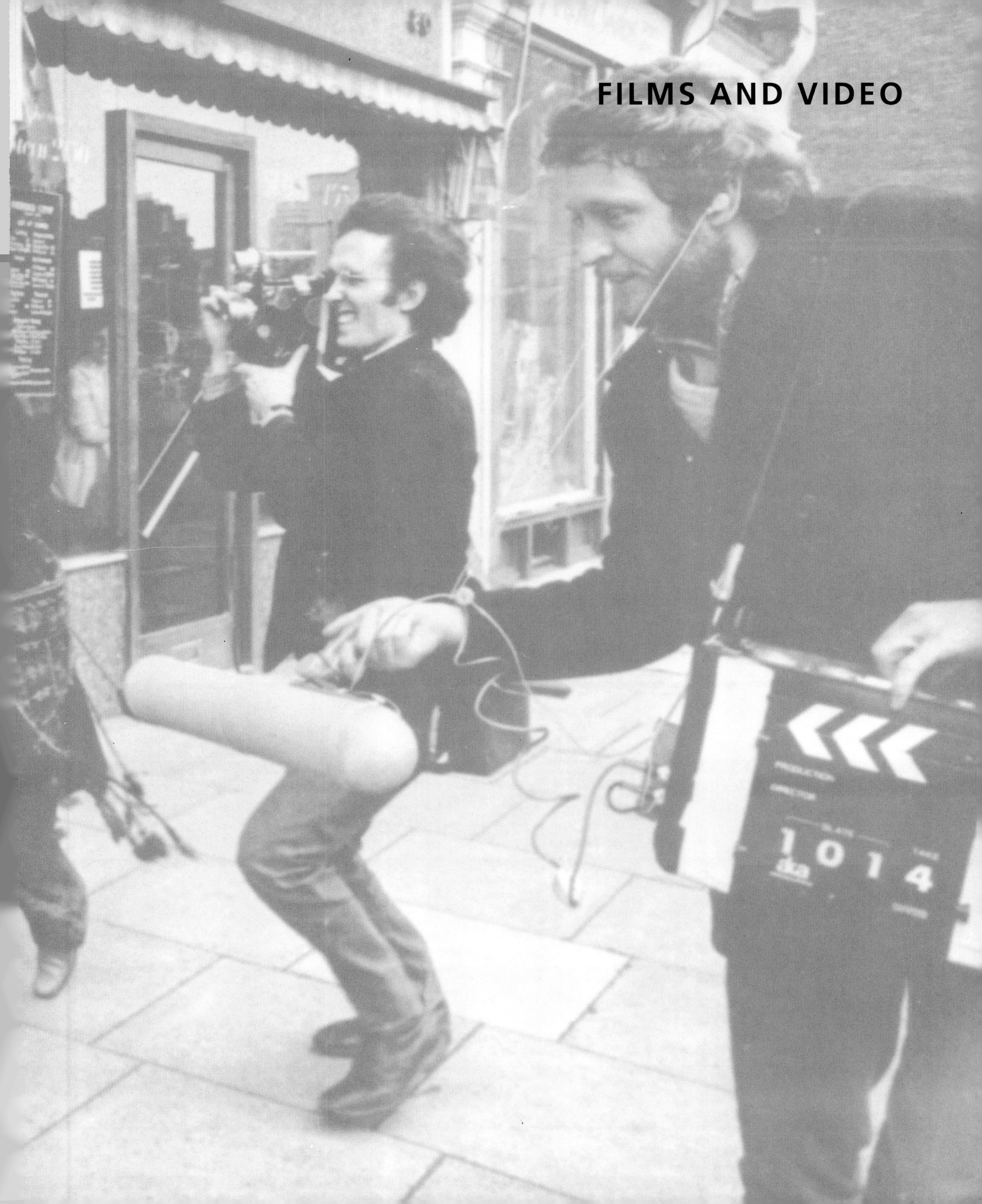

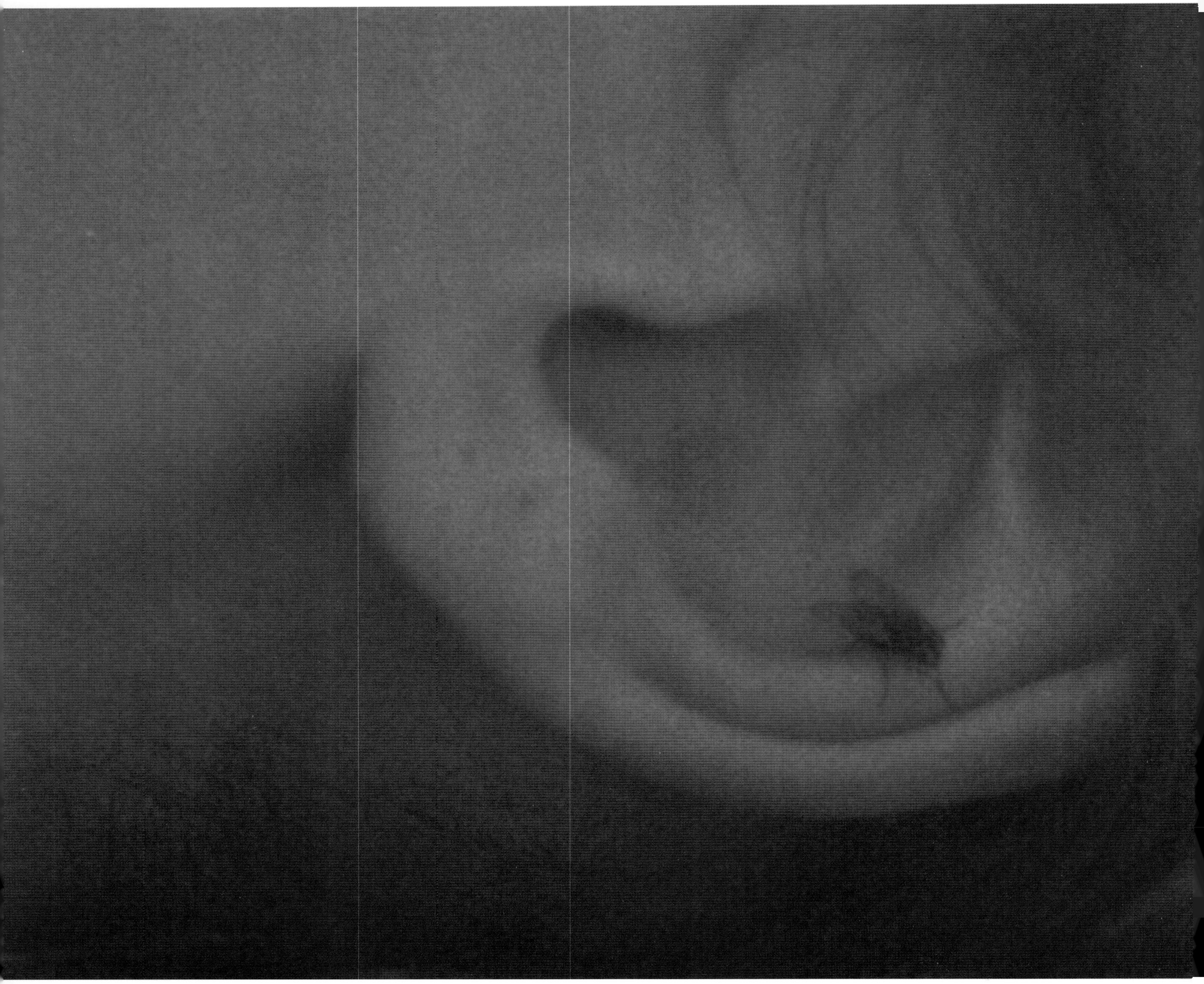

FIGURE 10.1
FRAME FROM *FLY*, 1970

Erotic Conceptualism: The Films of Yoko Ono

CHRISSIE ILES

The films of Yoko Ono occupy a unique position in the history of experimental film. Deeply rooted in the radical intermedia practices of the early 1960s American avant-garde, they emerged from the world of art rather than film at a moment when the definitions of both were being strongly called into question. Ono's films are an anomaly. Within the context of art, their firm grounding in the philosophical and aesthetic tenets of Fluxus sets them apart from films produced at the end of the sixties and beginning of the seventies by artists such as Robert Smithson, Bruce Nauman, and Joan Jonas. Ono's films are also markedly different from the films of Carolee Schneemann, another female artist based in New York during the 1960s who also worked in performance, painting, photography, and film. Yet, unlike Ono, Schneemann absorbed the personal, mythopoeic language of American avant-garde film, through her close friendship with Stan Brakhage.

Within the context of avant-garde film, Ono's early films, like other Fluxus films, predicted the structural films that emerged at the end of the 1960s in reaction to the expressionism of underground and earlier avant-garde film. Her later films also have a resonance with the work of Michael Snow, whose films, in particular *Wavelength* (1966–67), both she and John Lennon admired. Yet her work in film, as in other media, folds a personal, political, and emotional questioning inside a cool, cerebral form, which sets it apart from the intellectual rigor of structural film and the drier aspects of seventies Conceptual Art, as well as from the expressionistic performance and filmmaking of the sixties.

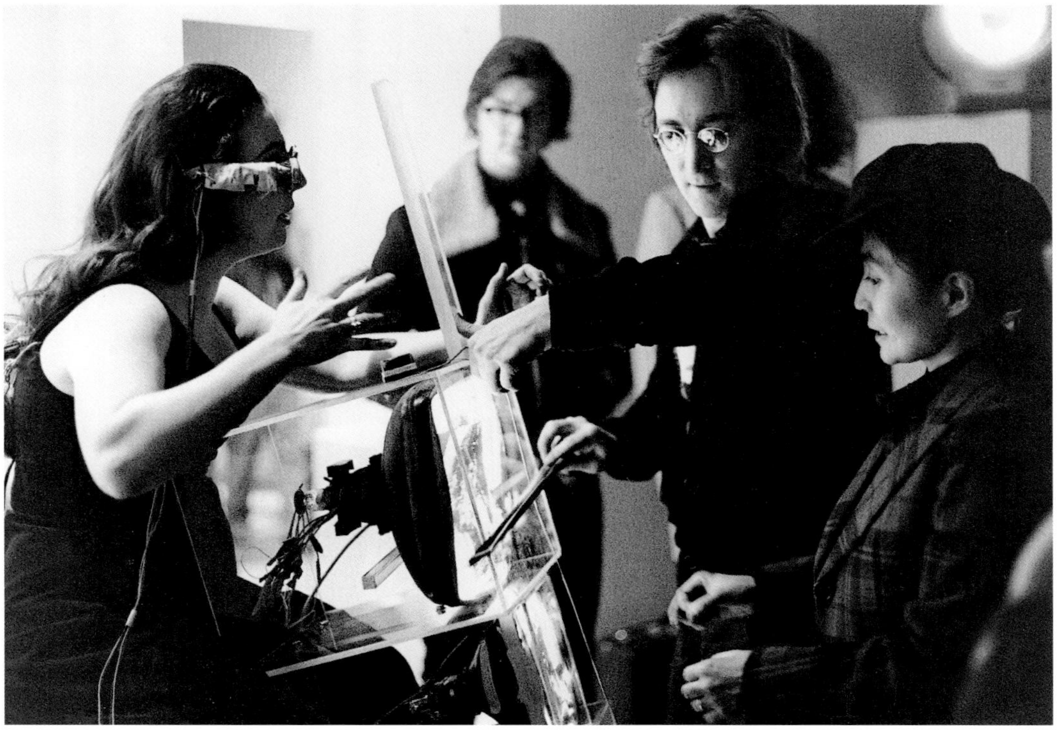

FIGURE 10.2
CHARLOTTE MOORMAN PERFORMING NAM JUNE PAIK'S ***TV GLASSES*** AND ***TV CELLO***, WITH LENNON AND ONO AT GALERIA BONINO, NEW YORK, 1971

Ono's association with filmmaking began in the early 1960s in Tokyo and New York, where she knew Japanese avant-garde filmmakers Teshigahara Hiroshi, Yoji Kuri and Takahiko Iimura, for whose films *Aos* (an animated film by Kuri) and *Ai* (Love; 1962–63, by Iimura) she composed and performed soundtracks. Her association in New York with George Maciunas, the central figure of Fluxus, led to a close friendship with filmmaker and cofounder of the Film-Maker's Cinematheque Jonas Mekas.[1] This gave her and Lennon a strong connection to the New York avant-garde film community. Ono and later Lennon were friends with Andy Warhol, who was close to Mekas and strongly influenced by the films of Jack Smith. Although his interest in celebrity and his pop sensibility were anathema to many of the late sixties sculptors working with film, it perfectly fitted with Ono's proto-Pop, Fluxus background and the couple's celebrity status.[2]

In addition to this conducive environment, Ono's long experience in music and performance made the transition into the time-based, collaborative process of filmmaking in 1966 easy to effect. Her films can be divided into three groups: the Fluxus films made and distributed with the help of Maciunas in 1966; her collaborative films made with Lennon between 1968 and 1971; and a number of film scores including a group of texts titled *Six Film Scripts by Yoko Ono*, made in Tokyo in June 1964: *The Walk to the Taj Mahal*, *Mona Lisa and Her Smile*, *Film Script 3*, *Film Script 4*, *Film Script 5*, and *Omnibus Film* (Anthology 20). As Ono explains in her introduction to the scores, they were intended to be made into films by others, and indeed "became a reality only when they were repeated and realized by other filmmakers." The conceptual and performative underpinnings of Ono's thinking are further made evident in the instructions for *Omnibus Film*:

> 1) Give a print of the same film to many directors.
>
> 2) Ask each one to re-edit the print without leaving out any of the material in such a way that it will be unnoticed that the print was re-edited.
>
> 3) Show all the versions together omnibus style.

In another group, titled *Thirteen Film Scores*, written in London in 1968, Ono included another version of *The Walk to the Taj Mahal*, titled *Film No. 1/A Walk to Taj Mahal*, whose instructions for the camera ("it should make the audience feel as though they are the ones who are walking in the snow and go up into the sky") evoke the film *Apotheosis*, made two years later. The thirteen scores also include other scores for films not realized as films (*Film No. 2/Watch*; *Film No. 3/Toilet Thoughts*), as well as scores for films both already made (*Film No. 4/Bottoms*) or about to be made (*Film No. 5/Rape [or Chase]*).

All Ono's films are fundamentally conceptual, and are characterized by the same concerns that underpin her work in other media: the body, duration, ephemerality, seriality, measurement, language, an active engagement of the viewer as participant, a performative structure, attention to the properties of the material, and a break with the autonomous work of art. Many of these tenets later characterized both Conceptual Art and structural film, for which Fluxus film is now acknowledged as an important precursor. In 1961, the Fluxus artist Henry Flynt wrote a definitive essay, "Concept Art," in which he gave the first definition of Conceptual Art; terming it "concept art" and "structure art," he linked it to the principles of experimental music being established by composers such as La Monte Young, with whom Ono was presenting concerts in her Chambers Street loft the year Flynt's text was written. Flynt's instructions in *Implications—Concept Art Version of Colored Sheet Music No. 1 3/14/61 (10/11/61)* evoke the filmmaking methods of Tony Conrad and later structural filmmakers such as Hollis Frampton, as well as the thinking of Conceptual artists, particularly Sol LeWitt:

> The axiom: a sheet of cheap, thin white typewriting paper
>
> The axiom implies statement 2: soak the axiom in inflammable liquid which does not leave solid residue when burned; then burn it on horizontal rectangular white fireproof surface—statement 2 is ashes (on surface)
>
> Statement 2 implies s. 3: make black and white photograph of s2 in white light...develop film—s. 3 is the negative
>
> ...melt s. 3 and cool in mould to form plastic doubly convex lens with small curvature; take color photograph of ashes' rectangle in yellow light using this lens; develop film—s. 4 is color negative....[3]

This extract from a sequence of instructions reveals both the prescience of Flynt's conceptual ideas, and the importance of the Fluxus context for Ono's first films.[4] Flynt's interest in seriality, ephemerality, and conceptual redefinitions of the "original" object (a photograph is burned to ashes, whose photographic image becomes a lens with which to photograph once again, and so on) echoed Ono's own definition of an artwork as capable of embodying several forms (a score, a performance, an object, and a film) and the idea of "event." It also paralleled her interest in burning and destruction as a demonstration of transience and temporality, the subject of her film *No. 1 (Match)* (1966), in which a match is filmed burning in slow motion (no. 42).

The importance of Flynt's text in relation to film, and to Ono's films in particular, lies in its resonance with the later conceptual use of photography by structural filmmakers such as Frampton, Morgan Fisher, Snow, and Larry Gottheim, to which Ono's use of the photographic image in *No. 1*, *Eyeblink* (1966), and *Erection* (1971; no. 49) is related. As Bart Testa has argued, the double impulse behind the invention of cinema was an analysis of the stopping of time in photography, and the subsequent reproduction of its flow.[5] *No. 1* and *Eyeblink* re-present this double impulse, intensified through the use of slow motion. Both films were made using a high-speed, fixed-frame scientific analysis film camera, to which Maciunas had gained access with the help of photographer and filmmaker Peter Moore.

Maciunas invited Ono and other artists associated with Fluxus to use the camera to make short films in a single session at Peter and Barbara Moore's New York apartment in January 1966, with Moore as cameraman. The camera's format defined the nature of the films Ono and the others produced, which was essentially photographic and taxonomic. The high-speed camera was intended to shoot scientific subjects and had a fixed-frame lens that could not be adjusted once set up, necessitating the filming of simple actions. The fast speed of 2,000 frames per second instead of the standard 24 allowed movements to be slowed down almost to a standstill. Ono chose as the subject of her films two fast actions—the burning of a match (*No. 1*) and the blink of her own eye (*Eyeblink*)—which could be slowed to the point of a nearly static photographic stillness, where they could be contemplated and analyzed by the human eye.

Since Leonardo da Vinci's first experiments with the camera obscura, the scientific nature of the film camera has been bound up with the subjective process of image-making. The characteristics of the camera used by Ono allowed the close observation of an action across time, treating the image scientifically in order to create an artistic statement. In *Eyeblink*, Ono's eye is seen looking directly at the camera as her eyelid slowly closes and opens, in a brief shot stretched to last thirty-five seconds. The simple action of blinking, like breathing, becomes a contemplative act, as the steady stare of the camera is returned by the human eye. The viewer is made intensely aware of both the presence of the apparatus and the process of looking.

The relentlessness of *Eyeblink*'s fixed-frame stare evokes Warhol's minimal black-and-white *Screen Test* films of the mid-1960s, in which subjects were asked to sit in front of the camera for three minutes in silence. Ono, by contrast, presented herself as the subject of the film as well as its author. Her dismantling of cinematic convention also led her to attach great importance to the ability of works to exist in the imagination, as well as on the screen itself. *No. 1* evokes a statement made by Ono the same year the film was made: "I think it is possible to see a chair as it is. But when you burn the chair, you suddenly realize that the chair in your mind did not burn or disappear."[6]

Ono's observation recalls LeWitt's famous statement in his "Paragraphs on Conceptual Art" (1967) that the idea is paramount, and that the realization of an object or image is an optional extension, or physical manifestation, of it. For Ono, the immaterial aspect of her work has a further meaning. Her use of whiteness, invisibility, transparency, silence, sky, and burning in her films and other works represents a means of transcending the physical object or world and moving into another level of consciousness. The slow motion of *No. 1* and *Eyeblink* allows the viewer to contemplate what is normally impossible to grasp visually; yet its purpose is not to capture a fleeting moment for eternity. Its insistence on the "now" of the extended image, slowing down the flow of conventional narrative time, is intended to shift the viewer's understanding of the image from representational subject to an abstract manifestation of consciousness.

Stimulated by her film session at the Moores' apartment, Ono made a third film independently later the same year in her own apartment, with the help of her husband Anthony Cox, using a conventional-speed 16mm camera. The taxonomical format of this, *No. 4* (*Fluxfilm #16*, also known as *Bottoms*, 1966; no. 43), Ono's best-known film, bears an important relationship to the nineteenth-century use of the new motion picture technology for the analysis and surveillance of the body in medicine and science. In *No. 4 (Fluxfilm #16)*, Ono filmed the naked buttocks of a group of Fluxus artists and friends, including Geoffrey Hendricks, Carolee Schneemann, James Tenney, and Ben Patterson, as they walked.

The rebellious, erotic, liberatory nature of the film, which reflects the tenor of Fluxus, acts in direct opposition to the nineteenth-century scientific treatment of the body as a "dynamic field of action in need of regulation and control."[7] One of the major uses of both the moving and still camera in the nineteenth century was to measure and regulate the human body. *No. 4 (Fluxfilm #16)* parodies the pseudoscientific role of the camera as an "objective" witness. Ono overturns the physiological determinism of nineteenth-century science and medicine. First, she documents a part of the body which has no special medical, physiological, or scientific significance, removing the option of "objective" value judgment. Second, she combines male and female buttocks in almost equal proportions within the same film, rejecting the traditional isolation of the female body as a subject of separate erotic observation, surveillance, and control. Third, the nudity of both sexes challenges the nineteenth-century anthropological racism by which it was only deemed acceptable for "primitive" peoples to be documented without clothes, later challenged by Eadweard Muybridge's taxonomical gridded studies of human motion, in which he documented movement using the male and female body, both clothed and naked.

In a second, longer, non-Fluxus version of *No. 4*, made in London soon afterward, Ono expanded the number of participants, aiming for 365, and included friends, acquaintances, and British artists including Richard Hamilton, John Latham, Jeff Nuttall, and Joe Tilson. The feature-length film also included a soundtrack of the participants' conversations and Ono being interviewed by the British press, which inserted another layer of meaning. Through the participants' descriptions of their experience, recorded out of sync with the actual images and mixed with Ono's interviews, the method of making the film and the individual personalities behind the body fragments are revealed. The construction of a special measuring instrument to ensure each set of but-

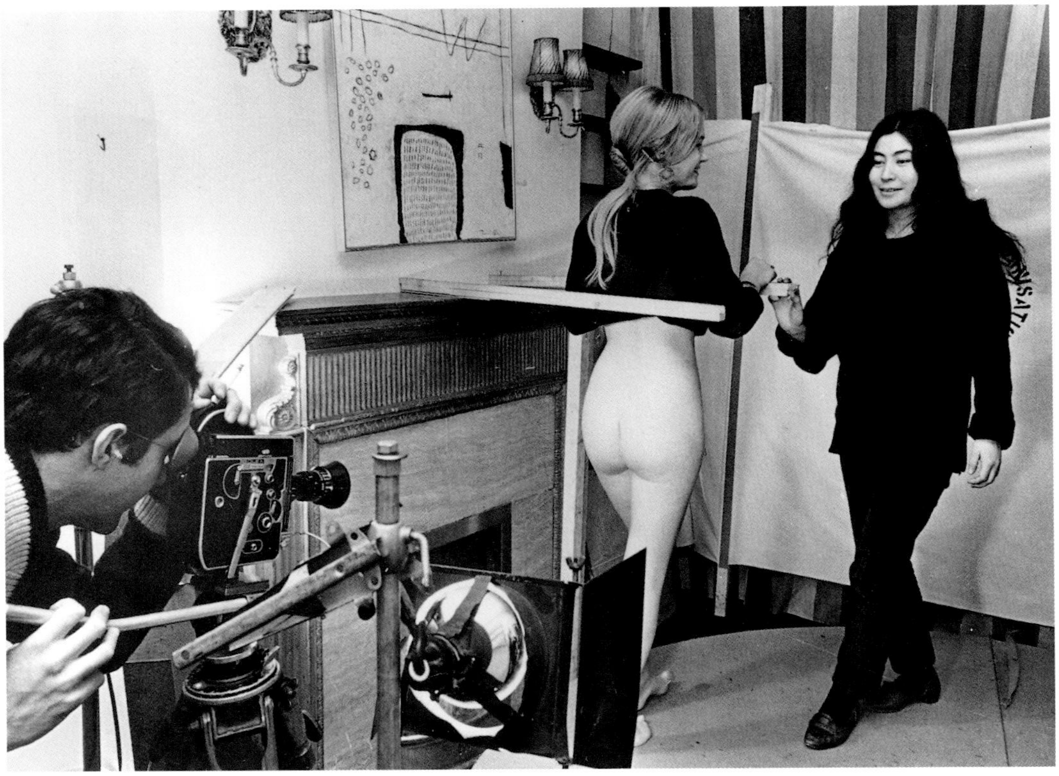

FIGURE 10.3
PRODUCTION STILL FROM
NO. 4 (BOTTOMS), 1966

tocks was in frame recalls the nineteenth-century grids used to make anthropological recordings of the human body, while rejecting their deterministic origin. It also echoes Conceptual Art's use of measurement and the grid to interrogate the conditions of representation (fig. 10.3).

For artists such as Sol LeWitt and Dan Graham, Eadweard Muybridge's gridded, serial photographic studies of motion were an important influence. In LeWitt's *Muybridge II (Schematic Representation)* (1964), movement is suggested by the progression of images seen as the viewer's eye moves along a horizontal enclosed wooden black box attached to the wall, looking through small holes in its front surface to observe black-and-white photographs of the same naked female body, getting closer in each frame until only her navel can be seen. The box, which evokes the voyeuristic nineteenth-century protocinematic optical devices such as the stereoscope, acts as a physical grid containing the individual "frames," and the space between one hole, or image, and the next makes visible the gap between one film frame and another.

Ono transforms Muybridge and LeWitt's narrative photographic structure into an atemporal sequence, a perpetual present in which singularity is achieved through a repetition of difference. LeWitt's observation that "Regular spacing might become a metric time element, a kind of regular beat or pulse"[8] parallels Ono's interest in the musical rhythm created by the repeated motion of the body. In *No. 4*, the endlessly different male and female bottoms form a grid of their own, each dividing the frame into the same four equal sections, whose abstract quality becomes more and more evident as the film progresses. Ono's grouping of male and female nakedness within the same film rejected the female-oriented cinematic eroticism of LeWitt and Muybridge's gridded works.

If Ono's first group of films made evident the process of their making and challenged the erotic oppressiveness of conventional cinematic structure, her second group of films, made after she had met John Lennon, developed this conceptual method in a more complex narrative form. Whereas during the 1960s avant-garde filmmakers often worked with musicians or conceived films around particular soundtracks, Ono and Lennon were able to combine their respective musical experience as composers and performers in equal measure, a unique situation that reinforced the singularity of their collaboration. They shared joint authorship of the shooting, editing, and production of each film, agreeing that the primary authorship would be determined by whoever had the original concept. Thus, Ono is credited as the author of *Film No. 5* (also known as *Smile*, 1968), *Rape* (1969), *Fly*, *Freedom*, and *Up Your Legs Forever* (all 1970), and Lennon of *Apotheosis* (1970) and *Erection* (1971).

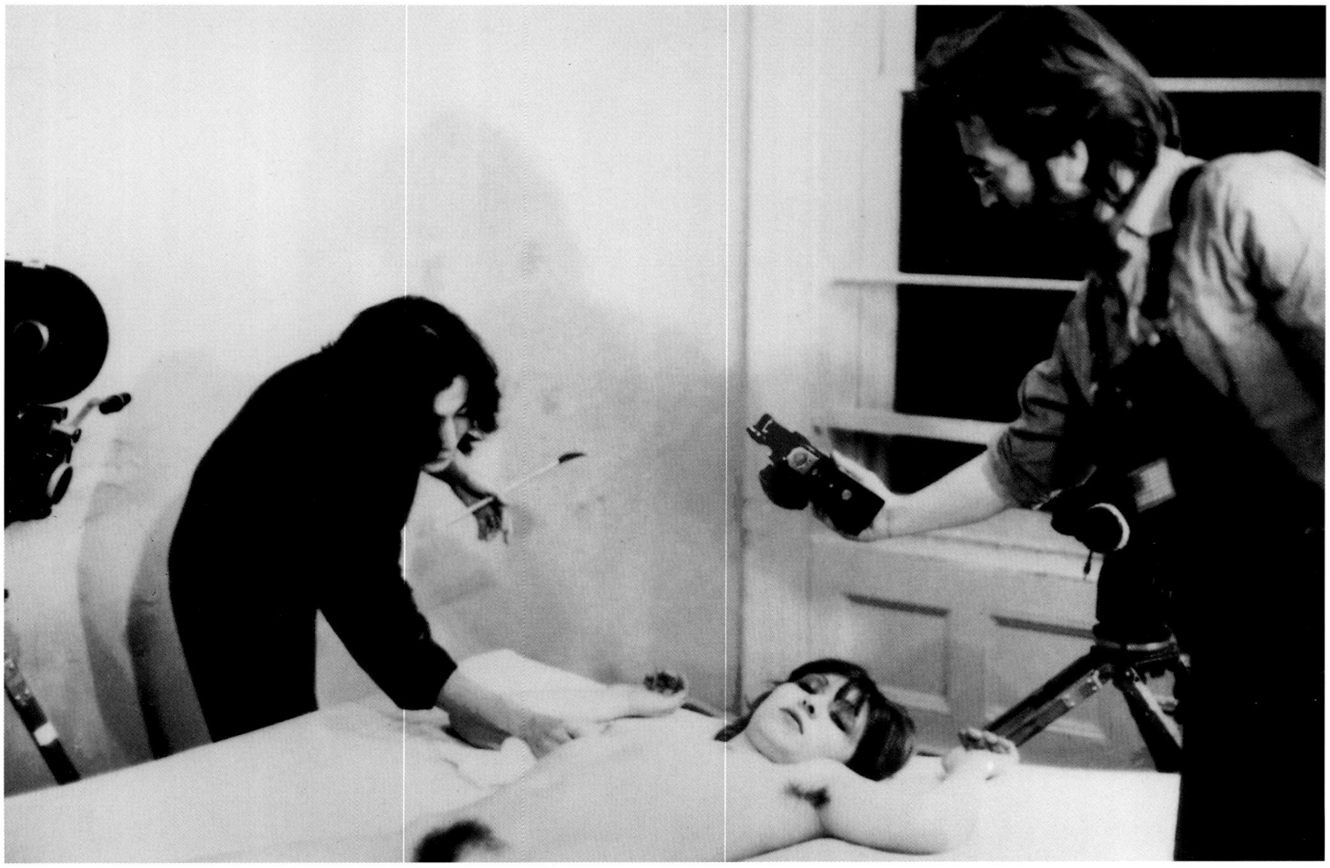

FIGURE 10.4
PRODUCTION STILL FROM
FLY, 1970

Ono and Lennon's collaborative films developed Ono's earlier concern with the body, women's rights, personal freedom, and political activism, which Lennon also embraced, within a broadly conceptual structure. In *Fly*, Ono expresses her own search for personal freedom, as well as a concern with the role of woman as passive object. A camera follows a fly as it alights on different parts of a woman's naked body, in extreme close-up (figs. 10.1, 10.4; no. 46). Ono describes her relationship to both the fly and the woman's naked body as autobiographical.[9] In this respect, *Fly* can be read as a metaphor for the split self. The fly, moving lightly over the surface of the body, represents the disembodied feminine imagination, anthropomorphized by Ono's vocal soundtrack in which she sings to herself, imagining herself to be the fly.

The woman's body, by contrast, lies inert and silent. Ono has described the still body as representing how she felt she had to behave in order to gain approval. If she became active, she encountered hostility, disapproval, and rejection. The film depicts the female self simultaneously as socially repressed and as liberated. The woman's apparently drugged state suggests, metaphorically, social control. By contrast, when the fly is filmed exploring parts of the woman's body—hair, lips, earlobe, pubic hair and vagina, nipple—it is as though Ono is exploring her own body, enjoying its erotic and physical power with the same lack of judgmental criticism expressed towards the naked buttocks in both versions of *No. 4*. Toward the end of the film, the camera draws back to reveal that the single fly is, in fact, several flies, which crawl over the woman's body, rendering it corpselike and repellent. The viewer's attitude towards the fly shifts from identification and empathy to disgust, in a clever symbolic restaging by Ono of the hostility expressed toward her active self, represented by the fly as her liberated alter ego. The viewer is suddenly implicated as her enemy. The voyeuristic low-angle camera shot of the woman's impassive naked body lying on the mattress, the pubic region suddenly prominent, hands the fly's (Ono's) enjoyment of the female body over to an invisible male oppressor. The shot evokes the composition of Marcel Duchamp's enigmatic *Given: 1). The Waterfall, 2) The Illuminating Gas* (*Etant Donnés*, 1946–66). In both cases, the woman's body is presented as a passive, lifeless object, whose life force has been drained, and therefore subdued.

In her one-minute film *Freedom* (1970; no. 47), made the same year, Ono reverses this deeply passive role, first expressed in her performance *Cut Piece* (1964; no. 30) in which she silently knelt on a stage while the audience was invited to come and cut away her clothing. In *Freedom*, Ono's pose, by contrast, is assertive. Standing rather than kneeling or lying, she has taken control of her own disrobing, presenting herself stripped down to her underwear. For one minute she tries to free her breasts from a purple bra, in a simple act of symbolic struggle for liberation. Lennon's brisk soundtrack reinforces the film's assertive message. Ono's political engagement with feminist issues was not superficial. In a text titled "The Feminization of Society" (1971; Anthology 24), she makes a passionate argument that both women and men be enabled to live a "real" existence, in which their individual personalities, as well as practical yet political issues such as childcare, can be seriously addressed. Ono's feminism had a strong impact on Lennon. His attempts to critique masculine sexuality were expressed in filmic terms in an ironic conceptual parody of its most classic symbol in his authored film *Erection*.

In the early seventies, Conceptual Art and structural film both used the serial photographic image to make visible the recording apparatus and to render time concrete. *Erection* similarly reveals the structure of its own making. On one level its composition conforms to the definition of structural film set out by the film scholar P. Adams Sitney, which includes a fixed camera position, a flicker effect, or the repetition of single shots.[10] On another, it echoes the format of Ono's early films, confirming James Peterson's argument that Fluxus films were important precursors of both Warhol's minimal films and structural film.[11] *Erection* is constructed from thousands of still photographs of a hotel being built in an empty lot in London over a period of eighteen months, collapsed into a twenty-minute pixellated film using a time-lapse dissolve. Although each photograph, taken hours or days apart, varies, sometimes almost imperceptibly, the subject and frontal viewpoint remain constant, allowing the viewer's attention to focus on deciphering the film's overall structure.

If the composition of *Erection* reverses the temporal structure of Ono's early slow-motion Fluxus films, the result is the same. Where *No. 1* and *Eyeblink* stretch a brief moment into several minutes, slowing the moving image almost to a standstill and revealing the film to be composed of single, static images, *Erection* compacts a year-long sequence of individual moments of time into twenty minutes. But the interval created by the dissolving of one static image into the next, at varying speeds, similarly reveals the

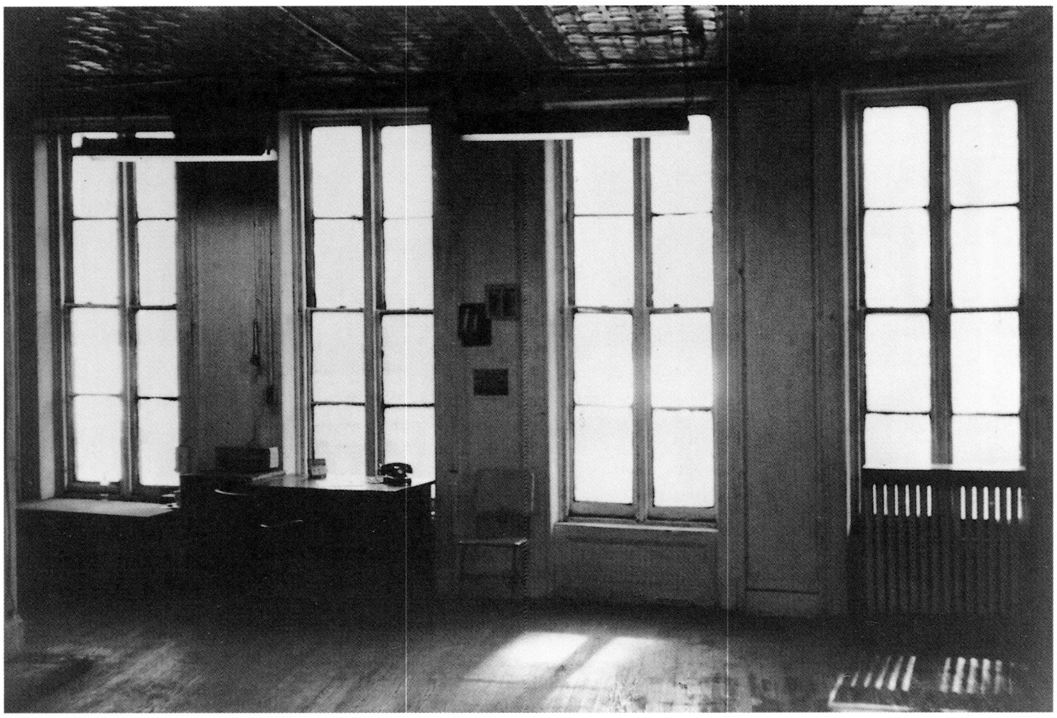

FIGURE 10.5
FRAME FROM MICHAEL SNOW, ***WAVELENGTH,*** 16MM FILM, 1966–67

passing of time as an illusion, underlined by the fact that the building's construction takes place over the impossibly short period of twenty minutes.

Peterson argues that in longer simple schematic films, the strategy of deliberate obscurity is often used to hold the viewers' attention as they attempt to decipher the developing sequence. In Ono and Lennon's *Apotheosis* (1970; no. 48), like Larry Gottheim's structural film *Fogline* of the same year, clouds and fog obscure the viewer's ability to determine anything specific before clearing, to reveal the sky and the landscape in a delicate diffusion of light. In *Erection*, the precise sequence of the building's construction is sometimes unclear. At certain moments in the film, the only evidence of time passing occurs in the subtle changes of light between one photograph and the next as the days and weeks are run together in an uneven sequence, evoking the similar marking of time through shifts in light in Michael Snow's *Wavelength* (1966–67; fig. 10.5), which Ono and Lennon knew and liked.

Sitney suggests that *Wavelength* was a complex reaction to the use of the fixed frame and zoom in the films of Warhol.[12] Warhol's minimal films from the early sixties had pared down their composition to a fixed-frame, single-shot format. *Erection*'s taxonomic recording of a specific place across a long period of time could be compared to Jackson Mac Low's score *Tree Movie* (1961, published 1964), and to Warhol's eight-hour minimal film *Empire* (1964), in which the Empire State Building was filmed in fixed frame by Jonas Mekas, over an eight-hour period from sunset to sunrise (fig. 10.6). However, although both films share a concern with temporality, unlike *Empire*, where stillness is suggested by an absence of movement in real time, *Erection* documents movement through stillness, capturing the development of the new building over time, from skeletal frame to completed structure, through still images. This difference in temporal representation is further underlined by a little-known, unrealized proposal by Warhol, related to *Erection* in concept. Warhol planned to make a six-month-long film called *Building*, which would show the destruction of one building and the erection of a new one, in real time. Where Warhol rejects the illusion of cinematic time, Ono and Lennon use the still photograph to make visible the illusion of movement.

Erection, like all of Ono and Lennon's films made after *No. 4*, differs from Warhol and structural films in one other, fundamental respect: its inclusion of a soundtrack. One of the central tenets of avant-garde film, from the mythopoeic films of Stan Brakhage to the minimal films of Warhol, was silence. Although some structural films used sound, often in the form of language, the image was usually foregrounded in silence. The sound in *Erection*, by contrast, inflects the conceptual nature of the film with a deeply emotional, almost hallucinatory quality. The particular character of the sound, different from any other avant-garde film soundtrack of the period, marks *Erection* as a bridge between the end of sixties psychedelia and the beginning of seventies Conceptualism. It also provides the erotic content of the film, which would otherwise exist purely as a verbal and visual pun.

Erection's soundtrack begins with a haunting percussive tapping, followed by a long cry by Lennon,

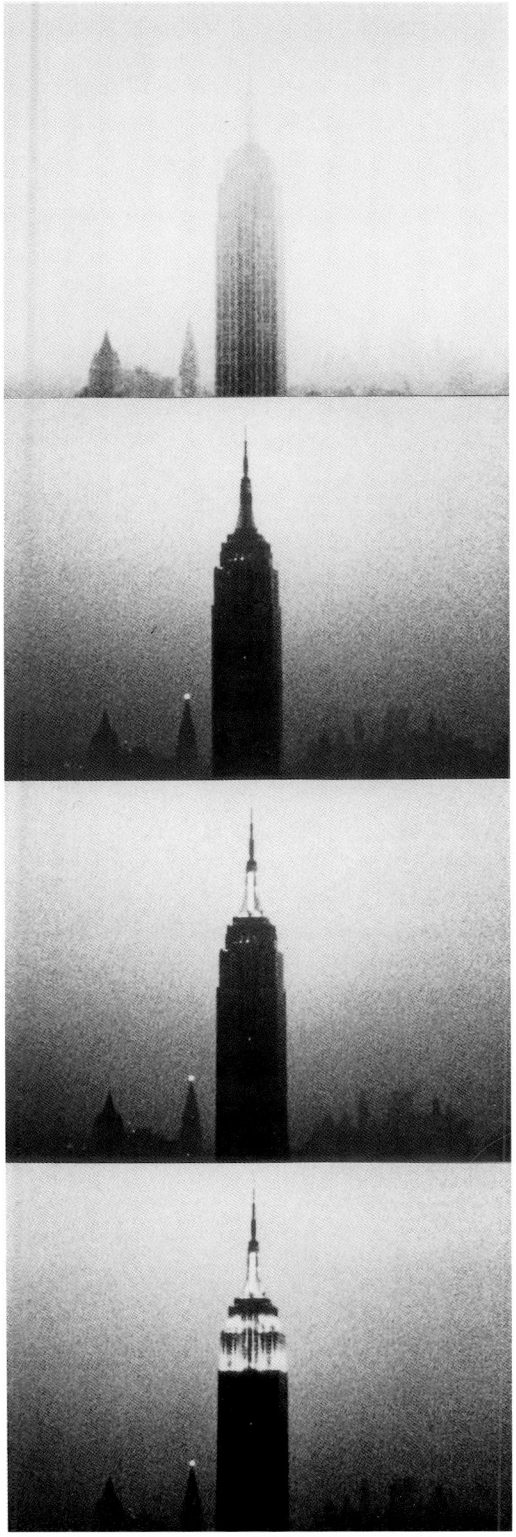

FIGURE 10.6
ANDY WARHOL, *EMPIRE*,
16MM FILM, 1964.
SELECTED FRAMES FROM
REEL 1. © 2000 THE
ANDY WARHOL MUSEUM,
PITTSBURGH, PENN.,
A MUSEUM OF THE
CARNEGIE INSTITUTE

sustained as a series of sung notes until it fades into its own echoes, meshing with a background shimmer of cymbals and other percussive instruments until the next wave of echoing cries appears. Ono and Lennon worked with the experimental musician Joe Jones to create a strongly psychedelic, abstract composition. The unreality of the disconnected dissolving images is heightened by the dreamlike sound, whose erotic sensuality and gradual crescendo and decrescendo shifts the viewer's attention between the conceptual meaning of the images and a suggestion of the act of lovemaking which the title implies. The erotic intensity of the soundtrack can be compared to Ono's soundtrack for Takahiko Iimura's film *Ai* (Love). The building becomes a metaphor for the male organ, filling out gradually until the climax of completion, whereupon daylight fades, Ono's voice subsides to sensual murmurs, and the viewer's anticipation is finally satisfied.

Lennon's symbolic presentation of the male, physical self as an instrument of measurement in *Erection* evokes Dan Graham's conceptual work *Detumescence* (1966/1969). Placing an advertisement in the magazine *National Tatler*, requesting a medical writer to describe the physiological and psychological characteristics of the postclimactic sexual state of the human male, Graham intended to distribute the resulting text within the art world as a poem. Positioning himself in the role of measurer, he used the magazine format as Lennon used the building in the film, as a site for the investigation of male sexual identity at one remove. This inquiry into the politics of the body reflected Ono's own quest for liberation in films such as *Fly* and *Freedom*. Situated between the conceptualism of artists such as LeWitt and Graham and the expressive minimalism of Warhol and Fluxus, Ono and Lennon's films mark an important conjunction between the proto–Conceptual Art of the early sixties, the Conceptual Art of the late sixties and early seventies, and the schematic inquiry of American structural film.

NOTES

1. In 1989 Jonas Mekas wrote a book titled *Mekasu no yūjin nikki: Renon, Yōko, Machūnasu* (Three Friends: John Lennon, Yoko Ono, George Maciunas—Conversations, Notes, Letters), trans. Kinoshita Tetsuo (Tokyo: Shōbunsha, 1989). Mekas also appeared with Ono and Lennon on a television program they hosted in 1971, *Free Time*. He interviewed Ono before he and Lennon wrapped her in white bandages, in a performance which echoed her earlier wrapping pieces such as *Sky Piece for Jesus Christ*, in which she wrapped members of an orchestra (no. 31). Further material exists in Jonas Mekas, "Bum-ba Bum-be"—conversations with John and Yoko, with an essay on rock and Yoko Ono by Richard Foreman, and Polaroid photos by John Lennon (unpublished manuscript).

2. David James's biography of Jonas Mekas, *To Free the Cinema: Jonas Mekas and the New York Underground* (Princeton: Princeton University Press, 1992), includes a photograph of Ono and Lennon with Mekas, Andy Warhol, Fred Hughes, and Pola Chapelle in George Maciunas's backyard at 80 Wooster Street, his home and the venue for Anthology Film Archives. The photograph was taken in 1971, after Ono and Lennon had completed several of their collaborative films.

3. Henry Flynt, "Essay: Concept Art" (1961) in La Monte Young, ed., *An Anthology*, 2d. ed. (New York: Heiner Friedrich, 1970), n.p. In Flynt's essay published in the second edition, quoted here, the word "statement" is substituted for the word "object" in the first edition of 1963.

4. Flynt's conceptual approach, deeply influenced by mathematics, was also echoed, although often in less rigorous terms, in the films of many of the Fluxus artists who made films alongside Ono. Only two of the forty-one Fluxfilms were made by artists who were known as filmmakers: George Landow and Paul Sharits. The others, including George Brecht, Nam June Paik, Robert Watts, Dick Higgins, Wolf Vostell and Joe Jones, and John Cale (who was part of the *Theater of Eternal Music* with Tony Conrad, La Monte Young, and Angus McLise before forming the legendary Velvet Underground), were using film as one of many other media to express their ideas.

5. Bart Testa, *Back and Forth: Early Cinema and the Avant-Garde*, exh. cat. (Toronto: Art Gallery of Ontario, 1992).

6. Ono, "To the Wesleyan People" (1966; Anthology 14).

7. Lisa Cartwright, *Screening the Body: Tracing Medicine's Visual Culture* (Minneapolis: University of Minnesota Press, 1995).

8. Lucy R. Lippard and John Chandler, "The Dematerialization of Art," *Art International* 12, no. 2 (February 1968).

9. Ono, speaking at an introduction to a screening of her films at the Whitney Museum of American Art, New York, 8 January 2000.

10. P. Adams Sitney, ed., *The Avant-Garde Film: A Reader of Theory and Criticism*, Anthology Film Archives, Series 3 (New York: New York University Press, 1978), xxv.

11. James Peterson, *Dreams of Chaos, Visions of Order: Understanding the American Avant-Garde Cinema* (Detroit: Wayne State University Press, 1994), 98. Peterson's chapter "Film That Insists on Its Shape: The Minimal Strain" provides an excellent analysis of the importance of Fluxus film in relation to structural film, and the parallel developments in systemic and conceptual art, music, and literature in the 1960s.

12. Sitney, xxv.

42 *No. 1 (Match),* 1966

(also known as *Fluxfilm 14*)
black and white, silent, 5 minutes

Yoko Ono made her first two films (*Match* and *Eyeblink*) on January 22, 1966, responding to an invitation by Fluxus impresario George Maciunas to experiment with a high-speed scientific film camera to which he had temporarily gained access. Other artists associated with Fluxus who took part in the project included Shiomi Mieko (Chieko), Joe Jones, and Pieter Vanderbeek. The filming took place in the apartment of photographer and film-maker Peter Moore on East 36th Street, New York, with Moore acting as cameraman. Ono used the extreme slow motion produced by the camera's filming rate of 2,000 frames per second, instead of the standard twenty-four, as a conceptual tool. Echoing the form of her performances and scores, a simple action—the striking of a match, the blink of an eye—became the subject of both films, in a rejection of conventional cinematic narrative and time.

In *No. 1*, a match is silently struck and left to burn, the slow motion expanding an action lasting a few seconds to several minutes. As the flame burns down we become aware of the passing of time, the ephemerality of the physical object, and the transience of human existence. *No. 1* re-presents in filmic terms one of Ono's earliest scores, *Lighting Piece* (1955), which was also realized as a performance (no. 1). All three can be defined as the same work in different forms. Like other Fluxus films made during the same period, *No. 1* radically challenges cinematic convention in its minimal structure. The ephemerality of the burning match reflects an interest in transience rooted in Zen, a discipline absorbed by Ono at an early age in Japan and adopted by many Fluxus artists, influenced by John Cage.

Ono's first two films belong to a group of forty-one films made by artists associated with Fluxus between 1962 and 1966, which were gathered by Maciunas into the anthology *Fluxfilms*. This anthology exists in several versions, and Maciunas often changed the order and selection of films.[1] An early forty-minute version is dated summer 1966, a longer, one-hundred-minute version was made in the winter of 1966, and in 1974, a sixty-four-minute version appeared. Jonas Mekas, filmmaker, director of Anthology Film Archives, and friend of both Maciunas and Ono, compiled the most complete version of the anthology since Maciunas's death in 1978, which includes thirty-seven of the forty-one films. Ono's films are included in all these versions. The numbers in Ono's "Fluxfilm" titles conform to Maciunas's initial numbering system for the anthology, although he repeatedly varied both the sequence and screening context of the films. Maciunas also broke up the Fluxfilms and transferred some, including those by Ono, to super-8mm to make film loops to present as *Flux Wallpaper*. These loops were displayed in environments by Ono and Lennon, including *Capsule by John & Yoko + Flux Space Center*, part of *Fluxfest Presentation of John Lennon & Yoko Ono +* (New York, 1970).

Ono's own numbering system for her films is inconsistent. *Eyeblink* is not numbered (it would logically be *No. 2*, but neither *No. 2* nor *No. 3* exists). *No. 4* exists in two variations, one a Fluxus film, conforming to the short, Fluxus form, the other a non-Fluxus film of eighty minutes. Ono numbered her films arbitrarily during 1966–68; *No. 5*, a non-Fluxus film, is her last numbered film, although several film scores are numbered up to *No. 13*.

CI

NOTES

1. See Maeva Aubert, *Flux Film*, trans. Pip Chodorov, booklet for the videotape edition of *Fluxfilm Anthology* (Paris: Re-Voir Editions, Paris, 1998), 26.

LITERATURE: Hendricks, *Fluxus Codex* (1988), 420; Haskell and Hanhardt, *Arias and Objects* (1991), 8; Hanhardt, *The Films of Yoko Ono*, exh. brochure. (1991); MacDonald, *A Critical Cinema* (1992), 140, 145; Iles, *Have You Seen the Horizon Lately?* exh. cat. (1997), 6–9; Aubert, *Flux Film* (1998), 34

PLATE 42
FILMSTRIP FROM ***NO. 1 (MATCH),*** 1966

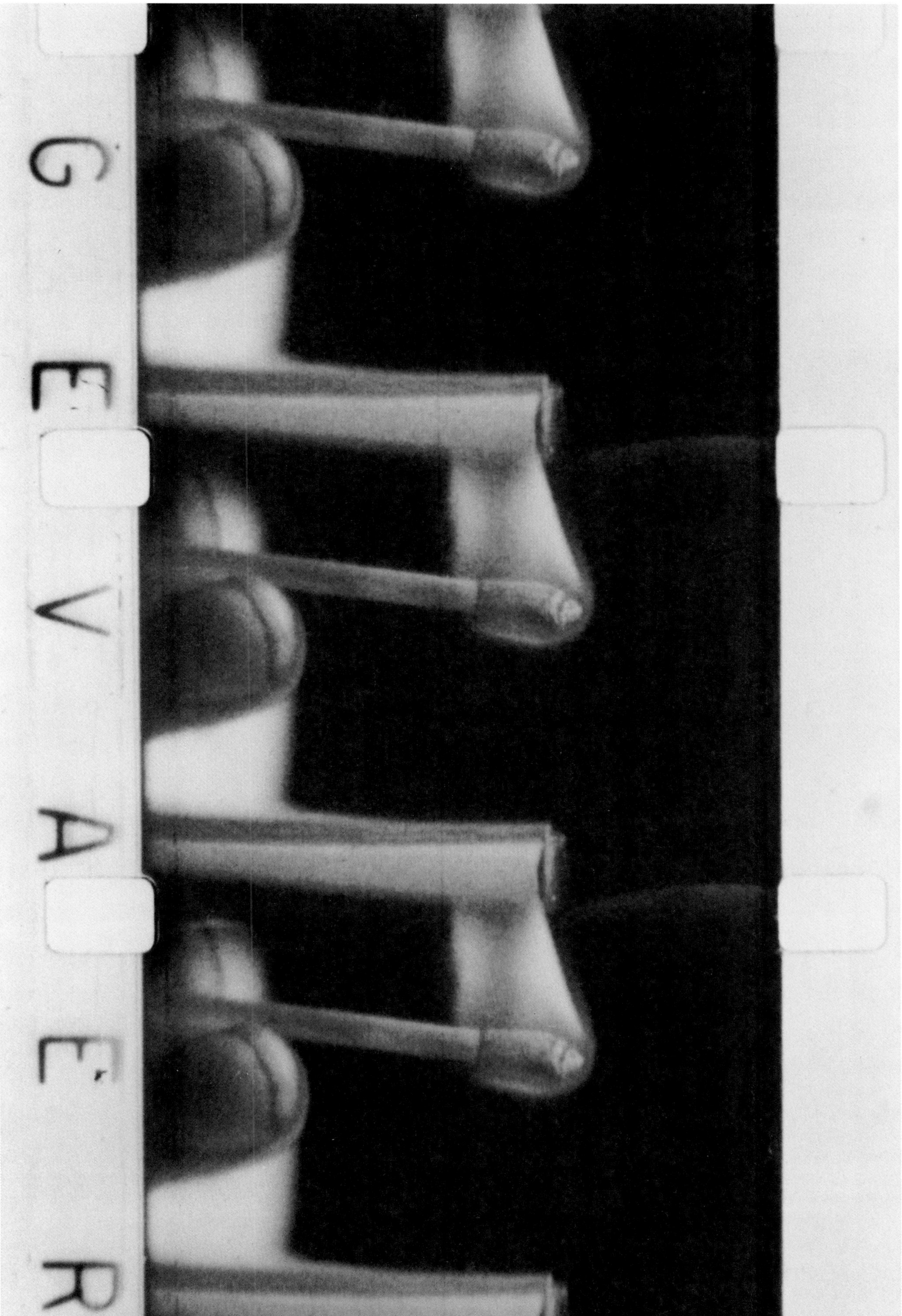
G E V A E R

43 *No. 4,* 1966

(also known as *Fluxfilm 16*)
16mm film, black and white, silent, 5½ minutes

No. 4 (Bottoms), 1966

16mm film, black and white, sound, 80 minutes

FILM NO. 4

BOTTOMS

String bottoms together in place of signatures
for petition for peace.

—From "Thirteen Film Scores by Yoko Ono, London, '68"

The first version of Ono's most famous film, popularly known as *Bottoms*, shows the naked, moving buttocks of a group of New York artists and friends, presented in sequence in close-up. Filmed in Ono's apartment at 1 West 100th Street, New York, with the assistance of her second husband Anthony Cox and Jeff Perkins, it includes the buttocks of Fluxus artists Geoffrey Hendricks, Ben Patterson, Philip Corner, Bici Hendricks, Jeff Perkins, and Pieter Vanderbeek, as well as those of Susannah Campbell, Cox, Ono's daughter Kyoko, Susan Pelland, Jerry Sablo, Carolee Schneemann, James Tenney, and Verne Williams. The film's form develops the seriality of her slow-motion Fluxfilms. The humorous, erotic, and rebellious tone of the film is pure Fluxus. George Maciunas's own work was full of references to toilets, bottoms, and "excreta fluxorum," and he used two stills from Ono's *No. 4* to make *Bottoms Wallpaper* (previously attributed as Ben Vautier's *Assholes Wallpaper*, 1973). In addition to its inclusion in the various versions of Fluxfilm anthology, *No. 4* was transferred by Maciunas to 8mm for both single-screen viewing and *Flux Wallpaper* film loop presentations. It appeared as an 8mm film loop in *Flux Year Box 2*. It was also featured in several subsequent film environments by Ono and John Lennon, including *Capsule by John and Yoko + Flux Space Center*, presented in New York in May 1970 as part of *Fluxfest Presentation of John Lennon & Yoko Ono +*, in which several 8mm loops of the film were projected on the walls, floor, and ceiling of a small enclosed space, or "capsule."

The longer version of *No. 4*, Ono's first non-Fluxus film, marks a transition in her filmmaking. She shot the film at the Belgravia house of Victor Musgrave, aided by Cox, during a long stay in London. Ono developed the structure of the earlier *No. 4* by expanding the number of bottoms (theoretically to 365, one for each day of the year), encouraging both friends and associates to participate by placing an advertisement in the newspaper, extending the film's length to eighty minutes, and including a soundtrack. A special turntable and measuring device were also constructed to ensure that each shot was framed correctly.

The irreverent Fluxus tenor of the short version of *No. 4* is modified by the conceptual, durational quality of the longer film, in which the soundtrack constructs a tangible narrative. Both films are radical, in formal and political terms, but there are important

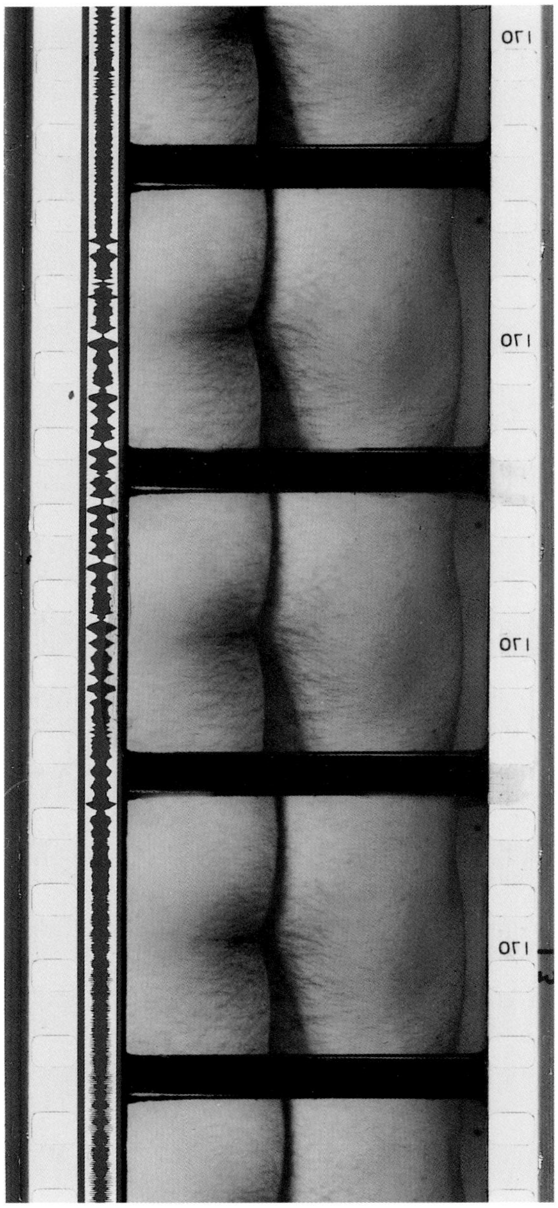

PLATE 43A
FILMSTRIP FROM ***NO. 4 (BOTTOMS)***, 1966

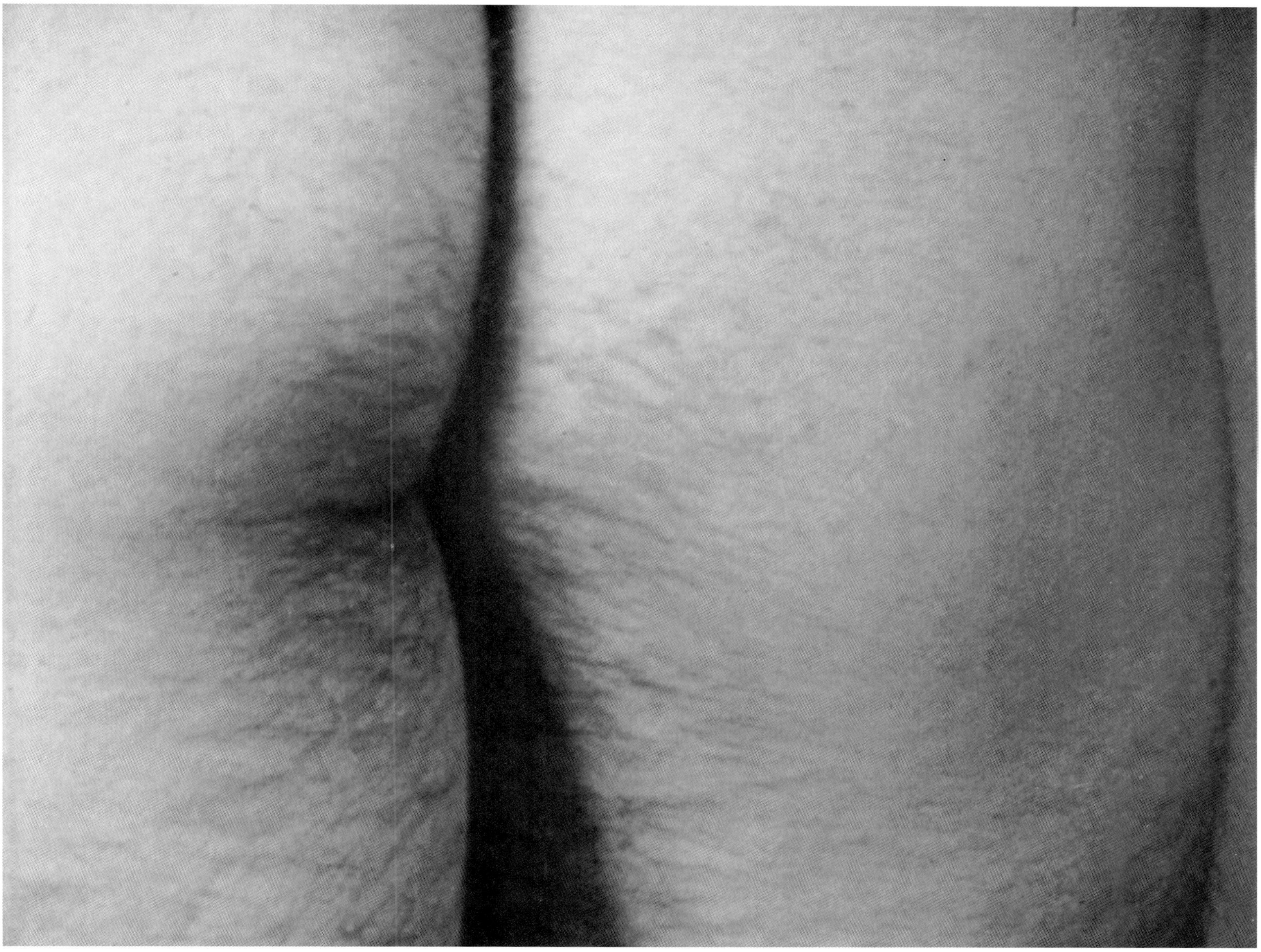

differences between them. Where the short, silent version transmits its meaning visually, through a single changing image by which differences in individual people are revealed solely through the body, the soundtrack of the longer version creates a more complex meaning. The commentary not only indicates a space beyond the frame, but reveals the personalities to whom the buttocks belong, shifting the emphasis from the visual to a more conventional filmic structure, involving a relationship between sound and image.

Ono described the filming process in terms of a "happening." The group-participatory nature of the film recalls group works by Ono in other media, such as *Shadow Piece*, performed in London in 1966, and the installation *Water Event*, presented as part of the exhibition *This Is Not Here* (Everson Museum of Art, 1971) by Ono and Lennon. It also prefigures her later collaborative films with Lennon, which adopt a narrative structure within which a conceptual idea is developed.

For Ono, one of the most important parts of the film was its rhythm, created by the constantly varying physical character and movement of each set of buttocks. The soundtrack both interrupts and reinforces that rhythm, while refusing the conventional match of sound with image. It includes enthusiastic, cautious, and intrigued reactions from participants and friends, descriptions of their experiences, and a press interview with Ono, contrasting with the monotonous, claustrophobic space of the screen, which the large images of naked male and female bottoms fill continuously, dividing it into four parts. The participants' conversations define the filming of their bodies as a social event, undermining the private, erotic intimacy of the conventional cinematic viewing experience of naked flesh.

The longer version of *No. 4* was privately screened, then banned in London by the British Board of Film Censors, a decision protested by Ono with a small, peaceful demonstration. A few weeks later, the Greater London Council Licensing Committee granted the film an X-rating certificate. For her London screenings in 1967, Ono created a film program containing her text "On Film No. 4 (in taking the bottoms of 365 saints of our time)" (Anthology 21) and "Questionnaire for Film No. 4," which were subsequently published in *Grapefruit*.
CI

FIRST SCREENING: 1966 (February 6) Film-Maker's Cinematheque, New York (short version); 1967 (August 8) Jacey Tatler Cinema, London (long version)

LITERATURE: Ono, "On Film No. 4" (1967); Hendricks, *Fluxus Codex* (1988), 420; Hanhardt, *Objects, Films*, exh. brochure (1989), 7–8; ———, *Arias and Objects* (1991), 99; ———, *The Films of Yoko Ono*, exh. brochure. (1991); MacDonald, *A Critical Cinema* (1992), 140–41, 146–49; Iles, *Have You Seen the Horizon Lately?* exh. cat. (1997), 108–21; Aubert, *Flux Film* (1998), 34

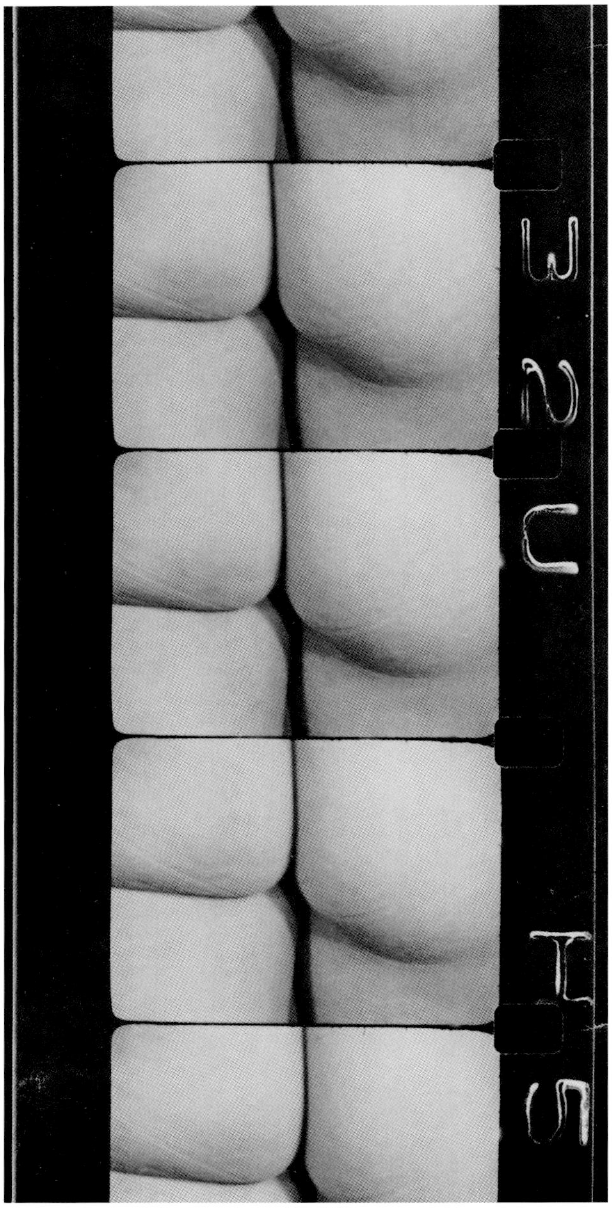

PLATE 43B
FILMSTRIP FROM ***NO. 4 (BOTTOMS)***, 1966

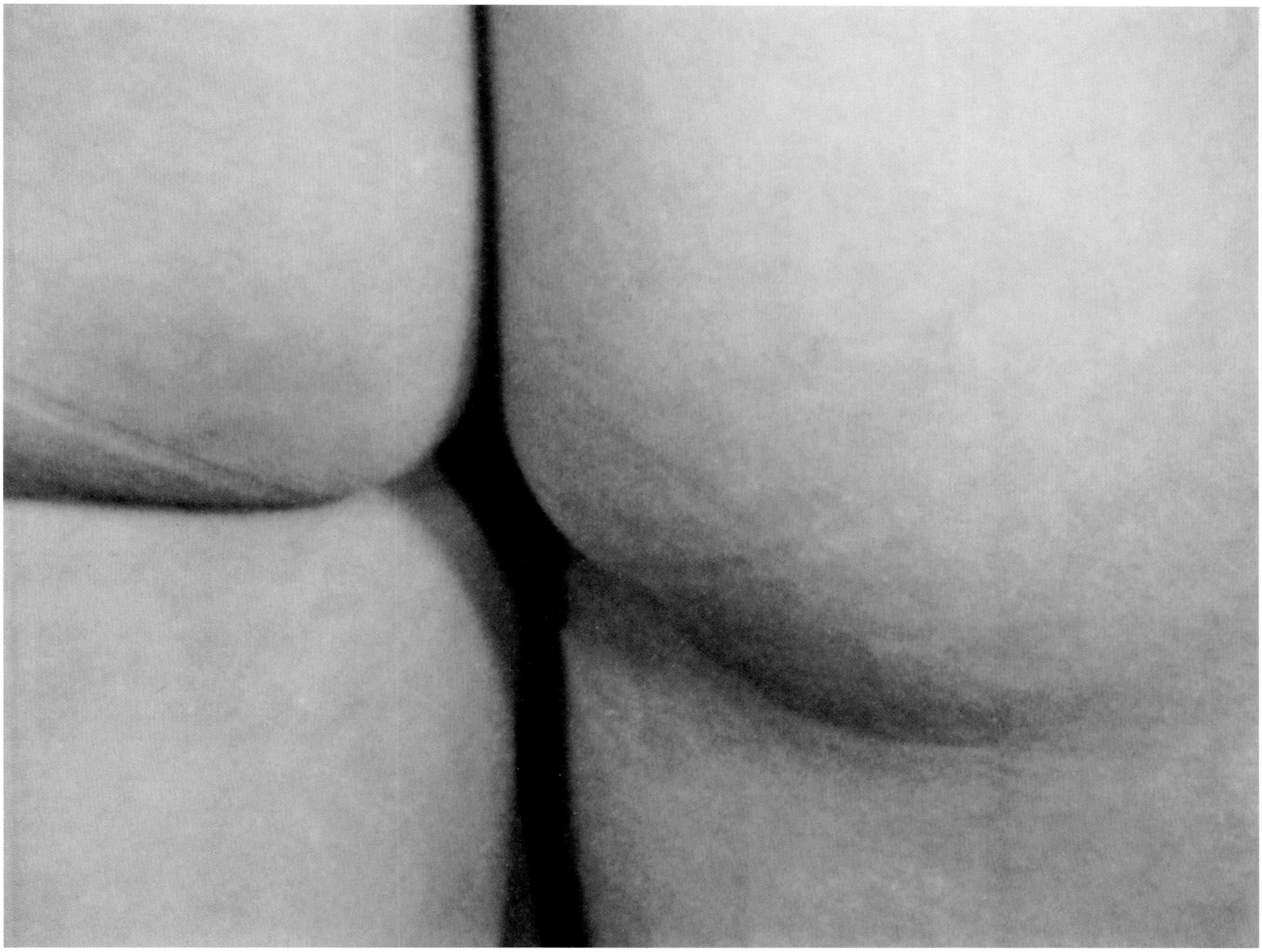

44 *Film No. 5 (Smile)*, 1968

16mm film, color, sound, 51 minutes

Film No. 5 (Smile) develops the format of Ono's first two Fluxus films (no. 42). It also relates to *Disappearing Music for Face* (*Fluxfilm 4*, 1966) by Shiomi Mieko (Chieko), made during the same filmmaking session at Peter Moore's apartment in New York, in which Ono's smile gradually disappears over several minutes. *Film No. 5* records the face of John Lennon for fifty-one minutes, in two single continuous shots; yet it differs from the earlier Fluxus films in several important respects. The high-speed camera used is slower, filming at 333 frames per second instead of the 2,000 frames per second of Maciunas's scientific camera; the film is in color rather than black and white; and it is shot outdoors instead of indoors, all of which suggests the everyday rather than the abstract. The content is also less "pure"; Lennon not only smiles but, particularly in the second shot, makes several other irreverent expressions, including putting his tongue out, blinking, and mouthing the word "ah." *Film No. 5* is an intimate portrait of Lennon rather than a conceptual film. In a statement titled "On Film No. 5 (also known as Smile) and Two Virgins" (1968; *Grapefruit*, 1971), Ono described *Film No. 5* and the accompanying film *Two Virgins*, made the same afternoon in their English garden, as being made "in the spirit of home movies...we were mainly concerned about the vibrations the films send out—the kind that were between us." She indicated that the films were also available on 8mm, "for people who'd like to have the film on their wall as a light-portrait."

Film No. 5 could be described as a distillation of Ono's earlier "ultimate" goal, stated in 1967, to "make a film which includes a smiling face snap of every single human being in the world."[1] Her statement had a political edge:

> We can also arrange it with a television network so that whenever you want to see faces of a particular location in the world, all you have to do is press a button and there it is. This way, if Johnson wants to see what sort of people he killed in Vietnam that day, he only has to turn the channel.[2]

The film expresses, in personal terms, the sense of unity and interconnectedness which her political statements, and installations such as *Half-A-Room* (1967; no. 20) and *Water Event* (1971; no. 6), also address.

Film No. 5 can be compared to Ono's *Self Portrait* (1965; fig. 7.3), a mirror into which the participant should smile, and the piece into which it evolved, *A Box of Smile* (1967; no. 22), a metal box whose inner mirror would reflect the participant's smile when opened. In 1970 George Maciunas made a work titled *Smile Machine for Yoko Ono*, which relates to both pieces.

CI

NOTES

1. Ono, "On Film No. 4" (1967; Anthology 21).
2. Ibid.

FIRST SCREENING: 1968 (November 14) *Chicago International Film Festival*

LITERATURE: Hanhardt, *Arias and Objects* (1991), 117; ———, *The Films of Yoko Ono*, exh. brochure. (1991); MacDonald, *A Critical Cinema* (1992), 141–42, 149–50

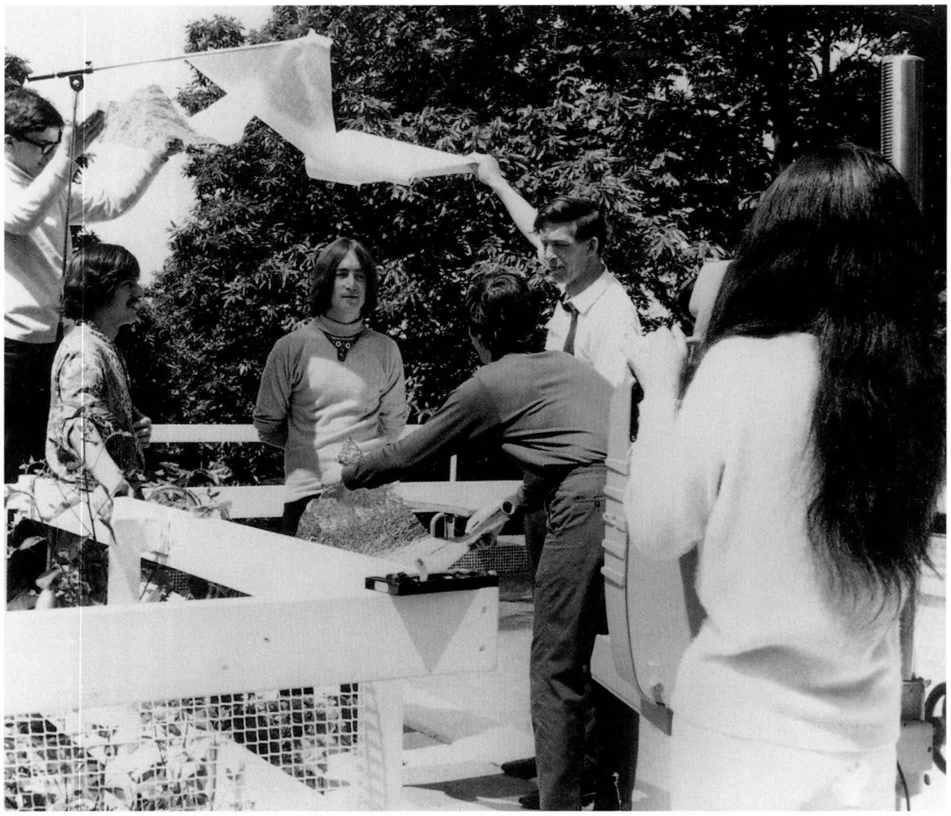

PLATE 44B
PRODUCTION STILL FROM
FILM NO. 5 (SMILE),
1968

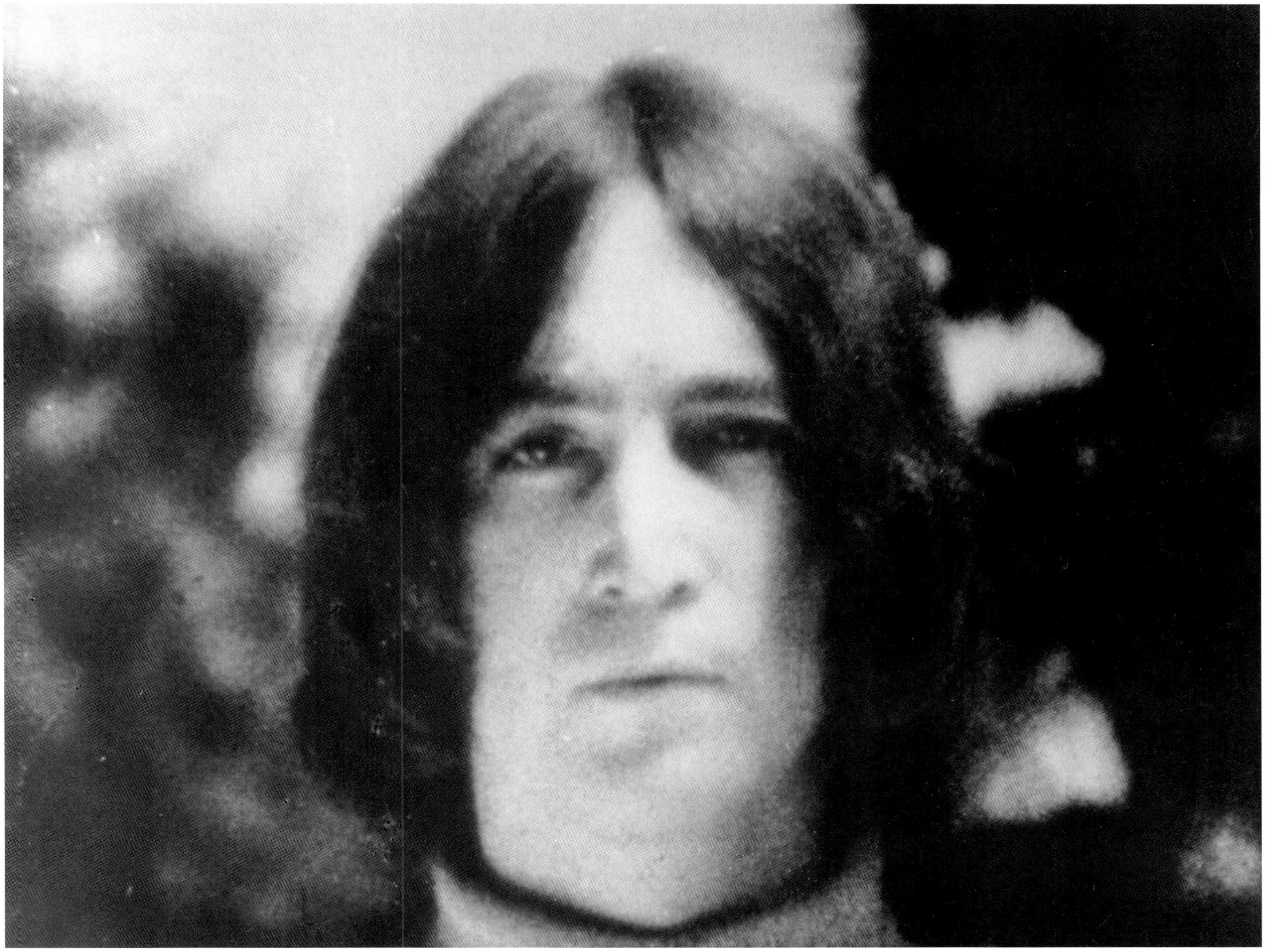

PLATE 44A
FRAME FROM *FILM NO. 5 (SMILE)*, 1968

45 *Rape*, 1969

16mm film, color, sound, 77 minutes
Directed in collaboration with John Lennon
Commissioned for Austrian television ORF

FILM NO. 5

RAPE (or CHASE)

Rape with camera. 1½ hr. colour synchronized sound.

A cameraman will chase a girl on a street with a camera persistently until he corners her in an alley, and, if possible, until she is in a falling position.

The cameraman will be taking a risk of offending the girl as the girl is somebody he picks up arbitrarily on the street, but there is a way to get around this.

Depending on the budget, the chase should be made with girls of different age, etc. May chase boys and men as well.

As the film progresses, and as it goes towards the end, the chase and the running should become slower and slower like in a dream, using a highspeed camera.

by yoko ono copyright '68

—From "Thirteen Film Scores by Yoko Ono, London, '68"

Following Ono's very public personal partnership with musician, songwriter, poet, artist, and Beatle John Lennon, the two artists began to collaborate on films, artworks, and music. Lennon displayed a deep understanding of conceptual ideas in his collaborations with Ono, combined with a wry sense of the absurd which meshed with both Ono's own humor and that of Maciunas and Fluxus. In each collaborative film, the authorship is assigned to whomever generated the initial concept.

Rape, made in London in 1969, is Ono's third film made with Lennon (following *Two Virgins*, 1968, and *Bed-In*, 1969). Its semi-documentary, narrative structure indicates a distancing from the Fluxus aesthetic, which had begun with the long version of *No. 4*. It also resonates with the conceptual, sociologically inflected performative ideas beginning to emerge in America during this period, expressed in works such as Vito Acconci's *Following Piece*, made in New York in the same year, in which Acconci followed strangers in the street. *Rape* had other overtones, reflecting the tension and fear felt by Ono and Lennon as the intrusive press and public attention generated by their fame became increasingly harder to bear.

In *Rape*, a two-man crew fix their camera on a Viennese girl walking through a cemetery in London, and begin to film her (fig. 14.21). At first she is flattered by the attention, asking if they think she is a film star, and halfheartedly rebuffs their attention in Italian, Hungarian, German, and, finally, English. She reproachfully asks them for a light for her cigarette. For the first two-thirds of the film, her irritation with the persistent film crew is modified by her desire for attention. It is only when the crew follows her onto the street and finally into her apartment, having colluded with her sister without her knowledge and gained access through a borrowed key, that she becomes increasingly angry and upset. Her level of tolerance toward the strangers also reflects a general female passivity which the fledgling women's movement of the sixties was beginning to address. Her inability to speak the language intensifies her isolation. The film, shot mainly in close-up with a hand-held camera, eventually traps her in a room, where she behaves like a cornered animal, lashing out at the camera. The flattering camera has become an intrusive weapon, invading her privacy and destroying her sense of autonomy. The film underlines Ono's feminism, which she continued to explore in two further films made the following year, *Fly* and *Freedom* (both 1970, nos. 46 and 47).

CI

FIRST SCREENING: 1969 (March 31) ORF TV, Vienna

LITERATURE: Mekas, *Movie Journal* (1972), 411–13; Lennon and Ono, *Filmmakers Newsletter* (June 1973); Hanhardt, *Objects, Films*, exh. brochure (1989), 7–10; ———, *Arias and Objects* (1991), 95; ———, *The Films of Yoko Ono*, exh. brochure. (1991); MacDonald, *A Critical Cinema* (1992), 142, 151–52; Iles, *Have You Seen the Horizon Lately?* exh. cat. (1997), 121–26

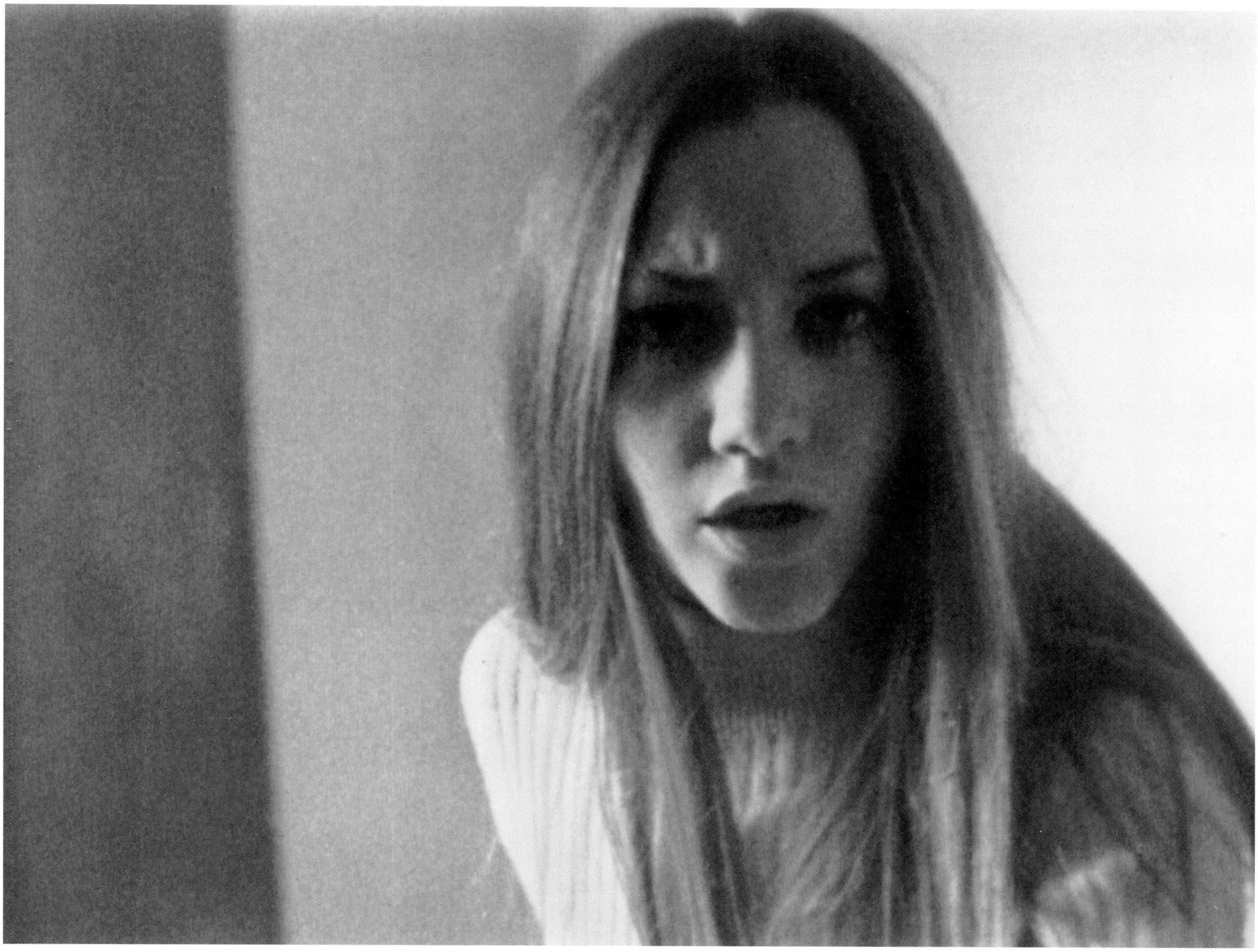

PLATE 45
FRAME FROM *RAPE*,
1969

46 *Fly,* 1970

16mm film, color, sound, 25 minutes

<u>FILM NO. 13</u>

<u>FLY</u> by Yoko Ono copyright '68

Let a fly walk on a woman's body from toe to head and fly out of the window.

—From "Thirteen Film Scores by Yoko Ono, London, '68"

In the same year that she made *Freedom* (no. 47), Ono made *Fly*, which likewise developed her concern with the body, women's rights, and her personal search for inner freedom. In *Fly*, the camera follows several flies in close-up as they alight on the naked body of a woman. For the majority of the film we see only one fly at a time, in extreme close-up shots of the woman's body as it walks briskly over its surface, nestling in the woman's hair and walking boldly into her parted legs, disappearing into her pubic hair. The woman remains unflinching, eyes closed, as the fly walks round the inside of her ear, across her lips, and perches on her nipple.

The fly's exploratory journey is accompanied by a vocal piece written and performed by Ono, whose extreme, disciplined singing matches the fly's movements so closely that it appears to describe the fly's persona. Ono has stated that both the woman's body and the fly are autobiographical.[1] Like her performance *Cut Piece* (1964; no. 30), the woman's body in *Fly* represented, for Ono, the state of stillness and passivity upon which she felt society insisted in order for approval to be attained. The fly, by contrast, represented the free spirit (embodied in the dual meaning implied by its name), and Ono imagined herself as a fly when composing and singing the vocal piece. The random movements of the fly dictate the path of the camera, whose extreme close-up shots frame the female body abstractly for much of the film, suggesting a landscape of flesh evocative of Walter Maas's *Geography of the Body* (ca. 1955). The viewer's attention constantly shifts between the movements of the fly and the part of the body across which it chooses to crawl. It obligingly selects all the major points of voyeuristic interest: parted legs, pubic hair, a nipple, an armpit of hair, an ear, mouth, and toes. Glimpses of the larger body give clues to the personality of the woman, revealing details such as painted finger- and toenails, red hair, and heavy mascara.

Once most of the body has been explored, the camera slowly opens out to reveal the complete body, lying splayed, corpselike, on a bed in an otherwise empty room. Another, unknown, dramatic narrative is suddenly implied. As Ono's soundtrack becomes more agitated, the flies are seen together for the first time, crawling across the body. The charm of following a single fly's journey in close-up is replaced by a sense of unease at the tawdry image of the fly-ridden, senseless female form. The role of the fly instantly shifts from a sympathetic personality, which Ono's complex and empathetic vocal soundtrack implies as female, to the standard negative association of flies with dirt and decay, and a sense of intrusion by the flies (evoking her and Lennon's film *Rape*, 1969; no. 45). On another level, the impassive naked body, the flies, and the movement of the camera away from the body and toward the sky outside the window suggest a metaphor for liberation, transience, and death. The transition from extreme close-up to the sky also echoes, in abbreviated terms, the structure of *Apotheosis* (1970; no. 48). Ono's focus on the minute details of a fly's behavior is typical of her Zen (and Fluxus) approach to small, everyday events, which are transformed into meaningful actions. *Fly* relates to pieces by Ono in other media, including scores, performances, music, and billboards (nos. 28, 41, 59).

CI

NOTES

1. Ono, introductory speech at film screening, Whitney Museum of American Art, 8 January 2000.

FIRST SCREENING: 1970 (December) *7¾ New York Film Festival*, Elgin Theater, New York

LITERATURE: Ono, *Crawdaddy* (5 December 1971); Mekas, *Movie Journal* (1972), 411–13; Lennon and Ono, *Filmmakers Newsletter* (June 1973); Hanhardt, *Objects, Films*, exh. brochure (1989), 7–9; ———, *Arias and Objects* (1991), 87; ———, *The Films of Yoko Ono*, exh. brochure. (1991); MacDonald, *A Critical Cinema* (1992), 153–55

PLATE 46B
FRAME FROM ***FLY***, 1970

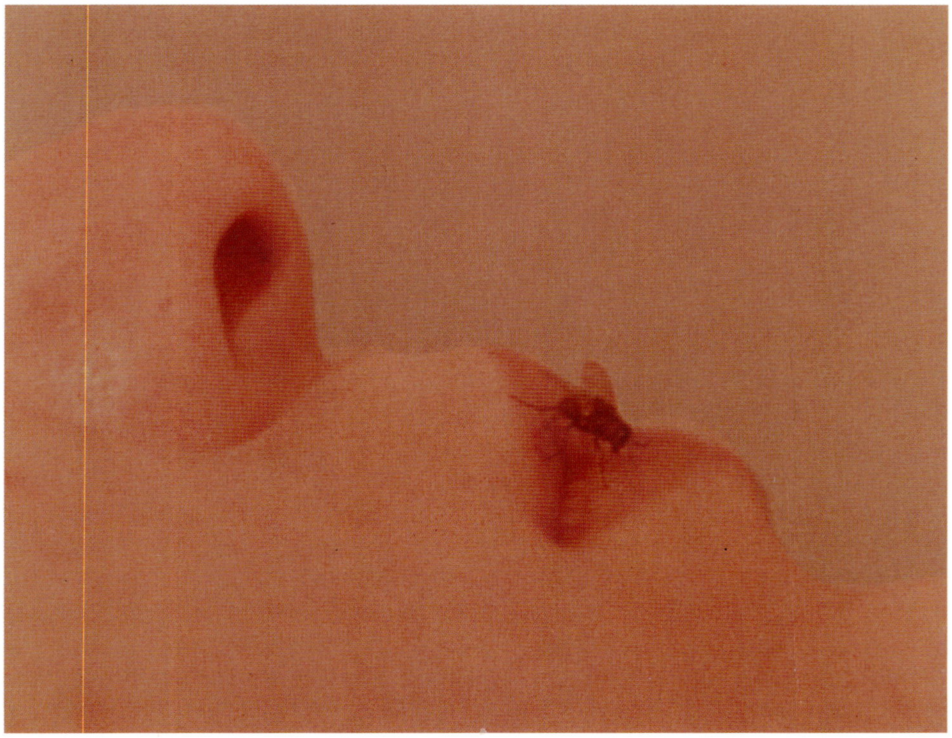

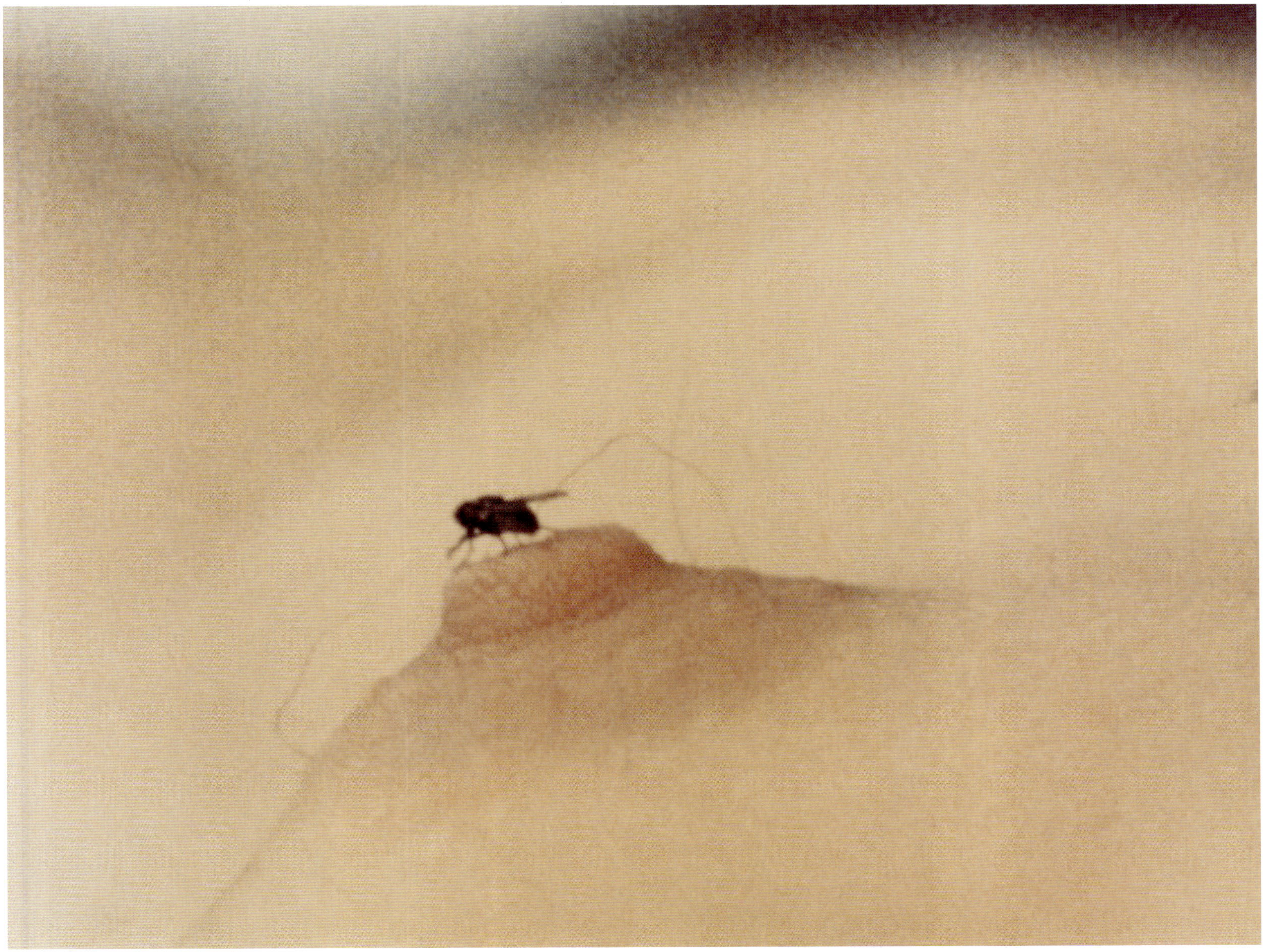

PLATE 46A

FRAME FROM *FLY*, 1970

47 *Freedom,* 1970

16mm film, color, sound, 1 minute
Soundtrack by John Lennon

Ono's succinct film *Freedom* is arguably the mirror opposite of her performance *Cut Piece* (1964), in which Ono knelt or sat passively on the stage while members of the audience were invited to come up and cut away her clothing, challenging their sense of personal responsibility when given permission to perform an essentially violent act (no. 30). *Cut Piece* externalized Ono's sense of helplessness in the face of social pressure to conform to a passive female stereotype, a role particularly prevalent in her native Japan. In *Freedom*, Ono stands stripped down to a purple bra in front of the camera. In contrast to *Cut Piece*, she has taken control of her own state of undress and pulls the front of her bra, trying to free her breasts from its restrictive hold. Her movements are slow, and deliberately theatrical. At one point she holds both hands out, exposing the stubborn bra fabric, as if demonstrating the difficulty of struggle. In her self-assertion, reinforced by Lennon's brisk soundtrack, Ono used the bra, an iconic symbol of the burgeoning women's movement, to stress the importance of freeing women from socially determined, restrictive roles through a liberation of the body. The difficulty in breaking the fabric of the bra evokes the struggle for emancipation in which women, including Ono, were engaged at the beginning of the seventies, and from which, it is implied, one can never be completely free. The lyrics of Ono's song *Sisters O Sisters* (1970) echo the sentiments expressed in the film:

> Freedom O Freedom
> That's what we fight for
> And yes, my dear sisters
> We must learn to fight

The film ends before we are able to discover whether the bra breaks. We are refused a final denouement precisely because it is the process of the struggle for liberation, and not the spectacle of the body, which forms both the subject and meaning of the film.
CI

FIRST SCREENING: 1970 (December) *7¾ New York Film Festival*, Elgin Theater, New York

LITERATURE: Mekas, *Movie Journal* (1972), 411–13; Lennon and Ono, *Filmmakers Newsletter* (June 1973); Hanhardt, *Objects, Films*, exh. brochure (1989), 7–9; ———, *Arias and Objects* (1991), 96; ———, *The Films of Yoko Ono*, exh. brochure. (1991); MacDonald, *A Critical Cinema* (1992), 155

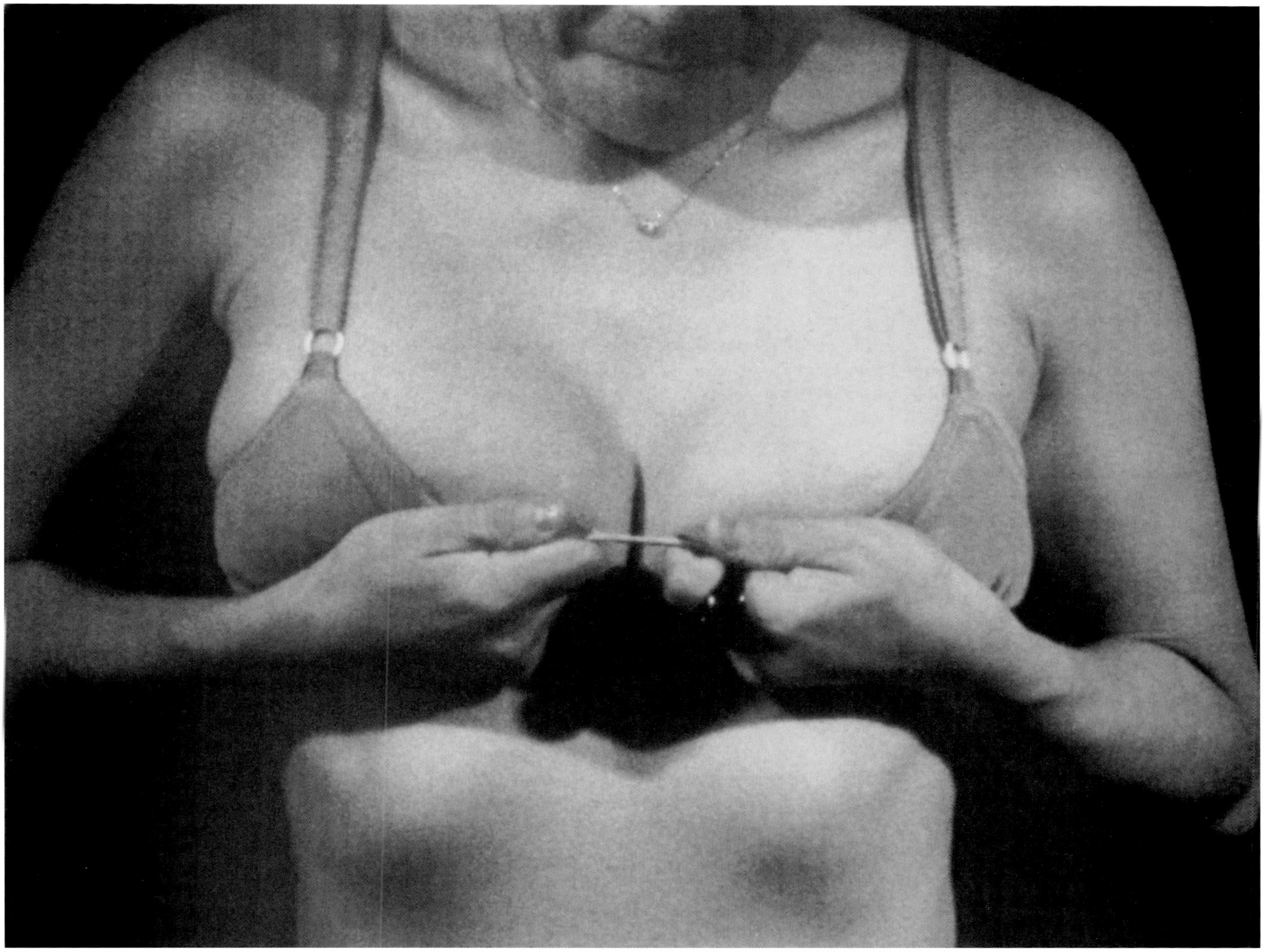

PLATE 47
FRAME FROM
FREEDOM, 1970

48 *Apotheosis,* 1970

John Lennon

16mm film, color, sound, 18½ minutes
Directed and produced by John Lennon and Yoko Ono

Apotheosis and *Erection* (1971; no. 49) demonstrate the singularity of Ono and Lennon's filmmaking and its relationship to the American avant-garde film of the late sixties and early seventies. Both artists were friends of Andy Warhol and the filmmaker and founder of Anthology Film Archives, Jonas Mekas. Both also admired the work of Michael Snow, and had been struck by his groundbreaking film *Wavelength* (1967), in which a fixed-frame camera moves gradually inward from a wide-angle shot of a Soho loft space to a close-up of a small photograph pinned to its far wall, over a period of forty-five minutes. At the beginning of the seventies, filmmakers were using conceptual ideas to explore both the material qualities of film and the process of its making. For artists and filmmakers, the environment beyond the gallery became important. *Apotheosis* and *Erection* take place in external rural and urban environments, and both comprise the filming of an action that occurs over a period of time whose end point is determined by the completion of the event.

The structure of *Apotheosis* could be described as a reversal of the method adopted in Snow's *Wavelength*. The film was made in winter, using a camera filming from a hot-air balloon, and despite its apparent seamlessness, is edited in three parts. The first part, lasting only a few seconds, shows the head and shoulders of Ono and Lennon in close-up, wrapped in coats and scarves, their mouths and noses muffled against the cold. Both stand silently in the square of a picturesque English village. In the next, longer section, the camera draws upward away from the square, showing rooftops, an aerial view of cars, people, buildings, the local church, and, as the village recedes, a patchwork of fields covered in snow.

As the sounds of the village die away a silence ensues, intensifying proportionally as the balloon rises. The silence is broken only by the distant barking of dogs far below, the occasional gunshot as someone hunting in the fields pursues his prey, and the sound of the hot air balloon's apparatus. The white landscape recedes as the balloon gently drifts further and further upward, until there is complete silence. In the third and final section, the balloon ascends into white clouds and the screen remains white for several minutes until the balloon re-emerges above the clouds, where the blue sky and winter sun can suddenly be seen. The journey ends with this dramatic, sublime image of a clear blue sky.

This collaborative film by Ono and Lennon is credited to Lennon, following their principle that whoever had the initial concept for the film would take the main credit. However, each film was collaboratively structured and executed, using cameramen and editors. The image of the sky had operated for Ono as a symbol of immateriality and freedom since her scores of the early 1960s. The sequence of *Apotheosis* can be read as a direct metaphor for liberation. Ono and Lennon made the film the year after *Rape*, and the same year as *Freedom* and *Fly*, all of which deal with a struggle for freedom in both political, feminist, and personal terms. Just as *Freedom* shows a personal struggle as yet unresolved, the title and sequence of *Apotheosis* suggest an acceptance of the concept of real freedom as a utopian fantasy.

CI

FIRST SCREENING: 1970 (December) *7¾ New York Film Festival*, Elgin Theater, New York

LITERATURE: Mekas, *Movie Journal* (1972), 411–13; Lennon and Ono, *Filmmakers Newsletter* (June 1973); Hanhardt, *Objects, Films*, exh. brochure (1989), 8; ———, *Arias and Objects* (1991), 63; ———, *The Films of Yoko Ono*, exh. brochure (1991); MacDonald, *A Critical Cinema* (1992), 153

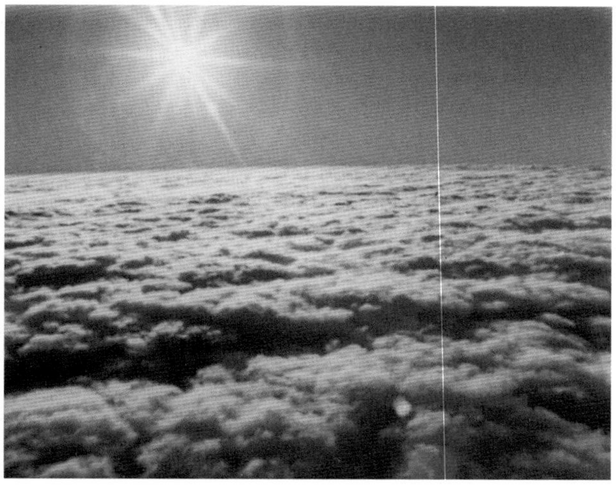

PLATES 48A–B
FRAMES FROM LENNON,
APOTHEOSIS, 1970

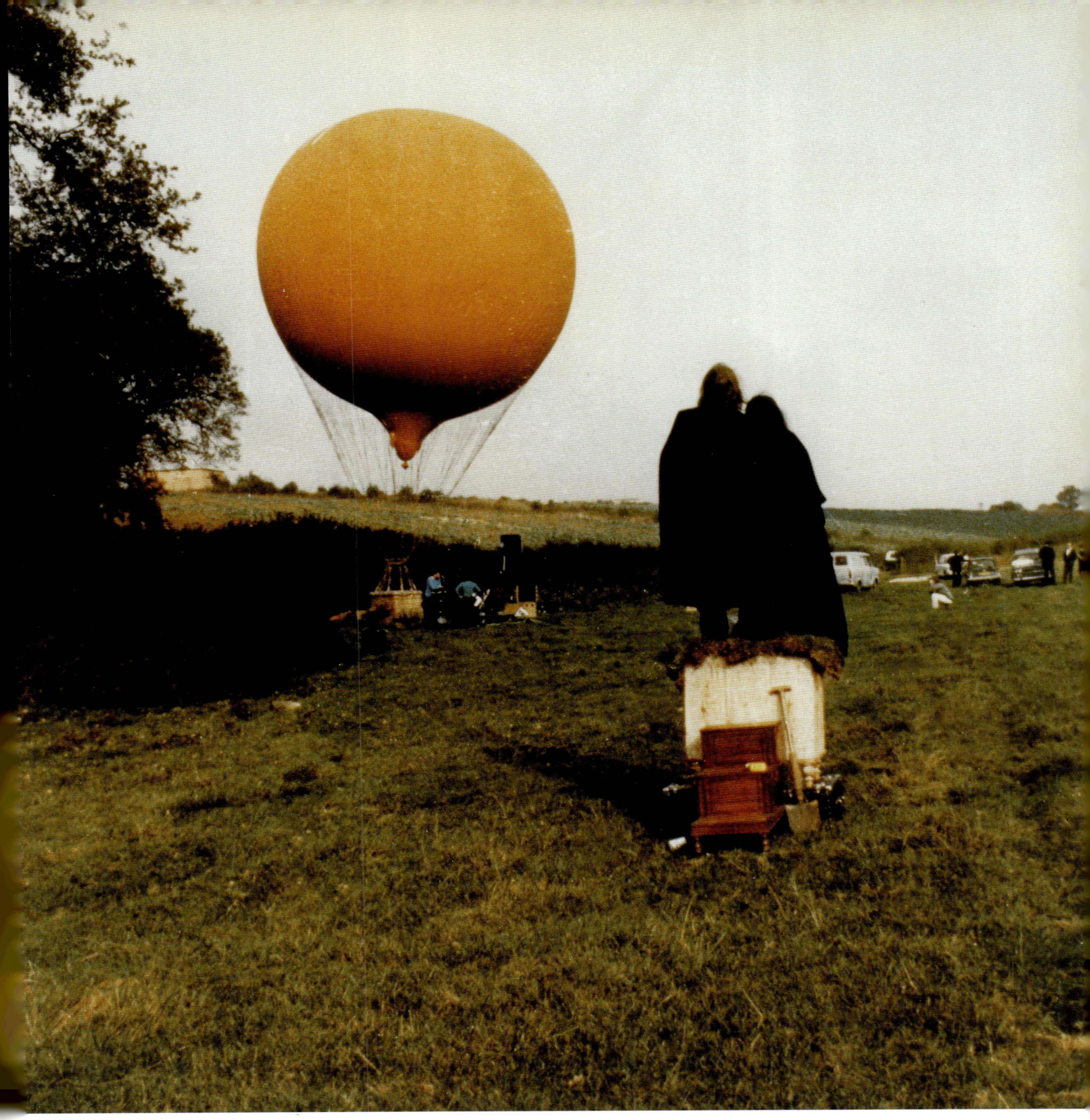

49 *Erection,* 1971

John Lennon

16mm film, color, sound, 20 minutes
Directed and produced by John Lennon and Yoko Ono
Still photography and direction of photography: Iain Macmillan
Titles by George Maciunas

The structure of this enigmatic film is related to both *Apotheosis* (1970; no. 48) and *No. 4 (Bottoms)* (1966; no. 43). *Erection* is constructed from a series of still photographs, taken over a period of a year with a fixed camera, of a hotel being built on an empty lot in London. The photographs, taken both hours and days apart, are run together in time-lapse dissolves. The first few images of the building site give way to a closer lens distance, which is then held until the end of the film. This subtle variation in distance reveals the informal quality of the film's construction. For the first half of the film, the sky and rows of Victorian workers' houses in the background are clearly visible. Cranes appear and disappear in a matter of seconds in front of them, laying the building's basic structure. After this initial flurry of activity, the building progresses at a less dramatic pace. The passing of time can be detected at times only by subtle changes in the light as the different days and weeks are run together, evoking the ephemeral changes in light so central to the meaning of Ono's shadow paintings. As the building gradually swells, our view of the other buildings is gradually obliterated. Towards the end of the film the light fades, and lights appear in various parts of the unfinished structure. As the walls are filled out by glass panels, which reflect the otherwise invisible cityscape beyond the film frame, the diagonal angle of the building asserts itself, and the perspective changes once again.

The dissolving sequence of still images, evoking both the use of still photographs in the work of structural filmmakers and the slide-dissolve artworks that artists began to make in the early 1970s, is accompanied by a dreamlike soundtrack by Lennon and Ono. Its erotic sensuality, gradual crescendo, and decrescendo suggest the act of lovemaking, which the film's title humorously implies. The building becomes a metaphor for the male organ, filling out gradually until the climax of completion, whereupon the daylight fades, Ono's voice subsides to a series of sensual murmurs, and the viewer's anticipation is finally satisfied. *Erection* reflects Lennon's interest in sexual politics (also explored in the film *Rape*, made two years earlier with Ono) and the role of the male body. The body plays a central role in all Ono's early films and in most of her collaborative films with Lennon, both taxonomically (bottoms—*No. 4*; legs—*Up Your Legs Forever*; the eye—*Eyeblink*; the mouth and face—*Smile*) and in narrative terms (*Freedom*, *Erection*, and *Fly*).

CI

LITERATURE: Mekas, *Movie Journal* (1972), 411–13; Lennon and Ono, *Filmmakers Newsletter* (June 1973); Hanhardt, *Objects, Films*, exh. brochure (1989), 8; ———, *Arias and Objects* (1991), 105; ———, *The Films of Yoko Ono*, exh. brochure. (1991); MacDonald, *A Critical Cinema* (1992), 143–44

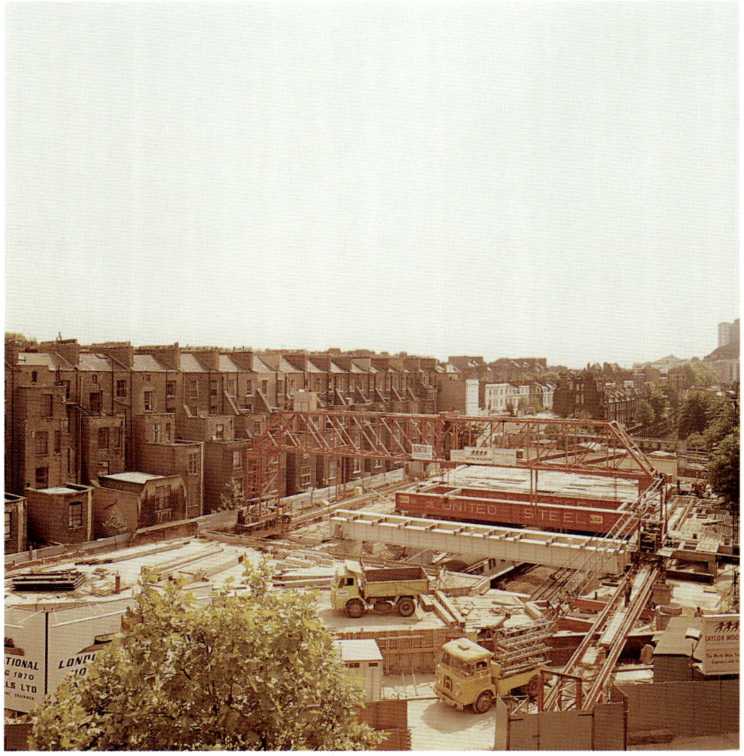

PLATES 49A–C
FRAMES FROM LENNON,
ERECTION, 1971

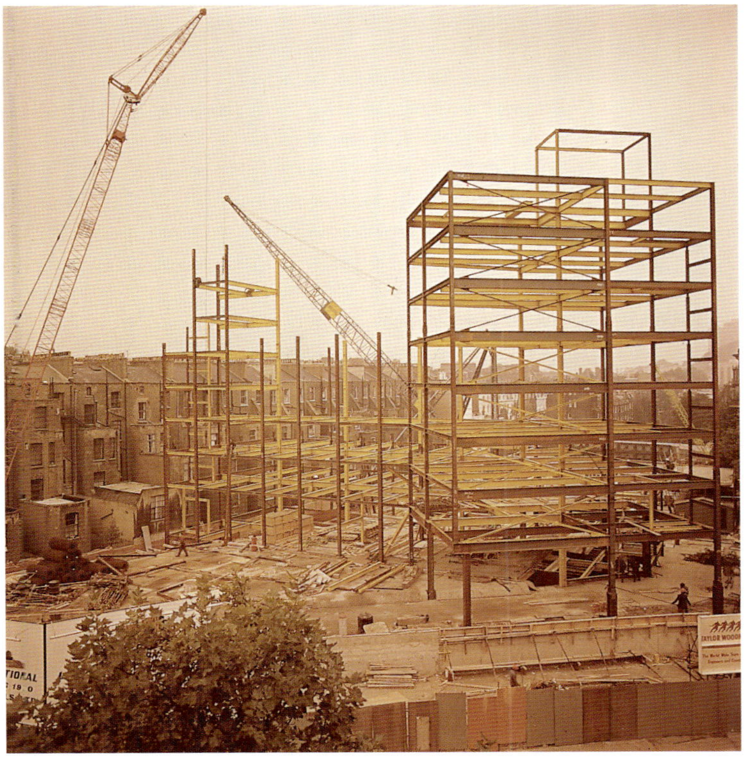

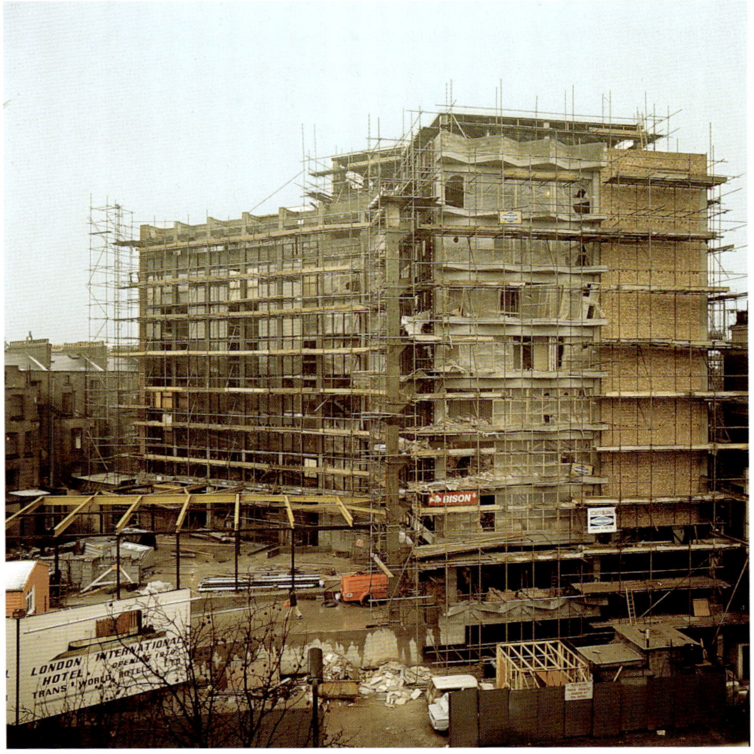
BISON
LONDON INTERNATIONAL
HOTEL
TRANS WORLD

50 *Sky TV,* 1966

closed circuit video installation
dimensions variable
Collection of the artist

Sky TV, one of the earliest video installations ever made, is Yoko Ono's only work in video art. A video camera placed on the roof or outside the window of the gallery transmits live images of the sky to a television set in the gallery. This piece was made just after the Sony Portapak was introduced on the market and before the advent of videotapes, at a time when all images on television were generated and controlled by commercial television broadcast companies. The ubiquitousness of surveillance camera video technology in our contemporary world makes it hard to appreciate the radicality and precociousness of *Sky TV*. The possibilities suggested by the ability to transmit an image in real time, using the instant-feedback properties of the video camera, were only just becoming apparent to both artists and the general public. The first artist to use the newly available video equipment to make art was the Korean-born Nam June Paik, who, along with Ono, was associated with the Fluxus group. Ono was close to Paik during the mid-1960s and participated in the avant-garde festival of Paik's collaborator, Charlotte Moorman. *Sky TV* anticipated the self-reflexive, instant-feedback video installations of the late 1960s and early 1970s. Significantly, Ono pointed the camera not at the viewer, but at the sky, implying that understanding could be achieved not by contemplating the self, but by considering an infinite world, beyond the ego.

Ono has used images of the sky in her work since the early 1960s. The sky was the subject of three scores (published in *Grapefruit*, 1964): *Painting to See the Skies* (1961), *Painting for the Skies* (1962) and *A Painting to See the Sky III* (1962), as well as *Sky Event for John Lennon* (1968; in *Grapefruit*, 1970). Cards inscribed with the word "sky" were "sold" through her *Sky Disperser* (1966; no. 17). *Sky TV* relates to her and Lennon's film *Apotheosis* (1970; no. 49) and, in particular, her *Painting to See the Skies* (1961), a canvas with a hole cut into it through which viewers could look at the sky.
CI

EXHIBITIONS: 1966 *Yoko at Indica*, Indica Gallery; 1992 *Color, Fly, Sky*, Museet for Samtidskunst, Roskilde; 1993 *Color, Fly, Sky*, Stiftung Starke; 1993 *Color, Fly, Sky*, Frauen Museum; 1997 *Have You Seen the Horizon Lately?* MOMA, Oxford

LITERATURE: Iles, *Have You Seen the Horizon Lately?* exh. cat. (1997), 98, 108

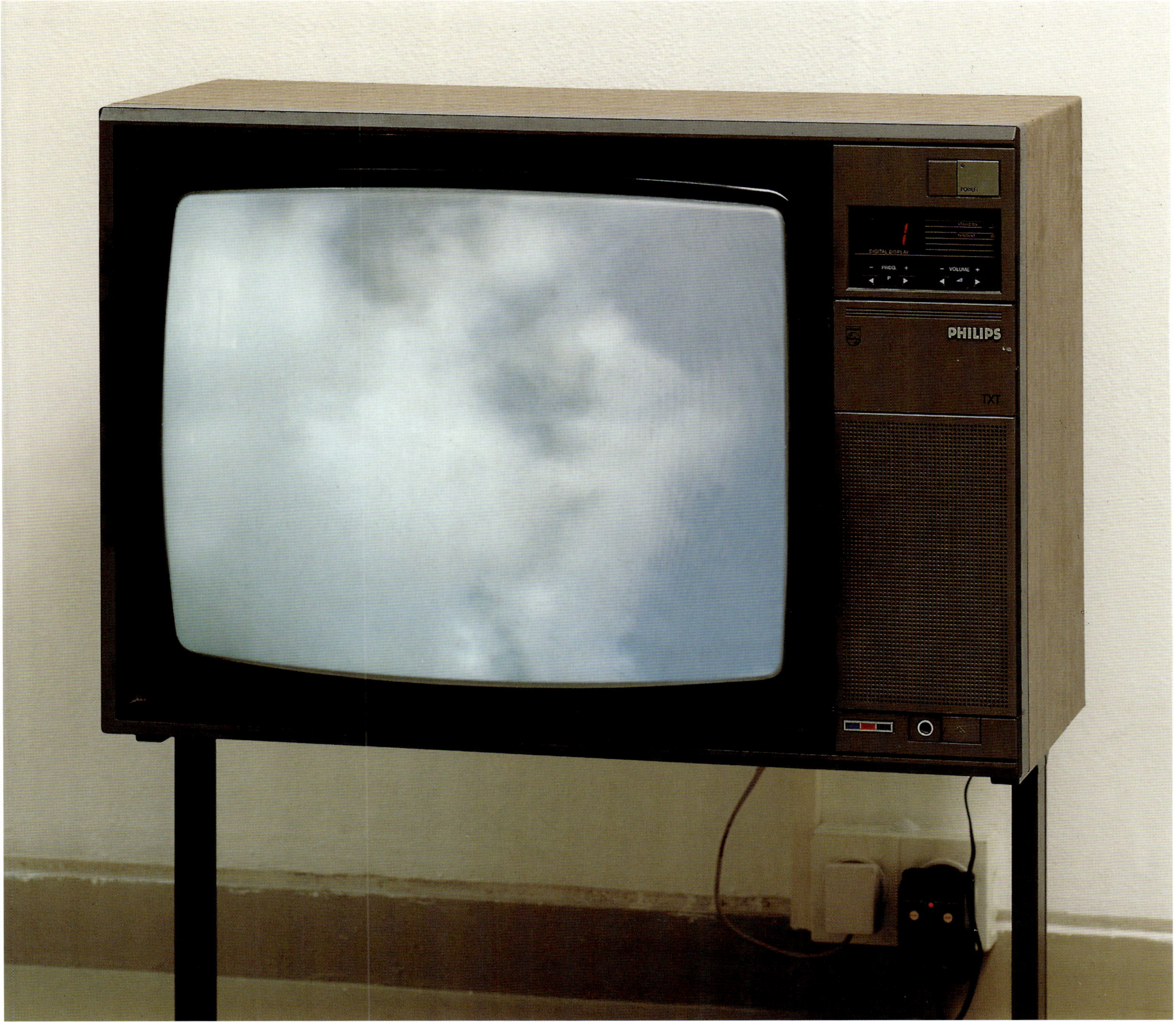

PLATE 50

SKY TV, 1966.
INSTALLATION VIEW,
THE ISRAEL MUSEUM,
JERUSALEM, 2000

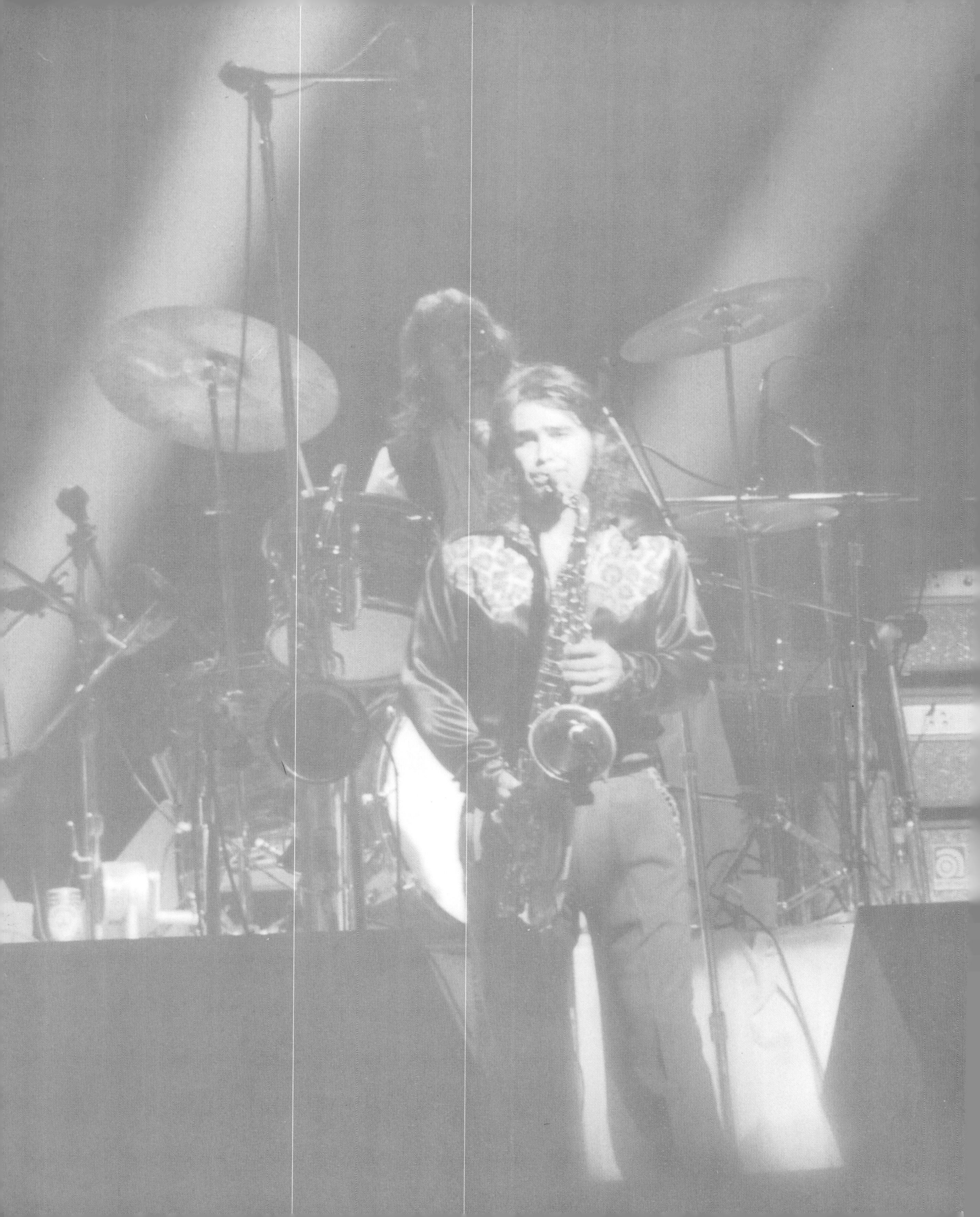

MUSIC

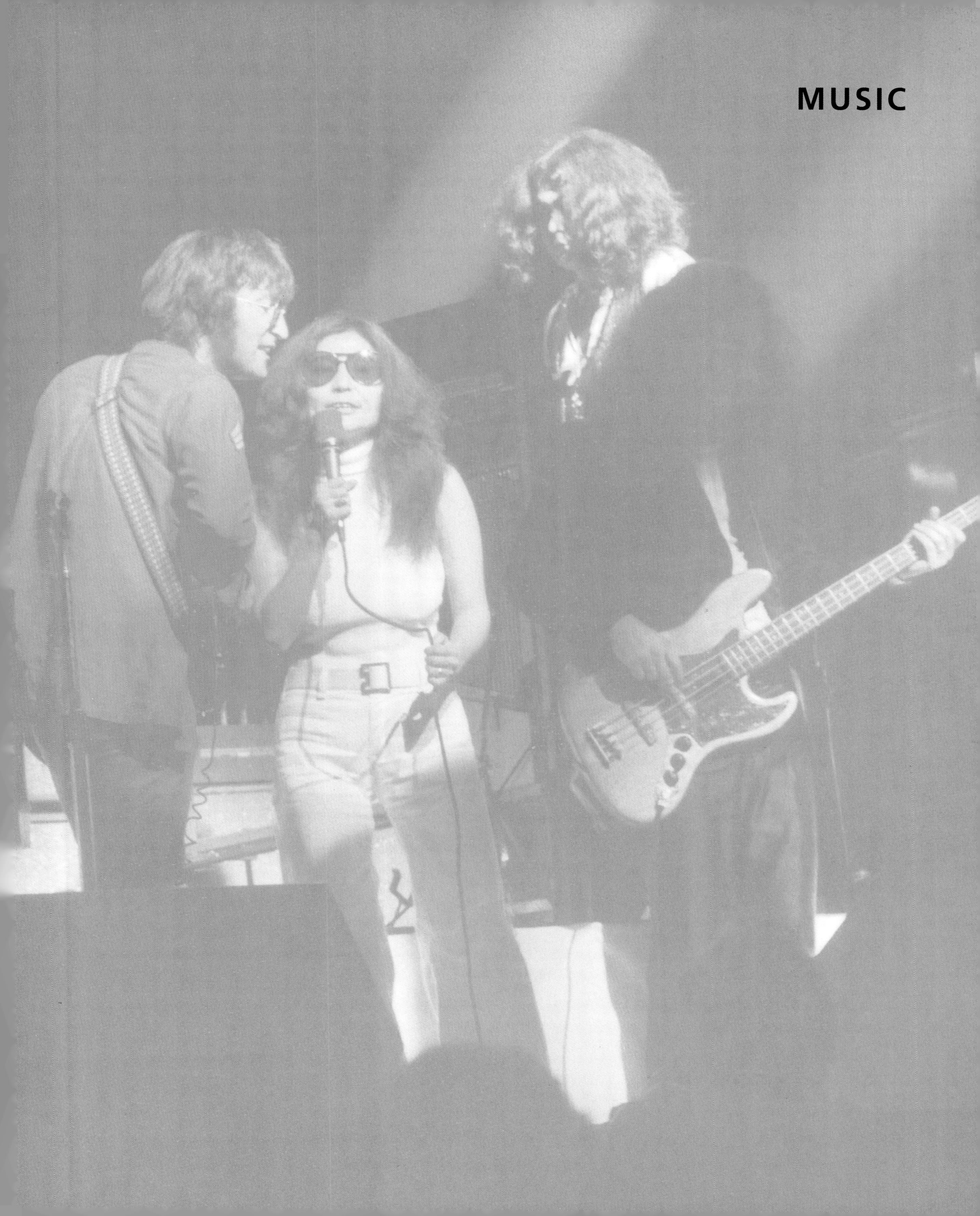

SECRET PIECE

Decide on one note that you want to play.
Play it with the following accompaniment:

The woods from 5 a.m. to 8 a.m.
in summer.

(The above is the later revision of the following original.)

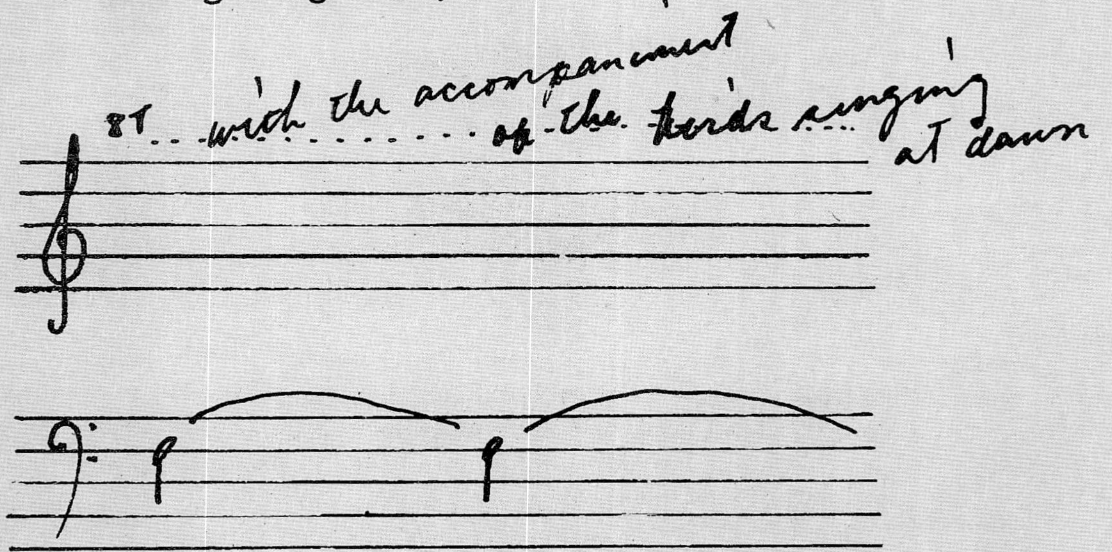

1953 summer

Music of the Mind from the Voice of Raw Soul

EDWARD M. GOMEZ

It was forty years ago today that Yoko Ono taught her band to play.

In the roughly four decades since Ono began publicly performing her music, her collaborators have included avant-gardists, rock-music luminaries, scores of veteran session musicians, and her own son and his post-punk, post-grunge pals. In varying configurations, they helped give memorable expression to Ono's evolving, sometimes startling, musical ideas. For as much as her work in many different media has been characterized by a poetic tone and point of view, it was in music and as a composer that Ono began her professional artistic career.

Poetry, music, objects, and actions or events seamlessly meld throughout Ono's multifaceted oeuvre. Still, many of her works are realizations of what the artist, like her Fluxus confrères, borrowing a music-composition term, called scores. Moreover, Ono has frequently noted that music has provided an essential, even therapeutic outlet through which she has poured unbridled emotion. Proving and re-proving her musical bona fides many times over the years, often in the face of harsh criticism, Ono has journeyed from the frontiers of avant-garde "art music" to the hook-laden grooves of mainstream pop. Along the way, she created, almost single-handedly, a not easily classifiable genre that is rock 'n' roll–and free-jazz-inflected—and that, in retrospect, has been acknowledged by critics and musicians alike as a seminal sound that helped pave the way for the rise of punk rock and its derivatives.

FIGURE 11.1
SECRET PIECE FROM
GRAPEFRUIT (1964)

From her upper-class mother, Isoko, Yoko learned about *ikebana* (flower arrangement) and various aspects of Japanese culture. "My mother, a 'nice girl' from a 'nice family,' had learned *shamisen*, *koto*, *ō-tsuzumi*, *ko-tsuzumi* and *nagauta*."[1] Ono Isoko also knew Japanese singing styles and could read Japanese musical scores. Yoko Ono has observed that Japanese written music, with its minimal indications of pitches and sound durations, resembles the instructions that typify her own mature work.[2]

As a youngster, Ono attended *kabuki* performances with her mother and heard the melancholy strains of popular *enka* songs on the radio. Her parents sent her to Jiyū Gakuen, a prestigious Tokyo school, where she began piano lessons at the age of four. Known for its music-centered curriculum, the school gave early starts to several notable Japanese composers. In a typical—and, for Ono, prescient—assignment, pupils were told to listen for and notate everyday sounds and noises.

Ono Yeisuke, Yoko's father, was an accomplished pianist who had dreamed of a career on the concert stage but whose family required him to become a banker. Ono continued the piano lessons until she was twelve or thirteen. "I was too shy to play the piano in front of my father…I would go and play in the next room, just to let him know that I was working."[3]

Ono's father routinely examined his daughter's hands for signs of her professional potential; eventually he concluded that she would never become a concert pianist. He discouraged Yoko when, at fourteen, she announced her desire to become a composer, believing, according to Ono, that music composition was "too hard for women."[4] She took up vocal training and became a fine singer of lieder but opted to study philosophy at Gakushūin University in Tokyo until her family moved to the United States. Yoko was then eighteen years old.

The Ono family settled in Scarsdale, New York. Yoko continued her education at nearby Sarah Lawrence College, although she was not previously aware of its renown in the arts. There, she studied poetry with Alastair Reid, music composition with the Viennese-trained André Singer, and English literature with Kathryn Mansell.[5]

Her education took place during a heady time in postwar music, when experimental composers redefined the nature of musical sound and brought convention-busting ideas into the sanctuary of the concert hall. By the mid-1950s, adventuresome composers looked for inspiration to the twelve-tone master Arnold Schönberg and, even more enthusiastically, to his student Anton Webern, the creator of short, spare, enigmatic pieces. Moving beyond Edgar Varèse's *musique concrète*, which had "established definitively that all possible aural sensations were now available for creative use as raw material,"[6] European composers such as Pierre Boulez and Karlheinz Stockhausen investigated the nature of sound itself in electronic music using tape recorders and newfangled instruments.

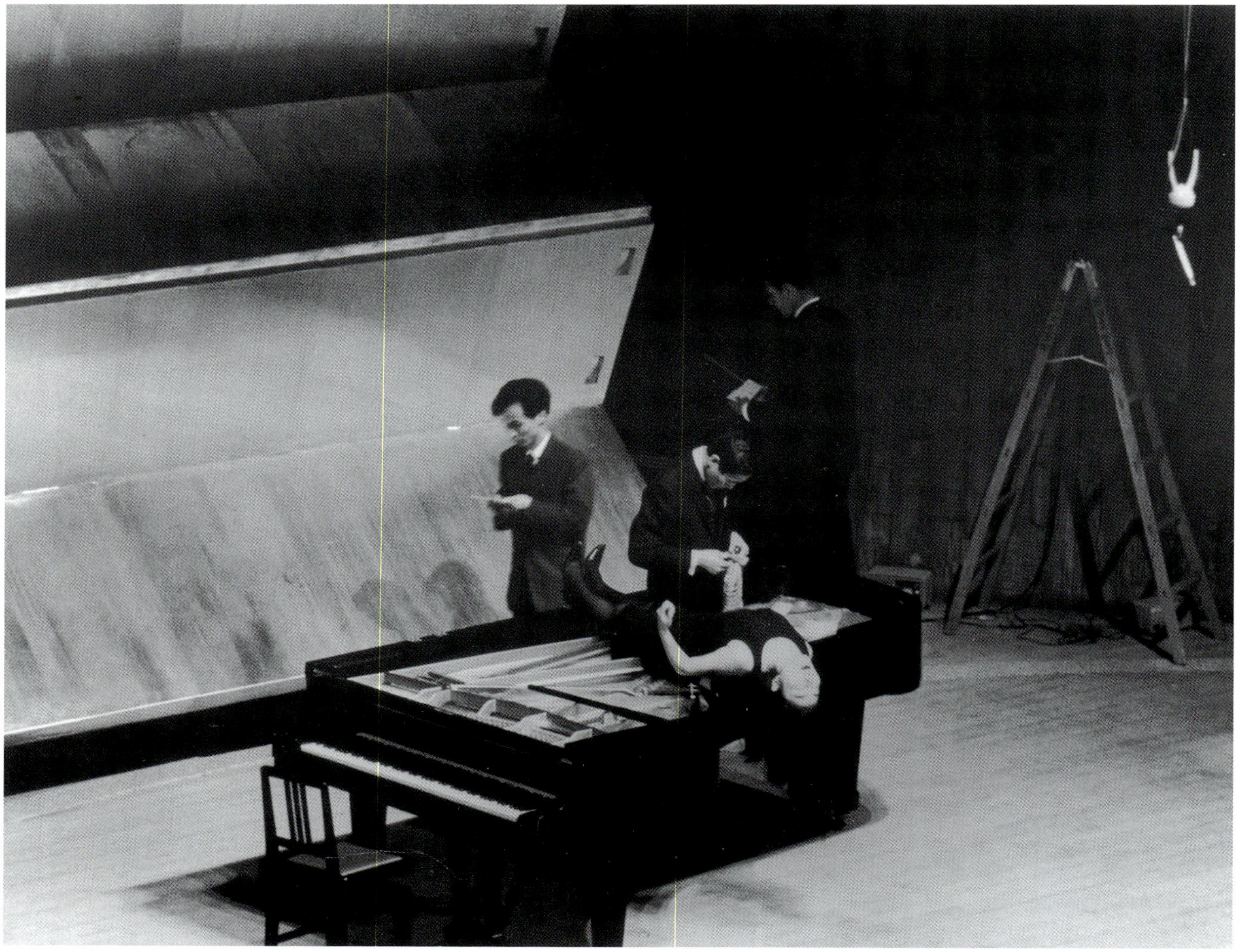

FIGURE 11.2
JOHN CAGE, ***MUSIC WALK***. PERFORMED BY CAGE, DAVID TUDOR, ONO, AND MAYUZUMI TOSHIRŌ, SŌGETSU ART CENTER, TOKYO, 1962

The postwar generation "wanted to make its own revolution in music," composer Aaron Copland wrote. They "accepted Schönberg's role as pioneer and innovator but rejected his structural procedures and his aesthetic."[7]

At Sarah Lawrence, Ono has said, "My heroes were the twelve-tone composers—Schönberg, Berg, those people—and I was just fascinated with what they could do. I wrote some twelve-tone songs, then my music went into [an] area that my teacher felt was really a bit off the track, and…he said, 'Well, look, there are some people who are doing things like what you do and they're called avant-garde.'"[8]

Echoing her childhood assignments, around this time Ono had attempted to use Western musical notation to capture "the storm of birds singing" that she woke up to each morning. But she found the system inadequate. This led her to devise her first instruction-based composition, *Secret Piece* (1953), published in 1964 in *Grapefruit* (fig. 11.1). It reads: "Decide on one note that you want to play. Play it with the following accompaniment: The woods from 5 a.m. to 8 a.m. in summer." Hand-drawn beneath this brief text, bass- and treble-clef staves appear without a time signature or measure-dividing lines, and two lonely, held half-notes on the bass F line hint at some sort of prolonged hum. Above the treble clef, Ono wrote: "With the accompaniment of the birds singing at dawn."

At first glance, this score is as cheeky as it is accurate within the limits of standard notation. *Secret Piece* suggests that birds will sing the unmarked, to-be-imagined melody in the blank treble clef against a do-it-yourself, droning rhythm in the bass. Blurring the line between music and poetry, it is simultaneously delicate, punchy, and clever. As an example of graphic art, it is eloquently austere.

The experimental composers whom Singer mentioned to Ono included Varèse, Henry Cowell, and John Cage. But no one at Sarah Lawrence personally introduced the young Japanese artist to Cage,[9] who would teach a course called "Composition" from 1956 to 1958 and another called "Experimental Composition" from 1958 to 1960 at the New School for Social Research in Manhattan.[10]

Cage urged his students to open their ears to everyday noises—roaring trucks, radio static, falling rain—and regard them as music. "We want to capture and control these sounds, to use them not as sound effects but as musical instruments," he advised.[11] Cage created Zen-inspired soundworks through the use of so-called chance operations. He made aleatory (from *alea*, Latin for "dice") compositions in which chance elements and randomness figured into their performances; their interpreters could or had to decide how long or in what order to play certain sections of a piece.

Against this creative backdrop, Ono left college and moved to New York in 1957 to pursue her artistic career. She supported herself through secretarial work and by giving lessons in traditional Japanese arts given at Japan Society. Ono was familiar with the Juilliard School of Music's library in Manhattan, where she had studied musical scores. During this period she met violinist Kobayashi Kenji and piano prodigy Ichiyanagi Toshi, Juilliard scholarship students from Japan who were already well-established in their homeland. Ichiyanagi became Ono's first husband. At the New School, Cage's students came to include the artists Allan Kaprow, George Brecht, and Al Hansen, and the poets Dick Higgins and Jackson Mac Low, among others. The composer Stefan Wolpe introduced Ichiyanagi and Ono to Cage, and once they attended one of his classes.[12]

In the late 1950s and early 1960s, Manhattan offered serious composers three main performance venues: Carnegie Hall, Carnegie Recital Hall, and Town Hall. Renting one was costly for struggling musicians. Ono longed for an affordable place where she could present her own works and those of other avant-gardists who had been "drawn like magnets to New York, and to each other."[13] Her search for a space led her to a warehouse district in downtown Manhattan, where she found a cold-water, fifth-floor walk-up loft at 112 Chambers Street for $50.50 a month. She took it and set up a studio-cum-living space in which she used orange crates as chairs and rearranged them into a bed at night. An acquaintance gave her an old piano.[14]

Ono's associates cautioned her against establishing a venue so far away from midtown Manhattan. Still, through the composer Richard Maxfield she and Ichiyanagi met the experimental composer La Monte Young, who later asked Ono to let him use her loft for some concerts he wished to organize. She agreed to do so, leading to a now-legendary series of experimental-music performances (lasting from December 1960 to June 1961) that featured Young, Maxfield, Ichiyanagi, Simone Forti, Henry Flynt, Robert Morris, and others. Ironically, Ono had to make a big effort to be included in Young's series—and put up with rumors that she was being supported by a "wealthy Chinese gentleman." In any case, she still proudly hoped to land Carnegie Recital Hall for her own major concert.[15] Ultimately, she did do an improvisation during another artist's concert in the loft series; in it, she used her long hair in a *kabuki*-dancelike movement to accompany her vocalizations.

On April 3, 1961, Ono was one of three Japanese composers on the bill at the Village Gate nightclub, along with Ichiyanagi and Mayuzumi Toshirō. She offered *Of a Grapefruit in the World of Park*, which mixed nursery-rhyme phrases with wild laughter, atonal music, and disjointed-sounding remarks ("I can smell metal in the air." "Dinner's ready." "The wind has stolen my key."). Her compositions then included everyday "real" sounds that Ono called "by-sound" or "insound."

Later that year, she appeared at Carnegie Recital Hall in her first major public performance. The promoter Norman Seaman agreed to present an Ono concert at the famed venue; via Seaman she contacted Charlotte Moorman, a classical cellist at Juilliard known for producing concerts, and engaged her services as production assistant. (The arrangement led to a lifelong friendship; until her death in 1992, Moorman championed Ono's music and regularly performed it in public.) To Ono's surprise, Moorman also intended to take part in the concert.

"It was her first avant-garde performance," Ono remembered, noting that Moorman willingly took instructions about how to stroke the cello and strike its strings. Others who took part in Ono's concert on November 24, 1961, included Brecht, Mac Low, Jonas Mekas, Yvonne Rainer, Young, and Maxfield (who was billed as "electronic technical assistant"). The program featured three works: *A Grapefruit in the World of Park*, *A Piece for Strawberries and Violin*, and *AOS—To David Tudor*. In *AOS—To David Tudor*, Ono wrapped two performers in gauze with bottles and cans dangling from them and instructed them to walk across the stage without making noise; she "made the stage very dim, so you had to strain your eyes," she explained, "because life is like that. You always have to strain to read other people's minds."

In the second work, "a performer stood up and sat down before a table stacked with dishes. Her action was accompanied by a rhythmic background of repeated syllables, a tape recording of moans and words spoken backwards, and an aria of high-pitched wails sung by Ono—a portent of the musical sound that later would become Ono's trademark."[16]

During the summer of 1961, Ichiyanagi returned to Japan, where he went on to enjoy considerable success. He urged Ono to join him and his fellow musicians there. Ono eventually headed to Tokyo and, from 1962 to 1964, stayed in Japan, where, along with Nam June Paik and local artists, she and Ichiyanagi became involved in the Tokyo Fluxus scene (see nos. 3, 27–29). She also worked with Ichiyanagi to bring Cage and David Tudor to Japan. Ono, Ichiyanagi, and other Japanese avant-gardists took part in Cage-Tudor performances there in 1962 (fig. 11.2).

By the early 1960s, Ono was also recording some of her compositions, which were often related to or realizations of her written instructional scores. For example, one score published in *Grapefruit* (1964) under "Music" reads:

> COUGH PIECE
>
> Keep coughing a year.
>
> 1961 winter

In a sound work with the same title, produced in 1963, an electronic rumble ebbs and flows through thirty-two and a half minutes of alternatingly soft and surging passages punctuated by the gentle clicking of what appear to be claves (rhythm sticks), and by the artist's occasional coughing. Ono's cough can sound intrusive at first, with its sudden shot of realism into the spare, swimming mix, but a listener soon hears it as a well-integrated musical element in an unfolding soundscape that lacks obvious cadences but immediately sustains an expansive, meditative mood. Ono, like early pioneers of electronic music and sound art, fused performance and composition in the making of her original recorded works. Now the tape recorder—primitive by today's standards and offering only a few tracks—had become not only a device for documenting a performance, but a vital tool in the making of the compositions it preserved.

When Ono returned to New York, she became increasingly active, making objects and short films, and staging events in the Fluxus milieu. Fluxus majordomo Maciunas encouraged her ideas. In September 1966, she was invited to take part in an avant-garde festival called *Destruction in Art Symposium (DIAS)* in London (no. 33). Thus far, her conceptual music, realized as performance events, reflected Ono's self-described "boredom with classical music and existing forms of art" and "desperate need" for "a new ritual to fill the void."[17] Buoyed by her acceptance by other avant-gardists, Ono continued to explore ephemeral sound rooted in raw emotion and the imagination. She called it "music of the mind" and presented audience-participation events based on this notion at *DIAS*.

"The sound you play in your mind is different than the sound that comes out," Ono said. "The sounds and music in your mind...exist without the physical limitations of the real world," she added, relating that she asked people at her "silent concerts" to create this music in their own minds.[18] Ono called attention to the "sounds you hear in silence... [when you] start to feel the environment and tension and people's vibrations...the sound of fear and darkness, like a child's fear that someone is behind him."[19] She outfitted dancers with contact microphones to capture such subtle emanations.

Remaining in London after *DIAS*, Ono made films and mounted solo gallery shows. Before she met

John Lennon in November 1966, she had experimented with tape recorders. Lennon had been integrating recorded-tape fragments played backward and other novel techniques into Beatles songs like "Tomorrow Never Knows" on the group's *Revolver* album (1966). When he met Ono, the Beatles were embarking on one of their richest periods of music-making, in which they would use the recording studio as a composing tool in groundbreaking ways. The results of their efforts would soon be heard in the multitracked textures of *Sgt. Pepper's Lonely Hearts Club Band* (1967), and in such songs as "Strawberry Fields Forever" (1967) and "I Am the Walrus" (1967).

From the start, Ono and Lennon's romantic partnership was an artistic one. "Yoko played me tapes I understood," Lennon said.[20] "I know it was very strange, and avant-garde music is a very tough thing to assimilate...but [I'd] heard the Beatles playing avant-garde music when nobody was looking for years." Ono, who was unfamiliar with the Beatles' music because of her long immersion in the avant-garde, appreciated the rock star's homemade recordings and films. Lennon said he had made "what would be termed 'far-out' tapes" for himself. There were very few people, he said, for whom he could play his tapes. "I played them to her and then we made *Two Virgins* a few hours later."

The May 1968 impromptu recording session that became the controversial *Unfinished Music No. 1: Two Virgins* album on the Beatles' Apple Records label (released in November) marked the beginning of Ono and Lennon's music-making dialogue.[21] A collage of electronic rumbling, whistling, music-hall piano, and random household noises punctuated by Ono's warbling, guttural outbursts, *Two Virgins* became as notorious for its unconventional—some said unlistenable—sound as it did for its creators' nude photo-portraits on its cover. *Two Virgins* can be heard as an essential link to "Revolution No. 9," the sound collage Lennon contributed to the Beatles' *White Album* (1968), which some Beatles fans never accepted.

In the early years of their partnership, despite divorces, Ono's miscarriage, a dubious drug bust, and the Beatles' very public breakup, the couple was extraordinarily productive. Documenting their lives and artistic activities, they made *Unfinished Music No. 2: Life with the Lions* (May 1969; no. 54)[22] and *Wedding Album* (October 1969; fig 1.24). The former LP included a live set that paired Lennon's swirling guitar feedback with Ono's expressionistic wailing, a recording of the heartbeat of the baby Ono had lost, and, in a Cagean turn, two minutes of silence. *Wedding Album* offered a long, playful exchange in which Ono and Lennon called out each other's names and a recording of their March 1969 *Bed-In for Peace* at the Amsterdam Hilton (no. 34). Its packaging, designed by John Kosh, was elaborate: a gatefold sleeve, photo and press-clip booklets, their line drawings, a facsimile of their marriage certificate, and a photo of a wedding-cake slice were all packed in a handsome white box.

These projects provided a warm-up for Lennon and Ono's work with an ensemble they would create in the era of rock-music "supergroups." "I had become so lonely doing mind music that I was ready to begin screaming again," Ono said, and she had a concept "for a band that would never exist...that didn't have a set number of members...that could accommodate anyone who wanted to play with it."[23] They called their group the Plastic Ono Band (no. 55).

In 1970, after undergoing primal-scream therapy with its creator, Dr. Arthur Janov, in California, Ono and Lennon returned to London to record John's first solo album, *John Lennon/Plastic Ono Band*. Both Janov's back-to-childhood, pain-purging method and Ono's influence are reflected in its raw sound and soul-baring themes, and in Lennon's screaming-tinged vocals in such songs as "Mother" and "Well, Well, Well."[24]

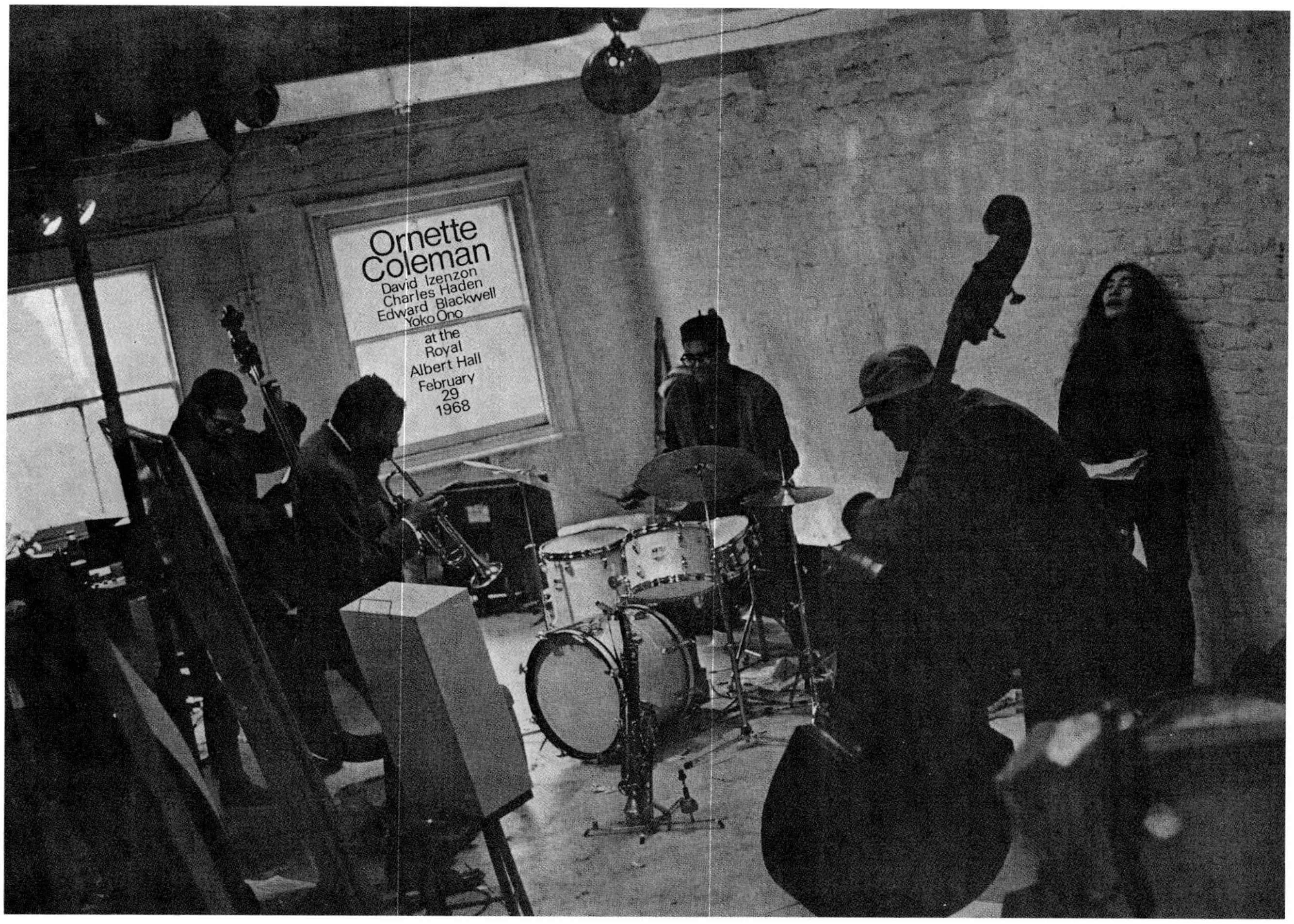

FIGURE 11.3
PROGRAM COVER FOR ORNETTE COLEMAN CONCERT WITH ONO, ROYAL ALBERT HALL, LONDON, 1968

Ono recalled that the "texture of [John's] album was set by the minimalist use of instruments" they had "carefully chosen" for it. By contrast, for her solo LP, backed by Lennon, Ringo Starr, and bassist Klaus Voorman, Ono delivered her signature screaming at full throttle in songs like "Why" and an assortment of raspy, groaning, deeply expressive vocals in "Why Not," "Touch Me," and "AOS." The last track, a rehearsal tape for a February 1968 performance with Ornette Coleman's avant-garde jazz ensemble at the Royal Albert Hall (fig. 11.3), showed Ono's detractors that her vocal style had a history—and some noteworthy admirers. With passages that climbed from near-whispers to climactic yelps, it was one of the most powerful pieces on an unusual record that still defies easy classification.

That *Yoko Ono/Plastic Ono Band*, the vital artistic companion to Lennon's disc, emerged at all was almost unexpected. "In those days, my performances were rarely recorded," Ono explained. "When I started to scream, I think [John] thought, 'Oh! I can do anything!' I would hear his guitar and think, 'Wow, I can answer that.'"[25] Ono was forced to scream louder than ever against amplified instruments; at times, the sound of her voice and Lennon's ferocious guitar work fused. Recording engineers routinely walked out during her jam sessions. Still, Ono took her improv tapes, sound effects, and other tape fragments that she concocted and developed richly textured soundscapes such as "Paper Shoes" and "Greenfield Morning I Pushed an Empty Baby Carriage All Over the City." These evocative sound poems blended train, bird, and dog-howl sounds into Ono's chanting voices, which were multitracked in overlapping waves.[26]

Ono has often said that rock music's 4/4 rhythm gave her "the beat, like a heartbeat," that she had been looking for—and that modern orchestral composers had lost. She had come from an ancient musical tradition that emphasized vocal pitch and a performance culture of subtle, symbolic, resonant gestures to investigate a pop-inflected musical language that emphasized melody, rhythm, and interpretation. She continued creating aural tapestries and exploring rock's rhythms and song forms in such solo albums as *Fly* (1971; no. 56), a companion release to Lennon's *Imagine*; *Approximately Infinite Universe* (1973; fig. 11.4); the feminist-themed *Feeling the Space* (1973); *Season of Glass* (1981; fig. 11.5); and several others. Critics and fans praised Ono's edgy contributions to the Lennon-Ono *Double Fantasy* album (1980), hearing in her vocals antecedents and affinities to the era's punk and new-wave styles. "Walking on Thin Ice" (no. 57), released a few months after Lennon's death in December 1980, reprised her legendary scream against a pounding rhythm of haunting minor chords; the *New York Times* judged the tightly produced record, which featured Lennon's "magnificent, over-the-top guitar solo," the number-one single of 1981.[27]

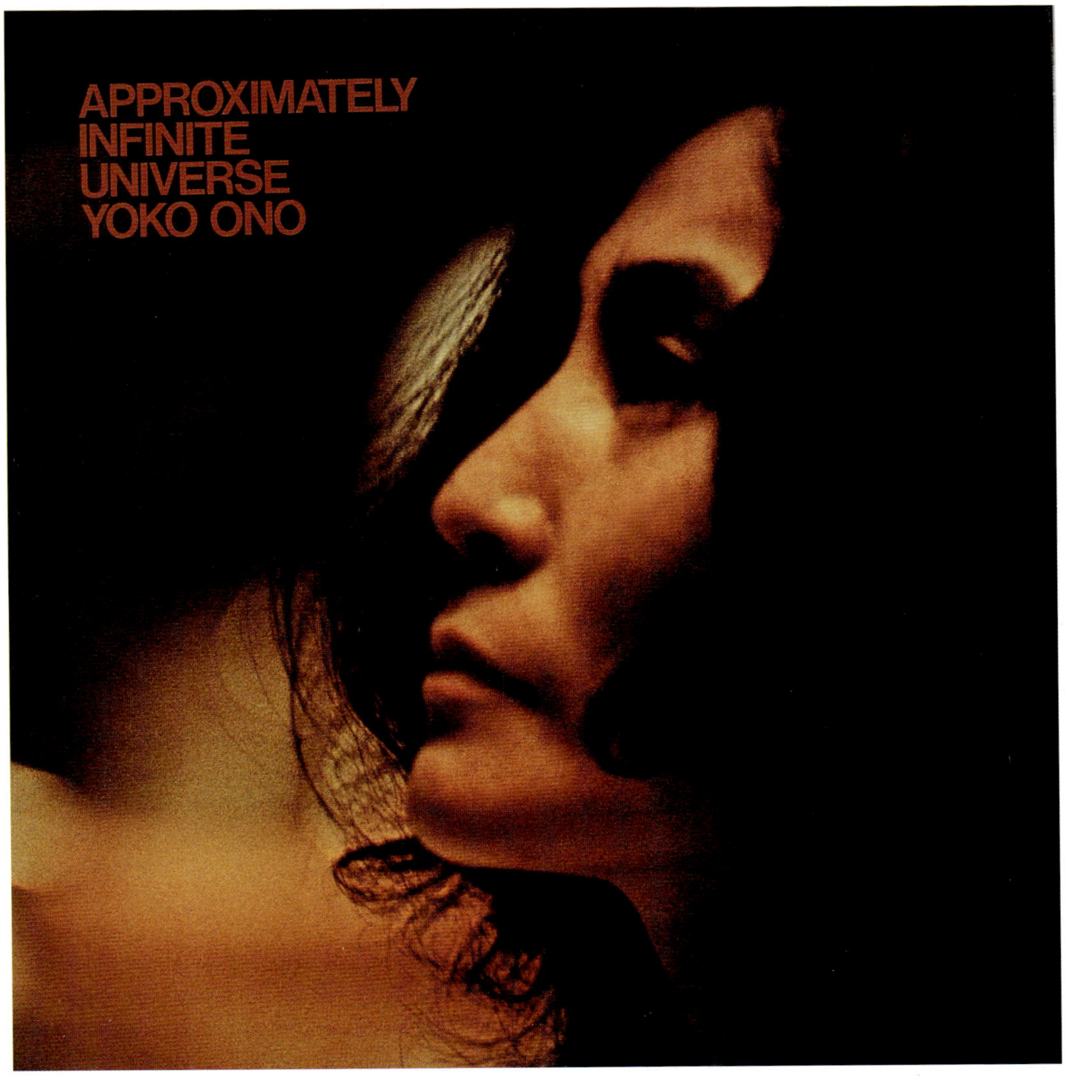

FIGURE 11.4
APPROXIMATELY INFINITE UNIVERSE, LP, 1973. FRONT COVER

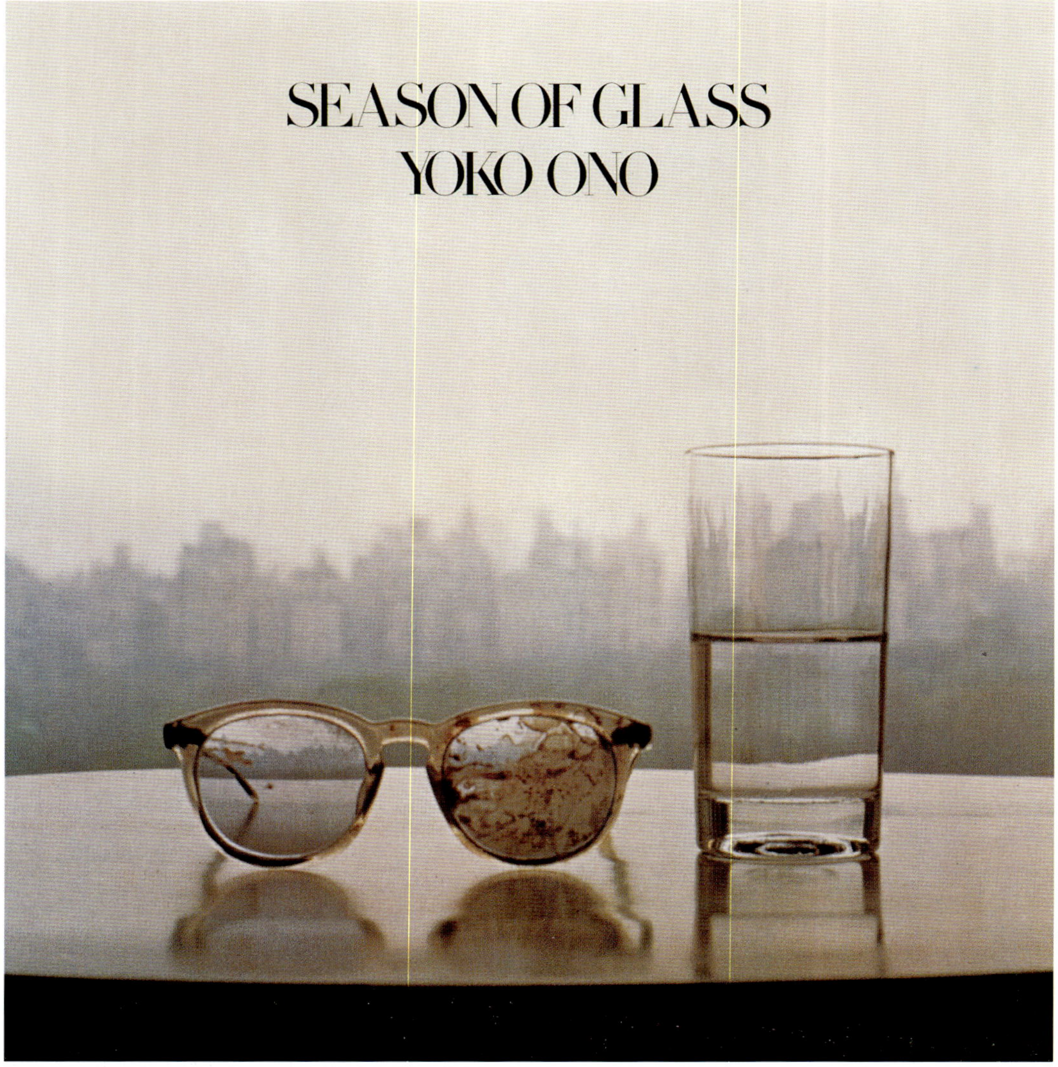

FIGURE 11.5
SEASON OF GLASS, LP, 1981. FRONT COVER

"Walking on Thin Ice" perfectly fused Ono's avant-garde vocals with more straightforward, dramatic singing and a contemporary dance-rock beat. With its air of impending danger, risk, and urgency, the song immediately grabs and holds the listener's attention, as Ono's clear, at first childlike voice, gives way to a thirty-two-measure-long passage of plaintive yelping that hits hard on the insistent 4/4 beat. As the song nears its end, Ono recites a mysterious anecdotal verse, and Lennon slices through a barrage of power chords as her yelps resurface in the mix, leading the rhythm charge to the fade.

Ono's feminism has long been a central aspect of her work. Early events like *Cut Piece* (1964; no. 30), when performed by the artist herself, alluded to a woman's vulnerability—public, personal, physical, psychological—in male-dominated society. In her music, Ono evoked a woman's concerns in the titles and moods of experimental or genre-bending musical compositions such as "Don't Worry Kyoko (Mummy's Only Looking for Her Hand in the Snow)" (1969) and "Greenfield Morning I Pushed an Empty Baby Carriage All Over the City," as well as, more directly, in many songs that she wrote, arranged, performed, and recorded in more conventional pop-rock formats. She sent out a feminist call to action with a finely crafted folk-song-cum-anthem, "Sisters O Sisters," which appeared on Lennon and Ono's *Sometime in New York City* album in 1972 and as the B side of Lennon's "Woman Is the Nigger of the World" single from that double-LP set. Ono's *Approximately Infinite Universe* (February 1973) explored a range of woman-centered emotion and issues in a variety of styles, from the explosive rock of the title song, which described a young woman's alienation and searching, to the intimate balladeering of "Shiranakatta (I Didn't Know)" and "What a Bastard the World Is," and the bluesy cooing of "I Have a Woman Inside My Soul." In November 1973, she released *Feeling the Space*, an album even more unabashedly feminist in message and again stylistically diverse. Among its songs, "Woman Power" offered a proud anthem, "Angry Young Woman" honored self-emancipation, and "Men, Men, Men," a coquettish ditty, teased its subjects—for a change—as sex objects.

In an era of prominent female singer-songwriters, including Carole King, Carly Simon, and Joni Mitchell, Ono's songs were unique for the honest examination of feelings and behavior rooted in personal pain or fear that they dared to present, and for their source: an "outsider" from the avant-garde art world working in the commercial, entertainment-driven realm of pop. Just as her personal and artistic partnership with Lennon inevitably had introduced her to a musical milieu whose members were unfamiliar with and even disparaged her avant-garde background, Ono's erstwhile comrades on art and music's fringe did not know what to make of her forays into pop-rock music. (Decades later, New Wave, post-minimalist "serious" or "classical" music, and various postmodern music-style fusions would reveal that Ono had helped pioneer art music's now-common intersection with pop-rock idioms, especially on the dance floor.)

Ono's music of the 1970s, like Mitchell's, was often unaffectedly introspective; like Janis Ian's "At Seventeen" (1975), in its emotion, it could also be unusually intense. Expressing anger and rage as much as love and whimsy, Ono's work in pop-rock modes was a precursor of the soul-scraping pop vernacular that such singer-songwriters as Alanis Morissette and Fiona Apple and their audiences would take for granted in the late 1990s.

For an artist who always had been uncompromisingly candid in her work, Ono's 1981 album *Season of Glass*, produced and released in response to Lennon's murder in December 1980, served as a deeply emotional—and inherently public—catharsis. Like "Walking on Thin Ice," which had been issued months earlier, *Season of Glass* was skillfully produced. It showcased Ono's stylistic range, from the bluesy hymn "Mother of the Universe" to the urgent, urban beat of "No, No, No," whose opening gunshot sounds unsettled some listeners. Ono was hurt, angry, confused, nostalgic, and afraid—and her new songs let the world know it. She provided the album's front-cover photo showing the bloodstained eyeglasses Lennon had worn on the night of his death, and a half-full glass of water. These simple objects had been set up in a ghostly poetic still life in front of a window in the couple's apartment, overlooking Central Park (fig. 11.5). With *Season of Glass*, grief and an inescapable chill wafted into Ono's music. In subsequent albums of the 1980s, Ono came to terms with her loss as she addressed environmental, survival, world-peace, and even maternal themes.

In 1995, the album *Rising* marked Ono's full-bodied return to her expressionistic-vocal style in spare, emotionally charged compositions based on simple chord sequences (no. 58). Featuring her guitarist son Sean Ono Lennon's band, IMA, Ono's first album in a decade and related concert tour were embraced by a post-punk, post-grunge audience that had learned—or now instinctively knew how—to appreciate her music in all its challenging originality.

Ono's music was a bridge—if not *the* bridge—between the avant-garde and rock. Heirs to her liberating, abstract-emotional vocal stylings (and feminist-in-music precedents) include performers as diverse as the singer Polystyrene of the British punk band X-Ray Spex, Lene Lovich, Cindy Wilson and Kate Pierson of the B-52's, Diamanda Galas, Courtney Love, and the 1990s Japanese popsters Cibo Matto. Ono's unorthodox singing style has shared affinities with everything from the disco diva Donna Summer's guttural cooing in "Love to Love You Baby" (1975) and the B-52's gleeful shrieking in "Rock Lobster" (1979) to Laurie Anderson's electro-stutter in "O Superman" (1982) and Madonna's sexy, groaning burps in "Bedtime Story" (1994).[28]

Ono, once a determined transcriber of bird song, became a confident performer, an accomplished composer in diverse genres, and a skilled record producer. "When I create, I'm obsessed with it, I'm driven by it," she has said. "The sheer joy and excitement surpasses all other considerations. A good composer knows what she wants to use—and eliminate—step by step, note by note, as she enters the sound world created by design and chance." It is in that realm of aural adventure and expressive possibilities that Ono has spent a lifetime charting her "music of the mind" in many forms and manners—and amplifying it for the world through an irrepressible voice of raw, unfettered soul.

NOTES

1. The *shamisen* is a three-string, banjolike instrument played with a triangular plectrum called a *bachi*. The thirteen-string *koto* is a kind of zither. The *ō-tsuzumi* and *ko-tsuzumi* are large and small hand drums. Derived from the *kabuki* theater, *nagauta* are chanted epic songs or ballads with *shamisen* and, often, drum or flute accompaniment.

2. Ono, interview with author, 3 November 1999. Ono's remarks in the text and in these notes are all from this interview, unless otherwise indicated.

3. Ono quoted in "Interview with Yoko Ono" in *The Guests Go in to Supper*, ed. Melody Sumner, Kathleen Burch, and Michael Sumner (Oakland, Calif.: Burning Books, 1986), 172.

4. Ibid.

5. See the 1955–56 Sarah Lawrence College course catalogue. Various pages kindly provided by Judith Schwartzstein of the school's public-affairs office.

6. Eric Salzman, *Twentieth-Century Music: An Introduction* (Englewood Cliffs, N.J.: Prentice-Hall, 1967), 150.

7. Aaron Copland, *The New Music, 1900–1960*, rev. ed. (New York: W. W. Norton, 1968), 171–73.

8. Ono quoted in "Interview with Yoko Ono," 173.

9. Ono set the record straight in an interview with the author:

> When I was at Sarah Lawrence...I had no idea about the existence of avant-garde composers in New York. André Singer, my music-composition teacher, told me the direction I was going in suggested I would be happier studying at a place like the New School for Social Research. He said there were some interesting composers in the avant-garde field in New York. He mentioned Henry Cowell, Edgar Varèse, and John Cage—just in passing. Maybe Lukas Foss, too. I didn't take much notice at the time. I only remembered it when I actually met all of those composers in New York. Toshi Ichiyanagi and I met Cage through Stephan Wolpe, a brilliant atonal composer.

10. Joseph Jacobs, "Crashing New York à la John Cage" in *Off Limits: Rutgers University and the Avant-Garde, 1957–1963*, exh. cat. (Newark: The Newark Museum, 1999), 66.

11. John Cage, *Silence* (1961; 10th ed., Middletown, Conn.: Wesleyan University Press, 1973), 3.

12. See Calvin Tomkins, *Off the Wall: Robert Rauschenberg and the Art World of Our Time* (New York: Doubleday, 1980), 149. Tomkins writes that "Ichiyanagi was the only musician in [Cage's] class," suggesting that he had been a regular student. But Ono recollected that "Toshi and I attended *one* lecture—that's all," and also debunked the misconception that she had been one of Cage's "disciples" who had studied with him at the New School. She never enrolled in his classes, nor did she attend them regularly as an unenrolled visitor, as some attendees reportedly did. See also Sumner, et al., 173, where Ono stated that, for Toshi at first, "Cage was a bit extreme for him. Then, later, he got into it, too."

13. Ono, e-mail to author, October–November 1999.

14. Coincidentally, another Japanese artist, the painter Katsura Yukiko, had been looking at the same space. When she turned it down, Ono jumped at the chance and took it.

15. Ono felt very upset that Young had not initially planned to include her as a performer in the concert series, despite the fact that finding and setting up a loft venue for such events had been her idea from the start—not to mention that she was struggling to pay for the space, too. Introduced merely as "the owner of the loft," Ono was also the brunt of a rumor that she "had a Chinese patron," an allusion to the sound of Young's last name.

16. Haskell and Hanhardt, "Introduction" in *Arias and Objects* (1991), 5.

17. Ono, e-mail to author, October–November 1999. See also Kate Pierson, "The Ballad of Yoko," *Rolling Stone* (19 March 1992): 17–18.

18. Ono quoted in Henry Edwards, "Yoko," *Crawdaddy* (29 August 1971): 34.

19. Ono quoted in Jonathan Cott, "Yoko Ono and Her Sixteen-Track Voice" in *The Ballad of John and Yoko* (1982), 121.

20. Quotations of Lennon in this paragraph from Jann Wenner, *Lennon Remembers: The Rolling Stone Interviews* (San Francisco: Straight Arrow Books, 1971), 69, 94.

21. Lennon famously quipped, "I played [Yoko]...all this far-out stuff, some comedy stuff, and some electronic music. She was suitably impressed, and then she said, 'Well, let's make one ourselves.'...It was midnight when we started *Two Virgins*, it was dawn when we finished, and then we made love at dawn. It was very beautiful" (ibid., 176).

22. *Unfinished Music No. 2: Life With the Lions* was the first release on Zapple Records, Apple's subsidiary for avant-garde music. George Harrison's *Electronic Sound* (1969) was its second—and last.

23. Ono quoted in Edwards, 34–35.

24. In various interviews, though, Lennon cautioned against listening more for the therapy than to the music he was making. Janov's therapy was inspired by a patient's account of the performance of Ralph Ortiz at *DIAS*, in which the artist moved around the stage in a diaper, drinking milk from a bottle and crying "Mummy! Daddy!" (see Iles, *Have You Seen the Horizon Lately?* exh. cat. [1997], 34–35).

25. Ono quoted in Pierson, 29.

26. Lennon has described how Ono took "half an inch" of tape, something that would normally be discarded, and was able to "create a symphony" (Wenner, 170–72). Ono also told the author that, during the pre-digital Plastic Ono Band sessions in 1970, she and Lennon literally unfurled long sections of her recording tape "across the room and back when we tried to crossfade the sounds of two separate trains, etc." She said, "John enjoyed participating in my experiments. I wanted to create a soundscape of spirits moving across the field of nowhere with the beat of the train, and the sound running with an improvisational casualness, like the wind. It reminded me of my all-time favorite *haiku* by Bashō: 'In the middle of my trip, I'm taken by illness, but my dream is still running, running in the wilderness.' This was his last poem."

27. Robert Palmer, "The Pop Life: A List of the Year's Best, Including Albums, Singles and EP's," *New York Times*, 30 December 1981, C9. See also Palmer, "The Pop Life: Yoko Ono on Her Own, 'Walking on Thin Ice,'" *New York Times*, 4 February 1981, C31.

28. For more on Ono's music as a bridge between genres see Edward M. Gomez, "Yoko Ono: A Scream Come True," *Oxymoron* 2 (1998): 36. On the meeting of avant-garde and rock music in the 1980s in particular, see Kyle Gann, "Techno Goes Post-classical: Any Similarity Purely Coincidental," *Village Voice*, 24 June 1997, 72. For an extraordinary recent example of an Ono vocal affinity, listen to the vocal acrobatics of pop singer Taylor Dayne in the remixes of "Naked Without You" (River North Records, 1999). Ono's early soundscape pieces share affinities with a vast range of other progressive rock artists' later, similar creations, including David Bowie's experiments on the albums *Low* (1977) and *"Heroes"* (1977), which feature chantlike, phonemes-only vocals.

51 *Voice Piece for Soprano,* 1961

instruction

VOICE PIECE FOR SOPRANO

Scream.

1. against the wind
2. against the wall
3. against the sky

1961 autumn

As a music-composition student in college, Ono admired the often atonal works of such modern composers as Arnold Schönberg, Anton Webern, and Alban Berg. Later, she found kindred spirits among experimental-music artists in New York's avant-garde. But Ono wanted to explore the voice as an instrument, and theory-driven music was not enough. "It was all just a head trip," she remarked in 1992. "The avant-garde guys didn't *use* the voice. They were just so cool, right? There was also [a] very asexual kind of atmosphere in the music. And I wanted to throw blood."[1]

EG

NOTES

1. Ono quoted in Mark Kemp, "She Who Laughs Last: Yoko Ono Reconsidered," *Option, Music Alternatives* (July–August 1992): 78.

LITERATURE: Haskell, *Arias and Objects* (1991), 28; Kemp, *Option, Music Alternatives* (July–August 1992); Gann, *Village Voice* (11 August 1992); O'Dair, *Rolling Stone* (13 November 1997)

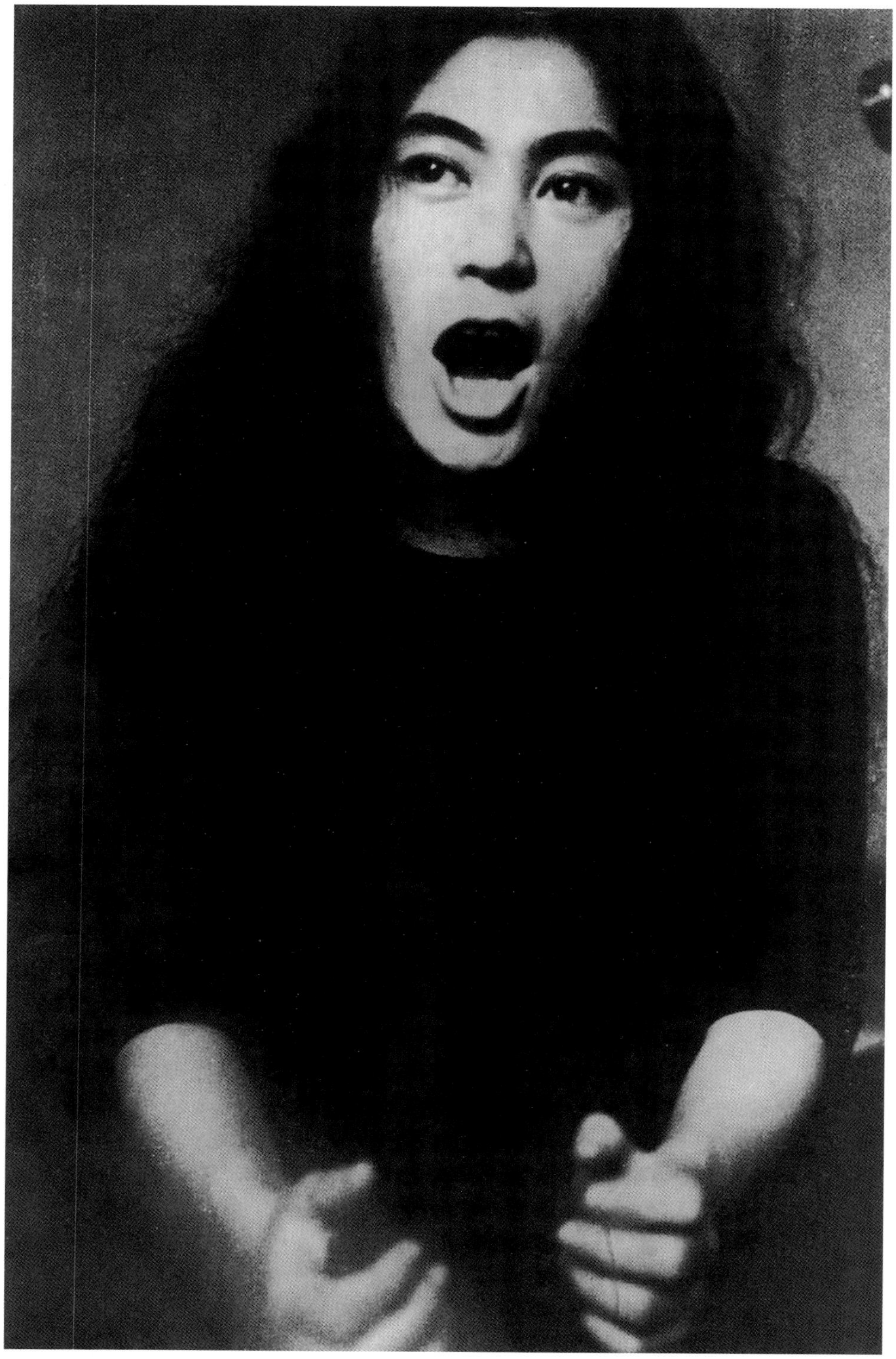

PLATE 51
VOICE PIECE FOR SOPRANO, 1961.
PERFORMED BY ONO

52 *Works by Yoko Ono,* 1961

Solo recital at Carnegie Recital Hall, New York, November 24

Ono's first major public solo concert of her experimental compositions was staged at Carnegie Recital Hall, a prestigious venue for serious composers. The concert was presented by Norman Seaman and produced by Charlotte Moorman, who also participated. Performers included experimental composers, dancers, poets, and artists in Ono's circle.

The program featured three works: *A Grapefruit in the World of Park*, *A Piece for Strawberries and Violin*, and *AOS—To David Tudor*.[1] Ono's high-pitched wailing, a tape recording of moans and words spoken backwards, performers acting out everyday gestures, and figures wrapped in gauze came together in a baffling spectacle charged with raw emotion. One review described Ono's "sighs, breathing, gasping, retching, and screaming—many tones of pain and pleasure mixed with a jibberish of foreign-sounding language that was no language at all."[2]

EG

NOTES

1. For Ono's scores for these performances, see *A Grapefruit in the World of Park* (1961; Anthology 5), and *Aos, the opera* (1961; Anthology 6). See also my essay, pp. 233.

2. Jill Johnston, "Life and Art," *Village Voice*, 7 December 1961, 10.

LITERATURE: Johnston, *Village Voice* (7 December 1961); Cott, *Rolling Stone* (18 March 1971), reprint, *The Ballad of John and Yoko* (1982), 121; Haskell and Hanhardt, *Arias and Objects* (1991), 5, 29

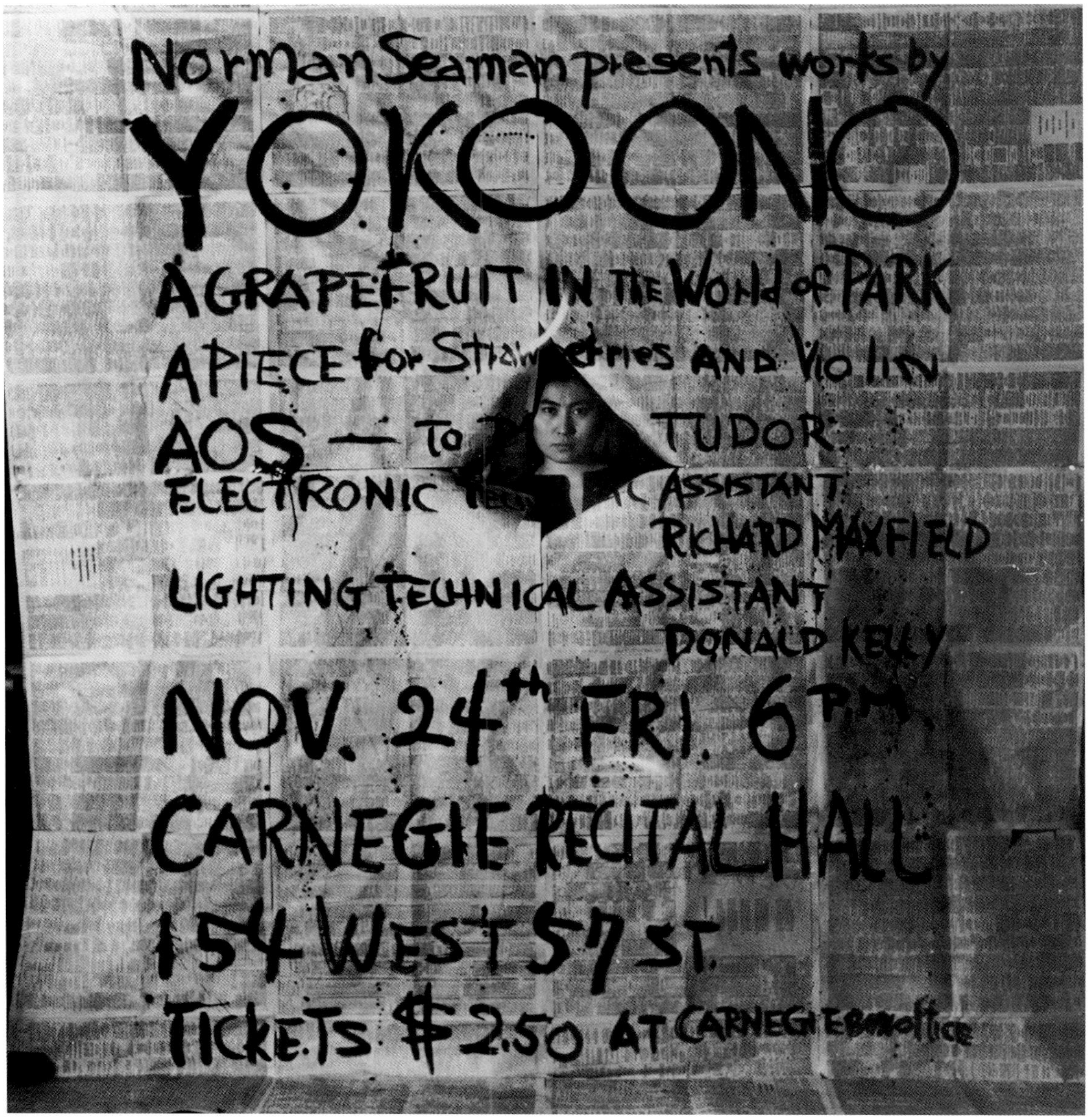

PLATE 52
PHOTOGRAPH BY GEORGE MACIUNAS, INTENDED AS POSTER FOR ***WORKS BY YOKO ONO*** (CARNEGIE RECITAL HALL), 1961.
THE GILBERT AND LILA SILVERMAN FLUXUS COLLECTION, DETROIT

53 *Unfinished Music No. 1: Two Virgins,* 1968

John Lennon and Yoko Ono

LP, Apple Records in assoc. with Track Records APCOR 2 (mono) and SAPCOR 2 (stereo) in U.K.; in assoc. with Tetragrammaton T5001 in U.S.

Two Virgins was the first album released on the Beatles' Apple label. Perhaps Ono and Lennon's most notorious project, it was meant to evoke the innocence, optimism, and freshness of its creators' budding romance. Instead, it instantly became controversial when executives at EMI and Capitol, the record companies with which the Beatles had long been associated and which distributed Apple Records in the United Kingdom and United States, learned that the couple planned to use their nude photo-portrait on the album's cover. EMI and Capitol refused to handle it, forcing Apple to find independent distributors—and to wrap the provocative cover in a brown-paper sleeve. (Still, police acting under local obscenity laws seized 30,000 copies of the disc in New Jersey in early 1969.) Verses from Genesis 2:21–25 were printed on the back of the outer sleeve, concluding with the line: "And they were both naked, the man and his wife, and were not ashamed."

Two Virgins was recorded at Lennon's home studio in Weybridge on May 20, 1968. A freewheeling sound collage, it features Lennon's piano tinkling and whistling, sputtering tape echoes, Ono's sporadic warbling, and assorted household noises. Its spirit was part *musique concrète* and part home movie. Ono's Conceptualist approach was evident in the record's title. *Unfinished Music*—recalling the subtitle of her 1966 Indica Gallery exhibition—suggested that listeners could use their imagination to complete its composition.

EG

LITERATURE: Wenner, *Lennon Remembers* (1971), 94, 175–76; Rockwell, *The Ballad of John and Yoko* (1982), 272–77; Robertson, *The Art & Music of John Lennon* (1993), 87–89

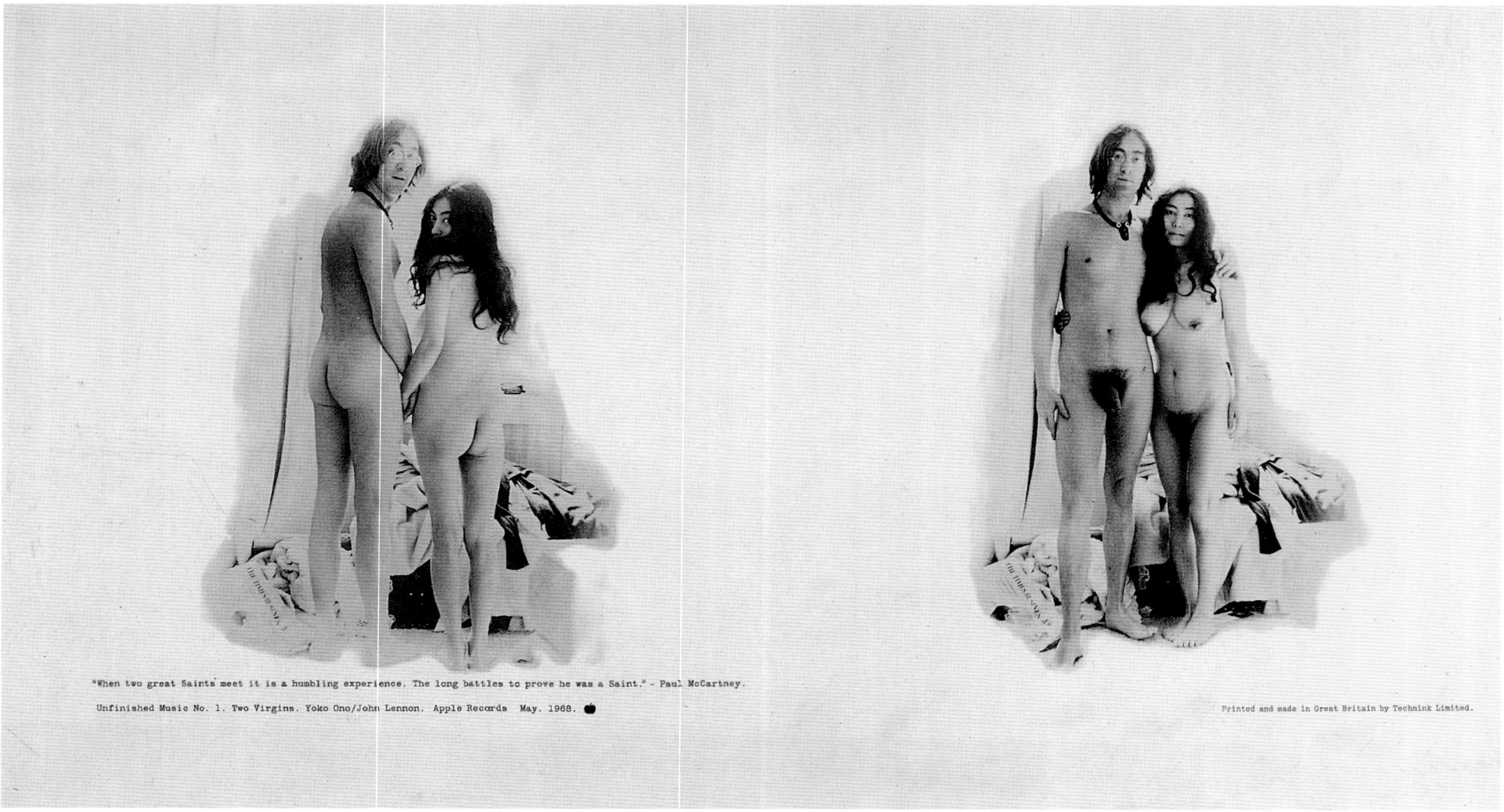

PLATE 53
LENNON AND ONO, ***UNFINISHED MUSIC NO. 1: TWO VIRGINS,*** LP, 1968. PRECUT SHEET FOR COVER JACKET

54 *Unfinished Music No. 2: Life with the Lions,* 1969

John Lennon and Yoko Ono

LP, Zapple Records 01 in U.K.; Apple Records ST3357 in U.S.

The documentary, life-as-art character of Ono's collaborations with Lennon was rooted in the avant-garde aesthetic that she knew well. It was evident in *Unfinished Music No. 2: Life with the Lions*, whose cover photos showed the couple in the London hospital where Ono miscarried a baby in November 1968, and during a drug bust a month earlier. ("'No comment'—George Martin," a remark from the Beatles' record producer, was printed on the back cover.) The LP included recordings of the miscarried baby's heartbeat, radio static, and two minutes of silence. It also featured a live performance in which Ono screamed against Lennon's guitar feedback.

Personal aspects of the couple's life would be documented again in *Wedding Album*, whose packaging and inclusions evoke the feel of real nuptial souvenirs and recall Fluxus-style multiples. And ultimately, *Season of Glass* offers heartbreaking testimony, not only through its wrenching musical content, but directly on its face: Ono's photographic still life of Lennon's broken, blood-stained glasses next to a half full/half empty glass of water on their apartment windowsill.

EG

LITERATURE: Rockwell, *The Ballad of John and Yoko* (1982), 276–77; Robertson, *The Art & Music of John Lennon* (1993), 97–98

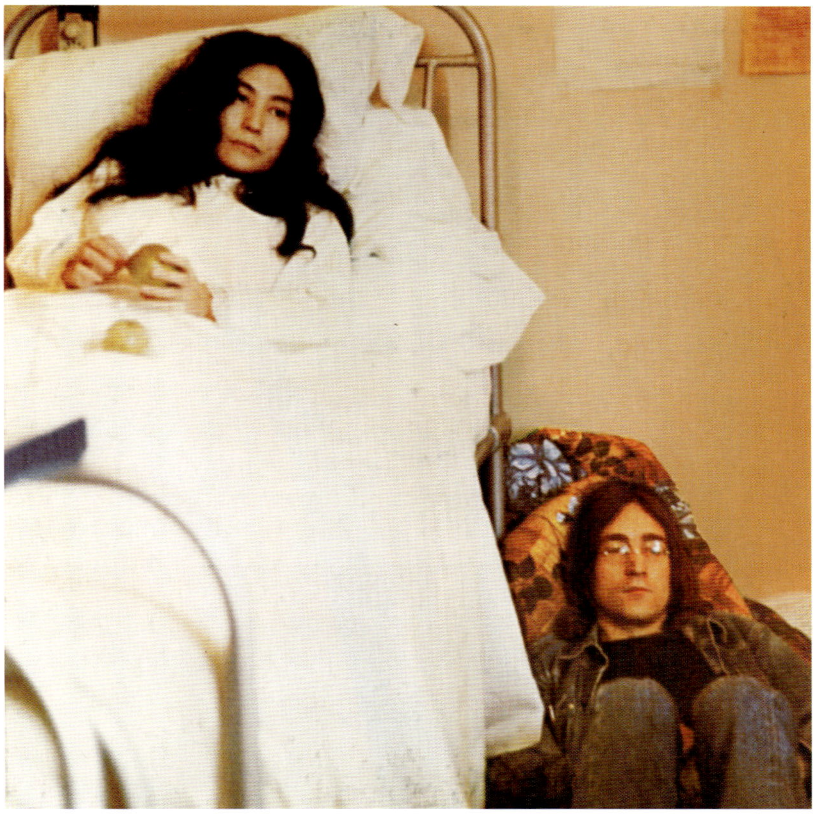

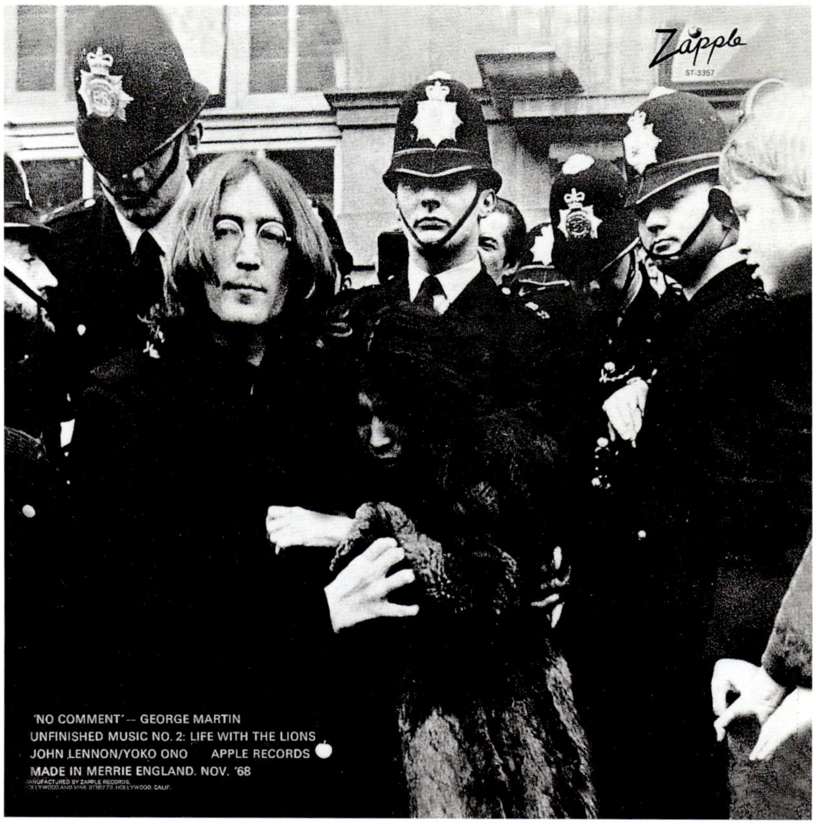

PLATE 54
LENNON AND ONO, ***UNFINISHED MUSIC NO. 2: LIFE WITH THE LIONS***, LP, 1969. FRONT COVER (TOP) AND BACK COVER (BOTTOM)

55 Plastic Ono Band

Plastic Ono Band exemplifies Ono's Conceptualist approach. Lennon once told a BBC radio host, "Plastic Ono Band was a concept of Yoko's...an imaginary band...a completely robot pop group."[1] Ono's sculpture, *Plastic Ono Band*, consisting of clear-acrylic boxes, microphones, and a tape recorder, appeared in early advertisements for the band and, in Lennon and Ono's absence, at a press party announcing the release of the single "Give Peace a Chance/ Remember Love" in July 1969. It is also shown on the sleeve of the U.K. release of the record (pl. 55a).

As Ono originally conceived it, Plastic Ono Band was an ensemble without any members. Initial ads bore the slogan, "You are the Plastic Ono Band." In the era of star-studded groups such as Cream and Led Zeppelin, this was a radical notion. In practice, Plastic Ono Band's membership varied from project to project, evoking the tradition of jazz pick-up bands with regularly changing lineups. For example, *Live Peace in Toronto* (1969), the first live recording credited to any Plastic Ono Band configuration, was taken from its performance at the *Toronto Rock 'n' Roll Revival* in September 1969. Band members, other than Ono and Lennon, were credited as Eric Clapton, guitar; Klaus Voorman, bass; and Alan White, drums. Ono's music, including a blistering version of "Don't Worry Kyoko," appeared on the LP's second side. "Now Yoko's gonna do her thing—all over ya!" Lennon says, introducing her set.

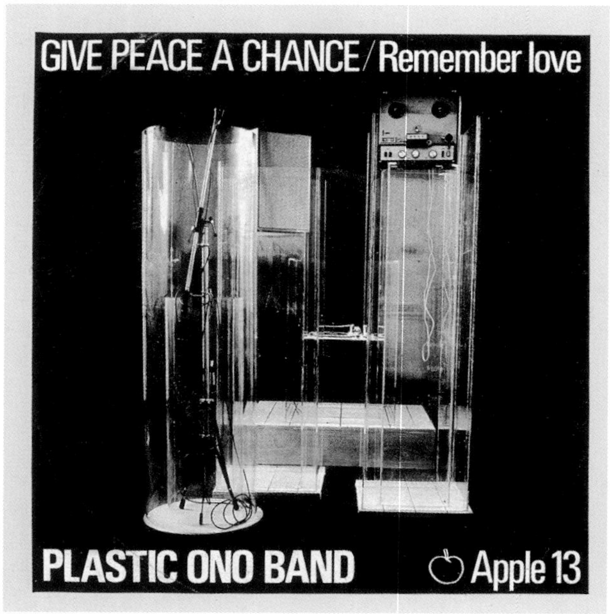

PLATE 55A
PLASTIC ONO BAND,
"GIVE PEACE A CHANCE"/
"REMEMBER LOVE,"
SINGLE RECORD, 1969.
FRONT COVER

From this point through 1973, Plastic Ono Band was credited on all of Yoko's records. Ono's songs appeared on the B sides of three Plastic Ono Band singles before December 1970, when Lennon and Ono released *John Lennon/Plastic Ono Band* and *Yoko Ono/ Plastic Ono Band*, their first solo albums, on the Beatles' Apple label.

Basic tracks for *Yoko Ono/Plastic Ono Band* unexpectedly emerged from Ono-directed jam sessions during the making of the *John Lennon/Plastic Ono Band* album. Lennon, Ono, and Phil Spector were credited as producers of the former Beatle's first solo LP; Lennon and Ono were billed as producers of her companion album. Ono created the five new compositions on her album from jam-session outtakes, sound effects, and on-the-spot experiments. "I did it note by note the way I wanted to; I enjoyed that," Ono has recalled. "Meticulous, hard work in the studio was something I had learned to cherish. There were no others standing around. It wasn't like the usual pop-rock sessions. There were only three of us—the engineer, John, and me. It was getting light outside when I finished making the album on the remix board. I felt like Madame Curie discovering a new sound world."[2]

For the two solo albums, critics cited the influence on their raw, soul-scraping sound of the primal-scream therapy the couple had undergone in California earlier that year. Most dismissed Ono's record as an oddity; some grasped its originality. In Britain, one critic noted: "Yoko breaks through more barriers with one scream than most musicians do in a lifetime."[3]

EG

NOTES

1. Ray Coleman, *Lennon: The Definitive Biography*, rev. ed. (New York: Harper Perennial, 1992), 550.

2. Ono, e-mail to author, October–November 1999.

3. Bill McAllister, "Togetherness: Mr. and Mrs. Lennon's Latest Records," *Record Mirror* (London), 19 December 1970, 5.

LITERATURE: Cott, *Rolling Stone* (18 March 1971), reprint, *The Ballad of John and Yoko* (1982), 113–25; Edwards, *Crawdaddy* (29 August 1971); Palmer, booklet in *Onobox* (1992); Robertson, *The Art & Music of John Lennon* (1993), 125–29; Grötz, *John Lennon*, exh. cat. (1995), 188–89

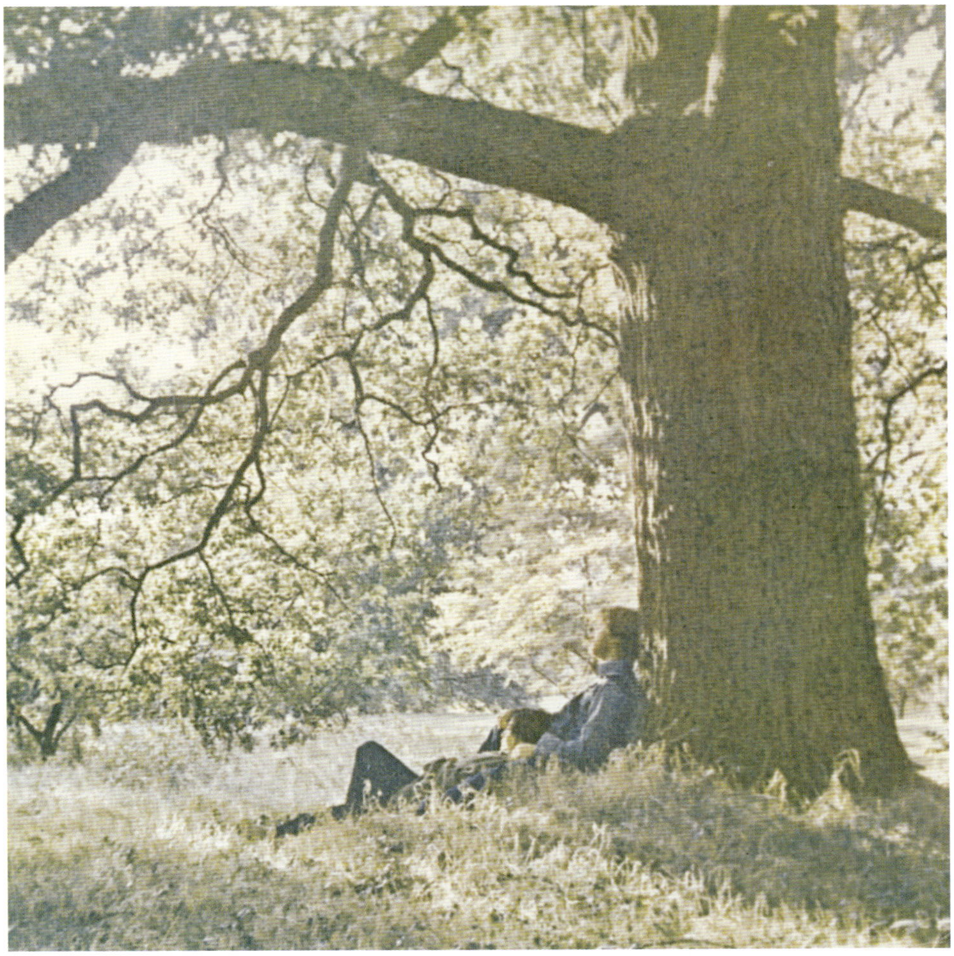

PLATE 55B

YOKO ONO / PLASTIC ONO BAND, LP, 1970.
FRONT COVER

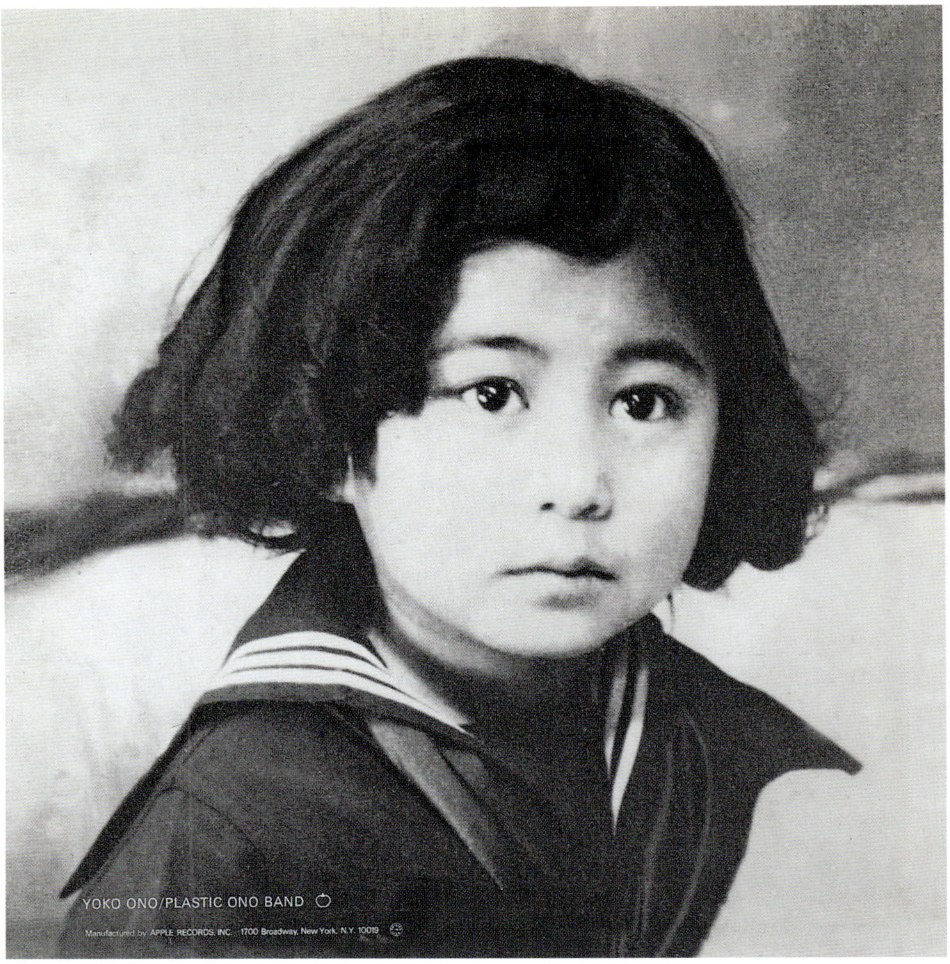

PLATE 55C

YOKO ONO / PLASTIC ONO BAND, LP, 1970.
BACK COVER

56 *Fly,* 1971

LP, Apple Records SAPTU 101/2 in U.K.; SVBB 3380 in U.S.

Backed by Lennon, Eric Clapton, Ringo Starr, Klaus Voorman, and top-rank session musicians, Ono recorded *Fly*, her first two-record album, in 1971, before and during the sessions for Lennon's *Imagine*. Both records were released in the United States in September of that year. *Fly* was billed a "Yoko Ono & Plastic Ono Band (with Joe Jones Tone Deaf Music Co.)" performance.

It showed Ono branching out to explore the expressive possibilities of her avant-garde vocalizations in a rhythmic, rock-music setting ("Midsummer New York" and "Mindtrain") and in that of more familiarly structured songs. Unexpectedly for listeners unfamiliar with her background in music composition, she wrote and sang with pop sureness in "Mrs. Lennon," a lush, moody ballad. "Don't Worry Kyoko (Mummy's Only Looking for Her Hand in the Snow)," which begins with Ono's sustained, warbling scream, and which had appeared as the B side to Lennon's "Cold Turkey" single (October 1969), appeared here, too. Side three contained three long, multitextured, experimental compositions, including "Air Male (Tone Deaf Jam)," the soundtrack of Lennon's film *Erection* (1971; no. 49); and the twenty-three-minute "Fly," the soundtrack of Ono's film of the same name (1970; no. 46).[1]

As with other records Ono was involved with (including Lennon's *Imagine*), the jacket and sleeve design extends her vanguard art practices and conceptualism. Fluxus helmsman George Maciunas, who helped design her Everson Museum exhibition this same year, designed the inside-cover collage, which incorporated photos from various sources, including from Ono's daughter, Kyoko (pl. 56c). Ono's whimsical drawings decorated the set's inner sleeves, and her liner notes thanked Fluxus artist Joe Jones, who was known for inventing unusual musical instruments. Her acknowledgment stated:

> joe built me 8 new instruments specially for this album which can play by themselves with minimum manipulation (turning switches only).

Some of Jones's inventions are pictured in the inside-cover photo. The package included a black-and-white photo poster of Ono, in close-up, wearing a hat and sunglasses; reflected in a sunglass lens is an image of Ono playing golf. The album's side-one and side-three record labels incorporated a photo of Ono's smiling face within the familiar apple motif.

EG

NOTES

1. For a detailed commentary on *Fly*, see Ono's original manuscript for publication in *Crawdaddy* (1971; Anthology 10).

LITERATURE: Cott, *Rolling Stone* (18 March 1971), reprint, *The Ballad of John and Yoko* (1982), 113–25; Edwards, *Crawdaddy* (29 August 1971); Palmer, *The Ballad of John and Yoko* (1982), 285–90; Palmer, booklet in *Onobox* (1992)

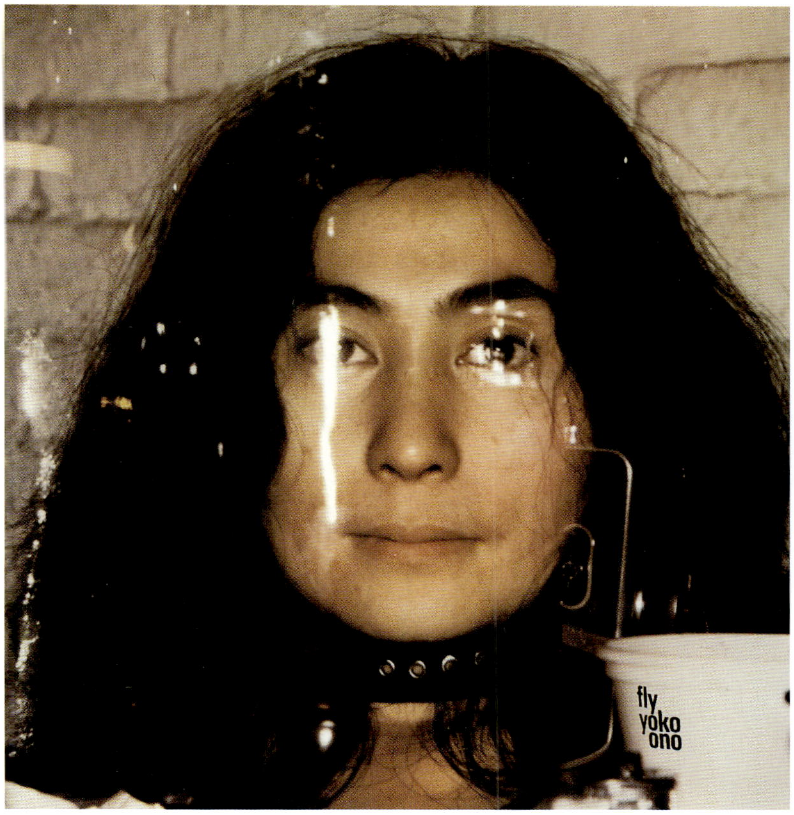

PLATE 56A
FLY, LP, 1971.
FRONT COVER

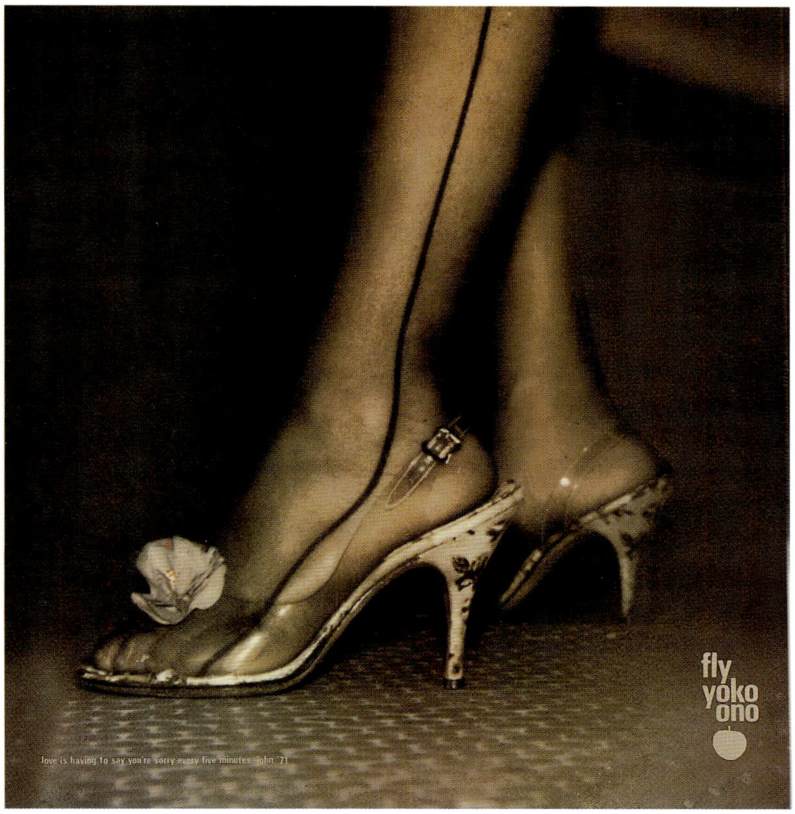

PLATE 56B
FLY, LP, 1971.
BACK COVER

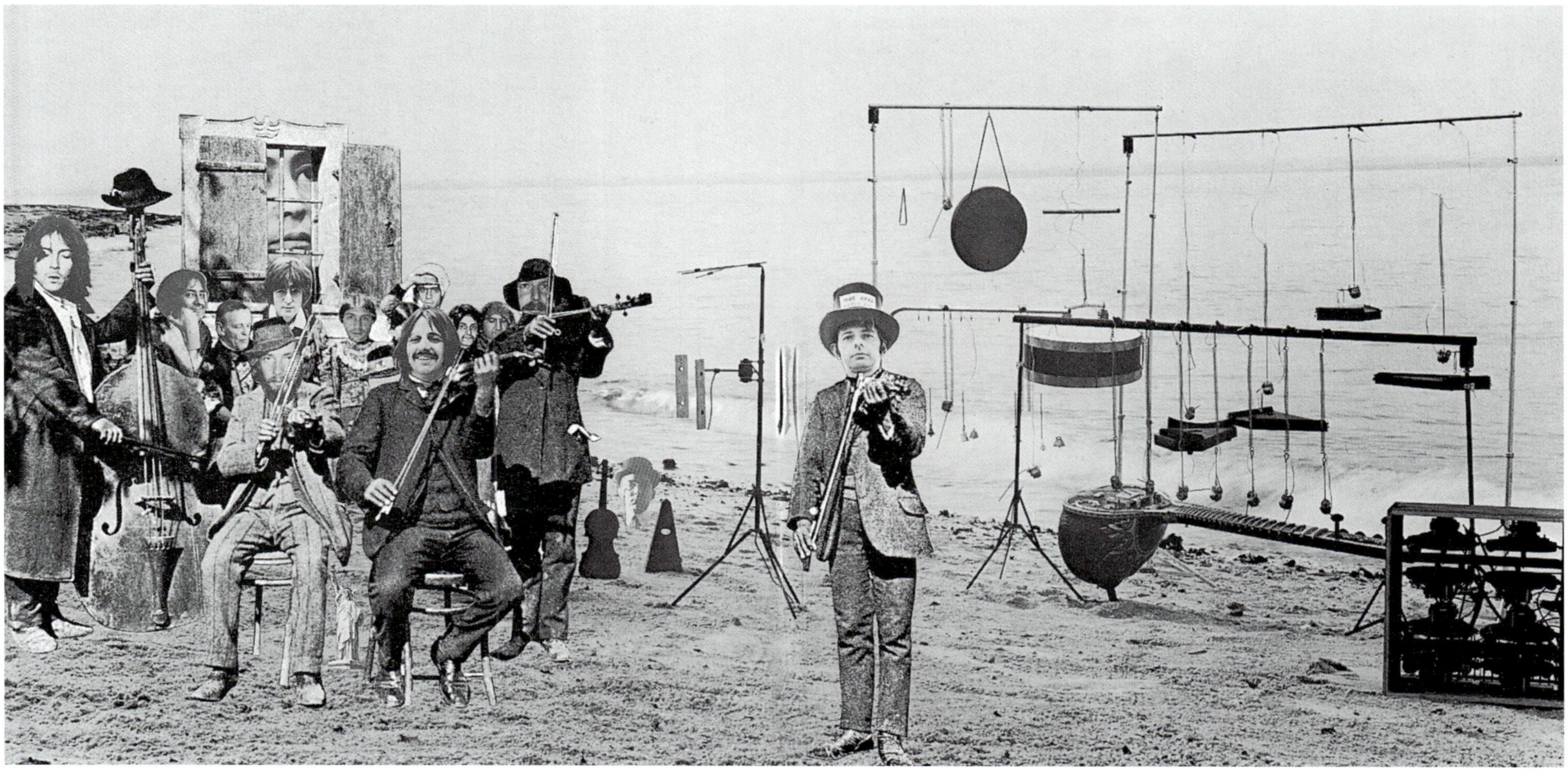

PLATE 56C
FLY, LP, 1971.
INNER SPREAD

57 *Walking on Thin Ice,* 1981

45 r.p.m. single, Geffen Records GEF49683 in U.S.;
K79202 in U.K.
music video, Rykodisc VVHS 0230 (released 1992)

Ono and Lennon had been working on "Walking on Thin Ice" the night Lennon was killed, in December 1980. The song emerged from the couple's flurry of composing and recording activity that led to their comeback album *Double Fantasy* (released in November 1980). Ono garnered unprecedentedly positive reviews for her contributions to that collaboration; "Walking on Thin Ice" was to have been included on her own follow-up, four-song EP, to have been called *Yoko Only*. Lennon spoke enthusiastically of his performance on the record, which featured the kind of vigorous, slashing guitar playing he had delivered on such early Plastic Ono Band recordings as "Cold Turkey," "Why," and "Don't Worry Kyoko."

Later, using home-movie clips, Ono created a visual montage to accompany the song. With images of the Lennons relaxing by a lake, playing with their son, and rolling about in a lovemaking embrace, Ono's video recalled the emotional intensity of their partnership. It was more voyeuristic than mawkish—and it spoke with the candor that had long characterized her music.
EG

LITERATURE: Sheff, *Playboy* (January 1981); Palmer, *New York Times* (4 February 1981); Occhigrosso, *Soho News* (11 February 1981); *Rolling Stone* (14 May 1981); Palmer, *New York Times* (30 December 1981); Divola, *People Weekly* (27 July 1992)

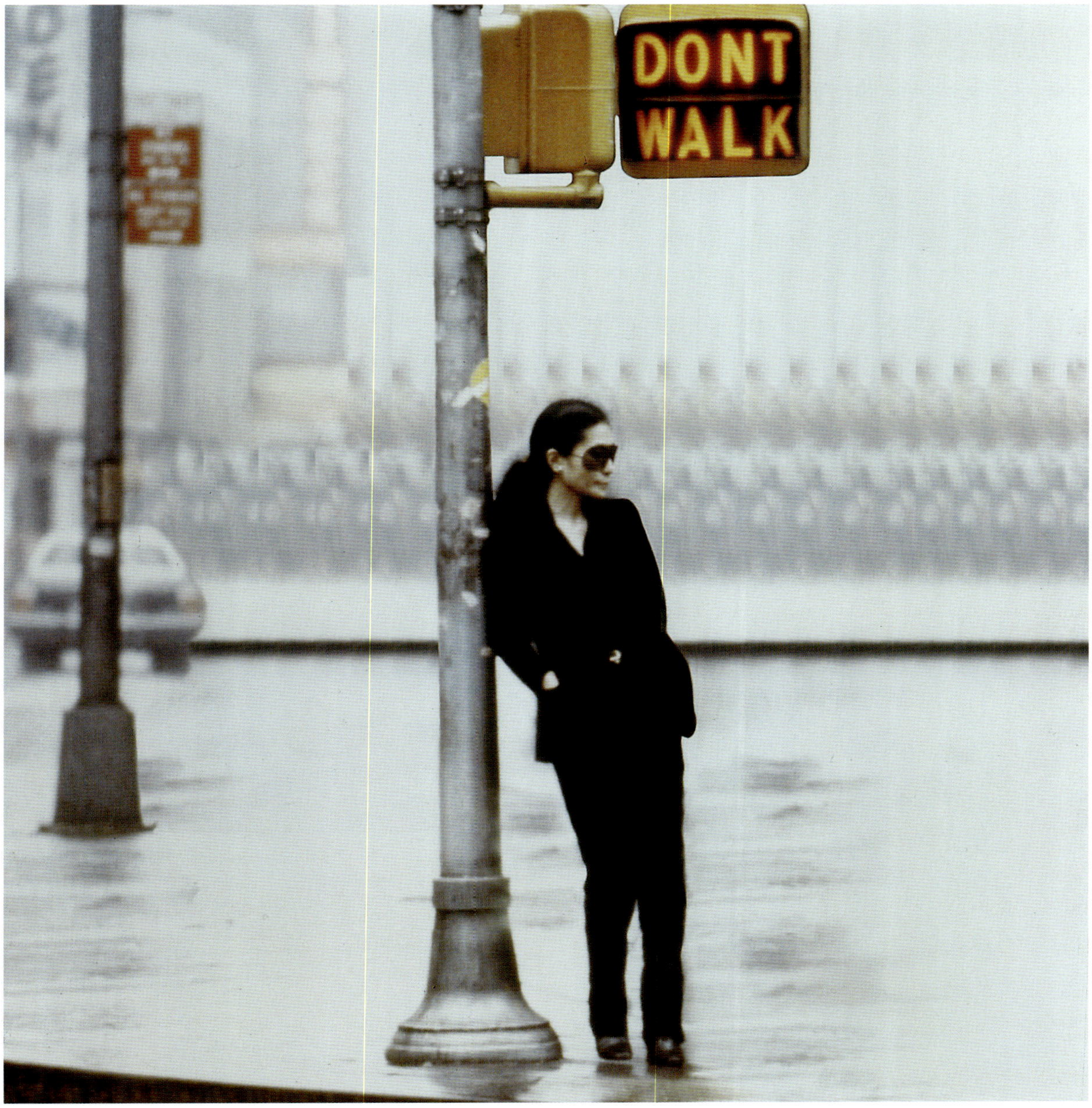

PLATE 57
COMPUTER-MANIPULATED IMAGE BASED ON PRODUCTION STILL FROM *WALKING ON THIN ICE*, VIDEO, 1981

58 *Rising*, 1995
Yoko Ono/IMA

CD, Capitol Records, CDP7243 8 35817 26

Almost a decade had passed between the release of Ono's last record album and *Rising*, issued in November 1995. With it, she unabashedly returned to the abstract vocalizations that had characterized her first solo recording twenty-five years earlier. In an era of AIDS and increasing urban violence, the album's spare, neatly arranged, but still spontaneous-sounding songs addressed some of Ono's enduring themes, such as fear, longing, pain, death, and hope in the face of despair. Critics praised Ono's production and performance, as well as the musicianship of back-up players Sean Ono Lennon, Timo Ellis, and Sam Koppelman. The record and a related concert tour the following year attracted a new generation of post-punk, post-grunge listeners (see Chronology, 1996, February 29). They found Ono's music less offputting than audiences of past decades and embraced its expression of intense, raw emotion. In the album's liner notes, Ono wrote: "The making of the album served as a purging of my anger, pain, and fear. I hope it will for you, too."
EG

LITERATURE: Christgau, *Village Voice* (14 November 1995); Fricke, *Rolling Stone* (30 November 1995); Gann and Powers, *Village Voice* (13 March 1996)

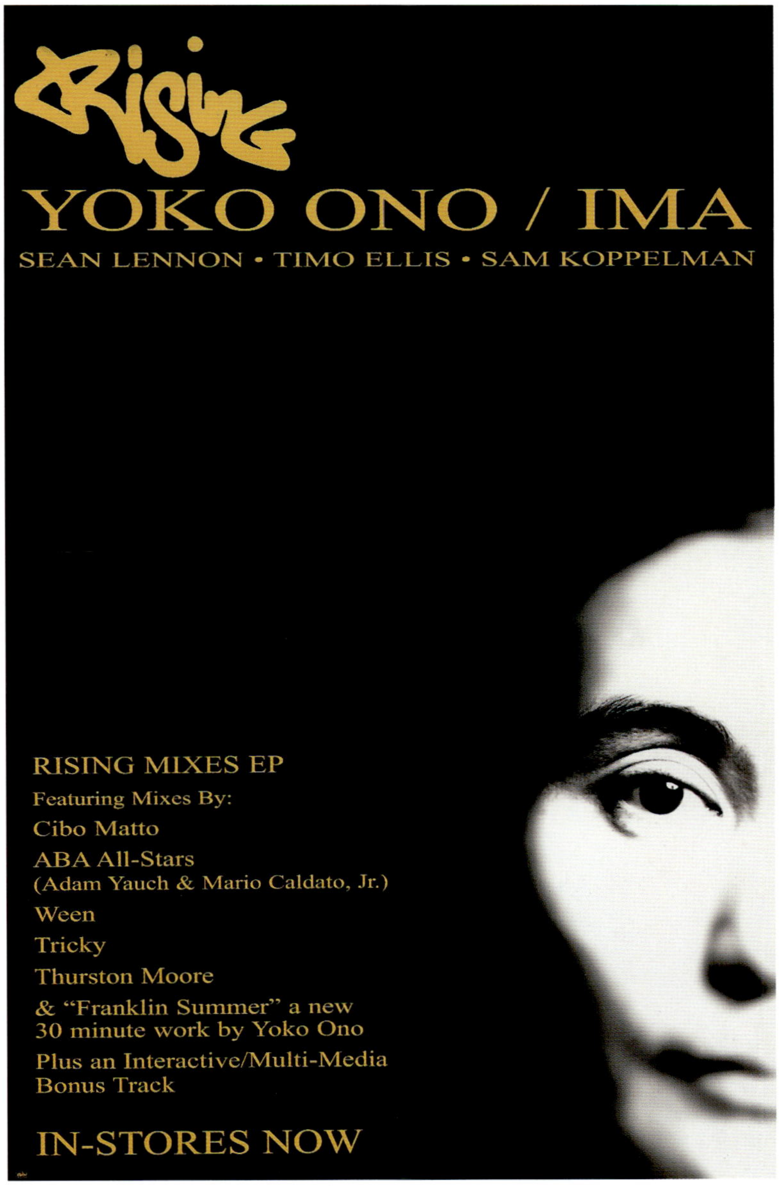

PLATE 58
POSTER, *RISING MIXES*,
1996

YOKO NOW

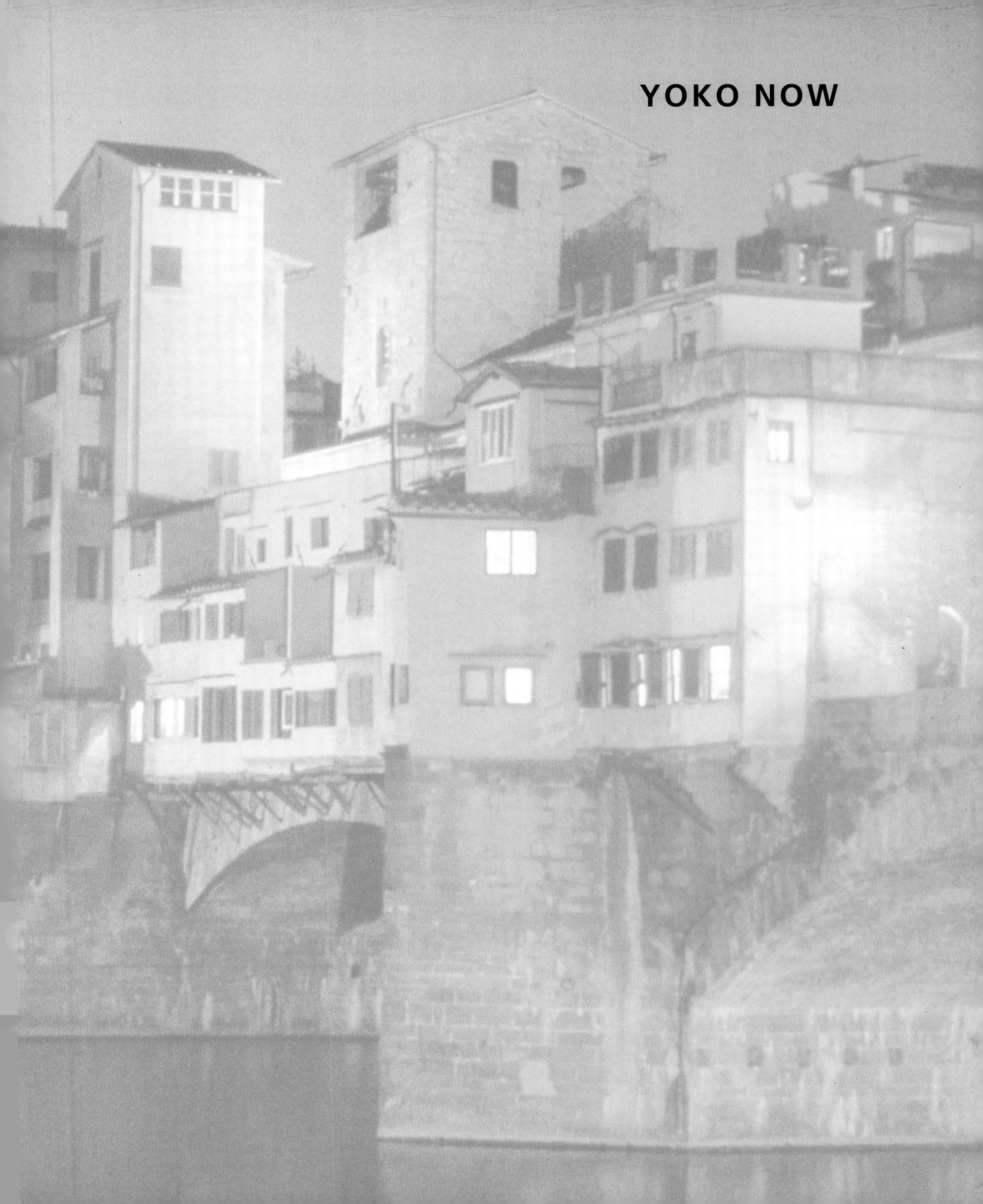

Bronze Age

ALEXANDRA MUNROE

In 1987, sixteen years after her legendary exhibition *This Is Not Here* at the Everson Museum of Art in Syracuse, Yoko Ono participated in an homage to John Cage on the occasion of his seventy-fifth birthday. For this show, organized by the Carl Solway Gallery in Cincinnati for the Chicago Art Fair, she made a bronze version of her 1966 work *White Chess Set* (no. 25). Like her earlier version, this new work presented an all-white chessboard with all-white pieces and alluded to the ideal of chess championed by Marcel Duchamp as "the landscape of the soul." With this homage work, Ono invoked the Duchamp-Cage legacy, which held the abstract, mental purity of chess akin to poetry and equal to art. But Ono's all-white game demanded the ultimate abstraction by leaving all but the first few moves to be played entirely in the mind. With minimal and conceptual means so typical of her art, she strips and upends the game to reveal its fundamental structure—an opposition defined by black versus white—to provoke a sage contemplation: How to proceed when the opponent is indistinguishable from one's self? Ono entitled her bronze work *Play It By Trust*.

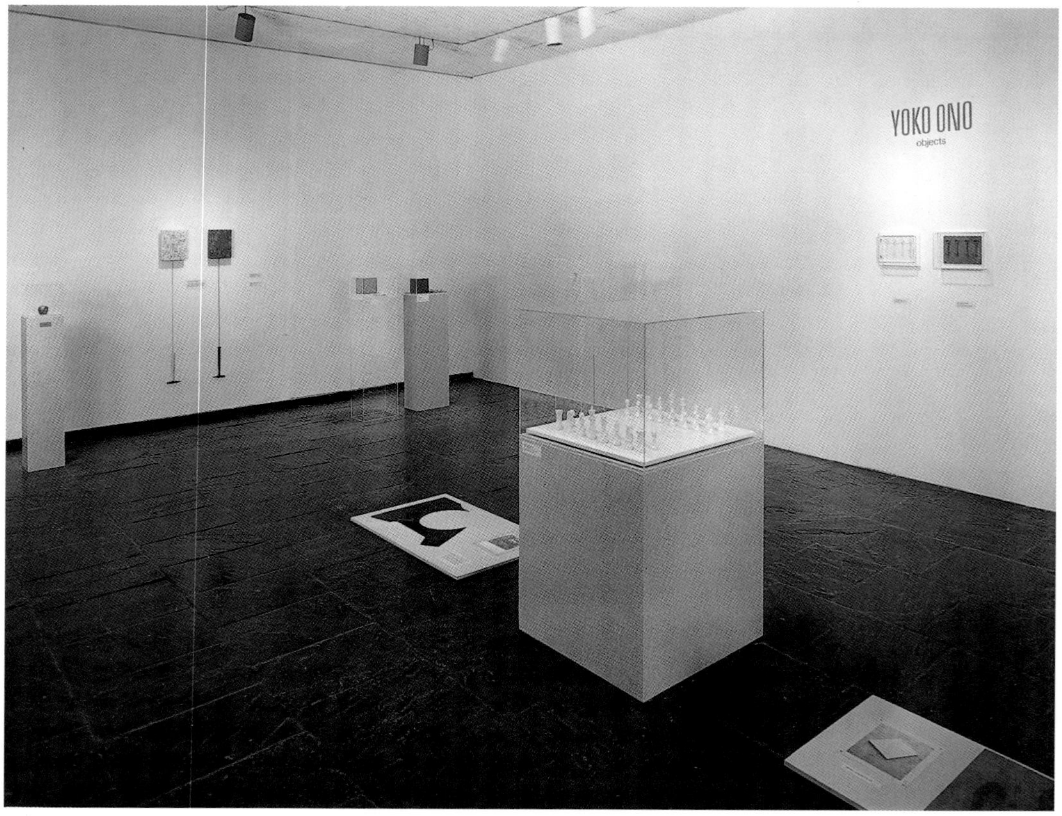

PLATE 59
INSTALLATION VIEW, WHITNEY MUSEUM OF AMERICAN ART, NEW YORK, 1989

Ono's participation in the Cage exhibition marked the beginning of a new period of her artistic activity. Around this time, the Whitney Museum of American Art invited her to show a selection of her early works together with a retrospective of her films. In the tradition of avant-garde exhibitions, Ono had often approached her shows—from her 1961 exhibition at AG Gallery in Manhattan to her Everson show in 1971—as an incentive to realize a new series or stage a new environment of concepts and events. For *Yoko Ono: Objects, Films*, which opened at the Whitney in February 1989, Ono created *Bronze Age*, her first new series of objects in several years (pl. 59).

As with *Play It By Trust*, she selected a group of works she had originally constructed in the 1960s—some from everyday objects like a needle, a hammer and nails, or silver spoons—and cast them all in a dark bronze, retaining the language of their inscriptions and titles. For example, the 1966 version of *Pointedness* (no. 12; pl. 60a) presented a sphere centered on a tall Plexiglas pedestal inscribed with the instruction:

> THIS SPHERE WILL BE A SHARP POINT WHEN
> IT GETS TO THE FAR CORNERS OF THE ROOM
> OF YOUR MIND

Ono's 1988 version presented the same form in radically altered materials: a bronze sphere on a patinated base on a Corian pedestal (pl. 60b). Even the fresh green apple of her 1966 *Apple* (no. 15) was replicated in bronze.

At the Whitney show, Ono placed the earlier versions, so fragile and ethereal, side by side with their heavy bronze casts in a dialogue that spoke as much to the paradox of permanence/impermanence as to the prevailing cultural attitudes of Reagan's America. Time present and time past coexist in this juxtaposition to tell a story, Ono suggests, "of change and survival." In an interview with critic Paul Taylor in the *New York Times* (February 5, 1989), Ono commented:

> There seemed like a shimmering air in the '60s when I made these pieces, and now the air is bronzified. Now it's the '80s, and bronze is very '80s in a way—solidity, commodity, all of that. For someone who went through the '60s revolution, there has of course been an incredible change.... I call the pieces petrified bronze. That freedom, all the hope and wishes are in some ways petrified.

Bronze continued to fascinate Ono. She willed lucidity from its dense mass while using its unyielding substance to reflect on the psychological and social violence of recent history. For her series *Family Album* (1993), she produced a number of everyday household objects marked with signs of violence and death—an unusually biographical reference within Ono's nonliteral art. A dressing mirror shat-

PLATE 60A
POINTEDNESS,
1964/1966 (CRYSTAL VERSION)

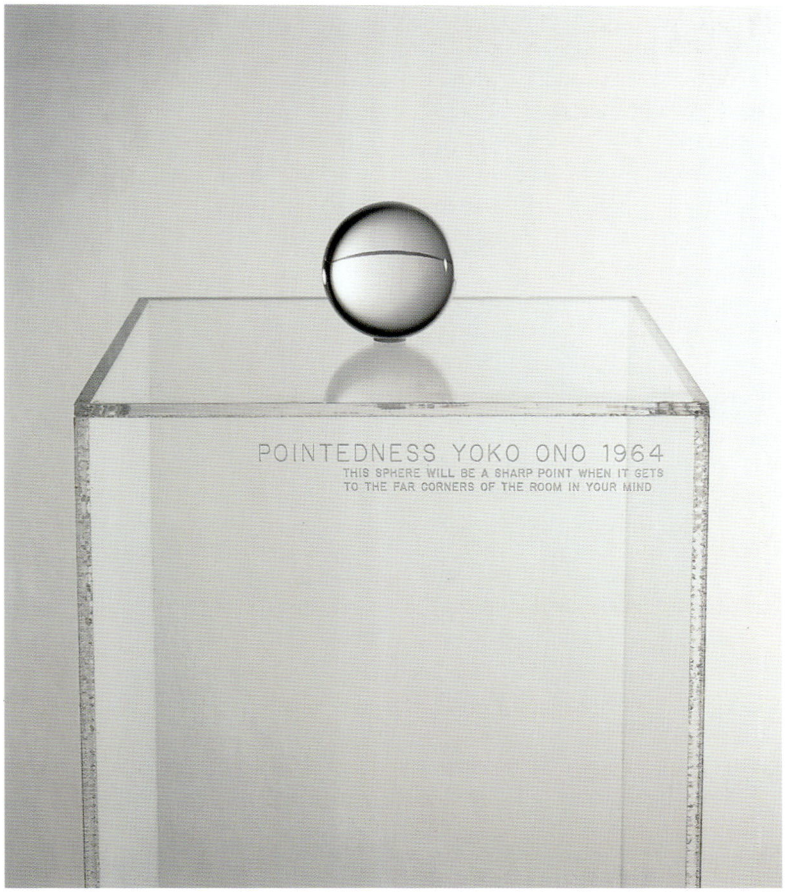

PLATE 60B
POINTEDNESS,
1964/1988 (BRONZE VERSION)

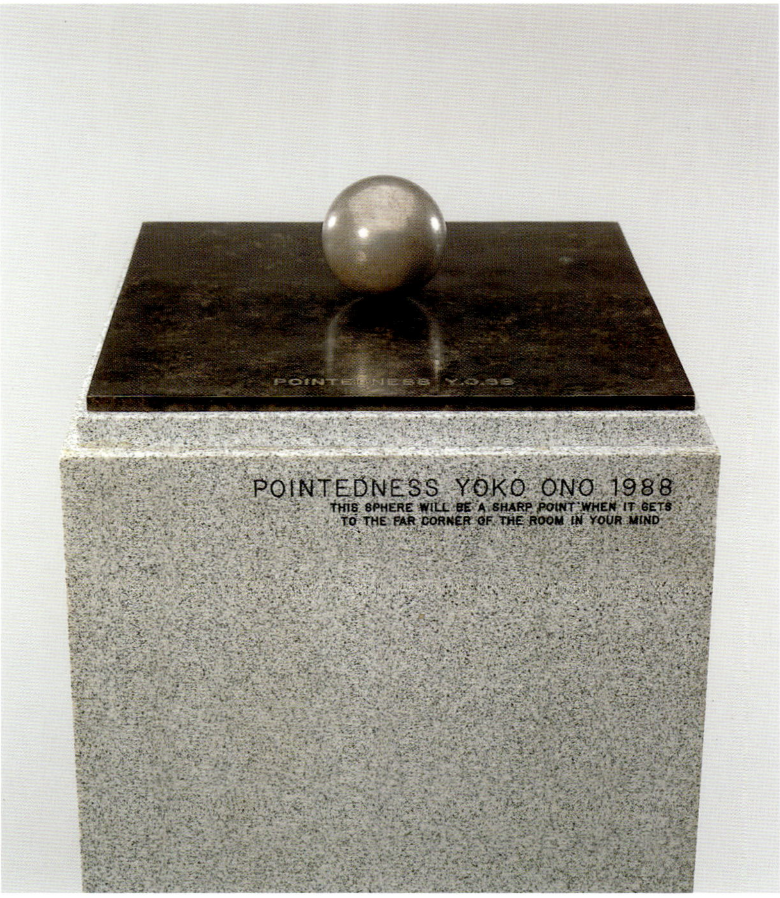

tered by a bullet hole, some bent hangers manipulated to abort a fetus, and a smashed baseball bat are cast in bronze and painted with a blood-red patina. In a related work, *Weight Object No. 5* (1990), she places a revolver on one side of a scale and balances it with a photograph of an anonymous family portrait (pl. 61). However specific, Ono's images of what she names "the history of violence" in *Family Album* call more to a shared memory of terror and are not politicized. The text for *Exhibit C: Box* (1993; pl. 62), which presents a solid bronze box form with blood seeping from its lid, reads:

> One day, quite suddenly, after so many
> years, blood started to flow out of the little
> black mind box I thought I had discarded.
>
> y.o. 1993 summer

The Whitney show and the works it introduced sparked renewed interest in Yoko Ono's art. At last, it seemed that critics and curators were looking at her work independent of her associations with either Fluxus or John Lennon. Beginning in 1989, aided by Jon Hendricks, who became Ono's curator and archivist that year, she participated in more and more exhibitions, both group and solo, in Europe, America, and Japan. Leading international curators, whose accounts follow here, sought her involvement in their projects and the marvelous spaces they offered—from the Spiral building in Aoyama, Tokyo, to a renovated convent in Valencia—inspired her to create on a larger and larger scale. Like the installation art of Robert Wilson or Robert Gober, Ono's room-size theaters of the 1990s make the viewer a protagonist in a constructed situation. In Ono's art, that imagined site gets erected, like a Noh drama of the afterlife, in a zone well beyond a worldly plane of existence. As in her all-white chess game, entering takes trust.

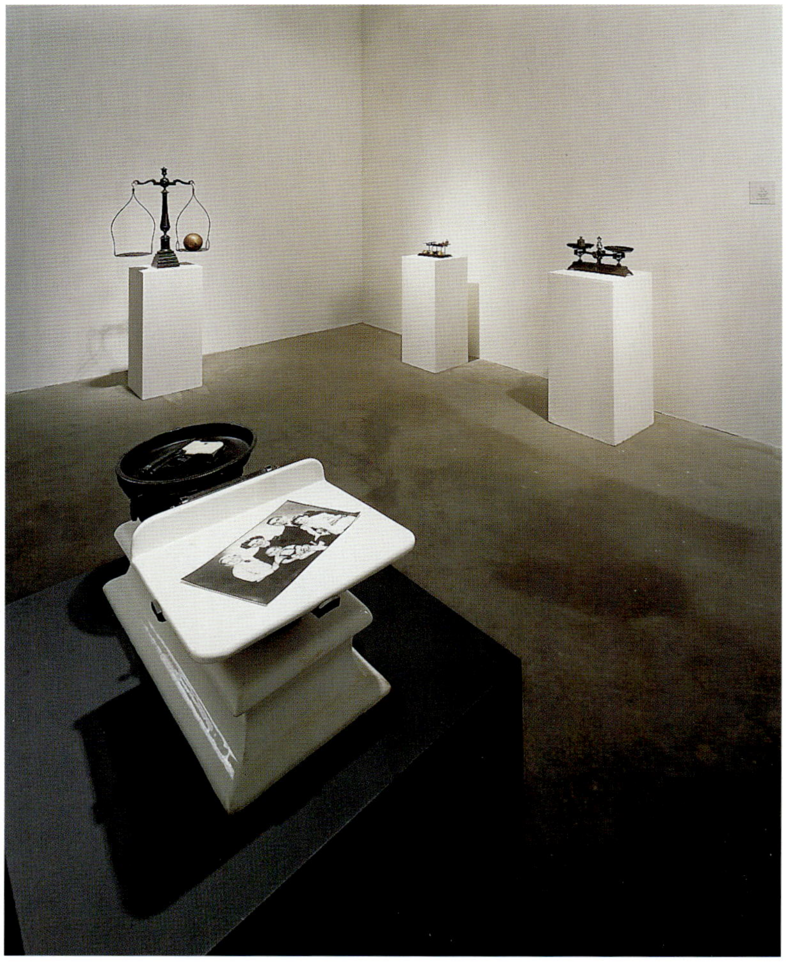

PLATE 61
WEIGHT OBJECTS,
1990. INSTALLATION VIEW, SHOSHANA WAYNE GALLERY, SANTA MONICA, 1993

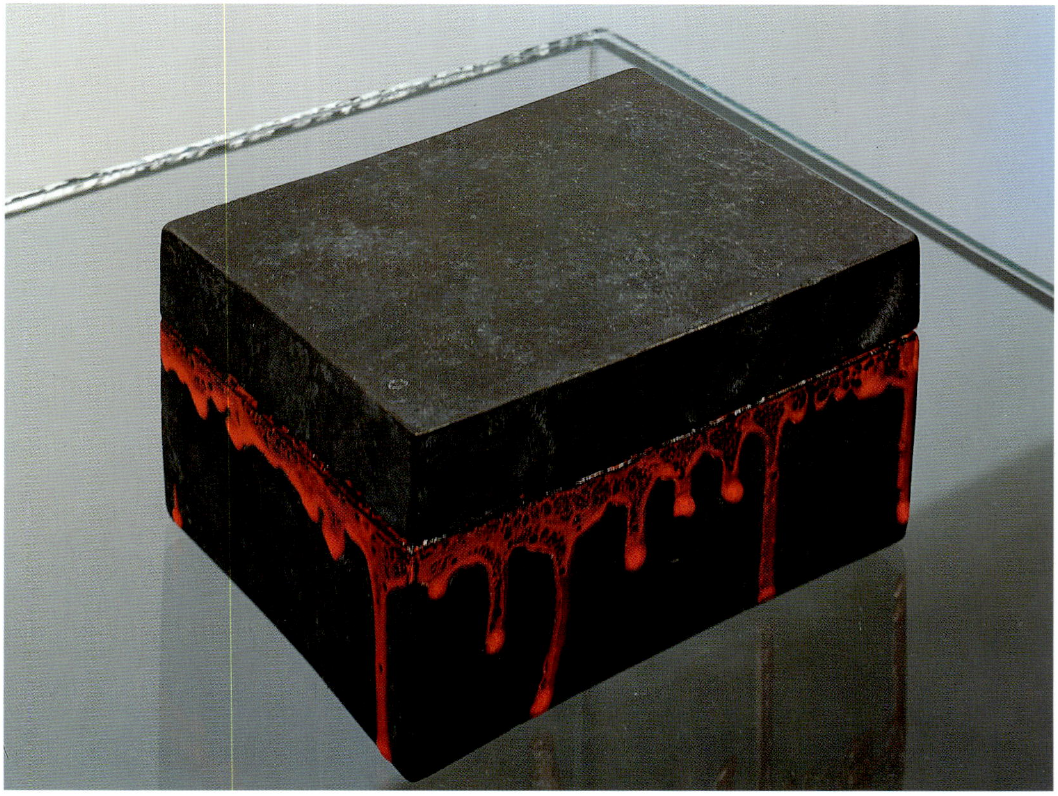

PLATE 62
FAMILY ALBUM, EXHIBIT C: BOX (MINDBOX), 1993.
PATINA AND PAINT ON BRONZE

When Idea Becomes Form

NANJŌ FUMIO

I first saw works of art by Yoko Ono in 1989, at her solo exhibition at the Whitney Museum of American Art in New York (pl. 59). From this relatively small show I carried away a distinct impression: the works I saw not only communicated a strong message, but also bespoke a poetic sensitivity.

The message they conveyed was not social and political but humanist and moralist—so full of implications as to unexpectedly alter our view on life, to make us think of the sky or landscape before our eyes, to prompt us to reflect on human emotions, if only for an instant in our everyday life. The poetry they intimated was not so much an epic as a *haiku* that expressed, with a minimal number of words, a fleeting moment in the seasons or nature as well as an insight into life itself. It was at once Japanese and global, for even if her expression was Japanese, its substance concerned something universal that any person in the world could think about and understand.

In 1993 in Japan, where the bubble economy had just burst, I drew up a plan for a lofty project to reexamine the way we humans live, entitled *Art Life 21: Re-Humanization*, for Tokyo's Spiral/Wacoal Art Center. While planning a series of exhibitions, I first thought of Yoko Ono, remembering the messages she had transmitted through her works and activities since the 1960s. One of them, of course, was the poetic message I received from the small works at the Whitney.

Some of her messages call for love and peace; others encourage us to see our life from different perspectives. But always at their heart is a call to us all to be human; and all are informed by Eastern wisdom and poetics transcending national boundaries.

I contacted the artist, explained the project's goals, and decided to exhibit *Endangered Species 2319–2322*, which was then traveling in Europe. *Endangered Species* is an installation work consisting of several elements (pls. 63a–c). The central components are four bronze human figures, to which are added twenty-two small two- and three-dimensional works. The human figures are identified by paper tags attached to them. One tag, for example, reads:

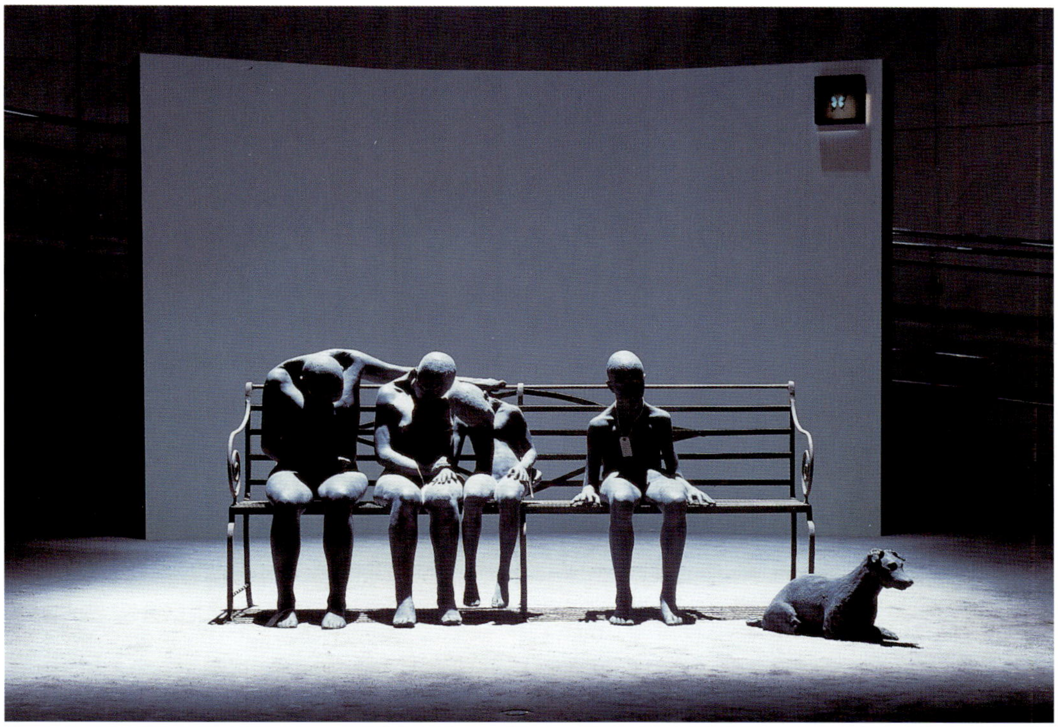

PLATES 63A–C
ENDANGERED SPECIES 2319–2322, 1992.
INSTALLATION VIEWS, SPIRAL / WACOAL ART CENTER, TOKYO, 1993

> No: 2321
> Sex: X
> Age: Unknown
> Section: Continent D
> Circa: BP 100

A plate on the wall explains in Japanese:

> These bodies (2319–2322), roughly dating from B.P. 50, were discovered in A.P. 100, on Continent D.
>
> The dreams and memories of Nos. 2319–2322 were also excavated at the same time.

In these documents, B.P. signifies "Before Peace," and A.P., "After Peace."

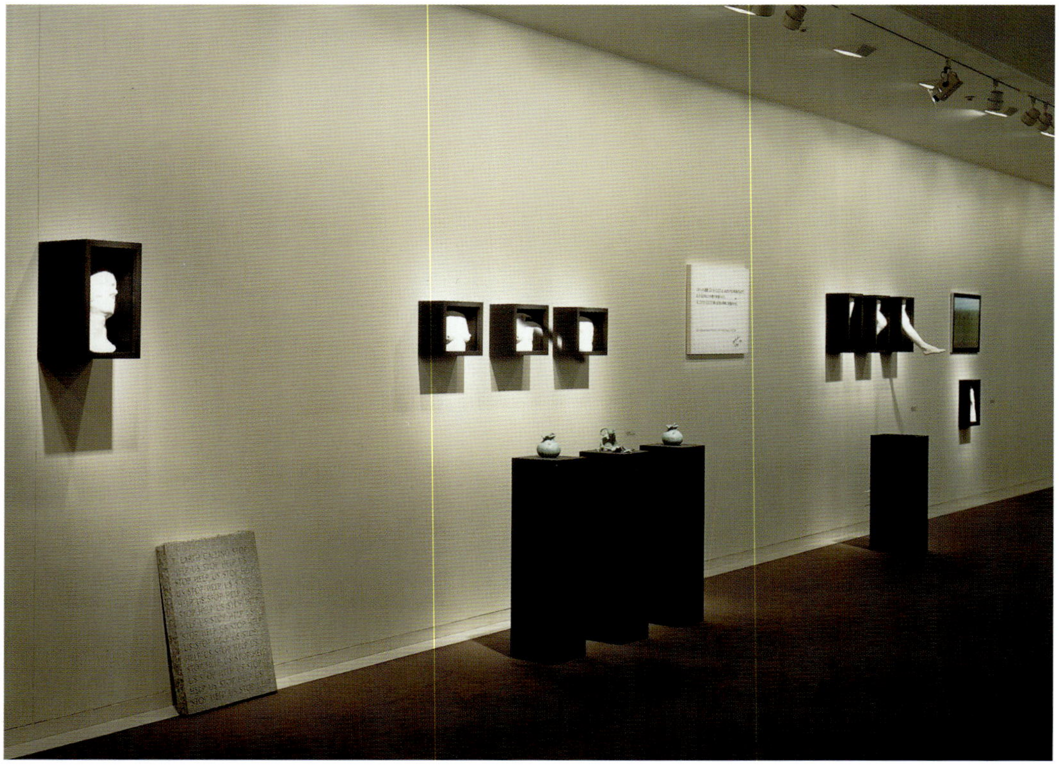

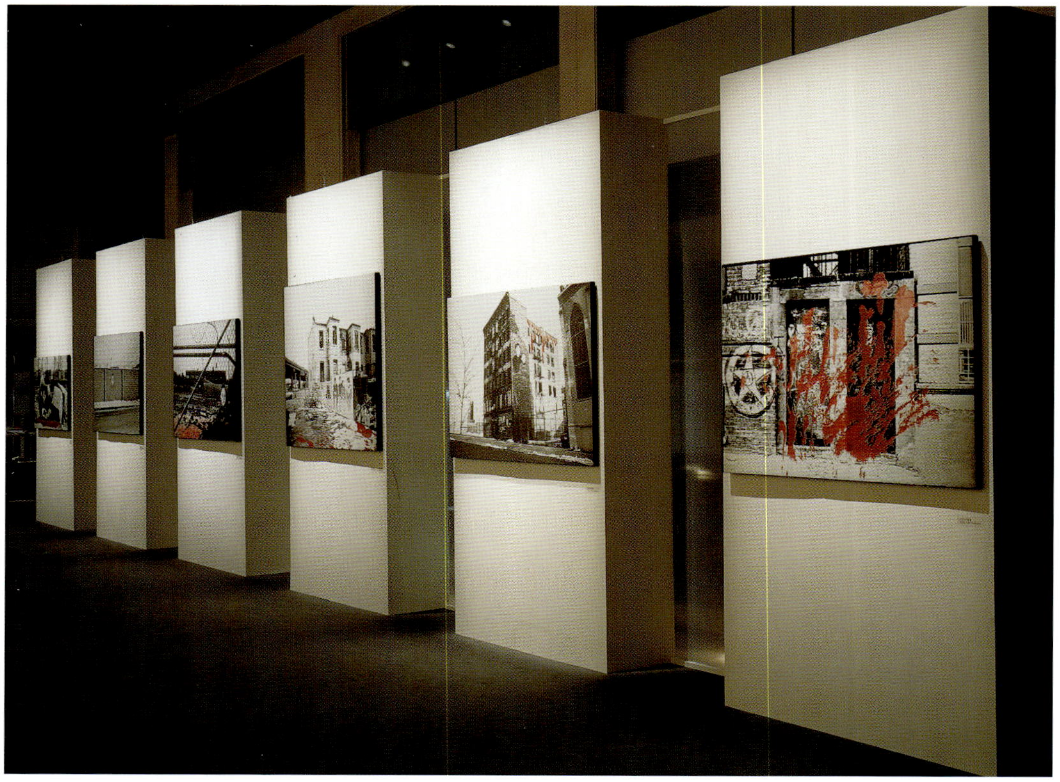

In other words, what we see in *Endangered Species* is a tragic portrait of a family, discovered 100 years after the advent of Peace. The fossilized family includes a husband and a wife with their children (a boy and a girl), who bear silent witness to some catastrophe that struck the species of humankind and the planet Earth in their lifetime. There is no indication whether this catastrophe was a third World War, a nuclear explosion, or an environmental disaster. Also excavated are the fear and anxiety they felt, together with the love and peace they longed for, as embodied in the fossilized "Thought Forms" (auxiliary pieces).

The image is tragic, yet not entirely hopeless, indicating the survival of humankind. That is to say, the work never implies the species' extinction, merely its endangerment at the time. Therein lies the hope of this work. A quite narrative creation, *Endangered Species* warns against human folly. Its clear message thus resonates with the artist's abiding pacifism, love for humankind, and affirmative stance.

Ono's exhibition became a central component of the Spiral program that projected a desire "to be human." The exhibition and especially the artist's lecture in her home country, coming as it did after her lengthy absence, attracted many young visitors. The installation will soon be seen by a greater audience at a new sculpture museum in Kirishima, Kagoshima Prefecture, which now owns the work.

In 1996, I had another occasion to work with Yoko Ono, when I was involved in a project to organize *The Internet 1996 World Exposition* in the ever-growing realm of the Internet. The project consisted of Web sites, or online "pavilions," put up by participating organizations. Among them was Dai Nippon Printing Co. Ltd., which decided to invite a few artists to show their works at the company's Web pavilion.

Asked to curate this virtual exhibition, I asked myself a simple question: What is the Internet? The Internet amounts to an ocean of information. If art were to evolve in such a space, it could be a kind of conceptualism, informed by a new way of thinking. What, then, would be best suited for the space would be an art based on message, on language; also, since it is possible to accommodate changes and display the process, a work of art in my virtual exhibition would be capable of incorporating a dimension of unfolding time. Based on these analyses, I concluded that Ono would be the best choice and solicited her contribution.

The resulting work was *Acorns: 100 Days with Yoko Ono* (pls. 64a–b). Every day, over a period of 100 days, the artist posted a poemlike message to the Web site on which interested viewers could then leave comments and responses; these in turn could be read by others. This was a sort of bulletin board that needed to be carefully designed and engineered: new materials would be added every day; the site must operate in both Japanese and English; and it should be easy for anyone to view comments and responses posted via e-mail. The whole project demanded new solutions in technology and systems, which were successfully devised and implemented.

Acorns: 100 Days with Yoko Ono displays characteristics of the artist's previous work, exemplifying the continuity of her thinking. It is in essence a language-based invitation or message that lightheartedly prompts readers to reexamine themselves and their lives from a different point of view. Internet technology made possible the work's innovation—to enable viewers to respond every day and make their messages available for perusal by the artist herself and others. Before this, it was impossible to display direct responses immediately on a real-time basis. *Acorns* was an imaginative marriage of Ono's conceptualism and message with the new media of the Internet.

I have worked with Yoko Ono only a few times, as outlined above. I would be gratified to know that I have, even tangentially, contributed to the development of her art. I will have yet further occasions to work with her for the Sydney Biennale 2000 and the Yokohama Triennale 2001.

What new messages will her works bring to us?

(Translated from the Japanese by Reiko Tomii)

Nanjō Fumio is an independent curator based in Tokyo.

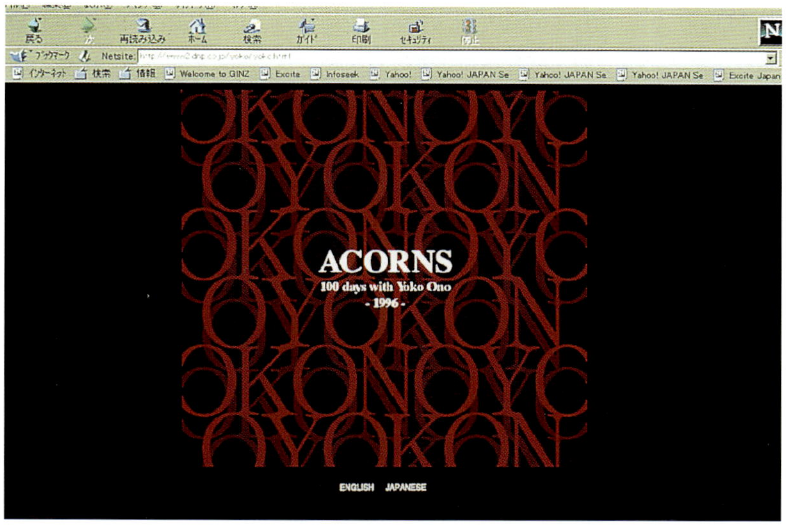

PLATE 64A
ACORNS: 100 DAYS WITH YOKO ONO, 1996.
INDEX PAGE

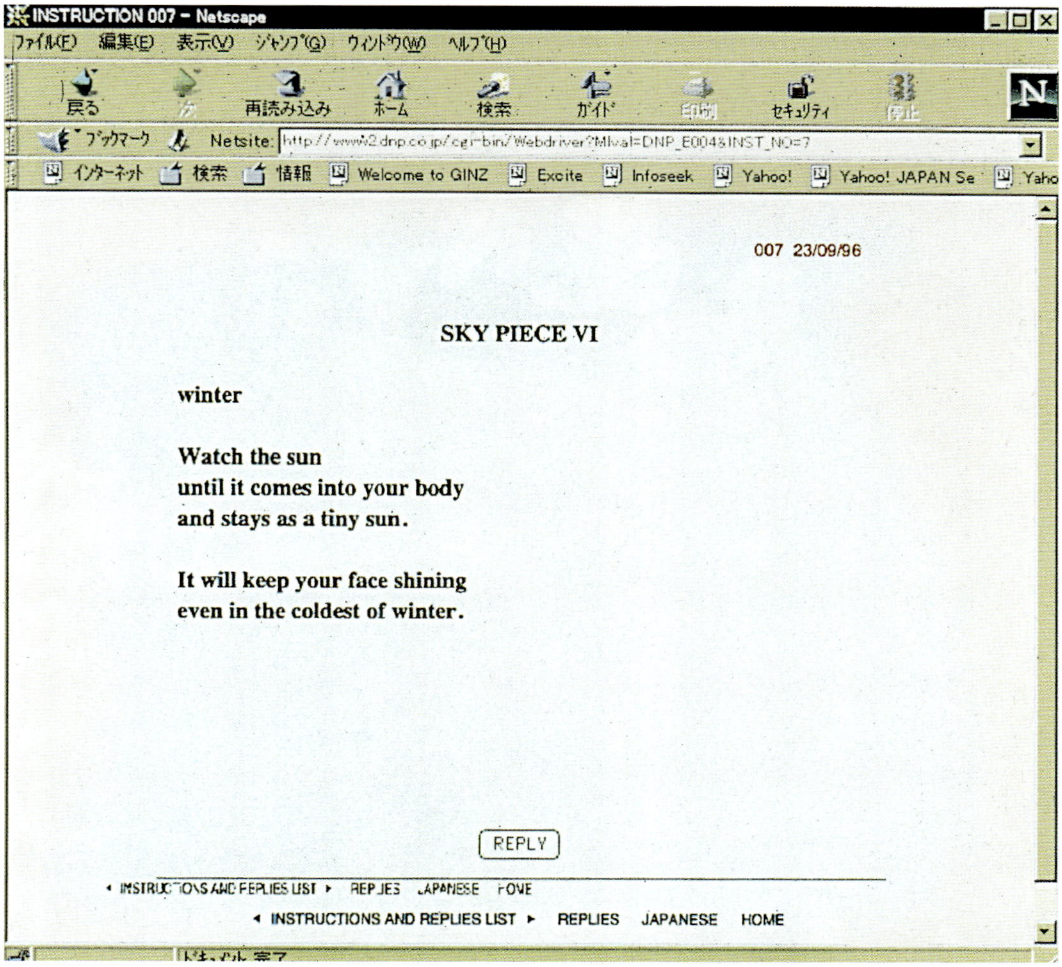

PLATE 64B
ACORNS: 100 DAYS WITH YOKO ONO, 1996.
INSTRUCTION, DAY 7
(SEPTEMBER 23)

Urban Space as Art Space:
A Celebration of Being Human

KAI BAUER

THE PLACE

Between 1992 and 1997, while I was commissioner of visual arts programming in Langenhagen—Hannover's "airport city"—we invited a number of contemporary artists whose works dealt with aspects of urban everyday living and its structures to participate in an exhibition series titled *vor ort—Kunst in städtischen Situationen*. The theme that faced the artists resulted from Langenhagen's special situation: the new center had been built within the space of a few years on a piece of land that connected five old villages. The new "downtown" included a city hall, office buildings, schools, a swimming pool, housing, and a shopping mall. In contrast to historically developed cities, cultural institutions and exhibition spaces had not been included in the pragmatic orientation of this "drawing-board city," precluding the presentation of any art forms that relied on the museum as display space. Therefore, the selection of artists focused on those whose works were defined by conceptual approaches or, rather, by positions that dealt with urban space as a place that invited interaction and that reflected structures of, and living conditions within, the city.

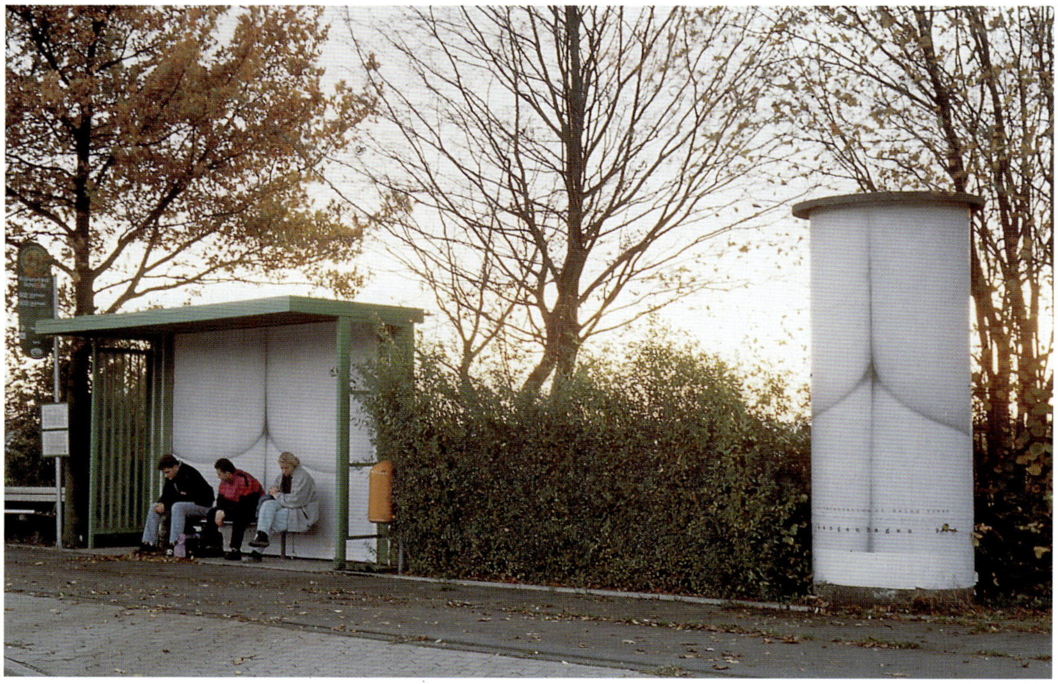

PLATE 65A
A CELEBRATION OF BEING HUMAN, 1994.
BUS STOP AND ADVERTISING COLUMN

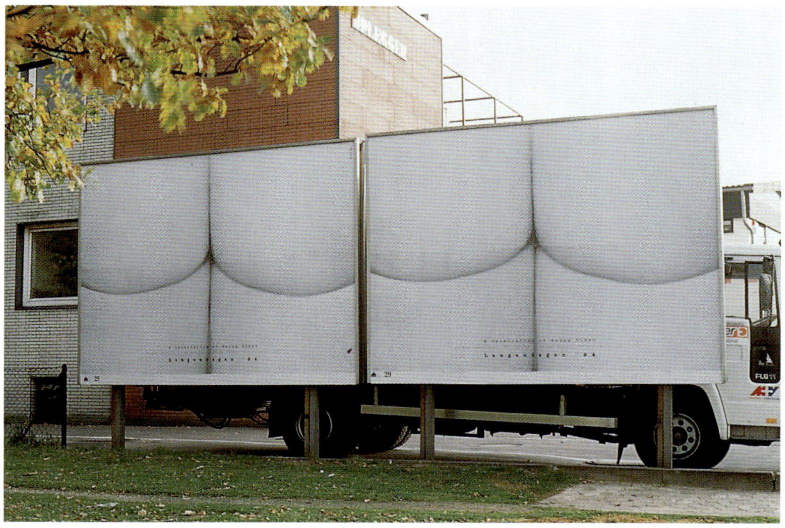

PLATE 65B
A CELEBRATION OF BEING HUMAN, 1994.
BILLBOARDS

THE CONCEPT

Yoko Ono's project for the *vor ort* series originated with a black-and-white photograph of human buttocks and a short, poemlike text:

> *A Celebration of Being Human*
>
> We are beautiful.
> We are fun.
> We are mammals without tails. y.o.
>
> Langenhagen '94

The photograph and text were accompanied by instructions for placing the text as a caption below the photograph with the motif (buttocks) appearing throughout the city of Langenhagen—on billboards and advertising columns, as well as in streetcars, shops, and public buildings (pls. 65a–c). At the same time, the image was supposed to be printed on a variety of objects, including umbrellas, T-shirts,

PLATE 65C
A CELEBRATION OF BEING HUMAN, 1994.
SIGN BANNERS

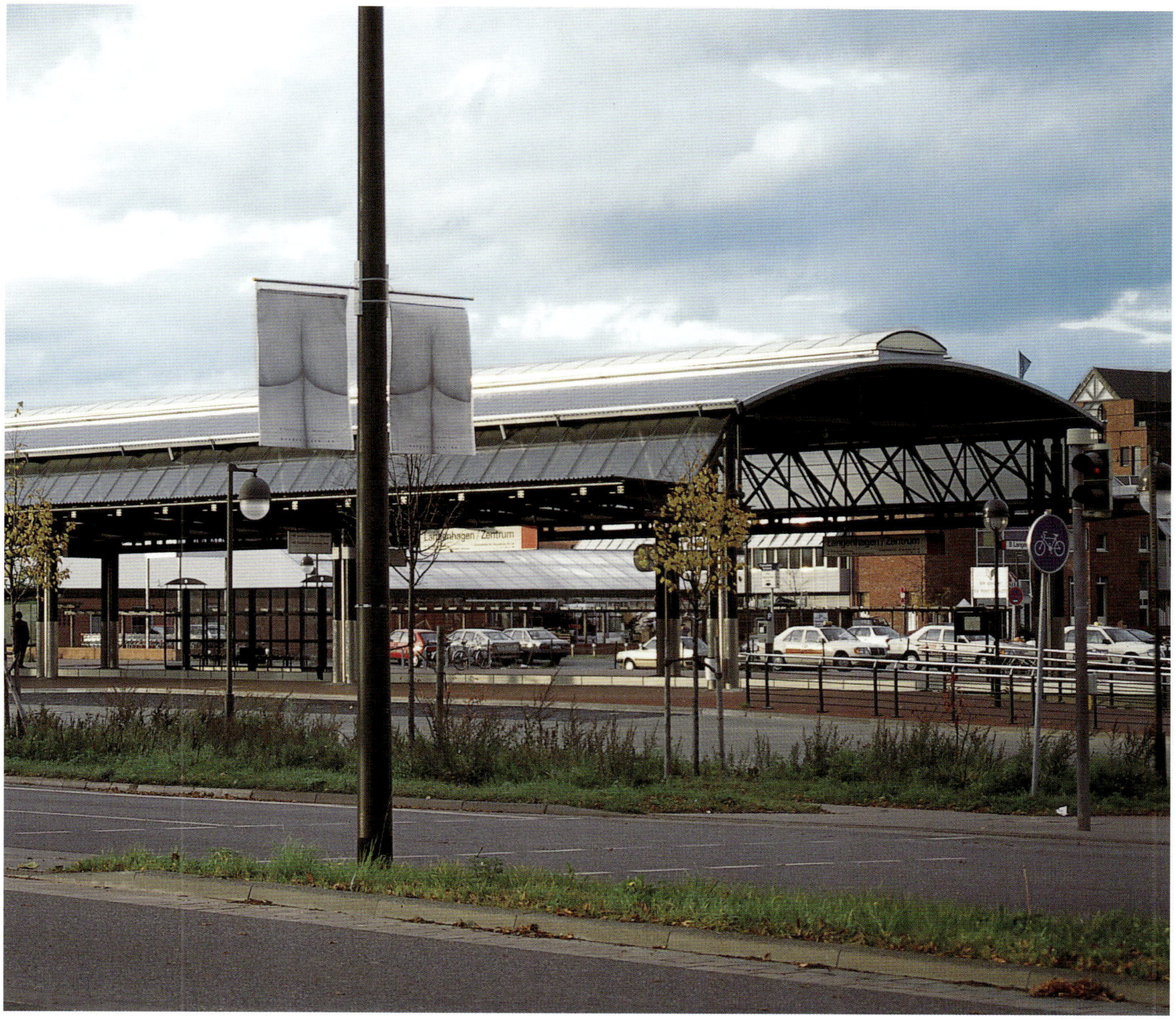

stickers, shopping bags, and postcards (pl. 65e). These would be handed to departing passengers at the Hannover-Langenhagen airport, with the idea that the motif would be carried around the world. This global aspect—widely proclaimed as a trademark of late-1990s art—was thus already conceptually present in Ono's idea for the *vor ort* series of 1994. The poetic notion of diffusion and dispersion harks back to Ono's artistic beginnings as a member of New York Fluxus and to the idea of the transitory nature of things, as well as the global dissemination of Fluxus ideas and products.

THE MOTIF

Similarly, the central motif in Ono's Langenhagen project takes up images from her film *No. 4 (Bottoms)* of 1966, although a new photograph was used as the motif for the Langenhagen project (no. 43). In contrast to the serial repetition in the film, the Langenhagen image was isolated and enlarged from a single shot. The detail emphasizes the graphic structure as well as the symbolic character of human buttocks. By showing only a detail of the original photograph, all further information about the image is eliminated, including any personal or eroticizing details, the person's gender, and the particular circumstance in which the picture was taken. Such technical manipulation liberates the motif from merely physical connotations. At the same time, however, the ambiguity of the image is enforced by its reproduction (either through offset printing or the more elaborate silkscreen technique) on various media and objects.

THE "YOKO ONO EFFECT": THE ARTIST AS PUBLIC FIGURE

With regard to the realization of the project, Yoko Ono's high degree of fame as a "pop icon" was an important catalyst. Recognizing the publicity potential, institutions, the media, and even political parties offered nearly unconditional support without even asking first for the actual content of the project and its artistic message. The mere announcement that Yoko Ono was planning a project for Langenhagen made involvement seem prestigious and appealing to the participating institutions and sponsors.

The actual presentation by Yoko Ono, however, showed her as a visual artist in the context of Fluxus, Conceptual Art, and the arts of the 1990s. Contrary to the public's expectations, appearances by the artist herself were limited to one press conference inside the Langenhagen airport terminal. While the artist became very much a part of daily life through the presence of her work, the public's access to the person, Yoko Ono, was only through the media and thus indirect. Coverage of her Langenhagen project, however, was distorted by stereotypical accounts that appealed to popular interest in the 1960s and Ono's publicized life. This blurring of reality and virtuality in the representation of the artist caused the public to lose confidence in the media, who were perceived as weak and confused.

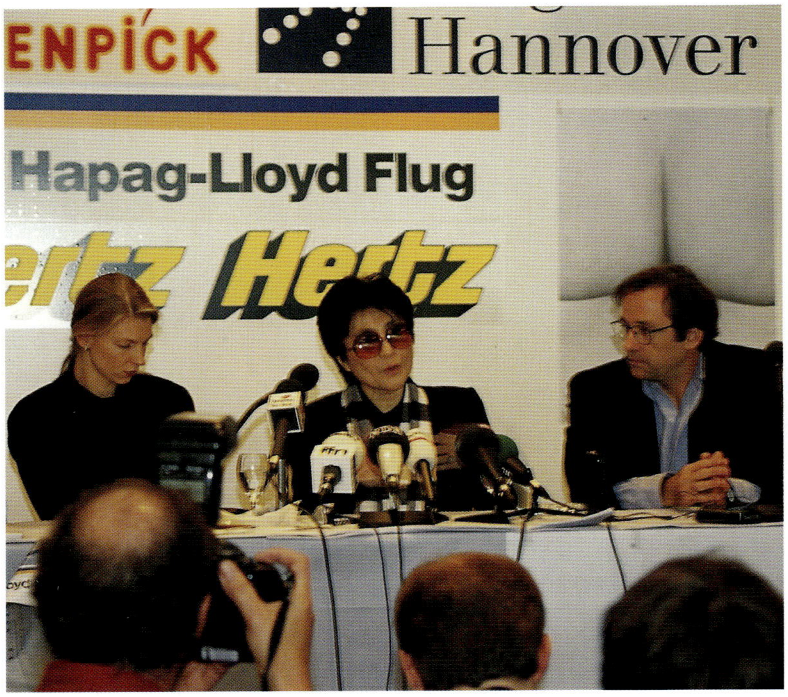

PLATE 65D
PRESS CONFERENCE FOR
A CELEBRATION OF BEING HUMAN, 1994.
YOKO ONO, CENTER,
AND JON HENDRICKS,
RIGHT

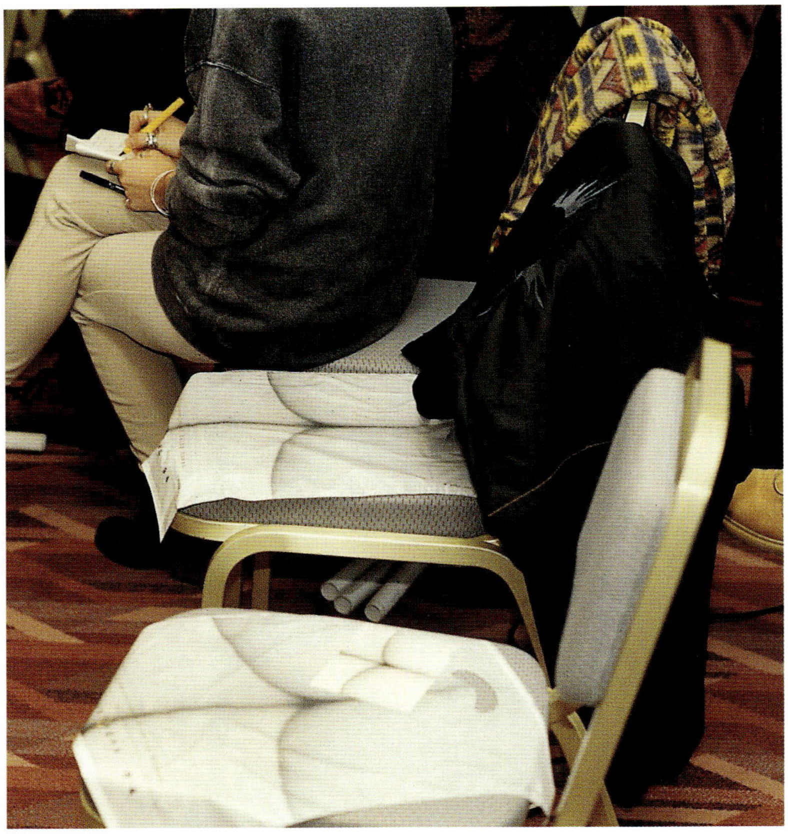

PLATE 65E
A CELEBRATION OF BEING HUMAN, 1994.
PLASTIC BAGS ON SEATS
AT PRESS CONFERENCE

THE PROJECT

Yoko Ono's concept can be seen as a kind of "software" programmed with various cycles of interdependent and, at times, competing systems. Suddenly, the whole city had become plastered with a recurring image. It occupied nearly all the billboards, sixty light-box advertisement panels, and a total of thirty advertising columns. Public advertising space in small towns is much more limited by law in Germany than, for instance, in France or the United States. In the fall of 1994, however, a happy circumstance facilitated the realization of Yoko Ono's project. A campaign for parliamentary elections had left behind numerous additional billboards. With the elections just over, the different parties agreed to make them available for the project. Overnight, hundreds of politicians' faces with their pretentious smiles radiating insincere optimism were replaced by Yoko Ono's poster image, resulting in a coherent visual density throughout the cityscape. The static aspect of the poster campaign was supplemented by mobile visual elements: 5,000 posters; 2,500 T-shirts; 25,000 shopping bags; 1,000 umbrellas; 30,000 postcards; and 5,000 stickers. These were distributed at shops, the weekly farmers' market, the local shopping mall, schools, and other public interior spaces. In addition, all local streetcars and buses (a total of nearly 200) running between Hannover and Langenhagen carried a peace message. The various items mentioned above were also distributed among departing passengers at the Hannover-Langenhagen airport so that the message "A Celebration of Being Human" would be carried throughout the world—much like the perfumed flies in *Museum of Modern [F]art* (1971), one of Yoko Ono's earlier works (no. 40).

In order to further increase the exposure and intensify the experience, a supplement with a full-page ad of the omnipresent image was inserted in the two local newspapers, *Hannoversche Allgemeine Zeitung* and *Langenhagener Echo*, at the beginning of the campaign (October 25, 1994). Anyone opening either newspaper at this time would have seen it. Sponsored by local stores, the page not only represented the essence of the Fluxus concept, it also occupied the same medium in which reviews of and reactions to the project could be read. This artistic implant in the dailies is just one example of how Yoko Ono's concept managed to dominate numerous sources of public information normally reserved for criticism, politics, or advertising. The media's difficulty in categorizing *A Celebration of Being Human* within art and culture, politics, or advertising is symptomatic of the subversive strategy behind the project and of its subtle effectiveness. The public's reactions were complex and diverse and evolved continuously throughout the ten-day campaign. Enthusiastic and amused reactions and comments stood in contrast to reactions of disapproval and lack of understanding. In some cases, the negative reactions resulted in hateful statements that accused the artist of sexism, pornography, or insult.

After a short interval, however, it became apparent that this spectacular project, precisely because of the controversy that surrounded it, became part of Langenhagen's history and ultimately contributed in its own way to the identity of this otherwise rather faceless small town.

(Translated from the German by Katharina Belting)

Kai Bauer, an independent curator based in Stuttgart, was commissioner of visual arts programming, Langenhagen, 1992–97.

The Interactive Field of Art

ACHILLE BONITO OLIVA

PLATE 66
INSTALLATION VIEW,
TWO ROOMS AT VENICE
BIENNALE, 1993

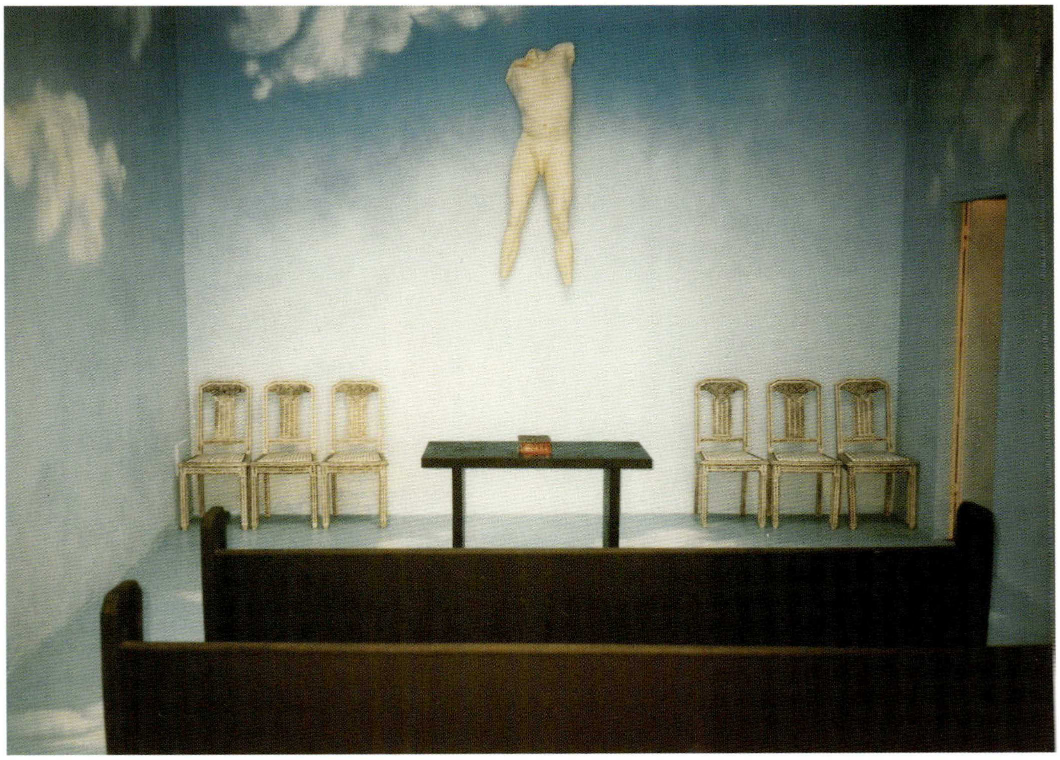

The group Fluxus has given to contemporary art an aesthetic and principled inheritance that has both linguistic and behavioral components. It has developed a productive strategy favoring the creative process above formal results, the concept above the object. An extreme cultural nomadism continues to characterize the perspective of these artists, who have worked on reducing geographical distances, defining existential common ground, and developing linguistic syncretism, interdisciplinary collaboration, and multimedia interactivity.

A founding member of this group, Yoko Ono has developed a creative strategy that is at once personal and contemporary, based on the creation of works and events. The result has always been a space made more intense and charged with the presence of the art and, at the same time, rendered habitable by the audience.

Certainly, Ono has always adhered to the idea of the complete work of art, one that expresses a synthesis of multiple languages. This is evident in her 1989 Whitney Museum exhibition in New York, which included a group of early works as well as works in bronze that reproduced, reinterpreted, or commented on the earlier versions (pl. 59).

The *Bronze Age* sculptures represent objects and scenes of urban life. The use of bronze indicates a desire on the part of the artist to use the weight of her material to contrast the frivolity of our materialistic age, with its domination by information technology. It is also an attempt to freeze the ephemeral forms of the everyday in the immobility of bronze.

In the 1990s Yoko Ono has brought to completion various projects formulated over recent decades. In these works, she uses multiple coded forms, such as crosses and coffins, which invoke life, death, and resurrection. Life and death become modular signals whose dramatic impact is neutralized by the serial silence of the object. One example is her installation for the special exhibition *Ubi Fluxus Ibi Motus: 1990–1962*, which I organized for the Venice Biennale in 1990. This revival of a project conceived in 1974 presented a long series of crosses, each with a mirrored disk at its center capturing a reflection of life. Again, *Ex It* (1997), an installation shown in Valencia and New York, displayed a series of coffins, each with a tree emerging from it—a token of the fertility of death (pls. 74a–b).

Death and suffering also took center stage in the installation *Two Rooms* at the Venice Biennale in 1993, where the nude torso of a man hung high on the wall was exhibited under the mild celestial color of a blue ceiling. This color was repeated as blue jigsaw-puzzle pieces which viewers were invited to take from a ceremonial font (pl. 66).

The body is another constant factor in Ono's oeuvre—whether nude or dressed, it is always a focus of fertility and beauty. That is how it is presented in a series of photographs transferred to canvas in *Mommy Was Beautiful*, exhibited in *Disidentico: Maschile femminile e oltre* (1998).

Several dimensions always coexist in the work of Yoko Ono: together, they give rise to a harmonious system of forms whose intimate conceptual nature is never directly approachable (as in Western art), but whose rarefied essence impregnates the space occupied by the work and the audience, in accordance with the canons of Asian art. Consider, for example, *Lighting Piece* (1955/1995), an outdoor installation projected onto the facades of historic buildings in Florence, coordinated by Stefania Miscetti (pls. 67a–b). The work documents the slow passage of time as a match is consumed by its own flame.

During a creative career spanning over forty years, Yoko Ono has always held to the idea of art as an interactive field, a concept that marks her as extremely contemporary in this global society, with its demands for communication and participation at the dawn of the new millennium. Within this interactive field, Ono has worked to lay the foundations for a kind of "vaporized architecture," one that is concretely defined by the presence of the work of art and at the same time opened up by the high degree of conceptualization that underpins the creative act.

A certain spatial-temporal nexus forms the basis of the architecture itself and the rooms in which, for example, *Blue Room Event* was created. The artist initiated this work, consisting of a series of texts, in 1966 (no. 5). In the 1990s, she displayed them on the walls of various museums, usually handwritten, as in her 1995 exhibition *3 Rooms*, at Galleria Civica di Arte Contemporanea in Trento (pl. 68).

The aesthetics engendered in these rooms are the fruit of a compositional and contemplative experience that promotes an all-important solidarity between the artist and her audience. Plenum and void echo each other simultaneously in space, while East and West coalesce in the muted reverberations of two cultures as they harmonize and together determine the ultimate effect of the rooms. Each room is the result of an architectonic persistence, a historical void spatially grasped by the artist, who recognizes and reaffirms the architectural context of the walls and selects one on which to mark her statement, "This room is bright blue."

Blue Room Event elaborates a dual discipline that involves the artist as producer and the audience as consumer. It confronts both with a spatial-temporal dimension consisting of past, present, and future. The acceptance, typically Eastern, of what already exists—the architecture—reveals the patient pliability of an artist who documents her present intervention with a handwritten text and a conceptual affirmation.

Brief, unambiguous phrases punctuate the barrenness of the rooms, infusing sense and formal rhythm bound up in the writing that signs its act of appropriation.

Yoko Ono's is an Eastern appropriation of a Western space, one aware of the possibility of injecting conceptual energy into the inertia of the architectural mass. This energy is unveiled, in all its potency, to the gaze of a nomadic public momentarily subjected to an unusual discipline, that of having to contemplate a void as if it were full, and having to consider the detail of the phrase isolated on the wall as its central focus. But the phrases overcome their isolation, they conceptually invade the void of the surrounding space with the fullness of their message, affirming that now the room is blue: the architecture yields to impregnation by the conceptual potency of the language of art.

Art evidently relies on an invasive procedure that tends to vaporize its effects in the sequential architecture of the rooms.

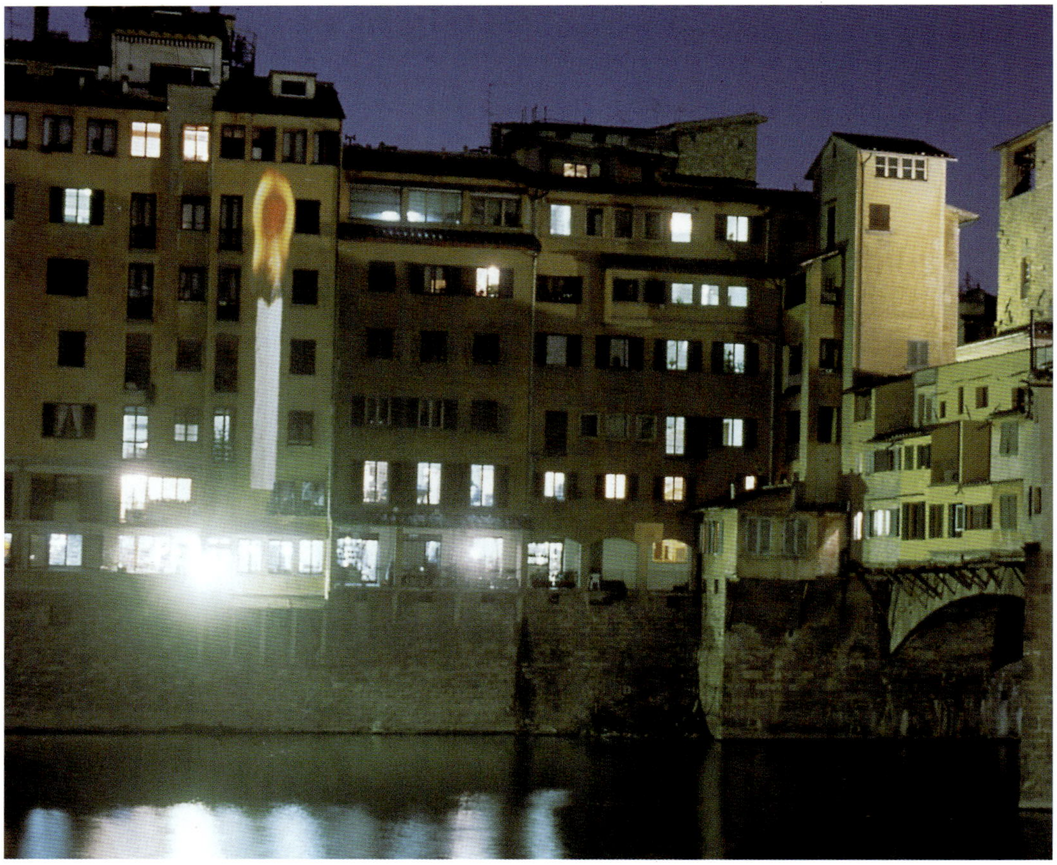

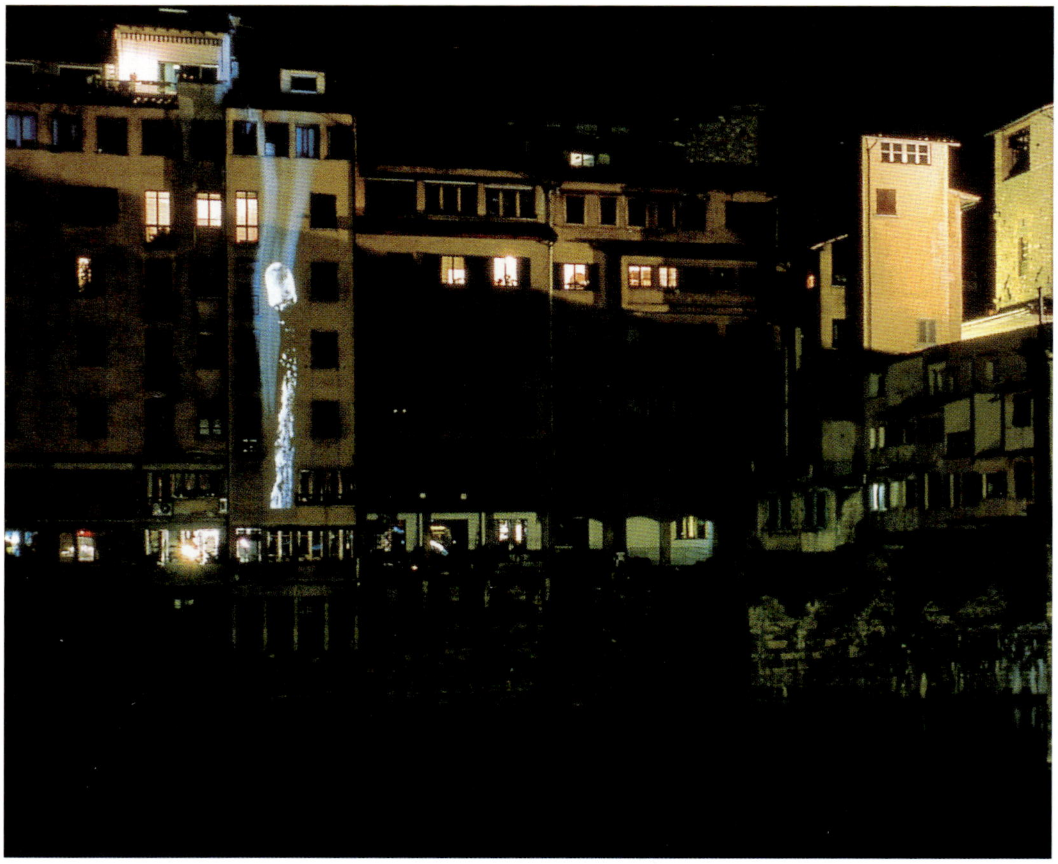

PLATES 67A–B
LIGHTING PIECE
AS PROJECTION EVENT
IN FLORENCE, 1995

The artistic overflows into the aesthetic, the visual form into the experience of the spectators, who find themselves enveloped effortlessly by the true installations that produce the maximum effect with an extraordinary economy of means. The economical use of the means of expression is a natural outcome of the mentality of an artist who is fully aware of the pervasive potency of the use of language and its capacity to take on the three-dimensional consistency of sculpture, as well as the two-dimensional form of painting and drawing.

The potency of the language is tautological and metaphorical, as well as geometric and atmospheric. It can alert us to the immobility of the floor and walls, underscore the static architecture of the rooms, and highlight the weightlessness of the clouds.

Yoko Ono develops a rarefied and rarefying aesthetic of space and time, one capable of toponymical indications ("This is the floor") and of demonstrable predictions ("This room glows in the dark while we are asleep"). Time and space become one, the fullness of presence and the void of absence enter into equilibrium, in the possibility of living the experience of art even after museum closing hours.

It is clear that the warmth of the writing produces a temperature all its own, perhaps stoked by the presence of the audience, but retaining its respective autonomy. This self-sufficiency of art is a product of the degree of resistance that art is capable of generating, irrespective of public acceptance; it is the artist's creation of an additional energy that reinvigorates life in the struggle against general entropy.

Yoko Ono makes use of preexisting architecture to initiate an active process of making and contemplating, one that relies not on the exemplary stillness of the form, but on the dynamic aspects of the contemplative and creative experience.

The artist cautions us, "This room slowly evaporates every day": it is a recognition of a temporal dynamic that spares neither art nor life. Yoko Ono's is an art of motion, one that brings her to the conclusion copied onto the wall: "Find other rooms which exist in this space."

There is no art without nomadism: the artist's journey is mirrored in that of the audience, which is drawn into the other rooms by the architectural void and by the fullness of the writing. The latter is supported in its role by the potential of the color blue, which denotes a crossing of boundaries and a sense of the infinite, the rarefying of a concept that does not recognize spatial limitations and architectural partitioning.

Each of the rooms requires a pause and visual reconnaissance, as well as a halt to gaze and a resumption of the journey. The boundary of the work is marked by the final affirmation ("Stay until the room is blue"), which is a negation of the first affirmation, "This room is bright blue."

The invitation to stay evidently implies the utmost degree of connectivity between space and time, as the necessity for contemplation makes clear with its focus on the development of the work and on its contemplative perception by the public. Ono aims at visually representing the dynamics of understanding, which cross the boundaries of aesthetics into philosophy: the possibility of rendering visible what lies beyond the spatial evidence of our conceptual notions of time.

Finally, Yoko Ono's entire creative career has always engaged the audience, as in a Zen dialogue that promotes an exchange of knowledge. But knowledge cannot be separated from experience, it cannot base itself on the proud logic of pure rationality: it always requires a focusing of different sense stimuli and mental disciplines. In this case, the discipline immediately demanded by Yoko Ono is the purification of space and the willingness to accept architectural nudity as the indispensable perceptual space of the individual consciousness.

In her work, Ono develops a certain kind of spiritual exercise that, far from mortifying the body, invites it to go for a physical and visual stroll. It totally deconstructs the context of the work and rigorously segregates its setting from all decorative elements and superstructure. Consequently, the public and the work directly face each other in a stripped-down intimacy that fosters the encounter and intensifies mutual contact. Through this process, space is cleansed by a philosophically ecological procedure, and the vaporization of art into the temporal dimension of the individual consciousness now becomes possible.

In conclusion, Yoko Ono produces an aesthetic intensification that annuls geographic and cultural distances and makes art and life coalesce within the architecture of the work. Her forms of expression are always many and varied, but the results are constant: the development of epistemological processes that, while remaining relative with respect to the experience of the individual, reveal themselves as absolutes with regard to the field of energy that radiates from their center.

(Translated from the Italian by Tom Di Salvo)

Achille Bonito Oliva, an independent curator based in Rome, was 1993 commissioner of the Venice Biennale.

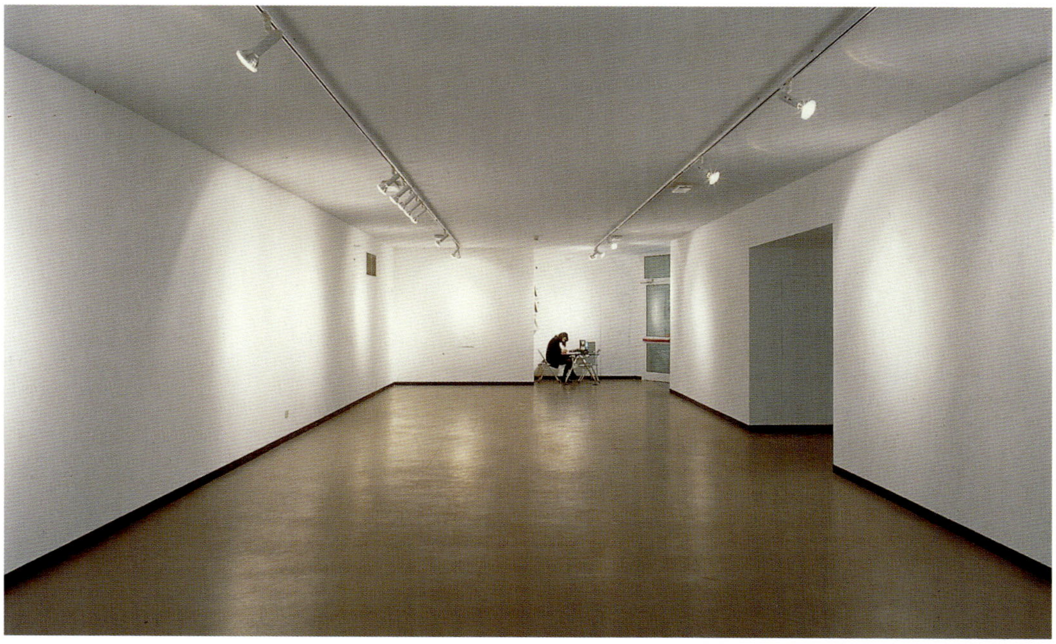

PLATE 68
BLUE ROOM EVENT,
1966. INSTALLATION VIEW, GALLERIA CIVICA DI ARTE CONTEMPORANEA, TRENTO, 1995

Yoko Ono's Conceptual Photography

LARS SCHWANDER

In *Conceptual Photography*, an exhibition I organized at Fotografisk Center (Copenhagen, 1997), Yoko Ono entered into a dialogue with photography as a medium. With a paradoxical blend of the abstract clarity of minimalism and the flesh and blood of artistic expression, she inductively sought out aspects of the very nature of photography. This is borne out in facets of the exhibition: the handwritten *Instructions for Photographs* (1961–71) blend in with such related themes as *Instructions for Films* and the new projects *Portrait of Nora*, *Vertical Memory*, *Horizontal Memory*, and *Toilet Thoughts—Film No. 3*, the last of which was originally published in her *Thirteen Film Scores* in 1968, but not realized until the exhibition (Anthology 22). What characterized the project was not a linear course of objective enclosure, but rather Yoko Ono's subjective and stringent approach to the material.

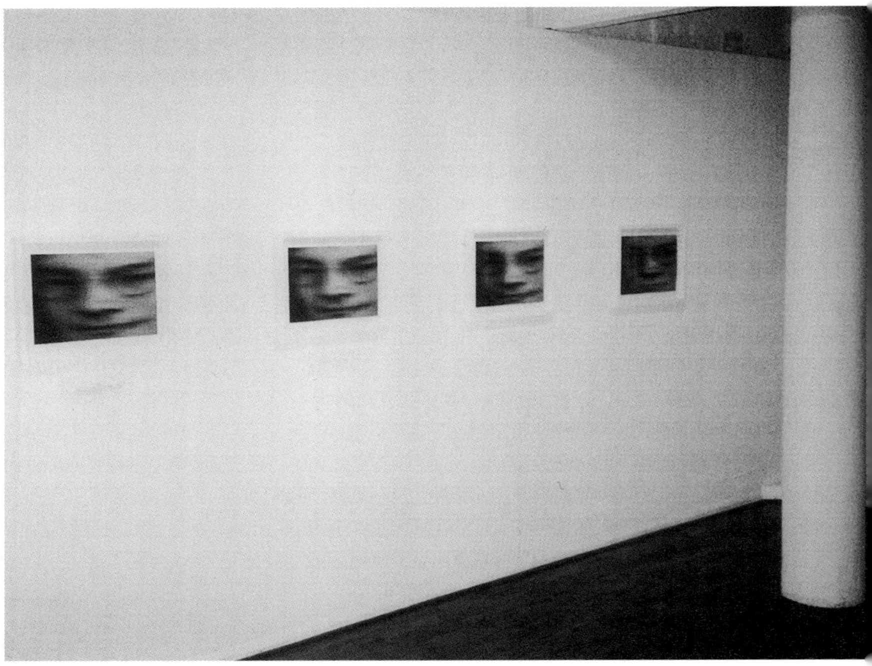

PLATE 69
VERTICAL MEMORY,
1997. INSTALLATION VIEW, MUSEUM OF MODERN ART, OXFORD, 1997

Conceptual Photography was concerned not only with photography as such, but also how the medium is perceived, the relationship between the observer (the Spectator, according to Roland Barthes) and the picture itself, a continuation of Yoko Ono's oeuvre. Recalling the classic book *Grapefruit* and its author's description, "a book of instructions," the essential—or basic—part of the actual exhibition is without doubt the series *Instructions for Photographs*. With these Ono shows her fundamental philosophy of art: art is not static and it demands that the audience take part, act—or even perform an event. This goes completely against the opinion that the creative act is over when the actual piece of art is finished. Her instructions force the Spectator to relate to the actual work of art.

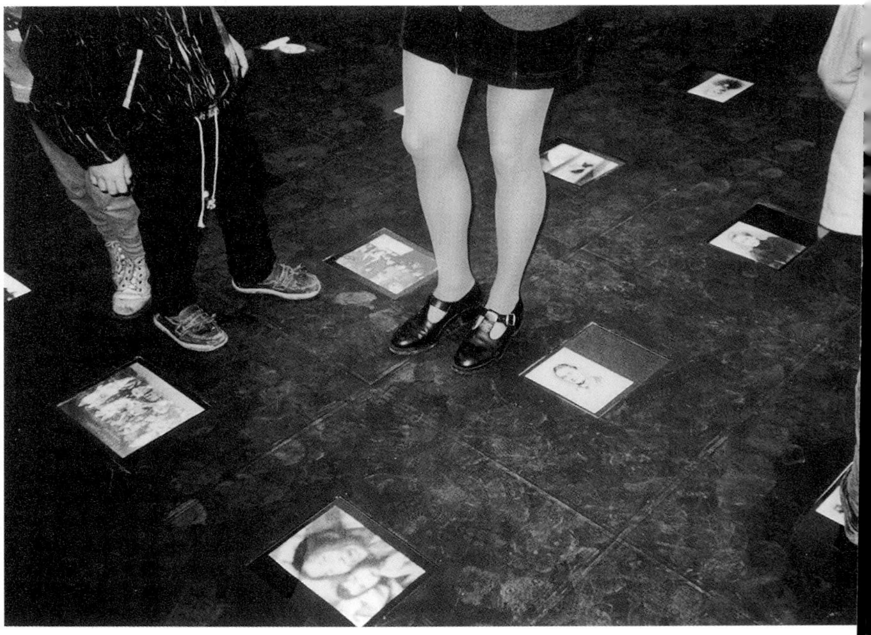

PLATE 70
HORIZONTAL MEMORY,
1997. INSTALLATION VIEW, KONSTHALLEN GÖTEBORG, 1997

Conceptual Photography bespeaks a process activated only in the meeting between the Spectator and the art, with the Spectator as creator of the photograph. *Vertical Memory* comprises twenty-one identical portraits accompanied by different texts (pl. 69). Each new context seems to displace the meaning of the picture. Each written fragment describes a woman's encounter—at times confrontational—with a different man in her life. This is represented as vertical movement because the woman, lying or sitting, looks upward at the men beginning from the birth experience:

> Doctor I
>
> I remember being born and looking into his eyes. He picked me up and slapped my bottom. I screamed.

And eventually ends up close (again) to the death experience:

> Attendant
>
> I saw a dark hole in a shape of an arch. I saw my body being slid into it. It looked like the arc I came out of at birth, I thought. I asked where it was going to take me to. The guy stood there looking at me without saying a word, as I lay down, It all seemed very familiar. What percentage of my life did I take it lying down? That was the last question I asked in my mind.

During this journey the female entity takes shape. The father figure is present for the first time as the child reaches the age of two and a half. He only looks down on her as she glances up. Under the gaze of these male figures—including Doctor II during the war, Doctor III who took out her appendix, Doctor IV who took her tonsils out, Doctor V (psychiatrist) who told her that her problem was that she was not dating, Doctor VI who took out her wisdom teeth, Doctor VII who performed abortions—Artists I through VI are all speechless (a silence more eloquent than words). The subject's life is completed by Priest, Doctor IX, and Attendant. The female entity's shape takes on a forceful resonance, maybe not so distant from the life of Yoko Ono herself, but at the same time illustrating in general the vulnerable situation of women.

The repeated picture is actually a computerized amalgamation of three photographs: of father Ono Yeisuke, husband John Lennon, and son Sean. This composite image creates a fictional person born from the creator herself. The words establish connections to the common lines of female destinies and the succession of conditions, but it is not an exposé of the artist's privacy. In this way the merged elements create Ono's *Vertical Memory*.

In *Horizontal Memory*—a work consisting of found photographs placed on the floor—the almost arbitrary choice of pictures provides an insight into the aesthetics of different historic times and places of origin (pl. 70). Even in the catalogue for the exhibition, the component pictures are placed arbitrarily, perhaps adding new dimensions. Whereas *Vertical Memory* is a completed work, *Horizontal Memory* has appeared in renewed constellations and expressions. The occupied floor space is sometimes a passage between two rooms, making it difficult, if not impossible, for the viewer not to step on the pictures. This was the case in 1997 at the Museum of Modern Art, Oxford, when new photographs were also added to the piece. The work's concept remains intact while the presentation evolves—just like the details of history itself.

It is Ono's expressed belief that the photographs should not be associated with the artist/photographer's self, that the creative act take place inside the Spectator, providing an opportunity to investigate the process of search within oneself—to open, enlarge, and widen the meaning of the mental process. It is very important for her to call attention to the misconception of the status of documentary photography as an "objective," "unstaged" process. For her all photography is staged, not only in the choice of situations, motifs, or angles but also in the connotations of the picture, which is not detached from the "art" photograph, as a nonintermediary register of reality.

It is as if the projects *Vertical Memory* and *Horizontal Memory* provide the material for a discussion about the character of experience, fictitious or real, in an extremely short prose form. *Horizontal Memory* is the reflective historic part, where you as a Spectator witness several appropriated images of nineteenth- and twentieth-century tableaux. Placed on the floor, this work can be seen only from above, with the Spectator looking downward. The photographs summon a variety of situations in the world, as a contemporary *Family of Man*. The dialectics may come into being because these old and new pictures hold glimpses of experience, what Roland Barthes would characterize as the *punctum* in a photograph, what moves you, as opposed to the more rational *studium*. Vulnerability exists in the selection of pictures, detached from the *eidos* of the situation.

Common to the portrait in *Vertical Memory* and the images in *Horizontal Memory* is that all of the photographs have to some extent been computer manipulated. A distance has been inserted, a difference, that may or may not make the Spectator doubt the degree of fiction and reality. The truth of photography is partially suspended. The composition of *Horizontal Memory* pretends to constitute reality.

Yoko Ono's work might at first seem to be a continuation of postmodernism, which has already taught us about the virtual insignificance of the real world. It has taught us how, with its blurred aesthetics, everything is possible in this new world of the arts. It has taught us that there is no single way of looking at contemporary art. Thus, a number of artists seem to work according to the following line of thinking: It does not matter whether something is real or not, so long as the image is present. This imaginary image has manifested itself within staged photography.

Whereas the defined staged photography is often based on the spectacular, or even cunning, Yoko Ono's approach to photography is far more discrete, or possibly more focused on the process. The pictures distance themselves—despite their qualitative character—from the actual finished piece. It is rather a physical and mental discipline, as it is expressed in Zen—*Conceptual Photography* through the "Zen camera of the mind," as Edward Putzar once expressed it:

> Zen-seeing is in effect a special relationship between the subject and the object; it is a constant realization of the fundamental nature of things, their suchness. It is perception based on the experience of satori, that is, with the experience of the non-Self. It is seeing with the original, unconditioned eye. (*Aperture* 17, no. 2, 1973)

The project *Conceptual Photography* is much deeper and far more complex than a commentary on the use of images. Ono seems to establish this mental practice for not just photography, but the act of looking and experiencing. A truly imaginary imagery. In *Position Piece*, dated summer 1963, she says:

> Position Piece
>
> Take one of the yoga positions
> and see the photo that you like
> for two days.
> Your position can be at any
> distance or direction from the photo.
> Destroy the photo after two days.
>
> 1963 summer y.o.

Ono's *Instructions for Photographs* series releases itself from photography's sacred "decisive moment." The artist disengages herself from the decisive moment as *Conceptual Photography*, as its practice removes itself from the objectification of images, and simultaneously removes photography from its existential part.

Finally, the exhibition also featured *Portrait of Nora*, a digitally manipulated (self-)portrait (pl. 71). The

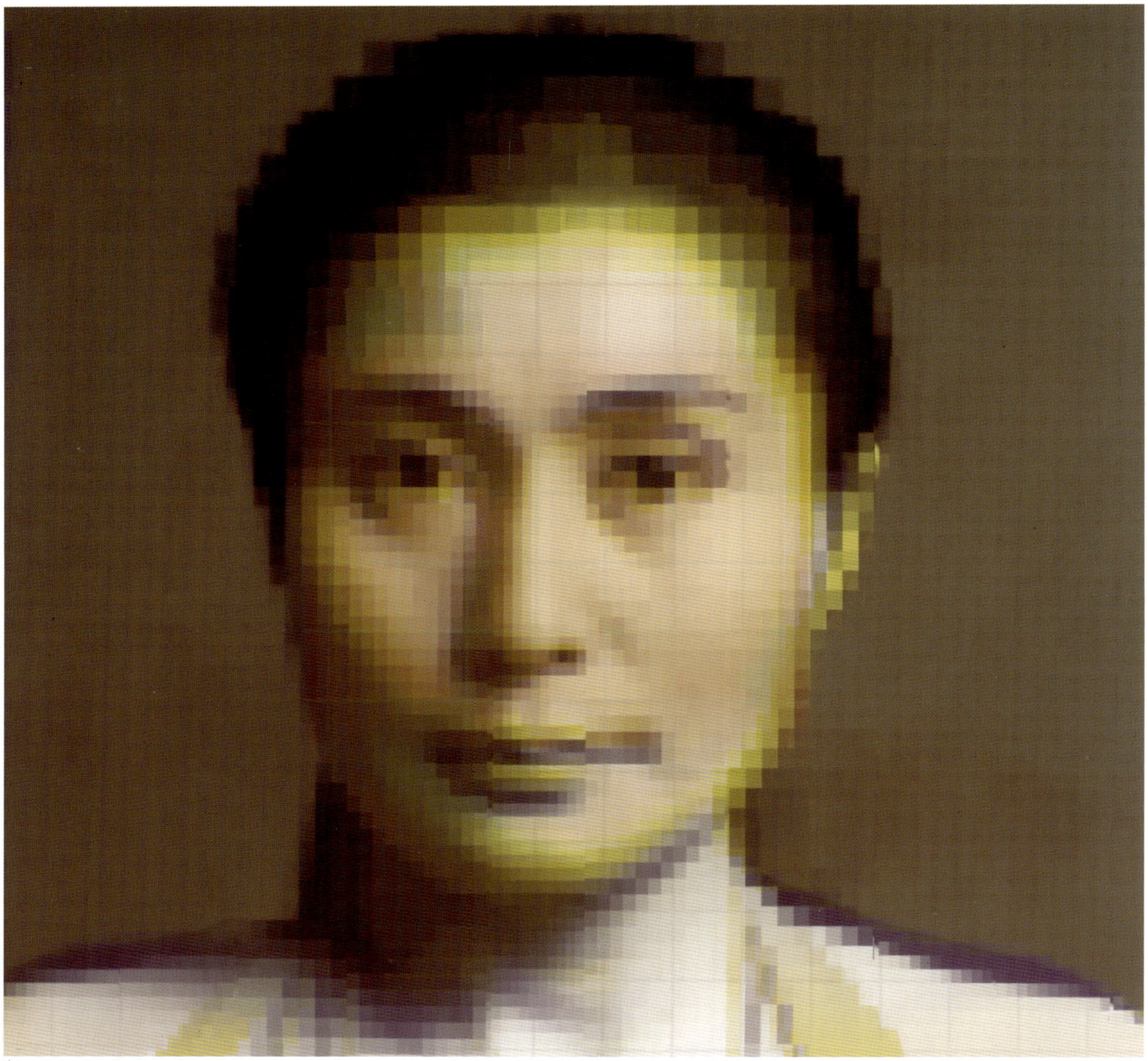

PLATE 71
PORTRAIT OF NORA,
1992. DIGITALLY MANIPULATED PHOTOGRAPH

reference is to the well-known liberated woman in Henrik Ibsen's *A Doll's House*. Nowadays she doesn't go out the door (leaving the man behind) but vanishes in bits and pieces in the electronic sign system. The portrait, as well as our history, is not trustworthy anymore; the world seems more or less manipulated, far away from our fathers' dreams and our mothers' memories. Here in the year 2000, memory in general might not be equivalent to photography as a medium. What we experience, what we see, hear, and feel seem to be a little distorted, a little distant from "reality."

(Translated from the Danish by Anders Kjærgaard)

Lars Schwander is director of Fotografisk Center, Copenhagen.

Seduction of the Gaze and Life Experience in the Work of Yoko Ono

PABLO J. RICO

In recent years, Yoko Ono has successfully developed new expressive and communicative strategies in her work, expanding the aesthetic palette of her artistic personality as she pushes the limits of her power to visually and emotionally seduce. In many instances, her new creations are a continuation of her most significant works and themes of the 1960s, although the staging and the writing are more compelling, increasing the power of the work to attract the viewers' gaze and provoke the deepest of reflections. In other instances, she works with new ideas and concerns born in the 1990s, which have the same passionate, evocative power. Ono has carved out one of the most fascinating creative territories to be found at the end of the century. Her conceptual intuition and aesthetic invention are already among the main referents of the art of the nascent century.

What are Yoko Ono's fundamental ideas? What are the existential concerns that anchor her answers to some of life's most disturbing questions? What instructions...for whose life? What words are keys to the imagination? In many works created by the artist in recent years we can find condensed this basic conceptual and experiential framework through which she invites us to develop deeper and wider levels of consciousness, to feel the world more than describing or thinking about it. I see among the ideas in Ono's work those of quiet remembrance; hopeful desire; the persistent, natural flow of things, free from anxiety; serene voyage and change; engaging life with trust; the equilibrium of our emotional balance; the surprises in the labyrinth of life; and the intransigence toward fanaticism, physical violence, and war.

It is interesting to note that, throughout her career, in many exhibitions, Yoko Ono has expressed all of these ethical commitments and ideas so important to her, insistently, pointedly, and with a compelling austerity that eschews a facile recourse to new technologies and spectacular packaging. Nature and the basic elements of our immediate environment have been her preferred materials. *En Trance—Ex It*, her concurrent exhibition in the Spanish cities of Valen-

PLATE 72A
CLEANING PIECE (RIVERBED), 1996/1997.
INSTALLATION VIEW,
THE ISRAEL MUSEUM,
JERUSALEM, 2000

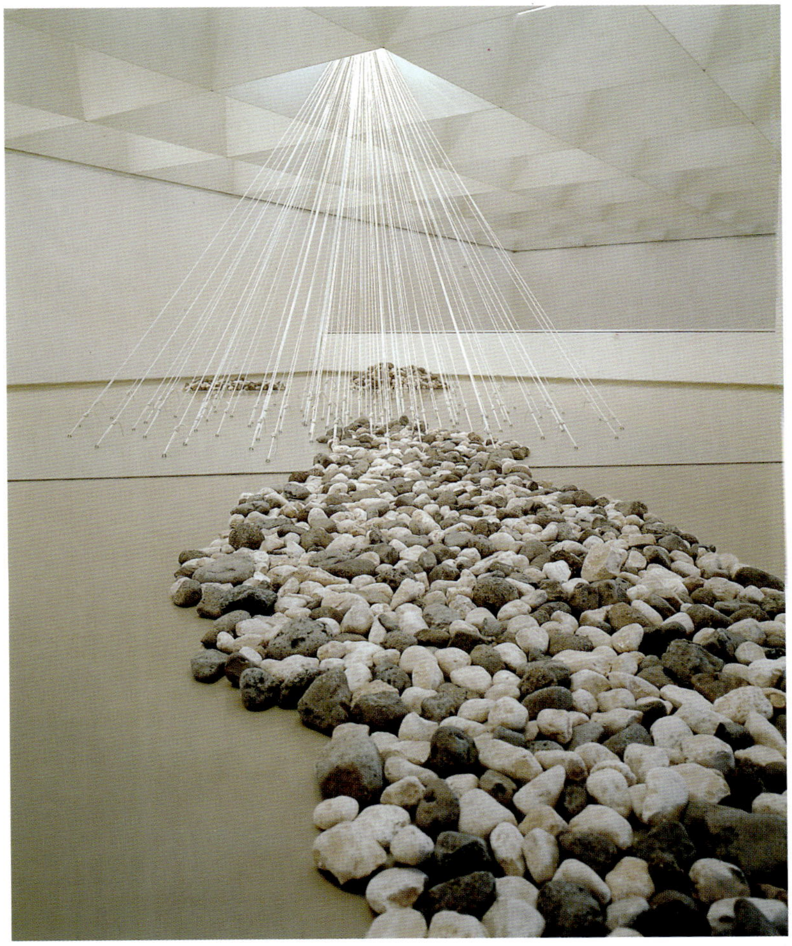

PLATE 72B
CLEANING PIECE, 1996.
INSTALLATION VIEW,
LONJA DEL PESCADO,
ALICANTE, 1997

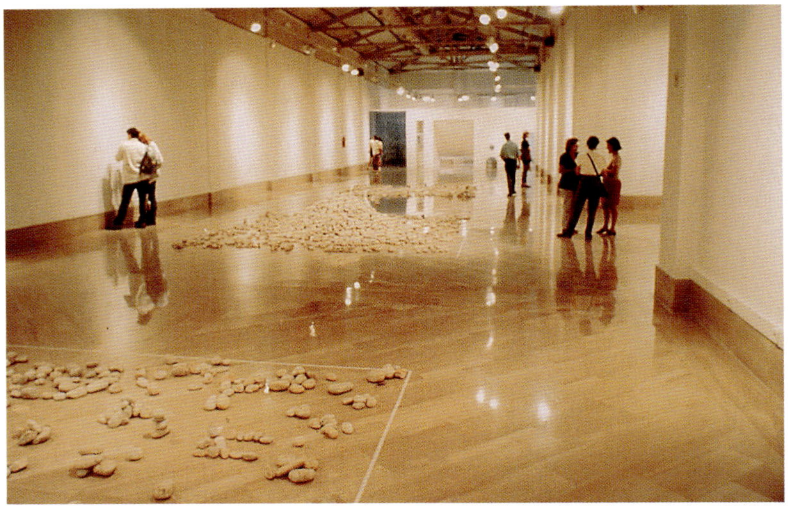

cia and Alicante, is one of the most representative instances of her recent trajectory. I would like to discuss below three of the works in that exhibition, for which I acted as co-curator.

While the earliest origins of *Cleaning Piece (Riverbed)* (pls. 72a–b) can be traced back to the 1960s, its most successful incarnation occurred in recent years. The environment created by this piece is successful in making us remember and explore our most private memories. A large expanse of stone is installed on the gallery floor. Sometimes it is shaped like a mountain; other times, as in the most recent versions, it looks like a riverbed, snaking into the distance, pebbles and stones rounded and washed by the waters of an ever-familiar, ever-present river. Our lives are like rivers; our memories are like these stones that sleep in the riverbed of life, which flows sometimes quietly, sometimes passionately.

Yoko Ono invites us to pause and contemplate this volume of stones, this trajectory of memories that are the best evidence of our existence. We are asked to recognize our past states of sadness and joy, remembered emotions, in the stones before us: to pick up some of the stones, identify them with a particular memory, and place them in small adjacent spaces—"the happiness space," "the sadness space"—where they will lose their status as existential fetishes and their dense melancholy. Thus washed by life itself, with the edge of burdensome melancholy smoothed away, these small river stones become splendid natural objects for contemplation, meditation, and aesthetic pleasure. Yoko Ono asks us, finally, to admire and compare their beauties.

Wish Tree is a splendid "machine" of and for desiring (pl. 73). That is the generic title of a series of works created by Ono in the 1990s using actual trees as the primary element and pillar of her conceptual project. The artist has referred often to her work as a way to create desire: "All my works are a form of wishing. Keep wishing while you participate." She has also often recounted how, as a child in Japan, she used to write her wishes on small pieces of paper that she would then tie to the branches of flowering trees in the courtyard of the temple.

Ono's "wish trees" are always old trees, with long lives and deep roots and, if possible, flowers and fruits that sweeten the air with their fragrance. For her exhibition in Spain, she chose a magnificent pomegranate tree, as evocative of the poetry and iconography of the Far East as of that of the West: the fruit of desire, the expression of divine eternity.

Yoko Ono asks that we, the audience, participate in this *Wish Tree* by desiring and wanting to desire, identifying our desires and daring to write them down on thin pieces of paper. We trust that they will come true if we tie them to the branches of the tree, thus letting our hope vibrate and flutter its wings (the "butterfly" effect) as these new white leaves and flowers slowly cover the tree of our desire. What is the smell of desire?

The last work that I will discuss here is *Ex It* (pls. 74a–b), a moving installation created by Ono for Valencia (she executed later versions for exhibitions in Brazil and Israel). This environment consists of one hundred simple, unadorned wooden coffins, sixty for men, thirty for women, and ten for children. The artist's instructions call for coarse, common coffins, such as those lined up on a field devastated by a catastrophe, a battle, a massacre. A tree grows out of an opening on each where normally one could see the face of the deceased. This extraordinary field of coffins moves and disturbs the audience, cutting across ideologies and religions. It is an inner forest sprouting in silence from silence itself in an atmosphere of sadness and desolation.

Movingly and directly, Yoko Ono reflects here on the human condition and the fragility of existence, on the uncertainty of regaining hope after the drama of death, and on the reclamation of anonymity. The title of the work seems to allude to the exit from life or to the abandonment of one's being, to losing one's proper name or the capacity to name things. Ono's wordplay signifies someone or something that has ceased to be who or what it was. A name? Someone who had the gift of calling things by their name? Words often display the spectacle of their own catastrophe, of a sacrifice from which new meanings and etymologies will emerge. Sometimes, words are broken or interrupted like human lives.

However, even though at first glance it may seem that this forest of trees can only evoke pain and sad-

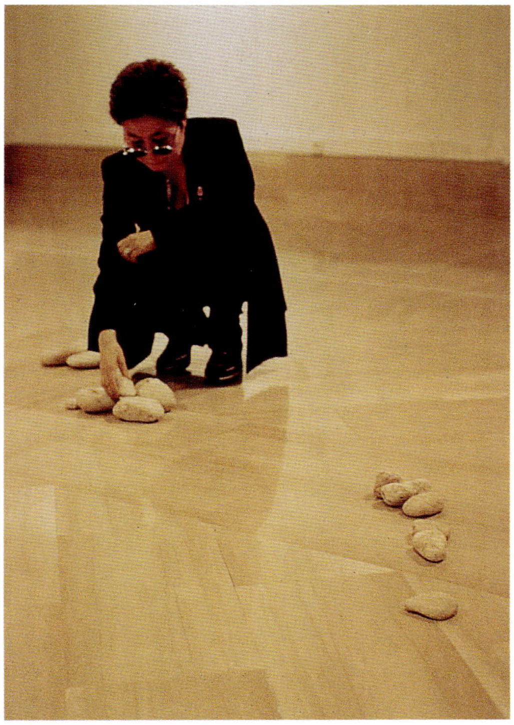

PLATE 72C (LEFT)
ONO PERFORMING
CLEANING PIECE,
LONJA DEL PESCADO,
ALICANTE, 1997

PLATE 73 (RIGHT)
WISH TREE, 1996.
INSTALLATION VIEW,
LONJA DEL PESCADO,
ALICANTE, 1997

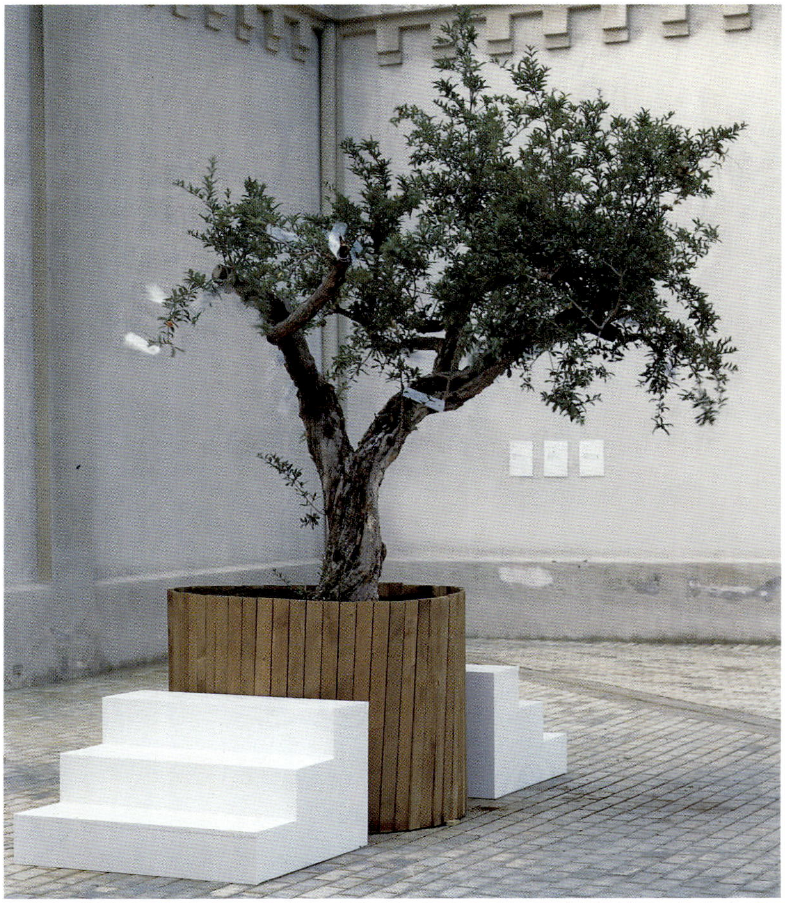

ness, I think that its chief message is a very different one. We also find hope in this environment, life and nature renewing themselves and offering us the possibility of penetrating the mystery of life and death, so close, with one following the other, that only a threshold of light separates them. Ono's acoustic environment reinforces this sensation with a strange background noise of whispers in which the sounds of birds, human voices, and the rustling of leaves are mingled in a magnificent sonata to dawn. Nature wakes up and renews itself. These seem to be the sounds of invisible dialogues, of distant echoes resonating inside the empty chamber of our memory as they move across it from the beginning of time.

Cleaning Piece, *Wish Tree*, *Ex It*: three works in which Yoko Ono fascinates and seduces us with the greatest ease, naturally, without artifice or distortion.

To seduce is to attract the gaze of the other, numbed by routine, by the undifferentiated generality of the conventional and the quotidian. To seduce is to surprise, to attract and possess the attention of the other without in fact either attracting or possessing. Seduction multiplies the wonders and clarity of truth, affects us almost effortlessly, without violence. The hypnotic light of the seducer of the gaze seems like an occult power, some kind of astral dimension flowing through systems that are different from the merely physical, surprising the spectators, inducing them to participate more actively in the pleasure of self-discovery and self-recognition in this new and unknown vision of the world whose delights they are experiencing.

Yoko Ono is a woman, an artist, luckily gifted with that rare light that commands attention just by offering itself. All artists know that their survival, their existential proof, depends almost exclusively on that unfathomable capacity to force the anonymous viewers tenderly glancing at their works to feel and imagine that they have in them everything they desire. I think that this is the essential condition of art and artists, their reason for being: to command attention and make people feel intensely human sensations. Those who maintained that "art is the work produced" or "art is the idea" were wrong: they were blinded and dazzled by the glitter of artifacts and fantasies. At the end of this century of living dangerously, I affirm with total conviction that "art is artists" and that nothing that is called art exists outside of them, without their will. I saw it in the eyes of Yoko Ono, at dusk, on a Mediterranean island.

(Translated from the Spanish by Ana Maria Simo)

Pablo J. Rico, an independent curator based in Mallorca, was the director of Fundació Joan Miró a Mallorca.

PLATE 74A
EX IT, 1997.
PREPARATORY DRAWING

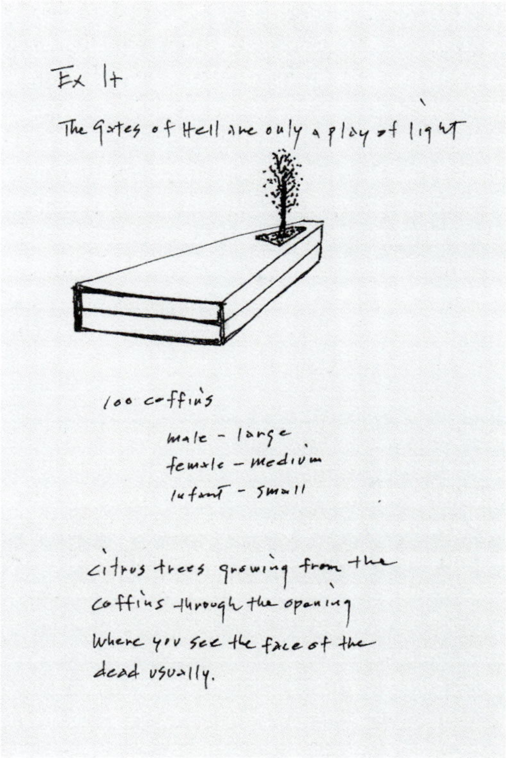

PLATE 74B
EX IT, 1997.
INSTALLATION VIEW,
L'ALMODÍ, VALENCIA,
1997

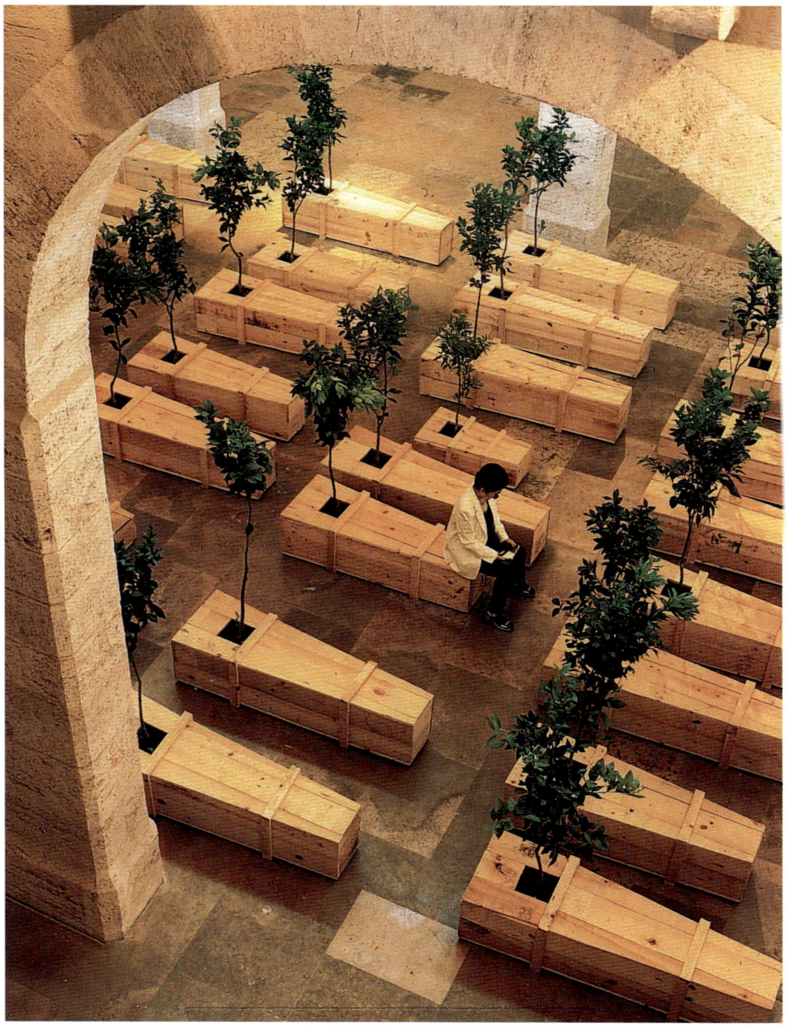

1 MESSAGE IS THE MEDIUM Y.O. '69

WAR IS OVER Y.O. '69

Published in *This Is Not Here*, exh. cat. (Syracuse: Everson Museum of Art, 1971)

Anthology: Writings by Yoko Ono

COMPILED BY JON HENDRICKS

INTRODUCTION

Yoko Ono's writings take a number of forms—some are on or about, others are the things themselves. Some explain, some ask questions of us. Frequently her writings lead us here and there, to a better understanding of ourselves and the world about us. Her writings can take the shape of advocacy—"Take off your pants before you fight, make that the rule" (1966) and *Message Is the Medium* (1969), flipping McLuhan's rally cry, and *War Is Over! if you want it* (1969), a powerful vehicle for direct change of attitude still in use thirty years after it was first declared.

Sometimes Ono is content to let a single verb function as the entire writing.

> *Fly* (1963)
> *Breathe* (1966)
> *Imagine* (1966)
> *Remember* (1999)
> *Touch* (1963)

Economy and minimalism become deep paths in the mind, guides, tools, enlighteners, metaphors for living, useful equipment.

> *Open Windows* (1997)
> *Open Window* (1999)

These two recent writings compel us to consider acting on the idea, and at the same time offer a statement of fact. They are, they can be. It is, it should be done.

Have You Seen the Horizon Lately? (1967) questions where we are and offers an opportunity of vision.

Ono can intentionally choose words that mean quite different things simultaneously. Within "The Word of a Fabricator" (1962), "The Word" is a message—it is also an affidavit, a declaration of truth. "A Fabricator" is a constructor, a maker. "A Fabricator" is also a liar, someone who fabricates the truth, so the title can read "the message of one who makes things," an advertisement; "the message of a not truthful person," a confession; "the true statement of an untruthful person," a dichotomy; or "the true statement of one who makes things," a guarantee. Each is possible, and when one explores the text that follows, one finds that all apply, and then some, for it is a manifesto of conceptualism, written to be published at the same time as her first exhibition of *Instructions for Paintings*, at Sōgetsu Art Center, Tokyo, May 1962.

Yoko Ono started writing at a young age. These early stories and journals acted as a witness to her thoughts and imagination. In this book we are only considering her art, so the works selected here all have an art bent—other writings can be considered another time. However, art encompasses a vast area of Ono's work: there is fertile soil to till. The earliest pieces selected date from 1950 and 1952: one architectural piece from a compilation titled "The Soundless Music" and two stories from "Seven Little Stories." The concepts in "A floating city" (1950) reemerge fifteen years later in expanded form in *Pieces Dedicated to George Maciunas, the Phantom Architect* (1965). Maciunas, a close friend of Ono's and the founder of the Fluxus movement, met her only in the winter of 1960–61 at the time of the Chambers Street loft concert events that she organized with La Monte Young. So with these pieces Ono incorporated early 1950s works into an expanded 1965 version, then in a revised form expanded them even further. The texts serve both as works in themselves and ideas for participatory sculptural works which followed. In 1969–70 Maciunas constructed a labyrinth of Ono's in the *John and Yoko Fluxfest* in New York. In her solo exhibition at the Everson Museum in Syrcuse the following October, Ono exhibited *AMAZE*, a transparent structure with a chamber in the center containing a toilet and see-through mirrored Plexiglas walls (no. 26). In 1991 she realized *En-Trance*, a gentle architectural structure which serves as a life metaphor and contains a slide and a tight mirrored corridor, among other elements.

In 1966 for *The Stone*, Ono wrote *Biography* and *Statement*, life experiences made into simple poetic metaphors. *Statement* is especially poignant: it relates to her 1960 poem, "the earth was covered," *Painting until It Becomes Marble*, and *Cut Piece* (no. 30) with its element of violation and prying, the feeling that others are continually trying to lay bare her self and then cut deeper into her soul. The films *Rape* (1969; no. 45), *Fly* (1970; no. 46), and the visual/verbal work *Vertical Memory* (1997; pl. 69) are works which also hold strong elements of violation—of the feeling of being used. They function as strong feminist statements, yet they are more complex. They are the thoughts of a radical, of someone who refused to conform to the dictates of the norm, be it class, nation, gender, religion, artistic form, or literary convention: a focused determination to do it her way. In *Biography*, sky becomes a metaphor for freedom, seaweeds have sexual connotations, and "snails, clouds, garbage cans, etc." seem to refer to male forms, while "schools" are the life experiences that we go through.

> *Old yellow notebook scribblings* translated Saturday September 25, 1999.
>
> The letter from my lover coming from overseas metamorphosed into a notice from a school to my sister. The only way I can redeem this tragic situation is to tear the notice up into pieces and rearrange the words to make it a poem.
>
> The above little scribbling of mine found recently in my old yellowed notebook under the pile of papers in the basement, expresses what I do in life and in my work. It is the essence of my work. Y. O.

2 *On Insound,* 1964

<u>On insound</u>
IN: like really in-within-inner-non-un-insane-crazed...
Insound is a practice rather than music.
Most of the insound pieces are spread by word of mouth.
The following is one of the insound pieces.

Stay in a room for a month.
Do not speak.
Do not see.
Whisper at the end of the month.

A word-of-mouth piece, a strip-tease piece and an audience piece will be performed in this concert.

Published in *Grapefruit* (Tokyo: Wunternaum Press, 1964); reprinted in program for *Contemporary American Avant-Garde Music Concert*, Yamaichi Hall, Kyoto, 20 July 1964

3 From *The Soundless Music,* 1950

"A floating city"

A floating city
The second level world
Upstairs on the clouds
Mountains and rain roaring underneath
Like Venice, we have to commute by
boat through air currents to visit
each other's floating houses.
Cloud gardens to watch all day.

Originally written in Japanese. Translation by Yoko Ono, published in *Grapefruit* (New York: Simon and Schuster, 1971); reprinted in *Yoko Ono: Ávores do Desejo Para o Brasil/Wish Trees for Brazil*, exh. cat. (Brasília: Teatro Nacional Claudio Santoro e Panteão de Pátria and Salvador: Museu de Arte Moderna da Bahia, 1998)

4 From *Poems by Yoko Ono,* 1960

"a greenfilled morning"

a greenfilled morning
women walked around with
empty baby carriages

"the earth was covered with clouds"

the earth was covered with clouds.
the breast of the dead woman was stabbed with thick nails.

the sound of the triton was lost.
the breast of the dead woman
was crammed with thick nails.

swarms of dogs extended the earth.
all lying, stretching, and sniffing
the smell of nails
at times.
some ruminating the flowers
and some
barking, barking, barking to
the core of sky.

the earth dozed to the placid wind.
the breast of the dead woman
was a well drained wound.

First and third of four poems. Published in "Program" for Department of Graphic Arts and Illustration, Pratt Institute, Brooklyn, New York, 23 March 1960. "the earth was covered with clouds" also published in "Two Poems" in *Campus* (Sarah Lawrence College), 25 April 1956

5 *A Grapefruit in the World of Park,* 1961

–1–

dark.

where is this?

this is the park

(but I smell metal in the air.
no, it's the clovers.
are they bleeding?
is this a room?
no, it's the sunset.

would you like to speak to the dead?

oh, no I only come here to peel the grapefruit.

is it too cold?

it's too warm, the sky's too high...people are turning
up their stomachs contentedly to the sky. your voice
sounds unusually small in the afternoon air. your minds
fly away between the clouds, and the dropping dews on the
cheeks is like the kisses of your lovers.

flush toilet

–2–

don't peel it.

is he the one who killed you?

everything seems so right in the park.

yes, doesn't it.

even the grapefruit.

oh, no, not the grapefruit.

yes, even the grapefruit.

do you want to peel it?

why don't you throw it away, it's wrinkled.

(it's wrinkled!)

it's wreeeeeeeeeekled......

let's count the hairs of the dead child
let's count the hairs of the dead child

room light

–3–

do you like clams?

I like clams, only it's hard to peel them though.

you peel clams?

oh, yes, you do. It's good for you they say.

I didn't know that. I must try that sometimes.

now, don't hurt your fingers.

no, I won't........

they look so juicy...now let's try

how is it?

I prefer metracal to clams, though, at least it's something different.
I should say.

–4–

dinner ready!

(did you hear that?)

(yes!)

(how ghastly!)

(sometimes it's too much isn't it?)

(yes, it's just too much for me)

let's count the hairs of the dead child
let's count the hairs of the dead child

nine.

baby carriage

–5–

I have to squeeze lemons.

yes, and we must live, we must do something, something constructive
I guess.

let's not leave the room let's stay. let's live longer so we can
drink tea together

that will be nice. but that's a dream.

six.

TWO (emphasize)

–6–

twenty-one

joe, joe, is that your tie flying in the sky?

oh, no, it's the lark isn't it?

but larks don't fly. (It's zipped into the sky)

who's Joe?

oh, I've never met him. but I know that he has long fingers.

long nails too?

no, just long fingers. and he can squeeze lemons very well.

I heard his voice once like fragments of broken mirror. it's
that we can't keep voices like we keep mushrooms.

–7–

one.

it's getting dark. the flowers are still white though.

(or are they waste papers?)

(is this the park?..........

(   )

(   )

look, that cloud is moving it was between those trees before, see?

cabbage.

–8–

one day his bones touched mine, I was happy.

you like bones?

yes, they make you feel comfortable, I guess.

(wipe your fingers on the grass.
it's sticky.
the lollipops are getting sandy.)

take off sweater.

–9–

do you like my baby carriages?

oh, it's simply wonderful! the curve, the shining wheels,
everything is just right. (is it empty!)

I shine it every day with vinegar, and take off the smell with
perfumes.

Yoko back.

–10–

did you know that I had to get this food all for ten dollars? what can you get with ten dollars for this many? i wanted to make it nicer, you know....not grapefruits and clams, anyway, but what can you do?....well, it makes you feel good to do something for others, I'm not complaining of being in charge of these things, but....are you listening? (giggle) you look so pale.....I guess it's this light or are you dead?

eighteen.

eighteennnnnnnn

ei...

Yoko wear sweater

chair upside down

hat bit come in

–11–

it's closing

(oh, it's closing.)

are you bleeding?

let's go. (let's not go.)

is it too wrinkled? (stop peeling!)

peas porridge hot

stop that. we're going now!

some like it hot—

does it still flush?

oh yes..yes.....I must remember that. it's so hard to keep track of things you know.

they all go.

are you going, mommy?

ook how you are perspiring. you'll catch cold, pussy. hurry and put on your sweater.

it's hot mommy, can't I have something to drink?

they're all gone, honey, now put on your jacket, too, it's getting chilly.

closing!

hat light out

–12–

three.

is the park gone? did it get tired of us?

the grapefruit is still shining on the table. the seeds, the pieces of hard skin.

I'm tired. do you have a lemonade?

is that your hair lying on the floor? or is that the grass? it's not isn't it? does it ever dry?

the room is filled with light. do you feel it?

the room is full of hairs.

the wind has stolen my hay.

(could we ever get out?)

where's my lemonade? don't I get a lemonade?

are you dead?

oh, no thank you. I only came here to peel you.

electronic metro—some tin and off

light out half

after electronic metronome

Unpublished typescript, possibly final performance script. Variation published in *Yoko Ono: To See the Skies*, exh. cat. (Milan: Mazotta, 1990)

6 *AOS, the opera,* 1961

AOS, the opera

The first scene: The environment should be completely dark. Any number of performers may have their own newspapers of any date, and of any language. The performer should read the newspapers by putting a match on, he should only read from the newspaper while his match is lit. The piece will end when all the performers finish reading their newspapers. The performer should start reading from whatever line that comes into his view. You may discontinue reading the newspaper when your match supply is out or you may go near another's light and try to read. The whole scene should be very quiet. Each one does not have to carry his own supply of matches, they can take matches from others, some may use flashlights.

The second scene: The environment should be completely dark. Bind any number of performers tightly with strings, from the head to the toe, so that it is impossible for them to move, two dancers should carry the performers one by one on the stage and pile them up, they may stop and rest and breathe whenever they wish to, the piled up performers should try their best to move around as much as possible and as quick as possible, without making any noise. The scene will end when all the performers are piled up on the stage. The performers may include the following movements in their movements if possible: pulling off other performers' clothing or shoes, flashing a light (flashlight) to see other performers, lighting a match to burn their skin, etc. The dancers may lie down and rest if they wish to, or light a cigarette, or eat, or read in order to rest during the labor (drink or read also).

The third scene: A tape of the performance of the first and the second scene, plus any number of tapes of any kind—may be voice of animals or other living things—should be all (should be all in voice) together. The scene will end when the first scene, second scene tape is over, though it may be played in any speed. The environment should be completely lighted.

The fourth scene: The environment should be completely dark. Several performers, not less than two, should have a discussion quietly, the contents of the discussion can be any one subject, the language they use can be any language or signal in voice, or otherwise. Examples of the possible subject: cooking, grammatical conjugation, mathematical or semantical problems, bird talk, etc. Two performers preferred and it should be extremely quiet. The performers may be seated in any posture, or position, they do not have to face each other, the posture or the position that they have selected should be unchanged until the end. The scene will end when the discussion is exhausted. The scene should have moving scenery as follows: Several dancers should be behind a large canvas put across the stage, they may use scissors, or other instruments to cut out holes on any place of the canvas and stick portions of their body, sticks, large poles, flashlights, matches, etc. Cigarettes, incense can be used also, the whole thing should be very quiet. A large bag which includes all the performers can be used also in place of the canvas.

The fifth scene: The environment should be completely dark. One of the performers should go on shouting until exhausted, the performer may use any violence against himself during the performance such as cutting hairs, banging head on the wall drinking liquor, drugs, etc.

Fin

Notes in connection with the Opera

The scenes can be played consecutively at one concert or it can be played separately, or the time can be set so that the whole Opera can be played by natural light. For an example, performing the scenes requiring darkness after dark, or performing the scenes requiring lightness after dawn and have an intermission until the next darkness.

Note when the performers are bound together, they can be bound together with toilet bowls, beer cans, typewriters, chairs, and ladders

Unpublished typed performance script. "Notes" typed on back of page one

7 ***Dear George...***, ca. June 1964

Dear George:

Most of my pieces are meant to be spread by word of mouth, therefore, do not have scores. This means is very important since the gradual change which occures in the piece by word spreading is also part of the piece. Paik suggested that I send you a piece he likes which is one of the word spreading pieces. I have thought over quite a bit about it, since he was right to suggest the piece because it is also one of the very few pieces that is easy to perform. But I think I will not change my mind about maintaining the piece as a word-spread piece.......*

*word-spread pieces are not included in this text

Published in *Grapefruit* (Tokyo: Wunternaum Press, 1964)

8 *Strip Tease Show,* early spring 1966

STRIP TEASE SHOW

by

YOKO ONO

The following script consists of a series of EVENTS that have been performed in Kyoto 1964, Tokyo 1964, Carnegie Hall 1965, and Wesleyan University 1966. The script is in two parts—the first of which are events that take place outside of the concert situation, and the second of which are events that constitute the actual performance, or, concert events. The first series of events is now being arranged into a gallery show to take place in New York this spring.

EVENTS OUTSIDE THE HALL

SALE OF THE TAPE OF THE SOUND OF SNOW FALLING AT DAWN

The tape, actually an unused recording tape in a box with the above title, will be sold by a performer to the audience priced accordingly by the length of tape they wish to purchase.

EXHIBITION OF IN-STRUCTURE

IN-STRUCTURE consists of works by Yoko Ono which are actually instructions for works of art.* Some of the IN-STRUCTURE may be instructions that have been completed or partially completed by other artists who have decided to follow the instructions. At present the following IN-STRUCTURES have been completed or are in process by the following artists: "Painting to See the Skies," "Blood Painting," "Eternal Time," "Sky Machine," "Telephone Piece," "Circle Event," "Painting to Hammer a Nail," "Self Portrait," and "Shadow Painting"—Geoffery Hendricks, Claes Oldenburg, Anthony Cox, Jeff Perkins, Isamu Noguchi, Minoru Niizuma, Mark di Suvero, John Cage and David Tudor. Some IN-STRUCTURES will actually be done at the time of exhibition.

EVENTS FOR PERFORMANCE IN THE CONCERT HALL OR AUDITORIUM

WHISPER

The word whisper printed in the center of single 8 x 10 card is passed around the audience

BAG PIECE

After the curtain has gone up (or — average time: 20'

if there is no curtain, at a designated time after the announcer announced the piece) two performers walk onto the stage.

Performers may be two males, two females, or a mixed couple.

Performers carry a bag large enough for both to get inside of.

Bag made of non-transparent material. Both performers get inside of bag.

Both remove all clothing while inside of bag.

Both put all clothing back on.

They come out of bag.

They exit with bag from stage.

TAPE PIECE

The voices of a comic act telling dirty jokes is sounded over the loudspeaker. — average time: 30'

The jokes may be in any language.

One, two or several people may tell the jokes.

In the case of many people this may be done simultaneously.

85 STRIP TEASE FOR THREE

86 First version for curtain: average time: 5'

87 Curtain rises to show three
88 chairs placed on stage.

89 Curtain descends.

90 Second version for no curtain: average time: 15'

91 Single performer places three
92 chairs on stage one at a time.
93 Performer removes chairs one at
94 a time.

95 FLY

96 The word FLY printed in the center
97 of a single 8 x 10 card is passed
98 around the audience

99 CUT PIECE

100 First version for single performer: average time: 30'

101 Performer sits on stage with pair
102 of scissors placed in front of him.

103 It is announced that members of the
104 audience may come on stage—one at
105 a time—to cut a small piece of the
106 performer's clothing to take with them.

107 Performer remains motionless
108 throughout the piece.

109 Piece ends at the performer's
110 option.

111 Second version for audience:

112 It is announced that members
113 of the audience may cut each other's
114 clothing.

115 The audience may cut as long
116 as they want.

117 **__________ PIECE FROM AOS

118 Theatre or auditorium is without average time: 20'
119 light.

120 It is announced that members of
121 audience must find their own means
122 of light for the ".....search...."

123 It is announced that a snake, butterfly,
124 rabbit, grapefruit or a body, or any
125 thing the announcer thought he wished
126 to see on the day of production, has
127 been released or hidden in the audience
128 and the audience must find it.

129 Two performers who have been tightly
130 bound together with rope then proceed
131 from one wing or side of stage to
132 the other wing or side and back as
133 quickly as possible and without
134 making any audible sound.

135 The two performers must be tightly
136 bound together, back to back, or
137 front to front, or side to side, or
138 with one performer upside down, or
139 in any position in which they may
140 be tightly bound together. Attached
141 to their bounds must be tin cans,
142 bottles or any objects that would
143 make noise upon movement.

144 CLOCK PIECE

145 Alarm clock is placed on stage and
146 set to ring at an undisclosed time.***

147 It is announced that the piece will
148 be finished when the alarm clock
149 rings.

----END------

*See THE WORKS OF YOKO ONO "Grapefruit," which are instructions for music, painting, event, object and poetry and "Saleslist 1965"

**The title of the piece is to be that word which the announcer has chosen to say has been released or hidden. Whatever it is, it should not actually be released or hidden, but only announced to that effect.

***In the performance at Sogetsu Kaikan, Tokyo, an alarm clock was used on which the face and hands had been removed so that it was impossible to know what time the clock had been set to.

ALTERNATE PIECES WHICH MAY BE USED IN THIS SHOW:

<u>RUBBING PIECE</u>

First version for one or many performers:

One, two, or many performers are instructed to rub themselves—or each other.

The piece ends when the performer(s) wish to stop.

Second version for audience:

It is announced to the members of the audience that they may rub each other.

The audience should rub as long as they want.

<u>TOUCH PIECE</u>

First & second versions exactly the same as Rubbing Piece only the word Touch is substituted for the word Rub.

<u>BREATHING PIECE</u>

First version for one or many performers:

One, or a number of performers sit on the stage.

It is announced that the members of the audience may come up on to the stage and listen to the body functions of the performer(s).

The piece ends when the performer(s) decide that it should end.

It is announced that the members of the audience may listen to each other's body functions.

The audience should listen as long as they want.

<u>WALL PIECE</u>*

First version for one or many performers:

One or a number of performers repeatedly knock his or their head(s) against the wall(s) on the stage or in the theatre or auditorium or place of performance.

The piece ends when the performers decide that it should end.

Second version for audience:

It is announced that the members of the audience may knock their heads against the wall(s) of the auditorium or theatre or audience area.

The audience should continue as long as they want.

*Performed at Wesleyan University in Place of <u>CLOCK PIECE</u>.

Self-published in New York, 1966

9 *9 Concert Pieces for John Cage,* December 15, 1966

To John
Since my pieces are meant to be spread by word-of-mouth, most pieces only have titles or very short instructions. Therefore, passing words as to how they were performed previously has become a habit.

My music is performed only to induce a situation in which people can listen to their own mind music. Therefore, maximus silence is required in presenting the pieces.
Also, every performance should be considered a rehearsal and unfinished.

There are 13 pieces here. Please select the 9 you like.

9 is a spiritual number which has a meaning of being unfinished.

Yoko Ono

Sweep Piece

Sweep.

by Yoko Ono

This was first performed 1962 in Tokyo, Sogetsu Art Center by Mizuno as simultaneous performance during 4 hour concert of works by Yoko Ono. It was performed again 1966 London, Jeanette Cochrane Theatre, as a solo piece by Yoko Ono, sweeping from one end of the stage to another.

Cut Piece

Cut.

by Yoko Ono

This piece was performed in Kyoto, Tokyo, New York and London. It is usually performed by Yoko Ono coming on the stage, and in a sitting form, placing a pair of scissors in front of her and asking the audience to come up on the stage, one by one, and cut a portion of her clothing (anywhere they like) and take it.

The performer, however, does not have to be a woman.

Beat Piece

Listen to a heart beat.

by Yoko Ono

This was performed first in 1965 at the East End Theatre, New York, by Nam June Paik, Shigeko Kubota, Tony Cox, Bill and MiMi Waring, and others.

Wind Piece

Make a way for the wind.

by Yoko Ono

This was first performed in 1962 Sogetsu Art Center, Tokyo, with a huge electric fan. In 1966, Wesleyan University, audience was asked to move their chairs a little and make one narrow aisle for the wind to pass through. No wind was created, with any special means.

Promise Piece

Promise.

by Yoko Ono

This was first performed in Jeanette Cochrane Theatre in London, 1966. Yoko Ono, as the last piece of the night, broke a vase on the stage and asked people to pick up the pieces and take them home, promising that they would all meet again in 10 years with the pieces and put the vase together again. Second performance was by Tony Cox in Tokyo calling Yoko Ono at the Plaza Hotel, New York, 1964, third performance by Yoko Ono in New York, 1962, calling Toshi Ichiyanagi in Tokyo, Kitazawa flat, and 4th performance by La Monte Young from Chinatown phone booth, New York, calling Yoko Ono at Chambers Street loft, 1961, all about future meetings. Call or write about future meetings or any other plans.

Whisper Piece

Whisper.

by Yoko Ono

This piece was originally called a telephone piece, and was the starting of the word-of-mouth pieces. It is usually performed by the performer whispering a word or a note into an audience's ear and asking to have it passed on until it reaches the last audience.

Hide piece

Hide.

1961 New York
by Yoko Ono

This piece was first performed in New York, Carnegie Recital Hall, 1961 by turning off the light completely in the concert hall including the stage, and Yoko Ono hiding in a large canvas sheet while La Monte Young and Joseph Byrd made soft voice accompaniment. In 1962, also in total darkness, in Tokyo, Sogetsu Art Center, Tone struggled to get out of the bag he was put in. (without accompaniment.) In London, Jeanetta Cochrane Theatre, 1966, Yoko Ono hid behind a 3 foot pole on the centre of the stage.

Breath Piece

Breathe.

by Yoko Ono

First performed at Wesleyan University, 1966. A large card with small lettering saying breathe, was passed three times among the audience.

Fly Piece

Fly.

by Yoko Ono

This piece was first performed in Tokyo, Naiqua Gallery, 1964, by Tony Cox, Nam June Paik, Shigeko Kubota, Akasegawa, Kosugi and others. Each person flying in his own way. It was performed again in London at Jeanette Cochrane Theatre, by the audience who came up on the stage and jumped off the different leveled ladders prepared for it.

QUESTION PIECE

QUESTION.

by Yoko Ono

This piece, which was first performed in Tokyo 1962, Sogetsu Art Center, by Tono Homei and Théo Lesoualch, was performed, at the time, in French. The piece is meant for a dialogue or a monologue of continuous questions answered only by questions. It was performed in English by Anthony Cox & Yoko Ono on Voice of America Radio Program, and in Japanese on NTV by 6 children who came to watch the TV show (both in 1964).

Disappearing Piece

Boil water.

by Yoko Ono

This piece was first performed in New York, 1966, by 5 people: Jeff Perkins, Pieter Vanderbeek, Tony Cox, George Maciunas and Yoko Ono for 1 audience. This was not deliberate but probably due to the subway strike in New York at that time. The water was boiled in a still, until it came out of the other side of the still, which took two hours. In London 1966, Mercury Theatre, the boiling of the water, the size of the pot (regular pot), etc. was announced on the stage. The actual boiling of the water was performed by Noa Latham at the Lathams' flat. The complete evaporation of the water was announced from the stage as the ending of the piece.

Clock Piece

by Yoko Ono

Usually a clock is placed on the center of the stage and audience is asked to wait until the alarm goes off.

Touch Piece

touch.

by Yoko Ono

This piece was performed many times in different places of Europe, United States and Japan. Usually, the lights are put off and the audience touch each other from 10 minutes to sometimes over two hours. In Nanzen temple in Kyoto, 1964, it lasted from evening till dawn. In London, people started to whistle the theme song of "Bridge on the River Kwai," which became a chorus.

Letter to John Cage is a holograph copy in the collection of the artist. *Hide Piece* reproduced from handwritten original in the artist's collection. Remaining texts are from vintage photocopies in the artist's collection of originals sent to Cage and now in John Cage *Notations* Collection, Northwestern University Music Library. "Beat Piece" published in *Notations* (New York: Something Else Press, 1969). Variation of thirteen texts published as "Record of 13 Concert Piece Performances" in *Grapefruit* (New York: Simon and Schuster, 1970)

10 *Fly—A Double Album,* 1971

FLY — A DOUBLE ALBUM

"Fly" is the last track of the record but it has been made the first just when my last album was finished and was out in the street. It was made in our bedroom in the Regency Hotel in New York on Xmas 1970 on a Nagra operated by John. I was thinking that I must make a soundtrack for my film FLY which was just near completion. Then John suggested maybe we should knock it off before the 10 o'clock news that night. It was that casual. We did it in one take, as most of my things are done.

I don't believe in doing things over. When I was painting one day it suddenly occurred to me that there is no line that you can go over. If you go over a line, the line that you went over is a totally new line.

When you use correctocopy to correct typing mistakes, you don't go over the wrong letters with the right letters. With the correctosheet you have to first go over the same line again with the exact wrong letters you typed before. Only then you can erase the mistakes and type over the correct letters. I'm always fascinated by this seemingly illogical fact.

It looks like there is some philosophical connection between these stories but I don't seem to be able to find the word for it now. But the point is I don't believe in doing things over, and unless it is a really bad take, I believe in the first take.

Another story: This is about a Japanese painter who was asked by his lord to do a painting. The lord waited a year and nothing has come of it. He sent a messenger to the painter. The painter came out and said, "Oh, o.k., just a minute" or something and did a one stroke painting while the messenger was waiting in the next room. The messenger returned with the painting and told the lord what had happened. The lord was very angry and arrested the painter. "You insulted me by making me wait for a whole year for the painting and on top of that, you used only a second to finish the painting. What was that!" something to that effect. The painter calmly replied, "Every day of the year that I was not painting, I was preparing for the painting, the painting may have been one stroke and it may have taken only a second to do it, but the whole year of pain and joy were in that stroke. The year was a necessary time."

I used to do things like fast five days before a concert to prepare my mind for the performance—because the performance was not my skill but the state of mind I was in at the time. Whenever I pick up a mike, I'm aware that every minute of 38 years goes into it, whether I like it or not.

What I did in "Fly" was what I wanted to do for 10 years, so I was very satisfied when I did it. I thought of making an album around this piece. It took almost a whole year after that to finally complete the album, though. Another Xmas is coming very soon. The winter is cold and tough—and you have to crawl a long way before you fly. Winter is age. Cold makes you go slow. Fly is a monologue in three stages.

Section one— monologue

Section two— monologue in a dialogue form: John played his guitar against the playback of my voice from section one. The guitar tape was then reversed and put together with my voice tape, so that the voice and the guitar ran in two opposite directions as separate monologues.

Section three—monologue in a trialogue form: John played his guitar against the reversed playback of tape section two. John's guitar tape made in this process was reversed and played while I did my voice. When the guitar tape was over and when my voice was still going, John played the radio against my voice.

Monologue is a reminiscence of my old days. I used to search for musicians who had the same state of mind as I to make musical dialogues with. But I had never met anyone who can really do that with me on the level that I was thinking of. Female artists for some reason, didn't have enough experience in expressing themselves with instruments—maybe they went for usage of a more direct instrument which was one's own body—and the male artists used to be caught in whatever brilliance they had possessed and were not free. So I ended up always in doing a monologue. John is the first person I met who knows how to be free, and that is why he plays such a very important role in all my pieces. For instance, you see that section 3 of Fly is a guitar solo with voice accompaniment rather than the other way around.

Most of the pieces in this album are centered around a dialogue between my voice and John's guitar. John and I crawl, roll, and fly together. John brought in musicians that are fine Samurais. John, as a rhythm guitarist, leads the rhythm track, he pushes them, drops them, chases them and frees them. He makes it easy for them to fly with me. Listen to Ringo and Jim Keltner's drumming, Klaus Voormann's bass, Chris Osborne's guitar and listen to the intricate conversation that goes between all of us in "Mind Train." Chris Osborne came from a guitar shop to sell a guitar to John. He stayed and played.

Thanks to John and the Plastic Ono Band. Thanks to Yoko's wisdom for allowing it to happen—rather than controlling note by note, to push her ego. Maybe she is a bit too proud about it, but let's not be too hard on her.

Note on Joe Jones Tone Deaf Music Co.:
I was always fascinated by the idea of making special instruments for special emotions—instruments that lead us to emotions arrived by their own motions rather than by our control. With those instruments, I wanted to explore emotions and vibrations which have not been explored as yet in music. I thought of building a house on the hill which makes different sounds by the wind that goes through different windows, doors and holes. (Re: Grapefruit: paperback edition out now!!!) Ten years ago I met Joe Jones who's been making such instruments almost unnoticed. This time, Joe built me 8 new instruments specially for this album which can play by themselves with minimum manipulation. (Turning switches only.)

I'm very happy about what happened with "Airmale" and "You" as a result of my session with Tone Deaf Co. "Airmale" is Yang and "You" is Yin. "Don't Count The Waves" is the water that connects the two Ying and Yang islands. "Airmale" expresses the delicateness of Male. "You" expresses the aggressiveness of female. "You" has all the feminine resentment, moan and animal satisfaction in it. Finally, there is just a wind blowing over a sand hill over white dried female bones, but still, with emotion. The wind created by tape feedback is what I always wanted to do a rock number with a tape loop of feedback as a riff. But this will do for now.

When I was in Sarah Lawrence, which was before I joined the avant-garde, and in London around 1967–8, which was when I was feeling very miserable, I composed many songs. "Mrs. Lennon" is in that category of songs, but unlike "Remember Love" and "Who Has Seen The Wind," I felt it was recorded very well. "Mrs. Lennon" was meant to be a joke on me, and also an anti-war song. The lyrics were made in 1969 and the music was finished this month in New York during the recording session.

"Midsummer New York" is about the deep insecurity I have in me that I associate with my life in New York before I met John. The lyrics were made last year, though I always wanted to make a song that uses the word "shaking" with a double meaning, since I discovered the usage of the word in rock songs in 1968.

This album roughly turned out to be:

1st and 2nd sides: Songs to dance to—Rock and songs with physical beat
3rd and 4th sides: Songs to listen to—mind music with mind beat

The Mind Music Section has number connections.

"Fly"—1, 2, and 3

"Airmale"—5

"Don't Count The Waves"—7

"You"—9

It is very important to know about numbers to understand the connections of the pieces, so I will quote the relevant lines from my writing called "On Number," and end this long introduction to the album.

ONE

One is an immobile number. One is found in our bodies often as fixed parts. We count ourselves as one but it might be better to count as half a pair or a half when you think of the fact that our reproductive organs can only function by meeting the other half.

One step is only half a move. Since we have two legs we have to take two steps or jump in order to move from one position to the next. One is before the cell splits in two. It is only mobile in the process of becoming two. One as a force is a point—which does not extend like a line. One constantly seeks for states of zero and two.

TWO

Two is a state that is mobile by nature. Like the footstep that goes one, two. It moves from one position to the next. Two as a force is a line. It extends and extends and unlike one, does not have to move to become mobile. Two is a state after splitting of the cell. Two constantly seeks for the state of one and three. We find two in our bodies quite often as a pair. Two is our heartbeat. After one and two, all the numbers are combinations of one and two. Therefore, there are actually only three basic states of numbers in the world: one, two and three, which is a combination of one and two.

THREE

Three is a number we cannot find in our bodies but we find it in nature around us. I call it a time number because we use it to divide time and the days. When the heart beats in three, it is when the heart is moving faster than what is natural. The heart beats one, two, one, two. And one number out of these repetitions of two gets abbreviated because of the speed. That is three. That means we set the time to the number which is one beat faster than our natural heartbeat. No wonder the culture is suffering from accelerated speed. The world will slow down if you dispense with clocks and watches and just follow your heartbeat.

The natural rhythm, when you don't check or control consciously, always goes slower (towards four) or faster (towards two) than a clock. Three is very fast and very mobile. It is a running rhythm as opposed to the walking rhythm of two, four and eight. Three as a force is a three dimensional point—an exclamation mark. Three will always seek for state of two or state of four. In three, two (which is a mobile number) and one (which is an immobile number) exist together equally. Paradox makes three extremely active towards inside, but not very active outside. While two is a travelling number, three is a whirling number (it moves forward spirally). After three, all numbers are combinations of states of one, two and three.

FIVE

Five is a number that very rarely exists on earth but exists very much in the sky (such as points of stars—but you know that even the five points of stars actually do not exist.) Unlike one (0 & 2), TWO (4 & 8) and three (6 & 9), five has no corresponding numbers in the series. In this sense it is very similar to 7.

In our bodies, it exists only on our hands and feet—as if that is the sign from the sky in us. The parts of our bodies where 5 exist are the only parts that have something to do with physical connections to things outside our bodies. Our hands reach to other things and our feet take us to other places with the help of a travelling number 2. 5 is a connection number—and just as the fingers do not work unless the thumb moves in an opposite direction from the rest of the fingers, five will be immobile unless it has different or opposite elements (one, two, and three) in it.

SEVEN

Seven is a conceptual number. Seven, like five, is a number you cannot find in our bodies (more so than five), or in the nature around us. I call it a conceptual number or number of music because we divide the musical scale into seven. (In time, we can only see it in the division of the week), and like five, it has no corresponding numbers.

NINE

Nine is a corresponding number of 3 and 6. Nine is superactive. Spatially, it is the closest of the numbers to circle. As a force it has a spirally forward movement as does three.

But despite all the words, music itself exists somewhere else and was made by pure instinct (that goes for me, too J.L.) and nothing else. Flashes of imagery and emotions.

Yoko Ono
Fall, '71
St. Regis Hotel, New York
For Crawdaddy

Original typed manuscript prepared for *Crawdaddy*; abridged and published as "Yoko Ono on 'Fly,'" *Crawdaddy* (5 December 1971)

11 *On Instructure,* 1964

On instructure
Something that emerged from instruction and yet not quite emerged—not quite structured—never quite structured...
like an unfinished church with a sky ceiling.

The instructures will be exhibited in the lobby.

Published in *Grapefruit* (Tokyo: Wunternaum Press, 1964); reprinted in program for *Contemporary American Avant-Garde Music Concert*, Yamaichi Hall, Kyoto, 20 July 1964

The Word of a Fabricator

I feel a strange attraction to the first man in human history who lied. How did he feel when he said he saw God, eternity, and heaven, for instance? Did he intend to deceive others while trembling from his own insecurity? Did he try to make the world of lies into a real world by deceiving others? Or did he believe that his fictional world actually existed somewhere in the Universe? Whatever his feelings were, I think it's interesting that he could not keep his lies to himself, and shared them with us.

Stylization is a materialization of the human desire to free oneself from the irrational rationality of life, hoping to extricate oneself from it by one's immersion in a fictional world and its order.

Medieval rituals interest me for that reason. Elaborate architecture, clothing, and various social conventions were attempts to make a detour to death by creating excessive dramas and illusions. At its bottom lay an endless pessimism that nothing but a fictional order could rescue us from death.

However, we now find ourselves in a "healthy" era, in which "fiction" is somewhat abhorred. In fact, we have contempt for any fictional act in the realm of consciousness. Even with his own set of rules, such as his belief, man cannot be satisfied without bringing the natural order into its structure and, by so doing, making it appear that his set of rules are equally real and valid as the law of nature.

It is hard not to notice the farce that, instead of legitimizing man's belief system, nature suddenly mutates into fiction as it is planted artificially into the framework of the man-made order.

Failing in the attempt to make the fabricated order appear equally real as nature, contemporary man has now gone to the opposite direction of placing men in a position equal to objects and plants. This is an attempt to raise men's stature to that of nature, by regarding nature's random operational characteristic as superior to men's own fictional order, and succumbing to and adopting random operation as men's own. It is the state of mind of wanting to become a weed and join the heartbeat of the Universe by entering the world of nothingness and blowing in a gentle wind.

This direction stems from one's optimism of thinking that as long as one discards one's consciousness, and leaves oneself in the hands of random operation, one could immediately turn into being a reed. This line of thought rubs me the wrong way.

It is too simplistic to think that one can reach the world of transcendence as long as one participates in the act of *gyo* and sweat. Is a human body worthy of such trust? We are talking about a body of a betrayer/l'étranger to the natural world, who carries the misfortune of being capable of even controlling the length of his life by will. We are talking about us, the contemporary men who are soaked to the bones with a fabricator called consciousness.

We, "the betrayer," are so invaded by the falsehood of consciousness we cannot even become random operational by using such a loose method as random operation. Instead, if we assign the most fictional rules, only then, may we possibly transcend our consciousness. My current interest is in such a world of fictional rules, the laws of the fabricator: to ask ourselves to imagine a perfect circle and a perfect line which exist only in our conceptual world: to assign ourselves to the nonsense act of counting the number of chimneys all over the world, and the repetition of those acts: to assign such set of rules to myself.

We can call these rituals a means to rationalize the irrationality in us, humans. The setting of such fictional rules and their enactment resemble the act of medieval stylization. Except here, they are rituals which cannot be shared in the physical world. One can say that they are rituals without the dignity of being real, a reality which even I could only acknowledge as fiction. The conceptual reality, as it were, becomes a concrete "matter" only when one destroys its conceptuality by asking others to enact it, as, otherwise, it cannot escape from staying "imaginary."

I wish not to be confused with the high-minded types who feel they have achieved Satori by becoming plantlike. I am still groping in the world of stickiness.

My attempt is not as serious as handing a knife to someone and trying to make my transcendence by asking the assistance of a force other than my own. It is nothing more than an obsessive act of the driven, attempting to make one's own fiction a reality by letting others cut off pieces of the romanticism that inevitably enwraps fiction. Thus, the conceptual reality finally becomes a concrete reality by an enactment of an intrusive, and therefore destructive, outside force.

I cannot stand the fact that everything is the accumulation of "distortion" owing to one's slanted view. I want the truth. I want to feel the truth by any possible means. I want someone or something to let me feel it. I can neither trust the plantlikeness of my body or the manipulation of my consciousness. I know no other way but to present the structure of a drama which assumes fiction as fiction, that is, as fabricated truth.

Published as "Kyokōsha no gen" in Japanese in *SAC Journal*, no. 24 (May 1962). Translation by Yoko Ono, 1999

13 *Letter to Ivan Karp* and *Reply from Ivan Karp,* 1965

Copy of letter sent to Ivan Karp Jan. 4, 1965

Jan. 4, 1965

Dear Ivan,

Thank you for seeing Tony Cox. Yes, it is necessary to sell the paintings, isn't it, if you have to spend $3000 for a show.

Why not have a strictly-for-the-artists preview opening 'to draw a circle'? We will invite only very selected artist-this is vulgar, but vulgarity can be very interesting. We will invite Bob Rauschenberg, Jasper Jones, etc. Some old artists such as Max Ernst, Marcel Duchamp, Isamu Noguchi are worth inviting.

I presume some of these artists are in Europe – such as Max Ernst – we will invite them with round-trip tickets, the expense of which you can add to the price of the painting. Because the painting, in short, will be a joint effort of these artists. They will be asked to bring means to draw a circle and to draw one on the painting – a blank canvas, that is. Drawing a circle shouldn't be so difficult a task for them, and the idea of making a trip to your gallery from wherever they are, just to draw a circle, is very nice, I think.

I think painting can be instructionalized. Artist, in this case, will only give instructions or diagrams for painting – and the painting will be more or less a do-it-yourself kit according to the instructions. The painting starts to exist only when a person follows the instructions to let the painting come to life. From there on, the painting goes through a life of transformation, by people adding their own efforts to the painting according to or, sometimes. against the given instructions, thus taking an active part in the existence of the painting.

Imagine the "nail painting" hanging in the Museum of Modern Art with instructions saying "hammer a nail on it", and people coming every day to hammer nails of various sizes, and the painting, thus, changing its face every moment.

–2–

They don't have to be a Rauschenberg or Jones to draw the circles, or to hammer the nails.

I can just see a Bronxville housewife saying to her guests "do add a circle to my painting before you have a drink", or a guest saying, "I was just admiring your painting by taking the previledge of adding another hole to it", etc. That is my dream, and something to come very much later, I suppose.

Because of the method – the instruction painting – many interesting things became possible – such as creating a visual object which is an interfusion of a physical and a non-physical objects, etc. You will see these instructions: long ones and short ones, in the painting section of my book. I hope many other instructions will come from people who take up this idea of painting. Soon there will be no need of artists, since people will start to write their own instructions or exchange them and paint.

But first, we should start with "drawing a circle", I think. We can also include the following paintings for the preview opening.

1) draw your shadow on the canvas.
2) make a hole on
3) hammer a nail
4) draw a flower
5) erase or cut until there is no canvas
etc.

Also, the canvas to start the painting does not have to be a blank canvas. They can be ready-made paintings on which we can draw circles, flowers, etc. Any painting will do. I can use from Da Vincci to Warhole, that is, if you can supply them for me instead of a blank canvas! I will enclose here two instructions based on the paintings of these two artists.

–3–

PAINTING – using "MONA LISA" (Da Vincci)

Hammer nails until it becomes only smile.

PAINTING – using "MARILYN MONROE" (Andy Warhole)

Hammer nails until the teeth are covered
Then erase the painting part.

Copyright Yoko Ono Jan. 4, 1965

Self-published, New York, 1965; partially reprinted in *Grapefruit* (New York: Simon and Schuster, 1970). Listed under "H. Letters" in *Ono's Sales List* (1965)

LEO
CASTELLI
4 E 77
NY 21

<u>Writer</u>

Dear Yoko,

Thank you so much for your urgent missive. It is indeed laden with pungent metaphysics and adventurous aesthetics. It seems now, however, after your clarifying and detailed exposition that the kind of show you have in mind fails to suit our temperament which is essentially restless, driven, aggressive, [redacted] fiercely Western and concrete -- not materialistic mind you -- perish the thought -- but terribly concrete. Max Ernst is very tired and doesn't want to travel. Most of the other famous characters despise each other and will not contribute to your panel. All Bronxville housewives go to Kootz and Findlay.

Alas then, from what you have proposed, you'll have to seek in other realms.

Cordially — Ivan

Self-published, New York, 1965. Listed under "H. Letters" in *Ono's Sales List* (1965).

14 *To the Wesleyan People*, January 23, 1966

YOKO ONO
1 WEST 100TH ST.
NEW YORK, 10025

JANUARY 23, 1966

To The Wesleyan People (who attended the meeting.)
-a footnote to my lecture of January 13th, 1966

When a violinist plays, which is incidental: the arm movement or the bow sound?

Try arm movement only.

If my music seems to require physical silence, that is because it requires concentration to yourself - and this requires inner silence which may lead to outer silence as well.

I think of my music more as a practice (gyo) than a music.

The only sound that exists to me is the sound of the mind. My works are only to induce music of the mind in people.

It is not possible to control a mind-time with a stopwatch or a metronome. In the mind-world, things spread out and go beyond time.

There is a wind that never dies.

****

My paintings, which are all instruction paintings (and meant for others to do), came after collage & assemblage (1915) and happening (1905) came into the art world. Considering the nature of my painting, any of the above three words or a new word can be used instead of the word, painting. But I like the old word painting because it immediately connects with "wall painting" painting, and it is nice and funny.

Among my instruction paintings, my interest is mainly in "painting to construct in your head". In your head, for instance, it is possible for a straight line to exist-not as a segment of a curve but as a straight line. Also, a line can be straight, curved and something else at the same time. A dot can exist as a 1,2,3,4,5,6, dimentional object all at the same time or at various times in different combinations as you wish to perceive. The movement of the molecule can be continuum and discontinuum at the same time. It can be with colour and/or without. There is no visual object that does not exist in comparison to or simultaneously with other objects, but these characteristics can be eliminated if you wish. A sunset can go on for days. You can eat up all the clouds in the sky. You can assemble a painting with a person in the North Pole over a phone, like playing chess. This painting method derives from as far back as the time of the Second World War when we had no food to eat, and my brother and I exchanged menus in the air.

There maybe a dream that two dream together, but there is no chair that two see together.

****

a a a a

I think it is possible to see a chair as it is. But when you burn the chair, you suddenly realize that the chair in your head did not burn or disappear.

The world of construction seems to be the most tangible, and therefore final. This made me nervous. I started to wonder if it were really so.

Isn't a construction a begining of a thing like a seed? Isn't it a segment of a larger totality, like an elephant's tail? Isn't it something just about to emerge-not quite structured - never quite structured... like an unfinished church with a sky ceiling? Therefore, the following works:

A venus made of plastic, except that her head is to be imagined.

A paper ball and a marble book, except that the final version is the fusion of these two objects which come into existance only in your head.

A marble sphere (actually existing) which, in your head, gradually becomes a sharp cone by the time it is extended to the far end of the room.

A garden covered with thick marble instead of snow-but like snow, which is to be appreciated only when you uncover the marble coating.

One thousand needles: imagine threading them with a straight thread.

****

I would like to see the sky machine on every corner of the street instead of the coke machine. We need more skies than coke.

****

Dance was once the way people communicated with God and godliness in people. Since when did dance become a pasted-face exhibitionism of dancers on the spotlighted stage? Can you not communicate if it is totally dark?

If people make it a habit to draw a somersault on every other street as they commute to their office, take off their pants before they fight, shake hands with strangers whenever they feel like, give flowers or part of their clothing on streets, subways, elevator, toilet, etc., and if politicians go through a tea house door (lowered, so people must bend very low to get through) before they discuss anything and spend a day watching the fountain water dance at the nearest park, the world business may slow down a little but we may have peace. To me this is dance.

*****

All my works in the other fields have an "Event bent" so to speak. People ask me why I call some works Event and others not. They also ask me why I do not call my Events, Happenings.

Event, to me, is not an assimilation of all the other arts as Happening seems to be, but an extrication from the various sensory perceptions. It is not "a get togetherness" as most happenings are, but a dealing with oneself. Also, it has no script as happenings do, though it has something that starts it moving - the closest word for it may be a "wish" or "hope".

At

oooooo

At a small dinner party last week, we suddenly discovered that our poet friend whom we admire very much was colour blind. Barbara Moore said, "That explains about his work. Usually people's eyes are blocked by colour and they can't see the thing."

After unblocking one's mind, by dispensing with visual, auditory, and kinetic perceptions, what will come out of us? Would there be anything? I wonder. And my Events are mostly spent in wonderment.

In Kyoto, at Nanzenji Temples the High Monk was kind to let me use one of the temples and the gardens for my Event. It is a temple with great history, and it was an unheard of honour for the Monk to give permission for such a use, especially, to a woman. The Event took place from evening till dawn. About fifty people came with the knowledge that it will last till dawn. The instruction was to watch the sky and to "touch". Some of them were just fast asleep until dawn. Some sat in the garden, some on the wide corridor, which is like a verandah. It was a beautiful full moon night, and the moon was so bright, that the mountains and the trees, which usually looked black under the moonlight, began to show their green. People talked about moonburn, moonbath, and about touching the sky. Two people, I noticed, were whispering all about their life story to each other. Once in a while, a restless person would come to me and ask if I was alright. I thought that was very amusing, because it was a very warm and peaceful July night, and there was no reason why I should not be alright. Probably he was starting to feel something happening to him, something that he did not yet know how to come with, the only way out for him was to come to me and ask if I was alright. I was a little nervous about people making cigarette holes on the national treasure floors and tatami, from being high on the moonlight, since most of the people were young modern Japanese and some French and Americans. But nothing like that happened. When the morning breeze started to come in, people quietly woke up their friends, and we took a bath, three at a time, in a bath especially prepared for us at that hour of day. The temple bath is made of huge stone, and it is very warm. After the bath, we had miso soup and onigiri (rice sandwich). Without my saying anything about it, people silently swept the room and mopped the corridor before leaving. I did not know most of them, as they were mostly Kyoto people, and they left without giving their names. I wonder who they were.

At another time, also in Kyoto, before the Nanzenji Event, I had a concert at Yamaichi Hall. It was called "The Strip-tease Show" (it was stripping of the mind). When I met the High Monk the next day, he seemed a bit dissatisfied.

"I went to your concert", he said.

"Thank you, did you like it?"

"Well, why did you have those three chairs on the stage and call it a strip-tease by three?"

"If it is a chair or stone or woman, it is the same thing, my Monk."

"Where is the music?"

"The music is in the mind, my Monk."

"But that is the same with what we are doing, aren't you an avant-garde composer?"

"That is a label which was put by others for convenience."

"For instance, does Toshiro Mayuzumi create music of your kind?"

"I can only speak for myself."

"Do you have many followers?"

"No, but I know of two men who know what I am doing. I am very thankful for that."

Though he is a High Monk he is extremely young, he may be younger than myself. I wonder what the Monk is doing now.

x x x x

Another Event that was memorable for me was "Fly", at Naiqua Gallery in Tokyo. People were asked to come prepared to fly in their own way. I did not attend.

***

People talk about happening. They say that art is headed towards that direction, that happening is assimilating the arts. I don't believe in collectivism of art nor in having only one direction in anything. I think it is nice to return to having many different arts, including happening, just as having many flowers. In fact, we could have more arts "smell", "weight", "taste", "cry", "anger" (competition of anger, that sort of thing), etc. People might say, that we never experience things separately, they are always in fusion, and that is why "the happening", which is a fusion of all sensory perceptions. Yes, I agree, but if that is so, it is all the more reason and challenge to create a sensory experience isolated from other sensory experiences, which is something rare in daily life. Art is not merely a duplication of life. To assimilate art in life, is different from art duplicating life.

But returning to having various divisions of art, does not mean, for instance, that one must use only sounds as means to create music. One may give instructions to watch the fire for 10 days in order to create music in the mind, or drink water once a month to create a vision in ones mind.

*

The mind is omnipresent, events in life never happen alone and the history is forever increasing its volume. The natural state of life and mind is complexity. At this point, what art can offer (if it can at all-to me it seems) is an absence of complexity, a vacuum through which you are led to a state of complete relaxation of mind. After that you may return to the complexity of life again, it may not be the same, or it may be, or you may never return, but that is your problem.

Mental richness should be worried just as physical richness. Didn't Christ say that it was like a camel trying to pass through a needle hole, for John Cage to go to heaven? I think it is nice to abandon what you have as much as possible, as many mental posessions as the physical ones, as they clutter your mind. It is nice to maintain poverty of environment, sound, thinking and belief. It is nice to keep oneself small, like a grain of rice, instead of expanding and make yourself dispensable, like paper. See little, hear little, and think little.

The body is the Bodhi Tree
The mind like a bright mirror standing
Take care to wipe it all the time
And allow no dust to cling. - Shen-hsiu

There never was a Bodhi Tree
Nor bright mirror standing
Fundamentally, not one thing exists
So where is the dust to cling? - Hui-neng

y.o.

Self-published as insert in *The Stone* (New York: Judson Gallery, 1966); reprinted in *Yoko at Indica*, exh. cat. (London: Indica Gallery, 1966) and *Grapefruit* (New York: Simon and Schuster, 1970)

15 *Some Notes on the Lisson Gallery Show,* October 1967

Some Notes on the Lisson Gallery Show y.o. October '67 London

I think of this show as an elephant's tail.

Life is only half a game. Molecules are always at the verge of half disappearing and half emerging.

Somebody said I should also put half-a-person in the show. But we are halves already.

Seng, Sung, Sang, Sing and Song were good musicians. The princess asked them to play for the concert of the midsummer night of the warmest day in Li-Fung. It was a tradition in Li-Fung for the best musicians to get together and play for the people all night and soothe the air from the heat. Seng said he would not play because he did not have enough time to prepare. Sung immediately went into an intensive and elaborate preparation. Sang did nothing. He wandered around the fields until the day came. On the night, Seng was not there. Sung's music overwhelmed people. Sang went on the stage, and when he sang, the warm wind went through his lungs and came out, transformed into the most beautiful music. It was the warm wind that made the music, he said. Sing did not even sing. He just stood on the stage and smiled, and the smile sent vibrations into people's mind, and they heard, they heard their minds tingling, and they smiled back. Do you know anything about Song? People say that he was too pure, and one day, he just suddenly turned into air and was assimilated into the skies.

It is sad that the air is the only thing we share. No matter how close we get to each other, there is always air between us. It is also nice that we share the air. No matter how far apart we are, the air links us.

The switch piece is meant to be mass-produced. By using this switch, you can dispense with a large part of language communication. Instead of shouting to your husband who is in the bath that the dinner is ready, you can turn on the light in the bathroom from the kitchen. Instead of calling your wife and telling her that you are coming home, you can just turn the light in her room from 500 miles away and she will know that you are on your way home, etc., etc. I would have a whole room of lights, like a light flower garden, and see which friends are tuning in.

When "Hammer A Nail" painting was exhibited at Indica Gallery, a person came and asked if it was alright to hammer a nail in the painting. I said it was alright if he pays 5 shillings. Instead of paying the 5 shillings, he asked if it was alright for him to hammer an imaginary nail in. That was John Lennon. I thought, so I met a guy who plays the same game I played. This time John suggested how about selling the other half of my half-a-matter objects in bottles. It was such a beautiul idea I decided to use it even though it was not mine.

Some practical and tangible future plans:

The light house is a phantom house that is built by sheer light. You set up prisms and at a certain time of the day, under a certain evening light which goes through the prisms, the light house appears in the middle of the field like an image, except that, with this image, you can actually go inside if you wanted to. The light house may not emerge every day, just as the sun doesn't shine every day.

The wind house is a house on a hill. The rooms and the windows are so constructed so it makes music, like a whistle, depending on the wind that goes through.

Moon-music: This is a well that is receptive to the moon-tide and makes music according to the tide. When we were fish, the sea-water surrounded us. When we came on ground, we carried the sea inside us. Our blood structure is 90% salt-water. There's a very strong tie between us and the moon-tide. They say that when you die a natural death it is invariably when the tide is low. You should have the moon-music in your house like you would have a clock. And when it sings, you will remember the connection.

TV to see the sky: This is a TV just to see the sky. Different channels for different skies, high-up sky, low sky, etc.

Published in *Yoko Ono at Lisson: Half-A-Wind Show*, exh. cat. (London: Lisson Gallery, 1967)

WHAT IS THE RELATIONSHIP BETWEEN THE WORLD AND THE ARTIST?

Many people believe that in this age, art is dead. They despise the artists who show in galleries and are caught up in the traditional art world. Artists themselves are beginning to lose their confidence. They don't know whether they are doing something that still has value in this day and age where the social problems are so vital and critical. I wondered myself about this. Why am I still an artist? And why am I not joining the violent revolutionaries? Then I realized that destruction is not my game. Violent revolutionaries are trying to destroy the establishment. That is good. But how? By killing? Killing is such an artless thing. All you need is a coke bottle in your hand and you can kill. But people who kill that way most often become the next establishment after they've killed the old. Because they are using the same method that the old establishment used to destroy. Violent revolutionaries' thinking is very close to establishment-type thinking and ways of solving problems.

I like to fight the establishment by using methods that are so far removed from establishment-type thinking that the establishment doesn't know how to fight back. For instance, they cannot stamp out John and Yoko events *Two Virgins, Bed Peace, Acorn Peace* and *War Is Over* poster event.

Artists are not here to destroy or to create. *Creating* is just as simple and artless a thing to do as *destroying*. Everyone on earth has creativity. Even a housewife can create a baby. Children are just as creative as the people whom society considers artists. Creative artists are just good enough to be considered children. Artists must not create more objects, the world is full of everything it needs. I'm bored with artists who make big lumps of sculpture and occupy a big space with them and think they have done something *creative* and allow people nothing but to applaud the lump. That is sheer narcissism. Why don't they at least let people touch them? Money and space are wasted on such projects when there are people starving and people who don't have enough space to sleep or breathe.

The job of an artist is not to destroy but to change the value of things. And by doing that, artists can change the world into a Utopia where there is total freedom for everybody. That can be achieved only when there is total communication in the world, Total communication equals peace. That is our aim. That is what artists can do for the world!

In order to change the value of things, you've got to know about life and the situation of the world. You have to be more than a child.

That is the difference between a child's work and an artist's work. That is the difference between an artist's work and a murderer's work. We are artists. Artist is just a frame of mind. Anybody can be an artist. It doesn't involve having a talent. It involves only having a certain frame of mind, an attitude, determination, and imagination that springs naturally out of the necessity of the situation.

Examples of today's living artists:

There was a temple in Japan called the Golden Temple. A man loved it very much as it was, and he couldn't stand the thought of anything happening to it. He felt the only way he could stop anything from happening to it was to burn it down, and he did. Now, the image of the temple was able to stay forever in his mind as a perfect form.

There was a man who made a counterfeit one thousand yen. It circulated with no trouble at all. The man travelled to another city and circulated another counterfeit one thousand yen. If he had made lots of counterfeit money he could have been discovered right away. But he wasn't interested in making lots of money. He wanted to have fun and play a subtle game. The police went wild and announced that if anybody found a counterfeit one thousand yen they would get two thousand yen as a reward if they came to the police station. This man changed the value of money by his actions.

In this very same sense, we have artists today whose works move beyond the gallery space and help change the world: Abbie Hoffman, Jerry Rubin, Paul Krassner, for instance, and many others. They radiate something that is sensitive and artistic in a very renaissance sense, when the majority of so-called artists these days are hardcore business-men. Message is the medium. There are only two classes left in our society. The class who communicates and the class who doesn't. Tomor-row I hope there will be just one. Total communication equals peace.

Men can destroy/Women can create/Artists revalue.

Y.O., Cannes Film Festival, May, 1971

Published in *This Is Not Here*, exh. cat. (Syracuse: Everson Museum of Art, 1971); reprinted in *Museum of Modern [F]art* (New York, 1971)

17 **Bronze Age**, 1988

BRONZE AGE

During my 1987 trip to the Soviet Union to attend a peace conference, I visited the beautifully restored Summer Palace just outside Leningrad. Each room had two photos on the wall side by side—one taken in the czarist period and the other taken just after the room was destroyed by the Nazis. The sepia photos of the palace in its heyday were dreamy; the black and white photos of the rooms after the Nazi destruction had no trace of the dream, and the restored rooms we walked through were brightly colored—maybe a touch too bright—like a rouged, old face. It was a story of change and survival. It was a story of all of us.

One day in New York, soon after the trip, I was eating spaghetti in an Italian restaurant with a friend. The friend casually suggested I should do some objects in bronze. The suggestion was so offensive to me that my smile froze and tears ran down my cheek. "This man doesn't know anything about my work," I thought. I realized then that I had an absolute fear of bronze. But why? Then the thought of the sixties flashed in my mind. The air definitely had a special shimmer then. We were breathless from the pride and joy of being alive. I remembered carrying a glass key to open the sky.

I thought I had moved forward right into the eighties and further. But part of me was still holding onto the sixties sky. The eighties is an age of commodity and solidity. We don't hug strangers on the street, and we are also not breathless. When the two big boys shake hands at the summit, maybe it's better that they exchange bronze keys rather than glass ones. In my mind, bronze started to have a warm shimmer instead of the dead weight I had associated it with. Bronze is OK, I thought. Eighties is OK. It has to do. One day, I would become a person who could handle bronze with grace and ease.

y.o. '88
New York

Published in *Yoko Ono: The Bronze Age*, exh. cat. (Bloomfield Hills, Mich.: Cranbrook Academy of Art Museum, 1989)

18 ***Wish Piece***, 1996

WISH PIECE
y.o. '96

Make a wish.
Write it down on a piece of paper.
Fold it and tie it around a branch of a Wish Tree.
Ask your friends to do the same.
Keep wishing
Until the branches are covered with wishes.

Self-published in New York, 1996

19 *Cleaning Piece,* 1996

CLEANING PIECE
y.o. '96

Make a numbered list of sadness in your life.
Pile up stones corresponding to those numbers.
Add a stone each time there is sadness.
Burn the list and appreciate
the mount of stones for its beauty.

Make a numbered list of happiness in your life.
Pile up stones corresponding to those numbers.
Add a stone each time there is happiness.
Compare the mount of stones
to the one of sadness.

Self-published in New York, 1996

20 *Six Film Scripts by Yoko Ono,* June 1964

SIX FILM SCRIPTS BY YOKO ONO
TOKYO, JUNE 1964

1- THE WALK TO THE TAJ MAHAL

2- MONA LISA & HER SMILE

3- FILM SCRIPT 3

4- FILM SCRIPT 4

5- FILM SCRIPT 5

6- OMNIBUS FILM

These scores were printed and made
available to whoever was interested
at the time or thereafter in making
their own version of the films, since
these films, by their nature, became
a reality only when they were repeated
and realized by other filmmakers.

A dream you dream alone may be a dream,
but a dream two people dream together
is a reality.

THE WALK TO THE TAJ MAHAL

1) The blind man or the
musician's version.
(ALL BLACK)

2) The deaf man or the
painter's version.
(WALK and RIDE of
PLACES—TIMES SQUARE,
GINZA, etc. by CARS,
MOTOR CYCLES)

3) The real picture—
winter scene.
(SNOW—in other words,
ALL WHITE) *

Music composed by Yoko Ono,
performed by the audience.
(1st version, WHITE FLOWERS
all silently picked)
(2nd version, no given music—
Just the sound of audience)

*can make SUMMER, AUTUMN,
& SPRING version by SUN-
GLARE, SKIES or COTTONS,
FLOWERS, ALL WHITE anyway)

note: any of the above
versions may be shown
independently.

MONA LISA & HER SMILE

Ask audience to stare
at a figure, (ANY FIGURE)
for a long time and then
immediately turn their
eyes to the screen and
see the reflection.

FILM SCRIPT 3

Ask audience to cut
the part of the image
on the screen that
they don't like.

Supply scissors.

FILM SCRIPT 4

Ask audience to stare
at the screen until
it becomes black.

FILM SCRIPT 5

Ask audience the
following:

1) not to look at
Rock Hudson, but
only Doris Day.

2) not to look at
any round objects
but only square
and angled objects—
if you look at a
round object watch
it until it becomes
square and angled.

3) not to look at
blue but only red—
if blue comes out
close eyes or do
something so you
do not see, if you
saw it, then make
believe that you
have not seen it.

OMNIBUS FILM

1) Give a print of
the same film to
many directors.

2) Ask each one
to re-edit the
print without
leaving out any
of the material
in such a way that
it will be unnoticed
that the print was
re-edited.

3) Show all the
versions together
omnibus style.

Self-published in Tokyo, 1964; reissued ca. 1968 as 14-page pamphlet

21 *On Film No. 4,* 1967

On Film No. 4 (in taking the bottoms of 365 saints of our time)

I wonder why men can get serious at all. They have this delicate long thing hanging outside their bodies, which goes up and down by its own will. First of all having it outside your body is terribly dangerous. If I were a man I would have a fantastic castration complex to the point that I wouldn't be able to do a thing. Second, the inconsistency of it, like carrying a chance time alarm or something. If I were a man I would always be laughing at myself. Humour is probably something the male of the species discovered through their own anatomy. But men are so serious. Why ? Why violence ? Why hatred ? Why war ? If people want to make war, they should make a colour war, and paint each other's city up during the night in pinks and greens. Men have an unusual talent for making a bore out of everything they touch. Art, painting, sculpture, like who wants a cast-iron woman, for instance.

The film world is becoming terribly aristocratic, too. It's professionalism all the way down the line. In any other field: painting, music, etc., people are starting to become iconoclastic. But in the film world—that's where nobody touches it except the director. The director carries the old mystery of the artist. He is creating a universe, a mood, he is unique, etc., etc. This film proves that anybody can be a director. A film-maker in San Francisco wrote to me and asked if he could make the San Francisco version of No. 4. That's OK with me. Somebody else wrote from New York, she wants to make a slow-motion version with her own behind. That's OK, too. I'm hoping that after seeing this film people will start to make their own home movies like crazy.

In 50 years or so, which is like 10 centuries from now, people will look at the film of the 60's. They will probably comment on Ingmar Bergman as meaningfully meaningful film-maker, Jean-Luc Godard as the meaningfully meaningless. Antonioni as meaninglessly meaningful, etc., etc. Then they would come to the No. 4 film and see a sudden swarm of exposed bottoms, that these bottoms, in fact belonged to people who represented the London scene. And I hope that they would see that the 60's was not only the age of achievements, but of laughter. This film, in fact, is like an aimless petition signed by people with their anuses. Next time we wish to make an appeal, we should send this film as the signature list.

My ultimate goal in film-making is to make a film which includes a smiling face snap of every single human being in the world. Of course, I cannot go around the whole world and take the shots myself. I need cooperation from something like the post offices of the world. If everybody would drop a snapshot of themselves and their families to the post office of their town, or allow themselves to be photographed by the nearest photographic studio, this would be soon accomplished. Of course, this film would need constant adding of footage. Probably nobody would like to see the whole film at once, so you can keep it in a library or something, and when you want to see some particular town's people's smiling faces you can go and check that section of film. We can also arrange it with a television network so that whenever you want to see faces of a particular location in the world, all you have to do is to press a button and there it is. This way, if Johnson wants to see what sort of people he killed in Vietnam that day, he only has to turn the channel. Before this you were just part of a figure in the newspapers, but after this you become a smiling face. And when you are born, you will know that if you wanted to, you will have in your life time to communicate with the whole world. That is more than most of us could ask for. Very soon, the age may come where we would not need photographs to communicate, like ESP, etc. it will happen soon, but that will be "After the Film Age."

Yoko Ono
London '67

Self-published as part of 16-page film program in London, 1967; reprinted in *Grapefruit* (New York: Simon and Schuster, Touchstone Book, 1971)

22 From *Thirteen Film Scores by Yoko Ono,* 1968

FILM NO. 3

TOILET THOUGHTS

Prepare 365 copies of a poster and paste them in bar toilets around the city.
Leave them for a week and take picture of all 365 copies.

Leave them again for a month and take pictures of them.

Go on until you are satisfied, or until the posters disappear.
Make a film by stringing all the pictures.

FILM NO. 6

A CONTEMPORARY SEXUAL MANUAL (366 sexual positions)

by yoko ono copyright '68

1½ hr. colour separate soundtrack. cast: a woman, a man and a child.

The whole film takes place in a bedroom with a large double bed in the center and a window at the foot of the bed.

The film is a family scene of a quiet couple and a four year old daughter lying on the bed for the whole night. All they do is just sleep, and the 366 sexual positions are all in the mind of the audience.

The delicate change of positions made by the threesome has a slow dance movement quality to it on one hand, and a comfortable domestic nature (scratching each other, etc.) on the other.

The contemporary sex, unlike what you see in blue films, reflects the complexity of our society, and it is subtle and multi-leveled. So in this film, you never see an obvious position as two people on top of each other, or actually making love in any form. They very rarely exchange words with each other and when they do, the sound is not synchronized so all you see is their mouth moving. But there is definitely an air of peaceful unity and coziness among the three.

There are occasional breaks that take place in the film: going to the toilet, for instance (in which case, all you see is one of them getting up and going out of the room and coming back).

The camera will start panning from under the bed, then the foot of the bed, gradually goes up, and finally up over their heads until the window at the foot of the bed starts to cover the whole screen. This camera movement can be compared to the moon rising and then disappearing at the other end in the time space of 1½ hr.

The soundtrack in contrast to the screen consists mainly of tragic conversations between a couple who are about to split, whimpering of a child, whispers, sighs and love groans. Also, a sound-tape from a Trafalgar Square soap-bubble happening comes in as if they are sounds in a dream of one of them, or of the three, while they sleep. At dawn, milkbottle rattling and bird sounds will come in, and the film will end with increasingly heavy bird sound.

FILM NO. 12

UP YOUR LEGS FOREVER

The camera work of the film should constantly go up, up, up non stop. Collect 367 pairs of legs and just go up the legs (from toes to the end of thighs) pair after pair and go on up until you run through the whole 367.

from 13 Film Scripts by Yoko Ono London '67

Self-published in London, 1968

23 *On Rape*, April 1969

ON RAPE

Violence is a sad wind that, if channeled carefully, could bring seeds, chairs and all things pleasant to us.

We are all would-be Presidents of the World, and kids kicking the sky that doesn't listen.

What would you do if you had only one penis and a one-way tube ticket when you want to fuck the whole nation in one come?

I know a professor of philosophy whose hobby is to quietly crush biscuit boxes in a supermarket.

Maybe you can send signed, plastic lighters to people in place of your penis. But then some people might take your lighter as a piece of sculpture and keep it up in their living-room shelf.

So we go on eating and feeding frustration every day, lick lollipops and stay being peeping-toms dreaming of becoming Jack-the-Ripper.

This film was shot by our cameraman, Nick, while we were in a hospital. Nick is a gentle-man, who prefers eating clouds and floating pies to shooting "Rape." Nevertheless it was shot.

And as John says: "A is for parrot, which we can plainly see."

Yoko Ono
April '69, London

Self-published in London, 1969; reprinted in *Grapefruit* (New York: Simon and Schuster, Touchstone Book, 1971)

24 *The Feminization of Society*, 1971

THE FEMINIZATION OF SOCIETY

The aim of the feminist movement should not just end with getting more jobs in the existing society, though we should definitely work on that as well. We have to keep on going until the whole of the female race is freed.

How are we going to go about this? This society is the very society that killed female freedom: the society that was built on female slavery. If we try to achieve our freedom within the framework of the existing social set-up, men, who run the society, will continue to make a token gesture of giving us a place in their world. Some of us will succeed in moving into elitist jobs, kicking our sisters on the way up. Others will resort to producing babies, or being conned into thinking that joining male perversions and madness is what equality is about: "join the army," "join the sexist trip," etc.

The major change in the contemporary woman's revolution is the issue of lesbianism. Lesbianism, to many, is a means of expressing rebellion toward the existing society through sexual freedom. It helps women realize that they don't necessarily have to rely on men for relationships. They have an alternative to spending 90% of their lives waiting for, finding and living for men. But if the alternative to that is finding a woman to replace the man in her life, and then build her life around another female or females, it isn't very liberating. Some sisters have learned to love women more deeply through lesbianism, but others have simply gone after their sisters in the same manner that the male chauvinists have.

The ultimate goal of female liberation is not just to escape from male oppression. How about liberating ourselves from our various mind trips such as ignorance, greed, masochism, fear of God, and social conventions? It's hard to so easily dismiss the importance of paternal influence in this society, at this time. Since we face the reality that, in this global village, there is very little choice but to coexist with men, we might as well find a way to do it and do it well.

We definitely need more positive participation by men in the care of our children. But how are we going to do this? We have to demand it. James Baldwin has said of this problem, "I can't give a performance all day in the office and come back and give a performance at home." He's right. How can we expect men to share the responsibility of childcare in the present social conditions where his job in the office is, to him, a mere "performance" and where he cannot relate to the role of childcare except as yet another "performance"? Contemporary men must go through major changes in their thinking before they volunteer to look after children, and before they even start to want to care.

Childcare is the most important issue for the future of our generation. It is no longer a pleasure for the majority of men and women in our society, because the whole society is geared towards living up to a Hollywood-cum–Madison Avenue image of men and women, and a way of life that has nothing to do with childcare. We are in a serious identity crisis. This society is driven by neurotic speed and force accelerated by greed, and frustration of not being able to live up to the image of men and women we have created for ourselves; the image has nothing to do with the reality of people. How could we be an eternal James Bond or Twiggy (false eyelashes, the never-had-a-baby-or-a-full-meal look) and raise three kids on the side? In such an image-driven culture, a piece of reality, such as a child, becomes a direct threat to our false existence.

The only game we play together with our children is star-chasing; sadly, not the stars in the sky, but the "STARS" who we think have achieved the standard of the dream image we have imposed on the human race. We cannot trust ourselves anymore, because we know that we are, well...too real. We are forever apologetic for being real. Excuse me for farting, excuse me for making love and smelling like a human being, instead of that odorless celluloid prince and princess image up there on the screen.

Most of us, women, hope that we can achieve our freedom within the existing social set-up, thinking that, somewhere, there must be a happy medium for men and women to share freedom and responsibility. But if we just took the time to observe the very function of our society, the greed-power-frustration syndrome, we would soon see that there is no happy medium to be achieved. We can, of course, aim to play the same game that men have played for centuries, and inch by inch, take over all the best jobs and eventually conquer the whole world, leaving an extremely bitter male stud-cum-slave class moaning and groaning underneath us. This is alright for an afternoon dream, but in reality, it would obviously be a drag.

Just as the blacks have in the past, women are going through an initial stage of revolution now. We are now at a stage where we are eager to compete with men on all levels. But women will inevitably arrive at the next stage, and realize the futility of trying to be like men. Women will realize themselves as they are, and not as beings comparative to or in response to men. As a result, the feminist revolution will take a more positive step in the society by offering a feminine direction.

In their past two thousand years of effort, men have shown us their failure in their method of running the world. Instead of falling into the same trap that men fell into, women can offer something that the society never had before because of male dominance. That is the feminine direction. What we can do is to take the current society, which contains both masculine and feminine characteristics, and bring out its feminine nature rather than its masculine force which is now at work. We must make more positive use of the feminine tendencies of the society which, up to now, have been either suppressed or dismissed as something harmful, impractical, irrelevant, and ultimately shameful.

I am proposing the feminization of society; the use of feminine nature as a positive force to change the world. We can change ourselves with feminine intelligence and awareness, into a basically organic, non-competitive society that is based on love rather than reasoning. The result will be a society of balance, peace, and contentment. We can evolve rather than revolt, come together, rather than claim independence, and feel rather than think. These are characteristics that are considered feminine; characteristics that men despise in women. But have men really done so well by avoiding the development of these characteristics within themselves?

Already, as I catch a glimpse of the new world, I see feminine wisdom working as a positive force. I refer to the feminine wisdom and awareness which is based on reality, intuition, and empirical thinking, rather than logistics and ideologies. The entire youth generation, their idiom and their dreams, are headed in a feminine direction. A more advanced field of communication, such as telepathy, is also a phenomenon which can only be developed in a highly feminine climate. The problem is that feminine tendency in the society has never been given a chance to blossom, whereas masculine tendency overwhelms it.

What we need now is the patience and natural wisdom of a pregnant woman, an awareness and acceptance of our natural resources, or what is left of them. Let's not kid ourselves and think of ourselves as an old and matured civilization. We are by no means mature. But that is alright. That is beautiful. Let's slow down and try to grow as organically, and healthfully, as a newborn infant. The aim of the female revolution will have to be a total one, eventually making it a revolution for the whole world. As mothers of the tribe, we share the guilt of the male chauvinists, and our faces are their mirrors as well. It's good to start now, since it's never too late to start from the start.

Originally prepared for *New York Times*; abridged and published under the same title on 23 February 1972. Unabridged version published as "Imagine: It's Never Toooo Late to Start from the Start" in *SunDance* (April/May, 1972). The version printed here reflects the abridged version published as liner notes in *Approximately Infinite Universe*, LP (1972) and CD (Rykodisc, 1997).

25 From *Seven Little Stories,* spring 1952

The Connection

Once we were fish
moving freely in the sea.
Our bodies were soft and swift
and we had no belongings.

Now that we crawled out of the sea
we are dry and full of cravings.
We wander city to city
carrying the memory of the sea
(but it isn't just a memory).

Listen very carefully and you will hear
the sea in your body.
You know, our blood is seawater
and we are all seacarriers.

Reincarnation

Mirror becomes a razor when it's broken.
A stick becomes a flute when it's loved.

First and third stories. Originally written in Japanese. Translation by Yoko Ono, published in *Grapefruit* (New York: Simon and Schuster, Touchstone Book, 1971)

26 *Biography/Statement,* 1966

Biography

born: bird year
early childhood: collected skys
adolescence: collected sea-weeds
late adolescence: gave birth to a grapefruit
collected snails, clouds, garbage
cans, etc. Have graduated many
schools specializing in these
subjects

at present: traveling as a private lecturer of the
above subjects and others

recipient of Hal Kaplow Award

Statement

People went on cutting the parts they do not like of me finally there was only the stone remained of me that was in me but they were still not satisfied and wanted to know what it's like in the stone.

y.o.

P.S. If the butterflies in your stomach die, send
yellow death announcements to your friends.

Published in *The Stone* (New York: Judson Gallery, 1966)

27 *Water Talk*, 1967

water talk

you are water
I'm water
we're all water in different containers
that's why it's so easy to meet
someday we'll evaporate together

but even after the water's gone
we'll probably point out to the containers
and say, "that's me there, that one."
we're container minders

Written for *Yoko Ono at Lisson: Half-A-Wind Show*, exh. cat. (London: Lisson Gallery, 1967), but unpublished; published in *Grapefruit* (New York: Simon and Schuster, 1970)

28 *Air Talk*, 1967

air talk

It's sad that the air is the only
thing we share.
No matter how close we get to each other,
there is always air between us.

It's also nice that we share the air.
No matter how far apart we are,
the air links us.

From "Some notes on the Lisson Gallery Show," published in *Yoko Ono at Lisson: Half-A-Wind Show*, exh. cat. (London: Lisson Gallery, 1967). Reprinted in *Grapefruit* (New York: Simon and Schuster, Touchstone Book, 1971)

ANTHOLOGY 2, 11
On Insound and *On Instructure*

Written as a statement and insight for the program of Yoko Ono's major events in Kyoto, July 1964, a few months before her return to New York (no. 29). It was during her July 20 concert at Yamaichi Hall that an *audience piece* which became known as *Cut Piece* was performed. This, together with other works, defined "insound." The "instructures" ("something that emerged from instruction") were exhibited in the lobby and were later described by the artist as a group of pedestals with materials on them with signs instructing the viewers to construct them with imaginary materials.

INSOUND

ANTHOLOGY 3

From *The Soundless Music*
This very early conceptual architecture text is an example of Ono's developing imagination when she was only seventeen years old. It was later incorporated into *Do It Yourself: Fluxfest Presents Yoko Ono & Dance Co.* in 1966.

ANTHOLOGY 4
From *Poems by Yoko Ono*

These poems were read at one of Ono's earliest public performances, March 23, 1960, at Pratt Institute in Brooklyn. The program, co-sponsored by Japan Society, included a demonstration of the folding and the unfolding of an origami swan and *Poem[s]* by Yoko Ono. The poems contain ideas that the artist included in several later works. The phrase "the breast of the dead woman was stabbed with thick nails" contains the concept used in the score *Painting to Hammer a Nail* (1961 winter): "Hammer a nail into a mirror...." In each example one can sense the pain inflicted on the artist. The first poem on the program, "a greenfilled morning," became *City Piece* (1961 winter), a poem of great loss and loneliness.

ANTHOLOGY 5
A Grapefruit in the World of Park

Several versions of *A Grapefruit in the World of Park* exist. The earliest published appeared in the 1950s in the Sarah Lawrence College publication, *The Campus*. This present version appears to be a final performance score. The work was first performed during *An Evening of Contemporary Japanese Music and Poetry* at the Village Gate, New York on April 3, 1961. The work was narrated and staged by Yoko Ono. Performers included David Tudor, Mayuzumi Toshirō, Ichiyanagi Toshi, Kobayashi Kenji, David Soyer, and (not listed on the program) John Cage and La Monte Young. In addition, Ono instructed David Johnson to go into the bathroom with a stopwatch and flush the toilet at certain intervals during the performance. A longer version of the work was presented in November at Ono's concert at Carnegie Recital Hall.

ANTHOLOGY 6
AOS, the opera

The Village Gate program for April 3, 1961, listed *AOS* by Yoko Ono, erroneously credited to Ichiyanagi, with vocals by Simone [Forti] Morris. An expanded version of *AOS, the opera*, programed as *AOS—To David Tudor*, was presented during Ono's concert at Carnegie Recital Hall, November 24, 1961. This extraordinary work was performed by a group of artists who became central to Fluxus in the following years, including Ay-O, George Brecht, Philip Corner, Jackson Mac Low, Jonas Mekas, La Monte Young, and Ono herself. Movements were performed by dancers who became founders of postmodern dance, including Yvonne Rainer and Trisha Brown. We have only recently located this script for *AOS, the opera* and this is its first publication. Another version of the script appears in *Strip Tease Show* (Anthology 8).

ANTHOLOGY 7
Dear George...

Yoko Ono's seminal book *Grapefruit* was originally to have been published by Fluxus as a Fluxus edition, part of the series of planned complete works by Fluxus artists. However, George Maciunas was overwhelmed by activities for Fluxus and was unable to publish many of his planned projects, so Ono published the book herself in Tokyo on July 4, 1964, using the imprint name "Wunternaum Press."

This text serves as an introduction to the 1964 edition of *Grapefruit* and outlines Ono's attitude about her performance works—a position expanded on in her text "To the Wesleyan People" (1966; Anthology 14).

ANTHOLOGY 8
Strip Tease Show

This plan for a concert and exhibition was prepared in early 1966 as a proposal for a possible touring concert of Ono's work. The plan was never realized.

In the early spring of 1966, Ono was engaged in realizing an environment entitled *The Stone* with several other artists at the Judson Gallery in New York. During this time plans were also discussed with the author for an exhibition at a prominent New York gallery, and although that show did not materialize, ideas for it were incorporated in her show at Indica Gallery in London later in 1966.

ANTHOLOGY 9
9 Concert Pieces for John Cage

This is a collection of thirteen performance pieces with notes on their performances. They were written out in response to a request by John Cage for scores to be published in a book titled *Notations* that he was editing, and that was eventually published by the Something Else Press, New York in 1969. This version of the pieces is dated December 15, 1966, and is the most informative of the various versions that exist. They are reproduced here together with a letter to John Cage that accompanied them.

ANTHOLOGY 10
Fly—A Double Album

It is unfortunately possible to include only a very few music scores and lyrics by Ono in this book, even though music is an integral part of her art and will figure prominently in the exhibition. *Fly* serves both as the soundtrack of her film of the same name and as a sound work on her double album *Fly*. The idea of "Fly," "Flight," "Flies," freedom, fleeing, appears frequently in Ono's work in a variety of forms, including a printed score, canvases, billboards and posters, and performances and installations with ladders and other objects. This text on the double album *Fly* must serve as an example of Ono's work with music.

INSTRUCTURE

ANTHOLOGY 12
The Word of a Fabricator

This was written for publication in *SAC Journal* to coincide with Ono's May 24, 1962 concert and exhibition at Sōgetsu Art Center in Tokyo (no. 27). The text serves as a manifesto for the radical *terrain vague* that Ono was entering. It was during this exhibition that she first showed her *Instructions For Paintings*—a group of perhaps thirty-four conceptual word paintings written with ink on paper and taped to the walls of the art center. The other works listed on the program were *Pieces for Chairs No. 1 to No. 10*, *Of A Grapefruit in the World of Park*, *A Piece for Strawberries and Violin*, *A Piano Piece to See the Skies*, *The Pulse*, *AOS—To David Tudor*, *Touch Poems*, and *Chance Poems*.

ANTHOLOGY 13
Letter to Ivan Karp and *Reply from Ivan Karp*

Ono has used the art form of letters on several occasions to put forward ideas not easily conveyed in other media. Letters are direct, invite a response, and by their nature they appear intimate. Yet as an art form, the letters published by Ono expose that implied intimacy. The letter *Dear George* (1964) was used as an introduction to *Grapefruit*. Ono's *copy of letter sent to Ivan Karp Jan. 4, 1965* is a provocative manifestation about her art, values, and something of an indictment of the art establishment as it existed at the time. Karp was director of the Leo Castelli Gallery in New York, by then perhaps the most powerful gallery of contemporary art in the world. During 1964, the Castelli Gallery exhibited Frank Stella, John Chamberlain, Jasper Johns, Roy Lichtenstein, Robert Rauschenberg, Richard Artschwager, Christo, Alex Hay, Robert Watts, Jack Twombly, Jack Tworkov, Scarpetta, E. F. Higgins, James Rosenquist, and Andy Warhol. Besides being the bastion of Pop, it was basically an exclusive all-male club. That Ono would dare to propose entrance elicited an amazed response from Ivan Karp: "the kind of show you have in mind fails to suit our temperament which is essentially restless, driven, aggressive, fiercely Western and concrete. . . ." It was this attitude on the part of many museum directors, curators, and critics, and gallerists during this period in American and Western Europe that blocked the exhibitions of women and minority artists as well as artists of non-European origin and training. Ono must have been very hurt by the response. She advertised copies of the correspondence in her 1965 *Ono's Sales List* in this way,

> H. Letters
> types:
> a) letter to Ivan Karp . . . . original . . . $300
> copies . . . 50c
>
> b) reply from Ivan Karp . . . . . original . . . 2c
> copies . . . 50c

clearly dismissing the attitude in Karp's response as basically worthless and contemptible.

ANTHOLOGY 14
To the Wesleyan People

Expanding on her philosophy of conceptualism that she first published in "The Word of a Fabricator" (1962) and *On Insound and On Instructure* (1964), Ono clearly states her ideas of "music of the mind" and "painting to construct in your head" in this text. "To the Wesleyan People" was first published in 1966 as a mimeographed insert in the publication accompanying the environment *The Stone*, presented at Judson Gallery, New York. It was reprinted that year in the publication *Yoko at Indica: Unfinished Paintings and Objects by Yoko Ono* for Indica Gallery, London, and subsequently in numerous editions of *Grapefruit* and exhibition catalogues.

ANTHOLOGY 15
Some Notes on the Lisson Gallery Show

Published in the catalogue for the London exhibition *Yoko Ono at Lisson: Half-A-Wind Show*, 1967, this text offers clues to two works in that show—*Switch Piece* and *Painting to Hammer a Nail*—and several ideas for future works. It is perhaps more significant because it does not attempt to explain the majority of the works in the exhibition. Instead, the text is an adjunct to the show—a kind of device to set the mind in a particular gear while thinking about the works in the show. These included Environments—*The Stone*, *The Blue Room*, *Half-A-Spring Room* (*Half-A-Room*), *Backyard*—and objects such as *Air Bottles* by John Lennon and Yoko Ono, Ono's *Three Spoons*, and *Mind Object: not to be appreciated until it's broken.*

ANTHOLOGY 16

What Is the Relationship Between the World and the Artist?

This text acts as a preface-manifesto to *Seven Texts* in the book *Museum of Modern [F]art* (1971). It was written earlier than those writings on ownership and flight, and serves as a bridge statement on the revolutionary role of the artist. It was written during an intense period of anger and frustration about the United States' war against Vietnam, and at racial and gender divisions and prejudice.

The *Seven Texts* which appear at the end of the book are concerned with the artist's attitude towards ownership (the "poverty of possessions") and freedom ("How to Fly—1. make sure that your mind is not clogged..."). One can view these texts as an adjunct to the accusations inherent in the sequential part of the book and a statement of position regarding values, art and the individual.

Museum of Modern [F]art: Yoko Ono One Woman Show is a conceptual artist's book. It is a sequential book about self, time, location, and participation. It is also a statement of gender exclusion. The work is an accusation against the art establishment as exemplified by the Museum of Modern Art, New York.

ANTHOLOGY 17

Bronze Age

In 1987 Ono began a series of bronze works referencing earlier works. Some of the pieces were fairly careful replicas of older works transformed with the use of the new material. Others were commentaries on or reversals of older works.

FILMS

ANTHOLOGY 20

Six Film Scripts by Yoko Ono

ANTHOLOGY 21

On Film No. 4

ANTHOLOGY 22

From ***Thirteen Film Scores by Yoko Ono***

ANTHOLOGY 23

On Rape

This section breaks down into two parts: two self-published collections of film scores from 1964 and 1968, and two texts on specific films. Ono's films and film scores are important aspects of the entire body of her art. And, as with her scores for Architecture, Painting, Dance etc., some are intended to be realized, others are intended to be seen only in the mind.

ON WOMEN

ANTHOLOGY 24

The Feminization of Society

The idea of women's liberation appears frequently in Ono's artworks. *Voice Piece for Soprano*, *Cut Piece*, the film and music *Fly*, *Rising*, *Painting to Hammer a Nail*, *Vertical Memory* are all strong feminist statements. As a woman, she has suffered the abuse of men—as an Asian woman artist working in an unfamiliar terrain, she has been the victim of extreme prejudice and intentional misunderstanding. "The Feminization of Society" is a manifesto for liberation.

CLOSING

ANTHOLOGY 25

From ***Seven Little Stories***

"The Connection" and "Reincarnation" are two early poems with themes of ownership, commonality, and balance that reemerge in her later writings. Compare, for example, "you know, our blood is seawater/and we are all seacarriers" with her 1967 work "Water Talk," which reads in part, "you are water/I'm water/we're all water in different containers."

ANTHOLOGY 26

Biography/Statement

Many of Ono's works contain elements of self or biography. These two texts were written for inclusion in *The Stone* (1966). Two recent works, *Vertical Memory* (1997; pl. 69) and *Portrait of Nora* (1992; pl. 71), contain strong autobiographical elements as well.

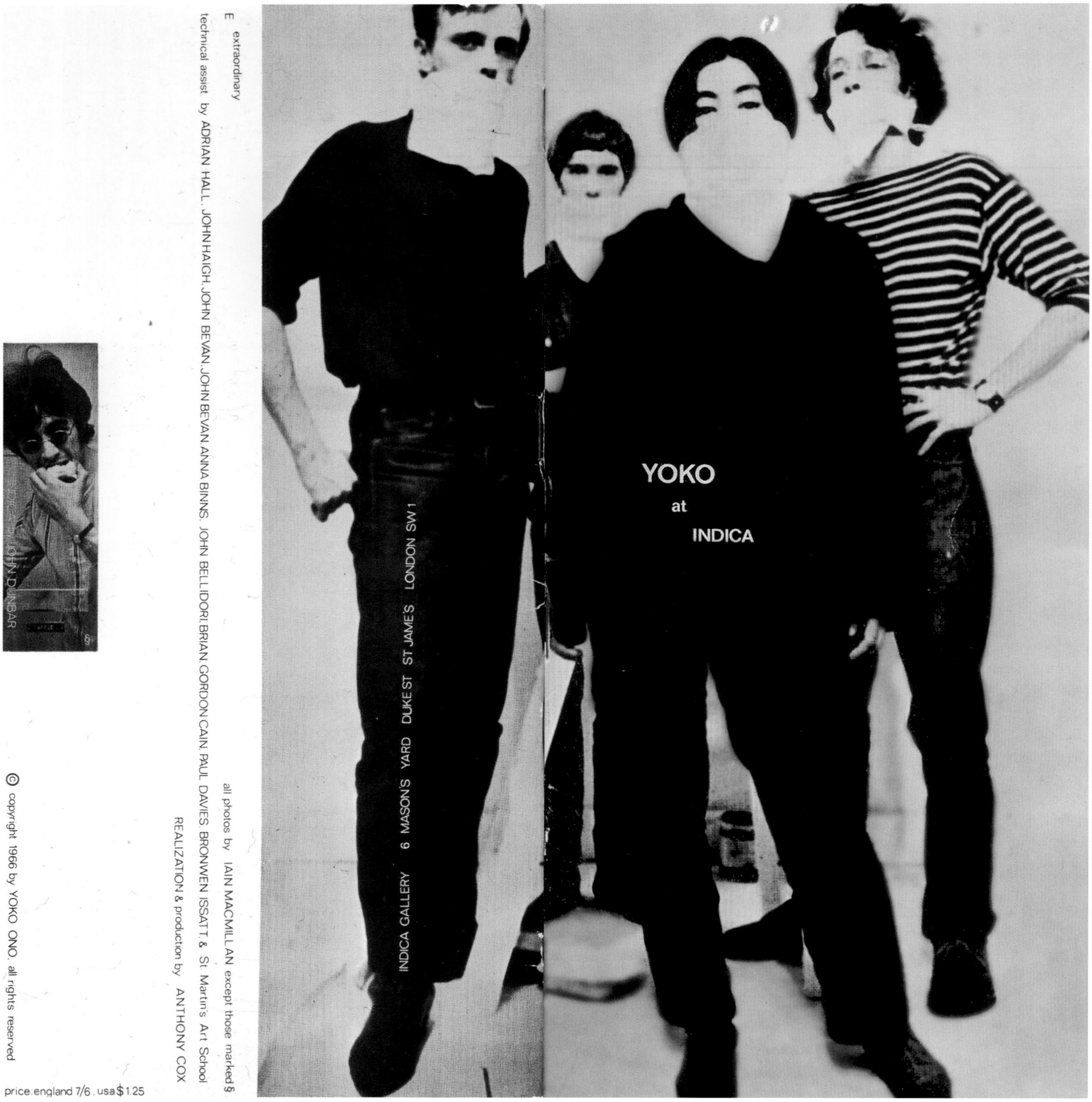

FIGURE 14.1
YOKO AT INDICA, EXH. CAT. (1966), FRONT AND BACK COVER

Chronology: Exhibitions, Concerts, Events, etc.

REIKO TOMII AND KEVIN CONCANNON

To map the artistic career of Yoko Ono is the task of the Chronology and Bibliography in the current volume. These compilations are by no means complete or exhaustive. History-writing is always a work in progress, shaped in an endless process of discovery, reflection, and reevaluation. In this sense, our Chronology and Bibliography constitute a new step in Yoko Ono studies, part of an ongoing exploration.

What makes our documentary project at once challenging and fascinating is the fact that the subject of this research has long been a public figure—each step of hers watched by the media, which generates ream upon ream of information on her. More importantly, in Ono's work, art and life are truly inseparable, to an extent that transcends the familiar avant-garde credo of mixing the two. In addition, Ono has often perceptively exploited the popular media to disseminate information on her works and ideas.

Another significant aspect of her career is that it spans the second half of the last century, and continues to flourish in full force entering the new century. During this time, the place of art in general, and the avant-garde in particular, within society has changed. Especially in the 1990s—the so-called decade of museums—the number of institutionally organized exhibitions and programs has dramatically increased worldwide, as have the information outlets that cover these events. In this information age, Ono's artistic activities have taken on an expanded dimension in an environment more accessible and conducive, and perhaps ever more public, than in the sixties.

Our goal has been to capture Ono's vast achievements that have taken place in this changing context as fully as possible within a limited space, while organizing clear and readable documents that will serve as a useful resource for further understanding and study of the artist's work. Focus is placed upon her exhibitions, concerts, and events, although certain activities (e.g., TV appearances and political protests) are selectively included to illuminate the breadth of her oeuvre.

Entries are ordered by date, with significant events highlighted. Each entry consists of: date; exhibition/concert/event title, where known, or descriptive caption; name of venue; and city. Narrative details are given to contextualize the artist's activities, where pertinent information has been uncovered during research. "Documents," where noted, comprise primary source materials that help substantiate captioned events, ranging from exhibition catalogues and concert programs to posters and flyers to newspaper ads and listings. Full citations of solo exhibition catalogues and select group exhibition catalogues can be found in the Bibliography.

This type of research project is never possible without the generous cooperation of many individuals and institutions. Our utmost appreciation goes to the artist herself, who generously opened her archives and clipping collections, responding patiently to our numerous queries. Equally vital was the assistance of Jon Hendricks, who shared with us his in-depth knowledge of the artist's work and assisted us in consulting the artist's archives and the Gilbert and Lila Silverman Fluxus Collection Archives, which he administers. Other individuals are separately acknowledged. Archives in which we have conducted research are listed in the Bibliography.

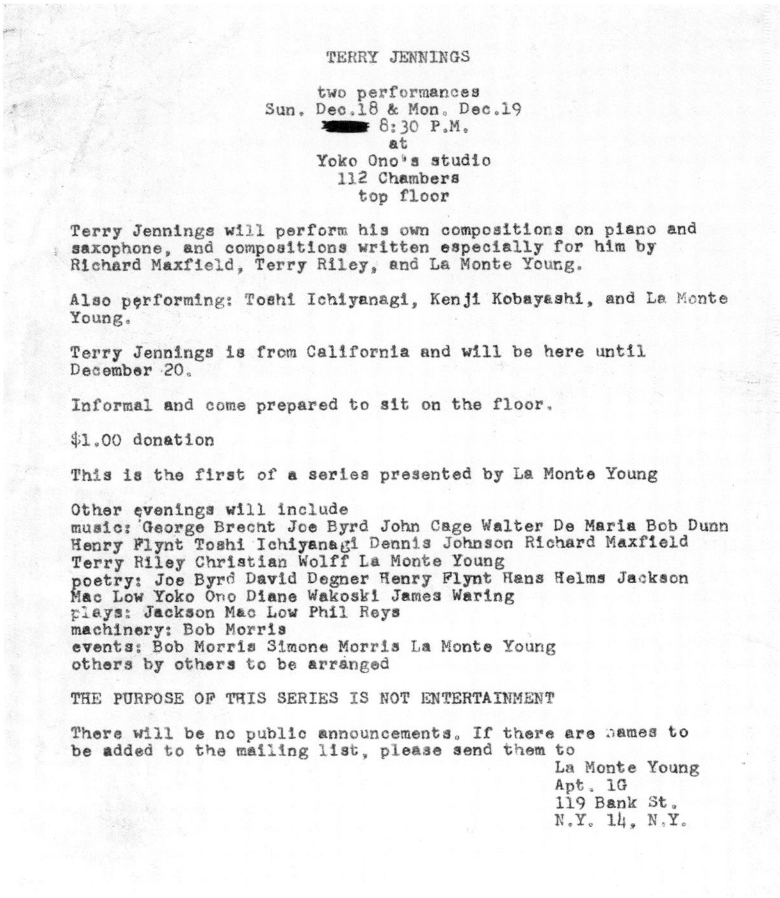

TERRY JENNINGS

two performances
Sun. Dec.18 & Mon. Dec.19
[redacted] 8:30 P.M.
at
Yoko Ono's studio
112 Chambers
top floor

Terry Jennings will perform his own compositions on piano and saxophone, and compositions written especially for him by Richard Maxfield, Terry Riley, and La Monte Young.

Also performing: Toshi Ichiyanagi, Kenji Kobayashi, and La Monte Young.

Terry Jennings is from California and will be here until December 20.

Informal and come prepared to sit on the floor.

$1.00 donation

This is the first of a series presented by La Monte Young

Other evenings will include
music: George Brecht Joe Byrd John Cage Walter De Maria Bob Dunn Henry Flynt Toshi Ichiyanagi Dennis Johnson Richard Maxfield Terry Riley Christian Wolff La Monte Young
poetry: Joe Byrd David Degner Henry Flynt Hans Helms Jackson Mac Low Yoko Ono Diane Wakoski James Waring
plays: Jackson Mac Low Phil Reys
machinery: Bob Morris
events: Bob Morris Simone Morris La Monte Young
others by others to be arranged

THE PURPOSE OF THIS SERIES IS NOT ENTERTAINMENT

There will be no public announcements. If there are names to be added to the mailing list, please send them to
La Monte Young
Apt. 1G
119 Bank St.
N.Y. 14, N.Y.

FIGURE 14.2
PROGRAM, "TERRY JENNINGS," 1960 FROM *CHAMBERS STREET LOFT SERIES*. THE GILBERT AND LILA SILVERMAN FLUXUS COLLECTION, DETROIT

1959–61

BIOGRAPHY: From 1956, lives with husband Ichiyanagi Toshi in New York at 426 Amsterdam Avenue; signs a lease for a Chambers Street loft in December 1960

Cultural programs, various venues
Ono, with Ichiyanagi Toshi, is employed by Beate Sirota Gordon of Japan Society, New York, to perform in cultural programs at universities, colleges, and various organizations, such as Brooklyn College and *Fine Art Festival* of Thiel College, Penn. Her demonstration includes the recitation of traditional poems, calligraphy, music, and origami; she also recites her own poems. In 1960, two such events are documented: March 23, at Memorial Hall, Pratt Institute, Brooklyn, cosponsored by Department of Graphic Arts and Illustration; and May 26, at Pi Eta Theater of Harvard University, Cambridge, sponsored by Japan Society of Boston. In both Ono also performs "unfolding" of origami.
DOCUMENTS: program for Pratt Institute; program for Harvard University

1960–62

December 1960–June 1961
Chambers Street Loft Series, Ono's loft at 112 Chambers Street, New York
During this period, Ono opens her top-floor loft for a series of events organized by La Monte Young and herself. Programs include:

- Terry Jennings (December 18–19, 1960; fig. 14.2)
- Ichiyanagi Toshi, *Music* (January 7–8, 1961)
- Henry Flynt, *Music and Poetry* (February 25–26, 1961)
- Joseph Byrd, *Music and Poetry* (March 4–5, 1961)
- Jackson Mac Low (April 8–9, 1961)
- Richard Maxfield (April 29–30, 1961
- *Compositions by La Monte Young* (May 19–20, 1961)
- Simone Morris, *Five Dance Constructions + Some Other Things* (May 26–27, 1961)
- Robert Morris, *An Environment* (June 3–7, 1961)
- Dennis Lindberg, *Blind: A Happening* (June 28–30, 1961).

Music of Phillip Corner is an addendum to the series in 1962 (January 26, 28). Extant programs do not include Ono's performance; however, Gordon recalls seeing Ono perform *Kitchen Piece* and *Smoke Piece* and Ono herself remembers performing *Pea Piece*, a piano piece, and a body-roll piece. Ono also performed in others' events.
DOCUMENTS: flyers

1961

April 3
An Evening of Contemporary Japanese Music and Poetry, The Village Gate, New York
Three-person concert. Presented by David Johnson, program includes music by Mayuzumi Toshirō and Ichiyanagi, and poetry by Ono. Ono stages and narrates *Of a Grapefruit in the World of Park*, accompanied by David Tudor, Mayuzumi, and Ichiyanagi (piano); La Mar Alsop and Kobayashi Kenji (violin); Jacob Glick (viola); and David Soyer (cello).
DOCUMENTS: program

June 16, 17–30
Paintings and Drawings by Yoko Ono, AG Gallery, New York
Solo exhibition (fig. 14.3). Previews on June 16, followed by a two-week run. In addition to *Instruction Paintings*, Ono also shows calligraphic works and other works on paper at the request of gallery co-owner George Maciunas (fig. 1.9). See no. 2.
DOCUMENTS: flyer

August 3
Montreal Festival
Performs *A Grapefruit in the World of Park* in "Concert No. 4" of *1ère Semaine Internationale de Musique Actuelle*, held at Comédie Canadienne.
DOCUMENTS: annotated program

November 24
Works by Yoko Ono, Carnegie Recital Hall, New York
Solo concert (figs. 1.11, 2.4, 14.4). Presented by Norman J. Seaman, program includes *A Grapefruit in the World of Park*, *A Piece for Strawberries and Violin*, and *AOS—To David Tudor*. Voice and instruments are provided by Ono, together with Ay-O, George Brecht, Philip Corner, Mac Low, Jonas Mekas, Yvonne Rainer, Young, Charlotte Moorman, and others, with movements by Patricia (Trisha) Brown, Rainer, and others. See no. 52.
DOCUMENTS: announcement card/program; poster; concert listing, *New York Times*, 19 November 1961, sec. 2 p. 14

1962

BIOGRAPHY: Goes back to Japan on March 3; lives in Tokyo until fall 1964
FILMS RELEASED: Takahiko Iimura, *Ai/Love* (soundtrack by Ono)

January 8
Benefit event for the publication of *An Anthology*, The Living Theater, New York
Ono's contribution to the program comprises her performance of *The Chair No. 1* as well as Ichiyanagi's *Mudai No. 1*. Lobby exhibition includes *Touch Poem* (fig. 14.5).
DOCUMENTS: program for January 8; flyer for January 8 and February 5

May 24
Sōgetsu Contemporary Series 15: Works of Yoko Ono, Sōgetsu Art Center (Sōgetsu Kaikan Hall), Tokyo
Solo recital-exhibition. Having returned to Tokyo, Ono

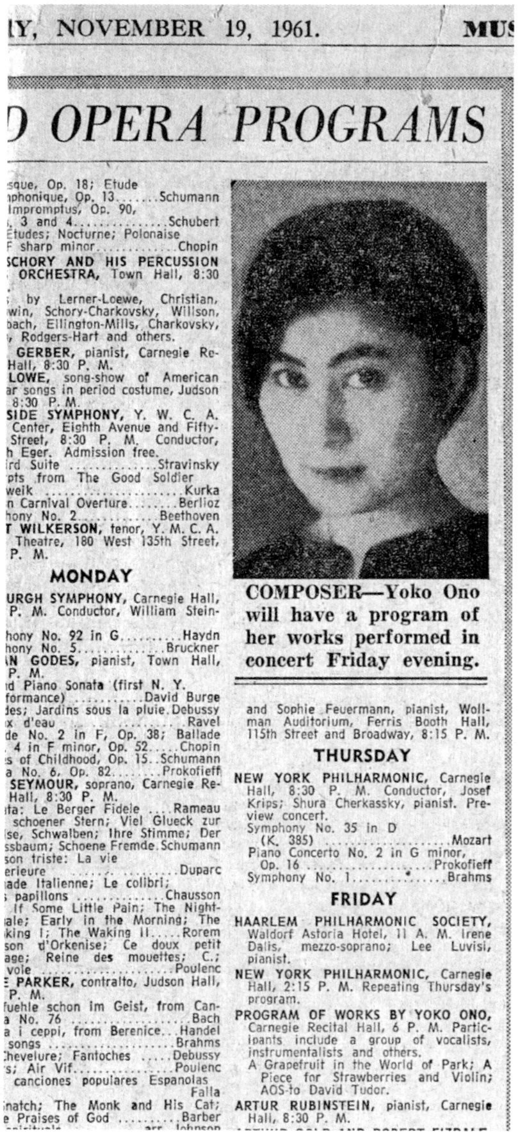

...Y, NOVEMBER 19, 1961. MU...

...D OPERA PROGRAMS

...sque, Op. 18; Etude
...phonique, Op. 13 .... Schumann
Impromptus, Op. 90,
... 3 and 4 .... Schubert
Études; Nocturne; Polonaise
F sharp minor .... Chopin
...SCHORY AND HIS PERCUSSION ORCHESTRA, Town Hall, 8:30
... by Lerner-Loewe, Christian, ...win, Schory-Charkovsky, Willson, ...bach, Ellington-Mills, Charkovsky, ... Rodgers-Hart and others.
... GERBER, pianist, Carnegie Re... Hall, 8:30 P. M.
... LOWE, song-show of American ...ar songs in period costume, Judson ... 8:30 P. M.
...SIDE SYMPHONY, Y. W. C. A. Center, Eighth Avenue and Fifty-... Street, 8:30 P. M. Conductor, ...h Eger. Admission free.
...ird Suite .... Stravinsky
...pts from The Good Soldier
...weik .... Kurka
...n Carnival Overture .... Berlioz
...hony No. 2 .... Beethoven
...T WILKERSON, tenor, Y. M. C. A. Theatre, 180 West 135th Street, ... P. M.

MONDAY

...URGH SYMPHONY, Carnegie Hall, ... P. M. Conductor, William Stein-...
...hony No. 92 in G .... Haydn
...hony No. 5 .... Bruckner
...N GODES, pianist, Town Hall, ... P. M.
...d Piano Sonata (first N. Y. ...formance) .... David Burge
...des; Jardins sous la pluie. Debussy
...x d'eau .... Ravel
...de No. 2 in F, Op. 38; Ballade ... 4 in F minor, Op. 52 ..... Chopin
...s of Childhood, Op. 15 .. Schumann
...a No. 6, Op. 82 .... Prokofieff
... SEYMOUR, soprano, Carnegie Re... Hall, 8:30 P. M.
...ta: Le Berger Fidele .... Rameau
... schoener Stern; Viel Glueck zur ...se, Schwalben; Ihre Stimme; Der ...ssbaum; Schoene Fremde. Schumann
...son triste: La vie ...erieure .... Duparc
...ade Italienne; Le colibri; ... papillons .... Chausson
... If Some Little Pain; The Night-...ale; Early in the Morning; The ...king I; The Waking II ..... Rorem
...son d'Orkenise; Ce doux petit ...age; Reine des mouettes; C.; ...vole .... Poulenc
... PARKER, contralto, Judson Hall, ... P. M.
...fuehle schon im Geist, from Can-...a No. 76 .... Bach
...a i ceppi, from Berenice ... Handel
... songs .... Brahms
...hevelure; Fantoches ..... Debussy
...s; Air Vif .... Poulenc
... canciones populares Espanolas ... Falla
...natch; The Monk and His Cat; ...e Praises of God .... Barber

COMPOSER—Yoko Ono will have a program of her works performed in concert Friday evening.

and Sophie Feuermann, pianist, Wollman Auditorium, Ferris Booth Hall, 115th Street and Broadway, 8:15 P. M.

THURSDAY

NEW YORK PHILHARMONIC, Carnegie Hall, 8:30 P. M. Conductor, Josef Krips; Shura Cherkassky, pianist. Preview concert.
Symphony No. 35 in D (K. 385) .... Mozart
Piano Concerto No. 2 in G minor, Op. 16 .... Prokofieff
Symphony No. 1 .... Brahms

FRIDAY

HAARLEM PHILHARMONIC SOCIETY, Waldorf Astoria Hotel, 11 A. M. Irene Dalis, mezzo-soprano; Lee Luvisi, pianist.
NEW YORK PHILHARMONIC, Carnegie Hall, 2:15 P. M. Repeating Thursday's program.
PROGRAM OF WORKS BY YOKO ONO, Carnegie Recital Hall, 6 P. M. Participants include a group of vocalists, instrumentalists and others.
A Grapefruit in the World of Park; A Piece for Strawberries and Violin; AOS-to David Tudor.
ARTUR RUBINSTEIN, pianist, Carnegie Hall, 8:30 P. M.

FIGURE 14.4
LISTING OF ***WORKS BY YOKO ONO***, IN *NEW YORK TIMES*

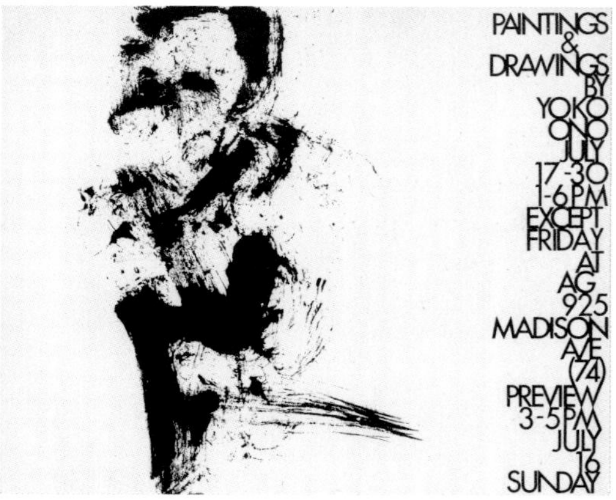

FIGURE 14.3
FLYER, ***PAINTINGS AND DRAWINGS BY YOKO ONO***, AG GALLERY, NEW YORK, 1961

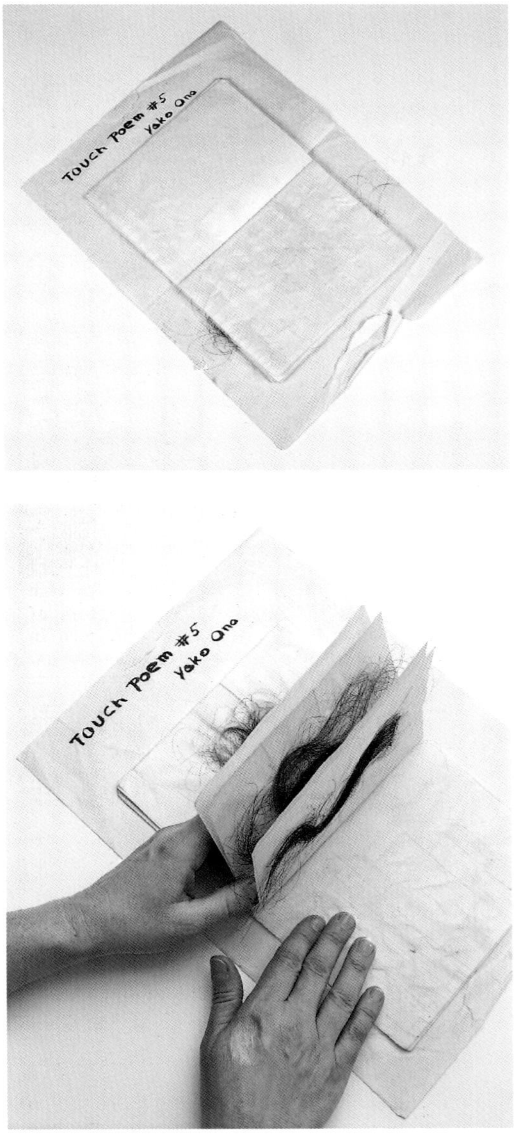

FIGURE 14.5
TOUCH POEM NO. 5,
CA. 1960. PAPER
AND HAIR

gives her first solo program in Japan (fig. 14.6). See nos. 1, 3, 27.
DOCUMENTS: program

May 28
Sōgetsu Contemporary Series 14: Kobayashi Kenji + Ichiyanagi Toshi, Duo Recital, Sōgetsu Art Center (Sōgetsu Kaikan Hall), Tokyo
Performs in Ichiyanagi's *The Pile*.

September 1, 9, 15
Fluxus internationale Festspiele Neuester Musik, lecture room at Städtischen Museums, Wiesbaden, Germany
First Fluxus concert series (fig. 2.5) includes *Ein Stück um den Himmel zu sehen* (Piece to See the Skies) in "Concert No. 2" (1st), *Der Puls* (The Pulse) in "Concert No. 6" (9th), and *Zwei Stücke* (Two Pieces) in "Concert No. 9" (15th). All performed by other artists. *News-Policy-Letter No. 2 (Fluxus Festival Only)*, dated July 12 lists Ono as member of "Festival Planning Committee." Hereafter Ono's name frequently appears in Fluxus documents.
DOCUMENTS: program; poster

October 9
Sōgetsu Contemporary Series 17: John Cage, Tokyo Bunka Kaikan Hall, Tokyo
Concert organized by Sōgetsu Art Center. Performs in the premiere of Cage's *Music Walk*, together with Cage, Tudor, Ichiyanagi, Takahashi Yūji, Kobayashi, Mayuzumi, and Takemitsu Tōru (fig. 11.2). During Cage and Tudor's Japanese tour in this month, Ono accompanies them as a performer in Tokyo, Sapporo, Kyoto (12th, Kaikan Daini Hall), and Osaka (17th, Midō Kaikan).
DOCUMENTS: program, printed in *SAC Journal*, no. 27 (October 1962)

October 10
Sōgetsu Contemporary Series 17: David Tudor, Tokyo Bunka Kaikan Hall, Tokyo
Concert organized by Sōgetsu Art Center. Ono (voice) and Tudor (piano), assisted by Cage, perform in the premiere of Cage's *Arias and Solo for Piano with Fontana Mix*.
DOCUMENTS: program, printed in *SAC Journal*, no. 27 (October 1962)

October 24
Sōgetsu Contemporary Series 19: Event of John Cage/David Tudor, Sōgetsu Art Center (Sōgetsu Kaikan Hall), Tokyo
Cage premieres *0′00″*, dedicated to Ichiyanagi and Ono; the couple perform in Young's *Poem*, together with Cage, Tudor, Kobayashi, Takahashi, Takemitsu, and Mayuzumi.
DOCUMENTS: program, printed in *SAC Journal*, no. 27 (October 1962)

October 26
Sapporo Contemporary Music Festival, Sapporo Shimin Kaikan Hall, Sapporo
As part of Sōgetsu Art Center's contemporary music project, a group of musicians are organized, including Ozawa Seiji, Kobayashi, Ichiyanagi, and Takahashi. The members participate in the music festival, with cooperation of Cage and Tudor. Ono performs with the group in the premiere of Ichiyanagi's *Sapporo*, conducted by Ozawa.
DOCUMENTS: announcement, printed in *SAC Journal*, no. 27 (October 1962)

November 25
Festum Fluxorum, Allé Scenen, Copenhagen
Program includes Ono's *The Pulse* in "Concert No. 3" for instrumental, vocal, and "action" music. Hereafter Fluxus concerts in Europe frequently include Ono's works performed by other artists.
DOCUMENTS: program

1963

BIOGRAPHY: Marries Anthony Cox; Kyoko Cox born on August 3 (fig. 14.7)

February 2–3
Festum Fluxorum Fluxus: Musik und Antimusik das Instrumentale Theater, Staatliche Kunstakademie, Düsseldorf
DOCUMENTS: poster (fig. 14.8)

1963–64

dates undetermined
During her stay in Japan, the following works by Ono are performed: *Question Piece* and *Palm Piece* by Ono and Anthony Cox for a radio program; *Question Piece* for Voice of America Japan in English; *Question Piece* by six children from the audience on Nippon TV; *Flower Event*; and *Shadow Event*.

1964

BIOGRAPHY: Issues the first edition of *Grapefruit* from Wunternaum Press on July 4 (see no. 4); moves back to New York in September
FILMS RELEASED: Kuri Yōji, *AOS* (voice by Ono)

January 26–27
Hi Red Center's *Shelter Plan*, Imperial Hotel, Tokyo
Together with Nam June Paik, designer Yokoo Tadanori, and others, participates in the event to take various body measurements to create "custom-made" shelters for purchase (fig. 1.12).

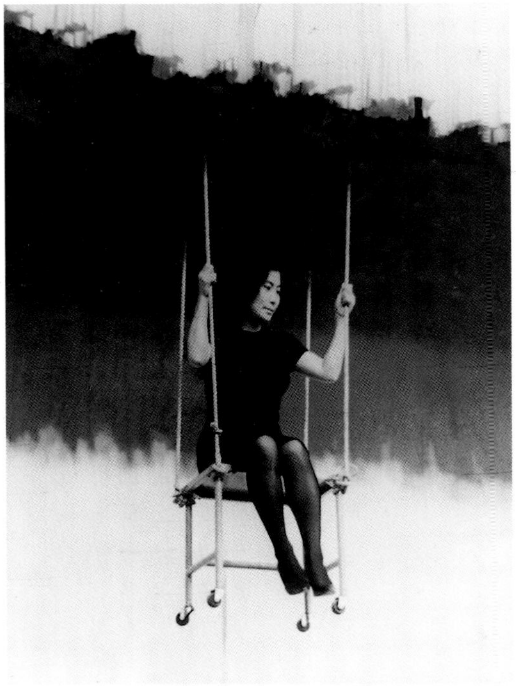

FIGURE 14.6
CHAIR PIECE (CHAIR ASCENSION),
SŌGETSU ART CENTER,
TOKYO, 1962

FIGURE 14.7

UNTITLED (BIRTH ANNOUNCEMENT),

1963. OFFSET ON PAPER

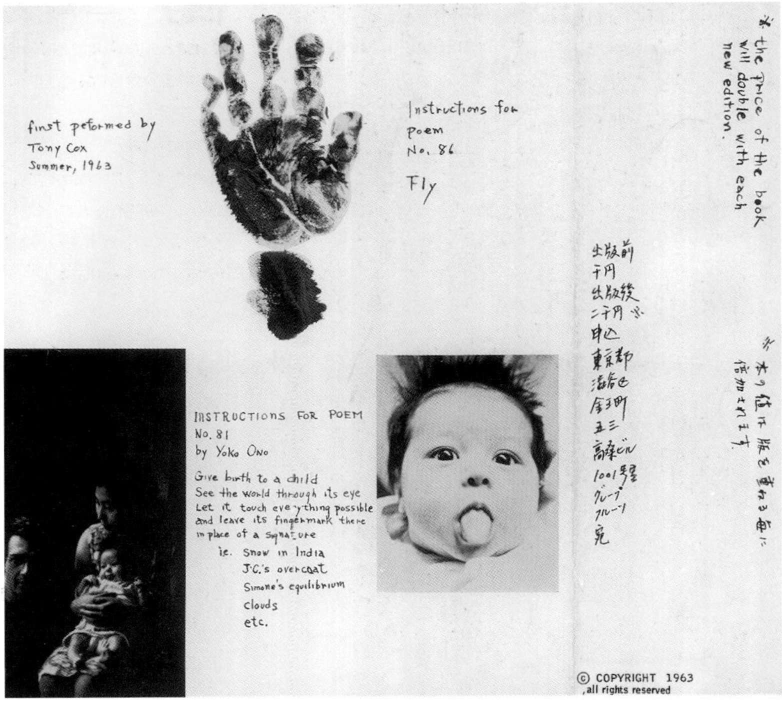

FIGURE 14.8

FLUXUS, ***FESTUM FLUXORUM FLUXUS,***

POSTER, 1963. THE GILBERT AND LILA SILVERMAN FLUXUS COLLECTION, DETROIT

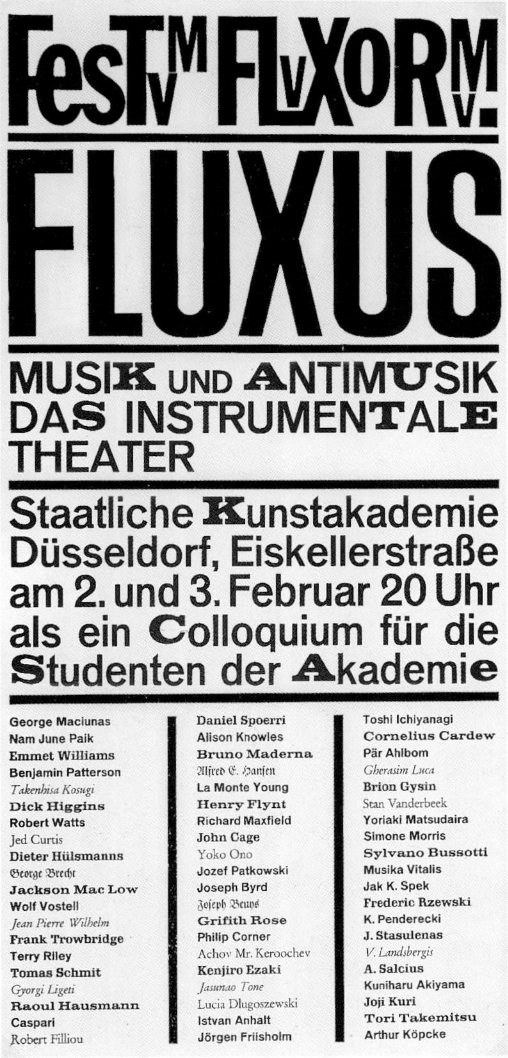

February 19

Perpetual Fluxus Festival, Washington Square Gallery, New York

Year-round program lists *Yoko Ono: From Grapefruit* (fig. 2.7). Event postponed.

DOCUMENTS: poster

March 33

***Touch Poem No. 3,* Nigeria, Africa**

Solo imaginary event, postcard. See no. 35.

April 25

***Fly,* Naiqua Gallery, Tokyo**

Solo event. Ono's work performed by attendees in her absence. See no. 28.

May 24, 31

***9 a.m. to 11 a.m.,* roofs of Naiqua Gallery (24th) and Ono's apartment (31st), Tokyo**

Solo event (figs. 1.16–17). Instruction reads: "Wash your ears well before attending." "Mornings" of three types (A. until sunrise; B. after sunrise; C. all morning) for eleven future dates are sold at varying prices (from ¥10 to ¥1000). Also known as *Morning Piece* (see 1965, September 12, 19, 26).

DOCUMENTS: typed flyers; handwritten "Notice" and "Oshirase"

May 29

Sōgetsu Contemporary Series: Works of Nam June Paik, Sōgetsu Art Center (Sōgetsu Kaikan Hall), Tokyo

Performs in Paik's concert.

DOCUMENTS: program

June

***Touch Piece,* Naiqua Gallery, Tokyo**

Solo event. A group of people including Ono sit in a circle and touch each other in silence. Nam June Paik joins from outside by serially ringing the gallery's telephone.

June 7, 14, 21

***3 Old Paintings of Yoko Ono,* Naiqua Gallery, Tokyo**

Solo imaginary event takes place in three parts between 5 and 11 a.m., with "no critics, art dealers, or dogs allowed." Presented: *Painting to See the Sky* (7th); *Painting to Shake Hands* (14th); *Smoke Painting* (21st).

DOCUMENTS: typed flyer

June 27

Fluxus Symphony Orchestra in Fluxus Concert, Carnegie Recital Hall, New York

Program lists *Questionnaire* at the end of "Part 1" and Ono and Shiomi Chieko's *Reply to Questionnaire* in the beginning of "Part 2." Performed by other artists.

DOCUMENTS: program in playing-card format

summer

***Morning Piece,* park in Tokyo**

Solo event. Ono and Cox sell "mornings" (see 1964, May 24, 31).

July 3

***Distillation Event,* Tokyo**

Solo event.

July 4

***Grapefruit* publication event, Tokyo**

Solo event. Upon publication of the first edition of *Grapefruit*, Ono and Cox sell books for ¥2,000 on the streets of the Ginza district.

July 20

***Contemporary American Avant-Garde Music Concert: Insound and Instructure,* Yamaichi Hall, Kyoto**

Solo event with Cox and Al Wonderlick. Marks the beginning of a three-day program in Kyoto (figs. 1.2, 14.9). Premiere of *Cut Piece* (see no. 30) and *Bag Piece* (see no. 31), among other performances.

DOCUMENTS: program; poster; ticket; three-event series ticket

July 21

***Evening till Dawn,* Nanzenji, Kyoto**

Solo event. Ono, together with Cox and Wonderlick, organize an event that lasts from 6 p.m. till the next morning. See no. 29.

DOCUMENTS: ticket

July 22

***Symposium: !* French Cancan Coffee House, Kyoto**

Solo event. See no. 29.

DOCUMENTS: ticket

August 11

***Yoko Ono Farewell Concert: Strip-Tease Show,* Sōgetsu Art Center (Sōgetsu Kaikan Hall), Tokyo**

Solo concert consists of three parts: "sprout," "motional," and "whisper," assisted by Cox and Jeff

FIGURE 14.9
POSTER FOR THREE KYOTO EVENTS, 1964. COLLECTION OF JON HENDRICKS

FIGURE 14.10
CUT PIECE, SŌGETSU ART CENTER, TOKYO, 1964 (SOURCE UNIDENTIFIED)

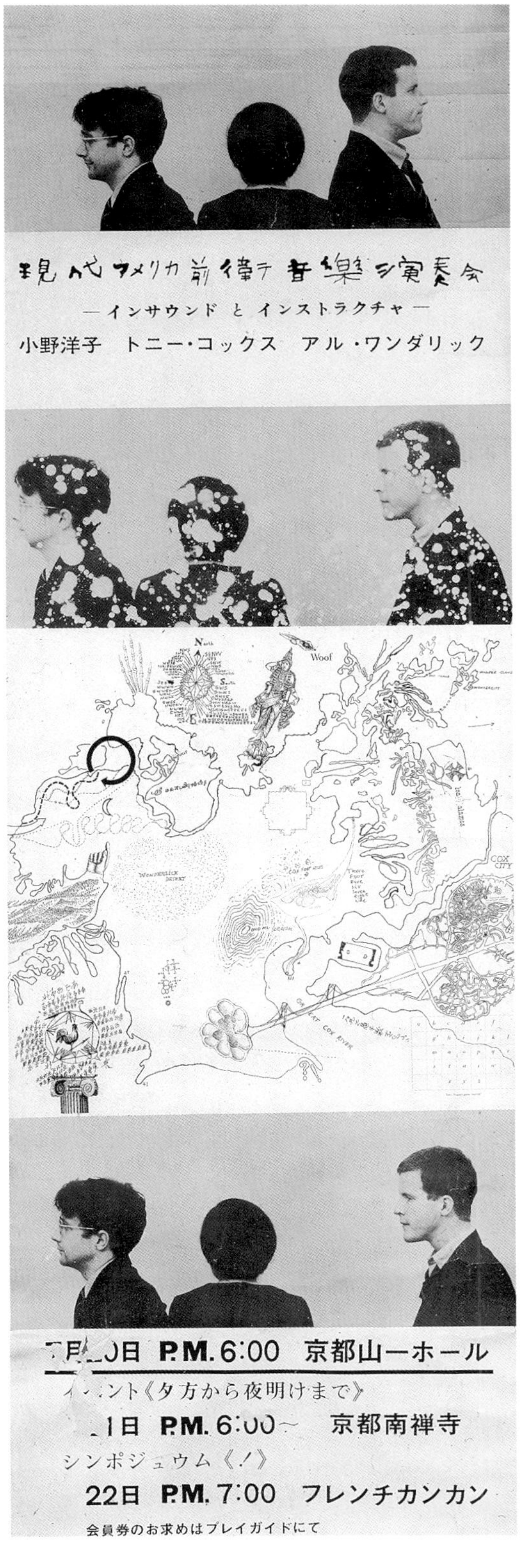

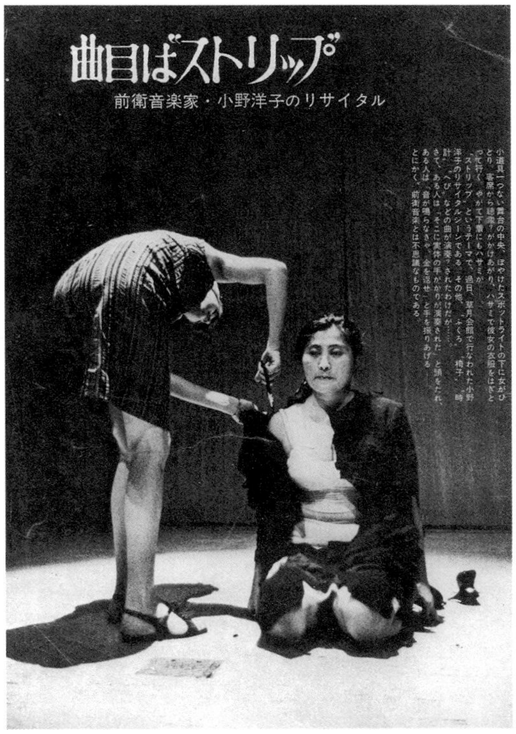

Perkins. Ono performed, among others, *Cut Piece* (fig. 14.10).
DOCUMENTS: announcement; press release (English); poster and ticket (Japanese)

September–October
Jury Event, Tokyo
Ono listed as a juror in the ad and application for a Tone-Prize competition conceived by musician-artist Yasunao Tone (fig. 9.2).

September 16
2nd New York Film Festival, Lincoln Center for the Performing Arts, New York
Returns to New York as interpreter for Teshigahara Hiroshi, whose film *Woman in the Dunes* is featured at the festival.

October 4
Nonfiction Theater, Nippon TV, Tokyo
Appears on a 10:15–10:45 p.m. program to explain her "eccentric conducts," which are "suitable to fill up the 'hollowness' of life."
DOCUMENTS: channel listing, *Yomiuri* (English), 4 October 1964, p. 7

Christmas time
Air Talk in New York
Solo postcard event. Instructs "keep smiling."

winter 1964–65
***Draw Circle Event*, New York**
Solo postcard event (fig. 14.11). Instructs "draw circle," answer the questionnaire, and send back to the artist at Empire State Building. Ono receives many responses, which the building's mail room staff hold for her.

1965

BIOGRAPHY: Lives in New York at 156 Prince Street, 37 Christopher Street, and 616 Hudson Street

early 1965 [?]
***Cut Out the Following Dotted Line*, New York**
Solo postcard event. Instructs "cut out the following dotted line" and return it to the artist at Empire State Building, where she briefly worked.

March 3–31
***Yoko Ono: Circle Event*, IsReal Gallery, New York**
Solo imaginary exhibition at a space that exists only in an advertisement. See no. 36.

March 21
***New Works of Yoko Ono*, Carnegie Recital Hall, New York**
Solo concert (fig. 14.12). Presented by Norman J. Seaman, it includes: *Bag Piece*; *Striptease for Three*; *Cut Piece*; * *Piece* [*missing word to be announced]; *Clock Piece*.
DOCUMENTS: flyer; program

April–May
***Hole Event*, IsReal Gallery, New York**
Solo imaginary exhibition at a space that exists only in an advertisement. See no. 36.

June 3
Concert by Moorman and Paik, Aachen
Touch Poem performed by Moorman and Paik. From 1965 until her death in 1991, Moorman regularly performs *Cut Piece* and *Touch Poem* in her concerts, including such two-person programs with Paik.
DOCUMENTS: program

June 15
Siebte Soiree, Galerie René Block, Berlin
Concert by Moorman (cello) and Paik (piano) includes *Touch Poem*.
DOCUMENTS: program

June 25
3° Festival Gruppo '70, Galleria Numero, Florence
Concert by Moorman and others includes *Touch Poem*.
DOCUMENTS: program

June 27
***Perpetual Flux Fest Presents Yoko Ono*, Cinematheque (at East End Theater), New York**
Solo event. Performs *Bag Piece* and premieres *Beat Piece* (fig. 2.9).
DOCUMENTS: ad, *Village Voice*, 24 June 1965, p. 23

August 30, September 1
First World Congress: Happenings, St. Mary's of the Harbor, New York
Octopus Allstars' feature presentation of Al Hansen's *Parisol 4 Marisol* also includes Ono's work.
DOCUMENTS: poster

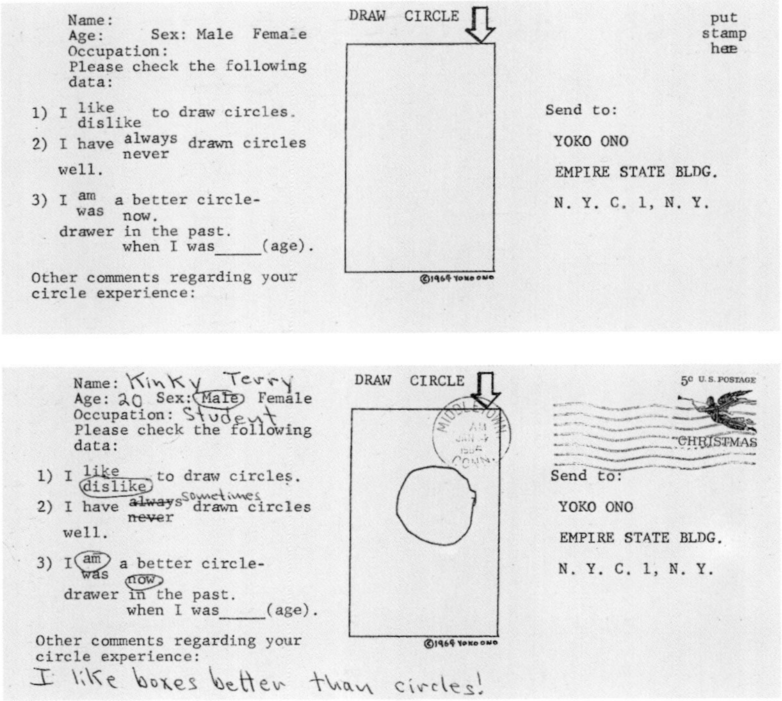

FIGURE 14.11
DRAW CIRCLE CARD,
1964–65. POSTCARDS

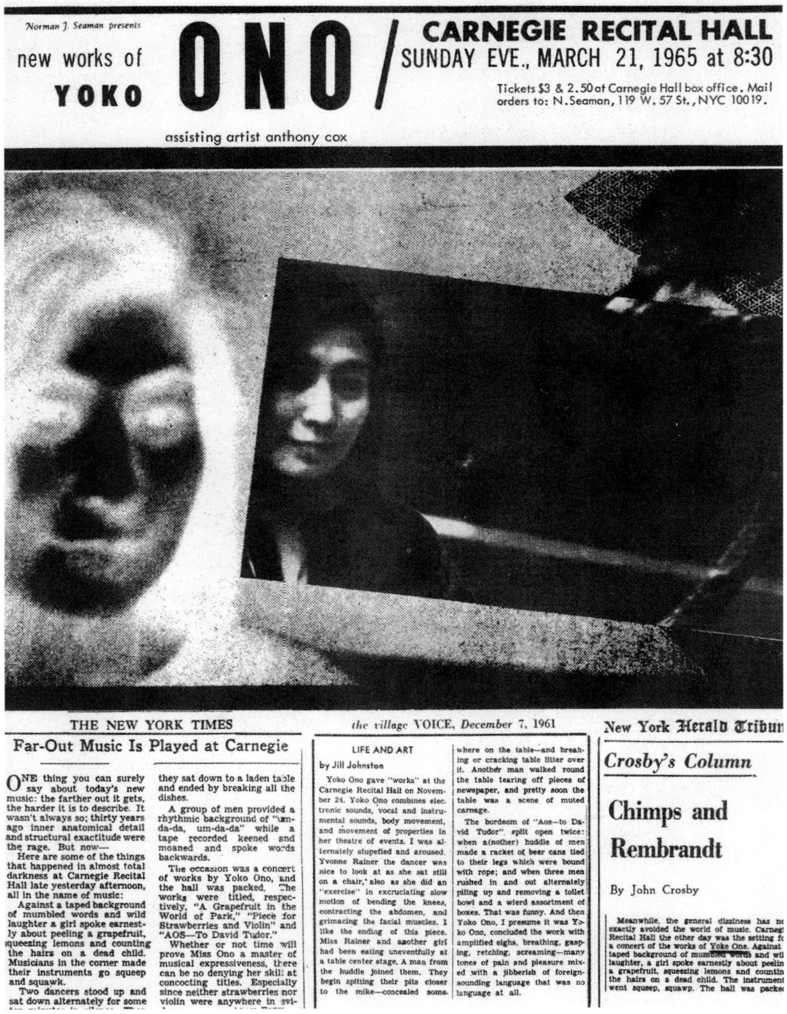

THE NEW YORK TIMES

Far-Out Music Is Played at Carnegie

ONE thing you can surely say about today's new music: the farther out it gets, the harder it is to describe. It wasn't always so; thirty years ago inner anatomical detail and structural exactitude were the rage. But now—

Here are some of the things that happened in almost total darkness at Carnegie Recital Hall late yesterday afternoon, all in the name of music:

Against a taped background of mumbled words and wild laughter a girl spoke earnestly about peeling a grapefruit, squeezing lemons and counting the hairs on a dead child. Musicians in the corner made their instruments go squeep and squawk.

Two dancers stood up and sat down alternately for some [...] they sat down to a laden table and ended by breaking all the dishes.

A group of men provided a rhythmic background of "um-da-da, um-da-da" while a tape recorded keened and moaned and spoke words backwards.

The occasion was a concert of works by Yoko Ono, and the hall was packed. The works were titled, respectively, "A Grapefruit in the World of Park," "Piece for Strawberries and Violin" and "AOS—To David Tudor."

Whether or not time will prove Miss Ono a master of musical expressiveness, there can be no denying her skill at concocting titles. Especially since neither strawberries nor violin were anywhere in evi-

the village VOICE, *December 7, 1961*

LIFE AND ART

by Jill Johnston

Yoko Ono gave "works" at the Carnegie Recital Hall on November 24. Yoko Ono combines electronic sounds, vocal and instrumental sounds, body movement, and movement of properties in her theatre of events. I was alternately stupefied and aroused. Yvonne Rainer the dancer was nice to look at as she sat still on a chair, also as she did an "exercise" in excruciating slow motion of bending the knees, contracting the abdomen, and grimacing the facial muscles. I like the ending of this piece. Miss Rainer and another girl had been eating uneventfully at a table center stage. A man from the huddle joined them. They begin spitting their pits closer to the mike—concealed somewhere on the table—and breaking or cracking table litter over it. Another man walked round the table tearing off pieces of newspaper, and pretty soon the table was a scene of muted carnage.

The bordeom of "Aos—to David Tudor" split open twice: when a(nother) huddle of men made a racket of beer cans tied to their legs which were bound with rope; and when three men rushed in and out alternately piling up and removing a toilet bowl and a wierd assortment of boxes. That was funny. And then Yoko Ono, I presume it was Yoko Ono, concluded the work with amplified sighs, breathing, gasping, retching, screaming—many tones of pain and pleasure mixed with a jibberish of foreign-sounding language that was no language at all.

New York Herald Tribun[e]

Crosby's Column

Chimps and Rembrandt

By John Crosby

Meanwhile, the general dizziness has n[ot] exactly avoided the world of music. Carneg[ie] Recital Hall the other day was the setting f[or] a concert of the works of Yoke One. Against [a] taped background of mumbled words and wil[d] laughter, a girl spoke earnestly about peelin[g] a grapefruit, squeezing lemons and countin[g] the hairs on a dead child. The instrument[s] went squeep, squawp. The hall was packe[d]

FIGURE 14.12
FLYER, *NEW WORKS OF YOKO ONO*, CARNEGIE RECITAL HALL, NEW YORK, 1965

September 2
3rd Annual New York Avant Garde Festival, Judson Hall, New York
First participation in Moorman's annual project. Performs *Touch Poem* for the festival's poetry program night.
DOCUMENTS: program; poster; ad, *Village Voice*, 26 August 1965, p. 15; ad, "Come to Participate in Yoko Ono's 'Touch Poem,'" *Village Voice*, 2 September 1965, p. 11; program/handout for *Touch Poem*

September 12, 19, 26
Morning Piece (1964) to George Maciunas, **roof of Ono's apartment building at 87 Christopher Street, New York**
See 1964, May 24, 31 (figs. 2.11–12).
DOCUMENTS: flyer; ad, *Village Voice*, 16 September 1965, p. 15

September 25
Fluxorchestra at Carnegie Recital Hall, **New York**
In Fluxus's "83rd concert" performs *4 Pieces for Orchestra to La Monte Young* and *Sky Piece for Jesus Christ* (see no. 32). *Touch Poem* also shown in a lobby exhibition.
DOCUMENTS: press release; poster; *Fluxorchestra Circular Letter No. 2*

October 3
Perpetual Fluxfest, New Cinematheque, New York
Listed in September to December program. Unrealized.
DOCUMENTS: poster

October 4
World Theatre, Cafe Au Go Go, New York
Work included in program of "experimental music & dance & theater" presented by H. Solomon and Steve Balkin.
DOCUMENTS: flyer; ad, *Village Voice*, 30 September 1965, p. 29

October 31
New Music at The Bridge, The Bridge, New York
Bicycle Piece for Orchestra performed by Rachel Gross.
DOCUMENTS: program; ad, *Village Voice*, 28 October 1965, p. 24

1966

BIOGRAPHY: Lives in New York at 1 West 100th Street and 99 Second Avenue; goes to London for *DIAS* in September and decides to stay; meets John Lennon at her solo exhibition at Indica Gallery
FILMS RELEASED: *Fluxfilms* (*No. 1, Eyeblink,* and *No. 4* by Ono; see nos. 42, 43)

January 1
Japanese Transitions, WBAI Radio, New York
Sings without accompaniment traditional, folk, and contemporary popular songs of Japan in their proper styles, commenting on the material she performs. One

of a series done with producer Ann McMillan beginning in 1965.
DOCUMENTS: radio listing, *New York Times*, 1 January 1966, p. 37

January 1–15
"Do It Yourself" Dance Festival, **various locations in New York**
Solo event. Newspaper ads solicit "donation 50¢/day, $3 series" and indicate "mail reservation only" (fig. 9.4). Thirteen-plus days' worth of instructions are given in "Do It Yourself: Fluxfest Presents Yoko Ono & Dance Co.," published in *3 newspaper eVenTs for the pRicE of $1* (Fluxus Newspaper No. 7), dated February 1, 1966 (fig. 2.13). They include four events with specific dates: February 3, 4, 8, and 12.
DOCUMENTS: ads, *Village Voice*, 23 and 30 December 1965

early January
Disappearing Piece, **Ono's apartment at 1 West 100th Street, New York**
One day during the subway strike (January 1–13) the instruction "Boil water" is performed for one audience member by five people: Perkins, Pieter Vanderbeek, Cox, Maciunas, and the artist. The event lasts two hours until the water evaporates. *Blue Room Event* also realized concurrently (see no. 5).

January 13
Avant Garde in Japan, **Davison Art Center Gallery, Wesleyan University, Middletown, Conn.**
Solo event. Performs *Wind Piece* and *Breath Piece*, and discusses her works. "To the Wesleyan People" written soon afterward (Anthology 14).

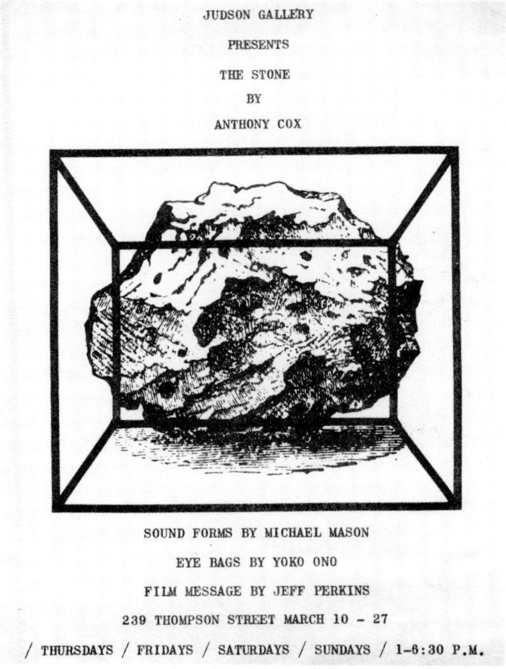

FIGURE 14.13
FLYER, *THE STONE*, JUDSON GALLERY, NEW YORK, 1966

January 14
Works by Behrman, Fine, Goldstein, Higgins, Kosugi, Lucier, Ono, Paik, Rot, Sahl, Tenney, Wolff, Judson Memorial Church, New York
Sky Machine shown and *Painting to Shake Hands at Judson* performed by Jon Hendricks.
DOCUMENTS: flyer; *Judson Newsnotes* (January 1966)

January 26, 29, February 1, 4
Animation: Films from Many Nations, The Museum of Modern Art, New York
"Program Number 3" includes Kuri Yōji's *AOS*. Cox distributes a card that lists "additional credit": "The title and the music of this film are taken from the opera, 'AOS to David Tudor,' by Yoko Ono. Voice performance by Yoko Ono."
DOCUMENTS: film program; "additional credit" card

February 4
Hide Piece, **Canal Street subway station, New York**
Solo event. As listed in "Do It Yourself: Fluxfest Presents Yoko Ono & Dance Co." (1966).

February 6
Fluxfilm Festival, Film-Maker's Cinematheque at 41st St. Theater, New York
Includes *No. 4*.
DOCUMENTS: ad, *Village Voice*, 3 February 1966, p. 22

March 10–27
The Stone by Anthony Cox, Sound Forms by Michael Mason, Eye Bags by Yoko Ono, Film Message by Jeff Perkins, **Judson Gallery, New York**
Collaborative environment (fig. 14.13). Additional credits include "air" by Hendricks and "technical assistance" by Ludwig Lanko.
DOCUMENTS: exh. cat.; flyer

March 31
April Fool's Dance: Models Ball, The Village Gate, New York
Benefit for the underground paper *East Village Other* includes *Painting to Shake Hands* performed by Ono.
DOCUMENTS: ad, *East Village Other*, 15 February–1 March 1966, p. 12

April–August
Blue Room Event, **Ono's apartment at 99 Second Avenue, New York**
Second realization of the event piece. See no. 5.

July 15–August
The Stone by Anthony Cox, Eye Bags by Yoko Ono, **The Paradox, New York**
Staged in an East Village restaurant's front room.
DOCUMENTS: poster; notice, *Village Voice*, 14 July 1966, p. 2; ads, *Village Voice*, 14 July 1966, pp. 2, 9, 15, 23; full-page ad, *East Village Other*, 15 July–1 August 1966, back cover; ad, *East Village Other*, 1–15 August 1966

September 9
4th Annual New York Avant Garde Festival, Central Park, New York
Includes *AOS* and *Cut Piece*. Two men perform *Cut Piece*.
DOCUMENTS: poster; press release

September 11–13, 15, 28–30
Destruction in Art Symposium (DIAS), **London**
Ono plays a major role in several events as part of *DIAS*. See no. 33 for individual programs. *London Look* article reports that one of her concerts also takes place in an "inflatable environment," which is set up at Battersea Park for *DIAS* press preview and remains through the month.
DOCUMENTS: program for *DIAS*; press release; program for *Two Evenings with Yoko Ono*, 28–29 September 1966; poster

September 30
Performance program, Gallery 101, Copenhagen
Paik and Moorman perform works by Ono, among others.

October 15
Launch party of *International Times*, Roundhouse, London
Performs *Touch Piece* ("touch the person next to you") for the inauguration of the London underground newspaper.

November 9–22
Yoko at Indica, **Indica Gallery, London**
Solo exhibition (fig. 14.14). Also billed as *Unfinished Paintings*, *Instruction Paintings*, and *Unfinished Paintings and Objects by Yoko Ono*. See nos. 7–9, 11–16, 19, 25.
DOCUMENTS: exh, cat.; poster; flyer

November 17
Music of the Mind, **Jeanetta Cochrane Theatre, London**
Solo concert. Presented by Michael White and The Traverse Theatre, it includes *A Grapefruit in the World of Park* and *Promise Piece (Mend Piece)*. Other works performed are *Hide Piece*, *Sweep Piece*, *Fly Piece*, *The Slipping Movement (Bicycles)*, and *Chorus for Bags*.
DOCUMENTS: poster; ad, *International Times*, 14–27 November 1966, p. 3

1967

FILMS RELEASED: *No. 4 (Bottoms)*

January 16–29
Unfinished Paintings and Objects, Camden Square, London
Solo exhibition. *International Times* ad (p. 13) announces a by-appointment viewing of works from Ono's Indica show and calls for volunteers for her film *No. 4*.

Spring
Evening with Yoko Ono, Leeds College of Art, Leeds, England
Solo event program.

March 10
Demonstration, outside British Board of Film Censors, London
Solo event. Protests the ban of film *No. 4*, also known as *Bottoms* (see no. 43), by delivering daffodils to the Board's office and also distributing the flowers to passersby (fig. 14.14). Newspapers report that the planned screening at Royal Albert Hall on April 27 is canceled. On March 31, Greater London Council Licensing Committee grants an X-rating certificate to *No. 4*. Royal Albert Hall officials nevertheless cancel Ono's booking in mid-April.

March 20
Scott Free, ITV, U.K.
Gives interview and shows clips of *No. 4*.

April 29
14-Hour Technicolour Dream, Alexandra Palace, London
All-night group event is part of Free Speech Weekend organized by London's Free University as a benefit for John Hopkins of *International Times*. Performs *Cut Piece*, with model Carol Mann.

May 28
Concert, The Electric Garden, London
Appears during opening weekend of new Covent Garden nightclub. Ono sends blindfolded women into the audience and communicates with audience members.

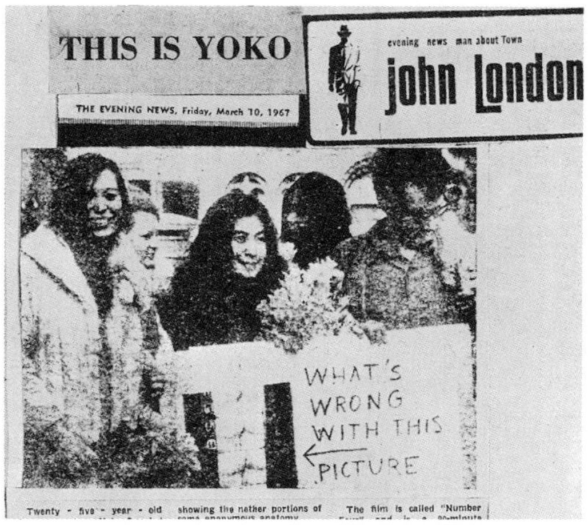
THIS IS YOKO
THE EVENING NEWS, Friday, March 10, 1967
evening news man about Town
john london

FIGURE 14.14
DEMONSTRATION FOR *NO. 4 (BOTTOMS)*.
NEWSPAPER CLIPPING REPRODUCED IN *THIS IS NOT HERE*, EXH. CAT. (1971)

May 31
Fluxfilme und Multiprojektionen, Galerie Tobies & Silex, Cologne
Includes *No. 4, 5'30"*. Two Fluxus films by Ono, *No. 1 (Match)* and *No. 4*, are included in the earlier version of *Fluxfilms* as #14 and #16. The subsequent version, distributed by Film-Makers' Cooperative in New York, includes Ono's *No. 4, 5'30"* as #16. Maciunas/Fluxus sends *Fluxfilms* anthology to be screened in Europe. It is also shown in *4th Annual Ann Arbor Film Festival* and wins a critics award in 1966.

June 4
***Be-In with Yoko Ono on a Kite-Flying Hill During the Day*, Hampstead Heath, London**
Solo event. Takes place as announced. "What's Happening" listing in *International Times* gives British Museum as rain venue.
DOCUMENTS: poster

June 6
Concert Fluxus, Galleria la Bertesca, Genoa

June 26
Concert Fluxus, Villa Cuccirelli, Milan

June 28
Flux Filme, Werkkunstschule Wuppertal, Wuppertal, Germany

July 5–August
Group exhibition, Robert Fraser Gallery, London
"Spectator participation" piece shown.

July 31
Projecteur de Films Fluxus, Galerie Ben Doute de Tout, Venice

August 3
***Lion Wrapping Event*, Trafalgar Square, London**
Solo event (fig. 14.15). Originally conceived in response to Indica Gallery viewers' unexpected intervention with *Wrapped Chair* (no. 19). During her exhibition there, Ono unsuccessfully attempted to cover the lion with paper (the police intervened, and the paper fell apart in the rain). This time, with police permission, Ono wraps and unwraps one of the four lion statues, using tarpaulins. The whole six-hour event is filmed.

August 8
***Film No. 4*, Jacey Tatler Cinema, London**
Solo film screening. Premiere of Ono's "film of many happy [365] endings," as a benefit for Institute of Contemporary Art. Regular screening begins on August 17.
DOCUMENTS: flyer; program; questionnaire; ad for August 17 screening

August 31–September 13
***Yoko Ono's Wrapping Event*, London**
Solo advertisement event. Published in *International Times*.

September 26
***Yoko Ono: Music of the Mind*, The Bluecoat Society of Arts, Liverpool**
Solo concert. Includes *The Fog Machine*, as part of *Goodnight Piece*.
DOCUMENTS: poster, program

September 27
Lecture, Liverpool College of Art, Liverpool

September 27–October 9
***Yoko Ono's 13 Days Do-It-Yourself Dance Festival*, London**
Solo event. Dance festival takes place "in your mind." One pound, or "a pound worth of flowers and 13 stamps," sent to Yoko Ono Dance Company at 25 Hanover Gate Mansions will result in 13 dance instruction cards mailed to the participant.
DOCUMENTS: promotional flyer

September 29–30
5th Annual New York Avant Garde Festival, John F. Kennedy Ferryboat at Whitehall Terminal, New York
twenty-four-hour performances includes *Water Piece* in Ono's absence.
DOCUMENTS: poster; program

October 11–November 14
***Yoko Ono at Lisson: Half-A-Wind Show*, Lisson Gallery, London**
Solo exhibition (fig. 14.16). Also listed as *1/2 Life*; *1/2 Life, 1/2 Space*; *Half-A-Spring Show*; *Half-A-Memory Show*; *Half-A-Sky Show*. See nos. 5, 10, 20, 24.
DOCUMENTS: exh. cat.; poster

October 14–15
***A Perception Weekend with Yoko Ono*, Midland Arts Centre, Birmingham, England**
Saturday–Sunday program includes special exhibition, screening of *No. 4*, and concert (14th); be-in and discussion with Cox moderated by Mario Amaya, editor of *Art and Artists* (15th).
DOCUMENTS: flyer; program

October 21
Concerto Fluxus, Liberia Rinascita, Modena

October 22
12 Evenings of Manipulations, Judson Gallery, New York
Ono listed as part of the last day's event in absentia.
DOCUMENTS: catalogue; program

December 2–28
Aktual Art International, Stanford Art Gallery, Stanford, Calif.
DOCUMENTS: exh. cat.

December 8
***Music of the Mind: Yoko Ono at Saville*, The Saville Theatre, London**
Solo concert (fig. 14.1). Includes *The Fog Machine*,

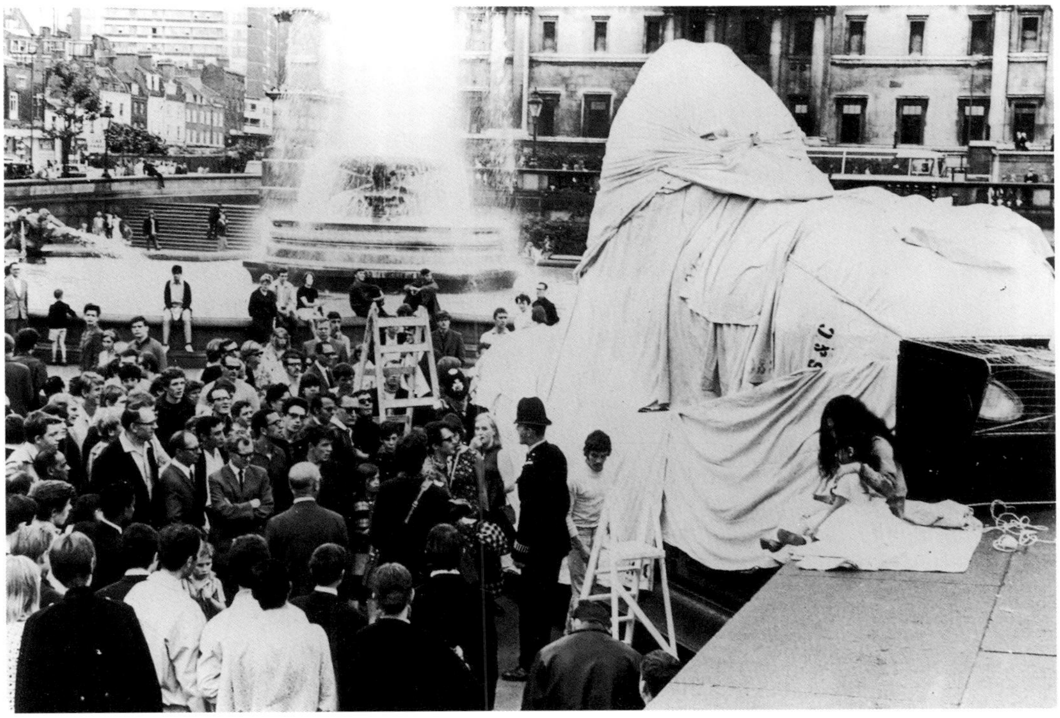

FIGURE 14.15 (ABOVE)
LION WRAPPING EVENT, TRAFALGAR SQUARE, LONDON, 1967

FIGURE 14.16 (BELOW)
FLYER, *YOKO ONO AT LISSON,* 1967

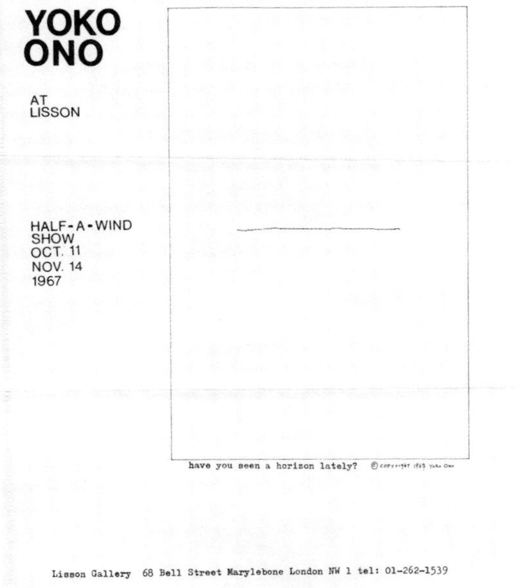

with *No. 4* screened in the Men's Room. Audience members are asked to bring a mirror.
DOCUMENTS: poster; flyer

December 8–13
***Evening with Yoko Ono,* University of Keele, Keele, England**
Screens *No. 4* and performs *Bag Piece* with Cox, followed by a discussion (undetermined day during the week).

December 15–January 15, 1968
Affiches Fluxus: De-Colllage, Libre Expression, Art Total, Bar le Provence, Nice

December 26
The Election of Miss Exprmnt, Casino, Knokke-le-Zoute, Belgium
Serves as a "contestant" in Jean-Jacques Lebel's Happening at the old beach front venue. A spoof of beauty contests, it mocks *EXPRMNT 4* (Fourth Experimental Film Contest, December 25, 1967–January 1, 1968), Royal Belgian Film Library's competition that refused to accept her *No. 4*. Also performs *Bag Piece* at the casino's entrance hall, staying in a black bag all day long.

date undetermined
Solo evening program at St. Martin's Art College, London

1968

FILMS RELEASED: *Film No. 5 (Smile)*; Ono and Lennon, *Two Virgins*
LP RECORDS RELEASED: Lennon and Ono, *Unfinished Music No. 1: Two Virgins* (see no. 53)

early January
Performance, La Contrescarpe, Paris
Solo event. On the way back from Knokke-le-Zoute to London, Ono stops in Paris to perform *Bag Piece* at the Latin Quarter café, arranged by Lebel.

early 1968
Lecture, Guildford School of Art, Guildford, England
Solo event. The artist Sue Coe remembers attending a program in which participants "were all blindfolded with sanitary napkins and sticking plaster."

February–March
Intermedia '68, upstate New York colleges
Moorman and Paik perform works by Ono, among other artists, at State University of New York at New Paltz (February 20), Albany (March 16), and Buffalo (March 19) as well as Rockland Community College (February 24) and Nazareth College of Rochester (March 12).
DOCUMENTS: poster

February 29
***Ornette Coleman,* Royal Albert Hall, London**
Performs *AOS* in guest appearance, accompanied by Coleman and his group (fig. 14.18).
DOCUMENTS: poster; flyer; program with Ono's handwritten instruction "To Ornette"

spring
Antiuniversity of London
Listed as giving "an irregular course" entitled "The Connection: To attempt to connect people to their own reality by means of brain sessions and ritual."
DOCUMENTS: course catalogue

May 28–June 1
***Yoko Ono: Water Show,* Arts Lab Center, London**
Solo exhibition.
DOCUMENTS: "What's Happening," listing in *International Times*, 17–30 May 1968

June 2–9
***Four Thoughts: Yoko Ono and John Lennon,* Arts Lab Center, London**
Two-person exhibition.
DOCUMENTS: "What's Happening," listing in *International Times*, 31 May–13 June 1968

June 15
Performance, Reardon Smith Lecture Theatre, Cardiff, Wales
Solo event. Organized by the local Group 56. A chauffeur-driven limousine is sent to some 200 people waiting in the lecture hall. It carries a photo of the artist, signed with her love, and the instruction: "Fly." Ono receives a photo of a £50 check in return from the organizer.

June 15
***Acorn Event,* Coventry Cathedral, Coventry, England**
Two-person event with John Lennon (fig. 14.19). They plant acorns and install a garden bench on the grounds, in a meadow in front of the cathedral ruins. The work is on view during *First National Sculpture Exhibition* at the site.
DOCUMENTS: exh. cat.

August 24
David Frost Show, ITV, U.K.
Appears with Lennon on the TV program and performs *Painting to Hammer a Nail In* with the show's guests. Frost also hammers a nail into the board.

September 14
6th Annual New York Avant Garde Festival: A Parade, Central Park West, New York
Participates in absentia.
DOCUMENTS: poster

November 14
Chicago International Film Festival
Premiere of *Two Virgins* and *Film No. 5*.

December 11
The Rolling Stones Rock and Roll Circus, Wembley Studio, London
Performs with Lennon in the all-star jam session.
DOCUMENTS: video

December 18
Alchemical Wedding, Albert Hall, London
In a benefit event organized by Jim Haynes for Arts Lab, Ono and Lennon make a featured appearance, performing *Bag Piece*. Haynes has the show videotaped.
DOCUMENTS: ticket, "Celebration in December," 18 December 1968

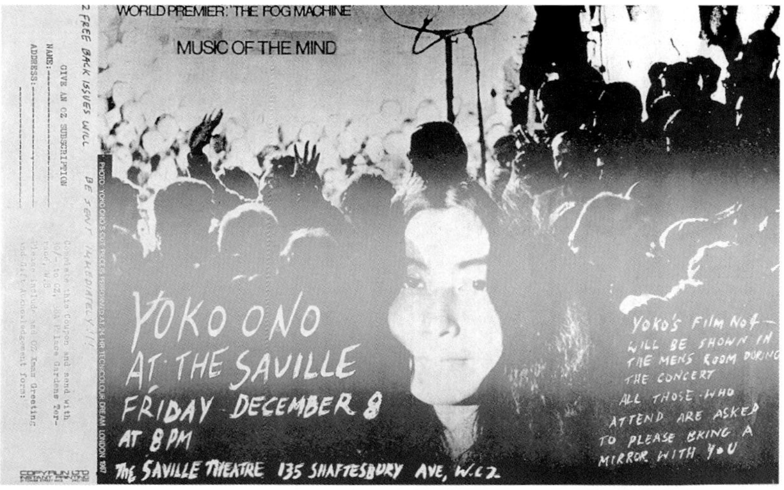

FIGURE 14.17
POSTER, *MUSIC OF THE MIND*, THE SAVILLE THEATRE, LONDON, 1967

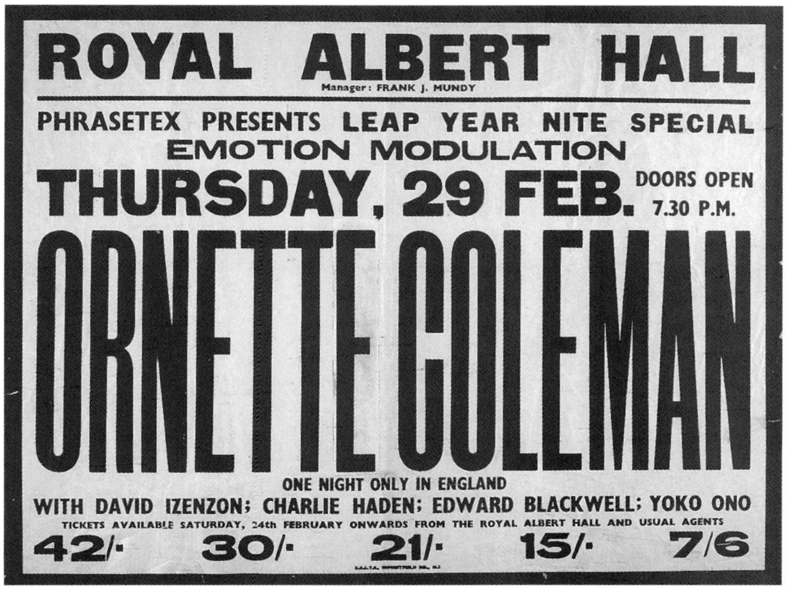

FIGURE 14.18
POSTER, ORNETTE COLEMAN CONCERT, ROYAL ALBERT HALL, LONDON, 1968

1969

BIOGRAPHY: Marries John Lennon in Gibraltar in March; Ono and Lennon form Bag Productions Ltd. in April
FILMS RELEASED: Ono and Lennon, *Rape*; Ono and Lennon, *Bed-In*
SINGLE RECORDS RELEASED: Plastic Ono Band, "Give Peace a Chance"/"Remember Love"; Plastic Ono Band, "Cold Turkey"/"Don't Worry Kyoko (Mummy's Only Looking for Her Hand in the Snow)"
LP RECORDS RELEASED: Lennon and Ono, *Unfinished Music No. 2: Life with the Lions* (see no. 54); Lennon and Ono, *Wedding Album*; Plastic Ono Band, *Live Peace in Toronto*

January 18
Fluxus-Filme, Auto-Fiat Gabriel, Wiesbaden, Germany

March 2
Natural Music, Lady Mitchell Hall, Cambridge, England
Lennon and Ono make their first concert appearance, in the international avant-garde jazz workshop produced by Nothing Doing in London in association with Cambridge University New Music Society. Other musicians include John Tchicai and Willem Breuker. The tape of Ono and Lennon's performance is included in *Unfinished Music No. 2*.

March 25–31
***Bed-In for Peace*, Amsterdam**
Two-person event. Following their marriage ceremony at Gibraltar on March 20, Lennon and Ono perform the seven-day event at Room 902 of the Amsterdam Hilton Hotel. See no. 34.

March 29
Concert Fluxus, La Capella, Triest

March 31
***Rape*, ORF TV, Vienna**
Two-person film screening. TV premiere of Ono and Lennon's film produced for the series *Underground* on Austria's national TV (fig. 14.20). They give a press conference at Sacher Hotel, where they perform *Bag Piece*. See no. 45.
DOCUMENTS: program brochure

April 3
The Eamonn Andrews Show, ITV, U.K.
Ono and Lennon perform *Bag Piece* and attempt to have host Andrews join them in the white bag.

mid April
***Acorns for Peace*, London**
Solo event. Ono and Lennon mail one acorn each to 96 world leaders, asking them to plant it for world peace.

April 25
9éme Rose d'Or de Montreux, Switzerland
Ono and Lennon attend screening of *Rape* at television festival.

May 26
***Bed-In*, Montreal**
Two-person event. Ono and Lennon arrive in Montreal via Bermuda and Toronto, and begin another *Bed-In* at Room 1742 of Queen Elizabeth Hotel (fig. 14.21). On June 1, they are visited by Allen Ginsberg, Phil Spector, and Timothy Leary, among others. The event ends on June 2.

June 2
Peace conference, University of Ottawa
Ono and Lennon participate in a panel discussion.

September 10
***Evening with John and Yoko*, New Cinema Club at Institute of Contemporary Arts, London**
Two-person event. *Two Virgins*, *Smile*, *John and Yoko Honeymoon*, *Self-Portrait*, and *Rape* are screened. Also listed in the program is guest appearance by Plastic Ono Band. Two people in a white bag, described in some accounts as the artists' stand-ins, are carted in and out during the program.

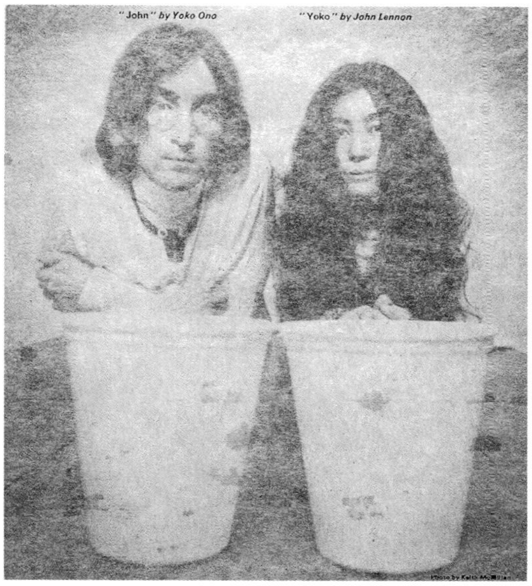

FIGURE 14.19 (LEFT)
CATALOGUE, *ACORN EVENT*, 1968

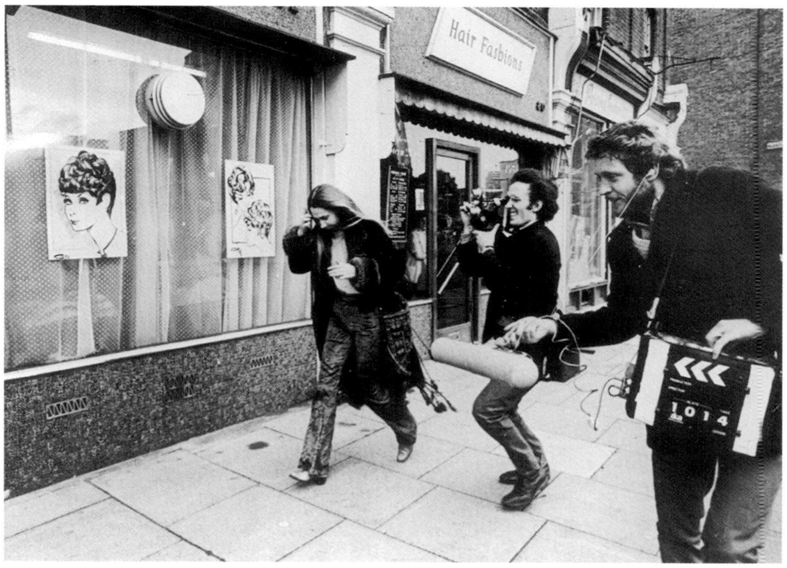

FIGURE 14.20 (RIGHT)
PRODUCTION STILL FROM *RAPE*, 1969

September 13
Toronto Rock 'n' Roll Revival, **College Stadium, Toronto**
Plastic Ono Band makes an impromptu appearance on the second day of the rock festival (also known as "Toronto Peace Festival"). Ono performs *Bag Piece* in a white bag during the first half of the band's performance, then sings "Don't Worry Kyoko" and "John, John (Let's Hope for Peace)."

September 28–October 4
7th Annual New York Avant Garde Festival: On Two Islands, Ward's Island and Mill Rock Island in East River, New York
Ono participates in absentia.
DOCUMENTS: poster

October 25
Outdoor film screening, St. Martin-in-the-Fields, London
Two-person film screening. *Smile* and *Two Virgins* shown on a large outdoor screen set up by Christian Aid for a Biafra famine benefit.

November 3, 10
Screenings of Ono and Ono-Lennon films, Institute of Contemporary Arts, London

December 15
Peace for Christmas, **Lyceum Ballroom, Covent Garden, London**
Concert of Plastic Ono Supergroup to benefit UNICEF. Ono plays "Don't Worry Kyoko."

War Is Over! **12 cities worldwide**
Two-person event (fig. 14.22). Ono and Lennon's billboard and poster campaign launched. See no. 39.

December 16
Phone calls to radio stations worldwide
Two-person event. Ono and Lennon phone in their peace message from Toronto to radio stations worldwide.

December 24
Sit-in and fasting, Rochester Cathedral, Kent, England
Comedian Dick Gregory, Ono, and Lennon attend the peace vigil outside the cathedral.

December 31
Announcement of "Year One A.P. [after peace]"
Two-person event with Lennon.

1970

BIOGRAPHY: Reissues *Grapefruit* (hardcover) through Simon and Schuster (U.S.), Peter Owen (U.K.), and Bärmeier & Nikel (West Germany); establishes Ono Music Ltd., music publishers
FILMS RELEASED: *Fly* (no. 46); *Freedom* (no. 47); *Up Your Legs Forever;* Ono and Lennon, *Apotheosis* (no. 28)
SINGLE RECORDS RELEASED: Lennon, "Instant Karma (We All Shine On)"/Ono, "Who Has Seen the Wind?"; Lennon, "Mother"/Ono, "Why"
LP RECORDS RELEASED: *Yoko Ono/Plastic Ono Band*

February 4
Rooftop ceremony, Black House, London
Ono and Lennon give their hair to Britain's Black Power leader Michael X to be auctioned for the causes of the Black movement and peace.

February 6
Grapefruit Publication Event, Lee Nordness Galleries, New York
Marks the publication of the new edition of *Grapefruit* on the opening of *John Lennon: Bag One* exhibition.

February 12 and 19
Top of the Pops, BBC1 TV
Plastic Ono Band's performance of "Instant Karma!" with a live audience (taped February 11) broadcast. Ono, blindfolded, performs instruction pieces.

April 1
April Fools' Day press release
Two-person event. Ono and Lennon announce they have entered a London clinic for dual sex-change operations

FIGURE 14.21
LENNON AND ONO, ***BED-IN***, MONTREAL, 1969

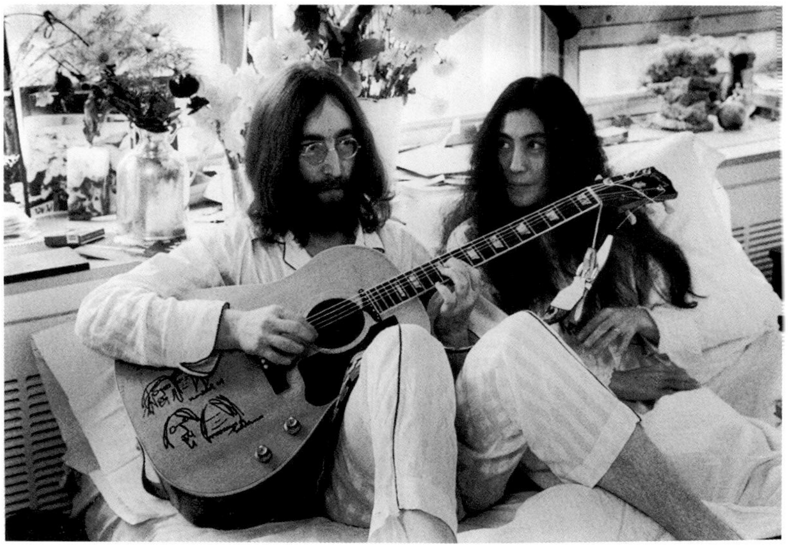

April 11–June 12
***Fluxfest Presentation of John Lennon & Yoko Ono +,* New York**
Two-person events realized by Fluxus (figs. 2.14, 14.23). In absence of the two principal artists, the program of a nine-week-long collaborative project at 80 Wooster Street (except for *Do It Yourself*) includes the following events, some of which do not appear to have been realized:

April 11:
Grapefruit Flux-Banquet (by Flux-chefs)

April 11–17:
Do It Yourself, by John & Yoko + Everybody,
Joe Jones Store, 18 N. Moore Street

April 18–24:
Tickets by John Lennon + Fluxtours

April 25–May 1:
Measure by John & Yoko + Hi Red Clinic + Fluxdoctors (by Hi Red Center unless otherwise noted)

May 2–8:
Blue Room by John & Yoko + Fluxliars

May 9–15:
Weight & Water by John & Yoko + Fluxfaucet

May 16–22:
Capsule by John & Yoko + Flux Space Center

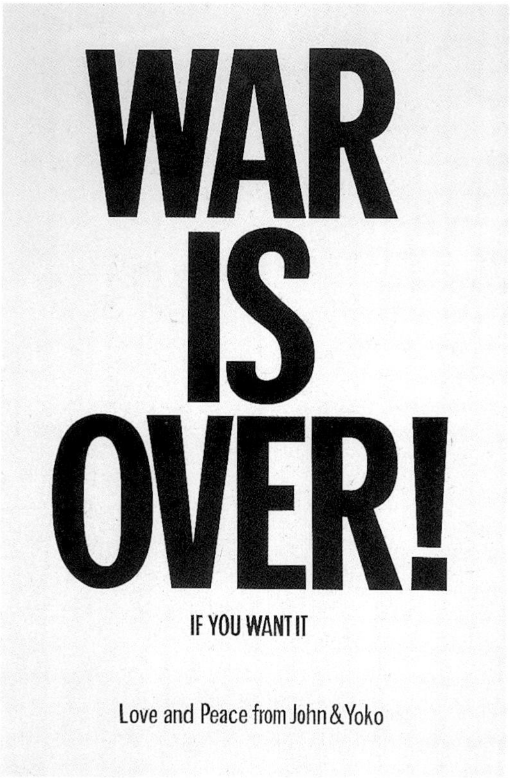

FIGURE 14.22
POSTER FOR *WAR IS OVER!* 1969

May 23–29:
Portrait of John Lennon as a Young Cloud by Yoko Ono + Everyparticipant

May 30–June 5:
The Store by John & Yoko + Fluxfactory

June 6–12:
Examination by John & Yoko + Fluxschool, with lectures on Saturday and Sunday

DOCUMENTS: press release; program; poster; flyer; *all photographs copyright nineteen seVenty by peTer mooRE* (1970); Ono, "Program: Fluxfest Presents Yoko Ono + John Lennon," eleven-page handwritten note to George Maciunas, Jean Brown Archives, The Getty Center for the History of Art and the Humanities, Los Angeles

November 6–January 6, 1971
Happening & Fluxus, Kölnischen Kunstverein, Cologne
Traveling survey exhibition.
DOCUMENTS: exh. cat.

November 15
Festum Fluxorum, Galerie Block in Forum Theater, Berlin
Includes *Cut Piece*, probably performed by Moorman.
DOCUMENTS: program

November 19–January 3, 1971
3→∞: New Multiple Art, Whitechapel Art Gallery, London
DOCUMENTS: exh. cat.

December 18–20
John and Yoko Film Festival, Elgin Theater, New York
Two-person film screening. Program includes *Fly*, *Up Your Legs Forever*, *Apotheosis*, *Rape*, and three other films. Benefit for Film-Makers Cinematheque.
DOCUMENTS: ad, *Village Voice*, 17 December 1970, p. 68

1971

BIOGRAPHY: Issues paperback editions of *Grapefruit* from Touchstone Paperback, Simon and Schuster (U.S.) and Sphere Books (U.K.); publishes *Museum of Modern [F]art*
FILMS RELEASED: Ono and Lennon, *Erection* (see no. 49); Ono and Lennon, *Imagine*; *The Museum of Modern Art Show*
SINGLE RECORDS RELEASED: Lennon, "Power to the People"/Ono, "Touch Me"; "Mrs. Lennon"/"Midsummer New York"; Lennon, Ono, and Plastic Ono Band, "Happy Xmas (War Is Over)"/"Listen, the Snow Is Falling"; Lennon, "Power to the People"/Ono, "Open Your Box" (U.K.)
LP RECORDS RELEASED: *Fly* (no. 56)

February 4
Film program, McAlister Auditorium, Tulane University, New Orleans
Two-person film screening. Two programs of Ono and Lennon films include *Rape*, *Smile*, and *Two Virgins*.

May 15
Cannes Film Festival
Ono and Lennon's *Apotheosis* presented in the program *Quinzain des réalisateurs* (Directors' fortnight). *Fly* also shown.

June 6
Concert, Filmore East, New York
Lennon and Ono perform with Frank Zappa and The Mothers of Invention

August 11
Protest demonstration, London
Ono and Lennon march with antigovernment protesters, decrying British policy toward Northern Ireland.

August 11–30
Art Spectrum, Alexandra Palace, London
Ono's *Miniature Piece* included in the Greater London presentation, part of seven concurrent exhibitions throughout the U.K., organized by Regional Arts Associations and Arts Council of Great Britain. Eleven Ono and Ono-Lennon films are shown daily.
DOCUMENTS: exh. cat.

September 5
Film showing, Alexandra Palace, London
Screening of five Ono and Ono-Lennon films, organized for *Art Spectrum London*, includes Ono's *Up Your Legs Forever*.

October 9–27
***This Is Not Here,* Everson Museum of Art, Syracuse, New York**
Solo exhibition (figs. 2.16, 14.24). Events in conjunction with the retrospective include: screenings of Ono and Ono-Lennon films (October 15–17, 19–22) and concert of Ono's music (October 23). See nos. 6, 18, 26.
DOCUMENTS: *Everson Catalogue Box*; newspaper-format exh. cat.; newspaper-format clippings anthology; folding invitation; film program

October 14
***Free Time,* WNET TV, New York**
Three-person event. Ono, Lennon, and Mekas perform her works, including *Fly*, in a 90-minute program, taped with live audience.

October 16
San Francisco International Film Festival
Sixteen-day (2nd–17th) program includes a special midnight screening of *The Films of John and Yoko Lennon*.

November 1
Group exhibition, Tyron Gallery, London
Opening of a show of animal drawings, including Ono's *Invisible Animals*. Later published in book *Milligan's Ark* to help Wildlife Youth Service.

November 6
The First Los Angeles International Film Exposition,

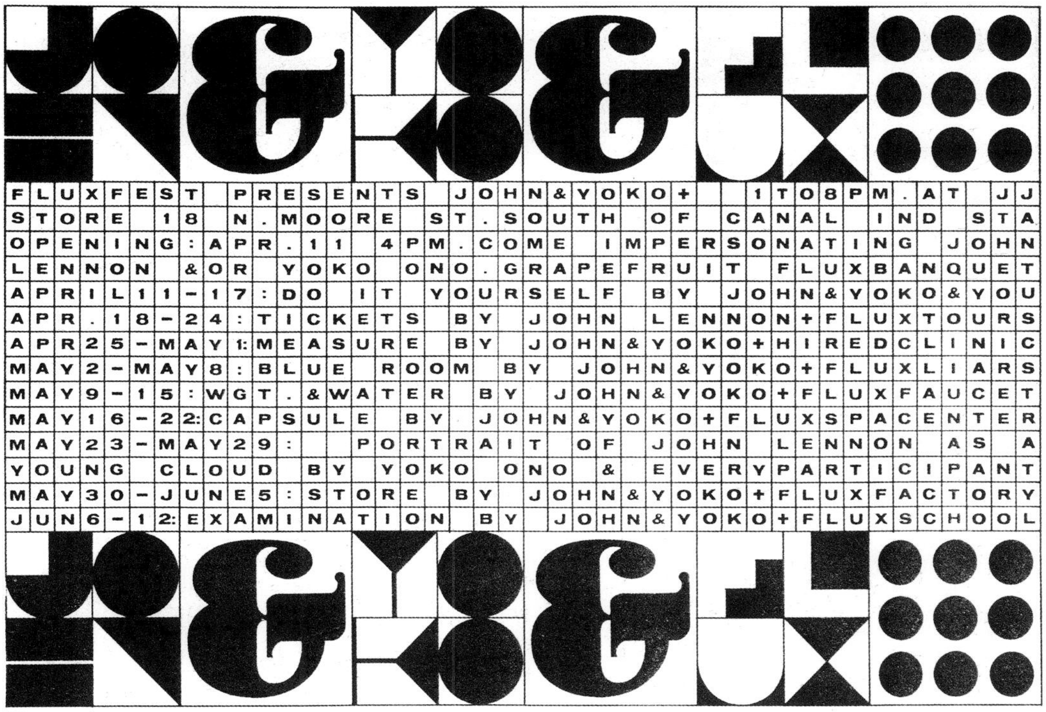

FIGURE 14.23
FLYER, ***FLUXFEST PRESENTATION OF JOHN LENNON & YOKO ONO +***, 1970

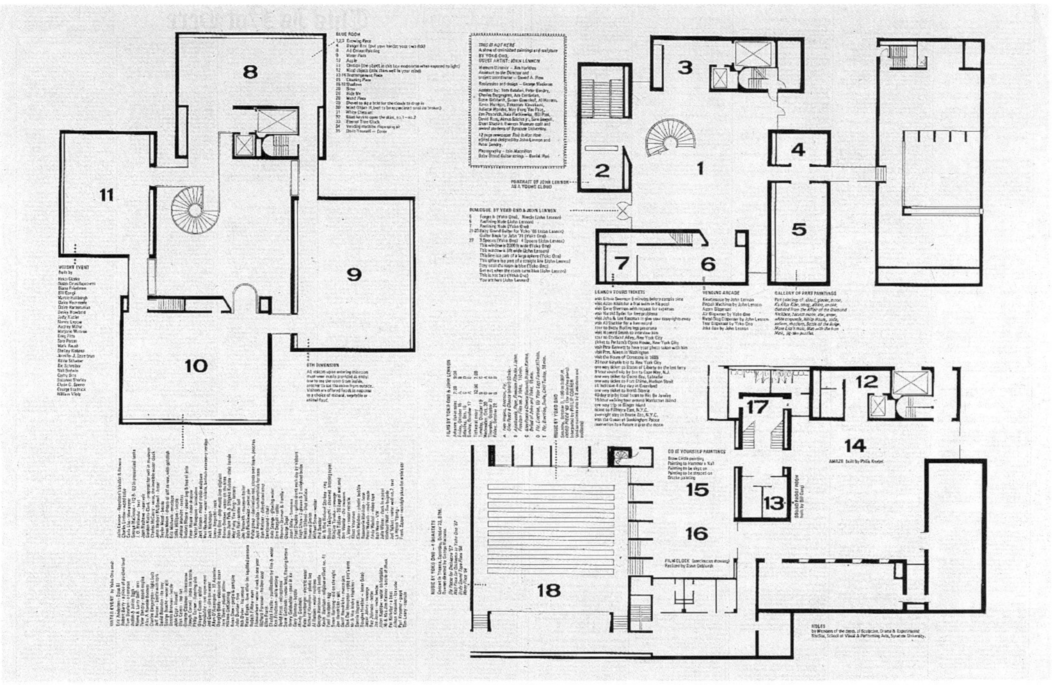

FIGURE 14.24
CATALOGUE AND FLOOR PLAN FOR ***THIS IS NOT HERE***, EVERSON MUSEUM, SYRACUSE, 1971

Grauman's Chinese Theater, Los Angeles
The Films of John and Yoko featured as part of the festival.

November 9
Woman's Hour, BBC Radio 2
Ono and Lennon, among others, appear to give a frank look at sex in special edition, "Oh No: Not That Again."

November 19
8th Annual New York Avant Garde Festival (Armory Show), 69th Regiment Armory, New York
Program lists Ono's *Human Maze*, *Shadow Painting*, *Coin Music*, and *Please Look at Me and I'm Only Small*.
DOCUMENTS: program; flyer; posters

early December
Rock Liberation Front
Declared by Ono, Lennon, Jerry Rubin, and David Peel. A letter about Bob Dylan signed by them published in *Village Voice*, December 2, p. 59.

December 1–15
Museum of Modern [F]art
Solo exhibition. Ono's "conceptual" exhibition takes place through ad, artist's book/catalogue, handbill, and film. See no. 40.

December 10–11
The John Sinclair Freedom Rally, Crisler Arena, University of Michigan at Ann Arbor
Ono and Lennon take top billing in the famous benefit concert, attended by an audience of 15,000, that campaigns for the release of political activist and rock manager sentenced to ten years in prison on minor drug charges. Subsequently, Michigan State Supreme Court orders Sinclair's release. A two-hour TV special is later aired on PBS (March 1972).
DOCUMENT: poster

December 17
Benefit concert for Attica State Prison, Apollo Theater, New York
Ono and Lennon make a cameo appearance to raise money for the families of those killed in a riot at the prison.

1972

BIOGRAPHY: Deportation order against Ono (dropped) and Lennon; supports Lennon's effort to gain U.S. residency (awarded in 1976)
FILMS RELEASED: Ono and Lennon, *Ten for Two: Sisters O Sisters*
SINGLE RECORDS RELEASED: Lennon, "Woman Is the Nigger of the World"/Ono, "Sisters O Sisters"; "Now or Never"/"Move On Fast"; "Mind Train"/"Listen, the Snow Is Falling" (U.K.)
LP RECORDS RELEASED: Lennon, Ono, and Plastic Ono Band with Elephant's Memory, *Some Time in New York City*

January 10
Concert by Earth Symphony, Alice Tully Hall, Lincoln Center, New York
Appears as a solo artist in a program organized by AWARE, a nonprofit arts organization. In her guest appearance, Ono conducts from her front-row seat, lacking a work permit in the U.S. Her contribution, in part assisted by Lennon, includes *Fan Piece* (a.k.a. *Wind Piece*: performance of Beethoven's "Fifth Symphony" accompanied by four huge fans blowing sheets of music out of sequence, which lasts until she finishes eating an apple); *Touch Piece*; and her instruction to the audience to exit the concert hall.

February 14–18
Mike Douglas Show, CBS
Ono and Lennon guest-host the popular afternoon talk show. Ono performs *Unfinished Painting*, *Touch Poem*, *Touch Poem for Group of People*, *Mend Piece*, "Love Calls," *Box of Smile*, and *Question Piece*. They also invite Ralph Nadar (14th), filmmaker Barbara Loden and Jerry Rubin (15th), Chuck Berry (16th), and Black Panther chairman Bobby Seale (17th), among others.

February [?]
Unjuried group show, Women's Interart Center, New York

March 20–29
***Films of John Lennon and Yoko Ono,* Whitney Museum of American Art, New York**
Two-person film screening. A selection of their films shown in Whitney's *New American Filmmakers Series*.

April 4
Carousel, WNET TV, New York
"This Is Not Here," produced by WCNY, Syracuse in conjunction with Ono's Everson exhibition, aired as the inaugural show of a thirteen-week arts series, sponsored by New York State Council on the Arts. (Aired on other public stations in New York on various dates.)

April 22
National Peace Action Coalition rally, New York
Ono and Lennon sing "Give Peace a Chance" in front of several thousand marchers protesting the Vietnam war in midtown Manhattan.

April 30
Concert by Moorman and Paik, Willard Straight Hall, Cornell University, Ithaca
Includes *Cut Piece* performed by Moorman.
DOCUMENTS: program

May
Radio program, New York
Ono and Lennon appear on Dick Gregory's program to discuss the racial implications of "Woman Is the Nigger of the World."

May 1
Opening of *Camden Arts Festival*, London
Collage of music by Lennon and Ono included in an exhibition at Roundhouse Gallery.

May 12–14
Film screening, Boarding House Theater, San Francisco
Program features films by Lennon and Ono, including *Erection*, *The Ballad of John and Yoko*, *Give Peace a Chance*, and *Apotheosis*.

May 14, 15, 17
Cannes Film Festival
Ono and Lennon's films, including *Bed-In*, offered. *Imagine*, *Fly*, *Freedom*, *Erection*, *Apotheosis*, and *Rape* are shown at local cinemas.

May 20
Antiwar demonstration, Duffy Square, New York
New York branch of National Peace Action Coalition organizes an evening rally. Ono and Lennon lead the crowd in singing "Give Peace a Chance."

June 30–October 8
Documenta 5, Museum Fridericianum, Kassel
Section entitled "Individual Mythologies, Self-Representation, Processes" includes Ono's works: *Painting to Hammer a Nail*, *Painting to Be Stepped On*, *Forget It*, *White Chess Set*, and *Painting to Let the Evening Light Go Through*. Her film *Fly* also presented in the film program.
DOCUMENTS: exh. cats.

August 25
National Organization of Women (NOW) gives a music award for "Positive Image of Women" to Ono and Lennon for "Woman Is the Nigger of the World" and "Sisters O Sisters."

August 30
One-to-One, Madison Square Garden, New York
Lennon and Ono give two appearances (afternoon and evening) with Elephant's Memory in a concert organized by WABC TV's Geraldo Rivera to aid mentally handicapped children (fig. 14.25). Other performers include Roberta Flack, Stevie Wonder, and Sha Na Na. ABC-TV later broadcasts "John Lennon and Yoko Ono Present the One-to-One Concert" on December 15.

September 16
Ken Dewey memorial, Dewey family farm, Far Hills, N.J.
Ono performs "silent lament" to Lennon's "air guitar," as part of memorial to artist-friend Ken Dewey.

October 1972–1973
Fluxshoe Exhibition, U.K.
Traveling exhibition and performances. Ono's work performed by others.
DOCUMENTS: exh. cats.; posters; programs

October 28
9th Annual New York Avant Garde Festival (A Riverboat Show Aboard the Alexander Hamilton), South Street Seaport Museum, New York
Includes Ono's *If It Fits You Can Have It* performed by others.
DOCUMENTS: poster

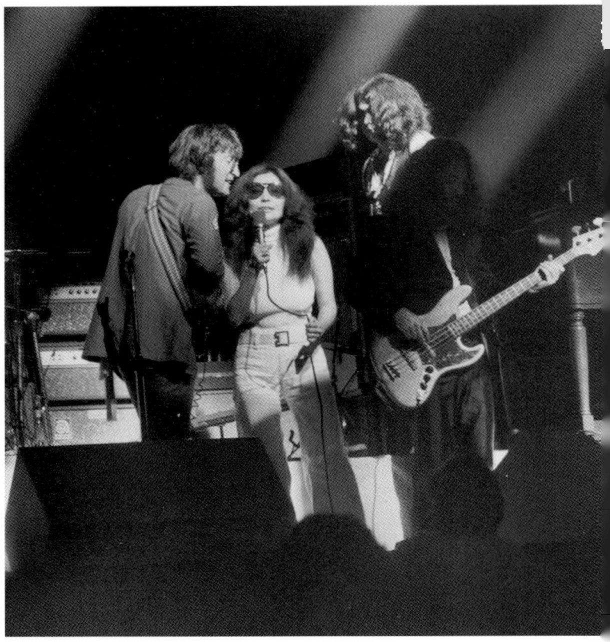

FIGURE 14.25
ONO AND LENNON PERFORMING, ***ONE-TO-ONE***, MADISON SQUARE GARDEN, NEW YORK, 1972

1973

BIOGRAPHY: Wins custody of Kyoko in March, but is unable to unite with her; moves into The Dakota apartment in May; separates from Lennon in October
SINGLE RECORDS RELEASED: "Death of Samantha"/"Yang Yang"; "Woman Power"/"Men, Men, Men"; "Run, Run, Run"/"Men, Men, Men" (U.K.); "Josei jōi banzai"/"Josei jōi banzai" (Pt. 2) (Cheers to women on top; Japan)
LP RECORDS RELEASED: *Approximately Infinite Universe* (fig. 14.26); *Feeling the Space*; *Welcome (The Many Sides of Yoko Ono)* (promotional, Japan)

January 11–24
Imagine, Whitney Museum of American Art, New York
Two-person film screening. Ono and Lennon's film premieres in New York as part of *New American Filmmakers Series*.
DOCUMENTS: ad, *Village Voice*, 18 January 1973, p. 75

April 1
Declaration of Nutopia, New York
Two-person event. At a press conference, Ono and Lennon declare the formation of Nutopia, a "conceptual country" with "no land, no boundaries, no passports, only people." Citizenship can be obtained when one declares his or her awareness of it.
DOCUMENTS: press release by Nutopian Embassy

May 20
Solo concert, Town Hall, New York
Ono's solo appearance, backed by Elephant's Memory, benefits WBAI public radio station.

June 1–4
First International Planning Conference, Lesley College, Cambridge, Mass.
NOW-organized event. In the second-night concert, Ono sings her songs, playing the piano, accompanied by Lennon's guitar; also sings at the closing ceremony.
DOCUMENTS: program

June 28
Demonstration, outside South Vietnamese Embassy, Washington, D.C.
Ono and Lennon take part in support of a political prisoner in Saigon.

June 29
Ono and Lennon attend the Watergate hearings and hold a press conference at the National Press Club.

September 16
Benefit concert, San Diego Stadium, San Diego
Ono appears with Plastic Ono Band in the concert organized for Sickle Cell Anemia Foundation in San Diego.

October 23–28
Solo concerts and events, Kenny's Castaways, New York
Plays solo, backed by Plastic Ono Superband.
DOCUMENTS: program

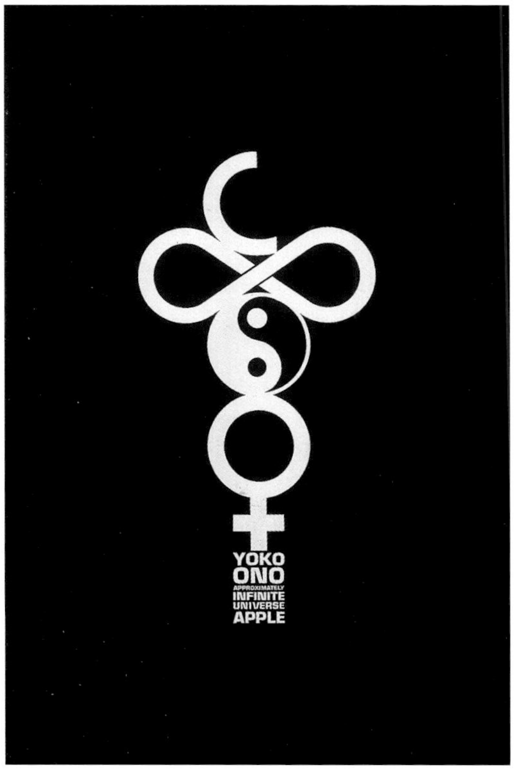

FIGURE 14.26
POSTER, ***APPROXIMATELY INFINITE UNIVERSE***, 1973

December 9
10th Annual New York Avant Garde Festival: On a Train of Penn Central Cars at Grand Central Station, **New York**
Event held around 20 Penn Central baggage cars on tracks 34 and 35. Ono contributes one railroad car with objects and texts (fig. 14.27).

December 23
The Artist as Prophet, Cathedral Church of St. John the Divine, New York
Ono and Lennon honored with Centennial Medal as part of the church's Sunday-in-Advent series.

December 25
Solo concert, Cathedral Church of St. John the Divine, New York
Accompanied by David Spinozza.

1974

SINGLE RECORDS RELEASED: "Yume o motō/Let's Have a Dream"/"It Happened" (Japan)

January 10
Women for Women, Town Hall, New York
Ono and her band, followed by the eight-woman band Isis, give a concert to inaugurate the weekly performing arts and lecture series of NOW from January 10 to February 14.
DOCUMENTS: flyer; program

February 1
Women Artists: History-Condition-Aspiration, Smithsonian Associates, Washington, D.C.
Gives a lecture for the lecture series.

August 10
One Step Festival, **Kōriyama, Fukushima Prefecture**
Ono participates with Plastic Ono Super Band in the eleven-day-long rock festival organized by a local environmental youth group (fig. 14.28). Ono also gives five solo concerts in Tokyo (11th, 12th), Nagoya (13th), Hiroshima (16th), and Osaka (19th), presented by Japan's veteran rock musician Uchida Yūya.
DOCUMENTS: program; poster

November 16
11th Annual New York Avant Garde Festival: At Shea Stadium, **New York**
Includes Ono's wish piece *46 Reflections*, consisting of crosses with mirrors, installed in the entire upper tier.
DOCUMENTS: poster; press release with Ono's instruction

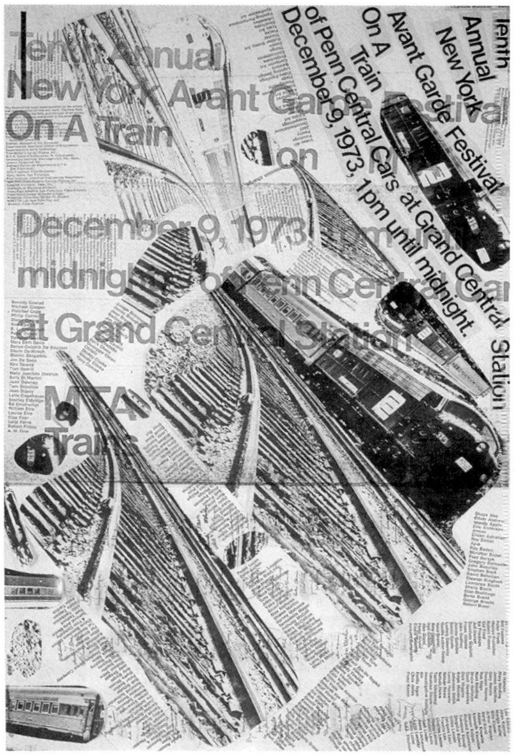

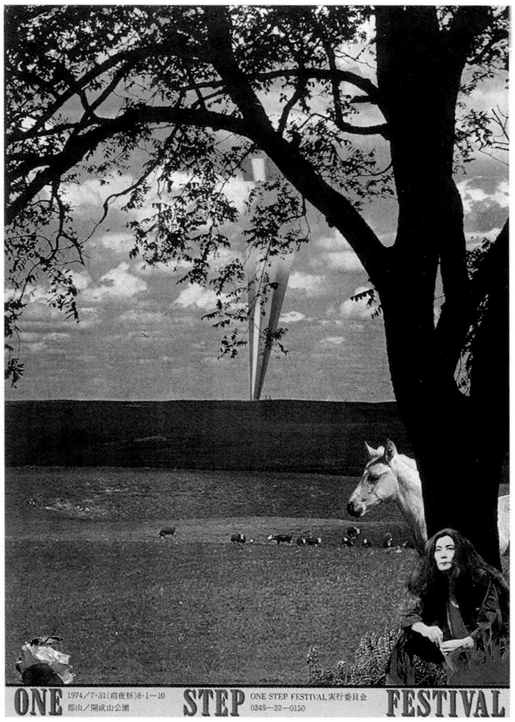

FIGURE 14.27 (TOP)
POSTER, ***10TH ANNUAL NEW YORK AVANT GARDE FESTIVAL***, 1973

FIGURE 14.28 (BOTTOM)
POSTER, ***ONE STEP FESTIVAL***, 1974

1975

BIOGRAPHY: Reunites with Lennon in January; Sean Taro Ono Lennon born on October 9

April 21
Fluxfest Presents: 12! Big Names! 80 Wooster Street, New York
Ono's name included among those projected onto screen (fig. 2.18).
DOCUMENTS: poster

September 27
12th Annual New York Avant Garde Festival: At Gateway National Recreation Area, Floyd Bennett Field, Brooklyn, New York
Includes Ono's *Wish Poem*, flower seeds planted on 7,000-foot runway in her absence.
DOCUMENTS: poster

December 31
Flux-New Year's Event, Clock Tower, New York
Including Ono's *Water Clock (Kiss)* (fig. 2.19).

1976

January 17–February 21
Fluxshow, Gallery A, Amsterdam

October 12–27
Fluxus Suggestion Show
DOCUMENTS: postcard announcement

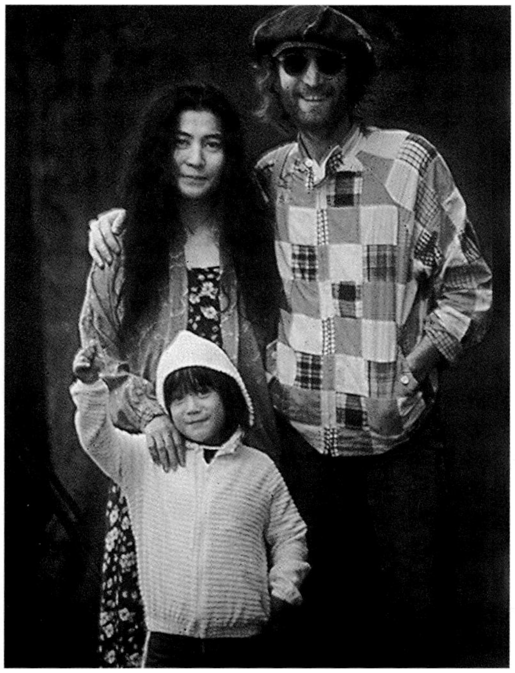

FIGURE 14.29
ONO, LENNON, AND SEAN IN JAPAN, 1979

1977

BIOGRAPHY: Visits Japan for four months with Lennon and Sean

March 20
Fluxus & Co., Cannaviello Studio d'Arte, Rome

April 5–20
Fluxfilms, Anthology Film Archives, New York

June 19
13th Annual New York Avant Garde Festival: At World Trade Center, New York
Program lists Ono and Lennon's sky-writing *Wish Poem*.
DOCUMENTS: poster

1978

May 20
14th Annual Avant Garde Festival/2nd Cambridge River Festival, Cambridge, Mass.
Includes Ono's *Wish Poem* with "48 reflective crosses."
DOCUMENTS: poster; press release

1979

BIOGRAPHY: Visits Japan with Lennon and Sean (fig. 14.29)

March 24
Flux-Concert, The Kitchen, New York
Includes Ono's *Wall Piece for Orchestra to Yoko Ono*.
DOCUMENTS: program; flyer

April
Fluxus International & Co., Elac, Lyons
Traveling exhibition.
DOCUMENTS: exh. cat.

April
Fluxus: The Most Radical and Experimental Art Movement of the Sixties, Galerie A, Amsterdam
DOCUMENTS: book

April 7–11
Fluxus, Caceres Museo Vostell Malpartida-España
Group exhibition as part of *SACOM 2 (Semana de Arte Contemporaneo Malpartida)*
DOCUMENT: flyer

May 27
"A Love Letter from John and Yoko to People Who Ask Us What When and Why"
Two-person event. Ono and Lennon run a full-page ad in *New York Times* and *Los Angeles Times*.

1980

BIOGRAPHY: Lennon murdered on December 8
SINGLE RECORDS RELEASED: Lennon, "Starting Over"/Ono, "Kiss, Kiss, Kiss"

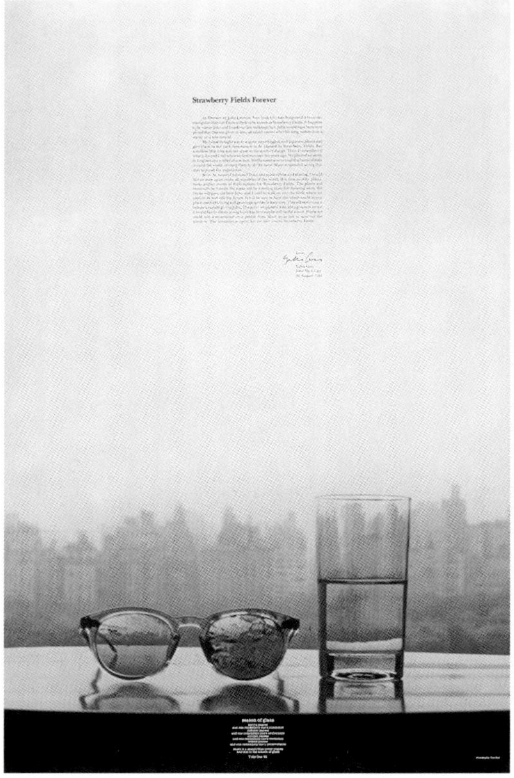

FIGURE 14.30
POSTER, "STRAWBERRY FIELDS FOREVER," 1981

LP RECORDS RELEASED: Lennon and Ono, *Double Fantasy*

July 20
15th Annual Avant Garde Festival of New York, Passenger Ship Terminal, 55th Street and 12th Avenue, Berths 5 and 6, New York
DOCUMENTS: poster; press release

December 14
At Ono's request, ten-minute silent vigil observed at 2 p.m. EST throughout the world in memory of Lennon, who was murdered six days before. Many radio stations worldwide also observe the silence. Following the vigil, a note from Ono widely reproduced by the media: BLESS YOU FOR YOUR TEARS AND PRAYERS. / I SAW JOHN SMILING IN THE SKY. / I SAW SORROW CHANGING INTO CLARITY. / I SAW ALL OF US BECOMING ONE MIND. / THANK YOU.

1981

VIDEOS RELEASED: *Walking on Thin Ice* (music video); *Woman* (music video)
SINGLE RECORDS RELEASED: "Walking on Thin Ice"/"It Happened" (see no. 57); "Walking on Thin Ice"/"It Happened/Hard Times Are Over" (cassette single, U.K.); Lennon, "Woman"/Ono, "Beautiful Boys"; Lennon, "Watching the Wheels"/Ono, "Yes, I'm Your Angel"; "No, No, No"/"Will You Touch Me";

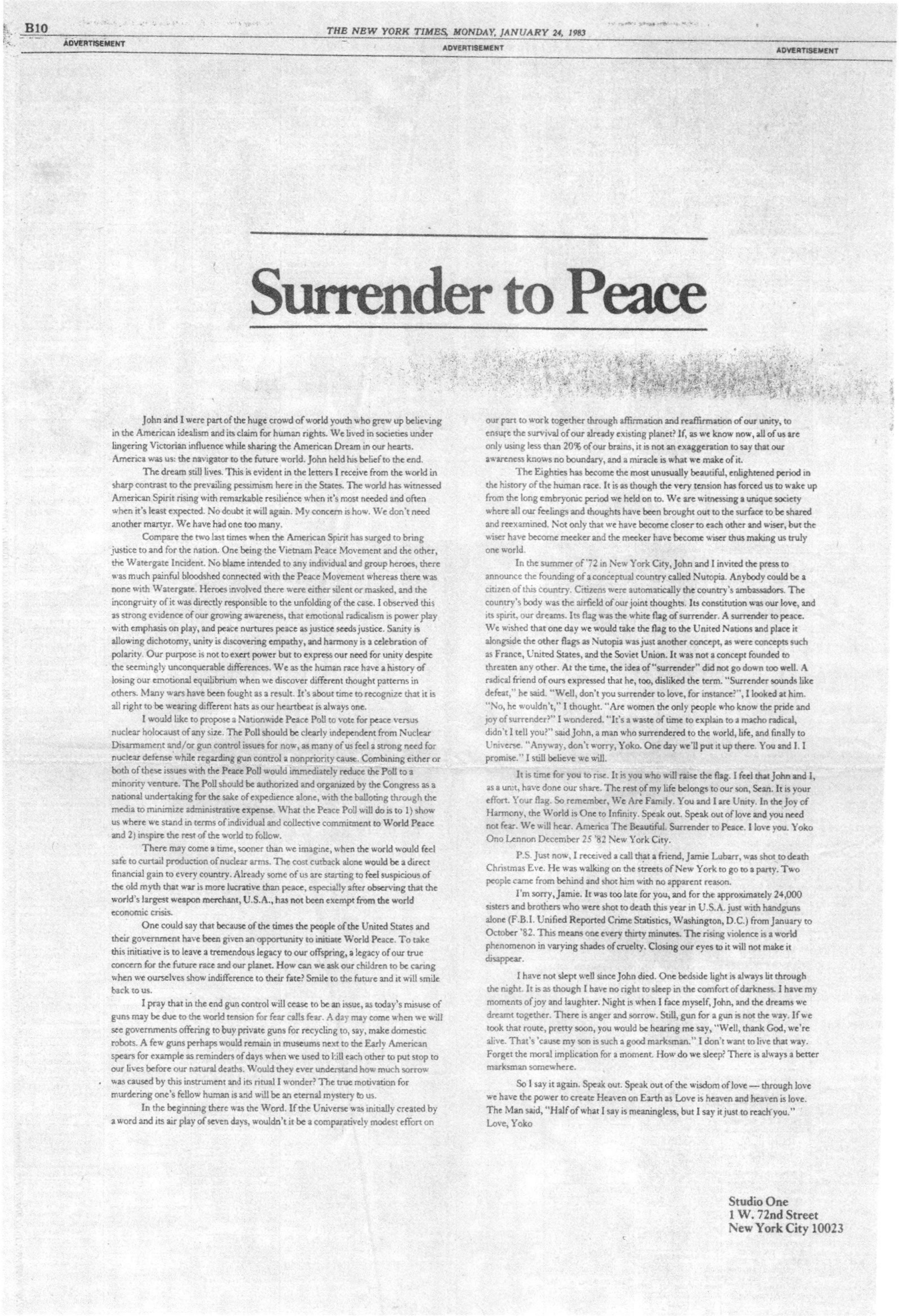

B10 THE NEW YORK TIMES, MONDAY, JANUARY 24, 1983

ADVERTISEMENT ADVERTISEMENT ADVERTISEMENT

Surrender to Peace

John and I were part of the huge crowd of world youth who grew up believing in the American idealism and its claim for human rights. We lived in societies under lingering Victorian influence while sharing the American Dream in our hearts. America was us: the navigator to the future world. John held his belief to the end.

The dream still lives. This is evident in the letters I receive from the world in sharp contrast to the prevailing pessimism here in the States. The world has witnessed American Spirit rising with remarkable resilience when it's most needed and often when it's least expected. No doubt it will again. My concern is how. We don't need another martyr. We have had one too many.

Compare the two last times when the American Spirit has surged to bring justice to and for the nation. One being the Vietnam Peace Movement and the other, the Watergate Incident. No blame intended to any individual and group heroes, there was much painful bloodshed connected with the Peace Movement whereas there was none with Watergate. Heroes involved there were either silent or masked, and the incongruity of it was directly responsible to the unfolding of the case. I observed this as strong evidence of our growing awareness, that emotional radicalism is power play with emphasis on play, and peace nurtures peace as justice seeds justice. Sanity is allowing dichotomy, unity is discovering empathy, and harmony is a celebration of polarity. Our purpose is not to exert power but to express our need for unity despite the seemingly unconquerable differences. We as the human race have a history of losing our emotional equilibrium when we discover different thought patterns in others. Many wars have been fought as a result. It's about time to recognize that it is all right to be wearing different hats as our heartbeat is always one.

I would like to propose a Nationwide Peace Poll to vote for peace versus nuclear holocaust of any size. The Poll should be clearly independent from Nuclear Disarmament and/or gun control issues for now, as many of us feel a strong need for nuclear defense while regarding gun control a nonpriority cause. Combining either or both of these issues with the Peace Poll would immediately reduce the Poll to a minority venture. The Poll should be authorized and organized by the Congress as a national undertaking for the sake of expedience alone, with the balloting through the media to minimize administrative expense. What the Peace Poll will do is to 1) show us where we stand in terms of individual and collective commitment to World Peace and 2) inspire the rest of the world to follow.

There may come a time, sooner than we imagine, when the world would feel safe to curtail production of nuclear arms. The cost cutback alone would be a direct financial gain to every country. Already some of us are starting to feel suspicious of the old myth that war is more lucrative than peace, especially after observing that the world's largest weapon merchant, U.S.A., has not been exempt from the world economic crisis.

One could say that because of the times the people of the United States and their government have been given an opportunity to initiate World Peace. To take this initiative is to leave a tremendous legacy to our offspring, a legacy of our true concern for the future race and our planet. How can we ask our children to be caring when we ourselves show indifference to their fate? Smile to the future and it will smile back to us.

I pray that in the end gun control will cease to be an issue, as today's misuse of guns may be due to the world tension for fear calls fear. A day may come when we will see governments offering to buy private guns for recycling to, say, make domestic robots. A few guns perhaps would remain in museums next to the Early American spears for example as reminders of days when we used to kill each other to put stop to our lives before our natural deaths. Would they ever understand how much sorrow was caused by this instrument and its ritual I wonder? The true motivation for murdering one's fellow human is and will be an eternal mystery to us.

In the beginning there was the Word. If the Universe was initially created by a word and its air play of seven days, wouldn't it be a comparatively modest effort on our part to work together through affirmation and reaffirmation of our unity, to ensure the survival of our already existing planet? If, as we know now, all of us are only using less than 20% of our brains, it is not an exaggeration to say that our awareness knows no boundary, and a miracle is what we make of it.

The Eighties has become the most unusually beautiful, enlightened period in the history of the human race. It is as though the very tension has forced us to wake up from the long embryonic period we held on to. We are witnessing a unique society where all our feelings and thoughts have been brought out to the surface to be shared and reexamined. Not only that we have become closer to each other and wiser, but the wiser have become meeker and the meeker have become wiser thus making us truly one world.

In the summer of '72 in New York City, John and I invited the press to announce the founding of a conceptual country called Nutopia. Anybody could be a citizen of this country. Citizens were automatically the country's ambassadors. The country's body was the airfield of our joint thoughts. Its constitution was our love, and its spirit, our dreams. Its flag was the white flag of surrender. A surrender to peace. We wished that one day we would take the flag to the United Nations and place it alongside the other flags as Nutopia was just another concept, as were concepts such as France, United States, and the Soviet Union. It was not a concept founded to threaten any other. At the time, the idea of "surrender" did not go down too well. A radical friend of ours expressed that he, too, disliked the term. "Surrender sounds like defeat," he said. "Well, don't you surrender to love, for instance?", I looked at him. "No, he wouldn't," I thought. "Are women the only people who know the pride and joy of surrender?" I wondered. "It's a waste of time to explain to a macho radical, didn't I tell you?" said John, a man who surrendered to the world, life, and finally to Universe. "Anyway, don't worry, Yoko. One day we'll put it up there. You and I. I promise." I still believe we will.

It is time for you to rise. It is you who will raise the flag. I feel that John and I, as a unit, have done our share. The rest of my life belongs to our son, Sean. It is your effort. Your flag. So remember, We Are Family. You and I are Unity. In the Joy of Harmony, the World is One to Infinity. Speak out. Speak out of love and you need not fear. We will hear. America The Beautiful. Surrender to Peace. I love you. Yoko Ono Lennon December 25 '82 New York City.

P.S. Just now, I received a call that a friend, Jamie Lubarr, was shot to death Christmas Eve. He was walking on the streets of New York to go to a party. Two people came from behind and shot him with no apparent reason.

I'm sorry, Jamie. It was too late for you, and for the approximately 24,000 sisters and brothers who were shot to death this year in U.S.A. just with handguns alone (F.B.I. Unified Reported Crime Statistics, Washington, D.C.) from January to October '82. This means one every thirty minutes. The rising violence is a world phenomenon in varying shades of cruelty. Closing our eyes to it will not make it disappear.

I have not slept well since John died. One bedside light is always lit through the night. It is as though I have no right to sleep in the comfort of darkness. I have my moments of joy and laughter. Night is when I face myself, John, and the dreams we dreamt together. There is anger and sorrow. Still, gun for a gun is not the way. If we took that route, pretty soon, you would be hearing me say, "Well, thank God, we're alive. That's 'cause my son is such a good marksman." I don't want to live that way. Forget the moral implication for a moment. How do we sleep? There is always a better marksman somewhere.

So I say it again. Speak out. Speak out of the wisdom of love — through love we have the power to create Heaven on Earth as Love is heaven and heaven is love. The Man said, "Half of what I say is meaningless, but I say it just to reach you."
Love, Yoko

Studio One
1 W. 72nd Street
New York City 10023

FIGURE 14.31
"SURRENDER TO PEACE,"
AD IN *NEW YORK TIMES,*
1983

"Goodbye Sadness"/"I Don't Know Why"; "Walking on Thin Ice"/"It Happened"/"Hard Times Are Over" (promotional 12"); "No, No, No"/"I Don't Know Why"/"She Gets Down on Her Knees" (promotional 12")
LP RECORDS RELEASED: *Season of Glass*

January 18
"In Gratitude"
Solo newspaper event. Runs a full-page ad in *New York Times* and other major international newspapers.

August 28
"Strawberry Fields Forever"
Solo newspaper event. Runs a full-page ad in *New York Times*.

September 20–November 1
Fluxus etc./The Gilbert and Lila Silverman Collection, Cranbrook Academy of Art Museum, Bloomfield Hills, Mich.
Traveling survey exhibition.
DOCUMENTS: exh. cats.

1982

VIDEOS RELEASED: *Goodbye Sadness* (music video)
SINGLE RECORDS RELEASED: "My Man"/"Let the Tears Dry"
LP RECORDS RELEASED: *It's Alright*

February 24
25th Grammy Awards, Shrine Auditorium, Los Angeles
Ono receives an "Album of the Year" award for her and Lennon's *Double Fantasy*.

August 23
Performance program, Moorman's apartment building roof, New York
Moorman performs *Cut Piece* and *Mend Piece*.

September 17–November 14
1962 Wiesbaden Fluxus 1982: Eine kleine Geschichete von Fluxus in drei Teilen, Museum Wiesbaden, Nassauischer Kunstverein, and Harlekin Art, Wiesbaden, Germany
Traveling group exhibition.
DOCUMENTS: exh. cat.

1983

SINGLE RECORDS RELEASED: "Never Say Goodbye"/"Loneliness"; "Never Say Goodbye"/"Loneliness" (remixed, 12")
LP RECORDS RELEASED: Lennon and Ono, *Heart Play—Unfinished Dialogue*

January 14–February 12
Mixed Grill, Grommet Gallery, New York

January 24
"Surrender to Peace"
Solo newspaper event. Runs a full-page ad in *New York Times* (fig. 14.31).

September 11–January 31, 1984
Give Peace a Chance: Music and the Struggle for Peace, The Peace Museum, Chicago
Group exhibition travels widely over several years.
DOCUMENTS: exh. cat.

1984

SINGLED RECORDS RELEASED: Lennon, "Nobody Told Me"/Ono, "Sanity"; Lennon, "I'm Stepping Out"/Ono, "Sleepless Night"; Lennon, "Borrowed Time"/Ono, "Your Hands"; Lennon, "Every Man Has a Woman Who Loves Him"/Ono, "It's Alright"; Lennon, "Borrowed Time"/Ono, "Your Hands"/Ono, "Never Say Goodbye" (12")
LP RECORDS RELEASED: Lennon and Ono, *Milk and Honey*

1985

SINGLE RECORDS RELEASED: "Hell in Paradise"
LP RECORDS RELEASED: *Starpeace*

February 2–23
Rain Dance, 292 Lafayette Street, New York
A benefit party and exhibition, organized and curated by Keith Haring for the U.S. Committee for UNICEF's African Emergency Relief Fund, includes *A Glass Key*.

October 9
Dedication ceremony, Strawberry Fields at Central Park, New York
The memorial to Lennon opens (also called "International Garden of Peace").

1986

February 28
Starpeace World Tour
Solo concert tour (fig. 14.32). Beginning in Brussels, it travels in Europe (West Berlin, Warsaw, Stockholm, Hamburg, Budapest, Ljyubliana, and London), followed by the shortened North American presentation in San Francisco (Warfield Theater, May 15), Montreal (Spectrum, May 20), and New York (Beacon Theater, May 22).
DOCUMENTS: program

June 15
Conspiracy for Hope, Giants Stadium, San Diego
Benefit concert for Amnesty International. Six-city tour ends with a twelve-hour concert which presents Ono, Sting, U2, and Lou Reed, among others.

October 24
Antinuclear march, near United Nations, New York
Ono and Rev. Jesse Jackson offer moral support to marchers who walked from Los Angeles to New York, stopping on their way to Washington, D.C.

1987

February 14–16
International Forum on Drastic Reductions of Nuclear Weapons for a Nuclear-Free World, Moscow
Ono attends a peace forum sponsored by the Soviet government, together with strategic studies experts and cultural figures.

April 21
Interrupted River, Joyce Theater, New York
Jennifer Muller/The Works premieres a dance piece, accompanied by Ono's music.

May 7–12
Tribute to John Cage, Chicago
Art-fair presentation of Carl Solway Gallery from Cincinnati, curated by Allan Kaprow. Includes *Play It By Trust*.
DOCUMENTS: catalogue box

November 7–January 3, 1988
Fluxus 25 Years, Williams College Museum of Art, Williamstown, Mass.
DOCUMENTS: exh. cat.

1988

January 23–March 13
Fluxus and Friends: Selection from the Alternative Traditions in the Contemporary Arts Collection, The University of Iowa Museum of Art, Iowa City
DOCUMENTS: exh. cat.

September 24–January 1989
Stationen der Moderne, Berlinische Galerie, Berlin
Includes *Painting to See the Skies*.

November 6–December 16
***Yoko Ono: Three Events,* Gallery of Art, University of Missouri at Kansas City**
Includes *Nail It*, *Play It By Trust*, and *Meno*.

November 17– March 10, 1989
Fluxus: Selections from The Gilbert and Lila Silverman Collection, The Museum of Modern Art Library, New York
Survey exhibition. Film screenings in conjunction with exhibition on November 14 and 15. Ono designs catalogue cover and poster (fig. 14.33).
DOCUMENTS: exh. cat.; poster

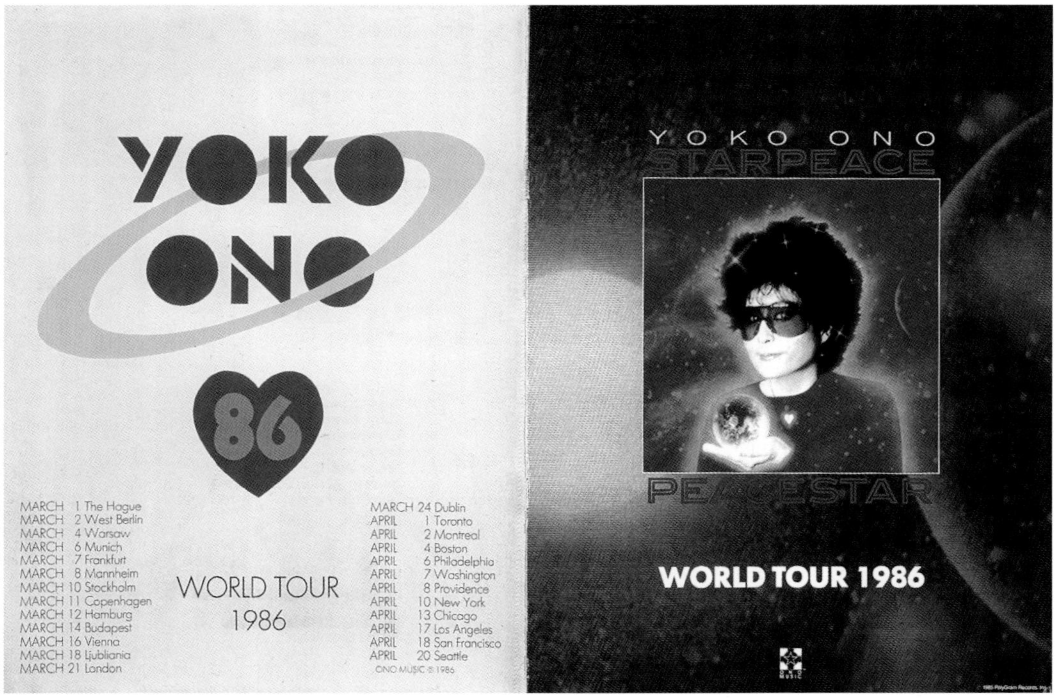

FIGURE 14.32
PROGRAM FOR
STARPEACE WORLD
TOUR, 1986

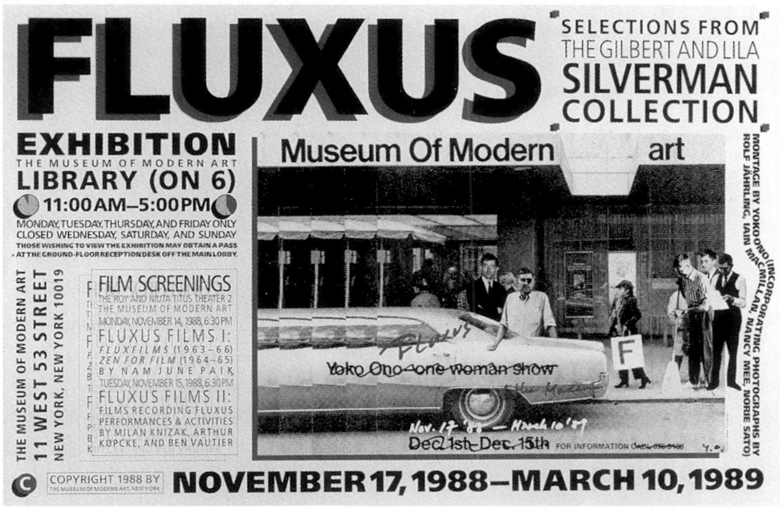

FIGURE 14.33
POSTER, *FLUXUS: SELECTIONS FROM THE GILBERT AND LILA SILVERMAN COLLECTION*, THE MUSEUM OF MODERN ART LIBRARY, NEW YORK, 1988. DESIGN BY ONO

1989

February 8–April 16
***Yoko Ono: Objects, Films,* Whitney Museum of American Art, New York**
Solo exhibition (pl. 59). Curated by Barbara Haskell and John G. Hanhardt. New bronze works included.
DOCUMENTS: exh. brochure

June 7–July 29
Happenings & Fluxus, Galerie 1900–2000, Galerie du Genie, and Galerie de Poche, Paris
Performs *Promise Piece* in conjunction with exhibition at Ecole Nationale des Beaux-Arts on June 7.
DOCUMENTS: exh. cat.

June 9
Performance, Ecole Nationale des Beaux-Arts, Paris
In support of the pro-democracy movement in Beijing, Ono performs *Promise Piece* by smashing a Chinese vase in front of 1,000 people, to whom she hands out pieces.

September 1–3
Intervalli tra Film, Video, Televisione: Yoko Ono, Alexander Kluge, Marina Abramovic, Silvie & Chérif Defraoui, Sellerio, Palermo
DOCUMENTS: exh. cat.

September 1–November 18
Images of Rock, Kusthallen Brandts Klaedefabrik, Odense, Denmark
Traveling group exhibition.
DOCUMENTS: exh. cat.

September 23–October 29
***Yoko Ono: The Bronze Age,* Cranbrook Academy of Art Museum, Bloomfield Hills, Mich.**
Solo exhibition (fig. 14.34). Curated by Jon Hendricks, who from this point plays a pivotal role with Samuel Havadtoy in the planning and realization of Ono's exhibitions and projects.
DOCUMENTS: exh. cat.; poster

October 7–15
Yoko Ono: The Bronze Age, FIAC, Grand Palais, Paris
Solo exhibition. Art-fair presentation of Galerie 1900–2000.
DOCUMENTS: exh. brochure

November 3–December 31
***Yoko Ono: The Bronze Age,* Carl Solway Gallery, Cincinnati**
Solo exhibition.

December 1–22
***Yoko Ono: The Bronze Age and Selected Unique Works,* Philip Samuels Fine Art, St. Louis**
Solo exhibition.
DOCUMENTS: checklist

December–January 1990
Fluxus & Co., Emily Harvey Gallery, New York

1990

January 19–March 11
***Currents: Yoko Ono,* The Institute of Contemporary Art, Boston**
Solo exhibition. Curated by David Ross. Includes *Painting to Hammer a Nail In* (cross version).
DOCUMENTS: exh. brochure

January 19–March 15, 1991
***Painting to Hammer a Nail In No. 4,* Judson Memorial Church, New York**
Solo event. Year-long participation piece at the church sanctuary (fig. 7.9).
DOCUMENTS: press release; handout

February 23–25, March 2–4, 9–11
***The Films of Yoko Ono,* Institute of Contemporary Art, Boston**
Solo film program. Curated by Hanhardt.
DOCUMENTS: program

March 18, 25
Fluxusfilms, Le Lieu-Centre en Art Actuel, Quebec
DOCUMENTS: press release

March 21–April 22
***Yoko Ono: In Facing,* Riverside Studios, London**
Solo exhibition. Curated by Hendricks. Ono gives public talk at the film theater on March 24 after the first of the film program series.
DOCUMENTS: exh. cat.

March 26–May 4
Fluxus: Selection from The Silverman Collection, Baxter Art Gallery, Portland School of Art, Portland, Maine
Includes *Painting to Hammer a Nail* (bed version) and several scores silkscreened onto gallery walls.

March 27–April 2
Yoko Ono: The Bronze Age, Stockholm Art Fair
Solo exhibition. Presentation by Lilla Galleriet from Mariefred, Sweden
DOCUMENTS: exh. cat.

May 21–July 14
***Yoko Ono: Fumie,* Sōgetsu Art Museum, Tokyo**
Solo exhibition (fig. 14.35). Curated by Watanabe Reiko. Ono's new calligraphic works included. Film program in conjunction with exhibition at Sōgetsu Hall (May 21–June 3).
DOCUMENTS: exh. cat.; poster

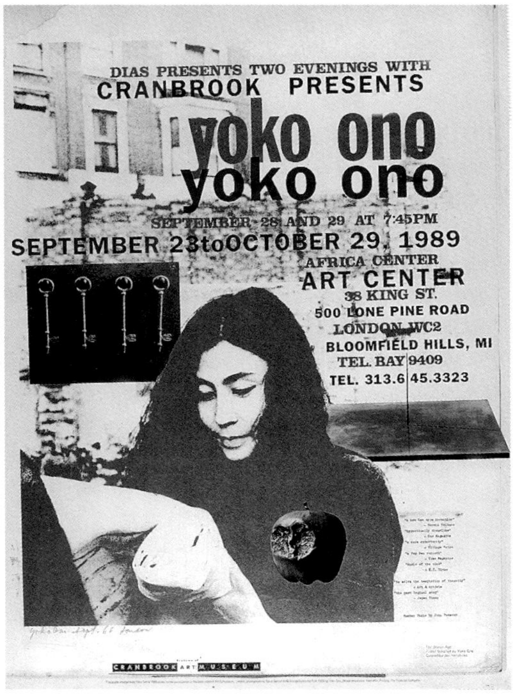

FIGURE 14.34
POSTER, *YOKO ONO: THE BRONZE AGE*, CRANBROOK ACADEMY OF ART MUSEUM, 1989

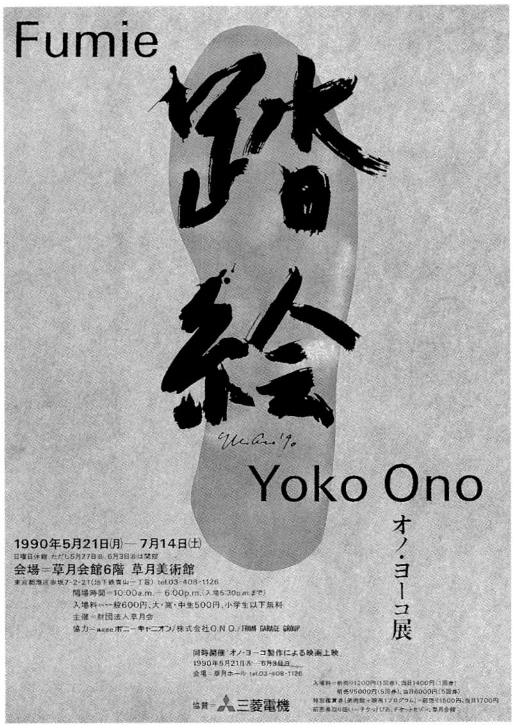

FIGURE 14.35 (LEFT)
POSTER, *YOKO ONO: FUMIE*, SŌGETSU ART MUSEUM, TOKYO, 1990. SHOWS DETAIL OF *PAINTING TO BE STEPPED ON II* (BRONZE VERSION), 1988

FIGURE 14.36 (RIGHT)
POSTER, *YOKO ONO: BIRCH MONOLOGUE*, PORIN TAIDEMUSEO, 1991. SHOWS ONO WITH *WISH PIECE* AT VENICE BIENNALE, 1990

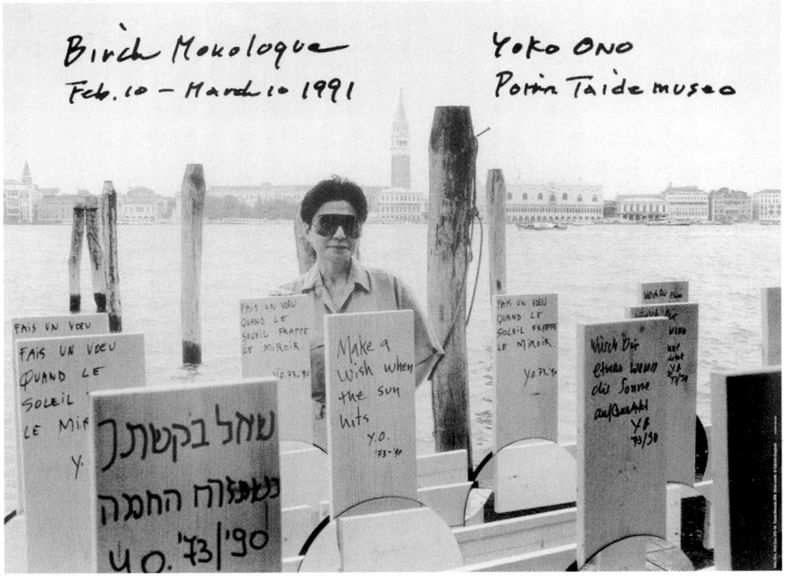

May 26–September 30
Venice Biennale
Special exhibition *Ubi Fluxus Ibi Motus: 1990–1962* (meaning "Where there is Fluxus there is movement") includes Ono's *Wish Piece* (see fig. 14.36). *Sky Piece for Jesus Christ* performed.
DOCUMENTS: exh. cat.

August 10–September 16
***Yoko Ono: En Trance,* Randers Kunstmuseum, Randers, Denmark**
Solo exhibition. Curated by Hendricks and Birgit Hessellund. *En Trance* realized for the first time.
DOCUMENTS: exh. cat.; poster

August 25–September 30
***Yoko Ono: Insound/Instructure,* Henie Onstad Arts Centre, Høvikodden, Norway**
Solo exhibition. Curated by Hendricks and Ina Blom. *Bastet* shown for the first time; *Blue Room Event* realized for the first time since 1971.
DOCUMENTS: exh. cat.; posters

September 21–November 3
Fluxus Subjektiv, Galerie Krinsinger, Vienna
DOCUMENTS: exh. cat.

October 6–November 3
Fluxus Closing In, Salvatore Ala, New York
Includes *Painting to Hammer a Nail* (toilet version).

October 23–November 24 (extended)
***Yoko Ono: To See the Skies,* Fondazione Mudima, Milan**
Solo exhibition. Curated by Gino Di Maggio and Hendricks.
DOCUMENTS: exh. cat.

November 9–December 31
***Yoko Ono: Painting to See the Skies,* Galerie Marika Malacorda, Geneva**
Solo exhibition.

November 15–January 6, 1991
Learn to Read Art: Artists' Books, Art Gallery of Hamilton, Hamilton, Ontario
DOCUMENTS: exh. cat.

1991

January 16–February
Works by Yoko Ono, Printed Matter Bookstore at DIA, New York
Solo exhibition.
DOCUMENTS: checklist

February 10–March 10
***Yoko Ono: Birch Monologue,* Porin Taidemuseo, Pori, Finland**
Solo exhibition (fig. 14.36). Curated by Hendricks and Marketta Seppala. *War Is Over!* signs hung on the side of museum building and Helsinki railroad station. Performs *Shadow Piece* on February 22.
DOCUMENTS: poster; postcards set

February 23–March 27
FluxAttitudes, Hallwalls Contemporary Arts Center, Buffalo, N.Y.
Traveling group exhibition.
DOCUMENTS: exh. cat.

February 28
Fluxus, S.E.M. Ensemble, Willow Place Auditorium series, Brooklyn
Includes *Sky Piece for Jesus Christ*.
DOCUMENTS: program

April 27–June 2
***Yoko Ono: Peace! Friður!,* The Reykjavík Municipal Art Museum**
Solo exhibition. Curated by Hendricks and Gunnar B. Kvaran. Previews on April 26 with performance of four *Shadow Pieces* and *Mend Piece* by Ono. *War Is Over!* sign hangs outside the museum.
DOCUMENTS: poster; postcard set

April 27–June 2
Fluxus, The Reykjavík Municipal Art Museum, Reykjavík, Iceland

May 3–16
***The Films of Yoko Ono,* org. The American Federation of Arts (AFA), New York**
Solo film retrospective, international tour. Curated by Hanhardt. Premieres at the Public Theater, New York.
DOCUMENTS: exh. brochure

May 25–July 7
Was ist Fluxus? Kunstmuseum Winterthur, Winterthur, Switzerland

June 11–October 27
The Cranbrook Collection: New and Notable Acquisitions, 1989–1991, Cranbrook Academy of Art Museum, Bloomfield Hills, Mich.

July 7–September 7
Yoko Ono and Fluxus, Pacific Film Archives & University Art Museum at Theater Gallery, University of California, Berkeley
DOCUMENTS: *University Art Museum* (July/August 1991)

September 1–29
***Homage to Nora: An Event in Three Stanzas,* Henie Onstad Art Centre, Høvikodden**
Solo event. Audience participation event curated by Per Hovdenakk.

September 13–December 15
Pop Art, Royal Academy, London
DOCUMENTS: exh. cat.

September 14–October 12
Social Sculpture, Vrej Baghoomian Gallery, New York
After group exhibition ends, Ono's *Play It By Trust* for twenty players remains on view until December 20.

September 30, October 1, 7, 8
Fluxfilms, Cranbrook Academy of Art, Bloomfield Hills, Mich.

October 12–November 24
Modernism and Beyond: Japanese Painting in the 20th Century, Fukuyama Museum of Art, Fukuyama, Japan
DOCUMENTS: exh. cat.

October 14, 15, 21, 22, 28, 29
Yoko Ono: Film Group I and II, Cranbrook Academy of Art, Bloomfield Hills, Mich.
Solo film program.

October 25
The Talking Drums, The Kitchen, New York
The Talking Drums' performance includes *Cut Piece*.
DOCUMENTS: concert program

November 19–February 1, 1992
Les couleurs de l'argent/Colors of Money, Musée de a Poste, Paris
Traveling group exhibition. Includes *Sky Dispenser*.
DOCUMENTS: exh. cat.

1992

CD'S RELEASED: *Onobox* (6-CD set); *Onobox Ultracase* (deluxe version); *Walking on Thin Ice* (compilation)

February 15
Memorial for Charlotte Moorman, Whitney Museum of American Art, New York
Ono performs *Promise Piece* in memory of the cellist/performance artist who frequently performed Ono's works.
DOCUMENTS: invitation

April 5
The Talking Drums: North American New Music Festival, Buffalo, N.Y.
The Talking Drums perform *Cut Piece*.

April 25–June 27
***Yoko Ono: Endangered Species 2319–2322,* Mary Boone Gallery, New York**
Solo exhibition.

May 20–July 10
The Power of the City/The City of Power, Whitney Museum of American Art at Federal Plaza, New York
DOCUMENTS: exh. cat.

June 13–November 8
***Yoko Ono: Endangered Species 2319–2322,* Stiftung Starke, Berlin**
Solo exhibition. Curated by Hendricks and Jörg Starke. Also includes *Blood Paintings*.
DOCUMENTS: exh. cat.; poster

August 22–November 29
***Yoko Ono: Color, Fly, Sky,* Museet for Samtidskunst, Roskilde, Denmark**
Solo exhibition (fig. 14.37). Curated by Hendricks and Marianne Beck. Travels to Stiftung Starke, Berlin (February 6–May 9, 1993); and Frauen Museum, Bonn (September 10–November 20, 1993).
DOCUMENTS: exh. cat.; poster (Roskilde and Berlin); five postcards

September 1–27
Fluxus Virus 1962–1992, "Temporäres Museum"–Kaufhof-Parkhaus, Kölnischer Kunstverin, and Moltkerei, Cologne
Traveling group exhibition.
DOCUMENTS: exh. cat.

September 18–November 14
Fluxus: A Conceptual Country, Franklin Furnace, New York
Traveling group exhibition. Related exhibitions include: *Ten Years on Broadway: Fluxus 1982–1992*, Emily Harvey Gallery; and *In and Around Fluxus: Film Festival and Fluxfilm Environments*, Anthology Film Archives (September 19–October 11).

October 16–November 9
Under the Influence of Fluxus, Plugin Gallery, Gallery 111 at University of Manitoba, and Melnychenko Gallery, Winnipeg
DOCUMENTS: exh. cat.

October 29–January 17, 1993
Fluxus: The Development of an Antidote, Galleri Stenström, Stockholm
DOCUMENTS: exh. cat.

November 1
Cagemusicircus! Symphony Space, New York
Memorial concert for John Cage includes performance of Cage's *0'00"* by Ono and Hendricks, dedicated to her and Ichiyanagi.

November
Excellent, several venues
Menu of Fluxus scores performed by chefs upon patrons' request at Wiesbaden/Erbenheim, Germany (22nd–24th); Judson Memorial Church, New York (24th); Nikolaj Kirke, Copenhagen (26th, 28th, 29th); and Malmö Kunsthalle, Sweden (27th).

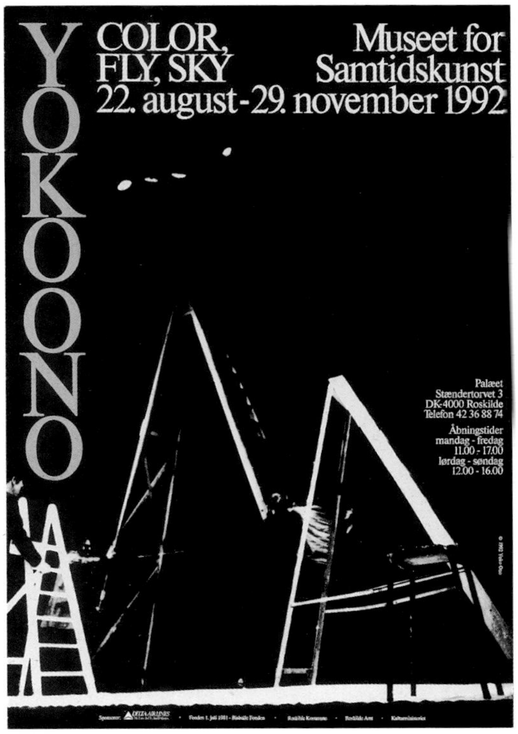

FIGURE 14.37
POSTER, ***YOKO ONO: COLOR, FLY, SKY,*** MUSEET FOR SAMTIDSKUNST, ROSKILDE, 1992. SHOWS ONO'S ***FLY,*** JEANETTA COCHRANE THEATRE, LONDON, 1966

1993

February–March
***Yoko Ono: A Piece of Sky,* Galleria Stefania Miscetti, Rome**
Solo exhibition.
DOCUMENTS: exh. cat.

14 February–June 6
In the Spirit of Fluxus, Walker Art Center, Minneapolis
Traveling group exhibition. Previews on February 13, when Ono's *Pants* is performed by Larry Miller and the audience. Related programs include screening of Ono's film on March 5, 12, and 19.
DOCUMENTS: exh. cat.

March 5
Fluxus: East of Moscow, Willow Place Auditorium, Brooklyn
S.E.M. Ensemble's concert includes Ono's *Sky Piece for Jesus Christ*.
DOCUMENTS: program

March 13–May
***Play It By Trust,* Galleria 56, Budapest**
Solo exhibition.

March 16–May 2
***Yoko Ono: Endangered Species 2319–2322,* Ludwig Museum, Budapest**
Solo exhibition. Curated by Samuel Havadtoy.
DOCUMENTS: exh. cat.

March 24
Downtown Ensemble, Renee Weiler Concert Hall, Greenwich House Music School, New York
Downtown Ensemble performs *Breath Piece*.

April 16–May 29
***Yoko Ono: Waiting for the Sunrise,* Shoshana Wayne Gallery, Santa Monica, Calif.**
Solo exhibition (pl. 61). *Family Album* shown first time.

May 1–June 12
Coming to Power: 25 Years of Sexually X-plicit Art by Women, David Zwirner, New York

May 1–June 12
The Design Show: Exhibition Invitations in the U.S.A. 1940–1992, Exit Art/The First World, New York
DOCUMENTS: exh. brochure

June 1–August 30
***Yoko Ono: Endangered Species 2319–2322,* Centre for Contemporary Art, Ujazdowski Castle, Warsaw**
Solo exhibition. Curated by Irena Groblewska.
DOCUMENTS: exh. brochure

June 14–October 10, 1993
Venice Biennale
Ono's *Two Rooms* shown in the special exhibition *Passage to Asia* (pl. 66).
DOCUMENTS: exh. cat.; puzzle pieces

June 15–September 5
***Family Album: Yoko Ono,* Stiftung Starke, Berlin**
Solo exhibition (pl. 62; fig. 14.38). Curated by Hendricks and Jörg Starke.
DOCUMENTS: exh. cat.; poster

September 12–November 28
Rolywholyover: A Circus, The Museum of Contemporary Art, Los Angeles
Traveling group exhibition.
DOCUMENTS: exh. cat.

September 29–October 31
***Glimpse: Works by Yoko Ono,* Cranbrook Academy of Art Museum, Bloomfield Hills, Mich.**
Solo exhibition. Curated by Hendricks and David D. J. Rau.
DOCUMENTS: exh. brochure; poster

October 7–25
***Yoko Ono: Endangered Species 2319–2322,* Wacoal Art Center/Spiral Garden, Tokyo**
Solo exhibition (pls. 63a–c). Curated by Nanjō Fumio. Part of the *Art Life 21: Re-Humanization* series in September 1993–March 1994 at the Spiral compound. See pp. 253–54.
DOCUMENTS: exh. brochure; poster

October 12
She Says, Joyce Theater, New York
Ono's music featured in one of three dance pieces premiered by Stephen Petronio Dance Company in a weeklong run.

November 16
Fluxus Concert, The Arts Club of Chicago
Includes *Wall Piece for Orchestra*.

1994

February 5–March 30
Japanese Art After 1945: Scream Against the Sky, Yokohama Museum of Art, Yokohama
Survey exhibition. Curated by Alexandra Munroe. Subtitle derives from Ono's musical piece (see no. 51). Ono's work prominently featured in "Conceptual Art" section.
DOCUMENTS: exh. cat.

February 5–March 12
***Yoko Ono,* Galerie A, Amsterdam**
Solo exhibition.

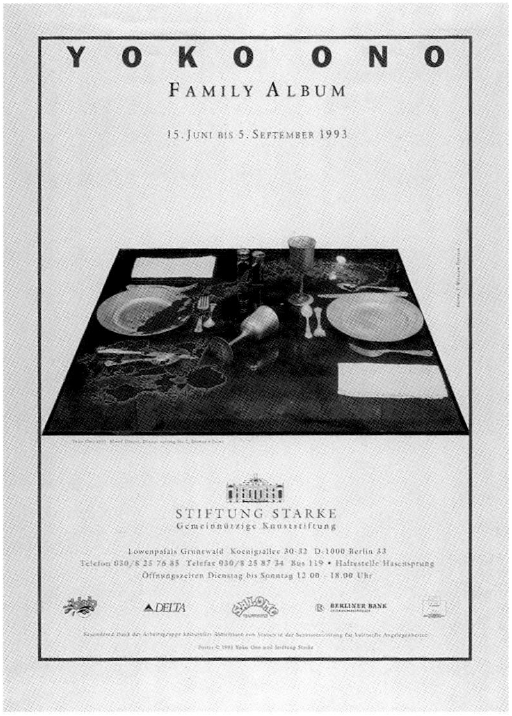

FIGURE 14.38
POSTER, ***FAMILY ALBUM: YOKO ONO***, STIFTUNG STARKE, BERLIN, 1993. SHOWS ***FAMILY ALBUM: EXHIBIT A, TABLE SETTING***, 1993

February 11–May 1
Outside the Frame: Performance and the Object, Cleveland Center for Contemporary Art, Cleveland
Traveling survey exhibition. Related performance series include *Sky Piece for Jesus Christ* and *Wall Piece for Orchestra* at Severance Hall on March 4.
DOCUMENTS: exh. cat.

5 days in February
Art Hotel: Sixty Rooms with a View, Amsterdam Hilton Hotel
International art fair, conceived by Cologne gallerist Gabriele Rivet, commemorates the twenty-fifth anniversary of Lennon and Ono's *Bed-In*.

February 26
Women in Fluxus, Willow Place Auditorium, Brooklyn
S.E.M. Ensemble's concert includes Ono's *Wall Piece for Orchestra*.
DOCUMENTS: program

March 3–April 17
***New York Rock,* WPA Theatre, New York**
Ono's off-Broadway musical premieres, directed by Phillip Oesterman (fig. 14.39).
DOCUMENTS: program; poster

March 29–June 19
Fluxbritannia: Aspects of the Fluxus Movement, 1962–1973, Tate Gallery, London
Includes public participation of *Imaginary Map Piece*.
DOCUMENTS: exh. brochure

April 1–30 (extended to May 14)
Not Knowing: Affinities in Eastern and Western Art, Gallery Schlesinger, New York

May 28–July 16
Worlds in a Box, org. South Bank Centre, London
Traveling group exhibition. Opens at City Art Centre, Edinburgh.
DOCUMENTS: exh. cat.

August 19
Performance program, Santa Barbara Museum of Art, Santa Barbara, Calif.
Ono's *Sky Piece for Jesus Christ* performed as part of Gala Preview Reception for *In the Spirit of Fluxus*.

August 21–October 30
Fluxus, Kunsthalle Basel, Basel
Traveling group exhibition.
DOCUMENTS: exh. cat.

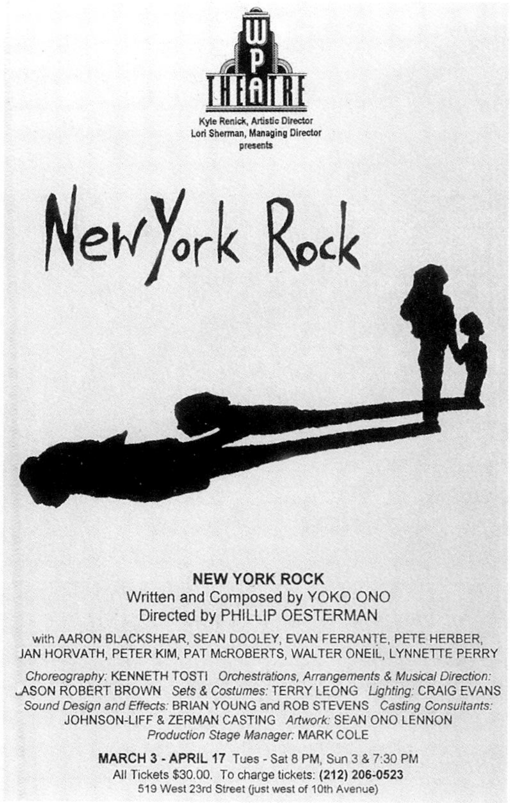

FIGURE 14.39
POSTER, *NEW YORK ROCK*, 1994

September 9
Lecture/performance/film showing, Santa Barbara Museum of Art, Santa Barbara, Calif.
In conjunction with *In the Spirit of Fluxus*, Ono's program includes participatory *Imaginary Map Piece*.

September 13–October 27
***Yoko Ono: Half-Full, Half-Empty,* Santa Barbara Contemporary Arts Forum**
Solo exhibition. Curated by Hendricks and Nancy Doll.
DOCUMENTS: poster

September 14–January 8, 1995
Japanese Art After 1945: Scream Against the Sky, Guggenheim Museum SoHo, New York
Survey exhibition traveled from Yokohama, Japan in modified form. Travels to San Francisco.
DOCUMENTS: book

October 1–November 19
Identity: The Logic of Appearance, Galerie Krinzinger, Vienna

October 25–November 15
***Yoko Ono: A Celebration of Being Human,* Langenhagen, Germany**
Solo event (pls. 65a–e; fig. 14.40). Curated by Kai Bauer and Hendricks, Ono's site-specific work is part of the series *vor ort: Kunst in städtischen Situationen* (For Town: Art in City Situations). See pp. 256–58.
DOCUMENTS: exh. cat.

November 9–January 23, 1995
Hors limites: L'art et la vie 1952–1994, Centre Georges Pompidou, Paris
Also film series *Cinéma vs. Performance* at Cinéma du Musée (November 9–December 22)
DOCUMENTS: film brochure

November 4–January 1, 1995
Neo-Dada: Redefining Art, 1958–62, org. The American Federation of Arts (AFA), New York
Traveling survey exhibition opens at Scottsdale Center for the Arts, Scottsdale, Ariz.
DOCUMENTS: exh. cat.

November 11–January 29, 1995
***Yoko Ono: Franklin Summer '94,* Galerie und Edition Hundertmark, Cologne**
Solo exhibition.

November 20–February 5, 1995
The Gold Show, Palo Alto Cultural Center, Palo Alto, Calif.
DOCUMENTS: exh. brochure

November 24
Performance program, Fundació Antoni Tàpies, Barcelona
Ono's *Conversation Piece* and *Cut Piece* performed in conjunction with *In the Spirit of Fluxus*.

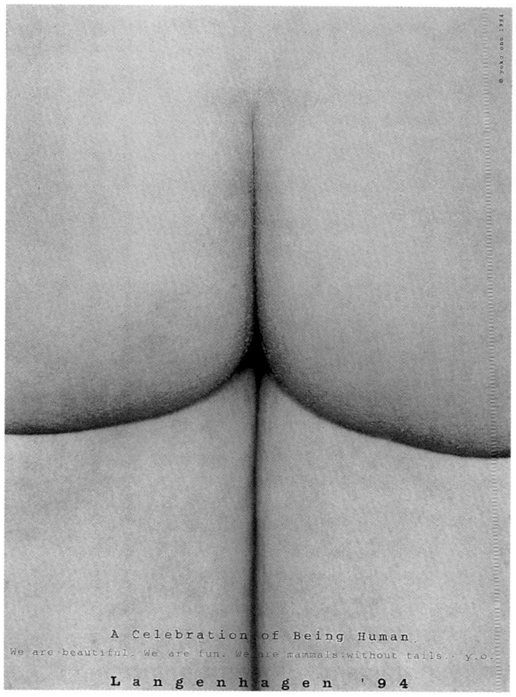

FIGURE 14.40
A CELEBRATION OF BEING HUMAN (POSTER VERSION), 1994

December 1–25
***Yoko Ono: Original Paintings and Sculptures,* The Frankel Collection, Palm Beach, Florida**
DOCUMENTS: poster

1995

CD'S RELEASED: Ono and IMA, *Rising* (see no. 58); *New York Rock (by Yoko Ono)*

January
***Yoko Ono: Lighting Piece,* Florence**
Solo event (pls. 67a–b). "Projected Art Event," organized by Studio Stefania Miscetti, takes place at Fortezza de Bassa.
DOCUMENTS: exh. cat.

January 30–March 10
Yoko Ono: Fluxus og Film, Nationalmuseet and Skoletjenesten, Copenhagen
Solo program.
DOCUMENTS: exh. cat.

February 3–April 1
Murder, Bergamot Station Arts Center, Santa Monica
Traveling group exhibition.
DOCUMENTS: exh. cat.

March 4–April 15
Endurance Art, Exit Art/The First World, New York
DOCUMENTS: press release

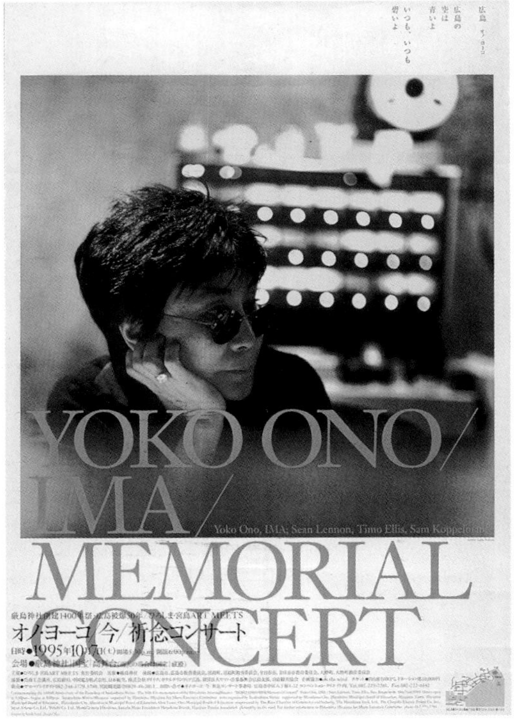

FIGURE 14.41
POSTER, ***YOKO ONO / IMA / MEMORIAL CONCERT***, 1995

March 7–12
13th Montreal International Festival of Films on Art
Ono's work included among 136 films from 22 countries.

May 9–June 18
***Yoko Ono: Sphere-9,* Fundació Pilar i Joan Miró, Majorca, Spain**
Solo exhibition. Curated by Hendricks with Jörg Starke and Havadtoy. *Two Rooms* and *Franklin Summer* drawings shown.
DOCUMENTS: exh. cat.

May 13–June 25
***Yoko Ono: 3 Rooms,* Galleria Civica di Arte Contemporanea, Trento, Italy**
Solo exhibition (pl. 68). Curated by Daniel Echer with Havadtoy and Hendricks. *Franklin Summer* drawings, *Play It By Trust*, and *Blue Room Event* shown. See Achille Bonito Oliva, pp. 259–61.
DOCUMENTS: exh. cat.; poster

June–August 27
L'Art du Tampon, Musée de la Poste, Paris
Rubber-stamp exhibition includes Ono's twelve stamps from *Everson Catalogue Box*.
DOCUMENTS: exh. cat.

July 13–September 13
***Yoko Ono: Sphere-9,* Stiftung Starke, Berlin**
Solo exhibition. Drawing series shown at gallery space in Kampinsky Hotel.

July 22–September 17
After Hiroshima: Message from Contemporary Art, Hiroshima City Art Museum of Contemporary Art
"Special Project for the 50th Anniversary of the Hiroshima A-Bombing" includes *Play It By Trust*. Ono also commissioned to create installation *Hako* (Box).
DOCUMENTS: exh. cat.

July 29–October 29
1968, National Gallery of Australia, Canberra
DOCUMENTS: exh. cat.

August 6
Ohayō Nippon, NHK TV, Japan
In commemoration of the 50th anniversary of A-bombing of Hiroshima, public network's morning program broadcasts Ono's song "Hiroshima Sky Is Always Blue," sung and recorded with Paul McCartney.

August 11–October 1
Action, Station, Exploring Open Systems..., Santa Monica Museum of Art, Santa Monica

September 9–October 21
Women on the Verge (Fluxus and Not), Elga Wimmer, New York
DOCUMENTS: exh. brochure

September 13
War Is Over! Museum in Progress, Vienna
Solo newspaper event published in *Der Standard*, p. 19. Curated by Hans-Ulrich Obrist.

September 30–December 10
Revolution: Art of the Sixties from Warhol to Beuys, Museum of Contemporary Art, Tokyo
Half-A-Room included.
DOCUMENTS: exh. cat.; poster

October 7
***Yoko Ono/IMA/Memorial Concert,* Itsukushima Shrine, Miyajima, Japan**
Solo concert (fig. 14.41). With son Sean Lennon's band IMA (meaning "now" in Japanese), commemorates the founding of Itsukushima Shrine near Hiroshima 1,400 years ago and the A-bombing of Hiroshima 50 years ago. Performance takes place at one of the shrine's National Treasure structures.
DOCUMENTS: program; poster

October 13
Aria for an Endangered Species, Diverse Works, Houston
A work in progress, dance piece by Several Dancers Core Performance Company is inspired by installation *Endangered Species 2319–2322*, with Ono's music and Ellen Bromberg's choreography.
DOCUMENTS: program

October 20–November 19
Breaking the Frame, Legion Arts/CSPS, Cedar Rapids

October 28–December 12
***Yoko Ono: Drawings from Franklin Summer and Blood Objects from Family Album,* Ubu Gallery, New York**
Solo exhibition.
DOCUMENTS: invitation with *Blood Object* (key)

November 17–January 13, 1996
Vast, N.A.M.E., Chicago
DOCUMENTS: exh. brochure

November 8–January 29, 1996
Das Menschenbild in der Werburg der 90er Jahre, Frauen Museum, Bonn, Germany
DOCUMENTS: exh. cat.

November 12
Intimate Portrait, Lifetime TV
Interview with Ono, produced and broadcast by Women's Cable Network. Documentary footage of her performance works included.

November 15–January 29, 1996
Building the Cranbrook Collection, Cranbrook Academy of Art Museum, Bloomfield Hills, Mich.

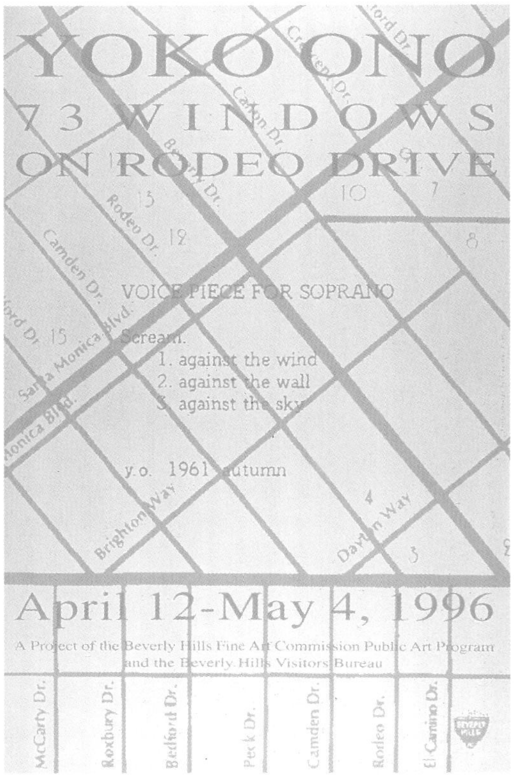

FIGURE 14.42
POSTER, ***YOKO ONO: 73 WINDOWS ON RODEO DRIVE***, 1996

December 1–January 2, 1996
Exhibit F, Blood Object from Family Album, Whitney Museum of American Art, New York
Single-work display.

1996

CD'S RELEASED: Ono and IMA, *Rising Mixes*

February 15–17
***Yoko Ono Film Festival: Smile Event,* Rome**
Solo event. In conjunction with Ono's film retrospective organized by AFA (1991), her work is projected in the evenings on a building facade at Piazza S. Apollinare, as the fourth of five events in the *Projected Artists* series, presented by Studio Stefania Miscetti & 2rc Edizioni d'Arte.
DOCUMENTS: program/catalogue

February 24–May 2
Reel Work: Artist Films and Videos of the 1970s, Museum of Contemporary Art, North Miami, Florida
DOCUMENTS: exh. cat.

February 29
***Yoko Ono/IMA,* 9:30 Club, Washington, D.C.**
Solo concert tour (fig. 14.42). With Sean Lennon's IMA. In North America and Europe, it travels to: The Knitting Factory, New York (March 6); Park West, Chicago (March 10); The Roxy, Los Angeles (March 13); Great American Music Hall, San Francisco (March 19); Crocodile Cafe, Seattle (March 21); Lee's Palace, Toronto (March 25); Paradise, Boston (May 10); Irving Plaza, New York (May 14); Milky Way, Amsterdam (May 25); Magazzini Generali, Milan (May 28); Bataclan, Paris (May 31); Metropole, Berlin (June 3); Markthalle, Hamburg (June 5); Astoria 2, London (June 8); *SummerStage*, Central Park, New York (July 6). Japanese leg includes: Club Quattro, Tokyo (June 22); Akasaka Blitz, Tokyo (June 25); Bottom Line, Nagoya (June 28); Shin-Osaka Mielparque Hall, Osaka (July 1).

March 19–April 6
A Grapefruit in the World of Park, Transmission Gallery, Glasgow
Group exhibition borrows its title from Ono's work.

April 10–June 9
Seamus Farrell, Daniel Faust, Raymond Hains, Richard Hoeck, Yoko Ono, Sturtevant, Rosemarie Trockel, La Criée-Centre d'Art Contemporain, Rennes, France
DOCUMENTS: exh. cat.

April 2–30
***Yoko Ono: The Blue Room Event Dedicated to Yoshiaki Tōno,* Gallery 360°, Tokyo**
DOCUMENTS: announcement; postcard set; multiple, *Spots on the Wall*

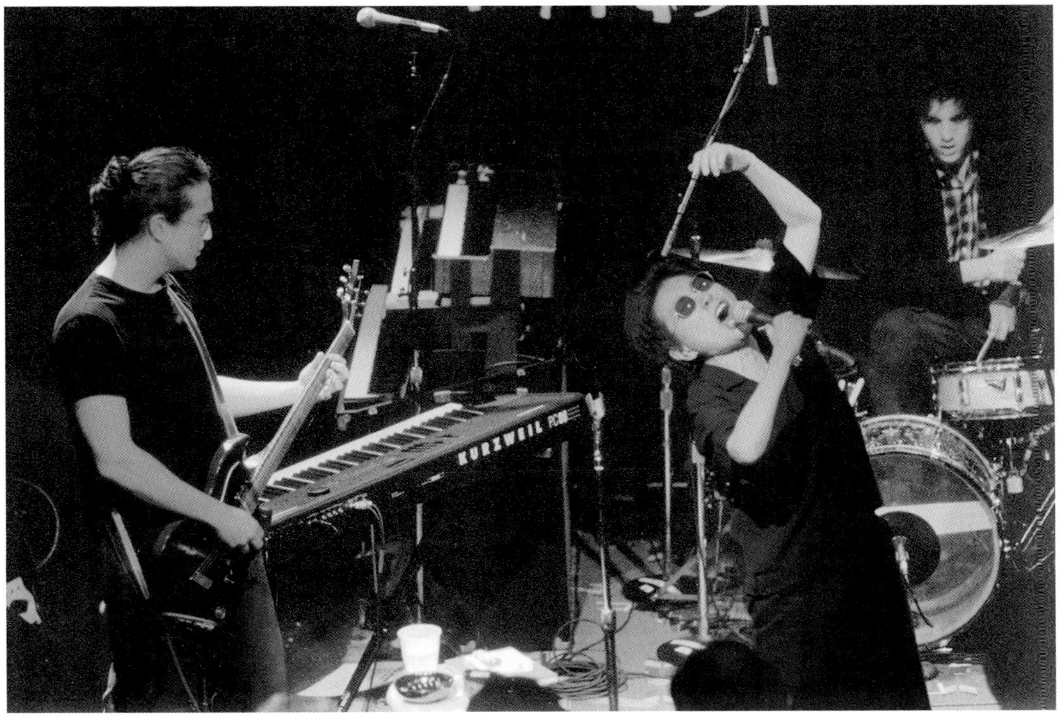

FIGURE 14.43
ONO AND SEAN LENNON PERFORMING, ***YOKO ONO/IMA,*** THE KNITTING FACTORY, NEW YORK, 1996

April 12–May 4
***Yoko Ono: 73 Windows on Rodeo Drive,* Beverly Hills, Calif.**
Solo exhibition (fig. 14.43). Curated by Hendricks and Joan Simon Menkes, organized by Beverly Hills Fine Arts Commission's Public Art Program and Beverly Hills Visitors Bureau. Ono's instruction pieces from *Grapefruit* placed across shop windows.
DOCUMENTS: poster

April 13–May 18
***Yoko Ono: Wishing Tree,* Shoshana Wayne Gallery, Santa Monica**
Solo exhibition. *Wish Tree* shown first time.

April 24–August 18
Sexual Politics: Judy Chicago's Dinner Party *in Feminist Art History*, Armand Hammer Museum of Art, University of California, Los Angeles
DOCUMENTS: exh. cat.

April 24–May 25
Women Draw, Gallery 128, New York

May 4–June 22
George Maciunas, Ubu Gallery, New York

May 17–June 22
Box, Fotouhi Cramer Gallery, New York

June 14
Internet program, http://pop.com
Ono talks live over the Internet, via RealAudio format.

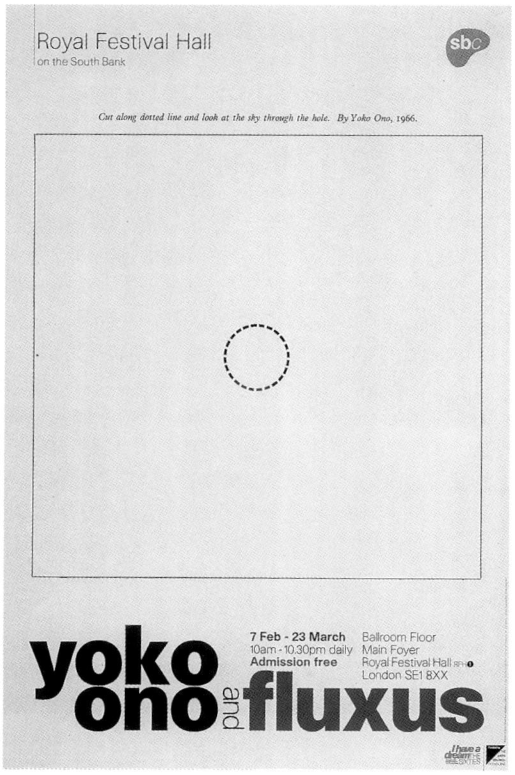

FIGURE 14.44
POSTER, ***YOKO ONO AND FLUXUS***, ROYAL FESTIVAL HALL, LONDON, 1997. SHOWS ONO'S ***CUT ALONG DOTTED LINE...***

June 16
Tibetan Freedom Concert, Polo Field, San Francisco
Appearance with IMA on the second day of the two-day event presented by Milarepa Fund and Bill Graham Presents. Participating groups include The Smashing Pumpkins, Beastie Boys, Sonic Youth, and Cibo Matto.
DOCUMENTS: poster

July 9
The Films of Yoko Ono, Films Charas, New York
Solo film program.

weekends of July 19–August 4
Fringe Festival of Contemporary Dance, Beacon Hill Studio Theater, Altanta
Several Dancers Core Performance Company's *Aria for an Endangered Species* presented.

July 18
***New York Story,* Theater in der Cristallerie, Wadgassen, Germany**
Ono's musical (*New York Rock*), directed by Gerald Uhlig, opens in Germany and runs July 19–28, August 5–9, 19–31.
DOCUMENTS: poster

August 26–October 26
***Yoko Ono: One Woman Show,* Web site of The Museum of Contemporary Art, Los Angeles (www.artcommotion.com)**
Solo exhibition. Based on *Museum of Modern [F]art*.

September 5–October 5
La Toilette de Venus: Women and Mirrors, CRG, New York

September 14–November 14
***Yoko Ono: Mindscapes,* Randers Kunstmuseum, Randers**
Solo exhibition. Curated by Hendricks.
DOCUMENTS: exh. cat.; poster

September 16–October 27
The Visible and the Invisible: Re-Presenting the Body in Contemporary Art and Society, Institute of International Visual Arts, London
For project at multiple "nonart" sites in London's Euston area, Ono contributes the billboard *A Celebration of Being Human*, next to "Peace Garden" of Religious Society of Friends (Quakers).
DOCUMENTS: exh. brochure

September 16–November 10
L'art du plastique, Ecole Nationale Supériure des Beaux-Arts, Paris

September 17-December 25
***Acorns: 100 Days with Yoko Ono,* www.park.org/Japan/DNP**
Solo event (pls. 64a–b). Curated by Nanjō Fumio. Interactive Internet project with "a new instruction every day" to "do it with Yoko on the Net!!!" See pp. 254–55.

October 18–December 23
***Yoko Ono: Fly,* Anderson Gallery, Virginia Commonwealth University, Richmond**
Solo exhibition. Curated by Jean Crutchfield. Lecture on October 19 and film screenings on October 19–20. See no. 41.
DOCUMENTS: exh. cats.; poster; postcards; T-shirt

October 26–January 4, 1997
The Subverted Object, Ubu Gallery, New York

October 30–November 4
European Art Forum Berlin
Solo exhibition. Presented by Ubu Gallery, New York.

December 22
S.E.M. Ensemble's concert, Thread Waxing Space, New York
Includes *Sky Piece for Jesus Christ*.
DOCUMENTS: program

1997

CD'S RELEASED: Ono's records reissued on CD from Rykodisc

January 9–March 8
***Yoko Ono,* Galeria 56, Budapest**
Solo exhibition. *Add Color Painting* included.

January 15–February 8
***The Films of Yoko,* Museo Nacional Centro de Arte Reina Sofia, Madrid**
Solo film program.

February 7–March 23
***Yoko Ono and Fluxus,* Royal Festival Hall/South Bank Centre, London**
Curated by Susan Copping and Hendricks (fig. 14.44).
DOCUMENTS: poster; postcard set; handouts

March 7–9, 14–17
Hiroshima, Norwalk Community-Technical College, Norwalk, Conn.
Preview workshop production of play by Ron Destro, with music by Ono.
DOCUMENTS: Program

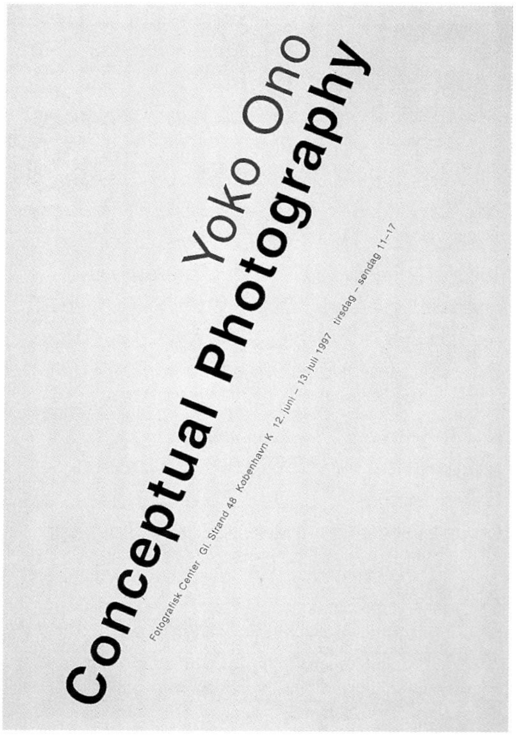

FIGURE 14.45
POSTER, ***CONCEPTUAL PHOTOGRAPHY,*** FOTOGRAFISK CENTER, COPENHAGEN, 1997

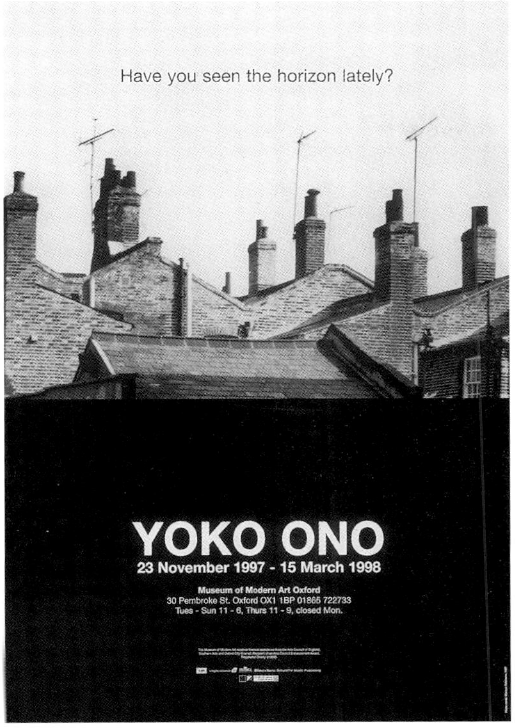

FIGURE 14.46
POSTER, *YOKO ONO: HAVE YOU SEEN THE HORIZON LATELY?*
MUSEUM OF MODERN ART, OXFORD, 1997

March 11
The Orchestra of the S.E.M. Ensemble, Paula Cooper Gallery, New York
Petr Kotik's group plays Ono's *Knock Piece*.
DOCUMENTS: program mailer

April 3
Benefit Concert for Dougie Bowne, Tramps, New York
Performs with Cibo Matto, Arto Lindsay, and Marc Ribot.

May 15–August 17
Diálogos Insólotos: Arte Objecto, Museo de Arte Moderno, Mexico City
Painting to Hammer a Nail In (office version) and *Mending Piece* included.
DOCUMENTS: exh. cat.

June 12–July 13
Yoko Ono: Conceptual Photography, Fotografisk Center, Copenhagen
Solo exhibition (pls. 69–71; fig. 14.45). Curated by Lars Schwander and Hendricks. Travels to: Konsthallen Göteborg, Sweden (September 27–November 9); Toldkammeret, Helsingör, Denmark (January 16–February 26, 1998). See pp. 262–64.
DOCUMENTS: exh. cat.; poster

June 14–25
Cartographers, The Museum of Contemporary Art and The Art Pavilion, Zagreb, Croatia
Imaginary Map Piece included.
DOCUMENTS: exh. cat.

June 15–July 27
Do It, org. Independent Curators Incorporated (ICI)
Opens at Palo Alto Cultural Center, Calif. and travels in North and South America through 2000. Includes *Wish Tree*.
DOCUMENTS: exh. cat.

June 23–July 25/June 26–August 10
Yoko Ono: En Trance–Ex It, Lonja del Pescado, Alicante/L'Almodí, Valencia, Spain
Solo exhibition (pls. 72b–c, 73, 74a–b). Curated by Hendricks and Pablo J. Rico. Travels to: Rufino Tamayo Museum, Mexico City (October 3–November 9; *Ex It* only); Instituto Cultural Cabañas, Guadalajara, Mexico (January 29–February 28, 1998; *Ex It* only); Museo de Monterrey, Mexico (June 11–August 9, 1998); Museo de Arte Moderno/Centro Cultural Recoleta, Buenos Aires, Argentina (October 15–November 5, 1998); Museo Nacional de Artes Visuales, Montevideo, Uruguay (November 26–December 20, 1998; *Ex It* only); MAC (Museo de Arte Contemporáneo)/Museo de la Solidaridad Salvador Allende, Santiago, Chile (September 2–October 3, 1999).
DOCUMENTS: exh. cat.

August 30–October 26
At the Threshold of the Visible: Minuscule and Small Scale Art from 1966–1996, org. Independent Curators Incorporated (ICI)
Traveling group exhibition. Opens at Herbert F. Johnson Museum of Art, Cornell University, Ithaca.
DOCUMENTS: exh. cat.

September 6–November 2
Yoko Ono: Have You Seen a Horizon Lately? The Contemporary Arts Center, Cincinnati
Solo exhibition. Curated by Hendricks.

September 11–November 2
The Shoe Show, Bedford Gallery, Dean Lesher Reginal Center for the Arts, Walnut Creek, Calif.

October 2–November 2
Hiroshima: A Play with Music, Joyce and Seward Johnson Theater, New York
Music by Ono.
DOCUMENTS: program; flyer

October 4–November 30
Public Notice, Exit Art, New York

October 23
Aria for an Endangered Species, La Sala, Arizona State University West, Phoenix
DOCUMENTS: program

October 24–present
Balance Piece, Kleine International Kustverein, Zürich
Solo window installation. Organized by Serge Ziegler.

November 22–January 4, 1998
4 Quartets: Sound In/Out, Chiesa del Carmine, Taormina, Italy
Part of *Taormina Arte '97: Cinema, Teatro, Musica*, the exhibition focuses on four musicians: John Cage, Giuseppe Shiari, Eugenio Miccini, and Ono.
DOCUMENTS: exh. cat.

November 23–March 15, 1998
Yoko Ono: Have You Seen the Horizon Lately? Museum of Modern Art, Oxford
Solo exhibition (fig. 14.46). Curated by Chrissie Iles. Travels to: The Fruitmarket Gallery, Edinburgh (April 4–May 30, 1998); Museum Villa Stuck, Munich (June 18–September 20, 1998); Ormeau Baths Gallery, Belfast (November 13–December 12, 1998); Firstsite, The Minories Art Gallery, Colchester, England (January 9–February 27, 1999); Helsinki City Art Museum (March 28– May 30, 1999); The Israel Museum, Jerusalem (November 26, 1999–March 25, 2000).
DOCUMENTS: exh. cat.; exh. cat. in German; posters (Oxford, Munich, Jerusalem)

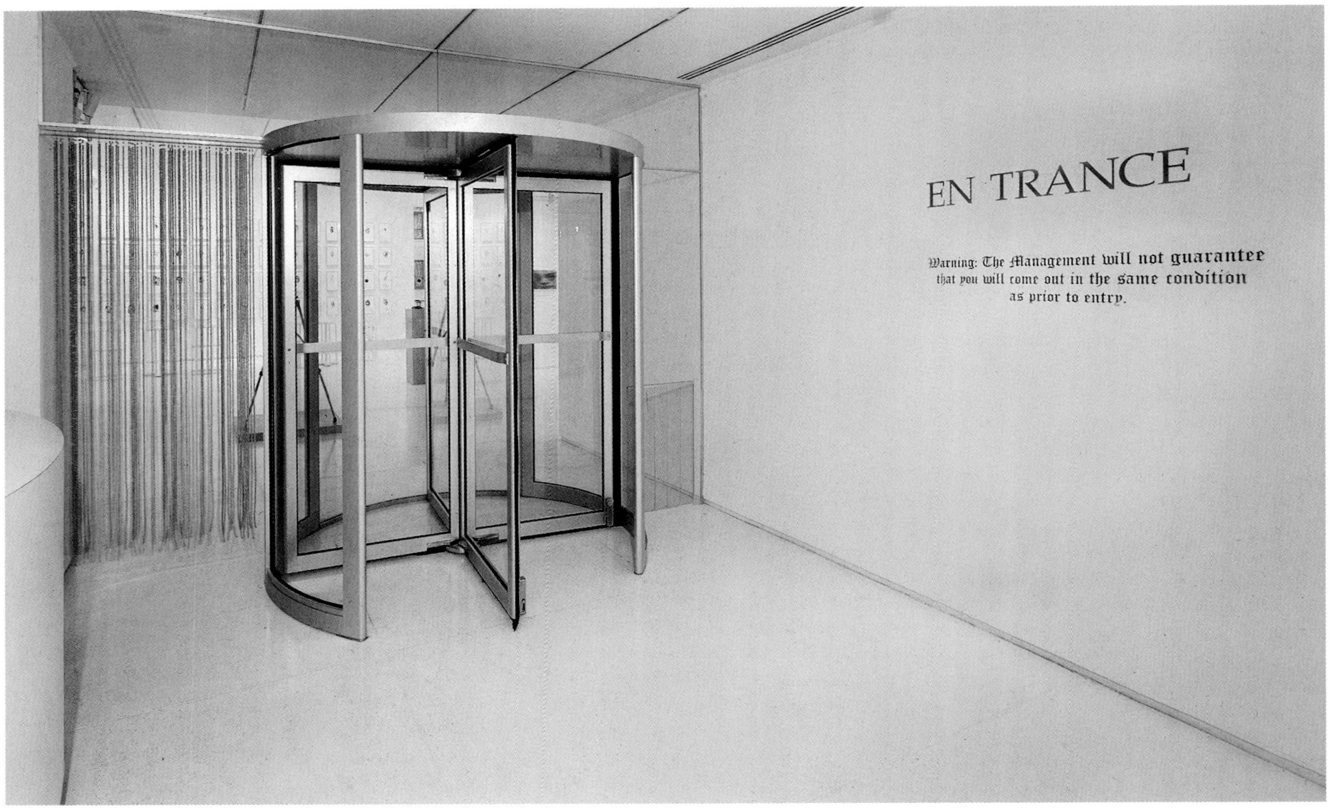

FIGURE 14.47
INSTALLATION VIEW, *YOKO ONO: EN TRANCE*, ANDRE EMMERICH GALLERY, NEW YORK, 1998

1998

January 30, 31
Aria for an Endangered Species, Rialto Center for the Performing Arts, Atlanta
Dance piece by Core Performance Company.
DOCUMENTS: program

February 8–May 10
Out of Actions: Between Performance and the Object, 1949–1979, The Museum of Contemporary Art, Los Angeles
Traveling survey exhibition.
DOCUMENTS: exh. cat.

March
Sarajevo Winter, square in downtown Sarajevo, Bosnia-Herzegovia
Organized by Museum of Contemporary Art, Zagreb

April 24–May 30
***Yoko Ono: En Trance*, Andre Emmerich Gallery, New York**
***Yoko Ono: Ex It*, Deitch Projects, New York**
Solo exhibitions (fig. 14.47).

May 9–June 20
***Yoko Ono: Crickets, Works from '58–'98*, Serge Ziegler Galerie, Zürich**
Solo exhibition. Includes *Crickets* and *Open Window*.
DOCUMENTS: postcards

May 21–June 27
Sixties in the 70's: A Decade in Neighborhood, Ubu Gallery, New York

May 23–July 26
Disidentico: Maschile femminile e oltre, Palazzo Braneiporte, Palermo
Traveling exhibition. Title translates: Dis-Identical: Male, Female, and Beyond.
DOCUMENTS: exh. cat.

May 24–November 8
Performance in the 1970s: Experiencing the Everyday, Walker Art Center, Minneapolis

May 28
***Lighting Piece*, Naples**
Solo event. Part of *Monumedia*, curated by Bonito Oliva and Franz Cerami; projected at Maschio Angioino.

May 29–September 13
Crossings: Kunst zum hören und sehen, Kunsthalle Wien, Vienna
Traveling group exhibition.
DOCUMENTS: exh. cat.

June 28–September 6
Double Trouble: The Patchett Collection, Museum of Contemporary Art, San Diego
Traveling group exhibition.

September 15–October 4
Beyond the Rainbow, Fundação Armando Alvares Penteado, São Paolo
DOCUMENTS: exh. cat.

October
Sanoja-Words-Paroles: An Exhibition of Artists' Poems, MUU Gallery, Helsinki
Traveling group exhibition.
DOCUMENTS: exh. cat.

October 17–November 29
Sōgetsu and Its Era, 1945–1970, Ashiya City Museum of Art and History, Japan
Traveling group exhibition.
DOCUMENTS: exh. cat.

October 21–November 29
***Yoko Ono: Wish Trees for Brazil*, Teatro Nacional Claudio Santoro e Pantheão da Pátria, Brasília**
Solo exhibition (fig. 14.48). Curated by Hendricks and Pablo J. Rico with Evandro Salles. Travels to: Museu de Arte Moderna da Bahia, Salvador (February 23–March 23, 1999).
DOCUMENTS: exh. cat.; poster

December 1–January 3, 1999
War Is Over! billboard, 47th Street and Broadway, New York

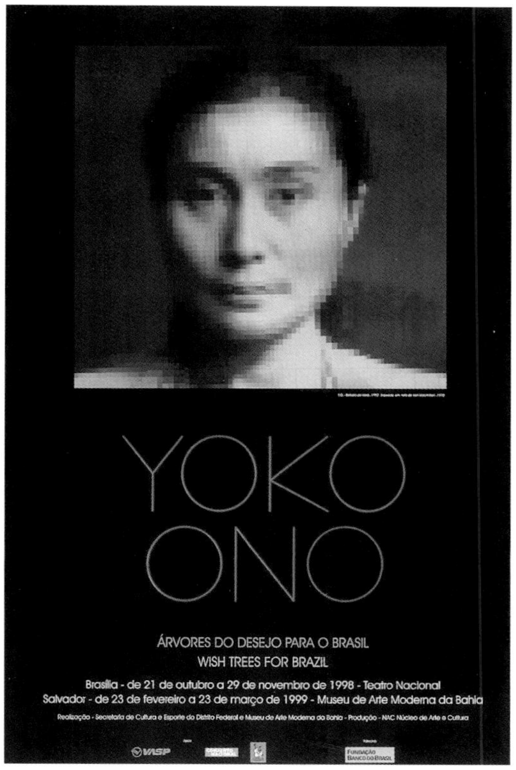

FIGURE 14.48
POSTER, *YOKO ONO: WISH TREE FOR BRAZIL*, TEATRO NACIONAL CLAUDIO SANTORO E PANTHEÃO DA PÁTRIA, BRASÍLIA, 1998

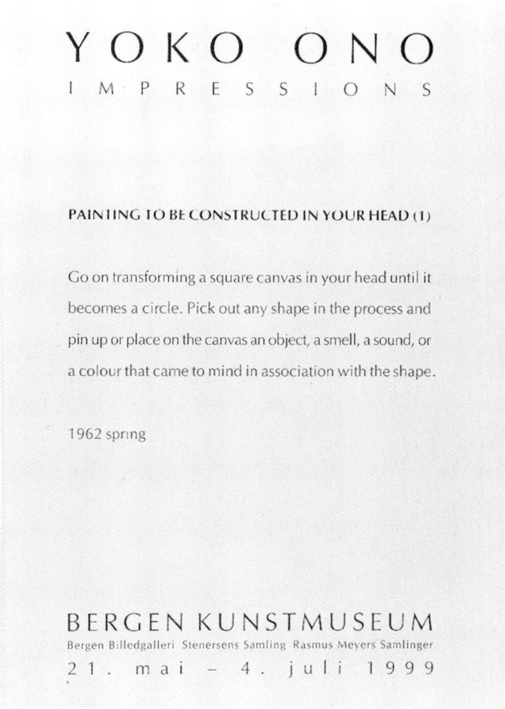

FIGURE 14.49
POSTER, *YOKO ONO: IMPRESSIONS*, BERGEN KUNSTMUSEUM, 1999

1999

January 28–March 28
Transmit: Fluxus, Mail Art, Networks, Queens Library Gallery, Jamaica, New York
DOCUMENTS: flyer

February 26
Concert, Tonic, New York
Special guest appearance in Cibo Matto's concert.

April 17–July 18
War Zones: Bearing Witness, Presentation House Gallery, North Vancouver
DOCUMENTS: postcard

April 28–August 29
Global Conceptualism: Points of Origin, 1950s–1980s, Queens Museum of Art, New York
Traveling survey exhibition. Ono included in both Japanese and North American sections.
DOCUMENTS: exh. cat.

May 9
***Yoko Ono,* Knitting Factory, New York**
Solo concert. Livecast on the Internet. Benefit for Kosovo Relief Fund.

May 21–July 4
***Yoko Ono: Impressions,* Bergen Kunstmuseum, Bergen, Norway**
Solo exhibition (fig. 14.49). Curated by Gunnar B. Kvaran. Instruction works also set up in art centers in Voss, Kvam, Odda, Balestrand, and Seljord.
DOCUMENTS: exh. cat.; poster

June 10
Concert, Bowery Ballroom, New York
Special guest appearance in Cibo Matto's concert.

June 10–July 10
Not There, Rena Bransten Gallery, San Francisco

August 21
Wish Tree of the North Land, NHK-BS2 TV, Japan
Documentary on Ono's *Impressions* exhibition in Bergen, Norway.

September 26–February 13, 2000
The American Century: Art and Culture, Whitney Museum of American Art, New York
DOCUMENTS: exh. cat.

November 17–January 15, 2000
***Yoko Ono: Open Window,* Umm El-Fachem Art Gallery, Umm El-Fachem, Israel**
Solo exhibition. Curated by Shlomit Shaked with Hendricks and Shoshana Blank. Trilingual "Open Window" billboard installed (English, Arabic, and Hebrew).
DOCUMENTS: exh. cat.; poster

December 5
The South Bank Show, ITV, U.K.
Ono interviewed by Melvyn Bragg.

ACKNOWLEDGMENTS

We thank Karla Merrifield and Curt Fritzeen for their kindness during our research at Studio One. Midori Yoshimoto provided indispensable assistance with Japanese sources. Many librarians and archivists who assisted in locating key documents and other bibliographic items include, among others: Jean Scott, Interlibrary Loan Office and Ray Bonis of Special Collections, Virginia Commonwealth University Libraries; Lynda Bunting and Beth Guynn, Getty Research Institute; Adrian Glew and Clare Storey, Tate Gallery Archives and Library, respectively; Barabara Moore, Bound and Unbound/The Charlotte Moorman Estate; Janis Ekdahl, Museum of Modern Art Library; Laura Kuhn, John Cage Trust; and Patti Owen, Sarah Lawrence College Archives.

We are also grateful to the following individuals for sharing their personal collections and recollections: Lynne A-man; Joseph Baranowski, Nazareth College; Ed Cardoni, Hallwalls, Buffalo; Joel Chadabe, Electronic Music Foundation; Sue Coe; Michael Colquhoun; Anthony Cox; Marsha Ewing, Instant Karma; Beate Sirota Gordon; Richard Joly, Onoweb; Joachim Kreck; Barbara Latham-Stevini; Jean-Jacques Lebel; Job (Marshall) Matusow; Albert Maysles; Barry Miles; Larry Miller; Nam June Paik; Jeff Perkins; Sara Seagull; Norman Seaman; Greg Schmidt, *Beatles Video Digest*; Steven Shaw, Kodansha International; Maruki Tamura; Shaun Usher, *Daily Mail*; Bill Wilson; Al Wunderlich; and Jud Yalkut.

Last but not least, we thank our spouses, Jeff Rothstein and Margo Crutchfield, for their support and patience.

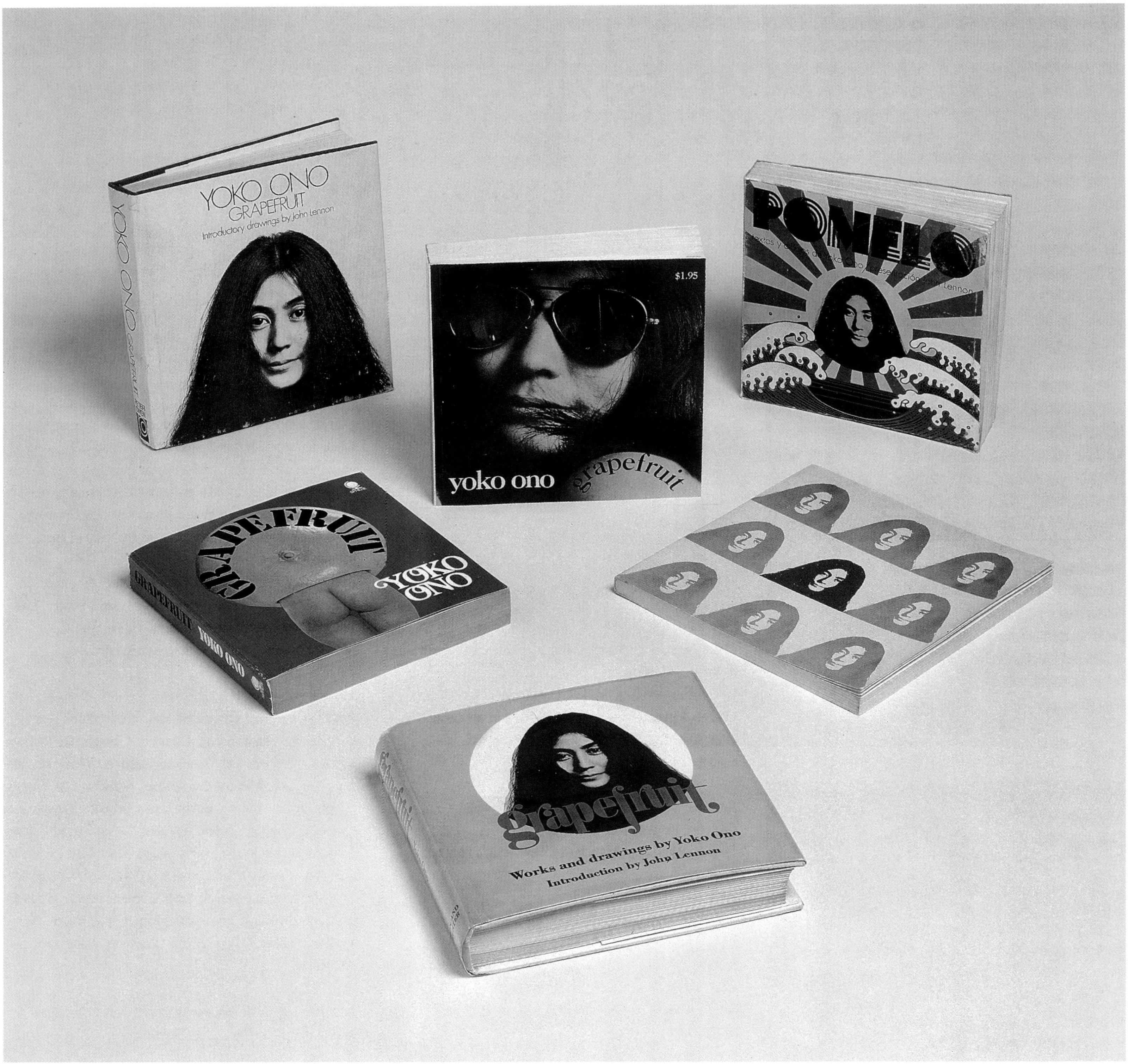

FIGURE 15.1
VARIOUS EDITIONS OF
GRAPEFRUIT

Bibliography

KEVIN CONCANNON AND REIKO TOMII

This bibliography is divided into two sections, "By Yoko Ono" and "On Yoko Ono," which are further grouped as follows:

By Yoko Ono
- A. Books
- B. Self-Published Scores, Statements, and Ephemera
- C. Artist's Pages and Publications Illustrated by the Artist
- D. Writings Published in Exhibition Catalogues and Programs
- E. Writings Published in Periodicals and Newspapers
- F. Interviews
- G. Films and Videos
- H. Discs and Other Sound Recordings
- I. Archives

On Yoko Ono
- A. Solo Exhibition Catalogues and Programs
- B. Group Exhibition Catalogues and Programs
- C. Books
- D. Art and Scholarly Periodicals
- E. Music Periodicals
- F. General Magazines and Newspapers
- G. Films and Videos

Entries are chronologically ordered in each category and further arranged as individually noted. Where no publisher is given, the material is self-published. Focus is given primarily to English sources, with some Japanese materials.

Books and articles in periodicals and newspapers may also be found under "By Yoko Ono, F. Interviews."

By Yoko Ono

A. Books

Alphabetically ordered by title in each year.

1964

Grapefruit. Tokyo: Wunternaum Press.

1969

"From 9 Concert Pieces for John Cage: Beat Piece." In *Notations*, ed. John Cage. New York: Something Else Press.

1970

Grapefruit. Frankfurt am Main: Bärmeier & Nikel.

Grapefruit. London: Peter Owen.

Grapefruit. New York: Simon and Schuster.

Pomelo. Buenos Aires: Ediciones de la Flor.

1971

Grapefruit. London: Sphere Books.

Grapefruit. New York: Simon and Schuster, Touchstone Book.

Museum of Modern [F]art. New York.

1981

Lennon, John, and Yoko Ono. *Songs from Double Fantasy/Season of Glass*. Winona, Minn.: Hal Leonard.

1982

Grapefruit/Gurēpufurūtsu bukku. Trans. Tagawa Ritsu. Tokyo: Shinshokan.

It's Alright (I See Rainbows). Winona, Minn.: Hal Leonard.

1986

Afterword to *Skywriting by Word of Mouth* by John Lennon. New York: Harper & Row.

Tada no atashi/Just Me! Ed. Takahiko Iimura. Tokyo: Kōdansha.

1988

"Forward." In *Imagine: John Lennon* by Andrew Solt and Sam Egan. New York: MacMillan.

1990

Foreword to *Ai: Japan Through John Lennon's Eyes: A Personal Sketchbook* by John Lennon. San Francisco: Cadence Books.

From the Blue Room Event 1966/1990. 16 postcards. Høvikodden, Norway: Henie Onstad Arts Centre.

1991

Shadow Pieces. Postcards. Reykjavík, Iceland: The Reykjavík Municipal Art Museum.

1992

Preface to *She's a Rebel: The History of Women in Rock and Roll* by Gillian Gaar. Seattle: Seal Press.

Yoko Ono: Calligraphy Suites. New York: Bag One Arts, Inc.

1993

Color, Fly, Sky/Summer '92: 5 Picture Postcards. Roskilde, Denmark: Museet for Samtidskunst.

Grapefruit Juice/Gurēpufurūtsu jūsu. Trans. Hae Shii. Tokyo: Kōdansha.

Hendricks, Jon, ed. *Instructions for Paintings by Yoko Ono: May 24, 1962*. Budapest: Galeria 56.

———, ed. *Paintings and Drawings by Yoko Ono: July 17–30, 1961, Preview July 16, Sunday*. Budapest: Galeria 56.

1994

New York Rock. London: Samuel French.

1995

Instruction Paintings. New York: Weatherhill.

"On the Exhibition in the Kunsthalle Bremen." In *John Lennon*, exh. cat. (1995).

Pennyviews. Santa Monica, Calif.: Turkey Press.

20 Postcards. Messina, Italy: Carte d'Arte.

1996

Aoi heya no ivento (Blue Room Event). Postcards. Tokyo: Gallery 360°.

Spots on the Wall. Tokyo: Gallery 360°.

"To the Wesleyan People (1966)." In *Theories and Documents of Contemporary Art: A Sourcebook of Artists' Writings*, ed. Kristine Stiles and Peter Selz. Berkeley: University of California Press.

1997

Yoko Ono. 8 postcards. London: Hayward Gallery and Royal Festival Hall.

1998

"Mid Air." In *AH Allen*. New York: A/C Editions.

"Birch Monologues." In *The Book: Sanoja—Words—Parole: An Exhibition of Artists' Poems*. Finland: Tapio Foundation.

"Sunday Bloody Sunday." In *Hidden Truths: Bloody Sunday 1972*, ed. Trisha Ziff. Santa Monica, Calif.: Smart Art Press.

1999

Introduction to *Real Love: The Drawings for Sean* by John Lennon. New York: Random House.

2000

Grapefruit. New York: Simon and Schuster.

B. Self-Published Scores, Statements, and Ephemera

Alphabetically ordered by title in each year.

1964

Six Film Scripts by Yoko Ono. Tokyo.

1965

Buy Now! Self Portrait by Yoko Ono. Flyer. New York: IsReal Gallery.

Cough Piece (1961 Winter). New York: Wunternaum Press.

Hide-and-Seek Piece (1964 Spring). New York: Wunternaum Press.

Line Piece to La Monte Young I (1964 Spring). New York: Wunternaum Press.

Ono's Sales List. New York.

Overtone Piece (1964 Spring). New York: Wunternaum Press.

Secret Piece (1953 Summer). New York: Wunternaum Press.

Send 5 Dollars for a Beautifully Framed Portrait of Mona Lisa by Yoko Ono. Flyer. New York: IsReal Gallery.

Tape Piece V (1963 Autumn). New York: Wunternaum Press.

Touch Poem. Performance program sheet, with *Morning Piece* ad. New York, 2 September.

Wall Piece for Orchestra to Yoko Ono (1962 Winter). New York: Wunternaum Press.

1966

Strip Tease Show. New York.

To the Wesleyan People. New York.

1967

Questionnaire for Film No. 4. London.

Send a Pound for Yoko Ono's 13 Days Do-It-Yourself Dance Festival to Be Held in London. London.

1968

Five Event Scores. London.

Thirteen Film Scores by Yoko Ono, London '68. London.

1969

Lennon, John, and Yoko Ono. "Fuck You." Unpublished sheet.

1971

To My Sisters, with Love. Broadside. New York.

1974

"Women for Women, NOW." Flyer for National Organization for Women.

1988

Addendum '88 (To the Wesleyan People). New York.

C. Artist's Pages and Publications Illustrated by the Artist

Alphabetically ordered by title in each year.

1962

Cover art. NHK Symphony Orchestra with Chorus, *Nirvāna Symphonie* by Mayuzumi Toshirō. New York: Time Records.

1963

"To George, Poem No. 18, October 29, 1961." In *An Anthology*. New York: La Monte Young and Jackson Mac Low.

1964

"Instruction for Poem No. 86." *ccV Tre*, Fluxus Newspaper No. 2 (February).

1965

"IsReal Gallery/Draw Circle Event." Advertisement. *New York Arts Calendar* 2, no. 6 (March): [64].

"IsReal Gallery/ Drill Hole Event." Advertisement. *New York Arts Calendar* 2, no. 7 (April–May): [74].

1966

"Do It Yourself Dance Piece (Swim in Your Sleep)." Advertisement. *Art and Artists* 1, no. 9 (December): 73.

"Do It Yourself Fluxfest Presents Yoko Ono & Dance Co." *3 newspaper eVenTs for the pRicE of $1*, Fluxus Newspaper No. 7 (February).

"Fountain Piece." Advertisement. *Art and Artists* 1, no. 7 (October): 44.

"Mouthpiece." Advertisement. *Art and Artists* 1, no. 8 (November): 39.

1967

"Letters" and "London Winter Orgasm Game." *Art and Artists* 2, no. 9 (December): 10 and 18–19.

1968

"Mend Piece for John" [multiple object]. *S.M.S. (Shit Must Stop)*: 5.

"On Paper." In *Nothing Doing in London Two*, ed. Anthony Barnett. London: Anthony Barnett/ The Curwen Press, n.p.

"Swim in Your Dreams as Far as You Can." Advertisement. *Promethean*.

1969

Ono, Yoko, and John Lennon. Front cover design. *Sculpture International* 3, no. 1 (October).

Ono, Yoko, and John Lennon. "War Is Over!" Advertisement. *New York Times*, 21 December, E16.

1971

"Invisible Animals." In *Milligan's Ark*, ed. Spike Milligan and Jack Hobbs. Walton-on-Thames, Surrey, U.K.: M & J Hobbs, 51.

"Museum of Modern [F]art: Yoko Ono One Woman Show." Advertisement. *Village Voice* (New York), 2 December, 25.

"Yoko Ono's 'Grapefruit' Game." *International Times* (London), 12–26 August, back cover.

1972

"Couple Event." *SunDance* (November–December): 7–8.

1995

"Passage (1994)." *Arshile*, no. 4 (1995): 69–93.

1996

"Franklin Summer." *Long Shot* 18 (1996): 30–34.

1997

Revelations. Broadside. Lexington, Ky.: The Literary Renaissance.

1998

"Vertical Memory." *Arshile*, no. 10: 51–93.

D. Writings Published in Exhibition Catalogues and Programs

Alphabetically ordered by title in each year.

1960

"Poems by Yoko Ono." In program for Japanese cultural demonstration, at Department of Graphic Arts & Illustration, Pratt Institute, Brooklyn, 23 March.

1964

"On Insound, On Instructure." In *Contemporary American Avant-Garde Music Concert*, program (1964).

Ono, Yoko, Anthony Cox, and Alfred Wonderlick. "Yoko Ono—Instruction Paintings." In *Yoko at Indica*, exh. cat. (1966).

1966

"On Circle Event," "Ads for Bagwear," "Forms to Be Filled Out for the Rental of Eye Bags" (also known as "Questionnaire"), and "Biography/Statement." In *The Stone*, exh. cat.

1967

"*Number Four* by Yoko Ono." In *Perception Weekend*, program.

"On Film No. 4." In *Yoko Ono: Film No. 4*, program and *Ono Film No. 4*, program.

"Some Notes on the Lisson Gallery Show." In *Yoko Ono at Lisson*, exh. cat.

1968

"Imaginary Film Series." In *Conceptual Photography*, exh. cat. (1997).

"On *Film No. 5* & *Two Virgins*." In *FIBA*, program.

Statement. In *"John" by Yoko Ono, "Yoko" by John Lennon*, exh. cat.

"To Ornette." In *Ornette Coleman at the Royal Albert Hall*, program. London: Royal Albert Hall.

1971

"On Numbers," "On Rooms and Footsteps," and "What Is the Relationship Between the World and the Artist?" In *This Is Not Here*, exh. cat.

1986

"*Starpeace* World Tour Statement." In *Star Peace World Tour*, program.

1989

"Bronze Age." In *The Bronze Age*, exh. cat. (Cranbrook).

1990

"Bastet." In *To See the Skies*, exh. cat.

"Hell in Paradise" (lyrics). In *Endangered Species*, exh. cat. (Starke 1992).

"In Facing" and "All My Works Are a Form of Wishing. Keep Wishing While You Participate." In *In Facing*, exh. cat.

"Mindscale 66 90." In *Glimpse*, exh. brochure (1993).

1991

"Play It By Trust '91." In *3 Rooms*, exh. cat. (1995).

1992

"A Homage to Nora—An Event in Three Stanzas." In *Homage to Nora*, exh. cat.

"SKYTALK with love to Denmark." In *Color, Fly, Sky*, exh. cat.

1993

"Endangered Species" and "Interception." In *Glimpse*, exh. brochure.

"A Piece of Sky." In *A Piece of Sky*, exh. cat.

Statement. In *Endangered Species 2319–2322*, exh. cat. (Wacoal).

1995

"Franklin Summer." In *3 Rooms*, exh. cat.

"Interception" (1993–95). In *Sphere-9*, exh. cat.

E. Writings Published in Periodicals and Newspapers

Chronologically ordered in each year.

1955

"Poem." *Campus* (Sarah Lawrence College), 4 May, 5.

"Marie." *Campus*, 11 May, 5.

"Three Poems." *Campus*, 28 September, 7.

"Of a Grapefruit in the World of Park." *Campus*, 26 October, 9.

1956

"Two Poems." *Campus*, 25 April, 5.

1962

"Kyokōsha no gen" (The Word of a fabricator). *SAC Journal*, no. 24 (May).

1966

[Ono, Yoko, and Anthony Cox]. "New York Is a Stone Summer Festival." Advertisement in "Village Bulletin Board." *Village Voice*, 14 July 1966, 2.

"Cannon Piece." *East Village Other* (New York), 15 August–1 September, 12.

1967

"Electric Garden." *International Times* (London), 29 May–2 June, 2.

"Yoko Ononism & Her Hairy Arseholes." *International Times* (London), 28 July–13 August.

"I Wonder Why." *ICA Bulletin* (August–September).

"Yoko Talks About It." *Rolling Stone* (21 December): 15–30.

1970

"Yoko Ono on Yoko Ono: On *Film No. 4*." *Film Culture*, no. 48/49 (winter–spring): 32–33.

1971

"'This Is Not Here' Show: 'Mikan no kaiga to chōkoku' ni tsuite" (On "Unfinished Painting and Sculpture") and "On 'Room and Footsteps'/'Heya to junro' ni tsuite." *Bijutsu techō*, no. 330 (January): 204–8 and 225–27.

Lennon, Yoko Ono. "Letters: We Can Work It Out." *Village Voice*, 8 July, 4.

Lennon, John, and Yoko Lennon. "Letters: The Turd Degree." *Village Voice*, 26 August, 4.

Ono, Yoko, and John Lennon. "Letters: Christgau, Superstar!" *Village Voice*, 7 October.

Lennon, John, and Yoko Ono Lennon. "Letters: Love Letter from Two Artists." *Post-Standard* (Syracuse), 7 October.

Lennon, Yoko Ono, and John Ono Lennon. "Letters: Yoko Explains Her Art: 'Bored with Artists Who Make Big Lumps.'" *Post-Standard* (Syracuse), 9 October, 4.

Ono, Yoko, John Lennon, David Peel, and Jerry Rubin (The Rock Liberation Front). "Dylan and Weberman: A Letter." *Village Voice*, 2 December, 59.

"Yoko on Fly." *Crawdaddy* (5 December): 14–15.

Lennon, John, and Yoko Ono. "Letter to the Editor: Peace and Love." *New York Times*, 28 December, 28.

1972

"O Sister O Sisters." *Ann Arbor Sun*, 4–18 February, 13.

"The Feminization of Society." *New York Times*, 23 February, 41.

"The Goals of Feminist Revolution." *Boston Globe*, 26 February.

Lennon, John and Yoko Lennon. "'Luck of the Irish': If They Don't Like It They Can Leave It." *Bard* (Berkeley, Calif.), 24 March.

"Imagine: It's Never Too Late to Start from the Start." *SunDance* (April–May): 67–69.

"Letters: Les We Forget." *Village Voice*, 6 April, 4.

"Letters: A Rock Star's Wife Is Not a Happy One." *Village Voice*, 20 April, 42.

Ono, Yoko, and John Lennon. "Imagine: Sometime in New York City." *SunDance* (August–September): 68.

1973

"John Lennon, Yoko Ono: Our Films." *Filmmakers Newsletter* 6, no. 8 (June): 25–27.

"Feeling the Space." *New York Times*, 24 August.

"Shake Hands with Yoko: The Space Between Us." *San Francisco Examiner-Chronicle*, 9 September.

"When I Was Seventeen." *New Ingenue* 15, no. 8 (December): 74–77.

"Going Out Guide: Train of Thought." *New York Times*, 8 December, 41.

1979

Lennon, John, and Yoko Ono. "A Love Letter from John and Yoko to People Who Ask Us What, When, and Why." Advertisement. *New York Times*, 27 May, E20.

1980

"Vigil: Yoko Ono Sends Her Blessings." *Times* (London), 17 December.

1981

Lennon, Yoko Ono. "In Gratitude." Advertisement. *New York Times*, 18 January, E24.

"Strawberry Fields Forever." Advertisement. *New York Times*, 28 August, A23.

1982

"Endpaper: December 8 '81." *Rolling Stone* (21 January): 84.

1983

Ono, Yoko, and John Lennon. [Everson Museum press conference transcript, part 1]. *Yoko Only*, no. 2: 13–14.

"Surrender to Peace." Advertisement. *New York Times*, 24 January, B10.

Lennon, Yoko Ono. "Ono Notice: In Apology and in Plea for Sanity." [Clipping from unidentified newspaper in MoMA's artist file].

1984

Ono, Yoko, and John Lennon. [Everson Museum press conference transcript, part 2]. *Yoko Only*, no. 3 (February): 8–9.

"Duckstown and Men-Sized Stones." *Berkeley Fiction Review*, no. 5 (spring): 31–39.

1985

[On the Lisson Gallery show]. *Yoko Only*, no. 8: 14–17.

[Open letter regarding 1968 Ornette Coleman concert]. *Yoko Only*, no. 8: 6–7.

1986

"Rainbow Revelation" and "A Crystal Ball." *Magical Blend: A Transformative Journey*, no. 12: 36 and 37.

Ono, Yoko, Rollo May, Leo Buscaglia, and Sarrel. "Dialogue." *Omni* (April): 16.

1987

Statement to Women's Action for Nuclear Disarmament (WAND). *Instant Karma*, no. 32: 3.

"Georgia Stone." *Yoko Only*, no. 17 (March): 4.

1990

"Painting to Hammer a Nail In." *Ear* 15 (March): 38–39.

"To Those Who Ask Why, Why, and Why." *Instant Karma*, no. 55: 3.

1997

Ono, Yoko, Ivor Davies, Gustav Metzger, Michael Gibbs, John Dunbar, Barry Miles, Genevieve Morgan, and Nicholas Logsdail. "Is That an Apple? Yoko Ono in London." *Art Monthly* (London), no. 212 (December–January 1998): 1–7.

Ono, Yoko, et al. "Friendly Legend: Allen Ginsberg in the Words of Those Who Knew and Loved Him." *Rolling Stone* (29 May): 40.

1998

"Linda McCartney Remembered." *Rolling Stone* (11 June): 31.

"Just Like Starting Over." *Daily Telegraph* (London), 24 October, 1.

1999

"Yoko Ono's Do It Yourself Dance Festival." Advertisement. *Bergens Tidende* (Bergen, Norway), 21 May–4 June 1999.

F. Interviews

Chronologically ordered in each year.

1967

Perry, Roger, and Tony Elliott. "Yoko Ono." *Unit* (December): 25–28.

1968

Turner, Robin. "In the Mad, Mad World of Yoko Ono." *Daily Express* (London), 5 July.

Pendennis. "Yoko Ono Speaks." *Observer* (London), 21 July.

Connolly, Ray. "Enigmatic Yoko Talks of Love, Loneliness, and Lennon." *Express & Star* (Wolverhampton, Staffordshire, U.K.), 28 October.

1969

Vincent, Pierre. "La paix organisée." *La Presse* (Montreal), 29 May.

Zec, Donald. "At the Bedside in Old Amsterdam." *Daily Mirror* (London), 31 May.

Yorke, Ritchie. "As Fans Mob Them, Lennon Admits Ringo's Right We Can't Tour Again." *New Musical Express* (London), 7 June, 3.

Dasi, Bibhavati. "'Guru' to Millions Practices Hard-Sell in Search of Peace." *Montreal Star*, 7 June, 25.

Chase, William D. "He Braves Bamboo-Stick Curtain to Interview Inscrutable Beatle." *Flint (Mich.) Journal*, 10 June.

Cochnar, Robert. "John, Yoko and Peace." *NEA (Newspaper Enterprise Association) Lively Arts Special*, 10 June.

Yalkut, Jud. "Film." *East Village Other* (New York), 25 June, 9–14.

Buckley, Jim. "In Bed with John and Yoko." *Screw* (27 June): 4–6, 12.

Sanders, Ellen. "Promoting Peace." *Los Angeles Free Press*, 11 July.

Childs, Charles. "Interview: John Lennon and Yoko Ono." *Penthouse* (October): 28–34.

Keene, Roger. "John and Yoko Plan Music, Peace World Conference." *Circus* (December): 15–18.

1970

Zeilig, Ken. "John Lennon and Yoko Ono Tell It Like It Is." *Los Angeles Free Press*, 23 January.

M[iles, Barry]. "John & Yoko: Give Em a Chance!" *Fusion* (20 February): 14–18.

Robinson, Richard. "The Last John and Yoko Interview." *Hit Parader* (August): 9–11.

Smith, Howard. "Scenes." *Village Voice* (New York), 17 December, 5-58, 60, 62, 64.

1971

Lennon, John. *Songs of John Lennon*. London: Wise Publishing.

Wenner, Jann. *Lennon Remembers: The Rolling Stone Interviews*. San Francisco: Straight Arrow Books.

"I Wanted to Say: Now, Mummy, Will You Love Me?" *Sun* (London), 12 March.

Vogel, Amos. "John & Yoko at Cannes: 'I Made a Glass Hammer.'" *Village Voice*, 24 June, 65, 74–75.

Blackburn, Robin, and Tariq Ali. "Lennon: The Working-Class Hero Turns Red." *Ramparts Magazine* (July): 43–49.

Crawford, Lynda. "Working Class Hero Bites Blintz." *Berkeley (Calif.) Barb*, 9–15 July.

Dillon, Barry. "What John and Yoko Told Me." *Southern Evening Echo*, 29 July, 18.

"The Hawaiian Actress Who Married the Man Who Won the Pools: An Interview with Yoko Ono and John Lennon." *Frendz with Oz* (London), 10 August, 6–7.

Mandelkau, Jamie, with William Bloom. "Interview Piece: Yoko Ono and *Grapefruit*." *International Times* (London), 12–26 August, 10–11.

Edwards, Henry. "Yoko the Filmmaker/Yoko the Recording Artist." *Crawdaddy* (29 August): 33–34.

Cowan, Liza, and Jan Alpert. "Pacifica Radio Interview, 11 September 1971." Los Angeles, Pacifica Radio Archives. Cassette tape.

1972

Iimura, Takahiko. "Ono Yōko: Kachi o tenkan shi, kisei gainen kara no dakkyaku o/An Interview with Yoko Ono by Takahiko Iimura" (Let's change values and flee from stereotypical concepts). *Bijutsu techō*, no. 350 (January): 202–29.

Blackburn, Robin, and Tariq Ali. "An Interview by British New Leftists: John and Yoko Lennon Rap About Jesus and Revolution." *Los Angeles Free Press*, 7 January, 3, 26–27.

Smith, Alan. "John and Yoko." *Hit Parader* (February): 31–33, 36–37, 44.

Gates, Jeremy. "'The Only Thing I Can't Do Without Is Yoko....'" *Lancashire Evening Telegraph* (Blackburn, Lancashire, U.K.), 27 April, Weekender section.

Vallee, Jean-François. "'Capitalism Killed the Beatles.'" *Record Mirror* (London), 29 April, 24.

———. "It's Your Message That Counts." *Record Mirror* (London), 6 May, 17.

Warhol, Andy, Paul Morrissey, and Glenn O'Brien. "John and Yoko: Sometime in New York and Sometime in the Big Apple." *Interview* (June): 6–8, 52.

St. Albin Greene, Daniel. "For the Lennons, Their Post-Beatle Mission Is to Perform as Reporters Who Sing." *National Observer* (Washington, D.C.), 3 June.

Skoler, Ron. "John & Yoko: Some Time in New York City." *Sounds* (London), 2 September, 18–23.

1973

Van Ness, Chris. "Yokospeak: An Interview with Ms. Ono." *Los Angeles Free Press*, 16 February, 5, 22.

Webb, Julie. "Approximately Yoko Ono." *New Musical Express* (London), 10 March.

Bockris-Wylie. "A Most Exclusive Session: Jammin with Edgar; Jawin with John and Yoko." *Drummer* (Philadelphia), 22 May.

Alterman, Loraine. "Yoko: How I Rescued John from Chauvinism." *Melody Maker* (London), 22 September, 13.

1974

Malawka, Alex. "Yoko Ono: Artist, Individual, Woman." *Aquarian* (Montclair, N.J.), 14 March, 16–17, 19.

1976

Interviews. In *The History of Syracuse Music*, vols. 7, 9. ECEIP Records 1015–18, LP.

1978

Interviews. In *The Beatle Tapes from the David Wigg Interviews*. PBR International 7005-6, LP.

1980

Occhiogrosso, Peter. "Yoko Ono: Here's the Rest of Me." *Soho News* (New York), 3–9 December, 9–11.

———. "Yoko Ono—A Wife and Partner." *Windsor (Ontario) Star*, 11 December.

———. "The Woman Who Changed John Lennon's Life." *Morning Herald* (Sydney, Australia), 11 December.

1981

Sheff, David. *The Playboy Interviews with John Lennon and Yoko Ono*. Ed. G. Barry Golson. New York: Playboy Press.

———. "Playboy Interview: John Lennon and Yoko Ono." *Playboy* (January): 75–114, 144.

Sholin, Dave. "John and Yoko on Marriage, Children, and Their Generation." *Ms.* (March): 58–64.

1983

Graustark, Barbara. "Life With and Without Lennon." *Ladies' Home Journal* (March): 118–20, 158–67.

Fass, Bob, and Cathie Revland. "Interview: Yoko Ono." *High Times* (May): 32–36.

Loder, Kurt. "Yoko Ono: 'Still in a State of Shock.'" *Rolling Stone* (20 June): 42.

Giuliano, Geoffrey. "Yoko Ono." *Playgirl* (July): 38–42, 114, 116.

Lennon, John and Yoko Ono. *Heart Play—Unfinished Dialogue*. Polydor 817-238-1-Y1, LP.

1984

McCabe, Peter, and Robert D. Schonfeld. *John Lennon: For the Record*. New York: Bantam Books.

Interviews. In *Reflections and Poetry*. Silhouette Records SM-10014, LP.

Tracy, Robert. "Yoko Only." *Mademoiselle* (October): 204–5, 263–64, 274.

Flanagan, Bill. "The Price You Pay: An Interview with Yoko Ono." *Record* (December): 28–35.

Hendel, Brian. "Yoko Ono: An Exclusive Conversation." *Yoko Only*, no. 7 (December–January 1985): 6–14.

1985

Gruen, Bob. "A Chat with Yoko Ono." *Rock Photo*: 78–85.

Torgoff, Martin. "Yoko Ono." *Interview* (January): 40–45.

1986

"Yoko Ono." In *The Guests Go in to Supper*, ed. Melody Sumner, Kathleen Burch, and Michael Sumner. Oakland, Calif.: Burning Books, 171–84.

Sumner, Melody, Kathleen Burch, and Michael Sumner. "An Interview with Yoko Ono." *Magical Blend: A Transformative Journey*, no. 12: 34–35.

1987

Fricke, David. "Yoko Ono: John and I Thought That Peace Could Only Be Gotten Through Peaceful Methods." *Rolling Stone* (15 November–10 December): 53–54.

1988

Harper, Hilliard. "Yoko Promotes Art for John's Sake." *Los Angeles Times*, 13 June, Calendar, 1.

1989

Esko, Ed, and Jessica Chambless. "Yoko Ono: A Woman Inside My Soul, February 1973." In *Meetings with Remarkable Men and Women: Interviews with Leading Thinkers on Health, Medicine, Ecology, Culture, Society, and Spirit*. Brookline, Mass.: East West Health Books.

Pinchbeck, Daniel. "Yoko Ono." *Splash* (February).

Sessums, Kevin. "Yoko: Life After Lennon." *Interview* (February): 76–81.

Gross, Terry. "The Ballad of Yoko Ono." *Applause* (June): 11–15.

"Press Conference" [at Cranbrook]. *Yoko Only*, no. 26 (fall): 8–12.

MacDonald, Scott. "Yoko Ono: Ideas on Film." With scripts. *Film Quarterly* 43, no. 1 (fall): 2–23.

The Lost Lennon Tapes Show 89-40: The John and Yoko Argument Interview, Autumn 1971. Culver City, Calif.: Westwood One Radio Networks, [for broadcast in week of] 25 September.

McLaren, Lee. "L'Evangile selon Sainte Yoko." *Rolling Stone*, French-language edition (December): 22.

1990

John and Yoko: The Interview. BBC Radio Collection BBCD 6002.

Interview. In *John Lennon—Testimony*. Magnum Music Group, CD.

"Yoko in London." Transcript of BBC2 TV interview, "The Late Show," 22 March. *Instant Karma*, no. 46: 41–43.

Appleyard, Brian. "An Ordinary Woman Made Myth." *Independent* (London), 29 March, 18.

Plaskin, Glenn. "Yoko." *Daily News Magazine* (New York), 6 May, 10–16, 31.

Movin, Lars. "Yoko Ono." *Copyright* (Copenhagen) (summer): 4–7.

1991

Casey, Michael. "Yoko Ono in Finland." *Form Function Finland*, no. 2: 52–54.

Watson, Gray, and Rob La Frenais. "The Poetry of the Personal: In Conversation with Yoko Ono." *Performance*, no. 63 (March): 8–15.

1992

MacDonald, Scott. "Yoko Ono." In *A Critical Cinema 2: Interviews with Independent Filmmakers*, 139–56. Berkeley: University of California Press.

"The Ballad of Yoko: The B-52's Kate Pierson Talks with Yoko Ono." *Rolling Stone* (19 March): 17–29.

Kemp, Mark. "She Who Laughs Last: Yoko Ono Reconsidered." *Option: Music Alternatives*, no. 45 (July–August): 74–81.

1993

Denk, Andreas. "Yoko." *Schnüss* (October): 16–19.

1994

Furlong, William, ed. "Yoko Ono." In *Audio Arts: Discourse and Practice in Contemporary Art, 96–97*. New York: Academy Editions.

Enright, Robert. "Instructions in the Marital Arts: A Conversation with Yoko Ono." *Border Crossings* 13, no. 1 (winter): 37.

Denk, Andreas. "Yoko Ono: 'Jeder muß etwas dazu tun....'" *Kunstforum International*, no. 125 (January–February): 278–85.

1995

McDonnell, Evelyn. "Oohhhh Yoko: For Years, Yoko Ono Has Been a Veteran of the Avant-Garde." *Interview* (December): 58–59.

1996

Giuliano, Geoffrey, and Brenda Giuliano. *The Lost Lennon Interviews*. Holbrook, Mass.: Adams Media Corporation.

Petros, George. "Yoko Ono." *Seconds*, no. 36: 16–27.

Huston, Johnny. "Yoko Ono: Everything That Rises...." *Puncture*, no. 35 (spring): 12–14.

Palmer, Robert. "Q & A: Yoko Ono." *Rolling Stone* (7 March): 18.

Cromelin, Richard. "Q & A with Yoko Ono and Sean Ono Lennon: After Some Difficult Years, They Decided to Give Music a Chance." *Los Angeles Times*, 13 March, F1.

Press, Joy. "A Life in Flux." *The Wire*, no. 146 (April): 18–24.

Katz, Larry. "'Rising' Popularity; Yoko Ono Wins Favor of Longtime Critics and Adulation from Alternative Rockers." *Boston Herald*, 9 May, 43.

"Big in Japan: Yoko Ono + Cibo Matto." *RayGun* (August).

"Perry Farrell and Yoko Ono Talk About Fame." *Mondo 2000*, no. 16 (winter 1996–1997): 90–97.

1997

Zollo, Paul. "Yoko Ono." In *Songwriters on Songwriting*. New York: DaCapo Press.

Swank, Michael. "In Flux with Yoko Ono." *F Newsmagazine* (May): 14–15, 20.

Masaoka, Miya. "Unfinished Music: A Conversation with Yoko Ono." *San Francisco Bay Guardian*, 27 August–2 September, 52–55.

Gaar, Gillian G. "Yoko Ono: Spoken Word Discography." *Goldmine* (7 November): 14–17, 176, 178, 182, 196, 223.

O'Dair, Barbara. "Yoko Ono." *Rolling Stone* (13 November): 114–15.

Jackson, Tina. "Yoko Ono Was Vilified in the Sixties...." *The Big Issue* (15–19 December): 17–18.

1998

Howitis: The John Lennon Anthology Yoko Ono Interview. Capitol Records DPRO 7087 6 13515 2 1, CD promo.

"Give Peace a Chance." *People Weekly* (6 July): 17.

Smith, Ethan. "Re: Fluxology." *New York* (21 September): 40–41ff.

1999

Jackson, Alan. "Cold Call." *Times* (London), 11 December.

Bracewell, Michael. "Imagine Yoko's Own Story." *Independent* (London), 12 December, 4–5, 7.

Suenobu Michi. "Jon Renon: Ono Yōko ga 20-nenme ni akasu shinjitsu" (John Lennon: Secrets revealed by Yoko Ono after 20 years). *Shūkan Asahi* (31 December–7 January 2000): 166–70. First installment, ongoing series of interviews.

G. Films and Videos

Alphabetically ordered by title in each year.

1966

No. 1, *Eyeblink*, and *No. 4*. In *Fluxfilm Anthology*. 150 min. Arthouse Inc., New York, 1997. Videocassette variation of original 8mm film.

1967

No. 4 (Bottoms). 16mm, 80 min.

Wrapping Event (unreleased). 16mm, 14 min.

1968

Film No. 5 (Smile). 16mm, 51 min.

Ono, Yoko, and John Lennon. *Two Virgins*. 16mm, 19 min.

1969

The Beatles. *Ballad of John and Yoko*. 16mm, 3 min. Apple Films, London. Promotional trailer.

Ono, Yoko, and John Lennon. *Bed-In*. 16mm, 61 min.

———. *Rape*. 16mm, 77 min.

1970

Ono, Yoko, and John Lennon. *Apotheosis*. 16mm, 18½ min.

Fly. 16mm, 25 min.

Freedom. 16mm, 1 min.

Up Your Legs Forever. 16mm, 70 min.

1971

Ono, Yoko, and John Lennon. *Erection*. 16mm, 20 min.

———. *Imagine*. 16mm, 70 min.

The Museum of Modern Art Show. 16mm, 7 min.

Ten for Two: Sisters O Sisters. 16mm, 4 min. excerpt. Prod. Yoko Ono and John Lennon; dir. Steve Gebhardt. 1971.

1981

Walking on Thin Ice. Video transferred to 16mm, 6 min.

Woman. Video transferred to 16mm, 3½ min.

1982

Goodbye Sadness. Video transferred to 16mm, 2½ min.

1990

Lennon, John, and Yoko Ono. *The Bed-In: All We Are Saying Is Give Peace a Chance*. 74 minutes. Picture Music International, Mississauga, Ontario. Videocassette.

1992

Onovideo. Rykovision Production, Rykodisc USA, Salem, Mass. Promotional videocassette.

H. Discs and Other Sound Recordings

Alphabetically ordered by title in each year. All records and CD's are U.S. releases unless otherwise noted. In 1997, Rykodisc reissued Ono's records on CD's, adding previously unreleased bonus tracks to each release. See original release for reissue data.

1) Solo Releases
a) Singles

1971

"Mrs. Lennon"/"Midsummer New York." Apple Records 1839.

1972

"Mind Train"/"Listen, the Snow Is Falling." Apple Records (U.K.) 41.

"Now or Never"/"Move On Fast." Apple Records 1853.

1973

"Death of Samantha"/"Yang Yang." Apple Records 1859.

"Josei jōi banzai" (Cheers to women on top)/"Josei jōi banzai" (Pt. 2). Apple Records (Japan) 10344.

"Run, Run, Run"/"Men, Men, Men." Apple Records (U.K.) 48.

"Woman Power"/"Men, Men, Men." Apple Records 1867.

1974

"Yume o motō (Let's have a dream)"/"It Happened." Odeon Records (Japan) EOR-10628.

1981

"Goodbye Sadness"/"I Don't Know Why." Geffen Records GEF-49849.

"No, No, No"/"I Don't Know Why"/"She Gets Down on Her Knees." Geffen Records PRO-A-975, promotional 12".

"No, No, No"/"Will You Touch Me." Geffen Records GEF-49802. 1981.

"Walking on Thin Ice"/"It Happened." Geffen Records GEF-49683.

"Walking on Thin Ice"/"It Happened"/"Hard Times Are Over." Geffen Records PRO-A-934, promotional 12".

"Walking on Thin Ice"/"It Happened"/"Hard Times Are Over." Geffen Records (U.K.) K-79202, cassette single.

1982
"My Man"/"Let the Tears Dry." Polydor Records PD-2224.

1983
"Never Say Goodbye"/"Loneliness." Polydor Records PD-810-556-7.
"Never Say Goodbye" (remix)/"Loneliness" (remix). Polydor Records PD-810-575-1, 12" single.

1985
"Hell in Paradise"/"Hell in Paradise" (instrumental). Polydor Records PD-883-445-7.
"Hell in Paradise" (club version)/(dub version)/(single version). Polydor Records PD-883-445-1 Y-1, 12" single.

1986
"Cape Clear" (vocal remix)/"Cape Clear" (instrumental remix)/"Walking on Thin Ice" (reedit). Polydor Records PD-883-872-1, 12" single.

1991
"Happy Xmas" (spoken word message, long version)/"Happy Xmas" (short version). Rykodisc VRCD ONO, promotional.

1997
"Listen, The Snow Is Falling." Self-published, Christmas card CD.

b) Albums and CD's

1970
Yoko Ono/Plastic Ono Band. Apple Records SW-3373. CD reissue: Rykodisc 10414.

1971
Fly. Apple Records SVBB-3380. CD reissue: Rykodisc 10415–16, 2-CD set.

1973
Approximately Infinite Universe. Apple Records SVBB-3399. CD reissue: Rykodisc 10417–18.
Feeling the Space. Apple Records SW-3412. CD reissue: Rykodisc 10419.
Welcome (The Many Sides of Yoko Ono). Apple Records (Japan) PRP-8026, promotional.

1981
Season of Glass. Geffen Records GHS-2004. CD reissue: Rykodisc 10421.

1982
It's Alright. Polydor Records PD-1-6364. CD reissue: Rykodisc 10422.

1985
Starpeace. Polydor Records 827-5301-Y1. CD reissue: Rykodisc 10423.

1992
Onobox. Rykodisc RCD-10224-29, 6-CD set with booklet.
Onobox Ultracase. Rykodisc RCD-10224-29, deluxe version.
Walking on Thin Ice. Rykodisc RCD 20230.

1995
Yoko Ono/IMA. *Rising*. Capitol CDP 7243 8 35817 2 6.

1996
Yoko Ono/IMA. *Rising Mixes*. Capitol CDP 7243 8 37268 0 6.
Yoko Ono/IMA. *Rising Mixes*. Capitol SPRO-11222, promotional 12".

1997
A Story. First released with *Onobox*. Rykodisc 10420.

2) With John Lennon
a) Singles
All singles Lennon A-side/Ono B-side unless otherwise noted.

1969
Plastic Ono Band. "Cold Turkey"/"Don't Worry Kyoko (Mummy's Only Looking for Her Hand in the Snow)." Apple Records 1813.
———. "Give Peace a Chance"/"Remember Love." Apple Records 1809.

1970
"Instant Karma!"/"Who Has Seen the Wind?" Apple Records 1818.
"Mother"/"Why." Apple Records 1827.

1971
Bill Elliot, "God Save Us"/Ono and Lennon as Elastic Oz Band, "Do the Oz." Apple Records 1835.
Ono, Lennon, and Harlem Community Choir, "Happy Xmas (War Is Over)"/"Listen, the Snow Is Falling." Apple Records 1842.
"Power to the People"/"Open Your Box." Apple Records (U.K.) 5892.
"Power to the People"/"Touch Me." Apple Records 1830.

1972
"Woman Is the Nigger of the World"/"Sisters O Sisters." Apple Records 1848.

1980
"Starting Over"/"Kiss, Kiss, Kiss." Geffen Records GEF-49604.

1981
"Watching the Wheels"/"Yes, I'm Your Angel." Geffen Records GEF-49695.
"Woman"/"Beautiful Boys." Geffen Records GEF-49644.

1982
Plastic Ono Band. "Happy Xmas (War Is Over)"/ Lennon, "Beautiful Boy (Darling Boy)." Geffen Records 7-29855.

1984
"Borrowed Time"/"Your Hands." Polydor Records PD-821-204-7.
Lennon, "Borrowed Time"/Ono, "Your Hands"/ Ono, "Never Say Goodbye." Polydor Records (U.K.) POSPX 701, 12" single.
"Every Man Has a Woman Who Loves Him"/"It's Alright." Polydor Records PD881-378-7.
"I'm Stepping Out"/"Sleepless Night." Polydor Records PD-821-107-7.
"Nobody Told Me"/"O Sanity." Polydor Records PD 817-254-7.

b) Albums
Exclusive of Lennon compilations.

1968
Unfinished Music No. 1: Two Virgins. Apple Records/Tetragrammaton T-5001. CD reissue: Rykodisc 10411.

1969
Plastic Ono Band. *Live Peace in Toronto*. Apple SW-3362.
Unfinished Music No. 2: Life with the Lions. Zapple ST-3357. CD reissue: Rykodisc 10412.
Wedding Album. Apple SMAX-3361. CD reissue: Rykodisc 10413.

1972
John & Yoko/Plastic Ono Band with Elephant's Memory. *Some Time in New York City*. Apple Records SVBB-3392.

1975
Vocals. In John Lennon, *Shaved Fish*. Apple Records SW-3421.

1980
Double Fantasy. Geffen Records GHS-2001.

1984
Milk and Honey. Polydor Records 817-160-1-Y1.

1986
Vocals. In *John Lennon: Live in New York City*. Capitol Records SV-12451.

1990
Readings from *Grapefruit*, jingle for *Radio Peace*, and other tracks. In *Let's Have a Dream: Omaggio a John Lennon*. Exh. cat. Rome: Palazzo delle Esposizioni, companion CD.

1991
"Oh My Love" (original version), "Happy Girl," "Somewhere in the Sky." In *The Lost Lennon Tapes (15 July 1991)*. Westwood One LT90-26, promotional LP.

3) With Other Artists

1962
Soundtrack. In Takahiko Iimura, *Ai/Love*, 16mm film, 10 min.

1964
Uncredited vocal by Ono in soundtrack by Ichiyanagi Toshi. In Kuri Yōji, *AOS*, film, 10 min., republished in *The Maniac Age* (Montvale, N.J.: Laserdisc Corporation of America, 1986).

1968
Vocals for "The Continuing Story of Bungalow Bill," "Birthday," "Revolution No. 9." In *The Beatles* (The White Album). Apple Records SWBO-101, LP.

1969
Uncredited voice in film soundtrack by Ichiyanagi Toshi. In Kuri Yōji, *Tragedy on the G-String*, film, 9 min., republished in *The Maniac Age*.

1970
Vocals for "Song for John: Let's Go On Flying"/"Snow Is Falling All the Time"/"Mum's Only Looking for Her Hand in the Snow." In *Aspen Magazine 7*, British Box (spring/summer), 8".
Vocals for 1968 and 1969 Christmas messages. In The Beatles, *The Beatles Christmas Album*. Apple Records LYN-2154, LP.

1972
Vocals for 4 tracks. In *Elephant's Memory*. Apple Records SMAS 3389, LP.

1990
Yoko Ono, Sean Lennon, Sano Motoharu, Hosono Haruomi, and Nonaka Eiki. *Happy Birthday, John: John Lennon 50th Birthday*. G.O.W. (Greening of the World) Label PCCY-00188.

1991
Yoko Ono, Sean Lennon, and Peace Choir. "Give Peace a Chance." Virgin America GPACD 1, CD single.

1992
"A Small Eternity with Yoko Ono" (remix). In Frank Zappa/The Mothers, *Playground Psychotics*. Rykodisc RCD 10557/58, 2-CD set.

1993
"Georgia Stone." In *A Chance Operation: The John Cage Tribute*. Koch International Classics 3-7238-2 Y6x2, 2-CD set with book.

1995
New York Rock (by Yoko Ono). Original cast recording. Capitol Records CDP 7243 8 29 843 2 0.

1996
"Whole Lotta Yoko." In *Rock and Roll Circus*. ABKCO 1268-2, CD with book.

1998
Soundtrack. In Laura Cottingham, *Not for Sale: Feminism and Art in the USA During the 1970s: A Video Essay by Laura Cottingham*. 90 min. Hawkeye Productions, New York. Videocassette.

I. Archives
Alphabetically ordered by holding institution or surname of individual's archives.

David Tudor Papers and Jean Brown Papers, The Getty Research Institute, Los Angeles
Jon Hendricks personal archives, New York
Jean-Jacques Lebel Archives, Paris
Charlotte Moorman Archives, New York
Artist Files, Museum of Modern Art Library, New York
John Cage Papers, Northwestern University Music Library, Chicago
Yoko Ono personal archives, New York
The Gilbert and Lila Silverman Fluxus Collection Foundation, Detroit
Artist Files, Tate Gallery Archives, London
Robert Watts Studio Archives, New York
William S. Wilson Archives, New York

On Yoko Ono

A. Solo Exhibition Catalogues and Programs
Alphabetically ordered by title in each year. All materials are exhibition catalogues, unless otherwise noted. For Ono's texts first published in exhibition catalogues and programs, see "By Yoko Ono, D. Published in Exhibition Catalogues and Programs."

1964
Gendai Amerika zen'ei ongaku ensōkai: Insaundo to insutorakuchua/Contemporary American Avant-Garde Music Concert: Insound and Instructure. Program. Kyoto: Yamaichi Hall.

1966
The Stone by Anthony Cox, Sound Forms by Michael Mason, Eye Bags by Yoko Ono, Film Message by Jeff Perkins. New York: Judson Gallery. Texts by Cox, Mason, Ono, Perkins.
Yoko at Indica. London: Indica Gallery. Texts by Ono; Ono, Anthony Cox, and Alfred Wonderlick.

1967
On Film No. 4. Program. London.
Perception Weekend with Yoko Ono. Program. Birmingham, U.K.: Cannon Hill Trust. Texts by Ono, Anthony Cox.
Yoko Ono: Film No. 4. Program. London.
Yoko Ono at Lisson: Half-A-Wind Show. London: Lisson Gallery. Text by Ono.

1968
Apotheosis. Program. London.
FIBA: New Professional Cinema Presents the Best Films of the Year (1968). Program for *No. 5* and *Two Virgins*. London: Film Bank Publications Ltd. Text by Ono.
Film No. 5/Two Virgins. Program. London.
"John" by Yoko Ono, "Yoko" by John Lennon. Coventry, U.K. Texts by Ono, Lennon, Anthony Fawcett.

1971
Everson Catalogue Box. New York. Designed and produced by George Maciunas. Contains *This Is Not Here*, 4-page cat.; *Grapefruit* (1971); multiple works by Ono and John Lennon.
This Is Not Here. 4-page newspaper-format cat. New York. Texts by Ono.
This Is Not Here. 12-page newspaper-format compilation of press clippings. Edited and designed by John Lennon and Peter Bendry.

1974
One Step Festival. Program. Kōriyama, Japan: One Step Festival Committee.
Yoko Ono & Plastic Ono Super Band. Program. Tokyo: Udo Artists, Inc. Texts by Ishizaka Keiichi, Michishita Masako, Sasaki Yōko, Yukawa Reiko.

1986
Yoko Ono Star Peace World Tour 1986. Souvenir tour program. New York. Text by Ono.

1989
Hendricks, Jon, ed. *Yoko Ono: The Bronze Age*. Bloomfield Hills, Mich.: Cranbrook Academy of Art Museum. Texts by Ono, Hendricks, George Maciunas, Roy Slade.
Yoko Ono: The Bronze Age. Paris: Galerie 1900–2000. Texts by Ono, anonymous author.
Haskell, Barbara, and John G. Hanhardt. *Yoko Ono: Objects, Films*. Exh. brochure. New York: Whitney Museum of American Art. Texts by Haskell, Hanhardt.

1990
Benglian, Ani. *The Films of Yoko Ono*. Exh. brochure. Boston: Institute of Contemporary Art.
Nolsen, Leslie. *Yoko Ono*. Exh. brochure. Boston: Institute of Contemporary Art.
Yoko Ono: The Bronze Age. Mariefred, Sweden: Lilla Galleriet.
Hendricks, Jon, and Birgit Hessellund, eds. *Yoko Ono: En Trance*. Randers, Denmark: Randers Kunstmuseum. Texts by Ono, Hessellund.
Yoko Ono: Fumie. Tokyo: Sōgetsu Art Museum. Texts by Ono, Akiyama Kuniharu, Takahiko Iimura, Watanabe Reiko, Yamaguchi Katsuhiro.

Hendricks, Jon, ed. *Yoko Ono: In Facing*. London: Riverside Studios. Texts by Ono, Sarah Kent, Michael O'Pray.
Hendricks, Jon, and Ina Blom, eds. *Yoko Ono: Insound/Instructure*. Høvikodden, Norway: Henie Onstad Arts Centre. Texts by Ono, Blom.
Hendricks, Jon, ed. *Yoko Ono: To See the Skies*. Exh. cat. for Fondazione Mudima, Milan. Milan: Mazzotta. Texts by Ono, Achille Bonito Oliva, Hendricks.

1991
Hanhardt, John G. *The Films of Yoko Ono*. Exh. brochure. New York: American Federation of Arts.

1992
Starke, Jörg, ed. *Endangered Species 2319–2322*. Berlin: Stiftung Starke. Texts by Ono.
Blom, Ina. *Homage to Nora*. Høvikodden, Norway: Henie Onstad Arts Centre. Texts by Ono, interview by Blom.
Les Films De Yoko Ono 1966–1982. Program for AFA-organized film exhibition. Geneva: Saint-Gervais Genève et le Centre d'Art Contemporain de Genève.
Hendricks, Jon, ed. *Yoko Ono: Color, Fly, Sky*. Roskilde, Denmark: Museet for Samtidkunst. Texts by Ono. Approx. 60 copies signed for the Berlin show: "Berlin Y.O. '93."

1993
Family Album: Yoko Ono. Exh. cat. for Stiftung Starke, Berlin. Budapest: Galeria 56.
Hendricks, Jon. *Glimpse: Works by Yoko Ono*. Exh. brochure. Bloomfield Hills, Mich.: Cranbrook Academy of Art Museum. Texts by Ono.
Yoko Ono: Endangered Species. Exh. brochure. Warsaw: Centre for Contemporary Arts, Ujazdowski Castle. Texts by Jon Hendricks and Bozena Uminska.
Yoko Ono: Endangered Species 2319–2322/Ono Yōko ten: Zetsumetsu ni mukatta shuzoku 2319–2322. Tokyo: Spiral/Wacoal Art Center. Texts by Ono, Asada Akira, Takahiko Iimura, Nanjō Fumio.
Yoko Ono: A Piece of Sky. Rome: Galleria Stefania Miscetti. Text by Ono, interview by Alessandra Mammi.

1994
Bauer, Kai, Michael Stephan, and Bettina Harborth, eds. *vor ort, Langenhagen 1994: Kunst in städtischen Situationen*. Three-person exh. cat. Text on Ono by Bauer.

1995
Movin, Lars. *Yoko Ono: Fluxus og Film*. Film festival cat. Copenhagen: Skoletjenesten og Nationalmuseet.
Yoko Ono/IMA/Memorial Concert/Ono Yōko/Ima/Kinen konsāto. Program. Hiroshima: Hiroshima Miyajimi Art Meets Executive Committee. Texts by Akasegawa Genpei, Akiko Iimura, Nam June Paik, Satō Kyōko, Yoshinaga Mototaka.
Fanicelli, Ida. *Yoko Ono: Lighting Piece*. Rome: Studio Stefania Miscetti.
Hendricks, Jon, Pablo J. Rico, and Pilar Baos, eds. *Yoko Ono: Sphere-9*. Mallorca: Fundació Pilar i Joan Miró a Mallorca. Texts by Ono, Rico.
Eccher, Danilo, ed. *Yoko Ono: 3 Rooms*. Exh. cat. for Galleria Civica di Arte Contemporanea, Trento. Milan: Skira. Texts by Ono, Achille Bonito Oliva, Eccher.

1996
Randers Kunstmuseum 3/96. Museum bulletin serves as cat. for *Mindscapes*. Randers, Denmark: Randers Kunstmuseum.
Yoko Ono: Fly. Richmond, Va.: Anderson Gallery. Text by Kevin Concannon.
Miscetti, Stefania, Simona Rossi, and Massimo Burgio, eds. *Yoko Ono: The Yoko Ono Film Festival Smile Event*. Rome: Studio Stefania Miscetti. Texts by Ono, Achille Bonito Oliva, John G. Hanhardt.

1997
Hendricks, Jon, ed. *Yoko Ono: Conceptual Photography*. Copenhagen, Denmark: Fotografisk Center. Texts by Ono, Lars Schwander.
Hendricks, Jon, and Pablo J. Rico, eds. *Yoko Ono: En Trance–Ex It*. Valencia, Spain: Consortium of Museums of the Community of Valencia. Texts by Ono, Hendricks, Rico.
Iles, Chrissie. *Yoko Ono: Have You Seen the Horizon Lately?* Oxford, U.K.: Museum of Modern Art.

1998
Hendricks, Jon and Pablo J. Rico, eds. *Avores do desejo para o Brasil/Wish Trees for Brasil*. Brasilia/Salvador: Teatro Nacional Claudio Santoro e Panteão de Pátria/Museu de Arte Moderna da Bahia. Texts by Ono, Hendricks, Rico.
Yoko Ono: Have You Seen the Horizon Lately? Munich: Museum Villa Stuck. German text by Jo-Anne Birnie Danzker.

1999
Kvaran, Gunnar B., ed. *Yoko Ono: Impressions*. Bergen, Norway: Bergen Art Museum. Texts by Ono, Kvaran
Shaked, Shlomit, ed. *Yoko Ono: Open Window*. Umm El-Fachem, Israel: Umm El-Fachem Art Gallery. Texts by Ono; Shaked.

B. Group Exhibition Catalogues and Programs

Alphabetically ordered by title in each year. "C. Books" below and "Documents" in the Chronology also include information on exhibition catalogues. For catalogues of exhibitions which do not include Ono's work that have textual references to Ono, see "C. Books."

1967
Berner, Jeff. *Aktual Art International*. Stanford, Calif.: Stanford University Department of Art and Architecture.
Hendricks, Jon, ed. *Manipulations*. New York: The Judson Gallery.

1970
Sohm, Hans, comp. *Happening & Fluxus: Materialien*. Cologne: Kölnischer Kunstverein.
McShine, Kynaston L. *Information*. New York: The Museum of Modern Art.
Campbell, Robin et al. *3→∞: New Multiple Art*. London: Whitechapel Art Gallery.

1971
Art Spectrum. London: Greater London Arts Association.

1972
Szeeman, Harald, et al. *Documenta 5*. Kassel, Germany: Documenta-GmbH.
Ehrenberg, Felipe, Terry Wright, and David Mayor, eds. *Fluxshoe*. Cullopton, Devon, U.K.: Beau Geste Press.

1979
Vautier, Ben, and Gino DiMaggio. *Fluxus International & Co.* Nice, France: Direction des Musées de Nice Action Culturelle Municipale.

1981
Hendricks, Jon. *Fluxus Etc.* Bloomfield Hills, Mich.: Cranbrook Academy of Art Museum.

1982
1962 Wiesbaden Fluxus 1982. Berlin: Harlekin Art & Berliner Künstlerprogramm des DAAD.

1983
Hendricks, Jon, ed. *Fluxus Etc., Addenda 1: The Gilbert and Lila Silverman Collection*. New York: Ink &.
Hendricks, Jon, ed. *Fluxus Etc./Addenda II*. Pasadena, Calif.: Baxter Art Gallery.
Philbin, Marianne, ed. *Give Peace a Chance*. Chicago: Chicago Review Press.

1987
Higgins, Dick, et al. *Fluxus: 25 Years*. Williamstown, Mass.: Williams College Museum of Art.
Kaprow, Allan, et al. *A Tribute to John Cage*. Cincinnati: Carl Solway Gallery.

1988
Phillpot, Clive, and Jon Hendricks. *Fluxus: Selections from the Gilbert and Lila Silverman Collection*. New York: The Museum of Modern Art.
Milman, Estera. *Fluxus and Friends: Selections from the Alternative Traditions in the Contemporary Arts Collection*, Iowa City: The University of Iowa Museum of Art.

1989
Dreyfuss, Charles. *Happenings and Fluxus*. Paris: Galerie 1900–2000.
Valentini, Valentina, ed. *Intervalli tra Film, Video, Televisione: Yoko Ono, Alexander Kluge, Marina Abramovic, Silvie & Chérif Defraoui*. Palermo: Sellerio.

1990
Fluxus Subjektiv. Vienna: Galerie Krinzinger.
Bonito Oliva, Achille, ed. *Ubi Fluxus Ibi Motus: 1990–1962*. Milan: Fondazione Mudima.

1991
Lauf, Cornelia, and Susan Hapgood, eds. *FluxAttitudes*. Gent, Belgium: Imschoot.
Edwards, Folke, et al. *Images of Rock/Rockens Bilder*. Göteborg: Göteborgs Konstmuseum.
Bronson, A. A., and John Goodwin. *Learn to Read Art*. Toronto: Art Metropole, 1991.
Les couleurs de l'argent/Colors of Money. Paris: Musée de la Poste.
Livingstone, Marco, et al. *Pop Art*. London: Royal Academy of Arts.

1992
Martin, Henry, ed. *Fluxers*. Bozen: Museion Museum für Moderne Kunst.
Hollevoet, Christel, et al. *The Power of the City/The City of Power*. New York: Whitney Museum of American Art.
Under the Influence of Fluxus. Winnipeg: Plugin Gallery.

1993
Herlin, Jean-Noël, et al. *The Design Show: Exhibition Invitations in the U.S.A. 1940–1992*. New York: Exit Art/The First World.
Armstrong, Elizabeth, and Joan Rothfuss. *In the Spirit of Fluxus*. Minneapolis: Walker Art Center.
Bonito Oliva, Achille, et al. *La Biennale di Venezia: 45. Esposizione Internationale d'Arte*. Venice: Edizioni La Biennale.

1994
Glew, Adrian, and Jon Hendricks. *Fluxbritannica: Aspects of the Fluxus Movement, 1962–1973*. Exh. brochure. London: Tate Gallery Archive Display.
Hapgood, Susan. *Neo-Dada: Redefining Art, 1958–62*. New York: American Federation of Arts.
Outside the Frame: Performance and the Object. Cleveland: Cleveland Center for Contemporary Art.
Worlds in a Box. London: South Bank Centre.

1995
Action Station: Exploring Open Systems. Exh. brochure. Santa Monica, Calif.: Santa Monica Museum of Art.
Pitzen, Marianne. *Das Menschenbild in der Werburg der 90er Jahre*. Bonn: Frauen Museum.
Hiroshima igo: Gendai bijutsu kara no messēji/After Hiroshima: Message from Contemporary Art. Hiroshima: Hiroshima City Art Museum of Contemporary Art.
L'Art du Tampon. Paris: SPADEM.
Yau, John. *Murder*. Santa Monica, Calif.: Smart Art Press.
Desmond, Michael. *1968*. Canberra: National Gallery of Australia.
Reboryūshon: Bijutsu no 60-nendai, Wōhōru kara Boisu made/Revolution: Art of the Sixties from Warhol to Beuys. Tokyo: Museum of Contemporary Art.
Fleck, Robert, ed. *Seamus Farrell, Daniel Faust, Raymond Hains, Richard Hoeck, Yoko Ono, Sturtevant, Rosemarie Trockel*. Rennes, France: La Criée-Centre d'Art Contemporain.

1997
Conzen, Ina. *Art Games: Die Schachteln der Fluxuskunstler*. Cologne: Oktagon.
Koscevic, Zelimir. *Cartographers*. Zagreb, Croatia: Museum of Contemporary Art.
Diálogos Insólotos: Arte Objeto. Ciudad de México: Museo De Arte Moderno.
Obrist, Hans-Ulrich, and Bruce Altshuler. *Do It*. New York: Independent Curators Incorporated.

1998
Além do Arco Íris: Beyond the Rainbow. São Paulo: Fundacao Armando Alvares Penteado (FAAP).
Artists' Recordworks. San Francisco: 871 Fine Arts.
The Book: Sanoja—Words—Paroles: An Exhibition of Artists' Poems. Finland: Tapio Foundation.
Bonito Oliva, Achile. *Disidentico: Maschile femminile e oltre*. Palermo: Panepinto Arte.
Schimel, Paul. *Out of Actions: Between Performance and the Object, 1959–1979*. Los Angeles: The Museum of Contemporary Art.
Sōgetsu to sono jidai, 1945–1970 (Sōgetsu and its era). Ashiya: Ashiya City Museum of Art and History.

1999
Phillips, Lisa. *The American Century: Art & Culture, 1950–2000*. New York: Whitney Museum of American Art.
Pichler, Cathrin, ed. *Crossings: Kunst zum hören und sehen*. Prague, Czech Republic: Galerie Rudolfinum.
Global Art—Rheinland 2000: Kunst-Welten in Dialog. Cologne: DuMont.
Farver, Jane, et al. *Global Conceptualism: Points of Origin, 1950s–1980s*. Queens: Queens Museum of Art.
Silberman, Robert, with Patricia McDonnell. *World Views: Maps and Art*. Minneapolis: University of Minnesota.

C. Books

Alphabetically ordered by the author in each year.

1965
Hansen, Al. *A Primer of Happenings & Time/Space Art*. New York: Something Else Press.

1966
Gruen, John. *The New Bohemia*. New York: Grosset & Dunlap.

1969
Bing, Erik. *Yoko Ono: Digte*. Copenhagen: Arena SUB-PUBlikationer.
Sturt-Penrose, Barrie. *The Art Scene*. London: Paul Hamlyn.

1970
John Lennon and Yoko: Their Love Book. Rev. ed. New York: M. F. Enterprises.

1972
Mekas, Jonas. *Movie Journal: The Rise of the New American Cinema, 1959–1971*. New York: Macmillan.

1973
Lippard, Lucy. *Six Years: The Dematerialization of the Art Object from 1966 to 1972*. New York: Praeger.

1974
Fong-Torres, Ben, ed. *The Rolling Stone Rock 'N' Roll Reader*, New York: Bantam Books.
Henri, Adrian. *Total Art: Environments, Happenings, and Performance*. New York: Oxford University Press.

1979
Goldberg, Roselee. *Performance: Live Art 1909 to the Present*. New York: Abrams.
Museum Moderner Kunst: Sammlung Hahn. Vienna: Gesellschaft der Freunde des Museum Moderner Kunst.

1980
Auslander, Philip. "A History of Fluxus Performance." Master's thesis, Hunter College, City University of New York.

1981
Fawcett, Anthony. *John Lennon: One Day at a Time*. New York: Grove Press.

1982
Cott, Jonathan, and Christine Doudna, eds. *The Ballad of John and Yoko*. Garden City, N.Y.: Doubleday, Rolling Stone Press Book.

1984

Akasegawa Genpei. *Tokyo mikisā keikaku: Hai reddo sentā chokusetsu kōdō no kiroku* (Tokyo Mixer Plans: Documents of Hi Red Center's direct actions). Tokyo: Parco.

Haynes, Jim. *Thanks for Coming: An Autobiography*. London: Faber and Faber.

1985

Akiyama Kuniharu, ed. *Bunka no shikakenin: Gendai bunka no jiba to tōshizu* (Cultural entrepreneurs: Fields and perspectives of contemporary culture). Tokyo: Seidosha.

Iimura Takahiko, *Yoko Ono/Ono Yōko: Hito to sakuhin* (The person and her work). Tokyo: Bunka Shuppankyoku.

1986

Hopkins, Jerry. *Yoko Ono*. New York: MacMillan.

1987

Jones, John. "Meeting Yoko Ono." In *The Lennon Companion: Twenty-Five Years of Comment*, ed. Elizabeth Thomson and David Gutman. New York: Schirmer Books.

Moore, Barbara. *Action Theatre: The Happenings of Ken Dewey*. New York: Franklin Furnace Archive.

Stiles, Kristine Elaine Dolan. "The Destruction in Art Symposium (DIAS): The Radical Cultural Project of Event-Structured Live Art." Ph.D. diss, University of California, Berkeley.

1988

Hendricks, Jon, ed. *Fluxus Codex*. New York: Abrams.

1989

Drucker, Hal, and Sid Lerner. *From the Desk of*. New York: Harcourt Brace Jovanovich.

Mekas, Jonas. *Mekasu no yūjin nikki: Renon, Yōko, Machūnasu* (Three Friends: John Lennon, Yoko Ono, George Maciunas—Conversations, Notes, Letters). Trans. Kinoshita Tetsuo. Tokyo: Shōbunsha.

1990

Coleman, Ray. *Lennon: The Definitive Biography*. Rev. ed. New York: Harper Perennial.

Friedman, Ken, ed. *Fluxus Performance Workbook*. Trondheim, Norway: El Djarida.

Goldberg, Marianne Linda. "Reconstructing Trisha Brown: Dances and Performance Pieces, 1960–1975." Ph.D. diss., New York University.

1991

Haskell, Barbara, and John G. Hanhardt. *Yoko Ono: Arias and Objects*. Salt Lake City: Peregrine Smith Books.

1992

Gaar, Gillian G. *She's a Rebel: The History of Women in Rock and Roll*. Seattle: Seal Press.

Palmer, Robert. "On Thin Ice: The Music of Yoko Ono." In booklet accompanying *Onobox*, CD set.

1993

Hendricks, Jon, ed. *Instructions for Paintings by Yoko Ono: May 24, 1962*. Budapest: Galeria 56.

———, ed. *Paintings and Drawings by Yoko Ono: July 17–30, 1961, Preview July 16, Sunday*. Budapest: Galeria 56.

MacDonald, Scott. "Yoko Ono: No. 4 (Bottoms)." In *Avant-Garde Film: Motion Studies*. New York: Cambridge University Press.

Moore, Barbara. "Theme and Variations." In *Contemporary Art*. Auction cat. London: Sotheby's.

Robertson, John. *The Art & Music of John Lennon*. New York: Citadel Press.

1994

Bad Girls. Exh. cat. New York: New Museum of Contemporary Art.

Contemporary Musicians: Profiles of the People in Music, Volume 11. Detroit: Gale Research.

Higgins, Hannah B. "Enversioning Fluxus: A Venture into Whose Fluxus Where and When." Ph.D. diss., University of Chicago.

McMullan, Jim, and Dick Gautier. *Musicians as Artists*. Boston: Charles E. Tuttle.

Morgan, Robert C. *Conceptual Art: An American Perspective*. Jefferson, N.C.: McFarland.

Munroe, Alexandra, ed. *Japanese Art After 1945: Scream Against the Sky*. New York: Abrams.

1995

Brownmiller, Susan. "Yoko and John." In *Rock She Wrote*, ed. Evelyn McDonnell and Ann Powers. London: Dell Publishing, Delta Book.

Hansen, Dorothee. "Performances." In *John Lennon: Drawings, Performances, Films*, ed. Wulf Herzogenrath and Dorothee Hansen. Exh. cat. Stuttgart: Cantz.

Kellein, Thomas, with essay by Jon Hendricks. *Fluxus*. New York: Thames and Hudson.

MacDonald, Scott. "Yoko Ono." In *Screen Writings: Scripts and Texts by Independent Filmmakers*. Berkeley: University of California Press.

Welch, Chuck, ed. *Eternal Network: A Mail Art Anthology*. Calgary: University of Calgary Press.

1996

Crow, Thomas. *Rise of the Sixties*. New York: Abrams.

Haring, Keith. *Keith Haring Journals*. New York: Viking Penguin.

Jarwood, Susan Anne. "Yoko Ono-Fluxus, Feminism and the Field of Power, or, Respectability, Radicalism, and Return." Master's thesis, University of Exeter.

Schwarz, Robert. *Minimalists*. London: Phaidon.

1997

Berger, Arion. "Yoko Ono." In *Trouble Girls: The Rolling Stone Book of Women in Rock*, ed. Barbara O'Dair. New York: Random House.

Green, Jonathon. *Days in the Life: Voices from the English Underground, 1961–1971*. London: Pimlico.

Woodall, James. *John Lennon und Yoko Ono*. Berlin: Rowohlt.

1998

Concannon, Kevin Christopher. "Yoko Ono's *Cut Piece* (1964): A Reconsideration." Master's thesis, Virginia Commonwealth University.

Engelhardt, Kristopher. "Yoko Ono." In *Beatles Undercover*. Burlington, Ontario, Canada: Collector's Guide.

Doris, David T. "Zen Vaudeville: A Medi(t)ation in the Margins of Fluxus." In *The Fluxus Reader*, ed. Ken Friedman. New York: Academy Editions.

Goldberg, RoseLee. *Performance: Live Art Since 1960*. New York: Abrams.

Gordon, Beate Sirota. *The Only Woman in the Room: A Memoir*. Tokyo: Kodansha International.

Guattari, Felix. "Jean-Jacques Lebel—Maler der Transversalität/Jean-Jacques Lebel—Painter of Transversality." In *Jean-Jacques Lebel: Bilder, Skulpturen, Installationen*. Exh. cat. Vienna: Museum Moderner Kunst Stiftung Ludwig Wien.

Palacios, Julian. *Lost in the Woods: Syd Barrett and the Pink Floyd*. London: Macmillan, Boxtree.

1999

Berndt, Katrin. "Yoko Ono, in Her Own Write: Ihr musikalisches Schaffen und der Einfluss von John Lennon." Master's thesis. Marburg, Germany: Tectum.

Green, Jonathon. *All Dressed Up: The Sixties and the Counterculture*. London: Pimlico.

Hübner, Klaus. *Yoko Ono: Leben auf dünnem Eis*. Munich: Econ & List Taschenbuch.

Kahn, Douglas. *Noise Water Meat: A History of Sound in the Arts*. Cambridge: MIT Press.

Uradomo, Stacey Mitsue. "Art Institutions in Perspective: Challenging Practices and Developing New Spaces: The Work of Yoko Ono, Judith Baca, and Jenny Holzer." Master's thesis, University of California, Riverside.

D. Art and Scholarly Periodicals

Chronologically ordered in each year; and further alphabetically arranged by author.

1961

Swenson, Gene R. [Review: Yoko Ono, "Smoke" Painting.] *Art News* 60, no. 5 (September).

1962

Fujimatsu Hiroshi. "Ten sen men, gaka no techō: Kyokō no kurokami" (Point line plane, a painter's notebook: Fictitious black hair). *Bijutsu techō*, no. 206 (July): 83.

Richie, Donald. "Tsumazuita saizensen: Ono Yōko no zen'ei shō" (Stumbling frontline: Yoko Ono's avant-garde show). *Geijutsu Shinchō* 13, no. 7 (July): 60–61.

Tōno Yoshiaki. "Chansu operēshon (gūzen sōsa)" (Chance operation). *Kamera geijutsu* (Camera art) 9, no. 7 (July): 126–29.

Haryū Ichirō. "Zen'ei bijutsu ni tsukaremashita" (I grew tired of avant-garde art). *Geijutsu Shinchō* 13, no. 8 (August): 148–53.

Ichiyanagi Toshi. "Saizen'ei no koe: Donarudo Richī eno hanron" (Voice of the most avant-garde: Objection to Donald Richie). *Geijutsu Shinchō* 13, no. 8 (August): 138–39.

1966

"Fluxus Shop." *Vaseline sTREet/Fluxus Presents Hi Red Center Street Cleaning Event*, Fluxus Newspaper No. 8 (May): back page.

Cox, Tony. "Instructive Auto-Destruction." *Art and Artists* 1, no. 5 (August): 16–20.

Special issue on "Auto-Destructive." *Art and Artists* 1, no. 5 (August).

Prosser, John. "DIAS: Photofeature." *Art and Artists* 1, no. 7 (October): 64–65.

"In View." *Art and Artists* 1, no. 8 (November): 7.

Hansen, Al. "London: Destruction in Art Symposium." *Arts Magazine* 41, no. 1 (November): 53–54.

Durgnat, Raymond. "Excerpts from Selected Papers Presented at the Destruction in Art Symposium." *Studio International*, no. 884 (December): 282–83.

Reichardt, Jasia. "Destruction in Art." *The Architectural Review*, no. 838 (December): 441–44.

1967

Overy, Paul. "Lincoln." *Artscanada* 24, no. 1 (January), supplement: 7.

"In View." *Art and Artists* 1, no. 12 (March): 68.

Wolfram, Eddie. "London: Does Yoko Ono Know?" *Art and Artists* 1, no. 12 (March): 42–45.

"In View." *Art and Artists* 2, no. 1 (April).

Davison, Kensington. "Private View." *Art and Artists* 2, no. 2 (May): 7.

Overy, Paul. "London." *Artscanada* 24, no. 6–7 (June–July): 10.

Tam, E. "Switched On." *Art and Artists* 2, no. 3 (June).

Special issue on *DIAS. Dé-coll/age* 6 (July).

"New in Town." *Continental Film Review* (August).

Reichard, Jasia. "Art Is Big, Round, and Good." *Studio International*, no. 892 (September): 80–81.

Durgnat, Raymond. "Film No. 4." *Films and Filming* 14, no. 1 (October): 24–25.

Wolfram, Eddie. "Well, Whatever Did?" *Art and Artists* 2, no. 7 (October): 36–39.

Pepys, Tom. "Never Too Late." *Dance and Dancers* 18, no. 11 (November).

Davison, Kensington. "Private View." *Art and Artists* 2, no. 9 (December).

1968

C. N. "Letters: Wit or Whimsy?" *Art and Artists* 2, no. 10 (January).

Apraxine, Pierre. "Exprmntl 4: Knokke." *Art and Artists* 2, no. 12 (March): 16–19.

Williams, Sheldon. "The Arts: Patterns in Today's Art: 1. Miniature Philosopher—The Trials of Yoko Ono." *The Contemporary Review* 212, no. 1228 (May): 263–69.

Lebel, Jean-Jacques. "On the Necessity of Violation." *The Drama Review* 13, no. 1 (fall): 89–105.

1969

"FIBA: Award/No. 5 and Two Virgins by Yoko Ono/Best Films of the Year 1968." *FIBA Actualité*, no. 1.

Alan, Mark. "John Lennon Tells: Why I'm in Love with a Married Woman." *Screen Life* 7, no. 2 (January): 48–50, 58.

Willard, Charlotte. "Violence and Art." *Art in America* 57, no.1 (January–February), 36–43.

"Concours de la Rose d'Or de Montreux emissions de variétés á la télévision." *Revue du Cinéma International*, no. 4 (June): 10–11.

1970

"Fluxfest Presentation of John Lennon & Yoko Ono + at 80 Wooster St. New York—1970." *all photographs copyright nineteen seVenty by peTer MooRE*, Fluxus Newspaper No. 9: 1–3.

Maciunas, George. "A Footnote." *Film Culture*, no. 48/49 (winter–spring): 32–33.

1971

Lambert, Jean-Clarence. "Yoko Ono." *Opus International*, no. 28 (November): 48.

1972

Benedikt, Michael. "Yoko Notes." *Art and Artists* 6, no. 10 (January): 26–29.

Wasserman, Emily. "Yoko Ono at Syracuse: 'This Is Not Here.'" *Artforum* 10, no. 5 (January): 69–73.

"Directory of U.K. Independent Film-Makers." *Cinema Rising*, no. 1 (April): 6.

"Jon Renon to Yōko Ono" (John Lennon and Yoko Ono). Special feature. *Bukku revyū/Book Review*, no. 1 (April). Texts by Akiyama Kuniharu, Kusamori Shin'ichi, John Lennon, Marshall McLuhan, Yoko Ono, Takiguchi Shūzō, and Jann Wenner.

Musgrave, Victor. "The Unknown Art Movement." *Art and Artists* 7, no. 1 (October): 12–14.

1982

Moore, Peter. "Fluxus Focus: Photographs by Peter Moore." *Artforum* 21, no. 2 (October): 33–37.

1984

Frank, Peter, and Ken Friedman. "Fluxus: A Post-Definitive History: Art Where Response Is the Heart of the Matter." *High Performance* 7, no. 3: 56–62, 83.

United Art Contractors. "Yoko Ono Be Our Patron." Advertisement. *Artforum* 22, no. 8 (April): 94.

1985

Nykopp, Lauri. "Fluxus Ja Ohikusemisen Taito" (Fluxus and a vanished skill). *Taide* (Finland) 26, no. 5: 13–15.

1987

Stiles, Kristine. "Synopsis of the Destruction in Art Symposium (DIAS) and Its Theoretical Significance (1)." *The Act* 1 (spring): 22–31.

1988

McKenna, Kristine. [Review: John Lennon, Imagine]. *American Film* 14 (October): 32–37.

1989

Hickok, Gloria Vando. "Yoko Ono: Wishes and Surprises." *Helicon Nine*, no. 20: 6–17.

Home, Stewart. "Towards an Acognitive Culture." *Smile*, no. 11: 3–4.

Westenholm, Margot. "Multimedia-Frau." *Pan*, no. 2: 10.

Stiles, Kristine. "Sticks and Stones: The Destruction in Art Symposium." *Arts Magazine* 63, no. 5 (January): 54–60.

Graw, Isabelle. "Yoko Ono." *Wolkenkratzer Art Journal*, no. 1 (January–February): 72–74.

Beasley, Conger Jr. [Review: Yoko Ono, The UMKC Gallery of Art, University of Missouri–Kansas City]. *New Art Examiner* 16, no. 6 (February): 56–57.

McCormick, Carlo. "Yoko Ono Solo." *Artforum* 27, no. 6 (February): 116–21.

Levin, Kim. "Ono: In Permanent Flux." *Connoisseur*, no. 926 (March): 36, 38.

MacDonald, Scott. "Putting All Your Eggs in One Basket: A Survey of Single-Shot Film." *Afterimage* 16, no. 8 (March): 10–16.

Chin, Daryl. "Walking on Thin Ice: The Films of Yoko Ono." *The Independent* (New York) 12, no. 3 (April): 19–23.

"Yoko on Her Own: Whitney Museum Shows Pioneering Conceptual Art and Films." *The Journal of Art* 1, no. 4 (4 April): 65, 67, 69.

Liu, Catherine. "Yoko Ono: Testimony to the Confusion About What Art Might Be in the World Today." *Flash Art*, no. 146 (May–June): 131.

Johnson, Ken. "Yoko Ono at the Whitney." *Art in America* 77, no. 6 (June): 167.

Altshuler, Bruce. "Fluxus Redux." *Arts Magazine* 64, no. 1 (September): 66–70.

Morgan, Robert C. "Idea, Concept, System." *Arts Magazine* 64, no. 1 (September): 61–65.
Birringer, Johannes. "Several Dancers Core: The First Move." *High Performance* (winter): 71.

1990
Cobilli Gigli, Nicoletta. "Yoko Ono, la vevoda di John Lennon, racconta: 'Le mie sculture ricordano Fluxus e i Beatles'—Ecco storia e prezzi" (Yoko Ono, John Lennon's widow says: "My sculptures recall Fluxus and the Beatles'—Here is the story and the prices." *Arte* (Italy), no. 204 (February): 146–48.
Kyriacou, Sotiris. "Review: Yoko Ono/Riverside Studios." *Artscribe* , no. No. 82 (summer): 72.
Schwander, Lars. "Yoko Ono Events and Objects." *Lund Art Press* 1, no. 4 (summer–autumn): 306–9.
Boogdanian, Dolores. "Honoring Conceptualism: A Suspicious Perception." *Whitewalls*, no. 26 (fall): 27–31.
Bauret, Gabriel. "Portraits." *Camera International* (France), no. 27 (winter): 66–83.

1991
Special issue on Fluxus concert/magazine events. *Ballade* (Oslo).
Saarinen, Veli-Matti. "Yokomaisuus Naytteilla" (Yoko's wealth on display)." *Taide* (Finland) 31, no. 2: 24–27, 66.
Ainardi, Dolène. "Galerie Marika Malacorda." *Art Press* (Geneva), no. 154 (January): 88.
Harris, Melissa. "'Fluxus Closing In': Salvatore Ala Gallery." *Artforum* 29, no. 5 (January), 128–29.
Daniels, Deiter. "Fluxus vor Fluxus" (Fluxus Before Fluxus) and "Fluxus und die Biennale di Venezia" (Fluxus and the Venice Biennale). *Kunstforum International*, no. 115 (September–October): 197–205 and 230–35.
"Klassentreffen" (Class Reunion). *Kunstforum International*, no. 115 (September–October): 236–55.

1992
Hubl, Michael. "Spurenelement" (Trace Element). *Kunstforum International*, no. 120: 97–107.
Smith, Owen. "Proto-Fluxus in the United States, 1959–1961: The Establishment of a Like-Minded Community of Artists." *Visible Language* 26, no. 1/2 (winter–spring): 45–57.
Stiles, Kristine. "Unbosoming Lennon: The Politics of Yoko Ono's Experience." *Art Criticism* 7, no. 2: 21–52.
"Fluxus: A Conceptual Country." Special issue. *Visible Language* 26, no. 1/2 (winter–spring).
Milman, Estera. "Historical Precedents, Trans-Historical Strategies, and the Myth of Democratization." *Visible Language* 26, no. 1/2 (winter–spring): 17–34.
Cornwell, Regina. "Interactive Art: Touching the 'Body in the Mind.'" *Discourse* 14, no. 2 (spring): 203–21.
"Yoko Ono's Promise Piece." *Ceramics Monthly* 40, no. 6 (June–August): 56.
Gomez, Edward M. "All Is Flux." *Art News* 91, no. 7 (September): 16.
MacDonald, Marie-Paule. "Urban Implication in the Work of David Hammons and Yoko Ono." *Parachute* (October–December): 26–32.
Wix, Gabriele. "Die Kunst der einfachen Geste (The art of the simple gesture)." *ART: Das Kunstmagazin*, no. 11 (November): 38–49.

1993
Mekkink, Mieke. "The Sky Is Not the Limit." *Ruimte* 10, no. 4: 26–31.
Andras, Edit. "Mi zajlik a muveszetben odaat, es mi kerul ide at?" (What's going on in art over there, and what gets here?). *Uj Muveszet* (Hungary) 4, no. 7 (July): 19–23.
Duncan, Michael. "Yoko Ono at Shoshana Wayne." *Art in America* 81, no. 11 (November): 139.

1994
Walsh, Meeka. "Framed by Women." *Border Crossings* 13, no. 1 (winter): 3.
Denk, Andreas. "Yoko Ono: 'Jeder muß etwas dazu tun....'" *Kunstforum International*, no. 125 (January–February): 278–85.
Johnston, Jill. "Flux Acts." *Art in America* 82, no. 6 (June): 70–79.
Woodard, Josef. "The Fame Game." *Artweek* 25, no. 19 (6 October): 19.
Hall, Charles. "Boxing Clever." *Art Review* (London) 46 (December–January 1995): 44–46.

1995
Kahn, Douglas. "Crash! Splash! Colliding and Colluding Arts." *Agenda* (Australia), no. 41 (March): 43–48.
Flannery, Ann. "Musicians Who Make Art." *Art & Antiques* 18, no. 4 (April): 59–61.
Mantegna, Giancarlo. "Yoko Ono: Camminando per l'aria sottile" (Yoko Ono: Walking on thin air). *Carte d'Arte Internazionale: Revista d'Arte Contemporanea*, no. 3 (September): 23–32.

1996
"Big Sounds, Little Sounds: To Ono." *Midwest* (New Zealand), no. 10: 54–58.
Wiens, Ann. "Vast at N.A.M.E." *New Art Examiner* 23, no. 6 (February): 41–42.
Schwendenwien, Jude. "Yoko Ono." *Sculpture* 15 (March): 56.
"They Don't Need Words, They Have Faces: Yoko Ono at the Knitting Factory; Jung Love." *Cue* (New York) 29, no. 10 (11 March): 63.
Gomez, Edward M. "Yoko Ono's Late Summer: A Pioneer Conceptual Artist Gets Back to Basics." *Art & Antiques* 19, no. 4 (April): 68–70.
Hainly, Bruce. "Oh Yoko!" *Artforum* 34, no. 8 (April): 23.
Millet, Catherine. "Jean-Jacques Lebel: Permanent Rebel." *Art Press* (Geneva), no. 213 (May): 20–27.
Frederiksen, Finn Terman. "Yoko Ono: Mindscapes." *Billedkunst* 4, no. 3 (15 October): 2–7.

1997
af Klintberg, Bengt. "Mr. Fluxus." *Index* (Sweden), no. 2: 36–40, 58–61.
Lindberg, Maria. "Collecting Piece II." *Paletten* (Sweden) 58, no. 2: 36–39.
Joselit, David. "Exhibiting Gender." *Art in America* 85, no. 1 (January): 36–39.
O'Dell, Kathy. "Fluxus Feminus." *The Drama Review* 41, no. 1 (spring): 43–60.
Osborne, Catherine. "Vomiting and Other Transgressions: Cette histoire n'est pas celle de Jubal Brown." *MIX* (Canada) 22, no. 4 (spring): 42–45.
Crowe, Ann Glenn. " Yoko Ono: Fly." *Art Papers* 21, no. 2 (March–April): 77.
Bolton, Wil. "Haphazard Documentation." *Make* (U.K.), no. 75 (April–May): 30.
Archer, Michael. "The Object of Art." *Art Monthly* (London), no. 208 (July–August): 13–15.
Mantegna, Gianfranco. "Mind Music." *Carte d'Arte Internazionale*, no. 6 (November): 69–72.
Carrera, Paul. "Yoko Ono: 'Have You Seen the Horizon Lately?' Museum of Modern Art, Oxford." *Orbit* (December–January 1998): 26.
Ono, Yoko, Ivor Davies, Gustav Metzger, Michael Gibbs, John Dunbar, Barry Miles, Genevieve Morgan, and Nicholas Logsdail. "Is That an Apple? Yoko Ono in London." *Art Monthly* (London), no. 212 (December–January 1998): 1–7.

1998
Gomez, Edward M. "Yoko: A Scream Come True." *Oxymoron* 2: 30-37.
Nixon, Mignon. "After Images." *October* 87 (winter): 115–30.
Roth, Moira. "A History of Performance." *Art Journal* 56, no. 4 (winter): 73-83.
Dimitrakaki, Angela. "Yoko Ono: Have You Seen the Horizon Lately?" *Third Text* (U.K.), no. 42 (spring): 99–104.
Ayers, Robert. "Out of Actions." *Art Monthly* (London), no. 214 (March): 1–4.
Heiser, Jorg. "Happening High Priestess." *Frieze* (U.K.), no. 39 (March–April): 48–49.
Manchester, Clare. "Let the Evening Light Come Through." *Make* (U.K.), no. 79 (March–May): 26.
Millard, Rosie. "Cutting Edge: It's the Thought That Counts." *Art Review* (London) 50 (April): 28–29.
"Do It." *Artichoke* (Canada) 10, no. 2 (summer): 10.
Ward, Frazer. "The Real Thing." *Frieze* (U.K.), no. 41 (June–August 1998): 46–48.
Jones, Ronald. "Yoko Ono: Andre Emmerich Gallery/Deitch Projects." *Artforum* 37, no. 2 (October): 121.
Blattner, Martin. "Yoko Ono: Have You Seen the Horizon Lately?" *Kunstforum International*, no. 142 (October–December): 436.
Wei, Lilly. "Yoko Ono at Andre Emmerich and Deitch." *Art in America* 86, no. 12 (December): 93.

1999
Buller, Rachel Epp. "Mail Order Art: The SMS Portfolios of 1968." *Oculus*: 2–11.
Concannon, Kevin. "Not for Sale: Yoko Ono's Discounted Advertising Art." *Athanor* 17: 77–85.
———. "Letters: The Ballad of Jones and Yoko." *Artforum* 37, no. 5 (January): 12–14.
"Ronald Jones Responds." *Artforum* 37, no. 5 (January): 14.
Hoffberg, Judith A. "Fluxus, Film and Sam: A Conversation with Jeff Perkins." *Umbrella* 22, no. 1 (April): 6–12.
Jeffreys, David. [Review: Yoko Ono, Firstsite, Minories Gallery, Colchester]. *The Burlington Magazine*, no. 1153 (April): 242–43.
Vetrocq, Marcia E. "Conceptualism: An Expanded View." *Art in America* 87, no. 7 (July): 72–77.
Cameron, Dan. "Best of the 90's." *Artforum* 38, no. 4 (December): 132.

E. Music Periodicals

Chronologically ordered in each year.

1969
"'The Ballad of John & Yoko.'" *Rolling Stone* (31 May).
"Beatles' Single Stirs Storm—Anti-Christ?" *Billboard* (7 June): 4.
Yorke, Ritchie. "Boosting Peace: John and Yoko in Canada." *Rolling Stone* (28 June).

1970
"John & Yoko's Christmas Gifts." *Rolling Stone* (21 January): 6.
Alverson, Charles. "Plastic: Wailing with Mrs. Lennon." *Rolling Stone* (7 February): 19.
Wenner, Jann. "Man of the Year." *Rolling Stone* (7 February): 24–25.
Yorke, Ritchie. "A Private Talk with John." *Rolling Stone* (7 February): 22–23.
Grossman, Loyd. "Beatles '75 or Six More Years of the Same, Bartender." *Fusion* (20 February): 12–13.
"Lennons Quit in Toronto Fest Tiff." *Billboard* (20 February): 3.
Sondheim, Alan. "Ballads of John & Yoko." *Fusion* (20 February): 8–11.
"Sour Grapefruit." *Record Mirror* (London) (27 June).

1971
Cott, Jonathan. "Yoko Ono and Her Sixteen-Track Voice." *Rolling Stone* (18 March): 24–26. Reprinted in *The Ballad of John and Yoko* (1982).
"Plastic Ono Band." *Hit Parader* (August): 25.
Somma, Robert. "The John and Yoko Show." *Fusion* (12 November): 26–28.
McAllister, Bill. "Togetherness: Bill McAllister on Mr. and Mrs. Lennon's Latest Records." *Record Mirror* (19 December).

1972
"Musical America: Earth Symphony (Eger)." *High Fidelity* (April): 27–28.
Holden, Stephen. "'Que Pasa, New York?' Indeed. What Do You Say About Artistic Suicide?" *Rolling Stone* (20 July).

1973
Werbin, Stuart. "Music: Lennons Discuss Deportation, Allen Klein, Beatles 'Reunion.'" *Rolling Stone* (10 May).
Snyder-Scumpy, Patrick. "People and Things That Went Before." *Crawdaddy* (June): 49–55.

1974
"Feeling the Space." *Circus* (February).
Cox, Pat. "Feeling the Space." *Crawdaddy* (March).
Schwartz, Mark. "John Lennon and Yoko Ono: Trouble in Nutopia." *Hit Parader*, (March): 14–16.

1976
Fawcett Anthony. "The Day John Lennon Stopped Believing in the Beatles." *Crawdaddy* (December): 32–36.

1980
Kozak, R. "Closeup." *Billboard* (6 December): 52.
Harrison, E. "Last LP Shows New Insights." *Billboard* (20 December): 28.

1981
Cohen, M. "John Lennon's Last." *High Fidelity* (February): 92.
Simels, S. "John Lennon/Yoko Ono." *Stereo Review* (March): 102–3.
"Random Notes." *Rolling Stone* (14 May).
"Record Reviews: Yoko Ono, *Season of Glass*." *Variety* (1 July): 69.
Holden, Stephen. "Yoko Ono: In Her Own Write." *Rolling Stone* (9 July): 55, 57.
"Records: Season of Glass." *High Fidelity* (September): 55ff.

1982
Grein, P. "Quincy Scores Five Grammys; Lennons Win with Fantasy LP." *Billboard* (6 March): 1ff.
Kirk, C. "No One Kept Up with the Jones on Granny Eve; Few Surprises; An Emotional Moment with Ono." *Variety* (13 October): 81–82.
"Polygram Inks Ono to Recording Pact." *Variety* (13 October): 174.

1983
Loder, Kurt. "Yoko Ono: It's Alright." *Rolling Stone* (20 January): 50–51.
"Records: It's Alright." *Creem* 14 (March): 50.
Sutherland, S. "$ Multi-Million Gift for Peace from Yoko." *Billboard* (5 November): 78.
"Ono Gives Proceeds of Real Estate Sales to Several Charities." *Variety* (9 November): 75.

1984
Berman, Leslie. [Review: Milk and Honey.] *High Fidelity* (April): 85–86.
Peel, Mark. "John/Yoko: Heart Play." *Stereo Review* (April): 86.
"Records: Milk and Honey." *Creem* (May): 57.
"Records: Every Man Has a Woman." *Creem* (November): 51–52.
Connelly, Christopher. "A Survival LP for Yoko Ono." *Rolling Stone* (8 November): 53–62.
Rowland, M. "Yoko Ono's Sweet Vindication." *Musician* (December): 58–62.

1985
Dauphin, E. "Yoko Ono: In & Out of the Danger Box." *Creem* (January): 32ff.
Bessman, J. "Ono Documentary Posed Audio Challenges; Sound Mixer Porath Describes Re-Tracking Adventure." *Billboard* (2 February): 39.
Berman, Leslie. "Yoko Ono on Her Own Merits." *High Fidelity* (April): 84–85.
"Reviews: Every Man Has a Woman Who Loves Him." *High Fidelity* (April): 84–85.
"Spotlight: Starpeace." *Record* (December): 60.
Bianculli, David. "Lennon Bio Set for TV: Will 'John and Yoko: A Love Story' Get Ono's Okay?" *Rolling Stone* (5 December): 20–21.

1986
Seidman, Tony. "Lennon's Last Concert Now a Video, LP." *Rolling Stone* (30 January): 10.
Moleski, L. "Ono to Tour for First Time in 12 Years." *Billboard* (22 February): 44.
"Media Cool." *Creem* (March): 64.
DeCurtis, Anthony. "Yoko Sets World Tour." *Rolling Stone* (13 March): 15.
Fricke, David. "Yoko's Shows Rock Europe: Stories, Music Combine for Moving, Emotional Concert." *Rolling Stone* (24 April): 19.
———. "Peace Gets a Chance: Yoko Ono Takes Her Music and Her Message to the People Behind the Iron Curtain." *Rolling Stone* (8 May): 45–46, 48, 94, 96.
Piccarella, John. [Review: John Lennon Live in New York City Video]. *High Fidelity* (June): 80.
"Concert Reviews." *Variety* (11 June): 72.
"Talent in Action." *Billboard* (14 June): 30.
Fricke, David. "Yoko: More Shows Possible." *Rolling Stone* (3 July): 14.
"Centerstage." *Creem* (September): 50.

1987

DeCurtis, Anthony. "Yoko Ono Attends Soviet Peace Parley." *Rolling Stone* (9 April): 14.

Fricke, David. "John Lennon and the Plastic Ono Band Varsity Stadium Toronto, September 13th, 1969." *Rolling Stone* (4 June): 67–138.

"Plastic Ono Band: John Lennon, Apple, Released October 1970." *Rolling Stone* (27 August): 52.

Yorke, Ritchie. "Ritchie Yorke: Remember When." *Canadian Composer* (September): 26–31.

Gaar, Gillian G. "Yoko Ono: Her Controversial Recording Career." *Goldmine* (9 October): 18–20.

1988

Hibbert, Tom. "Who the Hell Does Yoko Ono Think She Is?" *Q* (December): 5–7.

1990

A. D. "John Lennon: The Music." *Rolling Stone* (13–27 December): 128.

DeCurtis, Anthony. "The Legacy of John Lennon." *Rolling Stone* (13–27 December): 122–25, 128, 130.

1992

Gardner, Elysa. "Yoko in Retro." *Musician* (April): 25, 31.

Gaar, Gillian G. "Hip Before Her Time: Yoko Ono Revisited." *Goldmine* (1 May): 8–15, 156.

Fricke, David. "Yoko Ono: 'Fly' Girl Soars." *Rolling Stone* (14 May): 104.

"Quick Fixes: Onobox." *Stereo Review* (July): 74.

1994

Decker, Ed. "Yoko Ono: Singer, Composer, Artist." *Contemporary Musicians*: 179–80.

"Legit Reviews: Off Broadway." *Variety* (4 April 1994): 42.

1995

Fricke, David. "*Rising*, by Yoko Ono." *Rolling Stone* (30 November).

1996

"Spins: Rising." *Spin* (January): 86.

Shutkever, Paula. "Books: Write on Sisters!—'Rock She Wrote: Women Write About Rock, Pop, and Rap.'" *Vox* (March): 85.

"Spins: Rising Mixes." *Spin* (May): 109–10.

Gaar, Gillian G. "Approximately Infinite Ono." *Goldmine* (19 July): 64–82, 88.

"Live!" *Spin* (August): 38.

Hewitt, Ed. "Live & Kicking: Yoko Ono/IMA, Cibo Matto, John Zorn's Masada—Summerstage, Central Park, New York." *Puncture* (fall): 76–77.

Weisbard, Eric. "Live! Summer Concerts '96: Tibetan Freedom Concert." *Spin* (September): 62–64.

Cheshire, G. "Film Reviews: The Rolling Stones Rock and Roll Circus." *Variety* (7 October): 89.

1997

Dellar, Fred. "Time Machine, April 1967: Syd Barrett Wasn't Feeling At All Well." *Mojo* (April): 30–31.

"Concert Reviews: Yoko Ono at the Wigmore." *Musical Opinion* (fall): 105.

"Whistle, Tinkle, Wail: Yoko Ono Repels the Masses Again." *Spin* (September): 157.

Platts, Robin. "Unfinished Music: Yoko Ono Reissued." *Discoveries* (November): 34–37.

Gaar, Gillian G. "Seattle Hotel Gives Sleep a Chance with New Lennon Suite." *Goldmine* (7 November): 10.

Greenwald, Ted. [Reviews: Two Virgins, Life with the Lions, Wedding Album, Yoko Ono/Plastic Ono Band]. *Guitar Player* (December): 99.

1998

Leigh, Spencer. "Strange Days Indeed: Spencer Leigh Recalls Seeing Yoko Ono's Happening in Liverpool in 1967." *Beatles Unlimited Magazine* (January–February): 50–51.

Wiener, Jon. "Pop and Avant-Garde: The Case of John and Yoko." *Popular Music and Society* (spring): 1–16.

Smith, Geoff. "Composing after Cage: Permission Granted." *Musical Times* (fall): 5–8.

1999

"John Lennon & Yoko Ono." *Q* (March): 25.

F. General Magazines and Newspapers

Chronologically ordered in each year. Select articles as well as those referred to elsewhere in the book are listed below.

1961

McLean, Eric. "Novelty in Sound Motif of Festival." *Montreal Star*, 7 August, 6.

A. R. "Far-Out Music Is Played at Carnegie." *New York Times*, 25 November, 27.

Johnston, Jill. "Life and Art." *Village Voice* (New York), 7 December, 10.

1962

"Kemuri no chōkoku, moji no nai shishū: Shin-geijutsu 'hapuningu' to torikumu Nihon josei" (Smoke sculpture, book of of poems without letters: Japanese woman undertaking a new art of Happening), *Shūkan Yomiuri* (6 April): 68–70

"Daitanna kokoromi: Ono Yōko no ivento" (Bold experiment: Yoko Ono's event). *Asahi jānaru/Asahi Journal*, ([?] June): 45.

Thèo Lèsoualch, "Sakusha no inai kūhaku no go-jikan: Ono Yōko risaitaru no koto" (Five hours of void without the creator: On Yoko Ono's recital), *Nihon dokusho shinbun*, 9 July, 8

1964

"Kyokumoku wa "sutorippu": Zen'ei ongakuka Ono Yōko no risaitaru" (The piece's title is "strip": Recital of the avant-garde musician Yoko Ono)." [Clipping from unidentified weekly in the artist's archives].

"Zen'ei ongakuka no kimyō kiteretsuna shō" (Avant-garde musician's strange show). *Shūkan Shinchō* ([?] August): 17.

"Sutorippu wa geijutsu no kyūkyoku yo: Ono Yōko Tokyō ni najimezu Beikoku e dasshutsu (Strip is an ultimate art: Yoko Ono escapes to the U.S., unable to get acclimated in Tokyo)." *Tokyo shinbun*, evening edition, 8 August.

1965

DeMotte, Warren. "One Woman Many Arts." *Villager* (New York), 18 March, 4.

Ericson, Raymond. "An Event Is Not a Happening." *New York Times*, 21 March, sec. 2, 13.

DeMotte, Warren. "Yoko Ono Rides Again." *Villager*, 25 March, 8.

Wilcock, John. "The Village Square." *Village Voice*, 4 November, 2.

1966

Gustaitis, Rasa. "Experiencing an 'Experience' Inside a Black Bag." *New York Herald Tribune*, 20 March, 35.

Bourdon, David. "A New Direction." *Village Voice*, 24 March, 17.

McDarrah, Fred. "Avant Garde in Central Park." *Village Voice*, 15 September, 1, 16.

"'Beautiful, Jean-Jacques.'" *Time* (23 September): 37.

Cardew, Cornelius. "Yoko Ono." *Financial Times* (London), 29 September.

Day-Lewis, Sean. "'Music' with No Audible Sound." *Daily Telegraph and Morning Post* (London), 29 September.

Greville, Charles. "Bag Piece." *Daily Mail* (London), 29 September.

Amaya, Mario, "Destruction in Art," *London Life* (8 October).

Cox, Tony, and Jay Landesman. "Two Views of DIAS." *International Times*, 14–27 October.

"Ono-Woman Show." *International Times* (London), 14–27 October.

Amaya, Mario. "Games Mistress." *Financial Times* (London), 12 November.

"The Honourable Art of Selling an Apple for £200." *Daily Sketch* (London), 15 November, 4.

Lynton, Norbert. "Around the Galleries." *Guardian* (London), 19 November, 7.

Jordan, Brenda. "DIAS." *Resurgence* (November–December): 19.

1967

"A Nice Roll in the Stone." *Sunday Telegraph* (London), 1 January.

Campbell, Patrick. "Very Trendy." *Sunday Times* (London), 3 January, 12.

Farrell, Barry. "The Other Culture." *Life* (17 February): 86–88, 90, 92–93, 101–2.

Turnbull, Ivor. "The Strange Arts of Yoko Ono." *London Look* (18 March): cover, front matter, 28–33.

Ryan, Patrick. "Music at the Bottom of Our Garden." *Punch* (29 March): 443–44.

French, Abigail, and Judy Gemes. "Night Falls on the Garden?" *International Times* (London), 12 June, 12.

"Lion's Share of a 'Wrap-In.'" *Sun* (London), 4 August.

McNay, M. G. "Yoko Ono in Liverpool." *Guardian* (London), 27 September, 5.

Khan, Naseem. "Dance-Time with Yoko Ono." *Manchester (U.K.) Guardian*, 30 September.

Linscott, Gillian. "The High Priestess of the Happening." *Liverpool Daily Post*, 3 October.

Smith, Colin. "Be-In Was Beautiful—Then Row Started." *Birmingham (U.K.) Post*, 16 October.

Brett, Guy. "The Ways of Yoko Ono." *Times* (London), 18 November.

"Love It or Hate It, It's a Film You Can't Ignore." *Evening Sentinel* (Hanley, Staffordshire, U.K.), 15 December.

1968

Kington, Miles. "Power of the Saxophone." *Times* (London), 1 March, 12.

"Art's Hippiest Happening: 'Step Up and Strip Me Nude.'" *TAB: The Man's Pocket Magazine* (June): 65–68.

Rogers, Ken. "Yoko Gets Paid with a Photo of a Cheque." *Daily Mirror* (London), 8 July.

Chowen, Elizabeth. "Stripper in the Stalls Stops Pop Show." *Daily Mail*, 19 December.

Our Own Reporter. "A Happening That Just Happened." *Guardian* (London), 20 December.

1969

Mairowitz, David. "Alchemical Wedding." *International Times* (London), 1 January.

"The Happy Life of Yoko Ono." *Dapper* (March): 29–31.

Atkins, Ronald. "Jazz at Cambridge: Natural Music." *Guardian* (London), 3 March.

Rollin, Betty. "Top Pop Merger: Lennon/Ono, Inc." *Look* (18 March): 36–42.

Frischauer, Willi. "Brilliant! John and Yoko's TV Film Rape." *Evening Standard* (London), 1 April.

McEwen, Ritchie. "Lennon in a Sack in Sacher's." *Times* (London), 2 April.

"Acorns Galore for Lennon." *Daily Express* (London), 18 April.

"Lennons to Stage Bahamas Bed-In." *Dayton (Ohio) Daily News*, 25 May.

Dembart, Lee. "Lennon Sends Acorns Instead of Himself." *New York Post*, 24 May.

"Bahamas Too Hot for Beatle Bed-In." *Staten Island (New York) Advance*, 26 May.

"John Lennon, Wife Arrive in Toronto." *Pembroke (Ontario) Observer*, 26 May.

Winslow, Philip. "Bed-In Beatle Sells Peace Like Soap, Refrigerators." *Montreal Star*, 28 May.

"Beatle John Tangles with Triple Whammy." *Montreal Star*, 2 June.

"Hippies Call on Bedded Beatle." *St. John's (Newfoundland) News*, 4 June.

"Lennons Leave Montreal." *Calgary Albertan*, 4 June.

"Japanese Bed-in for Lennons?" *Toronto Daily Star*, 12 June.

Bott, Robert D. "Ah, Springs—Now We Have a 'Bed-In.'..." *Boston Herald Traveler*, 15 June.

Gleason, Ralph J. "On the Town, The Rolling Stones—A New Lineup." *San Francisco Chronicle*, 18 June.

"'Beatle' Support: Young Couple Holds Bed-In." *Philadelphia Inquirer*, 8 July.

Bott, Robert D. "Emergency Procedures in Case of Fire, Flood or Bed-in." *Houston Chronicle*, 13 July.

Baker, Robb. "John & Yoko: Rocking It." *Chicago Tribune*, 16 September.

"Boos, Whistles Greet Yoko Ono." *Herald Examiner* (Los Angeles), 16 September.

Yorke, Ritchie. "'It Was Bloody Marvelous': Lennon Will Do More Shows." *Detroit Free Press*, 3 October.

Gelmis, Joseph. "On Movies: A Bagful of John and Yoko." *Newsday* (Garden City, N.Y.), 4 October.

"Beatle 'Peace' Billboard Set for 11 Cities of World." *Philadelphia Daily News*, 15 December.

"Beatle Puts up Peace Signs." *Miami News*, 15 December.

"Cities Get the Lennon Message." *West Lancashire Evening Gazette* (Blackpool, Lancashire, U.K.), 15 December.

"John Lennons Convey Greetings Via Billboards." *New Tork Times*, 16 December, 54.

Herguth, Robert J. "Herguth's People." *Chicago Daily News*, 17 December.

"Look for Veto." *Cincinnati Enquirer*, 18 December.

Begley, Mary. "John, Yoko Send Greetings." *Los Angeles Tribune*, 21 December.

Emerson, Gloria. "Ads Act as Yule Cards for Some Britons." *New York Times*, 25 December, 4.

1970

"Beatle John Lennon Sells Peace." *Framingham (Mass.) News*, 7 January.

"Lennons to 'Sell' Peace in Campaign." *Champaign-Urbana Courier*, 10 January.

King, Paul. "John and Yoko Answer the Call-Up to Peace." *Los Angeles Times*, 18 January.

Brewer, James. "Now John and Yoko Plan a Peace Campaign That's Bluer Than Blue." *Liverpool Daily Post*, 5 February.

"Grapefruit." *Sunday Times* (London), 8 February.

"The Lennons at Home, Studying Grapefruit and Emily Brontë." *Evening Standard* (London), 18 February.

Cole, Peter. "Peter Cole's Beat: Peace—The Five-Letter Word Chairman Mao's Men Don't Like." *Evening News* (London), 18 February.

"Fake Disc of John and Yoko." *San Francisco Chronicle*, 24 April.

"Yoko Ono's Book Made for Burning." *Jersey Journal*, 27 April.

"Monkey Business." *Times* (London), 9 May.

"Beatle, Wife Promote Peace." *Sun* (Clearwater, Fla.), 22 May.

Harvey, Dona. "A Poetic Experience with Yoko." *Edmonton (Alberta, Canada) Journal*, 29 May.

Foyle, Christina. "Why Yoko's Literary Lunch Is Off." *Daily Mail*, 3 June.

Linscott, Gillian. "Read and Burn Says Yoko Ono." *Liverpool Daily Post*, 10 June.

Cook, Judith. "No-Poems: Yoko Ono in Her Own Rite." *Daily Mail*, 18 June.

"Launching the Lennons." *Daily Express* (London), 30 June.

Kaul, Donald. "Over the Coffee: Workings of an Idle Mind." *Des Moines Register*, 6 July.

Lyons, Leonard. "The Lyons Den." *New York Post*, 9 July.

Barber, Lynne. "Yoko's 'Grapefruit' Best Book Lennon Has Ever Burnt." *Evening Post* (Wellington Province, New Zealand), 22 July.

See, John. "Books: Oh No, Says Yoko to That Lennon Introduction." *Miami News*, 10 August.

Ireland, Alan. "'Grapefruit,' Book by Yoko Ono, Called Unusual in Tokyo Review." *Nichi Bei Times* (San Francisco, Calif.), 16 August.

1971

Fallowell, Duncan. "Playing Pictures." *Spectator* (London), 13 February.

"Yoko Entertains." *Evening Standard* (London), 21 June.

"Yoko Started Out Playing with Fire, Now Cools It with Ex-Beatle John." *Sunday Express* (Montreal), 1 July.

"The Fruits of Yoko." *Daily Mirror* (London), 3 July.

"Yoko Ono Is Now Author." *Mail* (West Hartelpool, Durham, U.K.), 10 July.

Hanauer, Joan. "Yoko Ono: An Artist in Grapefruit." *Detroit Free Press*, 11 July.

Ezard, John. "Segments." *Guardian* (London), 16 July.

"The Ono Show." *Times* (London), 20 July.

"Yoko—But Seriously." *Financial Times* (London), 20 July.

Faulconbridge, Sue. "Together—Just Yoko and John." *Liverpool Echo*, 27 July.

Drexler, Rosalyn. "Mellow Yellow Is the Color of My True Love's Grapefruit." *Village Voice*, 7 October, 20–24.

Glueck, Grace. "Art by Yoko Ono Shown at Museum in Syracuse." *New York Times*, 11 October, 48.
"250 Calls to Channel 13 Protest Nudity in Movie." *New York Times*, 16 October.
Alloway, Lawrence. "Art." *Nation* (8 November): 477–78.
Singleton, Donald. "Princess of Pop!: The Head for This Story Is in the Bag." *Daily News* (New York), 23 November, 42.

1972
Henahan, Donald. "Art Songs, 4 Big Fans and More." *New York Times*, 12 January, 34.
Hertzberg, Hendrik. "A Reporter at Large: Poetic Larks Bid Bald Eagle Welcome Swan of Liverpool." *New Yorker* (9 December): 138–52, 155–58, 161–62.

1973
"Yarō-domo yoku kikeyo!: Datō dansei mokuromu ribu sanka" (Guys, listen up!: A tribute to women's lib, aiming to overthrow men). *Hōchi shinbun*, 7 May.
Rockwell, John. "Pop Music: Yoko Ono's Contradictions." *New York Times*, 26 October.
Rose, Frank. "Riffs: Yoko Madness." *Village Voice*, 1 November, 49.

1974
Kaye, Lenny. "Sound Scene: Oh Yoko." *Cavalier* (April).

1980
Haberman, Clyde. "Silent Tribute to Lennon's Memory Is Observed Throughout the World." *New York Times*, 15 December, A1.
Hayter, Bryan. "Ritchie Yorke Led 69–70 Peace Campaign." *Erin (Ontario, Canada) Advocate*, 17 December.

1981
Instant Karma (Sault Sainte Marie, Mich.). Ed. Marsha Ewing. Fanzine published until 1994; online version since 1996.
Palmer, Robert. "The Pop Life: Yoko Ono on Her Own 'Walking on Thin Ice.'" *New York Times*, 4 February, C17.
Occhiogrosso, Peter. "Numero Ono." *Soho News* (New York), 11 February, 24–25.
Palmer, Robert. "The Pop Life." *New York Times*, 30 December, C9.

1983
Yoko Only (Toms River, N.J.). Ed. Brian Hendel. Fanzine published until 1992.

1986
Holden, Stephen. "Pop: Yoko Ono in Concert." *New York Times*, 25 May, sec. 1, pt. 2, 55.
"Yoko Returns to Montreal 'For Sentimental Reasons.'" *Toronto Star*, 25 May, D6.

1989
Taylor, Paul. "Yoko Ono's New Bronze Age at the Whitney." *New York Times*, 5 February, 31–34.
Perreault, John. "Yoko Ono at the Whitney: Age of Bronze." *Village Voice*, 7 February, 29–30.
Kimmelman, Michael. "Yoko Ono on Her Own, Storming the Barricades." *New York Times*, 10 February, C32.

1990
Wareham, Mark. "Yoko on Her Own." *Independent* (London), 23 March, 28.

1992
Divola, Barry. "Walking on Thin Ice: Yoko Ono." *People Weekly* (27 July).
Gann, Kyle. "The Part That Doesn't Fit Is Me: Yoko Ono, the Inventor of Downtown." *Village Voice*, 11 August, 69, 82.

1993
Stoffman, Judy. "Yoko Ono Exhibits Art in Budapest." *Toronto Star*, 17 March, B4.
Kearney, Syd. "Please Please Me with Beatles Suite." *Houston Chronicle*, 19 September, travel sec., 2.
Zwecker, Bill. "Yoko Takes a Swing at Baseball." *Chicago Sun-Times*, 1 October, 18.

1994
"Memories of John and Yoko's Visit: A Young Julian Stole Everyone's Drinks." *Ottowa Citizen*, 15 January, B4.
"Give Art a Chance." *Daily Telegraph* (London), 5 February, arts sec., 15.
Dannatt, Adrian. "Bedding Down at the Hilton, Adrian Dannatt Found Echoes of John and Yoko in an Avant-Garde Amsterdam Show." *Daily Telegraph* (London), 2 March, 18.

1995
Hess, Elizabeth. "Art: Body of Evidence." *Village Voice*, 14 November, 97.
Magee, Bill. "Visual Art Makes Its Bed in Shop Window—And Lies in It." *Herald* (Glasgow), 29 July, 7.

1996
Cromelin, Richard. "Q & A with Yoko Ono and Sean Ono Lennon; After Some Difficult Years, They Decided to Give Music a Chance." *Los Angeles Times*, 13 March, F1.
Selvin, Joel. "Yoko and Sean Share the Light; Widow and Son of John Lennon Make an Album and Go on Tour." *San Francisco Chronicle*, 17 March, 27.
Gann, Kyle, and Ann Powers. "Yokology." *Village Voice*, 19 March.
Fullerton, Elizabeth. "Grunge Grannie Yoko Ono Makes a Comeback." Reuters dispatch from London, 11 June.
Giorello, Sibbela C. "Yoko Ono's Work No Fly-by-Night Effort." *Richmond (Va.) Times-Dispatch*, 18 October, C1–4.
"Ono Vor-Ort 1994." *Hannoversche Allgemeine*, 25 October, special supplement.
Bird, Maryann. "People: Artful Yoko's Piece of Cheek." *Independent* (London), 28 October.
"Yoko Plasters Town with Bum Posters." *Toronto Star*, 1 November, C5.
Fox, Jim. "Faithful Flock to Beatles Shrine." *Ottowa Citizen*, 23 November, K8.
———. "Beatles Fans Make Montreal Pilgrimage." *Toronto Star*, 30 November, H11.

1995
Fowler, Rebecca. "Yoko and Paul End Their Feud." *Sunday Times* (London), 26 March.
"Yoko Ono's Exhibit Inspired by Birth." *USA Today*, 28 November, A7.

1996
Pareles, Jon. "A Rare Glimpse of Yoko Ono, Reaching Far Beyond Words." *New York Times*, 8 March, C4.
Kandel, Susan. "Opening New Windows on Yoko Ono's World." *Los Angeles Times*, 18 April, F11.
Laurence, Charles. "Yoko Ono Angers Church." *Daily Telegraph* (London), 18 May, 13.

1997
Joseph, Joe. "Sixties Rear View Gives Yoko Ono Fresh Exposure." *Times* (London), 8 February.
Windsor, John. "Imagine—A Blank Canvas, No Paint; Yoko Ono's Art, So Ridiculed by New York Critics in the Sixties, Has Finally Come of Age." *Independent* (London), 9 February, 7.
Kearney, Syd. "Love Nest for Beatles Fans; John and Yoko's Amsterdam Hotel Room Available for Weddings." *Houston Chronicle*, 10 August, travel sec., 5.
"Travel Advisory/Hotel: Instant Karma." *New York Times*, 10 August, sec. 5, 3.
"News, Tips & Bargains; Teeing Off a Trend: Weddings Away." *Los Angeles Times*, 17 August, travel sec., 3.
"Ono's Art Gets Marked; Visitor Faces Criminal Charges." *USA Today*, 5 November, D2.
"Ono Drops Charges Against Defacer of Paintings." *Gazette* (Montreal), 12 November, C10.
Higgins, Mike. "Yoko: The Godmother of Conceptual Art." *Independent* (London), 25 November, 6.
Feaver, William. "Ono, It's That Woman Again…." *Observer* (London), 7 December, 11.

1998
Greene, David A. "Come and Go: Yoko Ono." *Village Voice*, 19 May.
Levin, Kim. "Voice Choices: Art." *Village Voice*, 19 May.
"Hilton Takes Chance on New Slogan." *Toronto Star*, 29 September, D5.
"Hilton Owners in $10m Ad Link-Up." *Financial Times* (London), 2 October, 13.
Carter, Meg, and Kathy Marks. "John and Yoko Joined in Bed by Chris Evans." *Independent* (London), 7 December, 1.
Carpenter, Susan. "On the Street; Hey, Think Again." *Los Angeles Times*, 15 December, E2.

1999
Reed, Robert. "Action-Packed Guide to Contemporary Art." *Daily Yomiuri* (Tokyo), 18 March, 12.
Laurence, Jean-Christophe. "La suite du Bed-In 30 ans après." *La Presse* (Montreal), 22 May, D1, D3.
"Bed-In Turns 30." *Gazette* (Montreal), 27 May, B10.
Bist, David. "Queen E's Suite of Peace." *Gazette* (Montreal), 30 May, C3.
Davis, Barry. "Single Fantasy." *Jerusalem Post*, 25 November, Arts sec., 9.
"Ono Opens Exhibition." *Gazette* (Montreal), 29 November, B7.
Ronnen, Meir. "Ironies of Ono." *Jerusalem Post*, 17 December, B14.

G. Films and Videos

Alphabetically ordered by title in each year. Only those which are commercially available and in which Ono appears are listed below.

1965
Satan's Bed. Dir. Marshall Smith. Something Wierd Video, Seattle.

1966
Yoko Ono (Yoko Ono and Tony Cox Perform Cut Piece and Bag Piece for the Camera). 16mm, 4 min. WPI Film Library Job #97846, Chicago. Videocassette.

1970
Let It Be. Dir. Michael Lindsay-Hogg. 81 min. 1981. Videocasette of 1970 35mm film.

1971
Dynamite Chicken. Dir. Ernest Pintoff. 35mm, 76 min.

1984
Yoko Ono: Then and Now. Dir. Barbara Graustark. Polygram Records. Laserdisc.

1985
John and Yoko: A Love Story. Dir. Sandor Stern. 145 min. Horizon International Television. Videocassette.
John Lennon Live in New York City. 55 min. Pioneer Artists, Montvale, N.J. Videodisc.
Vain Glory. Dir. Tony Cox. 32 min. Videocassette.

1986
John Lennon: Imagine. 55 min. Sony Corporation of America Video LP. Videocassette.

1987
Dancing on the Edge of Success: An Interview with Choreographer Margaret Jenkins. Prod. I.V. Studios/Elizabeth Sher. 30 min. Videocassette.

1988
Imagine: John Lennon—The Definitive Film Portrait. Dir. Andrew Solt. 106 min. Warner Home Video, Burbank, Calif. Videocassette of 1971 35mm film.
Live Rock & Roll Revival, Toronto. Dir. D. A. Pennebaker. 56 min. HBO Video, New York. Videocassette.

1989
Grapefruit: The Story of John and Yoko. Dir. Cecelia Dougherty. 40 min. Video Data Bank, Chicago. Videocassette.

1990
John Cage: I Have Nothing to Say and I Am Saying It. Dir. Allan Miller. 59 min. Kultur, West Long Brach, N.J. Videocassette.

1991
Miller, Larry. *Some Fluxus*. 59 min. Electronic Arts Intermix, New York. Videocassette.

1992
The John Lennon Video Collection. 80 min. Picture Music International, Hollywood. Videocassette.

1993
Cut Piece: An Hommage [sic] *to Yoko Ono*. Dir. Lynn Hershman. 15 min. Hot-Wired Productions. Videocassette.
The Misfits: 30 Years of Fluxus. Dir. Lars Movin. 80 min. Electronic Arts Intermix, New York. Videocassette.

1994
"Art Hotel (Bed-In)." In *Zapp Magazine No. 1* 80 min. Amsterdam. Videocassette.
The Pink Floyd London 66–67. Dir. Peter Whitehead. Hathor/See for Miles Films, Maidenhead, Berkshire, U.K. Videocassette.

1995
Yoko Ono: New York Rock EPK. Dir. Peter Bogdanovitch. 9 min. Capitol Records, Hollywood. Promotional videocassette.
The Rolling Stones Rock and Roll Circus. Dir. Michael Lindsay-Hogg. 65 min. ABKCO Films, New York. Videocassette.

1996
The Beatles Anthology. Dir. Geoff Wonfor. 9 hr 53 min. Capitol Video, Hollywood. Videocassettes.
Happy Birthday to John Lennon. Dir. Jonas Mekas. 24 min. Arthouse, New York. Videocassette.
He Stands in the Desert Counting the Seconds of His Life. 124 min. Arthouse, New York. Videocassette.

1997
Beyond Life with Timothy Leary: The Documentary. Dir. Danny Schecter. 79 min. Polygram Video, New York. Videocassette.

1998
Miller, Larry. *Charlotte Resounding*. 40 min. Electronic Arts Intermix, New York. Videocassette.
Free Tibet. Dir. Sarah Pirozek. 90 min. MVP Home Entertainment, Canoga Park, Calif. Videocassette.
John Lennon Sweet Toronto. Dir. D. A. Pennebaker. 58 min. Pioneer Artists, Long Beach, Calif. DVD video, PA-98-584-D.
The Mike Douglas Show with John Lennon and Yoko Ono, Feburary 14–18, 1972. Rhino Home Video, Los Angeles. Videocassettes with book.
Music Scene: The Best of 1969–1970, Volume Five. Dir. Stan Harris. 60 min. MPI Home Video. Videocassette.

The Japan Society

FRIENDS OF JAPAN SOCIETY GALLERY

Mr. and Mrs. Peter A. Aron
Dr. and Mrs. Frederick Baekeland
William D. and Mary W. Baskett
Susan L. Beningson
Leon and Debra Black
Martha N. Blackwelder
Mary Griggs Burke
Mr. and Mrs. Willard G. Clark
Dr. Carmel and Babette Cohen
Charles T. Danziger
Peggy and Richard M. Danziger
Thomas C. Danziger
Carole Davenport
The Dillon Fund
Elaine Ehrenkranz
Mrs. Frederick L. Ehrman
Richard and Gail Elden
Margot Paul Ernst
Mr. Giuseppe Eskenazi
Mrs. Myron S. Falk, Jr.
Richard Fishbein and
Estelle Bender, M.D.
Mrs. Roger G. Gerry
Kurt A. Gitter, M.D. and
Alice Rae Yelen
Frederick L. Gordon
Mr. and Mrs. Richard L. Huber
Liza Hyde
Ryoichi Iida
Dr. and Mrs. Sebastian Izzard
Maurice M. Kawashima
Mr. and Mrs. Gilbert H. Kinney
Mr. and Mrs. James J. Lally
Leon Levy and Shelby White
Dr. Edmund and Dr. Julia Lewis
Mrs. Jean Chisholm Lindsey*
Mr. and Mrs. Leighton R. Longhi
Fergus McCaffrey
James Marinaccio
Morton H. Meyerson
Joan B. Mirviss and Robert J. Levine
Suzanne R. Mitchell
Klaus F. Naumann
Ann Richards Nitze
Halsey and Alice North
Wakako Ohara
Lea Sneider Poats
April Riddle
Howard and Mary Ann Rogers
Robert Rosenkranz
Patricia Salmon
Etsuya Sasazu
Diane Schafer
Carole Aoki and Frederick Schultz
Dr. Soshitsu Sen
Judy and Michael Steinhardt
Mr. and Mrs. John S. Wadsworth, Jr.
John C. Weber
Roger L. Weston
Mr. and Mrs. Hiroshi Yanagi
Koichi Yanagi
Mr. and Mrs. Takashi Yanagi
Eric J. Zetterquist

*Deceased

JAPAN SOCIETY BOARD OF DIRECTORS

Michael I. Sovern
Chairman

William Clark, Jr.
President

Hironori Aihara
E. Gerald Corrigan
Susan Dentzer
Robert E. Fallon
Jeffrey E. Garten
Carol Gluck
Maurice R. Greenberg
Richard L. Huber
Fred H. Langhammer
Richard S. Lanier
Robert MacNeil
Deryck C. Maughan
Katsuto Momii
Walter F. Mondale
Jiro Murase
Keisuke Nakasaki
Hugh Patrick
Peter G. Peterson
Keiichiro Shimakawa
Winthrop H. Smith, Jr.
Howard Stringer
James R. Thompson
Paul A. Volcker
Hiroshi Watanabe

ART ADVISORY COMMITTEE

Samuel Sachs, II, *Chairman*
Sondra Castile, *Advisor on Care and Handling*
Michael Cunningham
Barbara B. Ford
Mimi Gardner Gates
Richard S. Lanier
Sherman E. Lee
Thomas Lentz
Stephen L. Little
Miyeko Murase
Amy G. Poster
Valrae Reynolds
John M. Rosenfield
Emily J. Sano
Yoshiaki Shimizu
Kirk Varnedoe

Photography Credits

Courtesy Asahi Shimbun (fig. 3.1)

David Behl (pl. 59; fig. 7.10)
© YOKO ONO
Courtesy LENONO PHOTO ARCHIVE, New York

Courtesy Collection of Gilbert and Lila Silverman, Detroit (figs. 1.13)

Courtesy Kevin Concannon (pls. 36a, 36b, 38a, 38b, 38c; figs. 9.2, 9.4, 14.7)

Tony Cox (fig. 1.21, 7.1)
© YOKO ONO
Courtesy LENONO PHOTO ARCHIVE, New York

Dan Dennehy (pl. 2b)
Courtesy Walker Art Center, Minneapolis

Serge Domingie/Studio Stefania Miscetti (pls. 67a [and pp. 248–49], 67a, 67b)
Courtesy LENONO PHOTO ARCHIVE, New York

John Drysdale (fig. 10.3)
Courtesy LENONO PHOTO ARCHIVE, New York

Courtesy Galleria Civica di Arte Contemporanea, Trento (pl. 68)
Courtesy LENONO PHOTO ARCHIVE, New York

Courtesy The Gilbert and Lila Silverman Fluxus Collection, Detroit (pls. 3a, 3b, 3c; figs. 1.13, 2.3, 2.17, 2.18)

Phillip Greenberg (fig. 14.43)
Courtesy LENONO PHOTO ARCHIVE, New York

Thomas Haar, Honolulu (fig. 10.2)
© Thomas Haar

Nigel Hartnup (pl. 28b)
Courtesy LENONO PHOTO ARCHIVE, New York

Robert Hensleigh (pl. 24)
Courtesy The Gilbert and Lila Silverman Fluxus Collection, Detroit

Ruud Hoff (fig. 1.25)
Courtesy LENONO PHOTO ARCHIVE, New York

Graham Keen (figs. 1.1, 1.20, 6.7, 7.4)
© Graham Keen
Courtesy LENONO PHOTO ARCHIVE, New York

Annie Leibovitz/Contact Press Images (fig. 5.1)
© 2000 Annie Leibovitz/Contact Press Images

Courtesy LENONO PHOTO ARCHIVE (Pls. 30a, 34, 39a [and pp. 174–75], 39b, 40, 42, 43a, 43b, 44a, 44b, 45, 46a, 46b, 47, 48a, 48b, 51, 71; figs. 1.3, 1.4, 1.19, 1.26, 1.27, 10.1, 10.3, 10.4, 14.10, 14.14, 14.15, 14.20 [and pp. 198–99])

Oded Lobl (pls. 7, 10, 15, 17, 19, 20, 23, 50, 72a)
Courtesy Japan Society

George Maciunas (pls. 2a, 2c, 2d, 52; figs. 1.8, 1.9, 2.2, 2.4, 6.2 [and pp. 62–63], 6.3, 6.4, 6.5)
Courtesy The Gilbert and Lila Silverman Fluxus Collection, Detroit

Iain Macmillan (pls. 8, 14, 18, 25, 26, 49a, 49b, 49c; Figs. 1.22, 6.8, 6.9, 7.5, 7.6, 7.7, 7.8, 7.11, 7.13, 7.14, 7.19 [and pp. 90–91], 9.1)
© YOKO ONO
Courtesy LENONO PHOTO ARCHIVE, New York

Norman McBeath (pls. 5a, 5b, 5c, 5d)
© YOKO ONO
Courtesy LENONO PHOTO ARCHIVE, New York

Fred W. McDarrah, New York (fig. 7.9)
© Fred W. McDarrah

Richard Massey (jacket flaps, endpapers, and CD) © Richard Massey

Courtesy The Menil Collection, Houston (fig. 1.15)

Courtesy Michael Werner Gallery, New York and Cologne (fig. 1.23)

Larry Miller (fig. 2.21)
© Larry Miller, 1976

Courtesy Museum of Contemporary Art, Tokyo (fig. 1.12)

Courtesy The Museum of Modern Art, New York (fig. 1.14)

Courtesy Museum Wiesbaden, Wiesbaden (fig. 1.10)

Peter Moore (pls. 32a, 32b; fig. 2.12)
© Est. Peter Moore/VAGA, NY, NY

Peter Muscato (fig. 1.29)
Courtesy Andrea Rossen Gallery, New York

Courtesy Nanjō and Associates, Tokyo (pls. 64a, 64b)

William Nettles (pls. 61, 62)
© YOKO ONO
Courtesy LENONO PHOTO ARCHIVE, New York

Minoru Niizuma (pls. 30b, 30c; fig. 7.2)
Courtesy LENONO PHOTO ARCHIVE, New York

Niiyama Kenji (pls. 63a, 63b, 63c)
Courtesy Spiral/Wacoal Art Center, Tokyo

Tom Picton (pl. 33b)
Courtesy LENONO PHOTO ARCHIVE, New York

Tom Powell (fig. 14.47)
Courtesy LENONO PHOTO ARCHIVE, New York

John Prosser (fig. 1.18)
Courtesy LENONO PHOTO ARCHIVE, New York

Allen Radu (fig. 14.21)
Courtesy LENONO PHOTO ARCHIVE

Jeff Rothstein (fig. 14.25 [and pp. 228–29])
© Jeff Rothstein, New York

Courtesy Rutgers University Press, Newark (fig. 1.6)

Nishi F. Saimaru (fig. 14.29)
© 1990 Nishi F. Saimaru / YOKO ONO
Courtesy LENONO PHOTO ARCHIVE, New York

Stephen Salpukas (pl. 41)
Courtesy LENONO PHOTO ARCHIVE, New York

Lars Schwander (pls. 69, 70)
Courtesy Fotografisk Center, Copenhagen

Courtesy Shincho-sha, Tokyo (pl. 27b)

Jörg Starke (pl. 66)
Courtesy LENONO PHOTO ARCHIVE, New York

Michael Stephan (pls. 65a, 65b, 65c, 65d, 65e)
Courtesy Kai Bauer, Langenhagen

John Bigelow Taylor, New York (pls. 4, 6, 9, 11, 12, 13, 16, 21a, 21b, 22, 27a, 29, 33a, 53, 54a, 54b, 55a, 55b, 55c, 56a, 56b, 56c, 57, 58, 60a, 60b; figs. 1.16, 1.24, 1.30, 2.1, 2.5, 2.6, 2.7, 2.8, 2.9, 2.10, 2.11, 2.13, 2.15, 2.16, 2.18, 2.19, 2.27, 4.1, 4.2, 5.2, 6.6, 7.12, 7.15, 7.16, 7.17, 7.18, 8.1, 8.2, 8.3, 9.6, 11.1, 11.3, 11.4, 11.5, 14.1, 14.4, 14.5a, 14.5b, 14.8, 14.9, 14.11, 14.17, 14.18, 14.19, 14.22, 14.23, 14.24, 14.26, 14.27, 14.28, 14.30, 14.32, 14.33, 14.34, 14.35, 14.36, 14.37, 14.38, 14.39, 14.40, 14.41, 14.42, 14.44, 14.45, 14.46, 14.48, 14.49, 15.1; Anthology 2)
Courtesy YOKO ONO

Courtesy Yasunao Tone, New York (fig. 9.3)

Miguel Angel Valero (pls. 72b, 72c, 73, 74b; figs. 1.28, 7.21, 7.22)
Generalitat Valencia
Courtesy LENONO PHOTO ARCHIVE, New York

Courtesy *Village Voice*, New York (fig. 9.5)

Courtesy Vrej Baghoomian Gallery, New York (fig. 7.20)
Courtesy LENONO PHOTO ARCHIVE, New York

Courtesy The Andy Warhol Museum (fig. 10.7)
© 2000 The Andy Warhol Museum, Pittsburgh, PA, a museum of Carnegie Institute

Courtesy Whitney Museum of American Art (figs. 1.5, 10.5)
© 2000: Whitney Museum of American Art

Yoshioka Yasuhiro (pls. 1a, 1b, 27c [and pp 142–43], 27d, 27e, 31a, 31b, 31c; figs. 1.7, 11.2, 14.6)
© Sougetsu-Kai Foundation
Courtesy LENONO PHOTO ARCHIVE, New York

Materials Scanned by Big Pink, New York (pls. 28a, 35a, 35b, 37, 74a; figs. 1.2, 1.11, 1.17, 2.8, 2.13, 9.6, 11.3, 14.2, 14.3, 14.4, 14.12, 14.13, 14.16, 14.31; Anthology 1, Anthology 9, Anthology 13, Anthology 14)
Courtesy YOKO ONO

Every effort has been made to acknowledge correctly and contact the source and/or copyright holder of each picture, and Japan Society and Harry N. Abrams, Inc., apologize for any unintentional error or omissions, which will be corrected in future editions of this book.

Index

This Index is in two parts: an index of names and an index of works by the artist. Under WORKS BY YOKO ONO, page numbers for catalogue entries are given in bold.

Works by Yoko Ono